The Routledge Companion to the Study of Religion

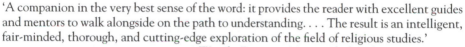

'A companion in the very best sense of the word: it provides the reader with excellent guides and mentors to walk alongside on the path to understanding. . . . The result is an intelligent, fair-minded, thorough, and cutting-edge exploration of the field of religious studies.'

Wendy Doniger, *Mircea Eliade Distinguished Service Professor of the History of Religions, University of Chicago*

'This is a very rich Companion to the Study of Religion. The survey of key approaches provides an excellent introduction for students and others, while the chapters show the reader why and where the study of religion is relevant to our contemporary situation.'

Willem B. Drees, *Professor of Philosophy of Religion and Ethics, Leiden University, the Netherlands*

The Routledge Companion to the Study of Religion is a major resource for everyone taking courses in religious studies. It begins by explaining the most important methodological approaches to religion – including psychology, philosophy, anthropology and comparative study – before moving on to explore a wide variety of critical issues, such as gender, science, fundamentalism, ritual and new religious movements. Written by renowned international specialists, and using clear and accessible language throughout, it is an excellent guide to the problems and questions found in exams and on courses.

- Surveys the history of religious studies and the key disciplinary approaches
- Highlights contemporary issues such as globalization, diaspora and politics
- Explains why the study of religion is relevant in today's world
- A valuable resource for courses at all levels

John R. Hinnells is Professor of the Comparative Study of Religions at Liverpool Hope University, and was previously professor at SOAS and the University of Manchester. His specialist research area is Zoroastrianism and the Parsis, on which he has written, among others, *The Zoroastrian Diaspora* (2005), *Zoroastrian and Parsi Studies* (2000) and *Zoroastrians in Britain* (1996). He is also the editor of various works, including *The New Penguin Handbook of Living Religions* (2000), *The Penguin Dictionary of Religions* (1997), *Who's Who of Religions* (1996) and the *Routledge Library of Religious Beliefs and Practices* series.

Contributors: Eric Sharpe, Robert Segal, David Ford, Peter Vardy, Donald Wiebe, Martin Riesebrodt, Mary Ellen Konieczny, Rosalind Hackett, Daniel Merkur, Douglas Allen, William E. Paden, Darlene Juschka, Kim Knott, Paul Heelas, Richard King, Judith Fox, Henry Munson, Paul Gifford, Garrett Green, Michael Barnes, George Moyser, Christopher Park, Thomas Dixon, Luther Martin, Mark Hulsether, Seán McLoughlin.

The Routledge Companion to the Study of Religion

Edited by John R. Hinnells

Routledge
Taylor & Francis Group

LONDON AND NEW YORK

First published 2005 by Routledge
2 Park Square, Milton Park, Abingdon, Oxon OX14 4RN

Simultaneously published in the USA and Canada
by Routledge
270 Madison Ave, New York, NY 10016

Routledge is an imprint of the Taylor & Francis Group

© 2005 John R. Hinnells for selection and editorial material; individual
contributors their contributions

Typeset in Goudy by
Florence Production Ltd, Stoodleigh, Devon
Printed and bound in Great Britain by
TJ International Ltd, Padstow, Cornwall

British Library Cataloguing in Publication Data
A catalogue record for this book is available from the British Library

Library of Congress Cataloging in Publication Data
The Routledge companion to the study of religion /
    edited by John Hinnells.
        p. cm.
    1. Religion – Study and teaching.   I. Hinnells, John R.   II. Title.

BL41.R685 2005
200'.71 – dc22   2004023489

ISBN 0–415–33310–5 (hbk)
ISBN 0–415–33311–3 (pbk)

Contents

Notes on contributors

Douglas Allen, Professor of Philosophy at the University of Maine, is author and editor of over ten books, including *Structure and Creativity of Religion* and other books focusing on phenomenology of religion. He served as President of the International Society for Asian and Comparative Philosophy (2000–3) and has had Fulbright and Smithsonian grants to India. His most recent book is *Myth and Religion in Mircea Eliade* (Routledge 2002).

Michael Barnes studied Theology at Heythrop College in the University of London and Indian Religions at the University of Oxford. After doctoral studies in Cambridge he now teaches Theology and Religious Studies at Heythrop and runs a small inter-faith centre in Southall, West London.

Thomas Dixon is a Lecturer in History at Lancaster University. His first book, *From Passions to Emotions: The Creation of a Secular Psychological Category* was published by Cambridge University Press in 2003. His teaching and research interests include topics in the histories of science, religion, ethics and political thought, especially in Britain and America from the eighteenth to the twentieth centuries.

David F. Ford is Regius Professor of Divinity at the University of Cambridge. He is the author of numerous books, including: *Theology: A Very Short Introduction* (2000), *Self and Salvation: Being Transformed* (1999), *The Shape of Living* (1997), *Meaning and Truth in 2 Corinthians* (1988, with Frances M. Young), *Jubilate: Theology in Praise* (1984, with Daniel W. Hardy) and *Barth and God's Story: Biblical Narrative and the Theological Method of Karl Barth in the Church Dogmatics* (1981). He also directs the Cambridge Interfaith Programme and is a member of the editorial board of *Modern Theology* and *Scottish Journal of Theology*.

Judith Fox is an independent academic who has researched South Asian new religious movements for over twenty years. In addition to journal articles and contributions to edited volumes, she has recently produced *Sahaja Yoga* (Richmond: Curzon Press 1999) and *Osho Rajneesh* (Salt Lake City: Signature Books 2002).

Paul Gifford teaches in the Department of the Study of Religions of the School of Oriental and African Studies (SOAS) at the University of London. He has published widely on Christianity in Africa, religion and development and on the role of scripture in religion.

Garrett Green is the Class of 1943 Professor of Religious Studies at Connecticut College (New London, Connecticut). He is the author of *Imagining God: Theology and the Religious Imagination* (1989, 1998) and *Theology, Hermeneutics, and Imagination: The Crisis of Interpretation at the End of Modernity* (2000).

Rosalind I. J. Hackett is a distinguished Professor in the Humanities at the University of Tennessee, Knoxville, where she teaches courses in Religious Studies and Anthropology. She has published widely on new religious movements in Africa (*New Religious Movements in Nigeria*, ed. 1987), as well as on religious pluralism (*Religion in Calabar*, 1989), art (*Art and Religion in Africa* 1996), religion in relation to human rights (*Religious Persecution as a U.S. Policy Issue*, co-edited, 1999), as well as gender, the media, conflict and violence. She is Vice President of the International Association for the History of Religions.

Paul Heelas, a Sociologist of Religion, has a longstanding interest in spirituality and religion in the West. Having published *The New Age Movement* (1996) and *Spiritualities of Life* (2005) (the latter together with Linda Woodhead), he is currently embarking on a volume which will complete his trilogy with Blackwell. His approach to the study of spirituality has gravitated from emphasizing the sacralization of the self to emphasizing the sacralization of life.

John R. Hinnells is Professor of the Comparative Study of Religions at Liverpool Hope University and was previously professor at SOAS and the University of Manchester. His specialist research area is Zoroastrianism and the Parsis, on which he has written, among others, *The Zoroastrian Diaspora* (2005), *Zoroastrian and Parsi Studies* (2000) and *Zoroastrians in Britain* (1996). He is also the editor of various works, including *The New Penguin Handbook of Living Religions* (2000), *The Penguin Dictionary of Religions* (1997), *Who's Who of Religions* (1996) and the *Routledge Library of Religious Beliefs and Practices* series.

Mark Hulsether is Associate Professor of Religious Studies and American Studies at the University of Tennessee, Knoxville. He is the author of *Building a Protestant Left: Christianity and Crisis Magazine, 1941–1993* and many articles on religion, culture and politics in the United States.

Darlene M. Juschka teaches in Women's Studies and Religious Studies at the University of Regina. She has recently published 'The Writing of Ethnography: Magical Realism and Michael Taussig' in *Journal for Cultural and Religious Theory* and has an edited volume *Feminism and the Study of Religion: A Reader* (Continuum, 2001).

Richard King is the author of four books including *Early Advaita Vedanta and Buddhism. The Mahayana Context of the Gaudapadiyakarika* (State University of New York Press, 1995), *Indian Philosophy. An Introduction to Hindu and Buddhist Thought* (Edinburgh and Georgetown University Presses, 1999/2000), *Orientalism and Religion. Postcolonial Theory, India and 'the Mystic East'* (London and New York: Routledge, 1999) and *Selling Spirituality The Silent Takeover of Religion* (co-authored with Dr Jeremy Carrette, Routledge 2004). Dr King has published numerous articles on Hindu and Buddhist thought, postcolonial approaches to the study of religion and the study of mysticism. He has served as Head of Religious Studies at Stirling and Derby Universities and is currently Associate Professor of Religious Studies at Vanderbilt University, Tennessee.

Kim Knott is Professor of Religious Studies at the University of Leeds, and Director of the Community Religions Project. Her current interests are in religion, locality and space, and research methods in the study of religions. She is author of *The Location of Religion: A Spatial Analysis* (Equinox, 2005), *Hinduism: A Very Short Introduction* (1998), and other books and articles on religions in Britain, new religious movements and gender and religion.

Mary Ellen Konieczny is a Ph.D. candidate in Sociology at the University of Chicago. Her dissertation, *The Spirit's Tether: Orthodoxy, Liberalism and Family among American Catholics*, is an ethnographic study exploring how religion shapes perceptions and practices of gender relations, sexuality and childrearing among middle-class Catholics. She has worked on the National Congregations Study, and her published papers include 'Resources, Race and Female-Headed Congregations in the United States' in the *Journal for the Scientific Study of Religion* (2000).

Dr Seán McLoughlin is Lecturer in South Asian, Islamic and Religious Studies in the Department of Theology and Religious Studies at the University of Leeds. He holds a Ph.D. in Social Anthropology (Manchester) and is author of various articles on the Muslim presence in Britain. His first book is *Representing Muslims: Religion, Ethnicity and the Politics of Identity* (Pluto Press, London).

Luther H. Martin is Professor of Religion at the University of Vermont. He is the author of *Hellenistic Religions* (1987) and of numerous articles in this area of his historical specialization. He has also published widely in the field of theory and method in the study of religion, most recently co-editing *Theorizing Religions Past: Archaeology, History, and Cognition* (2004). He is also co-editor of a series on *The Cognitive Science of Religion* (AltaMira Press).

Dan Merkur is a psychoanalyst in private practice in Toronto and a Research Reader in the Study of Religion at the University of Toronto. He has taught at five universities and published nine books in the history and/or psychoanalysis of religion, including *Psychoanalytic Approaches to Myth* (2004).

George Moyser is Professor and Chair of the Department of Political Science at the University of Vermont. He has published several books and numerous articles on the relationship of religion and politics including, *Politics and Religion in the Modern World* (Routledge), *Church and Politics in a Secular Age* (The Clarendon Press) and *Church and Politics Today* (T & T Clark).

Henry Munson is Professor of Anthropology at the University of Maine. He was a Visiting Scholar in Anthropology at Harvard University in 2003–4. He is the author of *The House of Si Abd Allah: The Oral History of a Moroccan Family* (1984), *Islam and Revolution in the Middle East* (1988) and *Religion and Power in Morocco* (1993). He is currently writing a book on the roots of Islamic militancy.

William E. Paden is Professor and Chair, Department of Religion, at the University of Vermont. He is the author of *Interpreting the Sacred: Ways of Viewing Religion*, and *Religious Worlds: The Comparative Study of Religion*, and numerous articles on theory and method.

Chris Park is a Professorial Fellow and Director of the Graduate School at Lancaster University, England. A graduate of the Universities of Ulster and Exeter, he has taught Geography at Lancaster for more than two decades, and has published widely within the environmental field, including the popular textbook *The Environment: Principles and Applications* (Routledge, 2nd edn 2001). His 1994 book *Sacred Worlds: An Introduction to Geography and Religion* (Routledge) is one of the few academic books that deal with the subject.

Martin Riesebrodt has been Professor of Sociology at the University of Chicago since 1990. Among his publications are *Pious Passion. The Emergence of Modern Fundamentalism in the United States and Iran*, translated by Don Reneau (1993), *Die Rückkehr der Religionen. Fundamentalismus und der Kampf der Kulturen* (2000) and *Max Webers Religionssystematik*, edited with Hans Kippenberg, (2001).

Robert A. Segal is Professor of Theories of Religion at the University of Lancaster, where he has taught since emigrating from the US in 1994. He is the author of *The Poimandres as Myth* (1986), *Religion and the Social Sciences* (1989), *Joseph Campbell* (rev. edn 1990), *Explaining and Interpreting Religion* (1992), *Theorizing about Myth* (1999), and *Myth: A Very Short Introduction* (2004). He is the editor of *The Gnostic Jung* (1992), *The Allure of Gnosticism* (1995), *The Myth and Ritual Theory* (1998), *Jung on Mythology* (1998), *Hero Myths* (2000) and the *Blackwell Companion to the Study of Religion* (forthcoming). He is also European Editor of *Religion*.

Eric J. Sharpe, in his early career, taught at the Universities of Lancaster and Manchester. In 1977 he was appointed to the First Chair of Religious Studies in Australia, at the University of Sydney, which he held until his retirement in 1996. His publications in the fields of religious studies and missiology include *Comparative Religion: A History* (1975), *Understanding Religion* (1983), *Karl Ludvig Reichelt, Missionary, Scholar and Pilgrim* (1984) and *Nathan Söderblom and the Study of Religion* (1990). Eric Sharpe died on 19 October, 2000, only days after completing his chapter in this book.

Peter Vardy is regarded as one of the leading experts on Religious and Values Education in Britain, Australia and New Zealand. He is the Vice Principal of Heythrop College, University of London where he lectures in Philosophy of Religion. He has published many books and articles, including *What is Truth?* (John Hunt Publishing) and *Being Human* (Darton Longman and Todd) and he has co-written *The Thinkers Guide to Evil* and *The Thinkers Guide to God* (John Hunt Publishing) with Julie Arliss. He is the series editor of *Fount Christian Thinkers* and consulting editor of *Dialogue Australasia*. Peter is a former President of the London Society for the Study of Religions and a member of the Society for the Study of Theology as well as a founder member of the British Society for Philosophy of Religion.

Donald Wiebe is Professor of the Philosophy of Religion in the Faculty of Divinity at Trinity College (University of Toronto). He is the author of *Religion and Truth: Towards an Alternative Paradigm for the Study of Religion* (1981), *The Irony of Theology and the Nature of Religious Thought* (1991), *Beyond Legitimation: Essays on the Problem of Religious Knowledge* (1994) and *The Politics of Religious Studies: The Continuing Conflict with Theology in the University* (1998) as well as numerous scholarly articles and reviews. He edits the series *Toronto Studies in Religion* for Peter Lang Press.

Introduction

Religions do not exist, nor are they studied, in a vacuum. While this book was being prepared major international events have rocked religions and societies: the attack on the Twin Towers in New York and on the Pentagon on 9/11; the war in Afghanistan, ever more brutal battles between Palestinians and Jews and the invasion of Iraq appear to have pitched three religions against each other Judaism, Christianity and Islam; bombs in Bali and Kenya, conflict in the Sudan, the opening up of the old Soviet Union to Christian missionaries – and to New Religious Movements – have given religions a huge, and often frightening, prominence on a global basis.

This book looks at the many perspectives from which religions may be viewed. It starts by looking at different answers to the question 'why study religion?'. It then considers how the study of religion(s) has developed – it is important to know how we got to where we are in a subject and how scholars have theorized about religion. The chapter by Eric Sharpe maps the historical picture of the growth of religious studies. Contrary to popular imagination there are many disciplines or approaches involved in the study of religions; each is discussed here in a separate chapter. The obvious routes are theology and religious studies, though there is much debate about the relationship between the two. In America there are indications of a growing difference, whereas in Britain the two appear to be coming closer together as can be seen in their respective chapters in this book (Ford and Wiebe). Authors were asked to look particularly at recent developments in their subjects; Rosalind Hackett exemplifies this in her chapter on anthropology by avoiding the all-too-common tour of nineteenth-century theorists. There are various social and/or scientific ways of studying religions – sociologically (Riesebrodt and Konieczny), anthropologically or by use of philosophy (Vardy) and through phenomenology (a term used by Allen slightly differently in religious studies from its use in 'straight' philosophy). 'Psychology of religion' is an umbrella term for a number of approaches, which are discussed in the article by Merkur. William Paden, author of two of the most widely used books on comparative religion, has authored the chapter on that subject here.

Whichever methodological approach one pursues, there are a number of key issues addressed by scholars involved with religions. Gender has obviously become a major topic (Juschka). Across many disciplines and subjects, postmodernism (Heelas) has become a way of addressing questions that simply cannot be ignored; in a similar manner, postcolonialism and Orientalism (King) have been influential in the reassessment of world-views. A question perhaps more specific to religious studies is that of the merits and problems of an 'insider's' perspective and understanding of a religion or culture, compared with that from the outside (Knott). In the 1960s and 1970s there was much debate on the processes of secularization, which contrasted with the growth of interest in spirituality, mysticism (King) and a proliferation of New Religious Movements (Fox). Contrary to what 'rationalist' approaches to society might have expected, fundamentalism (often a misused term), seems to have become more prominent in various cultures and countries (Munson). Old – and new – myths and rituals are interpenetrating and central to most religions and cultures (Segal). The question of authority is a major feature in many traditions, both in the sense of religious individuals and their charisma, and in terms of the established authorities and texts (Gifford). Of course, texts are not static; the words may not change, but their interpretation does – an issue at the heart of hermeneutics (Green). Religions do not exist in a vacuum, so six chapters then consider how religions have been involved in, interacted with or been seen through the prism of politics (Moyser), geography and geographical conditions (Park), advances in scientific discoveries and thought (Dixon), culture (Hulsether) and the arts (Hinnells). The chapter on religion and cognition by Martin looks at one of the most challenging forms of current approaches to religious studies. Back in the 1960s and 1970s international migration increased dramatically. It was assumed by many that migrants would, over a couple of generations, 'assimilate' and leave their religion behind. The reverse has happened, resulting in a growth in the study of diasporas around the globe (McLoughlin). As religions have met and interacted – and sometimes experienced tensions – so religious pluralism has become a question that many people have had to address (Barnes).

There have been numerous debates about definitions and presuppositions in the study of religion. Many scholars have questioned whether there is any such 'thing' as religion, there are only the religions. But some have gone further and questioned the value of the term 'religion' at all. In various languages, in Sanskrit for example, there is no word for 'religion'. Is 'religion' a Western construct imposed on various cultures as a part of intellectual imperialism? It has been said that 'words mean what we want them to'. My own opinion is that the word 'religion' is useful, but should be used with caution.

The ease of travel and large migrations to and from many countries have resulted in 'globalization', the interaction of cultures at a global level. 'The other' is encountered more often, more closely and by more people than ever before. Whereas some 'religions' were remote and exotic now they are part of the local scenery for many of us.

Students on many courses become fretful when studying theory and method. However, the more complex the subject, the more important such areas become. When that subject is one as full of sensitivities, presuppositions and prejudices as the study of religion is, then it is essential that, from the outset, the student is alerted to debates and doubts, and that key issues, motives, aims and beliefs are foregrounded – that is why my own assumptions and interests are articulated frankly and explicitly in the first chapter. I spent much time reflecting on the value of a section on the definition of important terms, for example 'religion'. But Mark Taylor has done just that (1998: 20) and for shorter articles students can consult my New Penguin Dictionary of Religions (1997). I thought this book should be on theoretical approaches and key issues at the heart of debate in the study of religions. There is no one 'right' way to study religions. One 'wrong way' is dogmatism – that does not appear in this volume. Not only are there different approaches, there are also different opinions and emphases – and much enthusiasm for the subjects (it is perhaps best to avoid the singular!). The publishers suggested that I indicate how the book may be used in courses. Had it been available during the forty years in which I taught the subject at undergraduate level, I would have woven a seminar around each chapter; if it were at (post)graduate level I would have required students to have read the relevant chapter before a lecture or seminar. However it is used I hope it is useful.

In planning the book authors were invited who are specialists and leaders in their field, on the basis that an introduction to a subject can be the most influential literature a student ever reads. In addition, it is often the person who has real command of the subject who is the person with the vision to give the best overview. Each author received the same authors brief on length, treatment of material and bibliography. Inevitably some kept more closely to the brief than others; equally inevitably some have different perceptions of what are the appropriate issues and levels for students in their first year of studying religions. Such are the facts of life for every editor. Nor is it necessarily a bad thing. The students using it will be different and it is foolish to invite senior scholars to contribute and then to put them all into a straightjacket. Furthermore, some topics are better handled in one way rather than another. But all authors have been willing to discuss and amend their text.

Inevitably, the moment a book is ready to go to press one thinks of missing subjects – I have already alerted the publishers to three additional topics for any second edition! The structure of the book follows broadly the structure of the introductory course I taught at the School of Oriental and African Studies in London University, some of the time with one of the contributors to the book Dr Judith Fox; she joined the course to the benefit and delight of both myself and the students. It has been amended in the light of discussion with Professors Rosalind Hackett and Don Wiebe in the early stages, and Professor Robert Segal has helped considerably on several occasions. I am indebted to all of them, although I take responsibility for any failings in the overall conception and execution of the book. The book has taken far longer to produce than the authors and I would have wished. In part that was due to family bereavement, to a series of major pieces of surgery and to a change of publisher. I am glad that the book is finally appearing with a publisher with whom I have worked for over thirty years.

I would like to dedicate my work in this book to Eric Sharpe, a long-standing close friend, who finished his chapter for this book only a few days before his death.

John R. Hinnells

Chapter 1

Why study religions?

John R. Hinnells

Introduction

Are the study of theology and religious studies only for religious people? If you are religious, should you not get on and practice your religion rather than study it? If you are studying religions, should you not get on with that – studying them – rather than discussing abstract theories and debates on methods? The answer to each of these questions is 'no'. Obviously many people do wish to study religion if they are religious, because they want to know more about their own religion, or be able to see their religion in the context of others. Some people find studying religion helps to develop their own spiritual journey, be they Christian, Jewish, Buddhist, Zoroastrian or whatever. Students in most fields object to starting a subject by lectures on theory and method. But it is necessary to be aware of the different disciplinary perspectives used, and to be alert to some of the key issues that affect basic presuppositions.

But why study religions if you are not religious and/or do not want to become religious? As a Professor of the comparative study of religion, the first question I am commonly asked when meeting people is – 'which religion do you belong to?'. Those who know me to be an atheist, often ask why I spend most of my life studying something I believe to be wrong? Indeed one might go further. I incline to the view that religions are dangerous because more people have been tortured and killed for religious reasons than for any other motive. Persecution, the torture and killing of heretics and people of other religions have been major themes running through much of world history. At a personal level a religion can be helpful, supportive and even joyous for many people. But equally many are tortured by feelings of guilt or shame because they cannot live according to the ideals of their religion, or cannot in conscience accept doctrines they are expected to hold.

Of course one does not have to agree with something in order to study it. Students of the Holocaust do not have to agree with Hitler and his followers. One can learn something about history, about oneself, from studying even evil forces. But why have whole departments of theology and religious studies? Why have such financial and human resources been invested in the subject if it is harmful or marginal, and for which one has no attachment? Increasingly sociology, psychology, history, philosophy departments in the twentieth and twenty-first centuries have moved religious studies towards the margins of their subject. One does not have to be ill to become a doctor but one does have to want to care for and aid the sick to be a doctor – why study religions if one does not wish to encourage people to be religious? Some universities have it in their constitution that they shall not teach or research religion – University College London and Liverpool are two examples in Britain.

Despite my own non-religious position, however, I want to argue that the study of religions is vital and not only for 'the Hitler principle' that one should never ignore forces for destruction (nor is it because religions have sometimes been forces for good), but because of the massive power that religions have wielded, something that no one can deny. I question whether one can understand any culture and history – political or social – without understanding the relevant religions. This is true not only of 'the Holy Roman Empire' or the Islamic conquest of Iran, i.e. in past history; it is true in the twenty-first century as well. Although the situation in Northern Ireland is complex it cannot be denied that there are strong religious motives involved in the conflict there; there is sectarian hatred. Christian Serbians were killing Muslims in the former Yugoslavia; Muslims in many countries believe that the West is anti-Muslim and many fear that if there is another World War it will be between Islam and the Christian world.

Originally my intention had been to write a standard survey of academic arguments for and against such studies. Obviously one only writes an Introduction to a book when all the material is in. Having read all the chapters it is clear that there are several scholarly and well-written articles in this book surveying the field. So I concluded that this should be a personal piece based on forty years of university teaching, also to make explicit my motive in producing the book and why it is structured with certain emphases. It means that most examples will be taken from my specialist field – the Parsis and their religion Zoroastrianism. There is no single argument for why and how one studies religions. Many readers will reject my arguments completely and that is perfectly reasonable; maybe where this book is used for a course an early seminar discussion on the subject may be 'why study religions?' The basic question to be addressed is: why should an atheist want to study religions? First, it is necessary at the start of a book of this nature to discuss what one means by the term 'religion'.

Defining religion

There have been endless discussions of the definition of 'religion'. Indeed recently some scholars have argued for avoiding the word 'religion' as meaningless and have argued instead for the term 'culture'. This introduction is not a place for extensive debate, but rather as a place for explaining where I am 'coming from' as editor of this book, but it would be a mistake not to indicate my position on this primary issue of saying what is meant by the word 'religion'. In my opinion there is no such thing as 'religion', there are only the religions, i.e. those people who identify themselves as members of a religious group, Christians, Muslims, etc. An act or thought is religious when the person concerned thinks they are practising their 'religion'. Organizations are religious when the people involved think they are functioning religiously. In some societies in East Asia a person may have, say, a Christian initiation, a Buddhist wedding and a Chinese funeral, in my understanding at the moment they are acting, say, in a Christian way then at that moment they are a Christian. Of course the boundaries of those groups are fluid – so some people who claim to be, say, Muslims are not accepted by the majority of that religion as being 'true' Muslims.

My general position in discussing religions is that people are what they believe they are. I am cautious about replacing 'religion' with 'culture' (Fitzgerald 2000, see also McCutcheon 2001) partly because that simply moves the debate on to the question of what is meant by 'culture'. But many others see culture as something that includes religion, but that also has much wider connotations. The Parsis, for example, have what they see as their culture in addition to their religion. The equivalent term is *Parsi panu* (Parsi-ness), and it includes non-religious dress (e.g. the Parsi style of a sari in contrast to the religious garments the sacred shirt and cord, *sudre* and *kusti*), drama (*nataks* – in Gujarati, rather bawdy but huge fun – and never on religious themes) and their own highly distinctive way of cooking *dhansak*. All these are Parsi favourites, common not only in the old country but also in the diaspora. They would interpret such items as parts of Parsi culture but not part of their Zoroastrian religion. Parsis who say they are not Zoroastrians (either because they are not religious or if they have converted to, say, Christianity) are still likely to enjoy *Parsi panu*. Some of my colleagues disagree with the use of the phrase 'the religious dimension' of a situation or event. I do not wish to imply that there is any 'thing' out there that is religious. But events, like people, are complex, and can have both religious and secular dimensions; having one does not exclude the other. An act is a religious act when the person involved believes it to be associated with their religion. A religious thought is a thought which the thinker thinks is Zoroastrian (Christian, etc.). Of course I recognize that the situation is far from clear-cut. What of 'cultures' that have no word for 'religion', as in Sanskrit, and where the term for a religion is anachronistic, for example the term 'Hinduism', which is a modern West-imposed label for a plethora of different groups, beliefs and practices across a large continent with some purely local phenomena. 'Hinduism' exists in the diaspora communities because of compliance with use of Western categories, e.g. to obtain charitable status. Ninian Smart's use of the term 'world views' has some merits, but prioritizes the belief aspect of religion that is inappropriate elsewhere, e.g. Parsis for whom 'religion' is to do with individual identity; it is something in the blood or genes, to do with community boundaries and associated practices but with little or no reference to beliefs. In the case of Zoroastrianism 'religion' is appropriate since there is a term (*den*) that it is reasonable to translate as 'religion'. All 'labels' have limitations and these must be accepted, so 'religion' is a useful but potentially misleading term.

Religions and politics

The former British Prime Minister, Margaret Thatcher, once argued strongly that religion was a private matter of belief (therefore bishops should not get involved in political debates as they were doing). But I believe that in this assertion she was completely wrong. Religions and religious leaders, have rarely been outside politics, be they Jesus, Muhammad or Gandhi. Christianity was a driving force in Spanish, Portuguese and British empire-building. With the first two there was a powerful urge for converts as well as fortunes. The British came to stress 'the white man's burden' of 'civilizing the natives' (though fortunes and converts were also welcome!).

Partition in South Asia in 1947 sought to create separate Muslim and Hindu nations. These countries have been to war, or on the brink of it, many times in the following decades (though, now that there are more Muslims in India than in Pakistan, the religious divisions no longer follow the original policy). The showing and sales of videos of the two Indian epics, the *Ramayana* and the *Mahabharata* stoked (probably unwittingly) the fires of Indian nationalism and the radical BJP (Bharatiya Janata Party) party came to power. A touchstone was the Hindu claim to the site of the mosque at Ayodhya, which they claimed was built over an important Hindu temple (Van der Veer). Many looked on in horror at the Hindu attacks on Muslims, the mob violence and the torching of Muslim homes in Bombay and Gujarat by Hindu militants in the early 1990s. The sorry tale of religious violence extends over all continents.

In the contemporary world the various religions seem to be even more prominent: the Israeli conviction that the land of Israel is God's gift to them and has led to attempts to eject or impose themselves over the Palestinians (who respond with suicide missions). The reason why it is thought American governments ignore Israel's breaking of UN resolutions is due to the powerful Jewish lobby in the US; rightly or wrongly many Muslims believe it be an anti-Islam stance. The Shah was overthrown in 1979 for various reasons, but a major factor was the popular uprising led by Ayatollah Khomeini on the grounds that American influence had become more important to the government than Islam. It is difficult to believe that the invasion of Iraq in 2003/4 is legitimately explained simply by the terrible massacre of thousands in the destruction of the Twin Towers in New York on 9/11. It is not only that there is little evidence of Iraqi Government involvement in al Qaeda activity; it is highly unlikely because Saddam Hussein was not a particular ally of a movement that opposed his secularizing tendencies. President Bush and Prime Minister Blair, both of whom have made public their Christian religious position, sought 'regime change' through invasion or 'a crusade' as Bush called it. For Muslims in many countries this was seen as a Christian assault on Islam and the consequences will almost certainly be with us for many years and may well have brought al Qaeda's ideology into Iraq and provoked more militant Muslims in many countries. Many fear it might bring nearer a war between the Christian 'West' and Islam.

Some writers suggest such acts are not the outcome of 'real' or 'true' Christianity/Islam, etc., rather they suggest this is people using a religion to justify their violence; it is not, they say, that religion is the cause of the problems. Even the fighting in Northern Ireland between Catholics and Protestants is often put down to other causes. Doubtless there are a variety of factors in most conflicts, but religions are often potent factors in the explosions of violence. Of course religions can also be at the forefront of movements for peace and justice; for example Gandhi's non-violent campaign; Archbishop Desmond Tutu in South Africa; the Reverend Martin Luther King with his dream in America; and the bishops' stand taken against the corrupt dictators in South America with 'Liberation theology'. How can anyone doubt the importance of studying religions when they are such potent forces?

Religion and culture

Is it possible to understand another culture without looking at the appropriate religion practiced there, be that in ancient Egypt or modern America? (It should be noted that the term 'culture' is a contested one, see Masuzawa in Taylor 1998: 70–93.) It is often difficult to say which came first, the religion or the values and ideals – but basically it does not matter; they are now part of an intricate network. In pre-modern times most artwork was produced for use in the relevant religion. How can one study the art without understanding its use and context? Whether the student/teacher/writer is religious or not, one cannot – should not – fail to study the religion of the culture. A study of the history of Gothic churches or of artefacts from Primal societies in North America or Africa or the Pacific without setting them in their religious context is inevitably going to fail to understand their importance and 'meaning'. The artist may or may not have been inspired by the religion of his region but it is important to know something of the culture in which the object was produced and used, and religions are commonly an important part of that culture.

In the contemporary world, interaction with other cultures is inevitable, with trade, in the news, when travelling or just watching television; meeting a different cultural tradition is inevitable for most people. To understand a religion, it is essential to have an awareness of the different sets of values and ideals, customs and ethical values. Even if the people one meets from the 'other' culture are not religious, nevertheless their principles, values and ideals will commonly have been formed by the religion of their culture. Although an atheist, I have no doubt that my value system has been formed by Christianity, specifically Anglican Christianity. My attitudes to gender relations, prioritizing one set of values over another, what I consider to be 'good and bad', have all been affected by my general background of which Christianity was a major part.

Racial and religious prejudices are major issues in the contemporary world. They are often interwoven so it is not clear whether someone is discriminated against for being, say, from Pakistan or because of prejudice against Islam, and either can be the excuse for violence. In the 1980s and 1990s I undertook a survey questionnaire among Zoroastrians in America, Australia, Britain, Canada, China, East Africa, Pakistan, and conducted a series of in-depth interviews with Zoroastrians in France and Germany. Many respondents believed that they had faced prejudice, especially in Canada, but there they said they had faced it mainly in obtaining a first job. Once you had shown that you were good at your work, they said, you were accepted. In America one-third of my respondents said that they had experienced discrimination, but what they feared even more was the threat of the 'melting pot' eroding their identity. Some scholars describe the 'melting pot' as a myth, and there have been different terms used, e.g. a 'salad bowl' of cultures. American respondents and informants thought that the 'melting pot' was a threatening reality. The countries in which most people said that they frequently faced discrimination were Germany and Britain – especially in schooling (Hinnells 2005). One major motive for me in pursuing the comparative study of religions (usually abbreviated, conveniently if unfortunately, to comparative religion) is to encourage knowledge and understanding between religions and cultures, based on the assumption that prejudice will be overcome if each knows more about the other. The media and many sections of society have stereotypical images of 'the other'. I hope that knowledge will result in understanding, and thereby better relations between peoples. Above all my 'quest' as a teacher is to enable students to 'see through the spectacles' of another culture. I do not believe that there is a block of knowledge that has to be conveyed. If someone can develop an empathetic understanding of one other culture, the result will be that they are more ready to empathize with other cultures as well. But am I wrong? Is it necessarily the case that the more you know about the other religion, the more you will think positively about people from that religion? Some might be alienated from it. Would people respect Hitler more if they knew more about him? Maybe my motives are 'woolly liberalism'. If I thought that, then I would feel I had wasted much of my academic life.

Some common presuppositions

Writers have a tendency to think that 'real' Islam is found in the Middle East and in Arabic texts; or 'real' Hinduism is found in Sanskrit texts. R. C. Zaehner, for example, wrote his widely used book *Hinduism*, without ever having been to India (when he went there he did not like it!). What resources he thought he needed to write about Hinduism were his books in his study and in the Bodleian library in Oxford. His methodological assumptions were shared by many of his contemporaries. Of course textual studies are important, both the 'sacred' texts but also their hermeneutical inter-pretation by later generations. One problem, however, is that these texts are commonly the domain of the intellectuals and the literary few – widespread literacy is a modern phenomena, and still not present in many countries. Archaeology can yield important information, but by definition most of the artefacts unearthed tend to be those which were most durable, costly and therefore often came from the domain of the wealthy and powerful, not from the wider population. That is one reason why in this chapter I have stressed the importance of studying various art forms both 'pop' and 'high' art. Meeting people from the religion studied can be very important (where possible) even if a student is studying ancient texts. It changes one's attitude when seeing how the religious literature is used. The study of religions needs to be 'polymethodic'.

There is a common tendency in religious studies to think of religions as monolithic wholes. It is now quite common to question if there is any such thing as Hinduism, but the same is less true of the study of other religions. For example, is there any such 'thing' as Christianity, or are there are many Christianities? Are Primitive Welsh Methodists a part of the same religion as the Russian Orthodox? Where does one draw the boundary of Christianity – does it include the Mormons or 'The Children of God' (now known as 'The Family'), a group which sought to express the love of God and Jesus through the practice of 'flirty fishing' following the Biblical injunction to become fishers of men (that practice has ceased but the movement remains active and some-what 'unconventional' – see Van Zandt). Some American tele-evangelists seem to be from a very different religion from that practised in St Peters in Rome – the Northern Ireland politician and preacher, the Reverend Ian Paisley, thinks so, judging by his tirades against the Pope. If a religious movement calls itself 'Christian' should it not be treated as part of Christianity – or one of the Christianities?

The new growth in religion: some key questions

In the 1960s many of us forecast that religions would gradually decline, especially, but not only, in the West – we were wrong! In studying religions it is important to ask why things happen and to understand why change comes about.

- In many Western cities, especially in America and the Middle East, but also in the new Russia, in Korea, in Mumbai, religious groups have become more promi-nent. Why?

- As far as Christianity is concerned, growth is pre-eminently among evangelicals and charismatic groups. Why?
- Whereas secularization was the theme of the 1960s and 1970s, there has been an increase in the number of New Religious Movements (NRMs). It is impossible to estimate the number of people involved, because many of the movements are small, and dual membership also happens. But the number of movements has increased. Why?
- The broad pattern of recruits to NRMs are middle aged, middle class, generally well educated – and often people who had sought but not found religious fulfilment in established religious groups. Why?
- The aspect of various religions that have become more prominent is what is labelled as 'fundamentalism'. Why?

In the 1970s and 1980s sociologists wrote from an entirely secular perspective about migration and diaspora groups in the West. The religion of the migrants and subsequent generations was ignored; they were simply labelled as Hindus, Muslims etc., but there was rarely any discussion of patterns of religious change and continuity, nothing about how Hinduism/Islam etc. have been shaped in the diaspora. Because the scholars were not themselves religious, they tended to look past the religion of the subjects they were writing about. The discussions were about prejudice, housing, working patterns – all, of course, issues of great importance, but writers ignored that which meant most for many migrants – religion.

There was another factor. Writing as someone involved in an aspect of government policy relating to migration in the 1960 and 1970s, frankly it was assumed that migrant's religions would fade over the years and generations as they assimilated. It was assumed that they had left their religion behind back in the old country. These ideas were completely wrong. Studies of transnational or diaspora communities at the turn of the millennium commonly found that migrants tend to be more religious after migration than they were before, because their religion gives them a stake of continuity in a sea of change. Further, recent studies are finding that what might be called the second generation's 'secular ethnicity' – their Pakistani/Indian/Bangladeshi, etc. culture is not as meaningful to the young, who prefer to see themselves as Muslims/Hindus/Zoroastrians, etc. (see for example Williams 2000; Hinnells 2005). Religion is becoming the marker that many young people are taking up. Further, there was an assumption that migrants and their youngsters would be more liberal than the orthodox people back in the old country. This is not necessarily so. The religions of people in South Asia move on (I am less familiar with the literature on South East and East Asians in America); their religions are dynamic and change or 'evolve'. There the changes are often greater than among people in the diaspora, for, in the latter, continuity matters in individual or group identity. An example of this would be the militancy among Sikhs in Britain, and especially in Canada, which was stronger than it was in India following the attack on the Golden Temple. The diaspora impacts on the old country. Since the 1970s the biggest source of income for Pakistan was money sent 'home' by families working overseas.

One common question in many religions is that of authority. To use a Parsi example again: in 1906 in a test case in the Bombay High Court it was decided that the offspring of a Parsi male married out of the community could be initiated, but not the offspring of an intermarried woman because Parsi society was a patrilineal one (there were also some caste-like debates). That judgement continues to be followed by most Parsis in post-colonial, independent India – and by many Parsis in the diaspora. Technically the authority of the High Priests (*Dasturs*) in India is within the walls of their temples (*Atash Bahrams*). But among the traditional/orthodox members in the diaspora their judgements carry considerable weight. These issues came to a head in the 1980s over an initiation in New York of a person neither of whose parents were Zoroastrians. When the furore erupted, opinions in America were evenly divided over whether the authority of a 1906 Bombay High Court judgement in the days of the British Raj, and of the priests 'back' in India, was binding over groups in the West in the third millennium. Lines of authority become complex as religious people adapt to new social, legal and cultural settings.

There is another vitally important factor in the study of religions in their diasporas, namely the implications of religious beliefs and practices of transnational groups for public policy in their new western homes. Some obvious examples are the implications for healthcare. Since attitudes to pain and suffering are different in different religions or cultures it can be essential that doctors and nurses are sensitive to, and are therefore knowledgeable about, values, and the priorities of their patients (Hinnells and Porter 1999; Helman 1994). The problems are even more acute in the case of psychiatric illness because what might seem 'abnormal' behaviour in one society may not in another (Rack 1982; Bhugra 1996; Littlewood and Lipsedge 1997; Honwana 1999 on the damage which 'Western' psychological practice can inflict on – in this case – African peoples who had experienced the trauma of the massacres in Mozambique). Perhaps the instance where informed sensitivity relating to religious/cultural values is of greatest need surrounds death and bereavement. Having 'a good death', the 'proper' treatment of the body and support for the bereaved all matter hugely to people of any culture. 'Doing the right thing' is emotionally vital and that commonly involves religious beliefs and practices even for those who do not consider themselves religious. (Spiro *et al.* 1996; Howarth and Jupp 1996; Irish *et al.* 1993, the last of these is particularly good on a wide range of minority groups in America, e.g. Native Americans.)

The presence of a huge range of religious groups be that in Australia, Britain, Canada or the USA and elsewhere has serious implications for social policy and national laws, problems both for the minorities and for governments because many religious traditions evolved outside a Western legal orbit (and others which have not, e.g. the Mormons and polygamy). The obvious example is concerning gender issues where some traditions are in conflict with Western concepts of human rights (Nesbitt 2001; Hawley 1994; Sahgal and Yuval Davis 1992; Gustafson and Juviler 1999). Policymakers concerned with schools and educational policy, crime and punishment all have a need to pay serious attention to the religions in their midst, the values, priorities and principles (see Haddad and Lummis 1987) especially at times such as the start of the twenty-first century, when Muslim feelings run high and where governments all too readily stigmatize minorities; when there is violence, invasion and wars; when there is a breakdown in aspects of human rights, for example the rights of prisoners. Ignoring religious issues and feelings can be exceedingly dangerous.

Change in the New World

Not only do religions change, so too do the countries to which people migrate. Perhaps the country which has changed the most is the USA. Prior to the Hart-Cellar Act of 1965 migration was only from Northern Europe and was mostly of English speakers. Gradually South and East Europeans were allowed in, but from the 1970s Asians were admitted, providing they fitted the criteria of US interests, admitting in particular the highly educated, especially scientists and people in the medical profession. There have long been migrants, many illegal, from Mexico to undertake menial tasks, but with the arrival of educated Asians, perceptions of 'the other' began to change. Black settlers from the days of slavery became accepted in a way hardly imaginable in the early 1960s; so that 'People of Color' can occupy places of high office. Attitudes to Asian cultures had changed briefly in the 1890s with the Parliament of World Religions in Chicago and in particular the teaching 'missions' of Swami Vivekananda. But it was mainly from the 1960s that interest in Asian religions began, with Rajneesh, the Maharishi, Reverend Moon and the work of the Krishna Consciousness movement. Many American cities have their China towns. In California there are 'villages' of nationalities, for example the Iranians settled near Los Angeles (in an area popularly known as 'Irangeles'). Refugees are not always the poor; many Iranians, for example, after the fall of the Shah brought their substantial wealth with them (see Naficy 1991). In the 1990s interest in 'Native' American religions grew. Hindu temples were built following the designs and bearing the images crafted by skilled traditional artists from India. The religious landscape of the US changed dramatically in some forty years (Eck 2000, 2002; Haddad 1991, 2000; Williams 1988, 2000; Warner and Wittner 1998).

In countries where there is substantial religious pluralism, inter-faith activity has been important. What has yet to be adequately studied is the impact of these activities. There are of course many benefits in developing active communications between groups, but I fear there may be problems not yet identified. On the Christian side it tends to be the Protestant churches who are involved, less so the Catholics who are numerically the biggest Christian denomination in the world. From the minority groups' side it tends to involve not necessarily the typical Hindu, Muslim, Zoroastrian, etc., rather those leaders whose linguistic and social skills enable them to interact with the 'outside world'. These 'gatekeepers' of the communities often emphasize the aspects of their religion that will find the most ready acceptance in the outside world, so with Zoroastrians they will emphasize the ancient (indeed the prophet Zoroaster's) emphasis on 'Good Thoughts, Good Words and Good Deeds' rather than, say, the purity laws. In time this sanitized version of the religion may impact back into the community. I read in one book of minutes from a Canadian Zoroastrian Group where the managing committee made a conscious decision to change the translation of an Avestan (roughly 'scriptural') text so that it would not offend Muslim guests. This is an issue which merits further study.

What of theology?

So far this chapter has focused on religious studies and comparative religion because this book is likely to be used mostly in the study of religions. For a member of any religion, its theology is important – the word is usually applied just to Christian thought, but there is comparable activity in most religions, certainly in Islam, Judaism and Zoroastrianism for example. (The late Ninian Smart often referred to Buddhology – and that may not be inappropriate.) 'Theologizing' is particularly important in many mystical groups, not least in Islam in the West (see Hinnells and Malik 2006). The Mullahs in Iraq and Iran have been prominent in recent times, exercising considerable influence over national politics with their teachings. For the billions of active religious people in the world, working out the implications of their crucial religious teachings for their daily life is of vital importance. Geography is far more important in the study of religions than is generally appreciated. Religious beliefs and ideas, symbols and practice, are naturally affected by social and geographical conditions in which the theology is elaborated. Religion in central New York is bound to have different symbols or images to cater for the different needs from those in a remote village in northern Scotland, which is in turn different in the deserts of Saudi Arabia or in India and Korea. I am fascinated by the differences between urban and rural patterns of religion. It is inevitable that if a theology is to be meaningful to a person, if it is 'to speak to that person', as many Christians would say, then it has to be different from that in a different environment. Such issues have probably been pursued more in the study of Buddhism, Hinduism or Islam than they have with Christianity (a notable exception is Ford 1997).

Can an atheist see the point in studying theology? Its value is that it addresses the big questions which many people want to ask – Who am I? Where do I come from? Where am I going? Why do the innocent suffer? What non-theologians often overlook with theology is the wide range of subjects involved – textual studies and languages, archaeology, philosophy, ethical issues, history and through applied theology there is an engagement with local communities. If theology was restricted to theological colleges and madrassas etc. the consequence would almost certainly be an increase in sectarian prejudice. But of course many people are religious, though they do not belong to a formal church yet they believe in a God. A lot of people outside the churches, the mosques, temples, etc. yearn for a 'spiritual' life and to them the study of theology and religious studies can be fulfilling. Secularism may be strong in Britain, but in many other countries religion is alive and well, not least in America.

The comparative study of religions

I am convinced by Max Müller's dictum: 'He who knows one knows none', that is if you only study one religion, you are not studying religion, but just, say, Christianity (or Zoroastrianism, or Islam, etc.). It is only through some element of comparison that we appreciate just what is, and is not, characteristic of religions generally and what is specific to that religion. The term 'comparative study of religion' is widely suspected, because it was used by particular Western academics, mainly in the nineteenth century, who were trying to prove that Christianity was superior to other religions. Some huge theories about 'religion' were constructed by writers who ranged widely across different religions – from the comfort of their armchairs and without the necessary first-hand knowledge of texts in the original language or without knowing people from that religion. The term 'comparative religion' has also been associated with superficiality because you cannot 'really' know much about a range of religions. But if comparative linguistics and comparative law, etc. are valid subjects then so, surely, 'the comparative study of religion' can be too. Of course I reject any idea of trying to compare to show the superiority of any one religion. When one is comparing it is essential to compare what is comparable, so should we compare the whole of one religion with the whole of another? In my study of the Parsi diaspora, it was helpful to compare the Parsi experience with that of Jews, or Hindus or Sikhs, etc. in that same context, which usually, but not necessarily, means in the same city or region. It has also been helpful to compare Parsis in different countries e.g. Britain, Canada and the US, or their experience in different cities in the US (e.g. Houston and Chicago). My theoretical question was 'how different is it being a religious Parsi, say, in Los Angeles or in London, or in Sydney or Hong Kong?' (Hinnells 2005). It is regrettable that there are not more comparative studies of diaspora religions in different countries so that we might discover what is, or are, *the* American (British/ Australian/Canadian) experience(s). It can also be helpful to compare the theology of different religions, e.g. on issues of attitudes to the body partly for doctors and nurses, or for the understanding of social groups (Law).

Obviously the comparative study of religion should not be concerned only with the modern world. Earlier in my career I was passionately interested in the Roman cult of Mithras (first to fourth centuries CE). In order to understand what was significant about Mithraism it was important to learn about contemporary religious beliefs and practices in the Roman Empire. There was such a rich diversity of religious cults; Mithraism shared features with some (e.g. early Christianity) and not with others. In fact the key breakthrough in the study of Mithraism came when Gordon and Beck began to look at the contemporary Roman ideas on astrology (Beck). By taking a blinkered look at just one cult, it would have been impossible to interpret the archaeological finds of temples and statues (especially difficult because there are virtually no Mithraic texts, only inscriptions and the comments of outsiders). One of the things which disturbs me about some work in New Testament studies and in research on Christianity's early developments is that so much of the evidence is looked at only through the lens of the Judaeo-Christian traditions. Can one really understand the development of the liturgy of the Mass/Eucharist/Lord's Supper without looking at the role of sacred meals in the contemporary Roman religions? Nothing exists in a vacuum. It seems odd that so many books and courses on the philosophy of religion look at key figures such as Hume and Kant without looking at their contemporary world; or studying the Biblical work of Bultmann without looking at the anti-Semitic culture in which he lived and worked and which many would say coloured his account of Judaism. Taking the context seriously, comparing other related phenomena, is crucial.

Bias

What of the theme of insider/outside? Can a person outside the religion really under-stand what it is like to be a Zoroastrian – or whatever? Even after thirty-five years of living with and studying Zoroastrians I think it is impossible for me to understand them and their religion fully. I may get close to it, but as an outsider my instincts, my basic thoughts and aspirations, etc. are, for better or worse, English. Ultimately we cannot change our basic conditioning; we cannot step outside our identity. We may – should – seek to go as far as possible in empathy and with understanding but we are all products of our own history.

It is vital that students and scholars should be conscious of their own motivations or biases – because we all have them. It is the ones we are not aware of that are the most dangerous: to illustrate the point with a story against myself. I am currently writing a book about the Parsis of Bombay in the days of the Raj. The book's structure seemed clear: defining key periods, important individual and social groupings; having worked on the history of temples, doctrinal changes, visited India many times over thirty years, and having worked with a high priest and each of us having the other as a house guest, I felt close to the community. Then a book came out which collected the oral histories of a broad spectrum of Parsis; some highly educated some not, some famous others not, about their personal private religious feelings (Kreyenbroek with Munshi 2001). It made me realize that with my atheistic attitude, despite my contacts with many Parsis, I had completely failed to look at the widespread belief in the miraculous powers of prayer; the importance of mantras to preserve people from misfortune and to bless and aid them in a project, i.e. the reality of miracles for many people. I had failed to look for what I don't believe in.

There is, of course, the alternative danger of being biased in favour of your subject. One can normally tell the denomination of a Church historian, or a theologian, from his/her writings. Authors rarely draw conclusions at variance with the teaching in their denomination. The same can be true of internal accounts of other religions, for example Orthodox and Liberal accounts of Judaism. There is often an honourable desire when making a university teaching appointment to look for someone who knows the tradition from the inside, be (s)he Muslim, Jewish, Sikh, Hindu, etc. Of course they can have a depth of insight that is beyond the outsider. But, as with Christianity, in principle the appointment should be solely on academic grounds. Many of those grounds, e.g. linguistic facility, may well make an insider the right appointment. But in recent years there have been difficult cases where such an appointee has been summoned to their religious council of elders and reprimanded for not teaching a particular perspective. There have been cases where an insider from one section of a religion has denied the others were true believers, but were heretics. This has happened in Christianity also when in recent years some theologians had papal support withdrawn and were not allowed to teach in a Catholic institution because they had 'deviated' from authorized Church teaching. There can be difficulties with insiders, as well as with outsiders.

Some time ago a publisher asked me to write a book on Zoroastrianism and the Parsis for English schools. It began to be used by Parsis in their Sunday schools and in some adult education classes. When the English edition lapsed, the Parsis in Bombay reprinted it and still sell it there and in some other centres around the world. At first it seemed to be the greatest possible compliment. Gradually however I began to worry. When I visited some communities my own words were coming back at me. With plant photography one must take great care never to break or destroy anything that is being photographed. How much greater care should one take with a living religion (especially one that is declining numerically at a great rate)? Should you affect the people you study? Can you get too close to your 'field'? Is it fanciful to think that you can avoid having an impact? What is the impact of a group of students going to a mosque or temple? Does it change an act of worship if there is an 'audience' of outsiders watching?

Using the right words

There are numerous debates about the meaning of key terms such as 'religion', 'culture', 'race', etc. This section is not about these important terms (a useful book for that is Taylor 1998), but rather it is concerned with terms that raise religious issues.

The first is to do with translations for key religious concepts. An obvious one is: should one write 'Allah', or 'God'? My vocabulary changes according to the audience. With Zoroastrians and students I use 'Ahura Mazda' (Pahlavi: Ohrmazd) rather than 'God'. The danger is of unconsciously importing Christian notions into the concept of the ultimate. However, if talking to the general public or perhaps in a lecture that is not essentially about theology the word 'God' may be appropriate, otherwise there are so many technical words that the listener (or reader) will switch off. But there are some technical words that it is essential to use because their obvious equivalent Western term would give a misleading impression. For example the terms 'spirit and flesh' are inappropriate for the Zoroastrian concepts of *menog* and *getig*. The *menog* is the invisible, intangible, the realm of the soul, *getig* is the visible and tangible world, but the *getig* world is not a subordinate or 'lower' world; it is almost the fulfillment of the *menog* – it is its manifestation. There is nothing of the Hellenistic 'spirit and flesh' dualism. A Zoroastrian could never make the connection 'the world, the flesh and the devil' for the *getig* world is the Good Creation of Ohrmazd. Misery, disease and death are the assault of the evil force, Ahriman, on the Good Creation; human duty is to fight evil and protect the Good Creation so that at the renovation *menog* and *getig* will come together to form the best of all possible worlds. Zoroastrians do not use the term 'the end of the world' for that would be Ohrmazd's defeat; instead they refer to the 'renovation', the time when all will be restored or refreshed and again becomes perfect as it was before the assault of evil. 'Spirit and flesh' therefore involve a different cosmology from *menog* and *getig*.

Sometimes scholars use Christian terms for concepts or practices in order to help the reader but it can lead to misrepresentation. For example, Zaehner uses the word 'sacrament' to describe one of the higher Zoroastrian ceremonies, the *Yasna* in which the *haoma* (*soma* in Hinduism) plant is pounded with pestle and mortar. The ceremony is led by two priests and can be performed at a time of death or for blessings. Laity may attend but rarely do so for the priests offer it on their behalf. This is Zaehner's description of the rite:

> The Haoma . . . is not only a plant . . . it is also a god, and the son of Ahura Mazdah. In the ritual the plant-god is ceremonially pounded in a mortar; the god, that is to say is sacrificed and offered up to his heavenly Father. Ideally Haoma is both priest and victim – the Son of God, then offering himself up to his heavenly Father. After the offering priest and faithful partake of the heavenly drink, and by partaking of it they are made to share in the immortality of the god. The sacrament is the earnest of everlasting life which all men will inherit in soul and body in the last days. The conception is strikingly similar to that of the Catholic Mass.
>
> (Zaehner 1959: 213)

Of course the Catholic convert, Zaehner, intended this as a very respectful account of the rite. But it bears no resemblance whatever to the Zoroastrian understanding of the ritual. There is a huge danger in failing to see the religion through the insider's spectacles.

An earlier writer, J. H. Moulton, is another good example of well-intentioned scholarly misrepresentation of another religion. Moulton was a Professor of New Testament Studies but took a keen interest in Zoroastrianism. He was also a Methodist Minister. In his Hibbert Lectures in 1912, he applied contemporary Protestant methods of Biblical scholarship to the study of Zoroastrianism. He applied the contemporary assumption that religions are divided between the priestly or prophetic forms; the former being associated with superstition and the latter with visionary, personal religious experience. He argued that since Zoroaster was clearly a prophet he could not have been a priest, so when Zoroaster refers to himself as a priest (which he explicitly did) then Moulton concluded he must have been speaking metaphorically. He concluded:

> That Zarathushtra is teacher and prophet is written large over every page of the Gathas [the poetic passages deriving from Zoroaster himself]. He is perpetually striving to persuade men of the truth of a great message, obedience to which will bring them everlasting life ... He has a revelation ... There is no room for sacerdotal functions as a really integral part of such a man's gospel; and of ritual or spells we hear as little as we expect to hear ...
>
> (p. 118)

A traditional Zoroastrian (or a Catholic Christian for that matter) would not make such a distinction between priestly and prophetic religion. These are but two examples of a widespread trend to impose Western ways of thinking, or methods of analysis, on non-Western phenomena. Misrepresentation does not arise only from prejudice against a religion, but can come equally from the well-intentioned scholar. Many scholars find it helpful to draw a typology of religions and these can be useful in classifying data, but they can also result in trying to fit data into a false dichotomy; it has to be 'either this, or that or that', etc. It rarely allows for 'this and that' – in Moulton's case either a prophet or a priest, but Zoroaster could be described as 'both ... and'.

Some of the most common words used in writing about religion are inappropriate or at least demand substantial clarification. 'Praying' and 'prayers' are words used in many religions, for example, in Christianity and Zoroastrianism. But the activities they refer to are somewhat different. In Western Christianity, prayers are in the vernacular and it is thought important to know what the words mean. Be the prayers intercessions or thanksgiving, there is an element of conversation with God. Prayers in Zoroastrianism are rather different. They should be in the ancient 'scriptural' Avestan language in which it is believed Zoroaster prayed to Ohrmazd. It does not matter if the worshipper does not understand them, indeed orthodox Parsi priests in India argue that it is unhelpful to understand the words, for if you do then you think about what they mean and thereby limit yourself to mere human conceptual thought. By praying in Avestan one seeks to share something of the visionary experience of the prophet, the purpose of prayer is to achieve direct experience of Ohrmazd in a trance-like state.

There are numerous terms in common usage which have presuppositions that merit questioning. The term 'faith community' implies that 'faith', i.e. a set of beliefs, is what defines a community and that is a Christian and intellectual understanding of the 'other'. For Jews and Parsis religion is to do with identity, a question of community boundaries, it is to do with who or what you are, something that is in the blood, the genes. For Parsis in particular, identity, far more than any set of beliefs, is what matters. For Muslims also it is a questionable term, since 'just' believing is inadequate, Islam is a way of life.

Another term in common usage which can cause religious offence is 'Old Testament'. Orthodox Jews object to it for it implies old, redundant, replaced. Most say that they have become accustomed to this Christian abuse of their scripture. Their preferred term though is 'Hebrew Bible'. The usual Christian reaction is to point out that a part (but only a very small part) is in Aramaic. But should students of religion use terms and phrases that can cause religious offence? The question becomes sharper when the word is used in the naming of university departments, of academic societies and books.

Conclusion

Whether one is religious or not, the study of religions is a key to understanding other cultures; religions have been powerful forces throughout history in any country, sometimes working for good and sometimes working to destroy. They have inspired some of the greatest and most noble of acts; equally they have inspired some of the most ruthless brutality. They have been the patrons – and the destroyers – of arts and cultures. But they are central to much social and political history. Scholars who have left religions out of their pictures when writing about various societies, be they Hindus in Britain or Muslims in America, are excluding a key element from their study. It is essential to know the values, ideals and priorities of those from another culture or religion with whom one comes into contact. Globalization makes such contact with 'the other' common. Religions might be compared to diamonds; they have many facets; they can be seen from many angles, but the pictures are too complex for any one writer to see the whole. This book looks at a range of approaches to these diamonds.

Bibliography

Beck, R. 1984, 'Mithraism Since Franz Cumont', in Temporini, H. and Haase, W. (eds), *Aufstieg und Niedergang der Romischen Welt*, II, 17, 4, Berlin: Walter De Gruyter, pp. 2002–115.

Bhugra, D. 1996, *Psychiatry and Religion: Context Consensus and Controversies*, London: Routledge.

Coward H., Hinnells, J. R. and Williams, R. B. (eds) 2000, *The South Asian Religious Diaspora in Britain, Canada, and the United States*, Albany: State University of New York Press.

Eck, D. 2000, 'Negotiating Hindu Identities in America', in Coward *et al.* 2000, pp. 219–37.

—— 2002, *A New Religious America*, San Francisco: Harper Collins.

Fitzgerald, T. 2000, *The Ideology of Religious Studies*, Oxford: Oxford University Press.

Ford, D. 1997, *The Modern Theologians: An Introduction to Christian Theology in the Twentieth Century*, Oxford: Blackwells.

Gustafson, C. and Juviler, P. (eds) 1999, *Religion and Human Rights: Competing Claims?*, New York: M. E. Sharpe publishers.

Haddad, Y. Y. 1991, *The Muslims of America*, New York: Oxford University Press.

—— 2000, 'At Home in the Hijra: South Asian Muslims in the United States', in Coward *et al.* 2000, pp. 239–58.

—— and Lummis, A. T. 1987, *Islamic Values in the United States*, New York: Oxford University Press.

Hawley, J. S. (ed.) 1994, *Fundamentalism & Gender*, New York: Oxford University Press.

Helman, C. G. 1984 (3rd edn 1994), *Culture, Health and Illness*, Oxford: Butterworth-Heinemann.

Hinnells, J. R. 1996, *Zoroastrianism and the Parsis*, Bombay: Zoroastrian Studies.

—— 1998, in Hinnells, *The New Penguin Handbook of Living Religions*, London: Penguin Books, pp. 819–47.

—— 2000, *Zoroastrian and Parsi Studies: Selected Works of John R. Hinnells*, Aldershot: Ashgate publishing (esp. chs 16–18 for this chapter).

—— 2005, *The Zoroastrian Diaspora: Religion and Migration*, Oxford: Oxford University Press.

—— and Malik, J. (eds), 2006, *Islamic Mysticism in the West*, Richmond: Curzon Press.

—— and Porter, R. (eds) 1999, *Religion Health and Suffering*, London: Kegan Paul International.

Honwana, A. M. 1999, 'Appeasing the Spirits: Healing Strategies in Post War Southern Mozambique', in Hinnells and Porter (eds) 1999, pp. 237–55.

Howarth, G. and Jupp, P. C. 1996, *Contemporary Issues in the Sociology of Death, Dying and Disposal*, Basingstoke: Macmillan Press.

Irish, D. P., Lundquist, K. F. and Nelsen, V. J. (eds) 1993, *Ethnic Variations in Dying, Death, and Grief*, Washington D.C.: Taylor & Francis.

Kreyenbroek, P. with Munshi, Shahnaz N. 2001, *Living Zoroastrianism: Urban Parsis Speak About Their Religion*, Richmond: Curzon Press.

Law, J. M. (ed.) 1995, *Religious Reflections on the Human Body*, Bloomington: Indiana University Press.

Littlewood, R. and Lipsedge, M. 1982 (3rd edn 1997), *Aliens and Alienists: Ethnic Minorities and Psychiatry*, London: Routledge.

McCutcheon, R. 2001, *Critics not Caretakers: Redescribing the Public Study of Religion*, Albany: State University of New York Press.

Melton, J. G. 1991, *The Encyclopaedia of American Religions*, New York: Triumph Books, (3 vols).

Moulton, J. H. 1913, *Early Zoroastrianism*, London: Williams and Norgate.

Naficy, H. 1991, 'The Poetics and Practice of Iranian Nostalgia in Exile', *Diaspora*, 1:3, pp. 285–302.

Nesbitt, P. D. (ed.) 2001, *Religion and Social Policy*, Walnut Creek/Lanham: Altamira Press.

Rack, P. 1982, *Race, Culture and Mental Disorder*, London: Tavistock Publications.

Sahgal, G. and Yuval-Davis, N. (eds) 1992, *Refusing Holy Orders: Women and Fundamentalism in Britain*, London: Virago.

Spiro, H. M., McCrea Curnen, M. and Wandel, L. P. (eds) 1996, *Facing Death: Where Culture Religion and Medicine Meet*, New Haven: Yale University Press.

Taylor, M. C. (ed.) 1998, *Critical Terms for Religious Studies*, Chicago: Chicago University Press.

Van de Veer, P. 1994, *Religious Nationalism: Hindus and Muslims in India*, Berkeley: University of California Press.

Van Zandt, D. E. 1991, *Living in the Children of God*, Princeton: Princeton University Press.

Warner, R. S. and Wittner, J. G. 1998, *Gatherings in Diaspora: Religious Communities and the New Immigration*, Philadelphia: Temple University Press.

Williams, R. B. 1988, *Religions of Immigrants from India and Pakistan*, Cambridge: Cambridge University Press.

—— 2000, 'Trajectories for Further Studies', in Coward *et al.* 2000, pp. 277–87.

Zaehner, R. C. 1959, 'Zoroastrianism' in Zaehner, R. C. (ed.), *Encyclopaedia of Living Faiths*, London: Hutchinson Books.

—— 1966, *Hinduism*, Oxford: Oxford University Press.

Chapter 2

The study of religion in historical perspective

Eric J. Sharpe

Motive, material, method

The academic study of anything requires that those involved should consider at least three questions: why, what and how? The first demands that we examine our *motive*; the second makes us consider our *material* – what do we accept as admissible evidence? The third, and most difficult, level of inquiry is concerned with *method*: how do we deal with the material we have at hand? How do we organise it, and with what end in view ('motive' again)? A century ago, it was not uncommon to speak in this connection of 'the science of religion' (German: *Religionswissenschaft*) – a form of words no longer current in English. What has been identified as the foundation document carried the title *Introduction to the Science of Religion* (Friedrich Max Müller 1873). According to Müller, such a science of religion was to be 'based on an impartial and truly scientific comparison of all, or at all events, of the most important religions of mankind' (1873: 34). It was, then, to be impartial and scientific by the standards of the age and based on the best material available at the time.

The history of the study of religion since the Enlightenment can never be told in full. There is simply too much of it, and it is subdivided in too many ways: by period, by geographical and cultural area and by the 'disciplines' cherished by most academics. The one history can be described as being made up of many smaller histories – for instance the history of the study of everything from Animism and Anabaptism to Zoroastrianism and Zen Buddhism. The field may be divided by subject matter; along national lines; depending on where in the world the tradition of study has been pursued; in relation to events in world and local history; and so on, virtually ad infinitum. No one can cover the whole of the area.

The words 'the study of religion' obviously convey different meanings to different people. For most of human history and in most cultures, they would have conveyed no meaning at all. To 'study' in the sense of standing back to take a coolly uncommitted view of anything, was not unknown in the ancient world, but it was uncommon, being cultivated by 'philosophers' – lovers of wisdom – but hardly elsewhere. Similarly, where what we call 'religion' is concerned: gods, goddesses, spirits, demons, ghosts and the rest, people knew and generally respected them (along with what it was hoped was the right way to please, or at least not to offend them); 'religion' they did not.

These supernatural beings – who were they? In the ancient world, they were envisaged in human terms: a hierarchy reaching all the way from a royal family down through nobles and artisans to mischief-makers: imps and demons of the sort who spread disease and curdle milk. There were the ghosts of the departed, still in many ways close at hand and with their remains buried nearby. (The unburied tended to turn into peculiarly nasty ghosts.) Sun, moon and stars watched; storms rampaged; forests and mountains brooded; powerful animals marked out their territories. 'Power' was perhaps the key to the world as archaic man saw it – power of heat over cold, light over darkness, life over death – and those who knew how to control that power became themselves powerful.

The process must have begun at some point in time, somewhere in the world, but we have no way of knowing when or where that point might have been (absolute origins of anything are always out of reach). When our records, such as they are, begin – numerical dates are worse than useless in such matters – we are already able to sense the presence of something or someone like a proto-shaman: at one and the same time a ruler and a servant of the spirits, a controller of rituals and an interpreter of laws and customs. From what we know of later shamanism, it would seem that such persons were servants of their respective societies by virtue of their knowledge of the spirit-world and their ability to establish and maintain contact with it. Shamanism 'proper' belongs in the context of hunter-gatherer societies, and as the structure of human societies changed, so too did the function of mediation between the tangible, everyday world and the unseen forces that were believed to control it.

The shaman was chosen and prepared for his (or in some cases, her) work, by aptitude, discipline and application, and by initiation – a pattern that survived most tenaciously in the trade guilds and those of the learned professions, which (untypically in the modern West) treasured their own past. In more complex societies – that of the agriculturalists and fisherfolk in their settled environments, that of the city-dwellers within their walls, and so on down to our own day and its bizarre preoccupation with economics – the functions of the shaman (serving the people by mediating between one order of being and another) have multiplied and diversified in an intriguing way.

This is not to say that the Pope or the Archbishop of Canterbury, or for that matter the Chief Rabbi or the Dalai Lama, or the Shankaracharya of Puri, are cryptoshamans: merely that their training on the one hand and their functions on the other, are of a kind one recognises. (How well or how indifferently individuals may fill high offices has no bearing on the question.) Each has a position in an ongoing tradition, and is responsible for its continuation. Here we have the first, and the dominant, sense in which what we call 'the study of religion' functions. It is appropriate to call this a *discipline* in the strictest sense, an apprenticeship in which a pupil (*discipulus*) is taught by a master (*magister*) inside the bounds of a system, within the frontiers of which both knew precisely what was to be taught to whom, and why. Since the wellbeing of individuals and societies depended in large measure on the maintenance of what it is perfectly proper to call 'law and order' much of what had to be learned was concerned with these concepts and their ramifications.

In many cultures, 'law' (in Sanskrit, *dharma*, in Hebrew, *torah* and in Latin, *religio*, even the much misunderstood Australian Aboriginal word 'dreaming') and 'religion' are almost synonymous. What one supposes began as habit hardened first into custom and eventually into law, on the basis of which boundaries could be set up and wars fought. In the ancient world, no one expected laws, or religions, to be all of one kind. The 'when in Rome . . .' principle was, and often still is, no more than common sense:

deities, like humans and animals, were to some extent territorial, and to pay one's respects to a *genius loci* was no more than courtesy. Customs differed in much the same way as languages differed, and normally even the learned would know very little of what went on outside the family. 'Study' was for the most part concerned only with the family's (tribe's, nation's) traditions, history, sacred places and the rituals associated with them. In time, as more of this material was committed to writing, the study of those writings assumed a central place in the student's apprenticeship: often through memorisation and constant repetition and chanting, in a setting in which the student's submissive obedience was simply taken for granted. This pattern of education is still operative today, though unevenly; generally speaking, Judaism, Islam, the ancient traditions of the East – varieties of Hinduism and Buddhism – have held fast to the method where instruction in the secular West has not.

What did the student make of other peoples' traditions, their deities, their rituals and their laws? In the ancient world, there were, roughly speaking, three alternatives: to ignore them altogether (the majority view), to observe them as curiosities, without taking them too seriously, and to condemn them as evil. Let us consider the second and third of these.

Greek and Roman 'philosophers' and historians were in many cases intrigued by the customs of the various peoples they met around the Mediterranean and as far afield as northern Europe. Perhaps they did not take their own national myths and rituals too seriously. At all events, the Greek and Roman historiographers, beginning with Herodotus (died approx. 420 BCE) showed a certain amount of interest in other people's behaviour where gods and the like were concerned. Berosus and Manetho (both third century BCE) wrote about ancient Egypt and Mesopotamia, Herodotus having previously written about the Persians. In the second century BCE Pausanias compiled an extensive and invaluable account of rituals and places of worship in his native Greece. The Romans for their part made fewer contributions, though special mention may be made of the accounts of the customs of the Celtic and Germanic tribes contained in 'war reports' like Caesar's *De bello Gallico* and Tacitus' *Germania*. Such writings as these (and there were many more) were compiled as information and entertainment, and to some extent propaganda: not as systematic accounts of anything. Tacitus 'studied' Celtic and Germanic tribes because they were troublesome to the Roman legions, and that was all.

The Hebraic attitude to such things could not have been more different. Israel knew all about 'the nations' and their deities, and trusted none of them. To the extent that other people's religion appears in the Hebrew Scriptures/Old Testament, it does so under a black cloud. Egypt and Mesopotamia – oppression. Canaan – apostasy. Persia – a brief glimpse of light. Rome – more oppression, this time apparently terminal, as the Temple was laid waste and the people scattered. Understanding? What was there to understand, except that the gods of the nations were impostors, small-time crooks, perhaps not without local influence, but entirely incapable of any act of creation. Least of all could they create a world, as Yahweh had done. They were mere 'idols', man-made and powerless. It is all summed up in two verses, 'For all the gods of the peoples are idols; but the Lord made the heavens' (Ps. 96:5); and 'The gods who did not make the heavens and the earth shall perish from the earth and from under the heavens' (Jer. 10:11).

There was the additional frightening possibility that 'idols' were nests of 'evil spirits' – unseen vermin whose existence was never properly explained, but whose malevolence no one in the ancient world seriously have doubted.

We find a partial relaxation of this uncompromising attitude in respect of the worship of natural phenomena – sun, moon and stars. These were at least God's creations, and not man-made objects, and may therefore be admired for the sake of their Creator, to whom ideally they ought to point the way. Human beings, however, are incorrigibly obtuse, and go off in pursuit of 'idols' even so. A classical statement of this attitude is to be found in Paul's Letter to the Romans (1:20–23):

> Ever since the creation of the world his invisible nature, namely, his eternal power and deity, has been clearly perceived in the things that have been made . . . [but to no avail] Claiming to be wise, they became fools, and exchanged the glory of the immortal God for images resembling mortal man or birds or animals or reptiles . . .

All of this carried over into early Christianity, later Judaism and later still, Islam. There is one God, who has created, and will ultimately judge, the world; he has made his will known to humanity through his servants the Prophets, though his power may be recognised in what he has created. To 'study' in this connection was to know and obey the will of God, as set forth in successive writings – historical records, prophecies, hymns, statutes and apocalyptic, visionary writings. We have no need to enter into further details, except to point out that in Judaism the heart of the matter is the Law (Torah) itself, in Christianity the person and work of Jesus Christ, and in Islam again the Law, as revealed afresh to Muhammad; in all three traditions, the dividing line between truth and falsehood was sharply marked (in some modern versions of Judaism and especially Christianity, it has grown less so, modernism and Islam meanwhile remaining largely irreconcilable).

All this stands out in sharp contrast to the spirit of detached inquiry we find in Greek philosophy. Where the Classical cultures had philosophers, the Judaeo-Christian-Muslim tradition had prophets and their disciples, whose business was less to inquire than to obey. The tension between them has been felt repeatedly in Western religious and intellectual history, and it is well that we recognise where it all began. On the one side there are the conservatives, who love and respect tradition and continuity; on the other there are the inquirers, the radicals, the freethinkers (or however else fashion may label them). The terminology is constantly changing, but today's alternatives would seem to be 'fundamentalist' (meaning conservative) and 'pluralist' (which may mean anything, but is obviously anti-fundamentalist).

What of the Orient in all this? Here we must be brief, but in the Hindu and Buddhist traditions, to 'study religion' has always meant to place oneself under spiritual guidance, either by private arrangement with a guru, or as a member of a community of monks or nuns. In either case, the disciple's relationship to a guru has always been paramount: to be accepted as a disciple, or a novice, is to be prepared to show unquestioning obedience to the guru in everything, however trivial or apparently unreasonable. Not until you have made your submission in faith (Sanskrit: *shraddha*) to a teacher, can you begin to be taught. *What* is to be taught, it is entirely up to the guru to decide. The process of teaching and learning is strictly one-way, from the guru to the disciple, whose role is generally limited to the asking of respectful questions and absorbing the teacher's answers, either in writing or (more often) by memorisation – a method still common enough in our own day, despite repeated attempts to discourage it.

We who live in the age of information, with every conceivable fact instantly available to anyone capable of pressing the right computer keys in the right order, find it hard to imagine a time when very little was known about our world and its inhabitants, and what little was known, had to be fitted into existing paradigms. At the end of the first millennium, the West divided religion into four categories, and only four: Christendom, Jewry, Islam and 'paganism' – an *omnium gatherum* for everything that did not sort under the first three. As to the study of religion, one studied within the framework of one's own tradition. To be sure, there was a certain curiosity value in other people's customs: travellers' tales have never lacked an audience, and although the genre invited exaggeration and a concentration on the previously unknown and the bizarre, world literature between the fifth and the fifteenth centuries (the 'dark ages' of Western culture) was full of fresh information concerning people's beliefs and customs, myths and rituals.

In his fascinating book *The Discoverers* (1983) Daniel Boorstin wrote that:

> The world we now view from the literate West – the vistas of time, the land and the seas, the heavenly bodies and our own bodies, the plants and animals, history and human societies past and present – had to be opened for us by countless Columbuses . . . .
>
> (p. xv)

Discoveries are not inventions. One discovers what is already there to be discovered; one invents what is *not* already there. Discovery is in a sense the archaeology of ideas, the finding afresh of what, somewhere and at some time, was once common knowledge but which the world has since forgotten. But having discovered, one has to find some way of incorporating the new information into one's existing frames of reference. In the Christian West, that meant in practice sorting each new wave of information into the categories set forth in the Bible, with occasional footnotes supplied by 'the ancients'. There were true and false gods and goddesses; there was the sin of idolatry; there were sacrifices offered to 'demons' and various related abominations. This was the only viable principle of measurement: by reference to the (so far) unquestioned and unquestionable data of revelation, as stated in Holy Writ and interpreted by the Holy Church. Not until the advent of evolutionary theory toward the end of the nineteenth century did the would-be student of religion have an alternative method to fall back upon.

'Discoveries' came thick and fast, once navigation had become a tolerably exact business, and exploration by sea (as distinct from the overland treks of antiquity) developed. Judaism and Islam were already known, though little understood – in Islam's case, against a background of fear fuelled by the Crusades. The Enlightenment (German, *Aufklärung*) was more interested in China and its (apparently) rational approach to religion than in alternative monotheism or pagan superstitions. Most of the Enlightenment's information about China came directly from the reports of Jesuit missionaries, among whom the first was Matteo Ricci (1552–1610), who idealised Chinese 'religion' as a system without 'priestcraft' (the bugbear of the Age of Reason), but in possession of high moral virtues. At much the same time other Jesuits were writing about the indigenous peoples of north America in similar terms; the phrase 'the noble savage' seems to have been coined by John Dryden (1631–1700) in his *Conquest of Granada* (1670), the point being that virtue can and does flourish beyond the boundaries of Western urban civilisation. The 'noble savage' was (or seemed to be) the antithesis of modern urban man – an image which has since proved remarkably resilient.

What manner of religion might 'the noble savage' have known and observed? On this point, the unorthodox Western intelligentsia in the seventeenth and especially the eighteenth century were of one mind. Ruling out supernatural revelation and its (supposed) manifestations as a matter of principle, but retaining a core of belief in a divine moral order, there was proposed a system of basic religion, resting on five 'common notions': that there is a God, a supreme power; that this power is to be worshipped; that the good order or disposition of the human faculties is the best part of divine worship; that vices and crimes must be eliminated through sorrow and repentance; and that there is a future life, in which virtue will be rewarded and vice punished. This was 'natural religion', later known as 'deism'. First formulated in the early seventeenth century by Lord Herbert of Cherbury (1583–1648) in his *De Veritate* (1624), and restated with variations ever since, 'natural religion' of this kind was passionately anti-ecclesiastical and contemptuous of rites and rituals, doctrines and dogmas, which it dismissed as 'priestcraft'. Its adherents long found access to faculties of theology/divinity practically impossible, but they were able to exercise an indirect influence on the study of religion from elsewhere in the academy.

The nineteenth century

Betweeen 1801 and 1901 the Western world passed through a time of unprecedented intellectual change. At the dawn of the century, Napoleon, having failed to conquer Egypt, was on the point of trying to impose his will on Europe; the formality of what Tom Paine called 'The Age of Reason' had begun to lose ground to those who valued the spontaneous more than the coolly calculated, and the natural more than the artificial. The Romantic movement (as it came to be called) left its mark on literature, music (where Beethoven and Berlioz were the greatest romantics of all) – and on both the practice and the study of religion. It did not begin in 1801. Romanticism had been years in the preparation among those for whom the dry categories of order for order's sake had no appeal.

Where the practice of religion in the West was concerned, little in 1801 differed greatly from what it had been a century earlier, except perhaps the new factor of Protestant revivalism which had begun with the Wesleys in England in the 1730s, and which in the nineteenth century was to lead to the Protestant missionary movement, and indirectly to the making available of vast quantities of material (of unequal value, naturally) for scholars to work on. Otherwise there were Protestants, Catholics and freethinkers; outside, there were Jews, Muslims and assorted pagans, about whom little was known other than by rumour and hearsay. A massive work like William Hurd's *New Universal History of the Religious Rites, Ceremonies and Customs of the Whole World*

(1788) is instructive in this regard, representing as it does what the educated but non-specialist reader might find of religious interest in the foundation year of the New South Wales penal colony. It was not the only compilation of its kind: the putting together of encyclopaedias was common enough in the eighteenth century. But it is instructive in its concentration on 'rites, ceremonies and customs', on the externals of religion in the non-Christian world. Often it was wildly inaccurate, sometimes to the modern reader (of whom I suspect I may be the only one) reminiscent of *Indiana Jones and the Temple of Doom*. In those days the heathen were expected to perform bizarre rituals and carry out abominable sacrifices in the name of their idols – the Bible said so! What else there might be behind the rituals, very few in the West knew.

The tide was about to turn, however. China, the West knew after a fashion. Before, almost until the end of the eighteenth century, India was a mystery within an enigma within a locked box. The Muslim north was known in part. Its official language was Persian before it was English; and it was through the medium of Persian that the West first gained a limited access to, first, Hindu laws (Halhed, *A Code of Gentoo Laws*, 1776, collected in Sanskrit, translated into Persian, then retranslated into English), and later, a number of *Upanishads*, this time from Sanskrit to Persian to Latin. Then in 1785 there appeared Charles Wilkins' translation of the *Bhagavadgita*, followed four years later by William Jones' translation of Kalidasa's play *Sakuntala* (1789), both this time directly from Sanskrit to English. No 'temple of doom' here. Instead, an India heavy with the scent of jasmine and sandalwood and a home, not of grotesque ceremonies but of timeless wisdom.

In the early years of the nineteenth century, while the fearsome figure of Napoleon was rampaging around Europe, India was coming to serve Europe and America as a landscape of the mind, and an antidote to the crass materialism that had emerged in the wake of the industrial revolution. This was not the 'real' India at all, but it served its purpose. And when it transpired that there was more to Indian thought than caste, cow-worship and suttee, India grasped and held the romantic imagination. One thing, however, was lacking: knowledge of Hindusm's most ancient scriptures, known collectively as the Veda (meaning knowledge), of which the oldest part, a collection of over a thousand ritual texts, was the *Rigveda*. Long kept secret from outsiders, its Sanskrit text was finally published, at the East India Company's expense, between 1849 and 1862, under the editorship of a German scholar working in Oxford, Friedrich Max Müller (1823–1900).

Müller was a pivotal figure in the study of religion in the West during the second half of the nineteenth century. He belonged firmly within the orbit of German Romanticism (his father wrote the poems set to music by Schubert as *Die schöne Müllerin* and *Winterreise*), he was a good friend of Ralph Waldo Emerson, and is said to have been a fine pianist. In religious terms he was (for want of a better word) a broad-church liberal Christian. One thing he was not: he was not a Darwinian.

Between 1801 and 1860 the raw material on which the study of religion is based multiplied at an extraordinary rate. What most of all captured the attention of a broader public was that involving the 'truth' of the Bible, and especially its chronology. We have no need to go into detail, though we may need to remind ourselves that in these years (before 1860), the study of religion sorted into two separate compartments: that which related to the world of the Bible (Egypt, Mesopotamia, Canaan, Iran, Greece and Rome); and that which did not (the rest), with Islam somewhere in between.

The Victorian anthropologists

Those who persist in believing 'the Victorian Age' to have been a time of smug self-satisfaction in matters of religion, delude themselves. For one thing, it was a very long period of time, and little of what was taken for granted in the 1830s still held good in 1900. No doubt there were smug and self-satisfied individuals, then as always, human nature being what it is. But with regard to religion, the second half of the nineteenth century saw practically everything called into question, somewhere, by someone. Then, as later, the chief focus of controversy was the word of the Bible: was it, or was it not, 'true' and therefore infallible, or at least authoritative? And if not, what leg has faith left to stand on?

On the negative side, some controversialists quite clearly said and wrote what they did chiefly to challenge the authority of the Church. The world could not have been created as described in Genesis, in 4004 BC. There had never been an Adam and Eve, a flood, a parting of the Red Sea. Further on, there had been no Virgin Birth, no Resurrection – the existence of Jesus himself was at least doubtful, and so on.

There was nothing new about this, battles having been fought over precisely this territory since the days of Lord Herbert of Cherbury and the deists in the early seventeenth century. But a blanket condemnation of 'miracles' and the supernatural was one thing; proposing a plausible alternative was another matter entirely. Before the middle years of the nineteenth century, though there was no shortage of fresh material, there was no comprehensive method with which to treat it, once one had abandoned the hard-and-fast 'truth-versus-falsehood' categories of Christian tradition. *Evolution* filled that gap from the 1880s on.

Say 'evolution' and one thinks at once of Charles Darwin and his epoch-making book *On the Origin of Species* (1859). Darwin had very little to say directly about religion, either for or against (Ellegård 1958). Some of his contemporaries were however less cautious. The most widely read of those writing in English was the popular philosopher Herbert Spencer (1820–1904), who took Darwin's biological theory and made it into a universal explanation of life on earth and its social institutions – government, language, literature, science, art and of course religion. All these things began with simple forms: *homo sapiens* had evolved out of something prior to and simpler than man (exactly what, no one knew, though the hunt for 'fossil man' was pursued with diligence); religion had therefore evolved out of something cruder than *Hymns Ancient and Modern*. What that 'something' might be, no one could possibly know (Trompf 1990). Conjecture was inevitable. Of the various theories put forward in the late nineteenth century, that labelled 'animism' has stood the test of time better than most. The term was launched by the Oxford anthropologist E. B. Tylor, in his important book *Primitive Culture* (1871), who declared that religion began with 'a belief in Spiritual Beings', prompted by reflection on the phenomena of dream and death. Suppose that I dream about my father, who died in 1957 (I do, as it happens): is that evidence that he is still alive in some other order of being? If majorities count, most of the world's population has always believed so. There is then at least some reason to inscribe 'animism' on religion's birth certificate, as indeed those wanting religion without revelation urged.

But might there perhaps be some even earlier stage, less explicit than animism? Tylor's successor at Oxford, R. R. Marett, thought there was, and called it 'preanimism', without dreams and reflections on the mystery of death, but with a sense of the uncanny and of supernatural power (Polynesian/Melanesian *mana*). Marett's book *The Threshold of Religion* (1909) set out the arguments.

A quite different attack on the animistic theory came from the Scottish man of letters Andrew Lang (1844–1912), who had begun as a classicist and specialist on Homer, was for a time a disciple of Tylor, but in the end struck out on his own. From his Tylorian years comes his first anthropological book, *Custom and Myth* (1884). *Myth, Ritual and Religion* (1887) marks a transition, and his mature position was stated in *The Making of Religion* (1898). Lang's final argument was that there was no way in which animism was capable of evolving into ethical monotheism. Again and again the anthropological evidence had recorded belief in 'high gods' – conceptions of a Supreme Being, divine rulers and creators – which the evolutionists had simply chosen to ignore or dismiss as proof of 'the missionaries' tampering with the evidence. Lang tried to let the evidence speak for itself. He never claimed to have cracked the code, merely that '. . . alongside of their magic, ghosts, worshipful stones . . . most of the very most backward races have a very much better God than many races a good deal higher in civilisation . . .' (Sharpe 1986: 63).

Lang was a public figure only in what he wrote. Having resigned his Oxford fellowship on his marriage, he held no farther academic position, living entirely by his pen. His versatility was extraordinary – historian, novelist, minor poet, psychic researcher, biographer, translator of Homer: he was sometimes ironical and often inaccurate, but never dull. His anthropological investigations were undertaken almost in his spare time, though he once confessed that given the opportunity, he might have devoted more time to anthropology. As it was, his hints and suggestions proved extremely fruitful. When he died in 1912, the Austrian ethnologist Wilhelm Schmidt had just published the first volume of his massive work *Der Ursprung der Gottesidee* (in the end twelve volumes in all), in which Lang's 'high gods' were taken very seriously indeed.

Another celebrated Scottish anthropologist to leave his mark on the study of religion was James George Frazer (1854–1951), still remembered as the tireless and unworldly author of *The Golden Bough* (1922), a compendium of practically everything sorting under what was then called 'primitive' religion, including folklore (domestic anthropology). For many years now, Frazer has been branded the archetypal 'armchair anthropologist', all of whose material was second-hand, having been raked together by casual observers whose motives were variable and whose accuracy was open to question. The criticism was justified up to a point, but Frazer did what he could to verify his sources, and was well aware of the risks he was running. In any case, the task of pulling together the growing bodies of evidence concerning archaic and vernacular religions needed to be undertaken by someone.

Frazer might well have become the first professor of comparative religion in the UK. In 1904 he was approached with a view to taking up such a post at the University of Manchester, but in the end declined, on the grounds that he was not a fit and proper person to instruct young men preparing for the Christian ministry. One wonders what might have become of the study of religion at Manchester, had Frazer's scruples been overcome!

The history of religion school

Between about 1890 and the outbreak of the first world war in 1914, a prominent position in Protestant religious scholarship was occupied by a group of fairly young biblical scholars, most of them Germans, known collectively as *die Religionsgeschichtliche Schule* (the history of religion (not 'religions') school). Their leaders were Wilhelm Bousset on the New Testament and Hermann Gunkel on the Old Testament side, and their chief theorist was Ernst Troeltsch (1865–1923), who, almost alone of the group, is still read today, thanks largely to his book *Die Absolutheit des Christentums und die Religionsgeschichte* (1902, belated Eng. tr. *The Absoluteness of Christianity and the History of Religions*, 1971). The principles of the movement were threefold: first, to focus on religion rather than on theology; second, to concentrate on popular expressions of religion rather than on high-level statements *about* religon; and thirdly, to examine closely the environment of the Old and New Testments, rather than merely treating them as the free-floating (and divinely inspired) texts of orthodox tradition. The productivity of the young men making up the movement was remarkable, though relatively little of their work found its way into English. The trouble was that, like the Deists of the seventeenth and eighteenth centuries, they were generally political radicals, socialists and populists at a time and in a country where socialism was held to be only one step removed from treason.

To the members of the school, the world or scholarship nevertheless owes a great deal, for liberating the study of the Bible from its dogmatic straitjacket, for opening up the worlds of 'later Judaism' and the Hellenistic mystery religions, and for demonstrating that conspicuous piety is no substitute for sound scholarship where the study of religion is concerned. Special mention may be made of their work on the religious traditions of ancient Iran, Egypt and Mesopotamia. Iran was important mainly because of the towering figure of the prophet Zoroaster/Zarathustra (perhaps c.1200 BCE), whose teachings seemed to anticipate those of the Judaeo-Christian tradition at a number of points, in particular eschatology (death, judgement and the future life). Also, there were myriad points of contact between Iran and India. There emerged a new label, 'Indo-European', as an alternative to 'Aryan' as a blanket term for everything from the languages of north India to those of northern Europe. (The sinister overtones of 'Aryan' as the equivalent of 'non-Jewish' came later.)

Other advances that were registered toward the end of the nineteenth century in the academic study of religion concerned Egypt and Mesopotamia, thanks in both cases to the decipherment of what had previously been unreadable scripts, hieroglyphic and cuneiform respectively. We cannot go into details, but in both cases sober history and wild surmise combined. In Egypt's case, speculation went all the way from the bizarre theories of the Mormons (invented before the hieroglyphs had been deciphered) to the Egyptian origins of monotheism, which Sigmund Freud wrote about and may even have believed in, and the universal diffusionism of the Australian Grafton Elliot Smith, which claimed Egypt as the cradle of the whole of western civilisation. A controversial expression of what came to be called 'pan-Babylonism' was a series of lectures on 'Babylon and the Bible' (*Babel und Bibel*), delivered in Berlin by Friedrich Delitzsch in 1902–5, which claimed that everything of value in the Old Testament was copied from Babylonian sources – the creation and flood narratives, the Sabbath, the notion of sin and much more.

The 'father' of the history of religion school (as distinct from its propagandists) had been the great historian Adolf (von) Harnack (1851–1930). In 1901 Harnack, also lecturing in Berlin, had argued *against* the widening of the theological curriculum to include non-biblical religions, chiefly on the grounds that the result would be dilettantism and superficiality. If comparative religion were to be taught at the universities, it should be in faculties of arts/humanities, and not under the aegis of theology. (Eventually, this was more or less what happened.) A somewhat different point of view was that of the Swedish scholar Nathan Söderblom (1866–1931), who argued in his Uppsala inaugural lecture of 1901 that there should be no artificial barrier between biblical religion and the rest, and that comparative religion (*religionshistoria*) should be an essential part of the theological curriculum. Three years later comparative religion in fact became an integral though subordinate part of the theological programme of the University of Manchester.

The trouble, though, was that often, the advocates of *Religionsgeschichte* (comparative religion) were at best indifferent and at worst hostile to theology as the churches understood it and the faculties taught it. And of course vice versa. Hence in most universities the study of 'other religions' came to be scattered around departments of history, anthropology, classics, Semitic studies and the like, and kept separate from theology. So it remained until the onset of 'the religious studies movement' in the 1960s.

Psychology and the mystics

The years around the turn of the nineteenth to twentieth century saw the emergence of many new 'sciences', among them 'the science of religion'. Within that science there were soon sub-sciences, of which the psychology of religion and the sociology of religion were the most significant. If two books were to be picked out as foundation documents of these sub-sciences, they might well be William James' *The Varieties of Religious Experience* (1977) on the psychological side, and Émile Durkheim's *The Elementary Forms of the Religious Life* (1915) on the sociological, though neither marks an absolute beginning. The difference between them is easily stated. Whereas the psychology of religion was, to begin with, concerned only with the individual's mental processes as they relate to religion, the sociology of religion saw (and still sees) religion as a collective, social phenomenon.

In both cases the formative years were the 1890s. This has nothing to do with the character of religion itself, which has always involved individuals and societies in equal measure. In psychology's case, the initial question concerned the mechanism by which the individual comes to experience sensations and feelings that he or she identifies as supernatural, and the consequences to which this may lead. The old alternatives had been divine inspiration on the one hand, and demonic deception on the other (speaking here in Judaeo-Christian terms). But suppose there were nothing supernatural involved. What then?

Interestingly enough, a number of the first psychologists of religion were Americans. Religious individualism was endemic in nineteenth-century America, especially among the heirs of the Enlightenment, such as Emerson and the New England Transcendentalists. 'Individualism ... was common enough in the Europe of the nineteenth century; in America, it was part of the very air men breathed' (Nisbet 1965: 4). This was due in part to the importance of the individual 'conversion experience' as the major criterion by which the genuineness of religion was judged. Sectarian extremism was also common, some parts of America even coming to resemble a menagerie of frequently warring sects. Add to this the impact of phenomena as diverse as exploration, industrialisation, migration, half-understood Darwinism and not least the Civil War, and it is not hard to grasp the fascinated energy with which intellectuals tackled religious questions. Here an important book was Andrew Dickson White's *A History of the Warfare of Science with Theology in Christendom* (1955). White, the first President of Cornell University, was writing too early to incorporate psychology into his account; he was not irreligious, but was passionately opposed to the imposition of 'theological' limits on free enquiry.

The first psychologists of religion in America are all but forgotten today – Granville Stanley Hall, James H. Leuba and Edwin D. Starbuck among them. Starbuck is worth a special mention as the first to work with questionnaires as a means of gathering material. How do you find out what people experience as 'religion'? Simple: ask them! The results of his enquiries took shape in his book *The Psychology of Religion* (1899). Starbuck also taught a course in the psychology of religion at Harvard in 1894–5. The major emphasis of his questionnaires was on 'religious experience' in general, and the experience of conversion in particular. The method as such was deeply flawed, but won approval as a means of breaking away from the crude choice between divine inspiration and demonic deception as explanations of 'the conversion experience'.

Starbuck's material was used (and duly acknowledged) by his Harvard teacher William James in preparation for the lectures delivered in Scotland and published in 1977 as *The Varieties of Religious Experience* – one of the few religious classics of the twentieth century. William James, (1842–1910), the elder brother of the novelist Henry James, came of Swedenborgian stock, though his personal religion was an undogmatic theism. He trained as a doctor, but never practised medicine. Then he became fascinated by the infant science of psychology, and for years worked on his one and only book, *The Principles of Psychology* (1890) – all his later publications were tidied-up lectures, *Varieties* being his unquestioned masterpiece.

James was writing (or rather, speaking) as what he called a 'radical empiricist', a pragmatist who was convinced that where religion was concerned, judgement is possible only on a basis of the results to which it leads – religion is what religion does, not what it claims to be able to do. He drew a famous distinction between two religious temperaments: that of the 'healthy-minded' – positive, optimistic, relatively unconcerned with the problem of evil – and that of 'the sick soul' – obsessed with the sense of its own unworthiness, inadequacy and (in Christian terms) sin. 'Let sanguine healthymindedness do its best with its strange power of living in the moment and ignoring and forgetting, still the evil background is really there to be thought of, and the skull will grin in at the banquet' (James 1977: 140).

James also anticipated in *Varieties* what in the 1960s was to become one of the bugbears of the study of religion, by introducing the subject of artificially induced 'religious' experience through drugs, even going so far as to experiment himself with nitrous oxide ('laughing gas') and to suggest that if there should be supernatural revelation, the 'neurotic' temperament might be better able to receive it than the well-adjusted.

There were major flaws in James' approach to his subject, and this may be the time to mention them briefly. One was entirely deliberate, namely, his exclusion of religion's social dimension from his inquiry: 'religion' he limited to 'the feelings, acts, and experiences of individual men in their solitude, so far as they apprehend themselves to stand in relation to whatever they may consider the divine' (James 1977: 31). How far individuals feel, act and experience because of the environment in which they live, with all its precedents, images, taboos, expectations and the rest, he does not discuss. More important was the assumption, shared by all those who have ever used questionnaire material, that the individual actually *knows*, fully consciously, what he or she believes and why – and this is not always safe, as Freud and Jung were shortly to show.

Lectures XVI and XVII in *Varieties*, James devoted to the subject of 'Mysticism', which we might perhaps characterise as religious experience at its most intensive. Wisely, he did not attempt to define this notoriously slippery word, but identified 'ineffability', 'noetic quality' (the quality of self-authenticating knowledge), 'transiency' and 'passivity' as a 'mystical group' of states of consciousness (James 1977: 380–2). Whether mysticism is therefore to be welcomed or avoided had long been disputed territory. *Mystik* had long been regarded by theologians (especially those of the Catholic tradition) as something entirely positive, a mark of divine favour; *Mysticismus* was the word used by German-speaking rationalists to denote irrationality and delusion in religion, in practically the same sense as 'enthusiasm'. The English language was in the unfortunate position of having only one word to cover both senses. Either way, 'mysticism' came in the years around the turn of the century to serve as a catch-all term for all that sorted under the categories of visions, voices, trances and what today we call 'altered states of consciousness'; but also to label religious intensity. At the back of all this was what was the mystic's desire to achieve oneness with the Ultimate Reality – or alternatively, a mental disorder of some kind, depending on one's presuppositions.

One cannot 'study' mystics, except to the extent that they are prepared to write or speak about their experiences. There was however no lack of such material, and beginning in the years around the turn of the century there appeared a number of significant works on the subject. The first of these was W. R. Inge's *Christian Mysticism* (1899), followed by, among others, James' *Varieties*, Nathan Söderblom's *Uppenbarelsereligion* (*The Religion of Revelation*, 1903, which drew the important distinction between theistic and non-theistic expressions of religious faith), Friedrich von Hügel's massive *The Mystical Element of Religion* (1908), Rufus Jones' *Studies in Mystical Religion* (1909) and Evelyn Underhill's *Mysticism* (1940). At the end of this line we may perhaps place J. B. Pratt's *The Religious Consciousness* (1920). It is perhaps worth noting that the last four authors mentioned were Roman Catholic, Quaker, uneasy Anglican and Unitarian respectively: clearly religious experience bore no particular relation to Christian denominationalism. Pratt's horizon was however wider: he had a lively interest in India, writing with regard to Buddhism that he had '. . . tried to enable the reader to understand a little *how it feels to be a Buddhist*' (Sharpe 1986: 115f. emphasis in original).

It was slightly ironical that Pratt's book should have been called *The Religious Consciousness*, since by the time it appeared, Freud, Jung and their respective bands of followers had most effectively called in question the very idea of consciousness as a decisive factor in human conduct. The new psychologists, wrote Sir John Adams in 1929, '. . . know exactly what they want and are quite clear about the way they propose to attain it. There is a lion in their path; they want that lion killed and decently buried. This lion is Consciousness . . .' (Sharpe 1986: 197). The Freudians, the Jungians and the rest of the psychoanalytical establishment did not pretend to scholarship in the area of religion, and some of their ventures into the field were quite bizarre; their profession was medicine, after all. But whereas Freud and his followers treated religion as part of the problem where mental health was concerned, the Jungians took a more positive view of religious mythology and symbolism. The psychoanalytical cause became fashionable in the years following the insanity of the First World War, not least in America, and cast a long shadow.

As an example, we may quote the case of the American anthropologist Margaret Mead (1902–1978), author of the celebrated *Coming of Age in Samoa* (1928), which proved, entirely to its author's satisfaction, that adolescence can be practically pain-free, once the sexual restraints imposed by society have been relaxed. Mead was a protegée of Franz Boas, a determined Freudian. Margaret Mead was no more than 23 when she did the field-work on which her book was based, and many years later one of her chief Samoan informants confessed that the girls who had supplied her with material had been pulling her leg (Freeman 1983). It did not matter. Her teacher Franz Boas wrote that: 'The results of her painstaking investigation confirm the suspicion long held by anthropologists, that much of what we ascribe to human nature is no more than a reaction to the restraints put upon us by civilisation' (Mead 1928: viii). 'Field-work' was of the essence, no matter how poorly equipped the investigator – an attitude which passed in the course of time to the study of religion.

Psychoanalysis aside, other issues divided students of religion in the early years of the twentieth century. Another relatively new science was the science of sociology – collective, rather than individual human behaviour. A key concept in this connection was 'holiness/sacredness' (the adjectives 'sacred' and 'holy' are generally interchangeable; 'the sacred' and 'the holy' are on the other hand abstractions).

There were two alternatives: on the psychological (and often the theological) side, what was up for investigation was 'what the individual does with his/her own solitariness'; on the sociological side, what communities do under the heading of 'religion'. At the time when William James was most influential, there was a strong current of thought flowing in precisely the opposite direction: toward the assessment of religion's social functions, past and present. Out of the second of these there emerged *the sociology of religion*, which over the years was to assume a more and more dominant role as an academic sub-discipline.

One can do sociology in two different but connected ways. First, as an evolutionary science. Although Darwin was first and foremost a biologist, it was not long before his admirers applied the evolutionary model to (among much else) the development of human societies. Here the prophetic voice was that of the popular philosopher Herbert Spencer (1820–1904), whose *First Principles* (1862) argued that 'the law of organic evolution is the law of all evolution' in every field of human activity, and not just in biology: 'this same advance from the simple to the complex, through successive differentiations, holds uniformly' (Spencer 1862: 148). Spencer held that the simplest, and therefore the earliest, form of religion had been the worship (or at least fear) of the dead, especially those who had been powerful during

their lifetimes: 'The rudimentary form of all religion is the propitiation of dead ancestors . . .' (Spencer 1901). This 'ghost theory' (as it came to be called) has the merit
of sometimes being at least partly true. Examples are not hard to come by. But it
leaves out too much to serve as a general theory of the origin of religion.

Shortly before Spencer's death, there had been published a centenary edition of an
influential book by the German theologian Friedrich Schleiermacher (1768–1834),
Über die Religion: Reden an die Gebildeten unter ihren Verachtern (1799; Eng. tr. *On
Religion: Speeches to its Cultured Despisers*, 1893). It was important on two counts:
first, because it argued that the only way to study religion adequately is not in terms
of the bloodless intellectual abstractions of 'natural religion' (which is in actual fact
neither natural nor religion), but in and through the religious beliefs and practices of
actual living human beings – a point made many years earlier by Charles de Brosses,
but taken insufficiently seriously since. And second, because to Schleiermacher, the
heart of religion was to be found, not in rules and regulations, hierarchies, hassocks
and hymnbooks, but in the individual's experience of (or sense of) and dependence
upon a power infinitely greater than his own. The reissue of Schleiermacher's *Über die
Religion* in 1899 could not have come at a more opportune moment. Darwinism was
all very well; the rule of law was an efficient sergeant-major in an unruly world, but
left little room for creative individuality. It was however Schleiermacher's editor
who made the greater long-term impression.

Rudolf Otto (1869–1937) was a philosopher and theologian by training and
temperament, with Indology as another area of interest and expertise. Today however
he tends to be remembered for only one book, *Das Heilige* (1917; Eng. tr. *The Idea
of the Holy*, 1923), which argued that what is essential in religion is the individual's
experience of 'the holy', even at one point requesting that the reader who has had
no such experience to read no further! But experience of what, precisely? Trying to
explain, Otto coined the word 'numinous' (*das Numinose*), a sense of the presence
of a *numen* (deity, supernatural being). This in its turn gives rise to a perception, or
apprehension, of a *mysterium* which is both *tremendum* (scary) and *fascinans*
(intriguing).

The words 'holy' and 'sacred' are adjectives, which need to be related to someone
or something if they are to make sense, and are not easily turned into nouns ('holy
scripture', 'holy mountain', 'holy day', 'sacred cow', 'sacred site' make sense as the
abstract nouns 'the holy' and 'the sacred' do not.

A few years before the appearance of Otto's book there appeared in France Émile
Durkheim's *Les Formes Élémentaires de la Vie Religieuse* (1912; Eng. tr. *The Elementary
Forms of the Religious Life*, 1915). Here we have the opposite argument: that (put
crudely) religion is a social phenomenon, resting not on the individual's feeling-
states but on the needs of the community. Families, tribes and nations set up symbols
of their own collective identity – from totem poles to national flags – which are
'sacred' through their associations.

On this view, every human community invents its own sacred symbols. The supernatural does not enter into it, the closest approximation being 'power' (the
Melanesian/Polynesian *mana* and similar power-words, which Durkheim mistakenly
believed to be impersonal, but which always turn out to be associated with spiritual
beings who possess them). It is therefore the community which decrees what is, and
what is not, 'sacred' in its own cultural terms.

The phenomenology of religion

Between the outbreak of the First World War in 1914 and the end of the second in 1945, the study of religion in the West became fragmented. The old idealism had been shattered in the trenches of the battlefield, and in 1920, religion itself, let alone the study of religion, seemed to have no future worth speaking of. On the Christian theological front, the tradition of scholarship was maintained by a very few idealists in the face of growing opposition from the disciples of Karl Barth, Emil Brunner and the other 'dialectical' theologians, in whose eyes 'religion' was as dust and ashes compared to the Gospel, and who declined to study it further. The conservatives were what they had always been: intent on doing battle with 'the world' on as many fronts as possible. Meanwhile, the anthropologists, Orientalists, philologists and the rest cultivated their respective gardens.

Comparative religion had been trying to compare religions as totalities, as systems, as competing solutions of the world's problems. This was unsound. Religions are totalities only in the pages of textbooks, and what believers actually believe, and how they believe, may bear little resemblance to what they are supposed to believe and do. The student, intent on examining religions and writing their histories, was faced with an impossible task. One alternative was to divide the field functionally, by themes and characteristics, and to attempt on that basis limited comparisons: prayer with prayer, sacrifice with sacrifice, images of deity with images of deity. In all this it was important to examine, not what the textbooks say, but what is actually there to be observed, the *phenomena* involved in the business of religion. The point had been made by Charles de Brosses in the 1760s and by Friedrich Schleiermacher in 1799: that the student of religion must concentrate, not on what people might do, ought to do or what the textbooks say they are supposed to do, but on what they actually do, and the ways in which they actually behave. But people do, and have done, so many things. How can anyone grasp the field as a whole?

It was with an eye to resolving this difficulty that the term 'the phenomenology of religion' was pressed into service. As we have said, limited comparisons were still possible, provided that they were based on either reliable information or careful observation. However, in the early years of the twentieth century, 'phenomenology' acquired another set of meanings, having to do less with the material than the mind-set of the observer. The name of the philosopher Edmund Husserl is often mentioned in this connection, though his contribution to the study of religion was at best indirect. 'Philosophical' phenomenology aimed at the elimination of sub-jectivity (and hence dogmatic bias) from the inquirer's process of thought. As such, the ideal was and is unattainable, and it was unfortunate that for a time in the 1970s, a few phenomenological catch-words (*epoché*, the suspension of judg-ment, and *eidetic vision*, the gift of seeing things as wholes, as well as 'phenomenology' itself) found their way into the vocabulary of the study of religion. In the inter-war years, the trend was best represented by the Dutch scholar Gerardus van der Leeuw (1890–1950), author of *Phänomenologie der Religion* (1933; Eng. tr. *Religion in Essence and Manifestation*, 1938).

Practically all the first phenomenologists of religion were Protestant Christian theologians – Chantepie de la Saussaye, Nathan Söderblom, Rudolf Otto, Edvard Lehmann, William Brede Kristensen ('. . . there exists no other religious reality than the faith of the believers . . .') and C. Jouco Bleeker. An exception was the enigmatic

German scholar Friedrich Heiler, whose chaotic book *Erscheinungsformen und Wesen der Religion* (1961) rounded off the series. In all these cases, phenomenology was a religious as much as a scholarly exercise. Those making up the between-the-wars generation of scholars we now call phenomenologists were deeply committed to the principle that the causes of sound learning and sound religion were not two causes, but one. The enemies of sound learning were all too often captive to *unsound* religion – unsound because (among other things) unhistorical and therefore almost inevitably authoritarian. Faced with such a configuration, one may distance oneself altogether from religious praxis; or one may try to bring the religious community (that is, the faculties of theology) round to one's way of thinking. Most opted for the first of these alternatives; the very few who chose the latter, though they won a few battles, ultimately lost the war – not because of the innate superiority of theological thinking, but due to the corrosive influence of secularisation on religious thought in general.

Tools of the trade

Over the past century or so, the study of religion has gradually acquired an extensive body of reference material for the use of students. The idea that it might be possible to bring together all the world's knowledge and publish it in encyclopaedia form belongs to the Enlightenment. Today we are more modest, but the genre has survived. As far as religion is concerned, an important landmark was James Hastings' *Encyclopaedia of Religion and Ethics* (1908–26); in German, there was *Die Religion in Geschichte und Gegenwart* (1909–13), a fourth edition is currently in preparation. The *Encyclopedia of Religion* (16 vols, edited by Mircea Eliade) appeared in the US in 1987. Given the new situation created by the Internet, it is unlikely that there will be any more.

Compact dictionaries and handbooks are by now legion, as are 'world religions' textbooks for student use. Special mention may be made of *The New Penguin Dictionary of Religions* (1997) and *The New Handbook of Living Religions* (1998), both edited by John R. Hinnells. On the textbook front, Ninian Smart's *The World's Religions* (1989, an updated version of a book first published in 1969 as *The Religious Experience of Mankind*) has proved an excellent *gradus ad parnassum* for generations of religious studies students.

Concerning scholarly journals, we must be brief. They have never been other than variable in quality, and though these days every effort is made to guard professional standards, the level of readability is often depressingly low. There is the additional factor that the fragmentation of the study of religion in recent years has resulted in more and more specialist journals, which can only be read with profit by fellow specialists. Among the best 'general' journals in English are *Religion* (UK/US), *Journal of the American Academy of Religion* (US), *Journal of Religion* (US) and *Numen* (international).

Congresses, conferences, consultations

In 1993 there was celebrated the centenary of the Chicago 'World's Parliament of Religions', though this time relabelled 'Parliament of World Religions' – a shift in meaning no one bothered to examine at all closely. Both were propaganda exercises, but for different causes: 1893 for religious oneness (monism), 1993 for religious diversity (pluralism). There would be little point in listing even a selection of the myriad conferences, congresses and consultations that have punctuated the years between, increasingly frequently since the advent of air travel in the 1960s. Opinions differ as to their importance, though it is probably true to say that the best are the smallest (the most satisfying conference I have ever attended numbered no more than thirty-five or so participants). It would however be churlish to deny their social function or the opportunity they provide for younger voices to make themselves heard among their peers.

Developments since the 1960s

In the immediate post-war years, where religion was studied seriously, the pattern was still largely that of the earlier part of the century. There was still the same broad alternative that there had been all century: most of those committed to the study of religion were equally committed to the community sponsoring it. Theology/divinity, in one or another form, was still dominant; independent studies were few and far between, and 'comparative religion' remained, as far as the West was concerned, something of a playground for liberal eccentrics. The world political scene was dominated by the threats and posturings of the 'Cold War', in which context it no longer seemed far-fetched to hope that the great world religions might some day make common cause against the common enemy of 'godless communism'; and by rapid decolonisation, beginning with India/Pakistan/Sri Lanka immediately after the war and sweeping through most of Africa (except, for the time being, the far south) soon thereafter. The Chinese Cultural Revolution, the Korean and Vietnam wars – these and many smaller conflicts all left their mark, even on such apparently arcane subjects as the study of religion. The creation of the State of Israel, and waves of Arab-Israeli conflict, left wounds which still today have not healed. The dismal record might be prolonged.

The consequences for the study of religion were profound, and lasting. Still in the 1950s it was simply taken for granted that religion was 'all about words', and since these had been written in a vast variety of languages, many of them no longer spoken, the student's first duty was to become as much of a philologist as possible in the time available, with a view to reading ancient texts 'in the original'. (Pre-literate societies were generally left to the anthropologists to deal with on their own functional terms.) Latin and perhaps Greek had been learned in secondary school; Hebrew, Arabic, Sanskrit, Pali, Mandarin and Japanese had not. The principle, however, still stood. The inevitable outcome was that the study of religion remained a sub-department of the study of (for the most part ancient) history, with a little philosophy added for good measure.

The times, however, were a-changing, and between 1960 and 1970 all these assumptions had been challenged. Certainly old style studies survived, for the time being, but the historical-philological approach was suffering greatly from the attentions, not of scholars, but of politicians and administrators (and their paymasters) whose sights were set at a different level, philology became problematical, as language teaching at the secondary level declined; 'history' even more so. The so-called 'educational' reforms which began in the 1960s in the West played their part. Most important, however, was the reading of the place of religion in history that emerged in the mid-to-late 1960s.

It is impossible in this connection to overlook the impact of the Second Vatican Council (1962–5), not only on the Roman Catholic Church, but on the whole of world Christianity. Vatican II (Second Vatican Council), in a manner of speaking, launched the idea of inter-religious dialogue on a poorly prepared world. A concept had found its *kairos*. Within a very few years, it became axiomatic that the study of religion could only justify itself on 'dialogical' principles – the assumption of course being that religion is far more than an aspect of ancient history. Once, it had been self-evident that the Western-trained historian should have the last word in all matters of importance. This was no longer as obvious as it had once been.

The reassessment began in the 1950s. An early expression was a little book by Huston Smith, *The Religions of Man* (1964), which expressed the hope that history might remember 'our years' '. . . not for the release of nuclear power nor the spread of Communism but as the time in which all the peoples of the world first had to take one another seriously' (Smith 1964). An important part of the 'taking seriously' process was the new readiness on the part of Western scholars to listen to the voices of people of other faiths explaining what they believed and why. Earlier this process had been haphazard, though the Chicago World's Parliament of Religions in 1893 had established the principle, and exotics like Radhakrishnan and Suzuki had continued the mission. The day of the vernacular (primitive, primal, pre-literate) religions, on the other hand, had still not dawned.

As to the object of the exercise, some controversy was caused when in 1958 the German scholar Friedrich Heiler, a passionate internationalist, declared at an international conference in Tokyo that the only worthy objective of the study of religion was 'true tolerance and co-operation on behalf of mankind' (Sharpe 1986: 272). For a number of years thereafter, the question of the 'pure *versus* applied' alternatives in the study of religion tended to dominate professional discussion. Although a mere recital of names would serve no purpose, the 'pure' camp was for the most part made up of classically trained historians and philologists, whose chief concerns were with history – and fairly remote history at that. In these circles, 'objectivity', in the sense of single-minded concentration on one's object of study (usually a text), was still an attainable ideal, and was contrasted with 'speculative' philosophy on the one hand, and with dogmatic theology on the other. This was scarcely a new point of view: rather it was the remnant of an old debate, prodded into life once more. 'Pure' scholarship could see no value in the study of religion unless it contributed directly to a better understanding among the nations.

Beginning in the mid-1960s, the ideal of scholarly objectivity began to be frozen out of the day-to-day study of religion. New words were coined, among them 'post-colonial' and 'post-modern', neither of which carried any very precise meaning, but both of which marked out a new territory. 'Deconstruction' was another neologism. All indicated extreme impatience with the intellectual and ideological past, with a history most of its advocates took little trouble to understand, and with every last form of idealism.

A forum for discussions of this order was provided by the new departments of (usually) religious studies that were founded between the late 1960s and the late

1970s. (Some tertiary institutions opted for other forms of words, 'religion studies', 'studies in religion' or whatever; a few retained the time-honoured 'comparative religion'.) Before the 1960s, despite the West's multifarious colonial involvements, little notice had been taken of what 'the natives' believed or did, and why; comparative religion had always been a cinderella subject in faculties of theology/divinity. But in the new post-war climate of opinion, it was decided that religion and it structures and functions world-wide, being far too important a matter to be left to the churches, was to be an object of study. By common consent, the pioneer department of religious studies was that founded at the University of Lancaster in 1967. Many others followed, the University of Sydney not until 1977, the University of Tromsø in Norway not before 1993. An important point was that the study of religion at university level should be entirely free from church (or other) sponsorship and control. There were to be no more heresy trials; every expression of religion was in principle open to investigation: there was to be no proselytism. As far as was humanly possible, every manifestation of religion was to be treated with 'sympathy' and 'understanding'.

Given these excellent principles, it was unfortunate that the one religious tradition frequently denied a fair hearing was . . . Christianity. Disillusion reached a new pitch of intensity during the 1960s; the Vietnam war was one obvious cause, post-colonial guilt was another, sexual (or gender) politics yet another. So it was that when the so-called 'new religious movements' (NRMs) in the vernacular, 'sects' or 'cults' – Transcendental Meditation (TM), International Society of Krishna Consciousness (ISKCON), the Unification Church and the rest – began to appear in the mid-to-late 1960s, they enjoyed immediate and in some cases lasting success.

The NRMs were extremely diverse in origin: some had their roots in the Hindu tradition (TM, ISKCON), others in Buddhism, one in Korean Shamanism (the 'Moonies'), others again in fringe Christianity (the Children of God). What all had in common was their clientèle and their basis in charismatic leadership. The old faculties of divinity/theology would have taken no notice of them: the new departments of religious studies quickly incorporated them into their curricula, as exercises in sociology, psychology – and in some cases, participant observation free from the discomfort that frequently attends fieldwork.

Religious studies and phenomenology

The post-war situation was one in which old patterns of belief and behaviour were being questioned and reshaped. The demise of colonialism had created a new international, intercultural and interreligious community, by no means 'one nation' but at least a world in which a degree of tolerance of one another's religious idiosyncrasies was a high priority. The sectarian squabbles and polemics of the past had, it was hoped, been laid to rest once and for all. There was a large element of left-leaning politics in what emerged in the late 1960s and early 1970s. Its chief ingredient was dogmatic egalitarianism: privilege based on accidents of birth is unacceptable, and no one can claim as a privilege what is not in principle open to everyone as a right. Religion, with all its hierarchies, resources, ranks and exclusivity, was an obvious target, as it had been since the Enlightenment. Christianity was an even more obvious target, given its place in Western, 'colonialist' and capitalist culture.

Other factors contributed. The Roman Catholics' Second Vatican Council (1962–5) had embraced the principles of religious freedom (*Dignitatis Humanae*) and improved inter-religious relations (*Ad Gentes, Nostra Aetate*), chiefly in the hope of righting the wrongs of anti-Semitism, but with far wider implications. Instead of confrontation, as in the past, 'dialogue' was now the order of the day, and inevitable, this gave a great boost to the intercultural study of religion. For some years, the incidence of ex-priests and ex-nuns in religious education (further impelled to move on by the 'anti-abortion, anti-contraception' decrees of the late 1960s) became unusually high.

Methods and methodologies

In recent years it has become more and more common for sessions, sections and sometimes whole conferences to be devoted to 'problems of method in the study of religion', the third of the Ms we mentioned at the outset. This in itself is evidence of widespread uncertainty in the field consequent on the erosion of old intellectual assumptions. The most successful of those known to the present writer was that held in Turku/Åbo, Finland, in August 1973. Others have been notably less worthwhile, though there would be little point in identifying them. A frequently recurring topic of late has been the age-old tension between theological and non-theological ways of studying religion, which seems no closer to a resolution now than it was a century ago. In 1996 I was privileged to be asked to present a 'position paper' on this subject to the American Academy of Religion. Poor health prevented me from attending, but my paper was duly discussed. In it, I am afraid that I quoted Omar Khayyam:

> Myself when young did eagerly frequent
> Doctor and Saint, and heard great Argument
> About it and about: but evermore
> Came out by the same Door as in I went.
>   (Song 27)

'Methods,' wrote Åke Hultkrantz some years ago, 'are the crutches of science'. The healthy have no need of them; the busy have little time for them. There is a danger that the 'second-order' student may spend so much time studying other people's methods (and quoting them at length, after the manner of social scientists) that there is little time left for the actual study of religion, let alone its practice.

Those who deplore what they see as the 're-theologising' of the study of religion deserve closer examination than we can give them here. One or two points may however be made. First, that (with the possible exception of the old USSR and its satellites) the study of religion had never been wholly 'de-theologised'; many and perhaps most of our intellectual forerunners were, as we say, 'believers'. They were not on the other hand obscurantists – prompting the reflection that the post-1960s generation is so far removed from genuine liberalism in religion as to be unable to acknowledge what it once was, namely, the ability to grasp more than one side of an argument and the reasons behind each.

It needs perhaps to be added that after about 1970, the meaning of 'theology' became more and more indistinct. What remained was 'theology as history of ideas' on the one hand, and 'theology as social ethics, with an occasional mention of God'.

Methodological issues

It is time to attempt an assessment of the study of religion after the years of discovery, progress and reappraisal (and of course conflict) we have passed in rapid review. What have we learned from our academic past? Sometimes the problems we face today seem substantially the problems our forebears wrestled with in the past, and our descendants will no doubt still be debating a century from now. Arguably the most persistent of these concerns the religious allegiance (or lack of it) of the student: does the student function best as an insider or as an outsider? To this one can only answer that the insider knows by experience what to the outsider is mere conjecture; the insider is allowed access to 'mysteries' which remain barred to the uninitiated. On the mundane level of such things as history and geography, on the other hand, the outsider may well be the better informed of the two. Whether the outsider can enter imaginatively into the insider's 'spiritual experience' is extremely doubtful. In many of today's secular societies, the issue may in any case be a red herring, since what the media unfailingly dub 'sectarian' (i.e. religious) conflict generally proves on closer examination to be a matter of territory and resources, history and ethnicity, rather than religion as such.

Another cardinal issue is that of secularisation, the process whereby religious ways of thinking and behaving are replaced by secular (from the Latin, *saeculum*, this world) substitutes. The process passes through three stages: *rejection* of religion and its replacement by secular authority, usually that of 'science'; *adaptation* of the old to the new values; and *reaction*, intransigent reaffirmation of the old ways in their entirety. It is at this third, reactive stage that there is created the much-maligned and much-feared phenomenon of fundamentalism and fundamentalists.

Fundamentalism and conservatism are not synonyms. A conservative is one who loves and respects the old ways and the old traditions, and is reluctant to see them change; a fundamentalist is one who tries to battle the corrosive influence of the new and to re-establish the absolute authority of a holy book (the Bible, the Qur'an, the Veda), a law, a community and its traditional values. The fundamentalist is permanently on the defensive, and may be given to paranoia in the face of real or imagined enemies. By its very nature, fundamentalism is a matter for semi-sociological research. Taking the longer view, despite the vast attention that has always been paid to the texts of holy scripture, their *functions* in the community remain imperfectly understood.

An overlapping subject for investigation is that of leadership. Fundamentalists seldom or never interpret scripture for themselves, but rely on the directives of a charismatic leader and the exegetical tradition of which he or she is part. The holy book is read (or listened to) selectively, after having been passed through the filter of a holy tradition – of which the individual fundamentalist generally remains unaware. The nature of religious community leadership then stands out as a matter of great importance, not least in the sectarian context.

Pluralism

Space permits only one last addition to the list of unfinished religious studies business: the issue of pluralism. Once, 'pluralism' meant no more than variety or diversity, and as such was an unremarkable fact of religious life. Recently, however, it has taken on a further, ideologically fuelled meaning: the unconditional right of every religious or other community to be itself and maintain its own traditions, practices and attitudes. Like every idealistic programme, that of pluralism (or in political terms, 'multiculturalism') is flawed. It tends to assume, for instance, that religious toleration and mutual acceptance is a normal and natural state of human affairs. History indicates otherwise. If, as we suggested at the beginning of this essay, religion and law are virtually inseparable in many societies (for instance Islam), a plurality of laws is as unacceptable as a plurality of gods was in ancient Israel, and for precisely the same reasons: peace and national cohesion.

Where religion is closely allied with nationalism and ethnicity, as it so often is, an extra dimension is added. Conformity is loyalty, dissent is potential or actual treachery – a totalitarian point of view reserved in secular societies for extremist politics. In educational terms, this has led in the West to the insistence that where religious studies are taught, such teaching must be ideologically sound, value-free (the old mirage of 'objectivity') and politically innocuous. Secular educators in pluralist societies may go so far as to forbid every expression of overt religiosity – public prayer in schools, the wearing of distinctive items of clothing, even the celebration of religious festivals, outside the circle of the faithful.

Clearly, the study of religion is not what it was to students of my generation. As the theologians have retreated – or at least redefined themselves – the social sciences have come to the fore. What are they hoping to 'understand'? Not as a rule the finer points of a Coptic text written two thousand years or so ago, or even an English or German text written less than a hundred years ago. The emphasis in departments of religious studies over the past thirty or so years has been tending more and more in the direction of contemporary issues, as pursued in departments of sociology and anthropology, where you use languages to communicate with the living, and not only to settle accounts with the dead.

It has become somewhat fashionable in recent years to call in question one of the basic assumptions of 1970s-style religious studies: that the student's business is to *understand* religious belief and behaviour, irrespective of time and place. The counter-claim now is that 'understanding' is in the blood, and not in the brain; you cannot pretend to understand what you were not *born* to understand, and to claim otherwise is arrogance and cultural neo-imperialism. Thus only women can understand women, only African Americans can understand African Americans, only gay people can understand other gay people, only Jews can understand Jews, and so on *ad infinitum*. So where the troubles of the study of religion initially had to do with gaining access to the material, later the problems shifted to method (what to do with it once you have it), now we are troubled as never before by motive: whose interests the study of religion is serving. The liberal ideal of disinterested scholarship pursued for its own sake is little mentioned in current debate.

In educational terms, it matters very little under what 'disciplinary' or administrative label the study of religion is pursued, provided that it is done with diligence and imagination by people who know what they are about, who are motivated by old-fashioned curiosity more than by the desire to score political points, beat a drum or make a career, and who respect the most frequently broken of the Ten Commandments, that which *orders* you not to bear false witness against your neighbour (whether alive or dead makes no difference). The history of the study of religion is the story of people of all ages and cultures and political affiliations, who believe certain things about the world in which they live (or have lived), and because of that belief, behave in certain ways. They have done all the things people have always done: they have celebrated times and seasons with music and dance, food and drink; they have waged war and made peace; they have wondered, as we all still wonder, what it all means and what, if anything, lies on the far side of death. The study of religion is about all of these things, and many more. Let no one pretend that he or she is unaffected by these matters. To those who make such claims, I am tempted to say: 'Sir, Madam, James, Jane – with respect, I do not believe you.' Because when all the dross has been cleared away, the fact of our mortality will remain to tantalise us until it is too late for it to matter.

Bibliography

Boorstin, D. J., *The Discoverers*. New York, Vintage Books, 1983.

Capps, W. H., *Religious Studies: The Making of a Discipline*. Minneapolis MN, Fortress Press, 1995.

Cook, S. A., *The Study of Religions*. London, A. & C. Black, 1914.

Daniel, G., *The Idea of Prehistory*. Harmondsworth, Penguin, 1964.

De Vries, J., *The Study of Religion: A Historical Approach*. trans. K. W. Bolle, New York, Harcourt, Brace & World, 1967.

Durkheim, É., *The Elementary Forms of the Religious Life*. Trans. J. W. Swain, London, George Allen & Unwin, 1915.

Eliade, M. (ed.), *Encyclopedia of Religion*. 16 vols, New York, Macmillan, 1987.

Ellegård, A., *Darwin and the General Reader*. Göteborg (Gothenburg, Sweden), Acta Universitatis Gothoburgensis 7, 1958.

Evans-Pritchard, E. E., *Theories of Primitive Religion*. Oxford, Clarendon Press, 1965.

Feldman, B. and Richardson, R. D., *The Rise of Modern Mythology, 1680–1860*. Bloomington, Indiana, Indiana University Press, 1972.

Frazer, J. G., *The Golden Bough*. Abridged edn, London, Macmillan, 1922.

Freeman, D., *Margaret Mead and Samoa: The Making and Unmaking of an Anthropological Myth*. Cambridge, Harvard University Press, 1983.

Hastings, J. (ed.), *Encyclopaedia of Religion and Ethics*. Edinburgh, T. & T. Clark, 1908–1926.

Heiler, F., *Erscheinungsformen und Wesen der Religion*. Stuttgart, publisher unknown, 1961.

Hinnells, J. R. (ed.), *The New Penguin Dictionary of Religions*. London, Penguin, 1997.

—— (ed.), *A New Handbook of Living Religions*. Harmondsworth, Penguin, 1998.

Hügel, F. von, *The Mystical Element of Religion*. 2 vols, London, Dent, 1908.

Hurd, W., *New Universal History of the Religious Rites, Ceremonies and Customs of the Whole World*. London, publisher unknown, 1788.

Inge, W. R., *Christian Mysticism*. London, Methuen, 1899.

James, W., *The Principles of Psychology*. 2 vols, New York, H. Holt & Co., 1890.

—— *The Varieties of Religious Experience*. The Gifford Lectures 1901–2, reprinted Glasgow, Collins, 1977.

Jones, R. M., *Studies in Mystical Religion*. London, Macmillan & Co., 1909.

Lang, A., *Custom and Myth*. London, Longmans & Co., 1884.

—— *Myth, Ritual and Religion*. 2 vols, London, Longmans & Co., 1887.

—— *The Making of Religion*. London, Longmans & Co., 1898.

Leeuw, G. van der, *Religion in Essence and Manifestation: A Study in Phenomenology*. Trans. J. E. Turner, London, George Allen & Unwin, 1938.

Marett, R. R., *The Threshold of Religion*. London, Methuen, 1909.

Mead, M., *Coming of Age in Samoa*. New York, Morrow, 1928.

Müller, M. F., *Introduction to the Science of Religion*. London, Longmans, Green and Co., 1873.

Nisbet, R. A., *Emile Durkheim*. Englewood Cliffs NJ, Prentice-Hall, 1965.

Otto, R., *The Idea of the Holy*. Trans. J. W. Harvey, London, Humphrey Milford, 1923.

Pratt, J. B., *The Religious Consciousness: A Psychological Study*. New York, Macmillan, 1920.

Schiele, F. M. (ed.), *Die Religion in Geschichte und Gegenwart*. 5 vols, Tübingen, publisher unknown, 1909–13.

Schleiermacher, F., *On Religion: Speeches to its Cultured Despisers*. Trans. John Oman, London, publisher unknown, 1893.

Schmidt, W., *The Origin and Growth of Religion: Facts and Theories*. London, Methuen, 1931.

Sharpe, E. J., *Understanding Religion*. London, Duckworth, 1983.

—— *Comparative Religion: A History*. London, Duckworth, 1975. Second edition, London, Duckworth, and La Salle, Open Court, 1986.

Smart, N., *The World's Religions*. Cambridge, Cambridge University Press, 1989.

Smith, H., *The Religions of Man*. New York, Harper & Row, 1964.

Spencer, H., *First Principles*. London, Williams & Norgate, 1862.

—— *Essays: Scientific, Political and Speculative*. 3 vols, London, Williams & Norgate, 1901.

Starbuck, E. D., *The Psychology of Religion: An Empirical Study of the Growth of Religious Consciousness*. London, Scott, 1899.

Trompf, G. W., *In Search of Origins*. London, Oriental University Press, 1990.

Underhill, E., *Mysticism: A Study in the Nature and Development of Man's Spiritual Consciousness*. 13th edn, London, Methuen, 1940.

Waardenburg, J., *Classical Approaches to the Study of Religion: Aims, Methods and Theories of Research*. 2 vols, The Hague and Paris, Mouton, 1973–4.

White, A. D., *A History of the Warfare of Science with Theology in Christendom*. 2 vols, London, Arco, 1955.

Part I

Key approaches to the study of religions

Chapter 3

Theories of religion

Robert A. Segal

Theories of religion go all the way back to the Presocratics. Modern theories come almost entirely from the modern disciplines of the social sciences: anthropology, sociology, psychology, and economics. Pre-social scientific theories came largely from philosophy and were speculative rather than empirical in nature. What John Beattie writes of modern anthropological theories of culture as a whole holds for theories of religion, and for theories from the other social sciences as well:

> Thus it was the reports of eighteenth- and nineteenth-century missionaries and travellers in Africa, North America, the Pacific and elsewhere that provided the raw material upon which the first anthropological works, written in the second half of the last century, were based. Before then, of course, there had been plenty of conjecturing about human institutions and their origins; to say nothing of earlier times, in the eighteenth century Hume, Adam Smith and Ferguson in Britain, and Montesquieu, Condorcet and others on the Continent, had written about primitive institutions. But although their speculations were often brilliant, these thinkers were not empirical scientists; their conclusions were not based on any kind of evidence which could be tested; rather, they were deductively argued from principles which were for the most part implicit in their own cultures. They were really philosophers and historians of Europe, not anthropologists.
>
> (Beattie 1964: 5–6)

Origin and function

A theory of religion is an answer to at least two questions: what is the origin and what is the function of religion? The term 'origin' is confusing because it can refer to either the historical or the recurrent beginning of religion. It can refer either to when and where religion first arose or to why religion arises whenever and wherever it arises. According to convention, nineteenth-century theories focused on the origin of religion, where twentieth-century theories have focused on the function of religion. But 'origin' here means historical origin. Nineteenth-century theories sought the recurrent origin of religion at least as much as any historical one, yet no more so than twentieth-century theories have done. Conversely, nineteenth-century theories were concerned as much with the function of religion as with the origin, and no less so than twentieth-century theories have been. Furthermore, the historical origin proposed by nineteenth-century theories was not that of a single time and place, such as the Garden of Eden, but that of the earliest *stage* of religion – any time and anywhere. Therefore even the 'historical' origin was as much recurrent as one-time.

The questions of recurrent origin and of function are connected, and few theories are concerned with only the recurrent origin or only the function. Ordinarily, the answer to both questions is a need, which religion arises and serves to fulfill. Theories differ over what that need is. Any theories that do concentrate on only the recurrent origin or on only the function typically either attribute the origin of religion to an accident or make the function a byproduct. Yet 'accident' and 'byproduct' really refer to the means, not the ends. Unless religion, however accidental its origin or coincidental its function, serves a need, it surely will not last and surely will not continually re-arise. Still, origin and function are distinct issues, and to argue on the basis of the sheer fulfillment of a need that religion arises *in order* to fulfill the need is to commit the fallacy of affirming the consequent.

The issues of origin and function can each be divided into two parts: not only *why* but also *how* religion arises or functions. In explaining the ends of religion, theories do not thereby automatically explain the means. Some theories explain how religion arises, others how religion functions, others both, still others neither.

For example, the Victorian anthropologist E. B. Tylor (1871), who epitomizes the purportedly nineteenth-century focus on origin, roots religion in observations by 'primitives' of, especially, the immobility of the dead and the appearance in dreams and visions of persons residing far away. The 'why' of origin is an innate need to explain these observations, which trigger the need rather than implant it. The 'how' of origin consists of the processes of observation, analogy, and generalization. Independently of one another, primitive peoples the world over create religion by these means and for this end. Later stages of humanity do not re-invent religion but instead inherit it from their primitive forebears. They perpetuate religion because it continues to satisfy in them, too, the need to explain observations. Similarly, religion changes not because the need changes but because believers revise their conceptions of god. Religion gives way to science not because the need changes but because science provides a better, or at least more persuasive, means of satisfying it. The 'why' of function is the same as the why of origin: a need to explain observations. The 'how' of function is the one issue that Tylor ignores.

Truth

Most twentieth-century theorists forswear the issue of the truth of religion as beyond the ken of the social sciences (see Segal 1989, ch. 7). One exception is the sociologist Peter Berger, who ever since *A Rumor of Angels* (1969) has been prepared to use his theory to confirm the truth of religion (see Segal 1992: 6–7, 16, 117–18). Most nineteenth-century theorists were not at all reluctant to take a stand on the issue of truth. But they based their assessment on philosophical grounds, not on social scientific ones. Instead of enlisting the origin and function of religion to assess the truth of religion, they assessed the truth on an independent basis and, if anything, let their conclusion about it guide their theorizing about origin and function (see Segal 1992: 15–17). They thereby circumvent the possibility of committing either the genetic fallacy or what I call the functionalist fallacy: arguing that either the origin or the function of religion refutes – necessarily refutes – the truth of it.

Theories from religious studies

The key divide in theories of religion is between those theories that hail from the social sciences and those that hail from religious studies itself. Social scientific theories deem the origin and function of religion nonreligious. The need that religion arises to fulfill can be for almost anything. It can be either physical – for example, for food, health, or prosperity – or intangible – for example, for explanation, as for Tylor, or for meaningfulness, as for Max Weber. The need can be on the part of individuals or on the part of society. In fulfilling the need, religion provides the means to a secular end.

By contrast, theories from religious studies deem the origin and function of religion distinctively religious: the need that religion arises to fulfill is for god. There really is but one theory of religion from religious studies. Adherents to it include F. Max Müller, C. P. Tiele, Gerardus van der Leeuw, Raffaele Pettazzoni, Joachim Wach, and Mircea Eliade.[1] For all of these 'religionists,' religion arises to provide contact with god. Like many social scientists, many religionists confine themselves to the issues of origin and function and shy away from the issue of truth. Just as social scientists entrust the issue of truth to philosophers, so religionists entrust it to theologians.

For religionists, human beings need contact with god as an end in itself: they need contact with god because they need contact with god. An encounter with god may yield peace of mind and other benefits, but the need is still for the encounter itself. The need is considered as fundamental as the need for food or water. Without that contact, humans may not die, but they will languish. Because the need is for god, nothing secular can substitute for religion. There may be secular, or seemingly secular, *expressions* of religion, but there are no secular *substitutes* for religion. Religionists consider the need for god not only distinctive but also universal. To demonstrate its universality, they point to the presence of religion even among professedly atheistic moderns.

Strictly speaking, there are two versions of the single religionist theory. One is the form just described: religion originates within human beings, who seek contact with god. The exemplar of this form is Eliade, who stresses the yearning for god or, so he prefers, the sacred: 'But since religious man cannot live except in an atmosphere impregnated with the sacred, we must expect to find a large number of techniques for consecrating space' (Eliade 1968: 28). Sacred places, or spaces, are one venue for encountering god. Religious sites, such as churches and mosques, are built on those spots where god is believed to have appeared – the assumption being that wherever god has once appeared, that god, even if formally omnipresent, is more likely to appear anew. Sacred times, or time, is the other venue for encountering god. Myths, which describe the creation by god of physical and social phenomena, carry one back to the time of creation, when, it is believed, god was closer at hand than god has been ever since: 'Now, what took place "in the beginning" was this: the divine or semidivine beings were active on earth ... Man desires to recover the active presence of the gods ... [T]he mythical time whose reactualization is periodically attempted is a time sanctified by the divine presence ...' (Eliade 1968: 92).

This version of the religionist theory bypasses the issue of the existence of god. The theory is committed to the existence of only the *need for* god, not to the existence of god. The catch is that if religionists claim that religion actually fulfills the need – and why else would they advocate religion? – then god must exist. Religionists thus prove to be theologians. Still, the emphasis is on the need itself.

The other version of the religionist theory, epitomized by Müller, roots religion not in the need for god but in the experience of god. However indispensable the experience of god may be for human fulfillment, religion originates not in the quest for god but in an unexpected encounter with god. Müller himself singles out the sun and other celestial phenomena as the occasion where god or, for Müller, the Infinite is encountered: 'Thus sunrise was the revelation of nature, awakening in the human mind that feeling of dependence, of helplessness, of hope, of joy and faith in higher powers, which is the source of all wisdom, the spring of all religion' (Müller 1867: 96).

The two versions of the religionist theory are compatible. The quest for an encounter with god may be fulfilled by an uninitiated encounter, and an uninitiated encounter can lead to a quest for further encounters. Still, the approaches differ. One starts with a need; the other, with an experience. Deriving religion from a need for god makes the religionist theory more easily comparable with social scientific theories, nearly all of which do the same.

Social scientific theories

Religionists commonly assert that social scientists, in making religion a means to a nonreligious end, are less interested in religion than they. This assertion is false. Social scientists are interested in religion for exactly its capacity to produce anthropological, sociological, psychological, and economic effects. Many social scientists consider religion a most important means of fulfilling whatever they consider its nonreligious functions. Some even make it the key means of doing so.

Moreover, for religion to function nonreligiously, it must be operating *as* religion. The nonreligious effect comes from a religious cause. The power that religion has, let us say, to goad adherents into accepting social inequality stems from the belief that god sanctions the inequality, that god will one day remedy the inequality, or that the inequality is a merely worldly matter. Without the belief, religion would have no social effect. Undeniably, the social sciences approve or disapprove of religion for only its anthropological, sociological, psychological, or economic consequences. Undeniably, religion is admired only when it inculcates culture, unites society, develops the mind, or spurs the economy, not when it makes contact with god. But the nonreligious benefit of religion presupposes the efficacy of religion as religion.

Put another way, religion for social scientists functions as an independent variable, or as the cause of something else. In *origin* religion is indisputably a dependent variable, or the effect of something else, as it, like anything else, must be, unless it creates itself *ex nihilo*. But in *function* religion is an independent variable. Even if it is the product of nonreligious causes, it is in turn the cause of nonreligious effects. If religion could not be an independent variable in its effect because it was a dependent variable in its origin, there would be few independent variables around.

Contemporary social scientific theories

Religionists often assert that contemporary social scientists, in contrast to earlier ones, have at last come round to seeing religion the way the religionists do. Contemporary social scientists are consequently embraced by religionists as belated converts. The figures embraced most effusively are Mary Douglas (1966, 1973), Victor

Turner (1967, 1968), Clifford Geertz (1973, 1983), Robert Bellah (1970), Peter Berger (1967, 1969), and Erik Erikson (1958, 1969). These social scientists are pitted against classical ones like Tylor (1871), Frazer (1922), Durkheim (1965), Malinowski (1925), Freud (1950), Jung (1938), and Marx and Engels (1957).

What is the difference between classical and contemporary social scientists? The difference cannot be over the importance of religion. Classical social scientists considered religion at least as important a phenomenon as any of their contemporary counterparts do. The power of religion is what impelled them to theorize about it. Similarly, the difference cannot be over the utility of religion. While for Frazer, Freud, and Marx, religion is incontestably harmful, for Tylor, Jung, and Durkheim it is most helpful. For Tylor and Jung, religion is one of the best, and for Durkheim, is the best, means of serving its beneficial functions. Contemporary social scientists grant religion no greater due.

The difference between contemporary and classical social scientists must be over the nature of the function that religion serves. In contrast to classical theorists, for whom the functions of religion are nonreligious, contemporary theorists purportedly take the function of religion to be religious. But do they? Where religionists attribute religion to a yearning for god, contemporary social scientists attribute it to a yearning for, most often, a meaningful life. Contact with god may be one of the best means of providing meaningfulness, but even if it were the sole means, it would still be a means to a nonreligious end. For Douglas, humans need cognitive meaningfulness: they need to organize their experiences. For Turner, Geertz, Bellah, Berger, and Erikson, humans need existential meaningfulness: they need to explain, endure, or justify their experiences. Existential meaningfulness as the function of religion is not even new and goes back to at least Weber, who, to be sure, limits the need for meaningfulness to the 'higher' religions (see Weber 1963, chs 8–13). But even if this function were new, the need would remain secular. In short, the divide between social scientific theories of religion and the religionist one remains (see Segal 1989, ch. 4).

The religionist argument

What is the case for the religionist theory? The case tends to be presented negatively. It appeals to the inadequacy of social scientific theories, which should in fact include contemporary theories. All social scientific theories are supposedly inadequate because, in deeming the origin and function of religion nonreligious, they necessarily miss the religious nature of religion. Only the religionist theory captures the religious nature of religion.

In actuality, social scientific theories do not miss the religious nature of religion. On the contrary, it is what they mean *by* religion. The religious nature of religion is the starting point of their theorizing. It is the datum to be theorized about. Far from somehow failing to perceive that adherents pray to god, sacrifice to god, and kill others in the name of god, social scientists take for granted that adherents do so. The question for social scientists is why they do so. The religious nature of religion may be the starting point of theorizing, but it is not the end point. If social scientists somehow missed, let alone denied, that Christians go to church, sing hymns, take sacraments, read the Bible, and devote their lives to God, and do all of these things because they believe in God, they would be left with nothing to explain. Religiosity, far from being overlooked, is the preoccupation of social scientists.

Against social scientists and others, religionist Eliade, in a famous passage, declares that 'a religious phenomenon will only be recognized as such if it is grasped as it own level, that is to say, if it is studied *as* something religious. To try to grasp the essence of such a phenomenon by means of physiology, psychology, sociology, economics, linguistics, art or any other is false' (Eliade 1963: xiii). But Eliade conflates description with explanation, not to mention description with metaphysics (essence). No social scientist fails to recognize religion as religion. That is why there exists the anthropology of *religion*, the sociology of *religion*, the psychology of *religion*, and the economics of *religion*. There would be no social scientific theories of *religion* if the distinctiveness of religion went unrecognized. But the *recognition* of religion as religion does not mean the *explanation* of religion as religion.

It is as believers in God that Christians go to church, but it is also, for example, as members of a group that they do so. While acknowledging the difference between a religious group and a team, a family, or a gang, sociologists explain religion in the same way that they explain a team, a family, and a gang: as a group.

At the same time no sociological account of religion can be exhaustive. There is a point at which any sociological account must cease – the point at which a religious group differs from any other kind of group. But to acknowledge a stopping point for sociology is not to concede a starting point. Sociology can account for religion to whatever extent religion does constitute a group. How fully religion constitutes a group, it is up to sociologists to establish. The more group-like they show religion to be, the more successful their account. Sociologists are to be commended, not condemned, for attempting to account as fully as possible for religion sociologically. Their inevitable inability to account for it entirely sociologically marks the limit, not the failure, of the sociology of religion.

Religionists would reply that the attempt to 'sociologize' is inherently futile, for the origin and function of religion can only be religious. Otherwise religion ceases to be religion and becomes society. But this conventional rejoinder, offered like a litany, misses the point. Nobody denies that religion consists of beliefs and practices directed toward god rather than toward the group. But Durkheim, for example, is not thereby barred from matching a believer's experience of possession by god with an individual's experience of participation in a group. Durkheim is not barred from asserting that the euphoria and power which individuals feel when they amass at once precede religious experience, parallel religious experience, and thereby account for religious experience. Participants, thinking their state of mind superhuman, attribute it to possession by god, but Durkheim attributes it to 'possession' by the group.

Still, Durkheim is not maintaining that religion originates exclusively through group experience. After all, the group is not itself god, just god-like. The concept of god and attendant practices must still be created.[2] Durkheim offers his account of religion as a necessary but not quite a sufficient one. What must yet be accounted for is precisely the step from group to god. But to concede that there is more to an account of religion than the group is not to concede that religiosity is all there is to an account. For Durkheim, religion is to be accounted for sociologically *and* 'religionistically' – with the sociological element predominant. For all other social scientists the same is true: a sociological, anthropological, psychological, or economic account of religion must be supplemented by a religionist one.

The final religionist rejoinder is the appeal to symmetry. If the effect is religion, the cause must be religionist. There must be a match between cause and effect. A sociological cause can produce only a sociological effect. Explained sociologically, the product is the group, not religion.

This rejoinder, like other ones, misses the point. Of course, there must be symmetry between cause and effect. Causes must be enough akin to their effects to be capable of producing them. But a sociological account of religion does not purport to account for the nonsociological aspects of religion, only for the sociological ones. To reply that the sociological aspects are aspects of the group and not of religion is to commit a double fallacy: excluding the middle and begging the question. A sociological account of religion is not an account of something *other than* religion. It is an account of aspects *of* religion. To limit religion to its religionist aspects is to beg the question at hand: what *is* the nature of religion?

To be sure, the claim that sociology can explain anything of *religious* beliefs and practices might seem to be asserting that sociology can explain something *nonsociological*. But this concern is misplaced. Sociology takes *seemingly* nonsociological aspects of religion and transforms them into sociological ones, which it only then accounts for. Durkheim matches atttributes of god – god's power, god's overwhelming presence, god's status as the source of values and institutions – with attributes of the group whose god it is. The symmetry between cause and effect is preserved by sociologizing the effect. A gap remains between the sociological cause and the religious effect: the group is still just a group, not a god. But symmetry is not intended to mean identity.

To take an example from another field, Freud contends that a believer's relationship to the believer's father matches the believer's relationship to god. He contends that believers' feelings toward their fathers precede their feelings toward god, parallel those feelings, and therefore cause the feelings. But he proposes only a necessary, if also a largely sufficient, cause of religion. No more than Durkheim does he propose, to use a redundancy, an altogether sufficient one. What must still be supplied is the step from father to god. The father for Freud, like the group for Durkheim, is god-like but not god. God may be human-like, but no human being is omnipotent, omniscient, or immortal. God is 'father' of the whole world, not just of a family. The adult conception of god may *derive from* a child's 'idolization' of the child's own father, but the conception transforms a god-like figure into a god. Even when Freud brashly declares that 'at bottom God is nothing other than an exalted father' (Freud 1950: 147), he is still distinguishing a human father from an exalted, deified father. The closer the link Freud draws between human father and god, the more convincing his account, but he, like Durkheim and all other social scientists, takes for granted a limit to the link, and does so even while ever trying to tighten that link. Again, symmetry does not mean identity.

The mind–body analogy

One way of exposing the fallacy in the religionist argument that only identity between cause and effect can account for the effect is to appeal to the grand philosophical issue of the relationship between the mind and the body. There are four possible relationships. (1) Only mind exists, and the body (matter) is an illusion (idealism).

(2) Only the body exists, and the mind (spirit) is an illusion (materialism, or reductionism). (3) Both mind and body, spirit and matter, exist, but they operate independently of each other (parallelism). (4) Both mind and body, spirit and matter, exist, and either one causally affects the other (interactionism). Alternatively, the two causally affect each other.

Religionists never go so far as to espouse the equivalent of idealism: claiming that only religiosity exists and that the mind, society, and culture are illusory. Rather, they assume as their options the equivalents of either parallelism or materialism/ reductionism. Parallelism clearly constitutes no threat, for it preserves religiosity. Religionists assume that the sole threat comes from materialism/reductionism, which they seek to counter by arguing that religion is other than mind, society, and culture. They often assume – falsely – that the social sciences are outright materialistic.

Religionists overlook the interactionist option. Interactionism grants religion partial autonomy but not immunity. On the one hand it does not, like reductionism, dissolve religion into sheer mind, society, or culture.[3] On the other hand it does not, like parallelism, preclude the impact of the mind, society, or culture on religion.

Nemeses of religionists like Durkheim, Freud, and Marx espouse interactionism rather than, as defined here, reductionism or, obviously, parallelism. They seek to *account for* religion, not to deny (reductionism) or to isolate (parallelism) it. If they denied religion (reductionism), they would have nothing to account for. If they isolated religion (parallelism), they would be unable to account for it. Because Durkheim, Freud, and Marx no more reduce religion entirely to society, mind, or economy than philosophical interactionists reduce the mind entirely to the body, they do not claim to be accounting wholly for it. They claim only to be accounting significantly for it. They claim that one cannot account for religion apart from society, mind, or economy. Furthermore, the interactionism is for them two-way: religion, here as an independent variable, accounts considerably for society, mind, and the economy, just as society, mind, and the economy account considerably for religion.

Postmodernism

A postmodern approach to religion might seem to offer religionists solace by its opposition to generalizations and therefore to theorizing, but in fact it does not. Religionists theorize as much as social scientists. Contrary to postmodernists, both sides vaunt precisely the universality of their formulations. Contrary to both religionists and social scientists, postmodernists insist that theories *cannot* apply universally, not merely that they *may* not – a point scarcely denied by theorists on either side.

The postmodern refutation of theory takes several forms. One form is the uncovering of the origin – the historical, one-time origin – of theories. The assumption is that a theory does not merely arise in a specific time and place but is bound by that time and space. Where, for most of us, testing may show that a theory is in fact limited in its applicability, postmodernists assume a priori that any theory is so limited, and on the grounds that it originates in a specific time and place. But how can the sheer origin of a theory undermine – necessarily undermine – the theory? The argument blatantly commits the genetic fallacy. Reducing the scope of theories to the occasion of their origin fails to allow theorists any capacity to think. It reduces theorists to mere mirrors of their times. It conflates discovery with invention, creativity with construction. For an example of this variety of the postmodern attack on theory, see many of the contributions to *Critical Terms for Religious Studies* (Taylor 1998).

Another form of the postmodern attack on theory comes from Derrida. Here theories are undermined by the presence of contrary currents in the texts that present the theories. The most brilliant application of Derridean deconstructionism to theories of religion is Tomoko Masuzawa's *In Search of Dreamtime*, the subtitle of which is *The Quest for the Origin of Religion*. Masuzawa assumes that classical theories of religion sought above all the historical, one-time origin of religion. She lumps religionist theories with social scientific ones and takes as her prime targets Durkheim, Freud, Eliade, and Müller. Against them, she argues that their own texts undermine their intentions. Like Pirandello's characters, their texts take on a life of their own.

For example, Durkheim's definition of the sacred as the ideal society is supposedly undermined by the continual appearance in *The Elementary Forms of the Religious Life* of another definition: the sacred as the opposite of the profane. Freud's attribution, in *Totem and Taboo*, of the origin of religion to the sons' rebellion against their tyrannical father is supposedly undercut by Freud's own characterization of this would-be historical deed as fantasy. Contemporary theorists of religion, epitomized by Eliade, may reject the quest for the origin of religion as unsolvable, but we are told that they remain obsessed with believers' own quest for the origin of everything, including religion. That quest is in turn undone by the locating of the origin of everything outside of history, in mythic time, and is undone still more by the attempt through myth to override history by recovering the past, by making the past present.

Masuzawa's argument is tenuous. As noted, classical theorists sought the recurrent more than the historical origin of religion. Declares Durkheim near the outset of his *Elementary Forms*:

> The study which we are undertaking is therefore a way of taking up again, *but under new conditions*, the old problem of the origin of religion. To be sure, if by origin we are to understand the very first beginning, the question has nothing scientific about it, and should be resolutely discarded. There was no given moment when religion began to exist, and there is consequently no need of finding a means of transporting ourselves thither in thought . . . But the problem which we raise is quite another one. What we want to do is to find a means of discerning the ever-present causes upon which the most essential forms of religious thought and practice depend.
>
> (Durkheim 1965: 20)

Even Freud, who in *Totem and Taboo* comes closest to seeking the historical origin of religion, seeks only the first stage of religion. Moreover, classical theorists, as noted, were as much after the function of religion as after the origin, recurrent or historical. Contemporary theorists are no different.

The presence in theories of inconsistencies argues for the provisional state of the theorizing, not for any systematic undermining of the effort. Furthermore, far more egregious inconsistencies in these theories have long been recognized. In Durkheim, sometimes society is the recurrent source of religion, but sometimes religion is the recurrent source of society. Freud himself sheepishly recognizes the seeming inconsistency between his account of religion in *Totem and Taboo* and his account of it in *The Future of an Illusion*. There may be irony, but no inconsistency, in Eliade's abandonment of the quest for the historical origin of religion on the one hand and his interpretation of myth as a return to the historical, or prehistorical, origin of everything in the world on the other.

Masuzawa's approach is postmodern in the conclusion she draws: that the quest for historical origin, for her the key concern of at least classical theorizing, must be abandoned, in which case, so presumably, must theorizing itself, at least of a classical variety. The rejection of historical origin is meant to be part of the deconstruction of epistemological foundations. The study of religion must acknowledge its fault lines.

But even suppose that all classical theorists outright failed in a common quest for the historical origin of religion. What would follow? That subsequent theorists dare not try? Does the failure of even all quests to date doom all future ones? Does the quest for the historical origin of religion become impossible rather than merely difficult and become improper rather than merely impossible?

The final postmodern rejection of theory derives from Foucault. Here the political end to which theories are put is sought – as if the use of a theory refutes the theory. This tactic commits what I dub the functionalist fallacy – the counterpart to the genetic fallacy. The fullest application of a Foucauldian analysis of religion is Russell McCutcheon's *Manufacturing Religion*. Rather than, like Masuzawa, attacking all theories of religion, McCutcheon attacks only the religionist theory. There is nothing postmodern in much of his attack, which concentrates on Eliade. Cataloguing standard objections, McCutcheon argues that Eliade attributes religion exclusively to a distinctively religious need, dismisses nonreligious needs as irrelevant by definition, and thereby isolates religion from the rest of life. McCutcheon is less Foucauldian than Marxist when he argues that religion arises to sanction oppression, as in using a myth of the origin of social inequality to justify the perpetuation of the inequality.

McCutcheon follows Foucault in targeting less religion than the religionist theory, or 'discourse,' targeting it for its political effects. He objects to Eliade's theory not simply because Eliade ignores the nonreligious origin and function of religion but even more because, in so doing, Eliade supposedly sanctions whatever political effect religion in fact has. McCutcheon denies that the political consequence is unintended. Citing Eliade's own well-documented alliance with the fascistic Romanian Iron Guard, he asserts that the conception of religion as otherworldly is a calculated method of masking how worldly in both origin and function religion really is. The religionist discourse 'manfactures' the theory of religion not merely to give religiosity autonomy, as has conventionally been argued, but to deflect attention away from the political origin and function of religion. McCutcheon even suggests that religionist theorists manufacture religion to benefit themselves: to give themselves a discipline and, with it, jobs. Knowledge is power, as Sophists back in fifth-century Athens proclaimed.

As delightfully iconoclastic as McCutcheon's claim is, he falls far short of proving it. One must do more than show that religion has a political side, and McCutcheon himself offers only a handful of examples. One must also show that religion has no religionist side, lest, as for even reductionists, the religionist theory still hold, albeit less than monopolistically. To do so, McCutcheon must account for all of religion nonreligiously. Showing who benefits from religion hardly suffices, for there can be multiple effects of religion, which, like much else in life, can be overdetermined. And the nonreligious effects can surely, as for Weber and other theorists, be coincidental rather than intentional. In trying to replace rather than to supplement a religionist account of religion with a political one, McCutcheon thus ventures beyond both classical and contemporary social scientific theorists, whose accounts of religion are, again, proffered as less than sufficient. Indeed, McCutcheon's one-sided view ventures beyond that of even some religionists, not all of whom insist, like Eliade, that religion is exclusively religionist in origin and function.

In postmodern fashion, McCutcheon ties his repudiation of the religionist theory to an opposition to theorizing itself. Somehow the attribution of religion to a spiritual need makes all religions the same – the prerequisite for a theory. Yet somehow the attribution of religion to a political need makes all religions different – and thereby impervious to generalization. When McCutcheon insists on 'contextualizing' religion, he means rooting religion not simply in political and other material conditions generally but in the material conditions particular to each religion. Yet his mechanical quest for the material beneficiary of each religion seemingly makes all religions the same. In place of the 'totalizing' religionist theory, he puts an equally totalizing materialist theory.

Postmodern criticisms of theories of religion arise in conspicuous ignorance of contemporary philosophy of social science and the sociology of natural science. Absent is the consideration of logical problems like those of induction, falsification, and relativism. Absent is the mention of the various alternatives proposed to the standard models of scientific explanation worked out by, above all, Carl Hempel, who himself allows for merely probabilistic explanations. Postmodernism dismisses theorizing per se, and on the most illogical of grounds, of which the worst is the one that 'we live in a postmodern world.'

In postmodern approaches to religion, one never encounters discussions of the ramifications of, above all, radical, contemporary sociology of science. For example, the Edinburgh 'strong programme' of David Bloor (1991), Barry Barnes, and Steven Shapin offers a comprehensive rationale for the activity that should make postmodernists salivate: the contextualizing of theories. According to the programme, the holding of all beliefs, true and rational ones no less than false and irrational ones, is to be accounted for sociologically rather than intellectually. Where McCutcheon and the contributors to *Critical Terms* (Taylor 1998) either ignore the issue of truth, limiting themselves to the issues of origin and function, or else conflate the issues, the Edinburgh sociologists distinguish the issues, take on truth as well as origin and function, and argue that all evaluations of scientific theories are dictated by nonintellectual factors. Would-be intellectual justifications purportedly mask sociological imperatives, including ideological ones. Epistemology becomes sociology. The boldness of this nonpostmodern approach to theorizing in science makes the postmodern approach to theorizing in religion rather tame.

Overall, theorizing about religion, whether by religionists or by social scientists, remains safe from the postmodern attack, just as social scientific theorizing about religion remains safe from the religionist attack. May social scientists continue to make sense of religion.

Notes

1   I exclude Rudolf Otto because he does not account for religion but instead simply defines religion as an encounter with god.

2   Furthermore, the group comes together in the first place for religious reasons – one of the circularites in Durkheim's argument. Thus Australian aboriginal clans, Durkheim's test case, amass to 'celebrate a religious ceremony' (Durkheim 1965: 246).

3   Reductionism here means complete, or eliminative, reductionism. The reduction is ontological. By contrast, the reduction in social scientific accounts of religion is only methodological. Social scientists deny not that religious beliefs and practices exist but that those beliefs and practices generate and sustain themselves. Religious beliefs and practices are not considered hallucinatory. The 'hallucination' is the assumption that they create and perpetuate themselves.

Bibliography

Beattie, John 1966 [1964] *Other Cultures*. London: Routledge & Kegan Paul; New York: Free Press.

Bellah, Robert N. 1970 *Beyond Belief*. New York: Harper & Row.

Berger, Peter L. 1967 *The Sacred Canopy*. Garden City, NY: Doubleday. (Also published as *The Social Reality of Religion*. London: Faber and Faber, 1969.)

—— 1969 *A Rumor of Angels*. Garden City, NY: Doubleday.

Bloor, David 1991 *Knowledge and Social Imagery*. 2nd edn (1st edn 1976). Chicago: University of Chicago Press.

Douglas, Mary 1966 *Purity and Danger*. New York and London: Routledge.

—— 1973 *Natural Symbols*. 2nd edn (1st edn 1970). New York: Vintage Books; London: Barrie and Jenkins.

Durkheim, Émile 1965 [1912] *The Elementary Forms of the Religious Life*, trans. Joseph Ward Swain. New York: Free Press.

Eliade, Mircea 1963 [1958] *Patterns in Comparative Religion*, trans. Rosemary Sheed. Cleveland: Meridian Books.

—— 1968 [1959] *The Sacred and the Profane*, trans. Willard R. Trask. New York: Harvest Books.

Erikson, Erik H. 1958 *Young Man Luther*. New York: Norton.

—— 1969 *Gandhi's Truth*. New York: Norton.

Frazer, James George 1890, 1900, 1911–15 *The Golden Bough*. Abridged edn 1922. London: Macmillan.

Freud, Sigmund 1950 *Totem and Taboo*, trans. James Strachey. London: Routledge & Kegan Paul.

—— 1964 [1961] *The Future of an Illusion*, trans. W. D. Robson-Scott, rev. James Strachey. Garden City, NY: Doubleday Anchor Books.

Geertz, Clifford 1973 *The Interpretation of Cultures*. New York: Basic Books.

—— 1983 *Local Knowledge*. New York: Basic Books.

Jung, C. G. 1938 *Psychology and Religion*. New Haven, CT: Yale University Press.

McCutcheon, Russell 1996 *Manufacturing Religion*. New York: Oxford University Press.

Malinowski, Bronislaw 1925 'Magic, Science and Religion,' in Joseph Needham, ed., *Science, Religion and Reality*. New York and London: Macmillan, pp. 20–84.

Marx, Karl, and Friedrich Engels 1957 *On Religion*. Moscow: Foreign Languages Publishing.

Masuzawa, Tomoko 1993 *In Search of Dreamtime*. Chicago: University of Chicago Press.

Müller, Friedrich Max 1867 'Comparative Mythology' (1856), in his *Chips from a German Workshop*. Vol. 2. London: Longmans, Green, pp. 1–141.

Segal, Robert A. 1989 *Religion and the Social Sciences*. Atlanta: Scholars Press.

—— 1992 *Explaining and Interpreting Religion*. New York: Peter Lang.

Taylor, Mark C., ed. 1998 *Critical Terms for Religious Studies*. Chicago: University of Chicago Press.

Turner, Victor H. 1967 *The Forest of Symbols*. Ithaca, NY: Cornell University Press.

—— 1968 *The Drums of Affliction*. Oxford: Clarendon Press.

Tylor, E. B. 1871 *Primitive Culture*. 2 vols. London: Murray.

Weber, Max 1963 *The Sociology of Religion*, trans. Ephraim Fischoff. Boston: Beacon Press.

Chapter 4

Theology

David F. Ford[1]

Definitions of theology and academic theology

Theology at its broadest is thinking about questions raised by, about and between the religions. The name 'theology' is not used in all religious traditions and is rejected by some. It is a term with its own history, which will be sketched below. Yet there is no other non-controversial term for what this chapter is about, so it is used here in full recognition of the disputes and diverse associations surrounding it. Theology has many analogues or comparable terms such as 'religious thought', 'religious philosophy', various technical terms for the teaching and deliberative dimension of particular religions and even 'wisdom'. Indeed, wisdom (though itself a complex idea with different meanings and analogues in different traditions) is perhaps the most comprehensive and least controversial term for what theology is about. Wisdom may embrace describing, understanding, explaining, knowing and deciding, not only regarding matters of empirical fact but also regarding values, norms, beliefs and the shaping of lives, communities and institutions. The broad definition of theology given above could be refined by reference to wisdom. The questions raised by, about and between the religions include some that are not necessarily theological, and many of these are formative for the disciplines covered in other chapters in this volume. One helpful (if still quite vague) further determination of the nature of theology by reference to wisdom is: at its broadest, theology is thinking and deliberating in relation to the religions with a view to wisdom.

This chapter is mainly about the narrower subject of academic theology as pursued in universities and other advanced teaching and research institutions, especially in settings variously called departments of religion, religious studies, theology and religious studies, theology or divinity. The primary focus is on this academic theology in its European history and its present situation in universities that are in continuity with that tradition and its expansion beyond Europe. There have been numerous traditions of theology (or its analogues) originating in other parts of the world and in various religious traditions, some of which are increasingly significant within contemporary universities; but an appropriate way of portraying academic theology within one chapter is to concentrate on its characteristics in the academic tradition that generated the field called in other chapters the study of religion or religious studies.

In that tradition, as will be seen, theology is an inherently controversial discipline because of its subject matter, because of its history, because of the relations of other disciplines to religious issues and because of the nature of modern universities and the societies that support them. Academic theology is distinguished from theology in general mainly by its relation to the various disciplines of the academy. So a preliminary definition of academic theology (and analogues of theology) is that it *seeks wisdom in relation to questions, such as those of meaning, truth, beauty and practice, which are raised by, about and between the religions and are pursued through engagement with a range of academic disciplines.*

The final preliminary definition to be considered is that of religion. This too is a contested concept, as other chapters in this volume make clear. For the purposes of this chapter it is sufficient to identify religion in a low-key, non-technical way through a number of generally accepted examples. Religion, it is assumed, includes such ways of shaping human life in communities and their associated traditions as are exemplified by Buddhism, Christianity, Hinduism, Islam and Judaism. This is not an exclusive definition; it simply limits the scope of reference of this chapter, while allowing that much of what it says could be applied to other instances of religion and to traditions (such as cultures, philosophical schools, or secular worldviews and ways of living) which might not be included in a particular definition of religion. It is also a definition that does not entail any particular position on such disputed matters as the essence, origin and function of religion.

Before focussing on the discipline of academic theology it is important first to say more about theology and its analogues in the broadest sense.

Theology beyond the academy

The religious communities mentioned in the definition above all place a high priority on learning and teaching. An immense amount of time and energy is spent on such activities as the study and interpretation of key texts, and instruction in tradition, prayer and ethics. Much learning happens through imitation, and the adoption of habits of thought, imagination, feeling and activity, which are assimilated through participation in a community's life. Such learning and teaching have been important in helping those traditions survive and develop over many generations.

It is, however, never simply a matter of repeating the past. The texts and commentators raise questions that require consideration afresh by each generation; each period and situation raises new issues; there are conflicts, splits and challenges from inside and outside the tradition. Even when the verdict is that what is received from the past ought to be repeated and imitated as closely as possible in the present, that is a decision which cannot be arrived at without some deliberation. Thinking about appropriate ways to understand and act in the context of a particular tradition comes under my broad definition of theology. Such thought is pervasive and usually informal, and teaching usually aims at turning its basic features into implicit, taken-for-granted assumptions in the light of which questions are faced and behaviour shaped. Yet, because of the many factors which prompt internal and external questioning, explicit thought may also be provoked, and theological inquiry, in the sense described above, may be generated. What is the right interpretation of this text? How should children be educated in this tradition? What is the right response to legal or political injustice? Does God exist? If so, what sort of God? What about death, creation, salvation, gender issues? What, if any, is the purpose of life? How should those with very different traditions and conceptions be treated? Such questions may give rise to theological inquiry.

Yet it is not only those who identify with a particular community and its traditions who ask such questions. Religions provoke inquiry in many beyond their own members; and some of their own members may dissociate themselves from their community but may still (sometimes even more energetically) pursue such questions. In addition, there are public debates about every major area of life – medicine, politics, economics, war, justice and so on – which raise religious issues and require deliberation and decision. Such debates display various types of theological thinking, both implicit and explicit.

Therefore theology in the broad sense is practised not only within religious communities but also by many who are beyond such communities or in an ambivalent relationship with them; and it is also present between religious communities and in public debates, both within and between nations.

Finally, theological questions arise at all levels of education. They may be focussed in religious or theological education, but, because of the considerations discussed above, they are also distributed through other subjects, and they are relevant to overall educational policy and practice.

Overall, it is important to remember that only a very small part of the theology going on in the world is taught and learnt in the university settings that are the main concern of this chapter.

Academic theology: early history in Europe

The Greek word *theologia* meant an account of the gods, and it was taken over by the early Christian church to refer to the biblical account of God's relationship to humanity. This close relationship to scripture was maintained through the Middle Ages in western Europe, when theology in the narrower sense of a specific discipline studied in universities arose with the development of universities in the early thirteenth century. It is significant that these universities themselves had many characteristics in common with Islamic institutions from which Christian scholars learnt a great deal.

Before the foundation of universities, theology had been nurtured in the many monasteries around Europe and in associated rural schools. Theology was there inseparable from the duties of worship and prayer, pervaded by the life of the cloister. In the cities the cathedral schools, founded for training diocesan clergy, were important theological centres. In addition, theology in the cities became part of the guild-oriented activity of a new rising class of freemen, both students and teachers, who responded favourably to new forms of argument and teaching and to the rediscovery of forgotten writings of the past. Here theology in schools (hence the label 'scholastic') was becoming a specialty subject for professional, philosophically trained dialecticians. Anselm of Canterbury (1033–1109), based in a monastery, brought fresh systematic and argumentative rigour to theology, and described it as 'faith seeking understanding'. Peter Abelard (1079–1142) represented the new sort of teacher and dialectician. In Paris, the new religious movement embodied in the Augustinian canons of St Victor mediated between the claims of the monastery and the schoolroom. This was an age of discovery, compilation and integration, which culminated in producing what became (in addition to the Bible) the standard theological text for discussion in the university schoolrooms of Europe during the next four centuries. This was the *Sentences* of Peter the Lombard (d. 1160), a collection of four books of the theological wisdom of Scripture and of the early Fathers of the church.

After the formal establishment of the first universities in the first part of the thirteenth century, scholastic theology developed under a new influence, the mendicant religious orders of Franciscans and Dominicans. Both flourished in the new University of Paris. Thomas Aquinas (1225–1274) among the Dominicans and Bonaventure (1221–1274) among the Franciscans developed distinctive ways of doing theology within the new universities. They drew on traditional monastic resources such as Augustine and Pseudo-Dionysius, and, especially in Thomas's case, on newly discovered texts of Aristotle as well. Their disputation-dominated educational environment produced several major theological syntheses, which remain classic texts. One persistently contentious issue remained the nature of theology. Whereas all agreed that it was a form of *sapientia* (wisdom) there was dispute about its status as a *scientia* (branch of rational knowledge relying on its own first principles).

In the later Middle Ages theology split into distinct 'ways' based on the religious orders. After 1450, as the Renaissance and other changes occurred in Europe, the dominance of Parisian theology was broken as many European universities established theology faculties. The largely Dominican faculty at Salamanca replaced Lombard's *Sentences* with Thomas Aquinas's *Summa Theologiae* as the basic text for classroom commentary. The Salamancan theologian Melchior Cano (1509–1560) produced a systematic treatise combining various kinds of authoritative texts, scriptural, scholastic and Renaissance humanist, including historical and scientific, covering the main theological *loci* (places). This gave birth to systematic theology in the modern sense.

By this time, humanist scholarship, especially represented by Desiderius Erasmus (1466–1536), together with the initiation of the Protestant Reformation by a professor at the University of Wittenberg, Martin Luther (1483–1546), had begun a reaction against a scholastic theology that had become highly specialised and abstruse. The humanist and Protestant emphasis was on recovering the original sense of scripture and of early Christian writers. They produced scholarly editions of the texts based on the best possible manuscript evidence, and they interpreted the 'plain sense' of the texts with the intention of approximating as near as possible to what the authors meant. The result in Protestant universities was that the main task of theology became the interpretation of scripture studied in Hebrew and Greek.

Catholic theology continued to be scholastic in form, with Thomas Aquinas dominant, though often understood through the medium of later interpreters and summaries in manuals. Polemics between Catholics and Protestants increasingly shaped both sides, as they developed systematic statements of their positions and counterpositions. A further dimension was apologetics defending theological positions against an increasing number of critiques and challenges, some of which made a sharp distinction between 'revealed' and 'natural' religion and theology. During the eighteenth century, theology began to lose its role as the 'leading science' whose word carried authority for other faculties. The rise of sovereign states, whose practical demands were less theological than legal, gave pre-eminence to the law faculties. These in turn were superseded by the 'new sciences' that entered the curriculum, studying the 'book of nature'. Many of the ideas that had most effect on later discussion of theological issues were generated by those outside theology faculties, whether Protestant or Catholic.

During these centuries, theology also became increasingly differentiated into branches. By the twentieth century the main branches had become: systematic (or dogmatic or doctrinal or constructive) theology; historical theology; biblical theology; moral theology (or theological ethics); philosophical theology; practical (or pastoral) theology and mystical theology (or spirituality).

Academic theology in the modern university

A formative event in the shaping of the modern academic tradition of Christian theology in the nineteenth and twentieth centuries was the foundation of the University of Berlin in 1809, which became for many the archetypal modern university (see Frei 1992: 95ff.). There was considerable debate about whether theology ought to be included in it. Some (such as the philosopher J.G. Fichte) argued that it had no place in a university committed to modern standards of rationality. The position which won was that of the theologian F.D.E. Schleiermacher, who affirmed the role of rationality in the university without allowing it either to dictate to theology or to be in competition with theology. He saw theology as a positive science or discipline (*Wissenschaft*), by which he meant that it was not included within any one theoretical discipline but that it related to several disciplines with a view to the practical task of educating those who would lead the Christian church. The usual pattern of theological faculties in the German university became that of the state overseeing and paying for a faculty which both owed allegiance to general standards of rationality (*Wissenschaft*) that presuppose academic freedom, and also was committed to training clergy for the state Protestant church. Two consequences of this make modern German theology a specially good focus through which to study the discipline in modernity.

First, it meant that theology was carried on in an environment where it was continually in engagement with and informed by other academic disciplines in their most advanced forms. Christianity became the religion that was most thoroughly examined, explained, critiqued and argued about in the nineteenth-century European university.

Second, the attempt to hold together the requirements of academy and church built into theology the tendency towards a tension between 'reason' and 'faith'. This tension is one way of approaching the task of describing basic types of modern Christian theology (see Frei 1992; Ford 2005; cf. below pp. 69–71). These types are of wider relevance than to the German or the Christian context, and developing them will provide a helpful framework later in this chapter.

The German pattern might be described as confessional theology (in the sense of theology according to the belief and practice of one religious community or 'confession' of faith) funded by the state. This continues to be the norm in Germany and other countries which follow its pattern, and some universities contain both Roman Catholic and Protestant faculties of theology. In addition, some German universities teach religious studies or 'history of religions', and there is a fluid situation as regards the relations with theology.

Elsewhere, different patterns have emerged. Those in North America and England exemplify the main contrasting ways in which the discipline is present in universities today.

In North America the tendency has been to separate theology from religious studies. Theology has often been understood as a confessional discipline (whereas the description given above includes confessional theology but is not limited to it) and has been largely taught in institutions affiliated to a Christian church or group of churches. The main location of theology has therefore been the 'seminary' or 'divinity school', sometimes attached as a professional school to a non-state university. Because of the separation of church and state, theology has rarely been taught, except as intellectual history, at state-funded universities, but many church-affiliated universities have departments of theology. Departments of religious studies exist in many state and private universities. These embody various understandings of the discipline, ranging from a few which integrate theology with religious studies, to others which define religious studies over against theology (a position that has been represented controversially by Don Wiebe, the author of Chapter 6). Judaism, numerically far smaller than Christianity, displays a comparable range of relationships in the institutionalisation of its theology or (to use a term which is preferred by many Jews) its religious thought (see pp. 73–4).

In Britain university theology has become largely state-funded, and has developed from being exclusively Christian and Anglican to embracing, first, other Christian traditions, and then, in the later twentieth century, other religions. Departments in British universities are called variously theology, religious studies, theology and religious studies, and divinity. Whatever the name, most now embrace both theology and religious studies.

Most universities in other parts of the world roughly correspond to the German (confessional theology), American (separation of theology and religious studies) or British (integration of theology with religious studies) models for the field, and both within countries and internationally there is a continuing debate about which is to be preferred. The next section will outline the main issues in the debate.

Theology in distinction from religious studies

Theology has advanced reasons why it should be separate from religious studies; religious studies has likewise had reasons for being separate from theology; and there have been advocates of integration who refuse to accept such separation. We will consider each set of reasons in turn, while recognizing that there are also those who interpret the reasons on one or both sides as rationalizations of religious, political or economic interests intent on maintaining or gaining power and influence.

Theology's reasons for favouring separation centre on three related considerations.

First, especially in the Abrahamic faiths (Judaism, Christianity and Islam) there is the role of God in knowing God, and of faith and commitment in doing theology. If theology includes knowing God (or analogues of God), and if knowing God depends on responding in faith and obedience (or on some other form of self-involving practice) to God's initiative, then surely those who are not believers cannot do theology?

Second, moving beyond the possible individualism of the first point, there is the relation of theology to a community and its tradition. If a particular theology is intrinsically connected to a particular community, then surely it can only be genuinely pursued in the context of that community? The logic of these points is to confine genuine theology to confessional faculties, seminaries, divinity schools or other institutions in affiliation with the community whose theology is being studied.

Third, there has been some theological suspicion of the very category of 'religion'. Whereas, for example, God in Jewish, Christian or Muslim belief can be understood as relating to and transcending all creation, religion has often been seen as one domain of human existence among others. The objection of theology to being paired with religious studies is that this constricts the scope of theology. The effect of the Enlightenment (not least through inventing the modern sense of the word 'religion') tended to be to privatize religion, so that it became a matter of private discretion with its proper sphere in human interiority. Where religion's public role was concerned, the tendency was to limit its power and to deny its contribution to public truth. Its competitors in the public sphere included not only nationalism, capitalism and communism, but also new understandings of the universe, humanity, history and society which were closely associated with various academic disciplines. When these disciplines focussed on their limited concepts of religion, theology did not find that they could do justice to its questions of meaning, truth, beauty and practice.

Religious studies in distinction from theology

Religious studies, for its part, has been aware that its origins in European and American universities lay partly in a desire for academic freedom for the study of religion without being answerable to religious authorities. Institutional separation from theology had a political point.

Academically, the key issue concerned knowledge and the methods which lead to it. The study of religion developed as a loose alliance of disciplines whose main concerns were elsewhere. It has never had a generally agreed method or set of methods, despite many proposals. In one of the most comprehensive accounts of the field, Walter H. Capps finds its fragile coherence in an Enlightenment tradition stemming from Descartes and Kant in its conception of knowledge and method (Capps 1995). Religious studies has focussed on questions such as the essence and origin of religion, the description and function of religion, the language of religion and the comparison of religions. But, in dealing with those questions through disciplines such as philosophy, psychology, sociology, phenomenology and anthropology, Capps suggests that the most fundamental feature of the field has been a broadly Kantian epistemology (if that can be taken as allowing for both empiricist and hermeneutical developments). The concern for academic autonomy in line with that tradition has often persuaded it to prefer separation from theology, except where theology (or its analogues) is willing to accept its terms. Capps is hospitable to theology, which is willing to find a role contributing to his conception of religious studies, but he also recognizes the need to go beyond his own paradigm. The next section offers one conception of how that might be achieved.

The question about knowledge and methods is a mirror-image of the problems, mentioned above, which theology has with religious studies. Religious studies has usually wanted to bracket out, for example, any conception of God being involved in the knowing that goes on in the field; and its pursuit of questions of meaning, truth, beauty and practice has tended to be limited to the methods of its constituent disciplines. It prefers to use such methods in rigorous pursuit of what can be known and justified to dealing with larger or more synthetic issues without those methods or beyond them. Overall, therefore, a basic concern of religious studies has been that of the academic integrity of the field.

Theology integrated with religious studies

Those who advocate the integration of theology with religious studies rarely suggest that all theology and religious studies should be institutionally combined. They recognize that religious communities will want to have their own academic institutions in which confessional theology (or its analogues) would be the norm; and that many universities will want to specialize in their religious studies (e.g. by focussing on a few disciplines such as sociology, anthropology or phenomenology) so as exclude theology as well as some other disciplines. There are many factors (historical, religious, political, economic, cultural) other than the overall conception of the field which help determine its shape in a particular institution. Their main point for integration is the academic case in principle for the inseparability of the two. One version of the case is as follows.

First, theology is not in competition with religious studies but needs it. If theology is to be rigorous in its pursuit of questions of meaning, truth, beauty and practice then it needs to draw on work in other disciplines. This will not just be a matter of using their results when they are congenial, but rather of entering into them from the inside and engaging both critically and constructively with their methods and results. Academic theology has done this much more thoroughly in some areas than in others. It has been most widely practised in relation to philosophy, textual scholarship and history. In each of these fields there are many practitioners who integrate their discipline with theology, and also many who do not. This gives rise to considerable debate about issues that are not likely to be conclusively resolved (a common situation in philosophy, textual interpretation and history). The argument is that for the health of the field it is desirable to have some settings where such debates can be carried on as fully as possible.

Second, theology is not just pursued by those who identify with a particular community, and it can be studied in many ways other than confessionally (see p. 63). Universities are obvious settings for those who wish to pursue theological questions in such ways. For the members of particular religious communities there can also be advantages in doing theology in dialogue with academics and students of other faith traditions and of none.

Third, religious studies need not be in competition with theology. Certain definitions of the field exclude certain definitions of theology (see above pp. 61–62), but other definitions of religious studies open it towards integration with theology. A key issue is how far questions intrinsic to the field may be pursued, and whether some answers to those questions are to be ruled out in advance. For example, is the question of truth concerning the reality of God as identified by a particular tradition allowed to be pursued and then answered in line with that tradition? If so, then the way is opened for critical and constructive theology within a religious studies milieu. If not, what reasons can be offered for cutting off inquiry and disallowing certain answers? Such cutting off and disallowing either appears arbitrary or it relies on criteria that are themselves widely contested and debated within the field. The irresolvability of the dispute over boundaries and criteria has been intensified by similar disputes, often bitter, in other disciplines with which religious studies and theology engage, such as literary studies, philosophy, history and the human sciences.

Fourth, the three main responsibilities of theology and religious studies can be argued to converge and so make integration appropriate for them in university settings. The first is their responsibility towards the academy and its disciplines. The requirement is excellence in the study and teaching of texts, history, laws, traditions, practices, institutions, ideas, the arts and so on, as these relate to religions in the past and the present. This involves standards set by peer groups, work within and collaboration between disciplines and a worldwide network of communication. The second is their responsibility towards religious communities. This includes the tasks of carrying out their academic responsibilities critically and constructively, educating members of religious communities as well as others, and providing forums where religious traditions can engage in study, dialogue and debate together. Universities have increasingly become centres of such interfaith engagement in which theological concerns with, for example, questions of truth and practice, go together with the use of a range of academic disciplines. The third is their responsibility to society and the realm of public life. Issues in politics, law, the media, education, medicine and family life often raise questions which require complex interdisciplinary, interreligious and international collaboration. These questions embrace theological as well as other matters.

Fifth, in the light of the above four points, the case for a fundamental dualism in the field is undermined. It is still appropriate to have institutions with particular emphases and commitments, but the overall intellectual and ethical 'ecology' of the field embraces theology and religious studies.

Types of Christian theology

How can the field of academic theology be described so as to do justice to the range of theologies and their different ways of relating to other disciplines? One typology worked out in relation to Christian theology is that of Frei (1992). It takes account of the importance of institutional contexts both historically and today. Frei takes the University of Berlin as his historical point of departure (see above pp. 65–6), and his typology also relates to the American situation of theology and religious studies. He recognizes that there are very different types of theology, some of which are more at home in universities than others. His typology therefore grows out of the academic tradition with which this chapter is mainly concerned and it is limited to Christian theology; but it can also be developed in relation to other religious traditions. Its attempt to do descriptive justice to the current state of the field results in allowing both for the separation of theology and religious studies and for their integration.

There are five types on a continuum, of which the two extremes will be described first.

Type I

This type gives complete priority to some contemporary philosophy, worldview, practical agenda or one or more academic disciplines. In its academic form it subjects

Christian theology to 'general criteria of intelligibility, coherence, and truth that it must share with other academic disciplines' (Frei 1992: 2). Immanuel Kant (1724–1804) is seen as the main historical exemplar of this in modernity. He applied his criteria of rationality and morality to theology and offered an understanding of religion 'within the bounds of reason alone'. In terms of the previous discussion, a Kantian Type 1 is in line with a conception of religious studies which insists on a particular set of epistemological criteria being met by any theology that is to be admitted to the academy. It therefore excludes other types of theology mentioned below. It also gives philosophy (of a particular type) priority as the main cognate discipline of theology.

Other versions of Type 1 use different external criteria to judge theology – for example, an ecological worldview, or a feminist ethic, or a political programme or an imaginative aesthetic.

Type 5

This type takes Christian theology as exclusively a matter of Christian self-description. It is the 'grammar of faith', its internal logic learnt like a new language through acquiring appropriate conceptual skills. It offers a scriptural understanding or a traditional theology or version of Christianity as something with its own integrity that is not to be judged by outside criteria. All reality is to be seen in Christian terms, and there is a radical rejection of other frameworks and worldviews. Examples include some types of fundamentalism (such as those seeing the Bible as inerrant and all-sufficient for theology) and also more sophisticated conceptions of a religion as a distinctive and embracing 'language game' or 'world of meaning'. In terms of the previous discussion, Type 5 is in line with a conception of theology which prefers separation from religious studies and other disciplines.

The two extremes of Types 1 and 5 can be seen to come together in their tendency to see everything in terms of some given framework (whether Christian or non-Christian) and to cut off the possibilities for dialogue across boundaries.

Types 2, 3 and 4

Between the two extremes come three types that in various ways incorporate dialogue.

Type 2 tries to correlate general meaning structures with what is specifically Christian. It interprets Christianity consistently in terms of some contemporary philosophy, idiom or concern, while trying to do justice to the distinctiveness of Christianity. One example is the German theologian Rudolf Bultmann (1884–1976), who reconceived the Christian Gospel in terms of existentialist philosophy. The overall integration is biased towards the general framework, and so this type is close to Type 1.

If Type 2 moves in the other direction towards a correlation which does not attempt a comprehensive integration, then it becomes Type 3. This non-systematic correlation is a thoroughly dialogical form of theology. Theological questions, methods and positions are continually being correlated with other questions, methods and positions. Theology can learn a great deal from other disciplines and positions without giving a single one overarching significance, and it is only from within the process of dialogue that judgements can be made. Schleiermacher is an example of this type, as is Paul Tillich (1886–1965) who correlated fundamental questions about life and history with the meaning offered by Christian symbols and ideas.

Type 4 gives priority to Christian self-description, letting that govern the applicability of general criteria of meaning, truth and practice in Christian theology, yet nevertheless engaging with a range of disciplines and with other worldviews and theological positions in *ad hoc* ways. It does not go to the extreme of Type 5, but still insists that no other framework should be able to dictate how to understand the main contents of Christian faith. It is 'faith seeking understanding', basically trusting the main lines of classic Christian testimony to God and the Gospel, but also open to a wide range of dialogues – not least because God is seen as involved with all reality. The Swiss theologian Karl Barth is of this type, resisting the assimilation of Christian faith to Western culture and ideologies, especially that of the Nazis. Type 4 sees Type 3 as inherently unstable: there can be no neutral standpoint from which to carry on dialogues, and therefore there has to be a basic commitment for or against Christian faith – which yet needs to be tested in encounter with other positions. A favoured cognate discipline of this type of theology as practised in Britain and North America is the more descriptive (rather than explanatory) types of social science.

Assessment of the types

Any complex theology is not likely to fit neatly into a single type, and the purpose here is not to set up neat pigeonholes enabling all theologians to be labelled. Many will display subtle blends and uncategorizable positions which resist easy description. Rather, the aim is to portray a range of types which spans the field and enables a judgement about theology in relation to other disciplines, including those embraced in religious studies. The judgement is that, while Type 5 is likely to be least at home in the university and Type 1 least at home in the Christian community, Types 2, 3 and 4 can, in different ways and with different points of tension, be at home in both. There are Christian communities that would exclude the first four types, and there are universities that would exclude the last four types, but these ways of drawing boundaries are controversial and many institutions are more inclusive. The practical conclusion is that an overview of the discipline of theology, as it has developed in universities carrying forward the European tradition, argues for a definition that can embrace all five types. This in turn supports the argument above in the previous section that it makes academic as well as theological sense to see the field as whole, embracing theology and religious studies. The different types of theology construe the field very variously, and particular institutions and traditions need to take fundamental decisions about which types they embrace – but that is the case in many other fields too.

Beyond Christian theology

The above typology has been deliberately tradition-specific. The next question is whether something like those types do justice to the other religious traditions which are the examples being used in this chapter: Judaism, Islam, Hinduism and Buddhism. There was a blossoming of the study of these and other religious traditions in the universities of Europe and the US in the nineteenth century, though apart from the special case of Judaism the study was mostly outside theological faculties. A major factor in the rise of the field of religious studies was an attempt to do fuller academic justice to religions other than Christianity. From a standpoint at the beginning of the twenty-first century it is possible to see that attempt as having two main phases, the second still in progress and provoking much debate.

The first phase involved the establishment of religious studies over against theology (usually against confessional Christian theology). The main concern was for properly academic study through disciplines such as the others described in this Companion.

The second phase has accompanied the multiplication of universities around the world and the growth of the study of theology and religious studies in them. The last half of the twentieth century has seen an unprecedented expansion in higher education and of the disciplines and subdisciplines that study religions. One crucial feature of this second phase has been that considerable numbers of academics and students in universities now study their own religion as well as the religions of others. This has led to debates similar to those which have surrounded Christian theology in the European tradition. How far is it appropriate to be a Jew and pursue critical and constructive Jewish thought in a university? If a Buddhist academic is discussing ethical issues, how far is it appropriate to develop Buddhist positions? Increasingly, the answer has been that it is appropriate; then the debate moves on to consider the criteria of appropriateness. But, once it is granted that members of traditions can contribute in such ways to academic discussions and utilize a range of disciplines in doing so, then what has been defined above as academic theology is being practised. The result is that the type of religious studies which defined itself against Christian confessional theology is now being challenged to 're-theologize'. Can it recognize the academic validity of inquiries, debates and dialogues which are theological (in the sense of seeking wisdom about questions of meaning, truth, beauty and practice relating to the religions and the issues they raise), which use various academic disciplines, and which relate to other traditions besides Christianity?

The impetus towards such theology has been strengthened by suspicion directed towards the ways in which religions have been studied by Western academics. For example, the accounts of Judaism by non-Jews (especially Christians) have been subjected to thorough critique (especially by Jews); Islam, Buddhism and Hinduism have struggled to resist the imposition of 'orientalist' identities projected by Western scholars; and Christians have often judged accounts of their faith to be distorted by post-Enlightenment academic presuppositions and criteria. In particular there has been a rejection of 'ideologies of neutrality' and associated positions such as the dichotomy between fact from value, or the separation of knowledge from ethics and faith. The key point has been: 'no one stands nowhere', and it is desirable that religious traditions (together with genders, races, classes and cultures) have their own academic voices that can speak from where they stand. Huge questions of epistemology, ethics, theology and the meaning of 'academic' are at stake here and are likely to remain in contention; but once they have been raised they are hard to suppress, and many institutions have created the settings for pursuing them. One such setting is the integrated field of theology and religious studies.

The typology suggested by Frei is an attempt to devise a conception of the field that fits such a setting. It is applicable to religions besides Christianity insofar as each is a tradition (or set of traditions) whose traditional identity can be rethought and developed in the present according to the five types. For example, there are those who assimilate Buddhist ideas and practices to a variety of non-Buddhist frameworks (Type 1); others are 'fundamentalist', or convinced of the self-sufficiency of a particular set of traditional Buddhist ideas and practices (Type 5); and others arrive at more dialogical identities which balance differently between those extremes (Types 2, 3 and 4).

Yet each of the sample religions with which this chapter is concerned has a distinctive history in relation to theology or its analogues. In line with this chapter's limited scope (focussing on theology in the university tradition begun in western Europe in the Middle Ages, continued today in research universities that are successors to that tradition in and beyond Europe and America, and concerned especially with the relation between theology and religious studies) it is not possible to discuss the history of each tradition in detail. What are offered below are some considerations from the standpoint of each of the five traditions as they take part in theology and religious studies in contemporary universities. Most space is given to Judaism as the tradition which has, besides Christianity, been most intensively engaged with academic study and thought in the universities of Europe, North America and more recently Israel.

Judaism

The term 'theology' is often considered suspect among Jewish thinkers. This is partly because theology is sometimes seen as being about the inner life of God, which has not usually been a Jewish concern. Partly it has been a reaction of a minority against oppressive and dominant confessional theology: it has not been safe for Jews to condone public or university theological talk, since Christians (or others) could use it to seek domination or to proselytize. Partly, too, theology has been seen as abstractive, intellectualizing and even dogmatizing (in the bad sense) instead of practice-oriented discussion about community-specific behaviour. Perhaps the most acceptable term is Jewish religious thought.

The main institution for articulating Jewish religious thought has been the rabbinic academy, whose origins are in the 'yeshivah', a centre of learning and discussion going back to the Mishnaic period in Palestine, and continuing in the Talmudic academies of Palestine and Babylonia, and later in centres spread around the diaspora. The discourse of these centres combined study of biblical texts (with a view to expounding both its plain sense and also its relevance to traditional and current issues), ethical discussion, jurisprudence, literary interpretation, folk science and much else. The rabbinic academy is still the normative institution for the religious thought of most orthodox Jewish communities, and there are equivalents in other forms of Judaism – for example, rabbinical seminaries, Jewish colleges and other institutes.

There have been other non-university centres of Jewish religious thought besides the rabbinical academies. Beginning in the late Persian or Second Temple period, sages, and later rabbis and textual scholars, included devotees of the esoteric circles that generated Jewish mystical practice and literature or 'kabbalah'. These kabbalistic circles conducted 'theology' in the sense of studying the inner life of God, or at least those dimensions of God that are processual and descend into levels of human consciousness. Hasidism is a large, popular movement of lived kabbalah, and some contemporary Jewish academics are paying increasing attention to kabbalistic study.

One influential tradition in Jewish thought has been sustained by intellectuals, scientists and statesmen working in a succession of empires and civilizations – Persian, Greek, Roman, Islamic, Christian, modern European and American. They have been social and cultural brokers in statecraft, finance, medicine, the sciences and scholarship, and have produced much sophisticated and often influential thinking which mediates between Jewish and non-Jewish interests and understandings and which might be categorized under Types 2, 3 and 4 above. Examples include Moses Maimonides (1125–1204) in medieval Spain, the Jewish doctors, mystics, scientists, scholars and diplomats of Renaissance Italy, the Jewish intelligentsia in twentieth century New York, and communities of lively religious thought which flourish outside the universities in Israel.

Jews were long excluded from the Christian-dominated university tradition of Europe, but since their entry into these academic settings they have, considering their small numbers, been disproportionately influential in many disciplines. Some have approximated to Types 1 and 2 above, attempting to accommodate Jewish religious traditions to the categories of Western thought. This was developed in German universities in the nineteenth century, Moses Mendelssohn (1729–1786) being a major figure. Others studied Judaism according to the canons of *Wissenschaft* (see p. 63), with a strong historicist tendency. This tradition, known in German as *Wissenschaft des Judentums*, remains the strongest influence on Jewish academic religious study. At its heart is the study of Jewish texts by explaining how and in which contexts they were composed, and what their sentences meant to those who composed and received them. This study is 'theological' in the sense used in this chapter insofar as it sometimes argues that the religious meaning of the texts is exhausted by what can be elicited through its methods.

Out of this tradition of *Wissenschaft* have come more complex forms of interaction, brokerage or dialogue with various types of academic inquiry, perhaps best labelled 'humanistic Jewish studies'. The study of texts has been opened up by such approaches as hermeneutical theory, structuralism and deconstruction, and the range of human and natural sciences has been related to Jewish concerns. In terms of the types above, it has most affinities with Type 3, but relates happily to any of the first four.

Finally, a recent development has called itself 'postcritical' or 'postliberal', sometimes welcoming the label 'Jewish theology'. Influenced by literary studies, postmodernism, and twentieth-century Jewish philosophies originating in Germany, France and America, these thinkers try to integrate three elements: philosophical inquiry; academic studies of texts, society and history; and traditional forms of rabbinic text study and practice. Its main affinities are with Type 4 in its concern to maintain a community-specific identity while learning from a wide range of dialogues – including dialogues with other religious traditions.

Islam

Islamic theology shares some of the strategies and concerns of Christian and Jewish discourse about God, since all three traditions are rooted in ancient Semitic narratives of a just and merciful Creator, and have historically evolved under the influence of Greek thought. For some three centuries after the death of the Prophet Muhammad (632 CE) the theology of the new religion was stimulated by encounters with several eastern Christian traditions, a debt which was later to be repaid when Avicenna, Ghazali and Averroes exercised profound influence on theologians of the Latin west in the Middle Ages. In spite of these convergences, however, the term 'theology' has no one Arabic equivalent, and theology in the sense used in this chapter has been pursued across many of the traditional Islamic disciplines.

One such subject area is Islamic jurispurdence (*usul al-fiqh*), which incorporates discussions of moral liability, natural law, the status of non-Muslims and other topics which received exhaustive treatment of a theological nature.

Sufism, Islam's highly diversified mystical and esoteric expression, also included systematic expositions of doctrine and cosmology in which mystical and exoteric teachings were juxtaposed, frequently in order to justify speculative or mystical insights to literalists.

A further discipline of great historic moment was Islamic philosophy (*falsafa* or *hikma*), which inherited late Greek philosophical syntheses and developed them into multiple religious systems. Many of these were regarded as too unscriptural and were therefore frequently confined to the status of private belief systems among elite circles.

Interacting with all these disciplines was *kalam*, conventionally translated as 'Islamic theology'. This is primarily a scriptural enterprise, applying forms of reasoning of Greek origin to the frequently enigmatic data of revelation. Ghazali (d. 1111) and Shahrastani (d. 1153) incorporated aspects of the *falsafa* tradition to shape *kalam* into a highly complex and rigorous Islamic worldview. Their tradition, known as Ash'arism, is still taught as Islam's orthodoxy in most Muslim countries. Orthodox status is also accorded to Maturidism, a theology which prevails among Muslims in the Indian subcontinent, Turkey, Uzbekistan and the Balkans. The debates between these schools are due mostly to the greater weight attached to rationality by Maturidism over against the comparatively more scriptural Ash'arism.

There have been various institutional settings for these types of theology, perhaps the most distinguished being Al-Azhar University in Cairo. In the twentieth century there have been many new universities. Those in Saudi Arabia, for example, have rejected the forms of reasoning from scripture found in both Ash'arism and Maturidism in favour of a strict literalism. These 'fundamentalists' (*Salafis*) are in a polemical relationship with traditional institutions such as Al-Azhar, and it may be that this engagement has become a more significant and widespread activity than the engagement with the discourses of modernity. In terms of the types used in this chapter, the main debates are between a Type 4, which inhabits and interprets the Qur'an with the aid of traditional Greek-influenced rationality, and a Type 5, which finds the Qur'an self-sufficient.

So far there has been comparatively little Muslim theology analogous to Types 1, 2 or 3. This is partly because of the widespread acceptance of the divinely inspired status of the Qur'anic text, and a rejection of the relevance of text-critical method-ologies. There are some modern Muslim theologians open to post-Kantian approaches to metaphysics, found in more secular institutions such as Dar al-Ulum, a faculty of Cairo University or the Islamic Research Academy of Pakistan. Perhaps partly because the Qur'an contains comparatively little cosmological or other material that might clash with modern science, the defining controversies in modern Islam concern the extent of the relevance of medieval Islamic law to modern communities. So it is in matters of behaviour rather than belief that the greatest range of types is found.

It is in universities in the European tradition that some of the potentially most far-reaching developments are now taking place. Due to the establishment of large Muslim communities in Europe and North America, making it now the second largest religion in the West, Muslim scholars and theologians are increasingly present in faculties of theology and religious studies. The study of Islam has shifted there away from 'oriental studies', and new forms of dialogue and interpretation are being developed.

Hinduism and Buddhism

Hinduism and Buddhism both have long and complex intellectual traditions of thought in many genres and many types of institutions. As with the other religious traditions, the university plays only a small role in contributing to Hindu and Buddhist religious or theological thought in the sense of a pursuit of wisdom. 'Hinduism' and 'Buddhism' themselves are terms which became popular due to Western interpreters in the nineteenth century but which mask the deeply plural phenomena that more developed understanding of these traditions now suggests. Nineteenth century university studies often approached these from the angle of philology, with more systematic studies of the religious dimensions frequently shaped by colonial concerns. The earlier conceptualizations of Hinduism concentrated on the Sanskritic (Brahmanical or elitist) forms as representative, with continuing repercussions.

India in the twentieth century has been one of the most important countries for dialogue between religious traditions, including Hinduism, Buddhism, Christianity and Islam. This dialogue has been deeply affected by Hindu and Buddhist approaches that insisted not only on theoretical and doctrinal discussion and disputation, in which argument (*tarka*) based on textual exegesis (*mimamsa*) plays a prominent part (and where the argumentation has been vigorously intra- and inter-religious in both traditions), but also on experience or realization of the goal (*anubhava/saksat-kara*, *dhyana*, ultimately *moksa/nirvana*), in what is an integrated grasp of truth-in-life.

This in turn encouraged suspicion of Western academic study applied to religion, especially the stress on the 'objectivity' of truth and knowledge and the tendency to separate understanding from practice. In Indian universities, the secular constitution led to religious traditions being studied mainly in departments of philosophy in ways similar to the more 'neutralist' approaches to religious studies in the West, and this reinforced the alienation of universities from the more wisdom-oriented inquiries of those concerned with the contemporary development of religious traditions and dialogue between them. In other countries of the East, however, there are other patterns – in Thailand, for example, where Buddhism is for all practical purposes the state religion, the study of Buddhism is privileged in the universities.

The numbers of Hindus and Buddhists living in diaspora in the West, together with large numbers of Westerners who now practice versions of these faiths, has begun to transform the situation of Hinduism and Buddhism in Western universities, where the late twentieth century saw a blossoming of posts related to them. The pattern has been repeated of a move from 'oriental studies' to 'religious studies' to a pluralist situation where oriental studies and religious studies continue, but there are also Hindus, Buddhists and others engaged in deliberating about questions of meaning, truth, beauty and practice with a view to wisdom for the contemporary situation.

Christianity

So far, Christian theology has been dealt with mainly in its history as a discipline, its relation to religious studies and its types. The contemporary situation of Christian theology is described using the five types in Ford 2005.

Of the traditions described above, the closest parallel is with Judaism, and there are analogies in Christian theology for most of the strands in Jewish theology. There is rapid growth at present in studies and constructive contributions to 'theology and . . .' topics, the accompanying fields including notably philosophy, ethics, politics (leading to 'theologies of liberation'), the natural and human sciences, culture and the arts, gender (leading to feminist and womanist theologies), race, education, other religions and postmodernity. The German and other European and North American academic traditions continue strongly, but the most obvious new development in the twentieth century has been that of theological traditions in other countries and cultures. African, Asian, Latin American and Antipodean theologies have all emerged (often displaying acute tensions between the types described above), and many of these are networked in transregional movements.

At the same time, major church traditions have undergone theological trans-formations, most noticeably the Roman Catholic Church through the Second Vatican Council. At present the Orthodox Church in countries formerly Communist is having to come to intellectual (and other) terms with exposure to massive global and local pressures; and the Pentecostal movement (reckoned to number over 300 million) is beginning to develop its own academic theology. Between the churches there have developed ecumenical theologies and theologies advocating or undergirding common action for justice, peace and ecological issues. As with other religious traditions, the spread of education has meant that far more members of churches are able to engage with theology, and there are local and international networks with university-educated laypeople addressing theological issues in relation to the Bible, tradition, and contemporary understanding and living.

The future of theology

Viewed globally, the vitality of theology in the twentieth century was unprecedented: the numbers of institutions, students, teachers, researchers, forms of theology and publications expanded vastly. It is unlikely that this vitality will diminish. Questions of meaning, truth, beauty and practice relating to the religions will continue to be relevant (and controversial), and the continuing rate of change in most areas of life will require that responses to those questions be constantly reimagined, rethought and reapplied. Higher education is likely to continue to expand, and there is no sign that the increase in numbers in members of the major religions is slowing. The convergence of such factors point to a healthy future, at least in quantitative terms.

Theology in universities is likely to continue according to a variety of patterns, such as the three mainly discussed in this chapter. Quantitatively, the main setting for theology or religious thought will continue to be institutions committed to particular religious traditions. There will also continue to be university settings in which religious studies is pursued without theology. My speculation is that the nature of the field, including its responsibilities towards academic disciplines, religious communities and public discourse, will also lead to an increase in places where theology and religious studies are integrated. The history of the field in recent centuries has not seen new forms superseding old ones (religious studies did not eliminate theology in universities) but the addition of new forms and the diversifying of old ones. Beyond the integration of theology and religious studies, further diversification is imaginable as theology engages more fully with different religions and disciplines and attempts to serve the search for wisdom through each.

Within the university it is perhaps the theological commitment to wisdom that is most important and also most controversial. Seeking wisdom through pursuing fundamental questions in the context of dialogue between radical commitments is never likely to sit easily within universities. Yet in a world where the religions, for better and for worse, shape the lives of billions of people, there is a strong case for universities encouraging theological questioning and dialogue as part of their intellectual life.

Note

1   I am indebted to four other scholars who are joint authors of parts of this chapter: John Montag, SJ on the early history of theology in Europe, Timothy Winter on Islam, Julius Lipner on Hinduism and Buddhism (all from the University of Cambridge); and Peter Ochs on Judaism (University of Virginia).

Bibliography

Capps, Walter H., *Religious Studies. The Making of a Discipline* (Fortress Press, Minneapolis 1995). Surveys the field well, but pays little attention to theology except as part of comparing religions.

de Lange, Nicholas, *Judaism* (Oxford University Press, Oxford and New York 1986). A lucid overview, with chapters on theology and eschatology but other chapters on further aspects of thought (Torah and tradition, law, ethics and mysticism), which are embraced in the definition of theology used in this chapter.

Ford, David F. (ed.), *The Modern Theologians. An Introduction to Christian Theology since 1918* 3rd edn (Blackwell, Oxford 2005). Covers the main Christian theologies of the period, both individual thinkers and movements, as well as the debates and critical questions about them.

Frei, Hans W., *Types of Christian Theology*, eds George Hunsinger and William C. Placher (Yale University Press, New Haven and London 1992). Offers a typology of modern theologies, sensitive to historical and institutional contexts.

Harvey, Peter, *An Introduction to Buddhism. Teachings, History and Practices* (Cambridge University Press, Cambridge 1990). Perceptive and comprehensive, especially good on religious thought and its relation to practice.

Keown, Damien, *Buddhism: A Very Short Introduction* (Oxford University Press, Oxford 1996). Brief, clear, interesting and reliable.

Lipner, Julius, *Hindus: their Religious Beliefs and Practices* (Routledge, London 1996). Perhaps the best comprehensive introduction to Hinduism.

Martin, R.C., Woodward, M. and Atmaja, D., *Defenders of Reason in Islam* (Oneworld, Oxford 1997). A perceptive up-to-date account of intellectual debates in Islam.

Montgomery Watt, W., *Islamic Philosophy and Theology* (Edinburgh University Press, Edinburgh 1985). Clear, accurate, descriptive, though elementary; mainly concentrating on the medieval period.

Pelikan, Jaroslav, *The Christian Tradition: A History of the Development of Doctrine* 5 vols (Chicago University Press, Chicago 1989). An exemplary historical theology.

Waines, David, *An Introduction to Islam* (Cambridge University Press, Cambridge 1995). Wide-ranging and especially strong on theology.

Chapter 5

Philosophy of religion

Peter Vardy

Philosophy of religion in the Western tradition uses reason to engage with central areas of religious belief – it is primarily concerned with religious truth claims and less concerned with the cultural or sociological understanding of religions, which are a matter for religious studies departments. For many people today, philosophy of religion provides a route to thinking deeply about questions of ultimate meaning and value without having to first adopt the faith assumptions of a particular religious group. However, it can also be disturbing and challenging for religious believers as it forces them to engage with issues they may not previously have considered in any depth. At the least, philosophy of religion keeps alive the great religious questions in a secular and post-modern age. The questions about whether there is a God or not, how language about God can be understood, what is means to claim truth and how the claimed existence of an all powerful and good God can be reconciled with a world full of suffering and evil are, arguably, the most important questions any individual can face and it is all too easy to neglect them.

Philosophy and theology have, over the centuries, been handmaids – mutually reinforcing and supporting each other. It is only since the early twentieth century that a divide opened up with many US and British philosophy departments increasingly having no interest in God or religious questions – however, it is important to recognise that this is a new phenomena. Most of the greatest philosophers have had a profound interest in metaphysical questions – questions about the nature of ultimate reality, the nature of being and the existence or non-existence of God. Philosophy of religion is the modern subject that uses the rational tools of philosophical enquiry to examine religious issues and religious claims.

A distinction needs to be made between philosophy of religion and philosophical theology although the boundaries between them are not clear. Philosophical theology uses philosophy within the assumptions of religious faith – it does not tend to challenge the basic faith assumptions but uses philosophy in the service of faith. The great Islamic Kalam school of philosophy is a good example of traditional philosophical theology. It derived from the world's greatest centres of philosophy and learning in Baghdad and Cairo in the eighth to the tenth century of the Christian era, when Europe was in the mud of the dark ages. It was Islamic philosophical theology that preserved the works of possibly the greatest philosopher of all time – Aristotle (384–322 BCE). Aristotle's works had largely been lost in the West and were re-imported into the University of Paris (the greatest Western university at the time) shortly before the medieval Christian writers such as the great thirteenth-century figures St Albert the Great (1206–1280) and St Thomas Aquinas (1224–1274) used Aristotle to provide a philosophical understanding of Christianity.

Philosophy of religion, by contrast, tends to stand outside faith assumptions and to examine religious claims from a neutral and dispassionate standpoint. There are no claims that are not subject to scrutiny and no assumptions that cannot be challenged. In Europe, philosophy of religion tends to be dominant. This is not surprising since there is a difference of priority between the US and Europe. In the US, religious belief is taken for granted much more than in Europe. In Europe there is a much greater degree of scepticism about religion and, therefore, a neutral standpoint is the one most likely to command interest and support, as it has few preconceptions and none that depend on a faith or cultural background.

There is also a difference between Catholic and Protestant Christians in their attitudes to philosophy of religion. In the Catholic Christian tradition, philosophy and theology have always been compulsory fields of study for anyone entering the priesthood. It is not considered possible to do good theology without being trained in philosophy, and philosophy without theology is held to be a limited discipline. The two go together. In the Catholic tradition the concentration tends to be on the great thinkers of the past (such as St Augustine (354–430) and St Thomas Aquinas who will be considered later) whereas in the Protestant tradition more modern figures tend to dominate. Many Protestants, however, would be less comfortable with the study of philosophy and some, at least, would consider that studying philosophy of religion should be avoided as it risks undermining faith. They would accept philosophical theology but would reject philosophy of religion precisely because it may challenge the fundamental assumptions of their belief system.

Three different ways that philosophy of religion attempts to prove the existence of God are worth considering.

Traditional arguments for the existence of God

In the Catholic tradition natural theology is theology based on reason and, therefore, on philosophy, whereas revealed theology is based on revelation. Nothing in revelation is held to contradict reason, but revelation can go further than reason. Philosophic argument can, it is held, arrive at the existence of God and basic knowledge about God's attributes but revelation is needed for doctrines like the incarnation or the Trinity. Natural theology is often held to start with proofs for the existence of God, of which the most famous are St Thomas Aquinas' 'Five Ways' of attempting to prove the existence of God.[1] Four of these five arguments derived from Aristotle. These are all *a posteriori* arguments, which means that they start from some features of the universe that can be experienced and then attempt to argue from them to the existence of God.

The starting points of the 'Five Ways' differ. They argue from:

1 Motion – in the universe we see things in motion and since it is not possible to have an infinite regress of causes, there must be a 'Prime Mover', something which is itself unmoved but causes everything else to move. This is God.
2 Causation – in the universe we see things and events caused by other things and other events. Since it is not possible to have an infinite regress, there must

be some uncaused cause, some cause which is not caused to come into existence by anything else and on which all other causes depend. This is God on whom all causes now depend.

3   Contingency – everything in the universe depends on something else, everything within the universe is contingent. The universe as a whole is the sum total of contingent things and is itself contingent. Since nothing can come from nothing, there must be something necessary, something that cannot not-exist and this necessary being is God on which the whole universe now depends.

4   From grades of perfection in things – some things are more perfect than others and this implies that there must be something supremely perfect – namely God.

5   Design – the universe is filled with purpose and everything in the universe is created with a sense of purpose. This points to the ultimate purpose of the universe – God.

All these arguments can be challenged, for although their starting points are widely held to be reasonable in that they start from readily accepted features of the world, the steps in the argument are, at least, debatable. For instance, the claim that there has to be an ultimate unmoved mover, an uncaused cause is frequently questioned. St Thomas Aquinas' arguments seek to arrive at a God who is '*de re* necessary', necessary in and of God's self and which cannot not exist and depends on nothing else for its existence. Both the Scottish philosopher David Hume (1711–1776) and the Prussian Immanuel Kant (1724–1804) rejected the very idea of anything which is necessary in and of itself – they held that the only sort of necessity is '*de dicto* necessity', necessity based on the way words are used. For instance 'Spinsters are female' is a *de dicto* necessary statement – it is necessarily true because of the way words are used. The word 'spinster' includes the idea of being female and it does not make sense to deny this statement because the meaning of words guarantees that the statement must be true. Hume and Kant, however, said that no existing thing can be necessary. Everything that exists may or may not exist, everything is contingent. Only propositions are necessary. So they reject the conclusion at which Aquinas tries to arrive as they argue that nothing – not even God – can exist necessarily.

Aquinas would reply to this by saying that everything in the universe is indeed contingent, everything may or may not exist. But that on which the universe depends is not like anything in the universe. God alone cannot not exist. God, therefore, is in a category of God's own. God is unlike anything in the universe as God is outside time and outside space. This leads to the key ideas in the Catholic Christian understanding of God – God is held to be wholly simple, timeless, spaceless and lacking in any potential. Everything in the universe is actual in that it exists but it has a whole array of potentialities. Human beings have a body, arms, legs, brain etc. – in this respect they are actual. However they also have a range of potentialities including the ability to walk, swim, run, love, learn, reproduce and many others. God is alone in having no potentialities God is fully actual. God is fully what it is to be God. To support this, Aquinas quotes from Exodus 3.14 when God reveals God's nature to Moses – God says 'I am who I am'. For Aquinas, this supports the idea that God is fully actual, fully what it is to be God. If God is outside time and space, it also follows that God has no body and cannot change in any way – God is therefore immutable.[2]

Modern versions of arguments for God's existence – the Kalam argument

Perhaps the most important of the modern arguments for the existence of God is put forward by the American philosopher, William Lane Craig.[3] Craig has put forward a new version of the so-called 'Kalam argument' – it is called this because it originated among Islamic philosophers of the Kalam school. This argument can be summarised in three statements:

1   Everything that begins to exist has a cause of its existence;
2   The universe began to exist;
3   Therefore, the universe has a cause for its existence.

It is difficult to prove the first of these claims, although one may feel that it is intuitively probable. Craig says: '. . . it is so intuitively obvious that I think scarcely anyone could sincerely believe it to be false'[4] yet some hold that at the micro-particle level there are uncaused events and, even if a single beginning could be shown not to have a cause, then premise 1 is false and the argument collapses. Paul Davies has argued that this assumption is false[5] as it appears that electrons can pass out of existence at one point and re-appear somewhere else. Craig has replied to this[6] saying that this does not affect the Kalam argument, as in modern physics a vacuum is not nothing, but rather a state of minimal energy. The electron fluctuations, he holds, are due to vacuum fluctuations and these electrons are not coming into existence from nothing as his critics maintain.

Craig puts forward a number of arguments to support premise 2 by maintaining that the universe must have begun to exist since an actual infinity is impossible. He argues, for instance:

1   An actual infinite cannot exist;
2   A beginningless temporal series of events is an actual infinite;
3   Therefore a beginningless series of events cannot exist.

The first of Craig's arguments in support of his first premise appeals to the idea of a library with an infinite number of red books and an infinite number of black books. If this library actually existed it would follow that there are as many red books as black books and as many red and black books together as there are red books. This, however, is absurd as the situation would arise that the subset of red books, which is half the total of red and black books, is both half the total and yet is equal to it. So, Craig maintains, an actual infinite is impossible – infinity is a possibility in the world of mathematical ideas but nowhere else. Craig is arguing that those who hold that the universe has existed for an actual infinite amount of time are mistaken since no such thing as an actual infinite can exist. This seems persuasive.

The real problem occurs with the claim that a beginningless temporal sequence is an actual infinite. Aristotle considered that there was a difference between an actual and a potential infinite – an actual infinite was one that existed at a particular time whereas a potential infinite was one that was never arrived at but which one could move towards through the passage of time. If Aristotle is right, then Craig is wrong, however, Craig's point is that the universe is actual and if the universe did not have a beginning then the universe is an actual infinite – and this is absurd.

Craig's second argument stems from the discovery of background radiation in the universe by Bell Laboratories scientists in 1965. This pointed to an initial explosive creation of the universe which has been termed the 'Big Bang'. The Big Bang seems to support the origin of the universe from a singularity when time, space, matter and energy all came into existence. However this is by no means proven and there may have been a preceding state (even if we do not know what it was), which would explain the eventual existence of the universe. We can express this by asking whether, if the universe began with a Big Bang, there was a preceding state of affairs that caused the Big Bang. This is problematic as in the first few hundred thousandths of a second after the singularity, time does not exist and no-one quite knows what happens. It may even be nonsensical to talk of a 'preceding' state of affairs as many scientists hold that time came into existence with matter immediately after the singularity and if this is accepted then there can be no preceding state.

At the Big Bang, the initial singularity exploded at a rate faster than the speed of light. Nuclear explosions took place, giving rise to concentrations of hydrogen and helium and some of the lithium found in inter-stellar space. After, perhaps, 300,000 years, the initial fireball dropped to a temperature a little below the present temperature of the sun allowing electrons to form orbits rounds atoms and releasing photons or light. This initial flash can today be measured as background radiation at microwave frequencies equivalent to a temperature of about 2.7 kelvin. (The kelvin scale begins at absolute zero, which is the lowest possible temperature and at this temperature all molecular activity stops. This temperature is equivalent to −273.16 degrees centigrade.)

The Big Bang theory of the origin of the universe is widely accepted and appears to explain a great deal. If this is true it would support the claim that the universe is not infinite. However, recent observations cast doubt on it and it is far from clear that the theory is adequate. Even if it is adequate, it seems that a great deal still remains to be explained that the conventional Big Bang theory cannot explain. The problems with the Big Bang theory include the following:

1   The Hubble Space Telescope has been measuring distances to other galaxies and these observations suggest that the universe is much younger than the Big Bang Theory implies. This is because the universe seems to be expanding much faster than previously assumed, this implies a cosmic age of as little as 8 billion years – about half the current estimate. On the other hand, some other data indicates that certain stars are at least 14 billion years old.

2   A group of astronomers who have become known as 'The Seven Samurai' have found evidence of what they call 'The Great Attractor', located near the southern constellations of Hydra and Cantaurus, which draw stars towards it. There seems no basis for such a 'great attractor' on the basis of the Big Bang Theory, which sees galaxies and stars flying apart after the initial explosion.

3   Big Bang theorists maintain that the initial explosion was extremely smooth – this is based on the uniformity of the background radiation left behind as throughout the universe this background radiation seems (according to current measurements) to be much the same. However, Margaret Geller, John Huchra and others at the Harvard-Smithsonian Centre for Astrophy have found a large number of galaxies about 500 million light years in length across the northern sky and, if these observations are accurate, then the smoothness and uniformity

of the Big Bang would seem to be questionable. If the Big Bang was *not* smooth, then questions arise as to why the variations occur and, indeed, whether there was a Big Bang in the first place.

There are a number of alternatives to the Big Bang Theory, including the idea of 'continuous creation' whereby matter is continually coming into existence perhaps in different parts of the universe. No certainty is possible. The Big Bang Theory remains at best a plausible theory, but no more than that at present and there is too much evidence against it to have any certainty. Even if the Big Bang Theory is accepted, it is compatible with two rival hypotheses:

1   The Oscillating Universe model. This holds that the universe goes through an infinite series of cycles, expanding and then contracting into a singularity before expanding again. If this is the case, then the universe does not need a beginning, as there would be an infinite series of 'big bangs' and an infinite series of contractions of the universe.
2   The Infinitely Expanding Universe model. This holds that there was an initial explosion from the singularity and the universe will keep expanding forever from this.

There is now some evidence that the Infinitely Expanding Universe model is more likely than the Oscillating model. *If* this is right – and it is still far from clear – this could point to the universe having had a beginning and thus support the Kalam argument's second premise. However there is no certainty. It must be recognised that science really cannot help to decide questions in philosophy. One problem with the Kalam argument is that the more it seems to rely on science, the more vulnerable it is to science offering alternative explanations.

It is also significant to note that all the arguments considered so far end up with the claim that there is a cause of the universe – the identification of this cause with God is, as with St Thomas Aquinas' arguments, problematic. It also depends on holding that God did not begin to exist (as clearly then one could ask what caused God?). God, to fulfil the requirements of the Kalam argument, needs to be the uncaused cause, the *de re* necessarily existent being – in other words the argument points to the sort of God whose essence included existence. As we have seen, Hume and Kant challenged the very idea of such a necessary being.

Modern arguments for God's existence – the religious experience argument

William P. Alston is one of the leading US philosophers of religion and he has argued, in a number of papers and books, for religious experience as a pointer to the existence of God.[7] Alston distinguishes between:

1   'Experiences of God', which, he says, can more generally be described as 'supposed experiences of God' where 'supposed' does not cast doubt on the authenticity of the experience but draws attention to the fact that many such claimed experiences may be interpretative;

2   Direct experiences of God, which excludes, for instance, being aware of God
     'through the beauties of nature, the words of the Bible or a sermon'.

Alston makes this distinction because he considers that these direct experiences are
most likely to be plausibly regarded as presentations of God to the individual (St Teresa
says that God 'presents Himself to the soul by a knowledge brighter than the sun').

What is more, Alston concentrates on non-sensory experiences as (since God
is purely spiritual) they have a greater chance of presenting God as God really is,
whereas sensory experiences are normally confined to objects in space and time.
Alston acknowledges that, for instance, Immanuel Kant argues that human beings
can only have sensory experiences as they can only experience things through their
five senses and, since God is not an object in space and time, God cannot be experienced by the individual. However Alston considers that this represents a lack of
imagination. As he says: 'Why should we suppose that the possibilities of experiential givenness, for human beings or otherwise, are exhausted by the powers of our
five senses?'. Animals, he claims, have senses wider than ours so: 'Why can't we
envisage presentations that do not stem from the activity of any physical sense organs,
as is apparently the case with mystical perception?'. Alston refers here to 'mystical
perception' rather than 'experience' as it involves something other than the normal
five senses. He advocates what he terms a 'perceptual model' of mystical experience
in which something presents itself to us. In a way it is a very simple form of perceptual awareness in which anything – a house, a book or a person – presents itself to
us in a similar way. Alston's causal theory of perception claims that religious experience is caused by the presence of God and subsequent members of the religious
community pick up the referent from those who went before.

Critics of Alston reject this view – they hold that religious belief does not rise
and fall with evidence in the way that Alston thinks it does. For instance, Richard
Gale says that he feels sorry for religious believers of the type that Alston describes,
because Gale considers that the beliefs of current religious believers would always be
vulnerable to new evidence and therefore these are constantly vulnerable to being
shown to be false. Against Gale, the Danish philosopher Soren Kierkegaard (1813–
1855) argued in the mid-nineteenth century that this is exactly the position that
religious believers are in. They are 'suspended over 70,000 fathoms', staking their
lives on an 'if' that may be false. This is why, for Kierkegaard, faith involves such
vulnerability.

Alston acknowledges freely that we may 'see' things differently depending on
our perceptual schemes and prior assumptions, but effectively he is claiming that
there is something to 'see', something that presents itself to us. The 'perceptual
model' relies on a 'theory of appearing' in which: '. . . perceiving X simply consists
in X's appearing to one, or being presented to one, as so-and-so. That's all there is
to it . . . .'

To perceive X is simply for X to appear to a person in a certain way. Alston says
there are three conditions that must be met if X is to appear:

1   X must exist;
2   X must make an important causal contribution to be experience of X; and
3   That perceiving X must give rise to beliefs about X.

Clearly, given these conditions, Alston recognises that to show that perceptual experiences are genuine would first mean showing that God exists (see 1 above). What he aims to show is the following:

1 Mystical experience is the right sort of perception to constitute a genuine perception of God if the other requirements are met; and
2 There is no bar in principle to these other requirements being satisfied if God does exist.

Crucially he says: 'This adds up to a defence of the thesis that it is quite possible that humans do sometimes perceive God if God is 'there' to be perceived. In other words, the thesis defended is that *if* God exists, then mystical experience is quite properly thought of as mystical perception.'

Alston takes this claim to be self-evident and feels that it cannot be denied unless one is to claim that all those who report such experiences of God are confused about them. Alston accepts that people's reports are not infallible, but still considers that they should be taken seriously. If a person considers that he/she is having an experience, then he or she is in the best position to judge this to be the case. Alston maintains that the only reason for rejecting the claims to experiences is that some people are sceptical about the claim that God exists. What, however, Alston does not do is to seek to show why such scepticism may not be well founded.

Alston acknowledges that believers make use of their prior frameworks but, then, he claims we do this with normal experience. If, he says, he sees his house from a great height (when in an airplane), he certainly sees his house and he may learn something new but it would basically be as he expected his house to look. Similarly when experiencing God, God is experienced as believers expect God to be experienced – there is no difference between ordinary experiences and religious ones.

Alston's claim, when analyzed, is very modest. All he really is establishing is that if one believes in God already then it is reasonable that mystical experiences should be taken as genuine. This, however, misses out the real issue that is the major part of the debate – which is *why* one should take experiences of God as any more veridical than experiences of the Loch Ness Monster or of UFOs.

However, as Richard Gale points out, supporters of religious experience hold that most religions and mystical experiences support their claims whereas the absence of such experiences does not serve to disconfirm what is claimed to be experienced. All that Alston may have demonstrated is that if one is a religious believer one may have grounds, from within a faith culture or perspective, to claim that religious experiences refer. However this does *not* serve to confirm why anyone should accept or reject the perspective in the first place – and this, surely, is what the argument from religious experience is intended to achieve.

Richard Swinburne, former Professor of Philosophy of Religion at the University of Oxford, seeks to argue for more than Alston.[8] Swinburne examines all the various arguments for the existence of God and maintains that none of them succeed in proving that God exists. However, when these arguments are put together they make a cumulative case that indicates that there is a reasonable probability that God exists. Given this probability, then Swinburne says it is reasonable to rely on two principles that point to the existence of God. These are:

1   The Principle of Credulity maintains that it is a principle of rationality that (in the absence of special considerations such as the person involved being unreliable or the conditions being such that any observation should be subject to doubt) if it seems to a person that X is present, then probably X is present. What one seems to perceive is probably so.
2   The Principle of Testimony maintains that, in the absence of special considerations, it is reasonable to believe that the experiences of others are probably as they report them.

Swinburne maintains that if we refuse to accept the first of these principles we land in a sceptical bog. Religious experiences should, therefore, be given initial credibility unless there is some evidence against them. The aim of the Principle of Credulity is to put the onus on the sceptic to show why reports of religious experience should not be accepted. This is important – all that the principle seeks to establish is initial credibility and that claims to religious experience should not be dismissed out of hand. The sceptic should, it is held, produce argument or evidence to show why claims to religious experience should not be accepted as valid – in the absence of such argument or evidence then the claims should be taken at their face value.

The Principle of Testimony simply relies on the inherent trustworthiness of other people. It asks us to believe reports of experiences unless we have some grounds for not doing so. If, for instance, a person is known to be unreliable, is on drugs, suffers from delusions or otherwise has a previous history that would cast doubt on his her or reliability, then we would be right to be suspicious of what we are told. However, if the person is apparently of sound mind, of reasonable intelligence and is generally reliable, then there is no reason, in principle, why we should not believe them.

Caroline Franks Davies builds on Swinburne's approach.[9] Effectively she and Swinburne work with a cumulative argument. They maintain that if all the arguments for and against the existence of God are considered, they are fairly evenly balanced. Some of the arguments strengthen the likelihood that God exists while others (for instance those concentrating on the problem of evil and suffering) make the existence of God less likely. If these are all taken together, then, it is held, it is neither highly probable or highly improbable that God exists; the scales of probability are evenly balanced. Given this situation, it is reasonable to rely on reports of religious experience to tip the scales in favour of belief that God exists.

It may be argued that neither Swinburne nor Davies give sufficient weight to counter arguments against belief in God[10] – for instance they give scant attention to the problem of evil and while their arguments may be persuasive to an existing believer, to an unbiased observer they would have rather less force. The existence of evil does significantly reduce the probability that the God of Christian theism exists – although how one balances the probability for and against God's existence will inevitably be a largely subjective matter about which opinions will differ.

Language about God

Based on philosophic analysis, as we have seen above, Aquinas and the Catholic tradition hold that it is possible to prove that God exists and that God is totally unlike anything in the universe as God is *de re* necessary, wholly simple, perfectly actual, timeless, spaceless and bodiless. It follows that using language about God is going to be exceptionally difficult as human language is derived from the spatio-temporal universe. How can language applied to things in space and time be applied to a God who is outside space and time? Moses Maimonidies (1125–1204), the great Jewish thinker who so influenced Aquinas and many medieval Christian thinkers, held to the Via Negativa – the negative way which claimed that God could not be talked about in positive language. It was only possible to say what God was not. He accepted the difficulties of using language about God. Aquinas rejected any univocal language – that is language about God that places God into the same sort of category as objects in the universe. To say that God is love is not to say that God loves like human beings do but more so, this would be to make God an anthropomorphic 'superman' type figure instead of having an entirely different order of existence to human beings.

Aquinas tackled the problem of language about God through the use of analogy and metaphor. As the whole created order depends on God for its existence, it is possible to use language drawn from this created order provided it is clearly recognised that the content of this language will be severely limited. It is true that God is love, but God does not love like human beings do – given that God is immutable, bodiless and outside space and time this would not be possible. God then loves in a timeless way which is largely unknowable. Analogy preserves the otherness of God but at the price of arguing that language about God has very little content.

Perhaps the best way of speaking of God, when God is understood as wholly simple, timeless and spaceless, is through metaphor. The Hebrew and Christian scriptures are full of metaphors about God – God is a rock, a vine, a strong tower, a mighty fortress, a loving father. None of these are to be taken literally. Metaphors reach out and seek to capture something of the reality of God. As Janet Martin Soskice says, metaphors refer to God without describing God in literal terms. They capture something of the reality of God by gesturing towards God.

This way of understanding God can also contribute to the problem of evil and moral theology. Something is good according to Aristotle if it fulfils its nature. This is a central plank in the Natural Law tradition of ethics in which acts are wrong if they go against the common human nature that all human beings are held to share. Ethics, however, forms a separate discipline from philosophy of religion, although the stance an individual takes on religious questions is likely to influence their perspective on ethics.

The wholly simple, timeless God and the everlasting God

Throughout more than two thousand years there has been a tension between the God of the philosophers and the God of the Christian and Jewish scriptures. Many attempts have been made to reconcile the two but almost always one will be given priority. In the Catholic Christian tradition, it is the *de re* necessary God that is given priority and the scriptures are then interpreted in the light of this understanding. It follows that whenever in the Bible God is described as doing any action that involves time or potential, this is treated not as being literally true but, at most, a metaphor. Thus when in Genesis Ch. 6, God is described as regretting making human beings because of the extent of their sin, Catholic philosophers would hold that this did not mean that God regretted in the way humans regret since this would involve a change in God. Any change in God is impossible since God is timeless and immutable. Similarly to claim that God walked in the garden with Adam or wrestled with Jacob is not to be taken literally as this would again involve change. Protestant philosophers and theologians, however, tend to start from a different starting point. They take their starting point from Martin Luther (1483–1456), John Calvin (1509–1564) and other Protestant reformers who gave pride of place to the Bible whereas philosophy (particularly the philosophy of St Thomas Aquinas) was largely rejected. Protestant theologians tend, therefore, to place God in time and to say that God is everlasting, without beginning and without end. If God is everlasting, time passes for God – the future is future and the past is past. 'A thousand ages in His sight are but an evening gone' as the hymn writer says, but nevertheless an evening has passed. God is not dominated by time as human beings are in their short lives, nor does God's character change with the passage of time but, nevertheless, time does pass for God.

Reformed epistemology

Epistemology is the branch of philosophy that is concerned with the study of the sources and basis for how human beings know things, it is therefore concerned with what underpins human claims to make true statements. One of the most significant modern movements in philosophy of religion comes from the US with the work of Alvin Plantinga. Plantinga is described as a 'reformed epistemologist' as he comes from the Protestant reformed Christian tradition and his work looks at how the claims of believers to know that God exists can be justified. He rejects attempts to argue for the existence of God (natural theology) as he considers that these arguments put reason into central place instead of revelation. God is held to have revealed truth to the world and it is this revelation that should be given precedence, not human reason, which is 'fallen' due to the sin of Adam and Eve as well as subsequent sin. Karl Barth (1886–1968), probably the greatest Protestant theologian of the twentieth century, said that of all the reasons for rejecting Catholicism, natural theology was the greatest as it relied on reason and not revelation. The Protestant tradition, and reformed epistemologists, rely on revelation having priority over reason.

Alvin Plantinga defines the set of beliefs a person holds together with the relations that hold between these beliefs as the person's 'noetic structure' (in other words all that they know and the way they know these things). Plantinga claims that the Christian religious believer sees the word correctly because they have accepted the Christian revelation and no justification is required for the basic Christian beliefs.[11] Plantinga calls this view 'Foundationalism'. The question then is whether a proposition is one that stands in need of evidence, or whether it is within the foundation of all that an individual knows. Put simply, this is asking whether belief in God requires justification or proof in the way that natural theology claims. Plantinga asks: 'Might it not be that my belief in God is itself in the foundations of my noetic structure?' If this is right, then there is no need to prove that God exists. This means that the believer in God is not required to justify his or her belief – this belief is foundational and requires no justification. The reformed epistemology holds that belief in God is 'properly basic' as it requires no justification and the believer has a 'properly ordered noetic structure', which means that their way of seeing and understanding the world is correct because they have been given the grace of God to see the world rightly. In the same way that I cannot prove that a tree is in front of me or that I am typing this with my hands or that I am in the presence of my eldest daughter in Boston when I meet her – nor does a believer require any proof for the existence of God, since God is so obvious to them when they read their Bible or pray that talk of justification is out of place. A believer does not, therefore, need proof that God exists.

This is an attractive position but it suffers from real difficulties. Christians may claim that their belief in God, their belief that Jesus is the son of God and that the Holy Spirit is the third person of the Divine Trinity is part of the foundations of their noetic structure and that they do not require justification for this. Muslims may claim that their belief in Allah and the Holy Prophet Mohammed is part of the foundations of their noetic structure and that they do not require justification for this. Buddhists may claim that that there is no God and that the Buddha's teaching about the transitory status of everything in the world and the route out of suffering and change does not require justification. In short, there are so many belief systems in the world, each of which can claim that their beliefs do not require justification, that reformed epistemology seems unsatisfactory. The reformed epistemologists may claim that they have been given God's grace to enable them to see the world correctly and that others are in error due, perhaps, to the effects of sin or the refusal of God's grace, but all this does is to retreat behind a claim to truth that cannot be justified.

Non-realism

Ludwig Wittgenstein (1889–1951)[12] was probably the great philosopher of the twentieth century and his influence has been profound. He argued that the whole subject of epistemology – the search for foundations for knowledge – rested on a mistake. Instead people are educated into a 'form of life', into a culture. Within this culture certain things are taken for granted and it simply does not make sense to doubt them. This applies, he argued, in the case of religious belief. Children are educated into the 'form of life' of their parents and are taught the language that expresses this form of life. Proofs are simply irrelevant. It is this basic approach that has given rise to non-realism.[13]

A growing approach to religious belief is found among some European philosophers of religion who have been influenced by Wittgenstein such as Don Cupitt, D.Z. Phillips[14] or Gareth Moore[15] who identify two problems with traditional approaches:

1   The arguments for the existence of God favoured by natural theology do not succeed. They are vulnerable to assumptions which may be persuasive to existing believers but will not be convincing to non-believers and, therefore, whilst they may help to support existing faith, they do not form the basis for belief. What is more, belief in God for most believers is not based on argument – rather believers share in a culture into which they are born and educated and philosophical proofs are irrelevant within these cultures.

2   Reformed Epistemology, with its dependence on revelation, does not succeed in establishing truth as so much depends on the community into which one is educated and the assumptions made in this community. Nevertheless non-realists

support reformed epistemologists in arguing that it is a mistake to look at foundations for faith.

To understand the non-realist approach it is first necessary to explain the difference between two theories of truth.

Realism is the theory of truth which holds that a statement is true if it corresponds to the state of affairs that it describes. Thus 'The mayor of Los Angeles is 56 years old' is true if (this means if and only if) there is a mayor of Los Angeles and this mayor is 56 years old. What makes the statement true is that it corresponds to the state of affairs which it describes. What would make the statement false is that it fails to correspond. Most people, most of the time, are realists. Realists affirm bivalence – this means that a statement is either true or false even though it cannot be known to be true or false. Thus the statement 'there are yellow frogs on a planet circling a star in the Milky Way galaxy' is either true or false depending on whether there is a planet circling one of the stars and depending on whether or not yellow frogs live there. There is at present no way of knowing whether or not this is the case, but the realist will say that either it is or it is not true or false depending on the state of affairs to which the statement is claimed to correspond. Most religious believers are realists – they maintain that their faith claims are true because they correspond to the state of affairs to which they refer. Thus Christians, Muslims and Jews will generally claim that their claim that 'God exists' is true because this claim corresponds to the existence of the God who created and sustains the world. Were it not for the existence of this being or spirit (whether timeless or everlasting) the claim that 'God exists' would be false.

The problem is that, if someone is a realist, they are vulnerable to challenge from the person who asks 'How do you know that your claim is true?' Natural theologians will reply 'wait a minute and we can show how this can be proved to be true'. Reformed epistemologists will respond 'We do not need proof, our claims are true because we have been given the grace to accept the revelation of God which guarantees the truth of our claims'. The trouble is that neither position is going to be convincing to non-believers. Non-realists claim they have the answer.

Non-realists reject all attempts to either prove that God exists or to show that God probably exists. Phillips argues that if the rationality of belief in God is to be shown, then 'belief in God is not a matter of believers entertaining a hypothesis'[16]. He mocks the probability approach saying that on this basis Psalm 139 would read 'If I ascend into heaven it is highly probable that thou art there: if I make my bed in hell, behold it is highly probable that thou art there also'.[17] Phillips therefore maintains that the probability approach argues for a 'method for establishing the rationality of religious belief . . . which actually distorts the religious belief'. What it is to have faith in God does not depend on philosophic argument at all, nor on showing that religious language corresponds to some independent state of affairs.

Non-realism is a theory of truth.[18] It holds that what makes a statement true is not correspondence but coherence – a statement is true if it coheres or 'fits in with' other true statements made within a particular 'form of life'. Non-realists maintain that people are educated into religious forms of life by their parents, their schools and the religious institutions that they attend. Within these forms of life certain statements are accepted as true without question. For the non-realist, truth rests not on correspondence to some state of affairs that is independent of language – instead truth depends on coherence within a particular form of life. In other words, within a particular religious form of life certain things are 'held fast' by what surrounds them; they are accepted as true without question. What makes them true is this acceptance. Truth is not something established by independent enquiry – instead truth rests on what is agreed. Truth, therefore, depends on agreement within a community and different and contradictory things may be true within different communities.

The non-realist will, therefore, agree with the reformed epistemologist that no justification is required for the existence of God or other central religious claims. They will agree that these statements are true – but they will differ about what makes them true. The reformed epistemologist will claim that these statements are true because they correspond to some independent state of affairs whereas non-realists will reject correspondence entirely and will instead maintain that they are true because they are accepted as true within the religious community concerned. As the Catholic theologian Gareth Moore puts it 'Religious truths are not discovered, they are made'[19] – in other words people live the story that their religion tells them and, to those who participate in a religion, this story is true. However what makes it true is not some state of affairs independent of the story but the story itself.

Thus within Islam it is true that there is one God and Mohammed is his prophet, within Catholicism it is true that God is Trinitarian, that Mary was assumed bodily into heaven and that the Pope, when speaking ex-Cathedra, is infallible. Within Judaism it is true that Abraham is the father of the Jewish nation and that God promised the land of Palestine to the descendents of Abraham. These claims do not conflict with each other since truth is internal to each form of life.

Non-realists claim that God is real and God exists – but they do not mean by this that there is a being or spirit called God who exists ontologically independent of the created universe that this God creates and sustains in existence. Instead 'God' is real and exists within the community of faith, within the form of life of those who worship, pray and place God at the centre of their lives. Jesus told his disciples that he would be present whenever two or three gathered in his name and, to the non-realist believer, this is true. When believers meet and speak of Jesus and pray to him Jesus is real and Jesus exists. Effectively 'God' and 'Jesus' are ideas that are created by communities of faith and that give those who have faith meaning and purpose. The key point is that, for non-realists, language about God does not refer any reality or state of affairs beyond itself, it is true because it is accepted and used by those within the community of faith.

The great advantages of the non-realist approach is that there is no need for justification of truth claims in religion. It recognises that religious faith claims are not held tentatively, that the community is recognised as central and that it can explain both how religious communities develop their truth claims (and decide, for instance, what is orthodoxy and what is heresy) over time. It also explains how different religions have such different truth claims. The disadvantage, from the point of view of many believers, is that it 'does violence' (to use an expression from Ludwig Wittgenstein) to what most ordinary believers say that they mean by their claims. Most believers consider, when they say that Jesus died on the cross and rose on the third day, that this is true because this is what actually happened. The non-realist, by contrast, will see this as being truth as this is part of the Christian story but, in the final analysis, the Christian story is a human creation.

The problem of evil

Possibly the greatest intellectual challenge to face the monotheist faiths (monotheism represents the claim that there is a single God who created, sustains and is inter-active within the universe) is the problem of evil. If God exists and is all powerful and wholly good, how can evil exist? If God is good, surely God would wish to get rid of evil and if God is omnipotent then surely God has the power to get rid of evil. Since evil clearly exists, critics will claim that either God does not exist or God is limited in some way (either by not being omnipotent or not being wholly good).

Various replies have been formulated to this challenge and they all revolve around the claim that God has good reason for either allowing evil to exist because of the need to give human beings freedom or else that evil is the means used by God to bring God's purposes about. These two approaches are generally referred to as the Augustinian and Irenaean approaches.

The fourth-century thinker St Augustine is possibly the most influential figure in Christian history apart from Jesus and St Paul. He has had a profound effect on both Catholic and Protestant theology and his approach to the problem of evil is of central importance.[20] Augustine argued against a group called the Manicheans who held that there were two cosmic forces in the universe – one good and one bad – and that these forces were engaged in a cosmic struggle. Manichean Christians saw themselves on the side of the force of good in a struggle against the forces of evil. The great advantage of this approach is that all evil can be regarded as stemming from the force of evil, and the good God can be absolved from responsibility. St Augustine recognised that this was not a Christian position and therefore sought to produce a theodicy which would justify and explain why the one, omnipotent God would allow evil to exist. His reply drew on the Hebrew scriptures and, in particular, the creation story of Genesis and also the philosophy of Aristotle.

The Genesis creation stories show God creating the earth and the first human beings perfect, and then disorder and evil entering the world as a result of the Fall – in other words as a result of the disobedience of Adam and Eve and the devil who, according to Augustine, was an angel who rebelled against God. God allowed human beings freedom but when he placed Adam and Eve in the garden of Eden he gave them one simple command – that they were not to eat of the tree in the middle of the garden. They disobeyed and because of this disobedience sin and evil not only entered the human world but Augustine saw this as having a cosmic effect. Natural evil – including death, disease, pain and suffering, entered the world as a result of the Fall. To us this may seem an extraordinary claim but Augustine held that the whole of creation was disrupted as a result of the disobedience of Adam and Eve. God, therefore, was not to blame for the Fall – the blame lies entirely on the first humans and also the misuse of Angelic freewill by the angel, Lucifer, who became the devil. Augustine argued that evil was not a positive thing, rather it was a priva-tion of goodness. It was where some good that should be present was absent. So if a seagull does not have a wing, it suffers a privation of the good it should have. If a human being cannot see, then this, also, is a privation. Anything that falls short of what it should be is to that extent suffering an evil. Humans suffer evils when they fall short physically of the perfect state that they should be in. However, humans can also use their freewill to act in ways that go against their common human nature and in this case they also fall short of what they should be, not this time due to evil that they suffer but due to moral evil which they freely choose to perform.

This provided the intellectual basis for Catholic moral theology which sees certain acts as 'intrinsically evil' as they go against the purpose of what it is to be human. Homosexuality or artificial birth control are, for instance, considered morally evil in the Catholic tradition as any action must be open to the possibility of procreation – since this is defined as the purpose of human genitalia. If genitalia are used for any purpose other than reproduction this use will be a morally wrong act. Moral evil, therefore, occurs when individuals use their free will to act in ways that are contrary to their God-given nature. Much, of course, will then depend on how human nature is defined.[21]

God allows evil to exist but does not cause evil. God allows evil because only if human beings are free can they choose to serve and to love God or to reject God and put self in the centre of their lives. God is not responsible for evil – human beings are. St Augustine, therefore, absolved God from responsibility for evil and puts the blame firmly on human beings.

St Thomas Aquinas follows this Augustinian approach except that, unlike Augustine, he did not blame natural evil on the Fall – instead he considered that anything that fulfils its purpose or nature is good. A volcano or tidal wave is not, therefore, a defect in creation caused by the Fall instead these things are part of a properly functioning universe and are good in that they fulfil their nature. Only when they are looked at from a purely human centred view may they appear to be evils. If one gets in the way of a lava stream from a volcano, then clearly suffering and probably death will result – but this does not make the volcano bad. The volcano is doing what it is intended to do.

The alternative, Irenaean approach to the problem of evil rejects the Fall as a literal event and instead sees God creating human beings in God's image but their having to move from this image to the likeness of God. This is based on a debatable reading of Genesis 1:26 in which God is said to have created human beings in God's image and likeness. Humans, in this view, have the potential to grow into the likeness of God by, for instance, developing the virtues including love, compassion, forgiveness, etc. but this potential is not realised in the 'raw' human state. Irenaeus separates 'image' and 'likeness' and holds that human beings are created in God's image but need to move to be like God – to say humans are created in the image of God means that they have the potential to grow to be like God but this potential is not actualised. John Hick, a modern Protestant theologian, has developed what has come to be called the 'Irenaean theodicy'[22] although Irenaeus never used it for this purpose. Hick argues that this world is a 'vale of soul making' and that human beings are created at an 'epistemic distance' from God – this means that they are created without a direct knowledge of God. The world is religiously ambiguous and created so that God's existence is not obvious – this is done in order to maintain human freedom and to allow each individual to choose to set out on a path towards God or to reject this possibility.

In this view, God creates evil and suffering deliberately and uses these as the means by which human beings are drawn closer to God. Through suffering and difficulties human beings can grow closer to God – they can move from image to the likeness of God, which is seen as the main task of life. Suffering is held to have positive advantages – a person can be leading a successful life, have a happy family and all may be going well, but then someone close to them may die, they may develop cancer, relationships may break down and they may be forced to reappraise what is really important in life. For some, suffering can provide a means to reorientate priorities and to focus on developing the virtues and seeking God rather than money, power and reputation. However, it can be argued against this that suffering can also destroy individuals and lead them away from God. Hick would reply to this by saying that suffering can provide the opportunity to grow closer to God, whether an individual takes advantage of this opportunity is only something that he or she can decide.

Conclusion

Perhaps the challenge of non-realism set above is the greatest challenge that modern believers and theologians have to face. Is the circle of religious language and practice a closed one where truth depends on internal coherence alone, or does this language refer beyond itself to a transcendent referent? The arguments for the circle being closed are strong – young people tend to be 'formed' into the religion of their parents and brought up into the cultural way of life of their community (which includes dress, diet and moral codes and the whole cultural understanding that makes up a religious form of life). This fits in well with the non-realist understanding and with the claim that religious truth is relative to the community to which one belongs. However most of the great religions would resist this idea and would maintain that their culture and beliefs are grounded in realist truth claims. Whether this is the case or not may be the central issue for religious studies and theology today to face – although, sadly, few academics in these areas seem to be aware of this philosophic challenge or to take it seriously.

Notes

1   Thomas Aquinas 'The Classical Cosmological Argument', in M. Peterson *et al.* 2001, pp. 184–7.
2   The best modern discussion of this understanding of God is by G. Hughes in *The Nature of God*, 1995.
3   W.L. Craig 1979.
4   W.L. Craig 1994, p. 92.
5   P. Davies 1984, p. 200.
6   W.L. Craig and Q. Smith 1993, p. 121–3.
7   W.P. Alston 'Perceiving God', in *Journal of Philosophy* 83 (1986), 655–666; also in Stump, E. and Murray, M. (eds) 1999, pp. 142–149; and in Plantinga, A. and Wolterstorff, N. 1984.
8   R. Swinburne 1991.
9   C.F. Davies 1989.
10 Cf. P. Vardy 1992.
11 A. Plantinga 1979, p. 12.
12 L. Wittgenstein 1986.
13 Although whether non-realists are faithful to Wittgenstein is highly debatable. Cf. F. McCutcheon 2001.
14 D.Z. Phillips 1988.

15   G. Moore 1988.
16   D.Z. Phillips 1988, p. 9.
17   D.Z. Phillips 1988, p. 10.
18   Realism and non-realism are dealt with in more detail in P. Vardy 2003a.
19   G. Moore 1988.
20   This is set out in P. Vardy and J. Arliss 2003a.
21   These issues are dealt with in more detail in P. Vardy 2003b.
22   John Hick 'An Irenaean Theodicy', in Stump, E. and Murray, M. 1999, pp. 222–227. Also John Hick 'Soul-Making and Suffering' in Adams, M.M. and Adams, R.M. 1990, Chapter 10.

Bibliography

Adams, M.M. and Adams, R.M. 1990, *The Problem of Evil*, Oxford, OUP.

Craig, W.L. 1979, *The Kalam Cosmological Argument*, London, Macmillan.

—— 1994, *Reasonable Faith*, Wheaton, Ill., Crossway.

—— and Smith, Q. 1993, *Theism, Atheism and the Big Bang Cosmology*, Oxford, Clarendon Press.

Davies, B. (ed.) 1998, *Philosophy of Religion: A Guide to the Subject*, London, Cassell.

—— (ed.) 2000, *Philosophy of Religion: A Guide and Anthology*, Oxford, OUP.

Davies, C.F. 1989, *The Evidential Force of Religious Experience*, Oxford, Clarendon Press.

Davies, P. 1984, *Superforce*, New York, Simon & Schuster.

Hick, J. (ed.) 1990, *Classical and Contemporary Readings in the Philosophy of Religion*, Englewood Cliffs, N.J., Prentice Hall.

Hughes, G. 1995, *The Nature of God*, London, Routledge.

Kierkegaard, S. 1954, *Fear and Trembling*, trans. Walter Lowrie, Princeton, Princeton University Press.

McCutcheon, F. 2001, *Religion Within the Limits of Language Alone*. Aldershot, Ashgate.

Mackie, J.L. 1992, *The Miracle of Theism: Arguments For and Against the Existence of God*, Oxford, Clarendon Press, Chapter 5.

Markham, I. 1998, *The Truth and Reality of God*, Edinburgh, T. & T. Clark.

Moore, G. 1988, *Believing in God*, Edinburgh, T. & T. Clarke.

Peterson, M. *et al.* (eds) 2001, *Philosophy of Religion: Selected Readings*, Oxford, OUP.

Phillips, D.Z. 1988, *Faith after Foundationalism*, London, Routledge.

Plantinga, A. 1979, 'Is belief in God rational?' in *Rationality and Religious Belief*, C. Delaney (ed.), Notre Dame, Ind., University of Notre Dame Press.

—— and Wolterstorff, N. (eds) 1984, *Faith and Rationality: Belief in God*. London, University of Notre Dame Press.

Stump, E. and Murray, M. 1999, *Philosophy of Religion: The Big Questions*, Oxford, Blackwell.

Swinburne, R. 1991, *The Existence of God*, Oxford, Clarendon Press.

Trigg, R. 1997, 'Theological realism and anti-realism' in *Companion to Philosophy of Religion* P. Quinn and C. Taliaferro (eds), London, Blackwell.

Vardy, P. 1992, *The Puzzle of Evil*, London, Fount.

—— 2003a, *What is Truth?*, London, John Hunt Publishing.

—— 2003b, *Being Human*, London, Darton, Longman & Todd.

—— and Arliss, J. 2003a, *The Thinkers Guide to Evil*, London, John Hunt Publishing.

—— and —— 2003b, *The Thinkers Guide to God*, London, John Hunt Publishing.

Wittgenstein, L. 1986, *On Certainty*, London, Harper Collins.

Chapter 6

Religious studies

Donald Wiebe

Including the notion of 'religious studies' as one discipline among many for description and analysis in a volume like this suggests that there is broad agreement among those who study religion in the modern Western university as to the meaning of the term. Unfortunately, this is not the case. There is a vast literature committed to providing an understanding of the nature and value of the enterprise, but, as I shall show, there is little agreement to be found among those who have put their hand to the task. Not only is the term 'religious studies' ambiguous with respect to the enterprise it designates, but the very idea of 'a discipline' is itself vigorously contested; and it is quite obvious that whether or not religious studies can justifiably be called a discipline depends wholly upon the understanding of 'discipline', which is operative. As one scholar has put it, the term is used with more passion than precision (Benson 1987: 91). There is, moreover, considerable debate about the nature of the modern university within which 'religious studies' as 'a discipline' exists, so that to equate 'religious studies' with 'the academic study of religion' provides little – if any – clarification as to the nature or structure of the enterprise beyond information about its institutional location. Indeed, depending upon the assumptions one makes about the *raison d'être* of the modern university, there is no guarantee that 'religious studies' as 'the academic study of religion' can even be clearly differentiated from the scholarly study of religion carried on in other institutions, including religious institutions. It is no surprise, therefore, that some who have attempted to set out the meaning of the term 'religious studies' have remarked that perhaps the clearest thing that can be said about it is that it 'appears to be the designation of choice for the academic study of religion in the college and university setting' (Olson 1990a: 549). There is, perhaps, equal agreement that this designation for the study of religion, 'legitimated' by virtue of inclusion in the curriculum of the university, came into use only after the Second World War; primarily since the 1960s. Providing a singular, overarching definition of 'religious studies' as it is carried out in the modern university, therefore, is hardly possible; at the very least, such an exercise is unlikely to be either persuasive or helpful. To understand 'religious studies' is to understand the diverse and nuanced way in which the term is used. And in a sense, one must follow the principle that to understand a concept it is important to be familiar with its history. This is not to say that no generalization is possible, but it does require that a thorough knowledge of the debate over the use of the term is essential before proposing one use of the concept over another. Much of this essay, therefore, will consist of a critical examination of the diverse ways in which the notion is understood in the reflective methodological literature in the field. Given the proliferation of relevant publications, however, this review cannot hope to be comprehensive. Accordingly, I restrict my analyses to Anglo-American (including Canadian) treatments of the subject, beginning with the attempts to provide a definitive statement on the notion in representative encyclopedias and encyclopedic dictionaries. Despite the diversity of views that will emerge in this analysis of the literature about the study of religion as it is currently carried out in colleges and universities, I shall attempt in the conclusion to draw out some warrantable generalizations about 'religious studies' that may assist those coming new to the field.

Encyclopedic treatments of 'religious studies' consider the term to refer to a new kind of study of religious phenomena – that is an exercise free from narrow ecclesiastical, if not also, more general religious interference or influence. Religious studies, that is, is often taken to be other than a religious quest or undertaking and, unlike earlier scholarly studies within the framework of the academy (colleges and universities), seems to work on the assumption of religion's status as a purely social phenomenon. There is agreement not only that there existed a scholarly study of religion in the university prior to the emergence of religious studies departments in the modern university, but also that it was religious or theological in character. ('Theology' is often used in the literature to refer not only to a particular discipline but also, more generally, to denote any kind of confessional or religious orientation.) Indeed, not only was it religious, it was parochial, exclusivist, and therefore sectarian and ideological. As I show here, however, the encyclopedia portraits are not internally coherent in their accounts of this enterprise and therefore leave much to be desired with respect to defining the term.

Those who consult the new *Encyclopedia of Religion* (Eliade 1987) for enlightenment on the notion of 'religious studies' (Vol. XII: 334) will find the cross-reference 'Study of Religion, article on Religious Studies as an Academic Discipline' (Vol. XIV) – an entry that consists of essays by Seymour Cain ('History of Study'), Eric J. Sharpe ('Methodological Issues'), and Thomas Benson ('Religious Studies as an Academic Discipline'), the last of which purports to trace 'the development of religious studies as part of the liberal arts curriculum of secular and sectarian institutions of higher learning during the latter half of the twentieth century' (64). According to Benson, religious studies is a scholarly or academic undertaking aimed at 'fostering critical understanding of religious traditions and values' (89) as opposed to a religious exercise designed to nurture faith. It is therefore a new enterprise, distinct from an earlier style of 'faith-based' study of religion in the university that is usually referred to as 'theology.'

Harold Remus, in the *Encyclopedia of the American Religious Experience* (1988, Vol. III), claims that the development of new academic disciplines, such as sociology, anthropology, and psychology, applied to the study of religion at the end of the nineteenth century, 'led eventually to the development of an academic field designated *religion* or *religious studies* that was dedicated in principle to the academic study of religion . . .' (1658). There is a clear line of demarcation, he insists, between this new discipline and its forerunner (the religiously committed study of religion). Religious studies, he warns, must not be confused with religious education which, like theology, is confessional in nature. 'Religious studies,' he writes, 'does not seek to inculcate religious doctrines or specific religious values, to strengthen or win

commitment to a religious tradition or institution, or to provide instruction preparatory to professional training for the ministry or rabbinate' (1653). For Remus,
therefore, religious studies cannot involve instruction *in* religion but can nevertheless
teach *about* religion (1657).

Alan Olson presents a similar picture of 'religious studies' in the *Encyclopedia of
Religious Education* (1990a), insisting that such studies are 'to be distinguished from theological studies programs at the some two hundred and fifty seminaries and divinity
schools in the United States and Canada' (549). For more than a century, he claims,
religious studies has been trying to differentiate itself from religious and theological
enterprises as a study that excludes personal belief. In his view, 'religious studies is meant
to identify an objective, scientific, non-biased study of religion as distinct from 'theological' and/or 'confessional' study for the purpose of increasing the faith, understanding, and institutional commitment of individual degree candidates in a particular
religion' (549–50). Thus, according to Olson, whereas the academic study of religion
in the US had been primarily in the care of religiously founded institutions until well
into the twentieth century – and, therefore, had been essentially religious in character
– by the 1950s it became more scientific and 'emerged as an important interdisciplinary,
polymethodological, and cross-cultural area of academic inquiry' (551).

The entry by Ninian Smart on 'Religious Studies in Higher Education' in John
Hinnells' *The New Penguin Dictionary of Religions* (1997) echoes Olson's description.
After acknowledging the existence of long-standing traditional approaches to the
study of religion in institutions of higher learning, Smart maintains that 'Religious
Studies as a new multidisciplinary subject incorporating history of religions, cross-
cultural topics, social-scientific approaches and ethical and philosophical reflections
. . . came to prominence chiefly in the 1960s and early 1970s' (420). The significance of the new 'discipline,' it is suggested, is that the academic study of religions
in the modern university made possible a variety of scholarly approaches different
from those sanctioned up to then by the traditional theological framework. Smart
argues that this shift of approach clearly broadened the scope of studies in religion.

Despite the advent of a new and clearly defined scholarly approach to religious
studies, that new study does not consistently reflect the neutral status of an objective science. Benson points to this, for example, arguing that even though admitting
religious studies results from secularizing forces in society, what lies behind the emergence of this new field is not primarily a scientific impulse. Religious studies programs,
he notes, have usually been created in response to student and community interests,
so that, even though such studies of religion are not as overtly religious as they once
were, they are nevertheless concerned with more than scientific knowledge, for they
are often touted as an important element in the 'liberal education' dedicated to the
cultivation of the self. As he puts it, religious studies is 'generally influenced by
pluralistic assumptions and [has] tended toward global perspectives on the nature and
history of religion' (1986: 89). As a consequence, religious studies, even while
bringing a broader curriculum to the religion department and considerably undermining the traditional seminary model, has unfortunately held the door open to 'a
crazy quilt of courses encompassing many disciplines, eras, regions, languages, and
methods of inquiry' (91) – including traditional seminary-type offerings of Christian
history, theology, biblical studies, religious ethics, religious thought, and religious
education. The survival of religious studies in the US, he suggests, is therefore tied

not to the social sciences but rather to the fate of the humanities which are, like theology in the past, directed not only toward providing knowledge about the human estate, but to the formation of the character of students. Recognizing this, Benson points to the vestigial religious overtones to 'religious studies' in the university context, noting that in the publicly funded university, the study of religion occasionally raises apprehension 'concerning church–state relations and the constitutional status of state-funded religious studies' (89). Objections to such studies in the public university context, he suggests, have eased in the light of court decisions that have distinguished teaching about religion (even with the overtones described) from religious indoctrination, implying that only self-ascribed sectarian religious education need be excluded from the field. In Benson's estimation, therefore, religious studies seems to connote a broadly liberal religious education directed toward the formation of character and the betterment of society rather than scientific study aimed at knowledge and explanation of religious phenomena. He admits that in the 1960s there was deep interest in gaining disciplinary status for religious studies, but not on the grounds of its being a science. Rather, such status was sought on the basis of scholarly interest in a common subject matter: 'the nature and diverse manifestations of religious experience' (91). But this, he declares, is not sufficient to warrant its recognition as a discipline, because it clearly does not have a method peculiar to itself. 'Religious studies are, perhaps, best understood,' he therefore concludes, 'as a community of disciplines gathered around the complex phenomenon of religious belief and practice' (92).

Although Remus argued for a line of demarcation between instruction *in* religion and teaching *about* religion, he also noted that such teaching *about* religion is of particular importance to liberal education (1988: 1658). And in so doing, he seems to suggest that religious studies is more than merely a scientific undertaking, despite his insistence that it is not the task of liberal education to make the university a religious place (1658). He claims, for example, that it is not only the emergence of the social sciences that provided an impetus to the development of this new field, but that a 'decline in institutional religions has also been a factor in enrolment in religious studies courses . . .' (1658), suggesting thereby that the new enterprise has become in some sense a surrogate religion. Courses available in the new departments, that is, provide students with 'opportunities to pursue some of the basic human issues – such as freedom, justice, love, evil, death – that universities were often bypassing in favor of technical and analytical study' (1659). Thus, although not intending to indoctrinate, the new religious studies department nevertheless constitutes an element in the student's search for meaning in life; it is not simply concerned with obtaining empirical and theoretical knowledge about religion.

Olson's demarcation of religious studies from a religio-theological study of religion is at least as ambiguous. For Olson, however, the reasons no such clear demarcation is possible are connected to the nature of science rather than to the nature of either religion or religious studies. A proper understanding of 'science,' Olson insists, will be seen to exclude all possibility of providing a fully naturalistic explanation for religion. 'Religious studies,' he writes, 'has greatly contributed to the growing awareness that *true science* does not have to do with the development of a monolithic discipline, but with the collective efforts of a community of scholars illuminating one or more facets of the truth' (1990a: 551, emphasis added). In an article on the university in the same encyclopedia (1990b), Olson's notion of religious studies is further clarified in his claim that the discipline is an important element in the humanities because it provides sustained attention to religious values, making knowledge alone an insufficient goal of the enterprise. Consequently for Olson – although he does not spell it out in great detail – a scientific study of religion that seeks to study religion wholly objectively is little more than an ideology of secular humanism.

The essay by Smart in Hinnells' *The New Penguin Dictionary of Religions* also acknowledges that the so-called new religious studies is not altogether new; in fact, it offers programs that often parallel those offered in divinity schools and departments of theology. It is acknowledged, moreover, that, at least in part, religious studies is fuelled by 'a growth in questing and questioning' rather than by the ideal of obtaining objective knowledge about religion (1995: 420–1). Thus, even though involving the sciences in the study of religion, the new religious studies is not unambiguously scientific in intent or in practice. Not only is it determined by a religious or theological agenda, it is also shaped, Smart argues, by other ideological agendas. Since its emergence in the 1960s it has been profoundly affected by newer, non-objectivist approaches to the understanding of human phenomena such as feminism and postmodernist theorizing (421). Smart then concludes by pointing out how important religious studies is to the humanities – and by implication – to the humanist (and 'liberal education') agenda: 'Religious Studies is in one sense a branch of social science but has also begun to play a vital role in the humanities, both because of its cross-cultural commitments and because of its serious consideration of diversity of human world-views' (421).

In light of this analysis of the encyclopedists' efforts to provide an account of 'religious studies' – of the academic study of religion in the university context – scholars will have to acknowledge, as does Adrian Cunningham (1990), that 'perhaps "religious" [in the phrase "religious studies"] may still carry hints of its earlier usage to describe adherents, and of the ambiguities of "religious education" . . .' (30). Michael Pye (1991) makes the same point more forcefully, arguing that 'the adjective "religious" can easily suggest, and sometimes may be intended to suggest, that these "studies" are supposed to be religious in orientation and not simply studies *of* religion . . .' (41). The term is often used, he maintains, to designate those subjects and activities which in the past have constituted theological enterprises, and must therefore be taken for 'camouflage for theology' (42).

The lack of clarity and precision in the encyclopedia definitions of 'religious studies' is not surprising for it reflects current practices in the discipline as it is observed in college and university departments. The character of that study is thoroughly analyzed in the ambitious state-of-the-art reviews of religious studies in Canadian universities directed by Harold Coward. Six volumes of the study have appeared between 1983 and 2001, covering the provinces of Alberta (Neufeldt 1983), Quebec (Rousseau and Despland 1988), Ontario (Remus *et al.* 1992), Manitoba and Saskatchewan (Badertscher *et al.* 1993), and British Columbia (Fraser 1995); and New Brunswick, Prince Edward Island, Nova Scotia, and Newfoundland (Bowlby 2001).

Although entitled '*The Study of Religion* in Canada/Sciences Religieuses au Canada,' the projected study is described in the editor's introduction to each volume as 'A State-of-the-Art Review of *religious studies* in Canada' (emphasis added), which seems to identify 'religious studies' in university departments very broadly with any and every type of study of religion carried on in institutions of higher learning. The ambiguity of the project description, in fact, provides Brian Fraser all the encouragement needed for dealing not only with the academic study of religion in the university setting but also with the religious and theological study of religion in other institutions in the province – including seminaries. Indeed, Fraser entitles his state-of-the-art review not 'Religious Studies in British Columbia' but *The Study of Religion in British Columbia* (1995), and makes it very clear early on in the volume that he believes the ambiguity of the project title leaves room for argument to the effect that the kinds of study carried on in these very different institutions are not only complementary but in some fundamental sense the same. 'In the other volumes in the Canadian Corporation for the Study of Religion (CCSR) series on the study of religion in Canada,' he writes, 'the focus has been on religious studies in the secular university, with minimal attention being paid to various approaches of theological studies' (viii). As there is only one department of religious studies in universities in British Columbia (UBC), and because Fraser works, as he puts it, from a 'vocational base in theological studies,' he chose 'to focus on the broader subject indicated by the original designation of the series as a whole, i.e., the study of religion' (viii-ix). A comprehensive review of the state-of-the-art in that province, he insists therefore, 'requires that appropriate attention be paid to both religious studies and theological studies' (ix). This, in his view, moreover, is not mandated simply by the fact that two radically different kinds of study of religion exist in institutions of higher education. It exists also because they have complementary interests, so that a proper study of 'religious studies' requires that this fact be recognized. According to Fraser, for example, both types of study of religion exact an element of commitment aside from that found in religious institutions; for while religious institutions of higher learning are committed to enhancing 'participation in and contribution to religious traditions and communities that govern the institutions in which the study takes place' (viii), the so-called neutral and non-advocative study of religion in the university is also directed toward results 'that intend to elucidate the questions of human existence that religions have always tried to confront' (viii). Religious studies, therefore, even though having 'nothing whatsoever to do with the professional training of ministers' (20), seems to be a kind of non-sectarian civil religion or general theology fit for 'a public and pluralistic institution' (viii) because it engages fundamental questions of meaning in human existence. His views in this regard are clearly exhibited in his praise for the work of the Centre for Studies in Religion and Society at the University of Victoria, which, he claims, emerged in part as 'the result of the need for an expanded view of studies in religion' (109) wherein the 'interdisciplinary nature of its commitment brings together the various voices of the scholarly worlds, while not ignoring the community at large, [to address] major challenges of global concern ...' (109). And it is in light of this kind of project that Fraser expresses the hope for an integration of the various approaches 'to the study of religion and the religions themselves[,] and for the development of a [university-based] doctoral program in *religious/theological studies*' (109, emphasis added).

Had Fraser consulted the first volume in this series, he would not have needed to provide justificatory argument for his study of religious and theological programs of study in British Columbia's religious institutions. For in Ronald W. Neufeldt's (1983) account of 'religious studies' in Alberta he acknowledges that some scholars 'expressed some opposition to the inclusion of theological colleges and bible colleges and institutions' (xi) but nevertheless in his study proceeded to support such an expanded notion of the field – as has every subsequent study. Neufeldt's justification for proceeding in this fashion is both practical and theoretical, and it is particularly symptomatic of the confusion that plagues the notion of religious studies as a new kind of academic undertaking. Among the practical reasons for including religious institutions in his account of religious studies in Alberta, Neufeldt cites the fact that 'particular courses in theological colleges are recognized by universities either as religious studies courses or as arts options' (xi), pointing to the practice that 'students from Bible colleges are sometimes given block credit for courses taken in a Bible college, or are exempted from taking introductory courses in religious studies in the universities' (xi). Although such practices suggest a profound confusion of the natures of the new study of religion on the one hand and theological studies on the other, Neufeldt supports the practice on theoretical grounds, none of which is persuasive. He insists, for example, that 'the confessional stance of a particular institution should not automatically be taken to mean that the programs and research in such institutions have no academic integrity at all,' as if that fact provides grounds for the integration of the two approaches to the study of religion in the university context. He suggests that the courses in the theological schools for which transfer credit is given, are all at the descriptive level and therefore not likely to differ greatly from the descriptive courses provided in university departments. Should this prove otherwise, however, Neufeldt is ready with further methodological argument. 'In effect,' he writes, 'the argument made here is for a humanities model for religious studies rather than [for] a model in which the predominant note is critical analysis and theory' (xii). And such a model, he claims (on the authority of Ninian Smart's analysis of religious studies in his *The Science of Religion and the Sociology of Knowledge* (1973)), shows religious studies to be open to aims beyond those of science; beyond merely seeking a theoretical account of religion. Neufeldt acknowledges that religious studies in Alberta is dominated by 'textual and theological/philosophical studies' (76), and while believing this needs correction through co-operation with cognate disciplines, nevertheless insists that the effort 'to hire scholars who are trained in other approaches to the study of religion' must not eclipse those trained in the theological traditions (77). For Neufeldt, evidently, religious studies is not clearly distinguishable from a study of religion that is itself a non-sectarian religious undertaking.

Les Sciences Religieuses au Québec depuis 1972 (1988), by Louis Rousseau and Michel Despland, traces the declining influence of the Roman Catholic Church on religious studies since 1960, but they point out that a claim to neutrality for religious studies cannot be made. Although they argue that the major societies and associations related to the field of religious studies show a marked move toward 'pluridisciplinarity,' they nevertheless maintain that theology and Christian studies still dominate departmental programs and scholarly research interests. Indeed, they argue that the situation in Quebec institutions is still extremely unfavourable to freedom of teaching and research, disrupting the claim that religious studies programs in the secular universities have eliminated theological approaches to the subject. According to Rousseau and Despland, therefore, the field of religious studies in Quebec integrates the approaches associated with theology and the sciences of religion; thus there is no indication of a decisive move from theology to the social scientific study of religion.

The Ontario volume (1992) by Harold Remus, William James, and Daniel Fraikin also fails to provide a clear analysis of the theology/religious studies problem. The authors, drawing on Charles Anderson's study in the early 1970s, suggest that universities drew a clear distinction between religious and secular study (58); but they erred in extending their history of the field to programs operating in Bible colleges, which, by definition, take a faith-based, rather than scientific approach to their curriculum and therefore were presenting not religious studies as much as theology. They reason, in part, that contemporary theology is discontinuous from its 'traditional' predecessor, therefore 'mak[ing] it possible for Ontario religious studies departments to offer such courses today' (33). That claim, however, is predicated on the assumption that religious studies is not reducible simply to the scientific study of religion. Consequently the authors maintain that students of religion must get on with the study of religion and stop the 'by now, sterile wrangling over the "theology-and-religious studies"' issue (33). Religion, they note, 'is studied in a number of academic fields other than theology and in ways that are helpful to religious studies scholars . . . [and that that] too, is "the state-of-the-art," in religious studies in general and in Ontario religious studies in particular' (34). Religious studies as a new hybrid discipline, it appears therefore, is also appropriately carried on in the context of the modern university.

The response of one theological reviewer of the Ontario study is particularly perceptive with respect to this religiously significant understanding of religious studies. Jean-Marc Laporte expresses gratitude for the authors' understanding of religious studies because it sees religious studies and theology as allies engaging 'the world and its problems' (1993: 249). The essential task of each, is identical – but that is largely because the fundamental task of religious studies has been assimilated to that of theology. This is lauded by Laporte, who writes: 'While the authors prize the academic objectivity of religious studies, they are far from advocating bloodless sterility. Professors of religious studies ought to respond to existential concerns and be free to disclose their own personal convictions in appropriate, non-proselytizing ways' (249). And this is not surprising for, as Laporte points out, the authors claim both that 'the matrix out of which religious studies emerged as a distinct reality is a theological one' and that 'the pioneers of this discipline in Ontario universities by and large did not make a clean break from their origins' (249).

The story of the rise of religious studies departments in the universities of Manitoba and Saskatchewan (Badertscher et al. 1993) reveals the same picture of religious origination and influence on the academic study of religion found in the other state-of-the-art studies, with the exception of the department at the University of Regina in Saskatchewan. As in Manitoba, claims Roland Miller, 'university education . . . grew out of a close association with an original perspective that viewed arts and theology as colleagues in the educational enterprise' (101). Theology consequently dominated the notion of religious studies, but only at the University of Saskatchewan (Saskatoon). The development of the department at the University of Regina, at first simply an extension of the department at the University of Saskatchewan, was radically different, even though it found itself involved with legally and financially autonomous, but academically integrated (federated), religious colleges. Nevertheless, its programs, Miller argues, 'grew out of a genuine recognition of the importance of the subject material and out of concern for a secular approach to its academic study' (83). The University of Regina, he continues, 'was interested in pursuing the direction that might be summed up by the phrase "science of religion," although those words do not appear in any of the materials' (83).

In *Religious Studies in Atlantic Canada* Paul W. R. Bowlby works with a definition of the field that excludes schools preparing people for professional work in religious institutions but includes religious colleges and universities that have accepted public funding and have to some degree, therefore, been secularized. Nevertheless, he is well aware that most of the departments of religion included in his study have evolved from departments of theology and that they have followed a conventional pattern of curriculum development, with particular emphasis on biblical and Christian studies. He maintains that these institutional structures have seen significant development (such as the introduction of comparative, social-scientific, and gender-critical approaches to the study of religion) yet also admits that the influence of Christianity on the field in this region of the country has hindered the advancement of 'religious studies' as a scientific discipline.

In all of the programs described in the Canadian studies, only that of the University of Regina is (in theory at least) purely cognitive in orientation. And its view about the nature of the discipline clearly places it in a minority. There were some early indications that religious studies would be identified primarily with a non-religious, scientific approach to understanding religion (Anderson 1972), but, as the state-of-the-art studies make clear, such views did not have a significant impact on the development of the field in Canada. Charles Davis's essay on 'The Reconvergence of Theology and Religious Studies' (1974–5) better captures the aims and desires of those involved in Canadian university departments of religion, as is clearly evident in the majority of the contributions to the more recent volume of essays, *Religious Studies: Issues, Prospects and Proposals* (1991), edited by Klaus Klostermaier and Larry Hurtado. While recognizing something new in contemporary religious studies, the editors nevertheless pointedly invited participants to the conference 'to consider the study of religion at public universities *as a continuation of the intellectual examination of religion which goes back over the ages*' (ix, emphasis added). This is also clearly evident in the character of the research activities of the majority of those who contribute to the Canadian journal *Studies in Religion/Sciences Religieuses*, whose pages are for the most part filled with religious and theological research rather than with scientific studies of religion (Riley 1984).

Although there are no other state-of-the-art reviews of the field of religious studies as extensive as that undertaken by the Canadians, the festschrift for Geoffrey Parrinder, edited by Ursula King and entitled *Turning Points in Religious Studies* (1990), provides a comparable one-volume review of the emergence, development, and current state of religious studies in the UK. This volume is of particular interest because it unequivocally presents itself as providing an account of religious studies as a new discipline, clearly distinguishable from the theological approaches to the study of religion that had until recently characterized university scholarship. As the fly-leaf notice about the volume puts it: 'Religious Studies was first introduced as *a new discipline* in various universities and colleges around the world in the 1960s. This discipline brought about a *reorientation of the study of religion*, created new perspectives, and influenced all sectors of education' (emphasis added). The clarity of this brief statement about a new discipline that has re-oriented scholarship in religion, however, is quickly effaced by the editor's general introduction to the essays intended to document both the emergence of the new discipline and the major turning points in its evolution. For King speaks here not of a *discipline*, but rather of a *field* of study which 'found wider recognition from the 1960s and 1970s onwards when the term "Religious Studies" came first into general use' (15). But as a field, religious studies cannot be characterized methodologically, for fields of study involve a multiplicity of disciplinary approaches to a particular subject matter of interest. Her introduction to the essays on the institutional growth of religious studies in the universities of England, Scotland, and Wales, moreover, compromises the claim that the so-called new discipline brought about a re-orientation of the study of religion already in existence prior to the 1960s. These essays, she writes, 'show how much the course of Religious Studies and the history of its programmes have been intertwined with and often curtailed by earlier institutional developments in the study of theology, so that it has often been difficult to maintain the distinctiveness of Religious Studies' (16). Having acknowledged this, King then goes on to claim that religious studies cannot really 'be fully understood without looking at the closely associated developments in religious education and practical issues in interfaith dialogue ...' (16), suggesting that religious studies is – and ought to be – more than an academic (scientific) discipline. Thus she includes in the volume not only essays on the development of the 'new discipline' but also on the role of religious studies in relation to developments in religious education, interreligious dialogue and philosophy of religion. For King, these 'concerns' characterize distinct approaches to the subject matter of religious studies and are therefore some of the disciplines that characterize the field as multidisciplinary; but all of them clearly reflect the traditional religious and theological concerns of the scholarly study of religion which 'Religious Studies' ought to have superseded. As Robert Jackson points out in his essay on 'Religious Studies and Developments in Religious Education' (1990), for example, religious education embodies not only a cognitive or scientific concern about religion, but also sees religion itself as a form of knowledge and a distinct realm of experience (107); and religious education, therefore, as directed to awakening 'a unique spiritual dimension of experience' in children (110). The *raison d'être* of religious education, therefore, is not only cognitive but formative; aimed at helping children exercise their spiritual curiosity, and encouraging 'in them an imaginative openness to the infinite possibilities of life' (110). W. Owen Cole's discussion of 'The New Educational Reform Act and Worship in County Schools of England and Wales' (1990) similarly confirms the judgement that religious education is concerned not only with gaining knowledge about religion but also with nurturing religious growth and development. As Cole puts it: 'Some kind of collective gathering is considered desirable by most teachers *for a number of purposes* including the collective exploration of and reflection upon values and beliefs ...' (129–30, emphasis added). The fact that philosophy holds the same kind of religious and theological import as one of the disciplines that make up the multidisciplinary enterprise of religious studies is clearly evident in Keith Ward's 'The Study of Truth and Dialogue in Religion' (1990). For Ward, philosophy's value to religious studies is to be found in its concerns with meaning and truth:

> Religious Studies is good for philosophy, since it keeps alive the questions of ultimate meaning and value which are its lifeblood. Philosophy is good for

Religious Studies, since it keeps alive the questions of truth and justification which preserve religion from complacent dogmatism. The discipline of Religious Studies now offers to philosophers a much wider and more informed basis for the investigation of meaning and truth in religion; and the most fruitful results are to be expected from the increasingly inter-disciplinary approach which is being adopted in British universities.

(230)

Interestingly (if not ironically), only Marcus Braybrooke – Chairman of the inter-faith movement 'World Congress of Faiths' – appears to assume that religious studies is a genuinely new approach to the study of religion. Braybrooke writes: 'The under-lying hope of the interfaith movement, *although not of the academic study of religions*, is that in some way religions are complementary or convergent' (1990: 138, emphasis added). He nevertheless seems to believe that a positive complementarity exists between religious studies and interfaith development. And Eleanor Nesbitt's article on Sikhism (1990) presents a similar proposal for encouraging a positive relationship between the modern student of religion and the religious devotee.

The descriptions of the emergence of religious studies in the universities in England (Adrian Cunningham), Scotland (Andrew F. Walls), and Wales (Cyril Williams), it must be noted, claim (or suggest) that it achieved status in the university as an autonomous discipline by virtue of its differentiation from religion and theology. Their claims, however, seem to be undermined by the editor of the volume in which they appear, for they are found in the context of numerous other contributions of the kind just described, as well as an essay by Ninian Smart – 'Concluding Reflections on Religious Studies in Global Perspective' (1990) – that argue a contrary case. It is true that neither Smart nor the other essayists argue specifically against undertaking sci-entific analyses of religion and religions. Smart does argue, however, against what he calls a scientifically purist stance in religious studies. As with the other essayists, Smart insists that religious studies can only properly be understood as a polymethodic and multidisciplinary enterprise which embraces 'as much as possible of the scholarship of all sorts going on in the world . . . [w]hether it is neutral and objective or religiously committed' (305, 300). As a non-purist study, religious studies, he claims, will triumph because it can 'be a force for permitting deeper conversations between religions, with-out reverting into a simple exchange of pieties' (305). In this light, it is ironic that Cunningham should remark, as I have already noted, that even though the designa-tion 'religious studies' for the study of religion carried on in university departments has an honourable history, 'perhaps "religious" may still carry hints of its earlier usage to describe adherents, and of ambiguities of "religious education," and it would be better for the university area to be simply called "religion"' (30).

Given Ninian Smart's widespread influence on the development of university studies of religion over the formative period under review here, not only in the UK but also in Canada, Australia, New Zealand, South Africa, and the US, it may be helpful to elaborate more fully his views on the nature and structure of 'religious studies.' In 'Some Thoughts on the Science of Religion' (1996), Smart clearly differ-entiates between the scientific study of religion and religious studies, with the former being associated with a multiplicity of disciplines, including history, comparative reli-gions, and other social scientific approaches to the study of religious phenomena

(16). It is possible, Smart admits, to take 'religious studies' to be fully described as the scientific study of religion, but he thinks such an understanding falls short of the view of that enterprise held by the majority of those engaged in it. Thus he argues for a broader view of 'religious studies' that will include not only scientific studies but also 'reflective studies' (19). By 'reflective studies' Smart means the examination of philosophical questions about the meaning and value of religion, in the same sense presented by Keith Ward (1990). Smart admits that such a reflective religious studies involves itself in 'presentational concerns,' by which he means engagement with the questions of truth and meaning, yet he denies that this amounts to merging religious studies with theology (19). This on two grounds: first, that which he calls 'extended pluralistic theologizing' is clearly distinguishable from traditional theology; and second, that 'certain reductionistic views of science are themselves ideological positions that are not clearly distinguishable from traditional theology' (20). He argues, therefore, that talk of the science of religion as the core of religious studies is wholly reasonable, but only if it remains non-reductionist. As such, the science of religion would then allow for critical reflection on the meaning, truth, and value of religion *insofar as* it is not simply identified with traditional theology, which, he claims, 'is tainted by arrogance, colonialism and a usual lack of pluralism' (19). As he puts it, '[i]f Religious Studies is to take on board reflective studies, and with that get involved with any presentational concerns with theology or ideology, it is only with Extended Pluralistic Theologizing . . . that it should blend' (19). For him, therefore, '[t]o be genuinely scientific and objective we need to be able to steer a middle channel between the Scylla of secret theology and the Charybdis of reductionism' (20), which requires a blend of non-reductionistic scientific studies of religion with reflective, extended theology. Both traditional theology and scientific purism are excluded.

In his contribution to Jon R. Stone's *The Craft of Religious Studies* (1998), Smart reiterates his concern about 'scientific purism,' even though he acknowledges that what is called modern religious studies arose only after the 1960s with the merger of the history of religions with the social sciences (18). The new discipline, he insists, must be both speculative and philosophically reflective, although he warns against its being used as mere 'clothing for a religious worldview' (24). It is little wonder, therefore, that Smart characterizes religious studies here as a quest (ix). But neither should it come as a surprise, therefore, that many in the academic world, as Smart himself puts it, have categorized religious studies 'as some form of tertiary Sunday School, . . . [and so] resist and despise it' (24). There is sufficient confusion about the notion of 'religious studies,' he judiciously notes, that 'the outside world in academia may be forgiven for misunderstanding what the field of Religious Studies is all about . . .' (24). But it does not appear to me that his own characterizations of the field have helped dispel the confusion; indeed, his own work seems to contribute to a view of religious studies as a religious exercise.

That this kind of confusion about the nature of religious studies exists in the American context is clearly acknowledged in the report of the Committee on 'Defining Scholarly Work' of the American Academy of Religion (AAR). In a report entitled 'Religious Studies and the Redefining Scholarship Project,' the committee notes:

> Religious Studies, however defined or wherever located, remains suspect in the eyes of many within the rest of the academy and continually finds itself marginalized or

otherwise obscured due to the fact and/or perception of blurred boundaries between studying religion and being religious, or between education about and education in religion.

(Myscofski and Pilgrim *et al.* 1993: 7)

The suspicion in which religious studies is held in the US academic context, therefore, is due primarily to the confusion of what is proposed as an academic (and therefore scientific) enterprise with a religious or theological undertaking. As in Canada and the UK, scholars in the US claim that a significant transformation in the nature of the study of religion in the university context occurred after the Second World War. In *God's People in the Ivory Tower: Religion in the Early American University* (1991), Robert S. Shepard claims that the study of religion in US colleges and universities briefly flirted with the idea of creating a science of religion but remained essentially a kind of 'Christian *Religionswissenschaft*' that was essentially moralistic and apologetic in intent and practice. As such it was unable

> to separate [itself] from the theological and professional concerns of the nascent university, particularly the rising seminary within the university. A theological agenda accompanied the entrance of comparative religion in American higher education despite the arguments, some rhetorical and some sincere, that the new discipline was objective, scientific, and appropriate as a liberal arts subject.
>
> (129)

Nevertheless, claims Shepard, the academic study of religion in US colleges and universities experienced a renaissance after the Second World War and within a very short period of time gained disciplinary status within the academic context. D. G. Hart (1992) comes to a similar conclusion in his analysis of the field of religious studies. While not unaware of the fact that the rapid growth of the field was stimulated by the cultural crisis generated by the Second World War, and that such studies were aimed at ensuring college and university students received an education that included 'values-training' and moral formation (209), he nonetheless insists that the development of the American Academy of Religion (AAR) transformed the field into a scientific discipline. These changes, he insists, constitute a watershed in the history of the study of religion in the US, because they involved the substitution of scientific explanations of religious phenomena for the earlier quest for religious, theological, and humanistic accounts of religion. 'The new methods of studying religion advocated by the AAR,' he writes, 'signalled the demise of [the] Protestant dominance [of the field] as professors of religion became increasingly uncomfortable with their religious identification . . . By striving to make their discipline more scientific, religion scholars not only embraced the ideals of the academy but also freed themselves from the Protestant establishment' (198). (Hart recapitulates the argument in his more recent book, *The University Gets Religion: Religious Studies in American Higher Education* (2000).)

Were this picture true, scholars would be hard-pressed to explain why the so-called new discipline is still held in suspicion by the rest of the academic and scientific community. What does account for the suspicion, however, is the fact that the notion of religious studies is not in fact carried out within a naturalistic and scientific frame-

work, but more nearly resembles the academic field as it first emerged in the US –
namely, as an inchoate enterprise not easily distinguishable from theology and characterized primarily by apologetic and moral concerns. This is clearly evident in the
review of the field produced for the AAR by Ray Hart, entitled 'Religious and
Theological Studies in American Higher Education' (1991), even though he admits
that the term 'religious studies' is now generally used to refer to 'the scholarly, neutral
and non-advocative study of multiple religious traditions' (716). Hart notes that many
in the AAR are extremely uncomfortable with 'the nomenclature that discriminates
"religious" from "theological studies"' (716), and points out that the members of the
Academy are divided between the terms 'study of religion' (gaining knowledge *about*
religion) and 'practice of religion' (*understanding* the truth of religion) (734, 778);
he then claims, however, that by far the majority of the members favor a style of
scholarship that combines the two activities, or one that at the very least eschews
a clear demarcation between them. Joseph Kitagawa's essays, 'The History of Religions
in America' (1959) and 'Humanistic and Theological History of Religion with Special
Reference to the North American Scene' (1983), strengthen Hart's contention
considerably. In the first essay, he maintains that the religious liberalism of the
World's Parliament of Religions served as the fundamental impetus for the establishment of the study of comparative religions – which later became religious studies
– in American universities, even though he acknowledges that the participants at
the Parliament meeting in 1893 for the most part gathered together representatives
of the world's faiths rather than scholars of religion. In drawing attention to this,
Kitagawa underlines the fact that the academic study of religion in the US has more
than one dimension; it has involved historical and social scientific analysis, but it
has also moved beyond what such analyses can provide. Consequently he distinguishes the 'History of Religions' (as a scientific enterprise) from the 'theological
History of Religions' – but with the implication that neither can do without the
other. And he insists that the *Religionswissenschaft* later destined to become 'religious
studies' is not simply scientific but rather 'religio-scientific,' being obliged to 'view
that data "religio-scientifically"' (1959: 21). In the second essay, Kitagawa suggests
that the scientific Enlightenment principles behind the scholarship of the members
of the International Association for the History of Religions (IAHR) have greatly
affected the development of the field in the US, and yet – in keeping with his earlier
analysis of *Religionswissenschaft* – he refers to the discipline as 'autonomous[,] situated between normative studies . . . and descriptive studies' (1983: 559). Unlike other
social sciences, then, for Kitagawa this discipline does not simply seek descriptions
or explanations of events and processes; rather, it enquires after the meaning of religious data and is therefore a mode of 'research' linking descriptive with normative
concerns (560). He contrasts this kind of study of religion with the more explicitly
normative 'theological History of Religions' cited in his earlier essay, but it is clear
that this 'humanistic History of Religions' also stands in contrast to the purely social-
scientific study of religion represented by scholars affiliated to the IAHR. As one
historian of the development of religious studies in the US puts it, despite the claim
of having become an independent scientific enterprise in addition to the other social
sciences, it has remained haunted by religious aspirations (Reuben 1996: 142). The
religious studies of the post-1960s, in particular has always been concerned with more
than scientific description and explanation of religion. As D. G. Hart echoes (1992:

207–8), post-1960s religious studies in the US is a discipline imbued with spiritual value; and the students of religion (as represented by the AAR) draw support from the humanities for their enterprise by stressing the spiritual relevance of their studies to the natural sciences.

The confusion that characterizes the post-war notion of 'religious studies' in the American context is rather clearly documented in Walter H. Capps's *Religious Studies: The Making of a Discipline* (1995). Although Capps refers to religious studies as an intellectual discipline which 'provides training and practice ... in directing and conducting inquiry regarding the subject of religion' (xiv), whereby the subject of religion can be made intelligible, he also claims that 'religious studies is a relatively new subject-field concerning whose intellectual composition there is as yet no consensus' (xv). He maintains that this is partly because the principal contributions to the field have been made by persons in other disciplines such as history and the social sciences, and because 'convictional goals' have affected the processes of interpretation applied. He states:

> the primary differentiation within religious studies derives less from the fact that historians, sociologists, anthropologists, psychologists, philosophers, theologians, and others are intensely involved in inquiry, and raise questions from within the frame of interests that belong to their respective vantage points, and much more from the fact that representations of all these fields and disciplines are interested in uncovering certain information about the subject *and pursue it via raising fundamental questions.*

> (xxii, emphasis added)

Cognitive and scientific inquiry, therefore, is secondary to the fundamental questions about meaning and value that provide a coherent framework within which the multiplicity of disciplines making up the field operate. Capps argues that it ought not to surprise anyone to see such a religious goal characterize this academic study. For, as he notes, not only was the historical and comparative study of religion established in the universities in the late nineteenth century and until the Second World War undertaken largely by scholars involved both in the study and the practice of religion (325), but one can also make a strong case that the subsequent flowering of the study of religion in the university context – and especially so in the US – was due to its character as a liberal theological undertaking. According to Capps, that is, it is largely because of the Tillichian conceptualization of the theological enterprise that students of religion gained 'forceful and clear access to the more inclusive cultural worlds, and in ways that could be sanctioned religiously and theologically' (290). He rejects the view that the perpetuation of theological reflection in the religious studies enterprise undermines its academic or scientific respectability (325). Instead, the student of religion must recognize that religious studies, insofar as it is merely the sum of the analytical and interpretive achievements of the various constituent fields of research, does not do full justice to the subject of religion. Furthermore, the polymethodic and multidisciplinary character of the academic study of religion today constitutes 'religious studies' only if all these fields are working together to show 'that religion has a necessary and proper place within the inventory of elements of which the scope of knowledge is comprised' (345). 'In sum,' he concludes broadly, 'religious studies recognizes that religion is not fully translatable into religious studies, and this is an analytical and interpretive truth' (347).

More recent work in America concurs with Capps's conclusion. In his introduction to *Critical Terms for Religious Studies* (1998), Mark C. Taylor claims both that prior to the 1960s religious studies was essentially a Christian (Protestant) undertaking and that the *raison d'être* of the new religious studies since that time is still essentially religious but neither particularly Protestant or Christian. At that time, 'departments and programs in religion tended to be either extensions of the chaplain's office, which was almost always Christian and usually Protestant, or affiliated with philosophy departments, which were primarily if not exclusively concerned with Western intellectual history;' whereas after the 1960s they are associated not with science, but rather with 'the flowering of the 1960s counter culture' (Taylor 1998a: 11). Although he admits that religious studies has been 'profoundly influenced by developments dating back to the Enlightenment' (10), its new incarnation in university departments in the US was predominantly influenced by multicultural sensibilities created by the civil rights and anti-war movements of the late 1950s and early 1960s. If the 'how' of religious studies has changed because of the increased influence of the social sciences in cultural studies during this period, he avers nevertheless that this has not altered the essence of the discipline; that is, even if a social scientific study of religion has somehow displaced the old theology, it has not displaced the fundamental religious concern that has always – and always will – characterize the field. Taylor notes elsewhere (1994) that it is precisely for this reason that religious studies is an academically suspect discipline in secular colleges and universities (1994: 950). Yet even though the field of religious studies became captive to other methodologies, he argues, it cannot be reduced to them (951), because the secular approach of the sciences absolutize their understanding of religion and are themselves, therefore, simply another form of theology.

For Taylor, there is no appropriate procedure for a comprehensive scientific study of religion, and religious studies must therefore be both multidisciplinary and multicultural. But if he seems to discern the complexity of his stance, he nevertheless does not assist the scholarly study under question by his fluid description. Postmodernism, he maintains, undermines all possibility of a fundamental method or comprehensive explanatory approach to the data of the field. Consequently its quarry cannot be cognition; rather it must seek to understand religion by applying a multiplicity of notions and concepts that might act as 'enabling constraints' (1998a: 16) for a discourse of a different kind: 'for exploring the territory of religion' (17) by means of a 'dialogue between religious studies and important work going on in other areas of the arts, humanities, and social sciences' (18). Such a religious studies, he point out, properly transcends scientific reductionism and, like the study of religion antedating it, recognizes that '[r]eligion . . . is not epiphenomenal but sui generis' (6; see also 1999: 4). Stated differently, scientific theory is not not-theological, as Taylor might express it, because theory itself is theo-logical and onto-theological in character, given that it is a search either for an 'overarching or underlying unity' that will coherently frame the data. As he puts it:

> The gaze of the theorist strives to reduce differences to identity and complexity to simplicity. When understood in this way, the shift from theology to theory

does not, as so many contemporary theorists think, escape God but exchanges overt faith for covert belief in the One in and through which all is understood.

(1999: 76)

The new post-1960s study of religion in the American context on this reading of the situation is not new in its fundamental orientation from the traditional study of religion in the university. The religious discourse of traditional studies is replaced not by scientific discourse but rather by a different form of religious discourse – namely, the discourse of 'responsible inquiry' that 'neither demands answers nor believes in progress but seeks to keep the future open by a relentless questioning that unsettles everything by settling nothing. To settle nothing is to leave nothing unanswered. Forever unanswered' (Taylor 1994: 963). This kind of 'responsible discourse,' it is quite apparent, is not primarily concerned with obtaining knowledge about religions and religion, but rather with the well-being of the individual.

That there is no general convergence of opinion about the nature of religious studies among students of religion in the Anglo-American university context is clearly demonstrated by the analyses of the various Canadian, British, and American views presented above. The same can be said about religious studies globally. Although a 'thick description' of the global situation cannot be given, I will nevertheless attempt a brief sketch of similar problems raised in 'religious studies' discussions elsewhere in the world. Eric J. Sharpe, for example, notes that although the study of religion in Australian universities and colleges was from its inception free from confessional attachments, '[that is] not to say ... that those involved in teaching these various programmes were without theological interests' (1986b: 249). He continues:

> On the whole, rather few [Australian students of religion] could be regarded as 'secular' scholars, and many held a form of dual citizenship, being 'theological' and 'scientific' at the same time ... All in all, the positions occupied by Australian scholars in the field by the late 1970s mirrored fairly accurately the divisions observable anywhere in the world ...
>
> (249)

In an essay entitled 'South Africa's Contribution to Religious Studies', Martin Prozesky claims that the discipline has made a significant contribution to society because of the peculiarity of its being both scientific and 'more than' science. The student of religion, he insists, must go beyond merely seeking an explanation of religious phenomena to 'a genuinely liberative practice' (Prozesky 1990: 18). According to Prozesky, the student of religion is able to do this because religion itself is a humanizing force, which, when properly understood, will have a transformative effect upon those who study it.

Another striking example is provided by Michael Pye, in his 'Religious Studies in Europe: Structures and Desiderata' (1991), where he points out that the ambiguities and confusions that plague the notion of 'religious studies' in the Anglo-American context also have their counterpart in Europe. He points out that in Germany, for example, 'the term *Religionswissenschaft* in the singular (science of religion, which for Pye is the same as religious studies) is rivalled in some universities by the plural *Religionswissenschaften* (sciences of religion) which tends to mean religious sciences with a religious motivation, including Catholic and Protestant theology' (41). The evidence, then, regarding the diversity of perceptions, claims, and proposals about 'religious studies' as an enterprise carried out in the context of the modern university cannot be ignored, and would seem to lead to only one conclusion – that 'religious studies,' as Michael Pye has suggested, is 'a flag of convenience' (1994: 52) used by scholars, programs, and institutions to 'legitimate' the aims, methods, and procedures they adopt in their study of religions. I do not think matters are quite this bleak, however, and, in concluding this discussion, I will attempt to set out what general agreements might be reached as to the meaning and use of the term 'religious studies' by those involved in an academic study of religion in the university.

The term 'religious studies' it appears from this discussion, is used in two quite different yet not wholly unconnected ways. In one sense, as the state-of-the-art reviews of 'religious studies' in Canada suggest, the term includes whatever study of religion and religions is undertaken in any post-secondary institution of education, whether religious or secular, and regardless of the methodology adopted. Here the term is often taken to be commensurate with 'the academic study of religion' and 'the scholarly study of religion,' which notions themselves are often used synonymously. In this case, then, as Michael Pye puts it, the notion of religious studies 'covers a multitude of possibilities' (1991: 42). The second, more common use of the term, however, is as a designation for a particular kind of approach to the study of religion with a particular aim, methodology, or style that distinguishes it from the type of study of religion antedating it. And when used in this sense, it still refers to the study of religion undertaken in the academy, but now designates an enterprise legitimated by the academy – here the modern research university – because it measures up to the received criteria of scientific study in the other university disciplines. Identification of religious studies with the academic study of religion in this instance, therefore, does not necessarily apply to all post-secondary research carried out under that rubric. 'Religious studies' as an academic undertaking, therefore, ought to connote a new kind of enterprise with respect to religions and religion, and might well be referred to as a discipline. The religious studies literature reviewed here, unfortunately, does not reveal general agreement among those engaged in the enterprise about the nature, structure, or intent of this activity, but neither does it allow inclusion of the multitude of possibilities contained in 'religious studies' merely as a designation of the institutional location in which those engaged in the study of religion are found.

Moreover, and to recall my initial thematic about the particularities of a discipline *qua* discipline, the notion of religious studies is further complicated by the fact that the very idea of disciplines in the university is under attack by postmodernist thinkers. And, as the foregoing discussion has made quite clear, religious studies is understood by many to be an enterprise involving a multiplicity of disciplines and is, therefore, polymethodical – and, consequently, without a method peculiar to itself. Nevertheless, most of those who have written on 'religious studies' seem agreed upon the nature of that study of religion that religious studies either complements or displaces: namely, a confessional – and therefore engaged – study of religion (usually Christian, and, more specifically, Protestant). There appears to be agreement, then, that it is the scientific element of religious studies that constitutes the newness of the modern study of religion; but there is still radical disagreement as to whether the scientific aspect of religious studies makes the new enterprise wholly discontinuous with the traditional study of religion, or whether it allows for a degree of comple-mentarity. One ought also, perhaps, to acknowledge that 'science' itself, like 'discipline,' is a seriously contested notion, which subject I might not venture to broach, did it not appear in the work of Mark C. Taylor cited above. For it is obvious that such a postmodern understanding of science admits a far broader range of intel-lectual activities than does modern science.

As designator of a particular type of study of religion, it appears that 'religious studies' is being used to refer to at least four distinct types of intellectual activity in college and university departments. Each differentiates itself from the confessional study of religion that characterized the university study of religion before the emer-gence of the new departments, although not all would deny at least some continuity with that earlier religio-theological study. I will provide here a brief characterization of each, moving from those that most overtly resemble the confessional approach to those that would deny all continuity with it.

The first of the activities designated 'religious studies' can be described as 'theology under new management.' This view is succinctly presented by Schubert M. Ogden, in his 'Theology in the University' (1986), in which he argues that theological inquiry is of the essence of the study of religion as a humanistic discipline (as distinct from a confessional undertaking) (121). If 'by "religious studies,"' he writes, 'is meant *a single field-encompassing field of study*, constituted by a single question for reflection, rather than simply many studies of religion, constituted by the multiple questions of other fields of study' (129, emphasis added), then it can only be constituted by focussing on 'the question as to the meaning and truth of religion as the primary way in which human beings make fully explicit the truth about ultimate reality disclosed by their spontaneous experience' (129). With the constitutive question of 'religious studies,' presented as indistinguishable from that of philosophical theology, Ogden insists that:

> either 'religious studies' designates a proper field of study constituted by the ques-tion as to the meaning of and truth of religion, and hence by the philosophical theological question as to the meaning and truth of all thinking and speaking about God or the ultimate, or else it is simply a loose way of speaking of what would be less misleadingly called 'studies of religion,' seeing that they are merely the several studies of religion already constituted by the constitutive questions of other fields of study such as philosophy, history, and the social sciences.
>
> (130)

Ronald F. Thiemann, in 'The Future of an Illusion: An Inquiry into the Contrast Between Theological and Religious Studies' (1990), promotes a similar interpreta-tion of the new religious studies, claiming that it, like all theologies – confessional theologies included – enquires 'after the dimension of universal human experience' (74) and therefore requires reflection on the question of the meaning and truth of religion determined to be a fundamental aspect of human existence (79). Similar views are expressed in M. Novak's *Ascent of the Mountain, Flight of the Dove: An Invitation to Religious Studies* (1971):

> [R]eligious studies are nothing more than a full articulation, through systematic, historical, and comparative reflection, of a person's way of life ... Religious

studies – then called 'theology' – used to be undertaken mainly in monasteries, seminaries, schools of divinity, church colleges . . . Today religious studies are pursued at secular universities in connection with programs of humanistic studies, with departments of the social sciences (psychology, sociology, anthropology), with institutes of African or Asian or Near Eastern studies, and even with investigations in the meaning and interpretation of the natural sciences (biology, physics, ecology).

(xii-xiii)

And in *Mended Speech: The Crisis of Religious Studies and Theology* (1982), P. Joseph Cahill provides a long, intricate argument in support of the claim that the humanistic study of religion – which he equates with the history of religions – and traditional theology are 'two disciplines in a coherent and intelligible field of religious studies' (5), a situation that makes possible the understanding of human religious experience by focussing attention on the element of belief and commitment central to all religions, and is used to justify his claim regarding the unity of the religious 'quest' (146, 158). '"Religious studies" as theology under new management,' given these accounts of it, is only marginally removed from the confessional theological studies it claims to replace. It is concerned with 'religious reality,' but deals with it in general philosophical and metaphysical terms rather than from a particular confessional (revelatory) point of view. An alternative theological understanding of religious studies is provided by Mark C. Taylor, whose work is discussed above. Since for Taylor theoretical science is itself essentially theological in character, reflection on the ultimate meaning of life can hardly be excluded from a proper understanding of religious studies on the grounds that it constitutes theology. And British theologian David Ford follows a similar line of postmodern thinking in this respect. The field of the study of religion, he argues, cannot appropriately be described by using the categories 'confessional' theology and 'neutral' religious studies, because in light of contemporary deconstructive criticism it is no longer possible to think any intellectual enterprise can be neutral. Consequently, religious studies, no less than theology, must make sure 'that questions of religious meaning, truth, practice, and beauty are given the academic significance that is due them . . .' (1999: 12). According to Ford, therefore, 'the academic study of religion' is appropriately institutionalized only in 'departments of theology *and* religious studies' because religious studies, like theology, 'must allow scope for intelligent faith leading to constructive and practical theologies' (18–19).

A second, distinct type of intellectual activity carried out under the banner of 'religious studies' might well be called 'religious studies as tertiary religious education.' The primary task of religious studies here is not that of seeking explanations of religion, nor that of providing the metaphysical justification for religion, but rather of providing for an 'experiential understanding' of religion. In this guise, religious studies is neither the scientific debunking of religion nor the confessional promulgation of it. Rather it is a humanistic appropriation of a range of human experience lending significance to our lives. In this sense, religious studies is not primarily directed to obtaining objective knowledge as it is concerned with the formation of the whole person. This view finds collective expression in Stephen Crites's 'Liberal Learning and the Religion Major' (1990), a report written on behalf of the 'AAR

Task Force on the Study in Depth in Religion,' undertaken in co-operation with a national review of 'Majors in the Arts and Sciences' initiated by the Association of American Colleges. 'The quest about religion,' according to Crites,

> plunges the student into the densest and most elusive issues of value, introduces the student into an ancient and enduring conversation, not always peaceful, about ultimately serious matters, engages the imagination of the student in the most daring imaginative ventures of human experience . . . For many students it is a disciplined encounter with an order of questioning that has affinities with their own struggles for personal identity. It is one way of joining the human race.
>
> (13)

Crites is quick to point out that the aim of the study of religion is not to convince students to join any particular religious tradition – which would be a form of sectarianism – but he nevertheless insists that the study of religion must aid students to discover that religion 'makes sense' and that this 'enlarges her or his own horizon of human possibility' (14).

Such a notion of religious studies really differs very little from the kind of religious education programs undertaken in modern, multicultural societies. Although religious education was at an earlier stage understood to involve the nurture of pupils in the dominant religious beliefs and traditions of a particular society, multiculturalism has forced a change of intention into the enterprise. And although education is clearly distinguished from nurture, the educational task, with respect to religion, is still seen to involve more than simply teaching students *about* religion. As John Hull (1984) puts it, with respect to religious education in the British school system, just as schools have a responsibility to prepare pupils for participation in a political democracy, so is there 'a role for the school in preparing pupils to take an informed and thoughtful part in a pluralistic society' (48), which requires a thoughtful study of the multiple religious traditions it embodies. And that 'thoughtful study,' he insists, involves more than the empirical and theoretical study of the traditions concerned. 'Religious education,' he writes,

> is a wider group of 'subjects' in which things like sensitivity training, moral education, personal relations and so on are set around religious studies as the periphery around the core. Religious education may thus be thought of as helping the pupil in his own quest for meaning. Religious studies is the inquiry after other peoples' meanings. The study of non-religious lifestyles is also a study of other peoples' meanings. So the question [of religious education] concerns the relation between my search for meaning and my study of other peoples' searches for meaning.
>
> (54)

For Hull, therefore, the plurality of subjects and activities involved in religious education is held together by 'the idea of informed existential dialogue' (54), which very much resembles the notion of religious studies represented in Crites's report to the AAR. And virtually the same conception of religious education holds sway in America, where scholars distinguish 'religion studies' from 'religious studies.' 'Religion studies,' argues Guntrum G. Bischoff, is appropriately intended to 'contribute to the student's growth in world-understanding and self-understanding' (1975: 132), an exercise clearly distinguishable from the religious instruction students receive in private religious communities. The task of such instruction is not merely to provide information about religion(s) but also to enable students to relate to a multicultural world. As Bischoff puts it:

> If we may define education generally as a process enabling a person to autonomously order his environment and himself into a meaningful world, and to relate himself to this world in a responsible way, we may define the primary educational objective of the public school as the enabling process which helps develop the young person's world-understanding and self-understanding.
>
> (129)

Religious studies, then, as Crites presents it in his report to the AAR, amount to a rather relaxed apology for religion in general, in the same sense as in programs of religious education. And accordingly, religious studies for Crites must actively engage the student in thinking through the question of the meaning of life, with the religious studies instructor engaged as facilitator in the process. And insofar as the teacher of religious studies is involved in that process of 'forming' the student, she or he takes the place of the religious educator and theologian.

The third, relatively widely held view of religious studies that can be discerned in the scholarly literature sees the enterprise to be essentially scientific. In this description, however, I am using the concept 'enterprise' as defined by Robert A. McCaughey (1984) – as 'any organized understanding of sufficient magnitude and duration to permit its participants to derive a measure of identity from it' (xiii). As 'scientific,' the enterprise is chiefly characterized by a cognitive intention, taking for granted that the natural and social sciences are the only legitimate models for the objective study of religion; but it does not itself constitute a distinct scientific discipline. The primarily cognitive focus in this version of religious studies clearly distinguishes it from the first two types described above. It is not that the earlier types of religious studies wholly reject the contributions made by the natural and social sciences to their understanding of religion, but just that the cognitive intention that informs the sciences is subordinated to religious commitments or theological assumptions; that it is placed in the service of other goals, such as the formation of character or the achievement of some form of (salvific) religious enlightenment. The earlier exercises are nevertheless 'academic enterprises,' because they are pursued by scholars in the context of the university, but they might be appropriately considered 'mixed genre enterprises' because they attempt to blend scientific and extra-scientific goals. Religious studies as a 'scientific enterprise,' however, is a naturalistic study of religion carried out in a wide array of complementary disciplines. And the review of the literature above provides evidence of the widely held view that the field is polymethodic and multidisciplinary – as does the volume in which this essay appears. Religious studies, in this view, is not a separate discipline but instead a general rubric for the empirical and scientific study of religion.

The fourth and final type of activity designated by 'religious studies' receiving some degree of general agreement among scholars in the field, is that it is a scientific discipline on a par with other scientific disciplines. There is some measure of agreement, that is, that the notion of religious studies as merely multidisciplinary and polymethodic is somehow incoherent, and that there ought to be a unifying principle guaranteeing methodological coherence and genuine complementarity in the multidisciplinary contributions to the understanding of religion. 'In this situation,' writes Michael Pye,

> there may arise the temptation to enjoy the flight to our personal interests in one specific religious tradition, to disappear entirely into some specialized philological, textual study, or to pursue just one or two analytical questions to the exclusion or at least the relative disregard of others. Such anarchy may seem attractive, but then it also implies the dissolution of 'religious studies' except as a flag of convenience.
>
> (1991: 52)

A search for what it is that might make of religious studies a discipline, rather than merely a disparate set of disciplines interested in one or other aspect of religion, has prompted a variety of answers, two of which I will set out briefly here. (In one sense, of course, this is simply not possible, because it would imply that religious studies is itself an autonomous discipline in addition to all the other disciplines of the so-called multidisciplinary exercise, which, it appears, would be paradoxical if not simply contradictory.) As has already been pointed out above, some scholars in the field believe the fundamental question of the truth of religion alone constitutes a unifying force among the many disciplines of the field. But this kind of approach, as I have also pointed out above, is religious and metaphysical rather than scientific, and therefore is not appropriately considered characteristic of a 'discipline' as that concept is employed in the modern research university. Others, however, have suggested naturalistic alternatives that might provide the kind of coherence needed to make of the many disciplines a coherent project. Michael Pye (1999), for example, has argued that religious studies can be understood as a disciplinary project on the basis of a judicial 'clustering' of the methodologies used by the various social sciences involved in the study of religion. Instead of the miscellaneous list of disciplines usually cited in descriptions of the field, he suggests that there are disciplines that 'correlate and integrate those features of academic (or in some languages "scientific") method which are particularly necessary in the study of religions' (195), which, 'clustered' together, make of religious studies a discipline. Pye lists three methodological strands, which, when integrated, make up the discipline: the relation between subject-matter and method; the relation between sources and method; and the methodological requirements. And he argues (not wholly persuasively) that a complete argument about what the clustering of these strands might look like is not necessary to understanding religious studies as a discipline. An alternative view of what makes religious studies a discipline is hinted at by Eric J. Sharpe in his history of the field (1986a). Attention in this regard, he suggests, must be paid to the role of theory in the academic study of religion in the late nineteenth century. The early history of the academic study of religion, he writes, involved independent theological, philosophical, and other scholarly approaches to the study of religion, and therefore lacked a single guiding principle of method to provide it coherence. However, argues Sharpe, unity was brought to the field with the application of theory to the understanding of religion because, as he puts it, it made it possible for 'the real focus of the study of religion ... to be located, not in transcendental philosophy, but in ... this-worldly categories' (24). Sharpe also points out that, as evolutionary theory became associated with simplistic notions of progress and fell into disrepute, the students of religion became interested in 'close and detailed studies in a limited area rather than in vast comparison and synthetic pattern-making' (174). Thus, with the demise of theory, the study of religion once again became multidisciplinary, without focus, and therefore lost its disciplinary quality. By implication, then, the disciplinary quality of the academic study of religion can only be found in theory, for it is only theory that can provide a coherent framework that can make sense of the contributions of the various disciplines.

In providing an account of the diversity of meanings of 'religious studies' alive and well in university education today, the task of this essay has been addressed. Yet one might reasonably raise the question as to whether all these usages are appropriate to the modern university – and if not, which ones are? The answer to these questions, of course, depends upon one's conception of the nature of the modern university and, concomitantly, of the academic vocation. It is clear that, if one thinks of the academic vocation as concerned not simply with gaining objective knowledge of the world in which we live but also with edification – and therefore with the formation and cultivation of character – the first two types of religious studies are not only appropriate to the university but also necessary. If however, the *raison d'être* of the modern university is the search for and dissemination of knowledge, and the skills involved in the process, then the task of religious studies must be purely cognitive, committed to the advancement of objective and neutral knowledge about religion and religions. In this kind of milieu, then, only the last two types of religious studies outlined would be appropriate, for that kind of religious studies scholarship is concerned simply with what advances knowledge. If, *per impossibile*, one conceives of the academic vocation as involving both tasks, all the types of religious studies outlined above are acceptable, even though it is clear that the first aspect of such an academic vocation would necessarily conflict with the second. The fact of the matter, however, is that the modern Western university is generally understood as essentially a research institution dedicated to the advancement of objective knowledge about the world and we can conclude, therefore, that 'religious studies' should be understood to refer to a purely scientific undertaking.

Bibliography

Anderson, Charles P., 1972 *Guide to Religious Studies in Canada*, (3rd edn), Toronto: Corporation for the Publication of Academic Studies in Canada.

Badertscher, John M., Gordon Harland, and Roland E. Miller, 1993 *Religious Studies in Manitoba and Saskatchewan*, Waterloo: Wilfrid Laurier University Press.

Benson, Thomas L., 1987 'Religious Studies as an Academic Discipline,' in Mircea Eliade (ed.), *Encyclopedia of Religion*, New York: Macmillan Press, Vol. XIV, pp. 88–92.

Bischoff, Guntrum G., 1975 'The Pedagogy of Religiology,' in Anne Carr and Nicholas Piediscalzi (eds), *Public Schools Religion-Studies: 1975*, Missoula: American Academy of Religion, pp. 127–35.

Bowlby, Paul, W. R., 2001 *Religious Studies in Atlantic Canada: A State-of-the-Art Review*, Waterloo: Wilfred Laurier University Press.

Braybrooke, Marcus, 1990 'Religious Studies and Interfaith Development,' in Ursula King (ed.), *Turning Points in Religious Studies*, Edinburgh: T. & T. Clark, pp. 132–41.

Cahill, Joseph, 1982 *Mended Speech: The Crisis of Religious Studies and Theology*, New York: Crossroad.

Cain, Seymour, 1987 'History of Study,' in Mircea Eliade (ed.), *The Encyclopedia of Religion*, New York: Macmillan Press, Vol. XIV, pp. 64–83.

Capps, Walter H., 1995 *Religious Studies: The Making of A Discipline*, Minneapolis: Fortress Press.

Cole, W. Owen, 1990 'The New Educational Reform Act and Worship in County Schools of England and Wales,' in Ursula King (ed.), *Turning Points in Religious Studies*, Edinburgh: T. & T. Clark, pp. 117–31.

Crites, Stephen (*et al.*), 1990 'Liberal Learning and the Religion Major' (an AAR Task Force on the Study in Depth of Religion), Syracuse: American Academy of Religion.

Cunningham, Adrian, 1990 'Religious Studies in the Universities: England,' in Ursula King (ed.), *Turning Points in Religious Studies*, Edinburgh: T. & T. Clark, pp. 21–31.

Davis, Charles, 1974–5 'The Reconvergence of Theology and Religious Studies,' *Studies in Religion*, 4, pp. 205–21.

Ford, David, 1999 *Theology: A Very Short Introduction*, Oxford: Oxford University Press.

Fraser, Brian J., 1995 *The Study of Religion in British Columbia: A State-of-the-Art Review*, Waterloo: Wilfrid Laurier University Press.

Hart, D. G., 1992 'American Learning and the Problem of Religious Studies,' in G. M. Marsden and B. J. Longfield (eds), *The Secularization of the Academy*, Oxford: Oxford University Press, pp. 195–233.

—— 2000 *The University Gets Religion: Religious Studies in American Higher Education*, Baltimore: Johns Hopkins University Press.

Hart, Ray, 1991 'Religious and Theological Studies in American Higher Education,' *Journal of the American Academy of Religion*, 69, pp. 715–827.

Hull, John, 1984 'Religious Education in a Pluralistic Society,' in John Hull, *Studies in Religion and Education*, London: The Falmer Press, pp. 45–55.

Jackson, Robert, 1990 'Religious Studies and Developments in Religious Education,' in Ursula King (ed.), *Turning Points in Religious Studies*, Edinburgh: T. & T. Clark, pp. 102–16.

King, Ursula (ed.), 1990 *Turning Points in Religious Studies*, Edinburgh: T. & T. Clark.

Kitagawa, Joseph M., 1959 'The History of Religions in America,' in Mircea Eliade and Joseph M. Kitagawa (eds), *The History of Religions: Essays in Methodology*, Chicago: University of Chicago Press, pp. 1–30.

—— 1983 'Humanistic and Theological History of Religion With Special Reference to the North American Scene,' in Peter Slater and Donald Wiebe (eds), *Traditions in Contact and Change: Selected Proceedings of the XIVth Congress of the International Association for the History of Religions*, Waterloo: Wilfrid Laurier University Press, pp. 553–63.

Klostermaier, Klaus K. and Larry W. Hurtado (eds), 1991 *Religious Studies: Issues, Prospects, and Proposals*, Winnipeg: University of Manitoba and Scholars Press.

Laporte, Jean-Marc, 1993 'Review of *Religious Studies in Ontario: A State-of-the-Art Review*,' Toronto Journal of Theology, 9/2, p. 249.

McCaughey, Robert A., 1984 *International Studies and Academic Enterprises: A Chapter in the Enclosure of American Learning*, New York: Columbia University Press.

Myscofski, Carol and Richard Pilgrim (*et al.*), 1993 'Religious Studies and the Redefining Scholarship Project: A Report of the AAR Committee on "Defining Scholarly Work",' *Religious Studies News*, 8/3, September, pp 7–8.

Nesbitt, Eleanor, 1990 'Sikhism,' in Ursula King (ed.), *Turning Points in Religious Studies*, Edinburgh: T. & T. Clark, pp. 168–79.

Neufeldt, Ron W., 1983 *Religious Studies in Alberta: A State-of-the-Art Review*, Waterloo: Wilfrid Laurier University Press.

Novak, Michael, 1971 *Ascent of the Mountain, Flight of the Dove: An Introduction to Religious Studies*, New York: Harper & Row.

Ogden, Schubert M., 1986 (1975) 'Theology in the University,' in Schubert M. Ogden, *On Theology*, San Francisco: Harper & Row, pp. 121–33.

Olson, Alan M., 1990a 'Religious Studies,' in *Encyclopedia of Religious Education*, Iris V. Cully and Kendig Brubaker Cully (eds), San Francisco: Harper & Row, pp. 549–51.

Olson, Alan M., 1990b 'University,' in *Encyclopedia of Religious Education*, Iris V. Cully and Kendig Brubaker Cully (eds), San Francisco: Harper & Row, pp. 673–4.

Prozesky, Martin, 1990 'South Africa's Contribution to Religious Studies,' *Journal of Theology of Southern Africa*, 70, pp. 9–20.

Pye, Michael, 1991 'Religious Studies in Europe: Structures and Desiderate,' in Klaus K. Klostermaier and Larry W. Hurtado (eds), *Religious Studies: Issues, Prospects and Proposals*, Winnipeg: University of Manitoba and Scholars Press, pp. 39–55.

—— 1994 'Religion: Shape and Shadow,' *Numen*, 41, pp. 51–75.

—— 1999 'Methodological Integration in the Study of Religions,' in Tore Ahlbäck (ed.), *Approaching Religion* (Vol. I), Åbo: Åbo Akademic University Press, pp. 189–205.

Remus, Harold E., 1988 'Religion as an Academic Discipline' (Part I: 'Origins, Nature and Changing Understandings'), in Charles H. Lippy, Peter M. Williams (eds), *Encyclopedia of the American Religious Experience*, Vol III, New York: Charles Scribners Sons, pp. 1653–65.

—— William Closson James, and Daniel Fraikin (eds), 1992 *Religious Studies in Ontario: A State-of-the-Art Review*, Waterloo: Wilfrid Laurier University Press.

Reuben, Julie, 1996 *The Making of the Modern University: Intellectual Transformation and the Marginalization of Morality*, Chicago: Chicago University Press.

Riley, Philip Boo, 1984 'Theology and/or Religious Studies: A Case Study of *Studies in Religion/Sciences Religieuses* 1971–1981,' in *Studies in Religion*, Vol. 13, pp 423–44.

Rousseau, Louis, and Michel Despland (eds), 1988 *Les sciences religieuses au Quèbec depuis 1972*, Waterloo: Wilfrid Laurier Press.

Sharpe, Eric J., 1986a *Comparative Religion: A History*, (2nd edn), London: Duckworth.

—— 1986b '"From Paris 1900 to Sydney 1985" (An Essay in Retrospect and Prospect),' in Victor C. Hayes (ed.), *Identity Issues and World Religions: Selected Proceedings of the Fifteenth Congress of the International Association for the History of Religions*, Redford Park: Flinders University Press, pp. 245–52.

—— 1987 'Methodological Issues', in Mircea Eliade (ed.), *Encyclopedia of Religion*, Vol XIV, pp. 84–8.

Shepard, Robert S., 1991 *God's People in the Ivory Tower: Religion in the Early American University*, New York: Carlson Publishing Inc.

Smart, Ninian, 1973 *The Science of Religion and the Sociology of Knowledge*, Princeton: Princeton University Press.

—— 1990 'Concluding Reflections: Religious Studies in Global Perspective,' in Ursula King (ed.), *Turning Points in Religious Studies*, Edinburgh: T. & T. Clark, pp. 299–306.

—— 1996 'Some Thoughts on the Science of Religion,' in Arvind Sharma (ed.), *The Sum of our Choices: Essays in Honor of Eric J. Sharpe*, Atlanta: Scholars Press, pp. 15–25.

—— 1997 'Religious Studies in Higher Education,' in John R. Hinnells (ed.), *The New Penguin Dictionary of Religions*, London: Penguin, pp. 420–1.

—— 1998 'Methods in My Life,' in Jon R. Stone (ed.), *The Craft of Religious Studies*, New York: St. Martin's Press, pp. 18–35.

—— 1999 'Foreward,' in Peter Connolly (ed.), *Approaches to the Study of Religion*, London: Cassell, pp. ix-xiv.

Taylor, Mark C., 1994 'Unsettling Issues,' *Journal of the American Academy of Religion*, Vol. LXII/4, pp. 949–963.

—— 1998a 'Introduction,' in Mark C. Taylor (ed.), *Critical Terms for Religious Studies*, Chicago: University of Chicago Press, pp. 1–19.

—— 1998b 'Retracings,' in Jon R. Stone (ed.), *The Craft of Religious Studies*, New York: St. Martin's Press, pp. 258–276.

—— 1999 *About Religion: Economics of Faith in Virtual Culture*, Chicago: University of Chicago Press.

Thiemann, Ronald F., 1990 'The Future of an Illusion: An Inquiry Into the Contrast Between Theological and Religious Studies,' *Theological Education*, 26/2, pp. 66–85.

Walls, Andrew F., 1990 'Religious Studies in the Universities: Scotland,' in Ursula King (ed.), *Turning Points in Religious Studies*, Edinburgh: T. & T. Clark, pp. 32–45.

Ward, Keith, 1990 'The Study of Truth and Dialogue in Religion,' in Ursula King (ed.), *Turning Points in Religious Studies*, Edinburgh: T. & T. Clark, pp. 221–231.

Williams, Cyril, 1990 'Religious Studies in the Universities: Wales,' in Ursula King (ed.) *Turning Points in Religious Studies*, Edinburgh: T. & T. Clark, pp. 46–56.

Further reading

McCutcheon, Russell, 1997 *Manufacturing Religion: The Discourse on Sui Generis Religion and the Politics of Nostalgia*, New York: Oxford Press.

McCutcheon, Russell and Willi Braun (eds), 1999 *Guide to the Study of Religion*, London: Cassell.

Preus, S., 1987 *Explaining Religion: Criticism and Theory from Bodin to Freud*, New Haven: Yale University Press.

Reuben, Julie, 1996 *The Making of the Modern University: Intellectual Transformation and the Marginalization of Morality*, Chicago: University of Chicago Press.

Sperber, Daniel, 1996 *Explaining Culture: A Naturalistic Approach*, Oxford: Blackwell.

Wiebe, Donald, 1999 *The Politics of Religious Studies: The Continuing Conflict with Theology in the Academy*, New York: St. Martin's Press.

Chapter 7

Sociology of religion

Martin Riesebrodt and Mary Ellen Konieczny

Until the end of the 1970s most sociologists of religion seemed rather confident about their understanding of religious phenomena. We all more-or-less knew that modern societies were undergoing a process of secularization. Of course, this process could take different forms in different societies depending on their institutional order or religious culture. Certainly, very few sociologists expected religion to totally disappear. Most assigned to religion a legitimate space in the private sphere. Many assumed that religious institutions would undergo a process of internal secularization and would increasingly adapt to the requirements of modern institutions while maintaining their religious symbolism. Others expected religious values to permeate modern societies, leaving behind traditional forms of religion. Some imagined that national ideologies or civil religions would functionally replace religious traditions. But hardly anybody was prepared for the dramatic resurgence of religion that we have witnessed over the last two decades in which religion has re-emerged as a relatively autonomous public force, a marker of ethnic identities, and a shaper of modern subjects and their ways of life.

The renewed global importance of religion from North America to Japan, from Africa to Korea, from Latin America to India and Sri Lanka, from Iran to Poland has had a profound impact on the sociology of religion. It not only provided the discipline with an opportunity to revive the empirical study of religious phenomena on a global scale – more importantly, it challenged its conventional theoretical perspectives. Social theorists had to cope with their own cognitive dissonance between their expectation of secularization on the one hand and the actual resurgence of religion on the other.

The two most typical reactions to this challenge have been denial and instant conversion. Some authors have simply insisted that their expectations of modernization and secularization are basically sound. Focusing on the resurgence of religion in 'third world' countries has allowed them to pretend that these revivals of religion are part of an ongoing 'modernization' process. Not surprisingly, many have taken pains to detect a 'Puritan spirit' or an 'inner-worldly asceticism' in such movements. Other authors have chosen the opposite route of instant conversion, denying any general trend towards secularization in the West and elsewhere. According to them, secularization or the 'disenchantment of the world' are not general trends related to social differentiation and the rationalizing effects of capitalism, science, and bureaucracy as most theories had assumed, but are just an effect of European-style religious monopolies. This present state of uncertainty and confusion in the sociology of religion offers a good opportunity to review the development of the discipline from its nineteenth century origins to the present, and to speculate about future directions it might take.

Three classical paradigms

The sociology of religion emerged from the philosophy of the Enlightenment on the one hand and its Romantic critique on the other. Although it attempts to make religion the object of scientific study, sociology has inherited certain presuppositions from the philosophical discourse that have shaped its perspectives on religion in different ways. In order to better understand the development of the sociology of religion, one has to consider how social scientific understandings of religion are informed by basic assumptions about Western modernity, the course of history, and the place of human beings in this world. Three classical paradigms had the strongest impact on the discipline: the approaches of Karl Marx, Émile Durkheim, and Max Weber.

Karl Marx (1818–1883)

For Marx, as for his teacher Hegel, history follows a logic through which human beings emancipate themselves from the realm of necessity to the realm of freedom and self-realization. However, for Marx, unlike Hegel, the engine of this development is not the dialectics of the 'world spirit' but that of the material conditions of existence. Human beings realize themselves in the process of the production and reproduction of their concrete lives. This takes place through actors' engagements in the technical and technological control of nature, in conjunction with the social relations through which humans exercise this process of control. An increasing control of nature leads to an increasing division of labor, creating class distinctions initially based upon gender. In particular the differentiation between manual and intellectual labor causes drastic inequality based on the ownership of private property. In early socioeconomic stages, 'nature' seems rather mysterious, whereas with increasing control of natural forces and increasing class differentiation, 'society' becomes more unfathomable.

In other words, modern science and technology have produced an unprecedented rational understanding and practical control through which nature has become widely demystified. However, capitalism has produced an extreme class differentiation between manual and intellectual labor as well as between owners of the means of production and workers. These social relations are usually not comprehended as they actually are, but are misunderstood, misrepresented, and mysticized.

The reasons for this mystification are manifold, but all based upon the alienating structures of modern socioeconomic relations. There are the privileged, who have an interest in legitimation. They produce and spread an ideology of self-justification, which is in part strategic – perhaps even cynical – and in part self-deluding. Then there are the workers, who are alienated from each other through competition, and deprived of their creativity and self-realization through the mechanical character of their work and the loss of control over its products. Finally, misrecognition lies in the very nature of commodity production itself, since the interaction between social actors appears in the form of an exchange relation between products.

For Marx, religion plays an obvious role in these processes. In early socioeconomic stages, religion consists mainly in a response to the mysteriousness of nature and expresses humanity's lack of understanding and control. But in more advanced stages, religion increasingly distorts the understanding of the true nature of social relations by expressing the alienation inscribed into class structures. Religion, by creating the illusion of a transcendental power of perfection, which demands submission to the *status quo*, also prevents social actors from collectively establishing a social order that would allow them to realize their full potential as social and creative human beings.

In order to overcome alienation, it is necessary but not sufficient to criticize religious consciousness. Rather, one has to overturn the class structure of capitalism and change the mode of production. Once this has happened, religion would disappear and people would be able to understand and control society as rationally as they do nature and they would be free to realize their true natures as social and creative beings.

Since for Marx religion does not represent the source of human alienation, but just expresses it, this approach does not pay much attention to the study of religion *per se*. Although the Marxian perspective that religions reflect the structures of social relations in which they appear holds true for all social scientists to a certain degree, a rather narrow reading of Marx has led to a long and unfortunate neglect of the study of religion in the Marxian tradition. Only recently have social scientists recaptured the fruitful aspects of the Marxian perspective while giving up the teleological view of history. Here the contributions of Jean and John Comaroff are especially important (Comaroff and Comaroff 1991, 1995).

Émile Durkheim (1858–1917)

While Marx's understanding of history and humanity is based on a model of human and social emancipation, Durkheim's is based on social order and its civilizing, moralizing, and socializing mission. According to Durkheim, human beings have a double nature consisting of body and soul. On the one hand, they are driven by bodily needs, following their egoistic natural drives and desires; on the other, they have souls, which are social and moral. The task of any social order is to keep the egoistic drives of individuals in check, and to transform these individuals into social and moral agents who conform to group norms (Durkheim 1914/1960).

Although civilization progresses for Durkheim, the basic problem stays in many respects the same. What changes is the division of labor, and with it, modes of thought and methods of social integration. An increasing division of labor, which according to Durkheim has been institutionalized not for its unforeseeable greater efficiency but for the social regulation of competition, makes people much more interdependent than they were in segmentary societies. Segmentary societies, then, need much stronger integration through beliefs and rituals than modern ones.

Nevertheless, any social order only works when people share the basic categories of thought and moral beliefs, and reinforce them through collective rituals. These shared beliefs and practices originate in religion, which is based on the distinction between sacred and profane. Categories of thought such as space, time, cause, and number originate in this distinction. Religion, therefore, is the source of thought and knowledge but – following Comte – Durkheim argues that with the progress of civilization other modes of thought, especially science, replace religion at least in part. However, this is only a difference in degree, not in kind; since scientific knowledge also becomes obligatory it is, so-to-speak, a higher form of religion. In addition science cannot replace the emotional side of religion, which attaches people to each other and to societies' symbols. This can be only generated by dense interaction in extraordinary and often ecstatic situations, such as public ceremonies.

Durkheim's understanding of religion assumes a basic identity between the political and the religious unit and appears to be heavily informed by the modern Western idea of the nation. Durkheim's theory directly jumps from tribal religion to civic religion – omitting all examples of religious pluralism, conflicts between and within religious traditions, and the disintegrative effects of religions. Durkheim suggests via his study of Australian 'totemism' that all societies need a unifying system of thought and symbols, norms and values, identifying nationalism as the new 'civic religion' adequate to modern industrial societies (1912/1995). However, for Durkheim also nationalism is only a necessary intermediary stage in the emergence of the positivist utopia of human universalism. Durkheim's understanding of religion has been the most dominant theoretical influence in sociology and anthropology.

Max Weber (1864–1920)

For Weber neither human emancipation nor social order and integration are the central points of departure. Neither does history have an intrinsic goal, nor does modernity's central problem lie in the control of egoistic individualism. For Weber, modern Western societies are not underregulated but rather overregulated. In the modern bureaucratic age there is hardly any space left to lead a meaningful life according to any principles other than utilitarian ones. Weber's central question, therefore, is how this modern rationalist system of external social control and internalized self-control has developed historically, and how modern individuals as cultural beings can respond to it with dignity and responsibility.

Weber's sociology of religion begins with an inquiry into the religious sources of modern capitalist culture, and ends with cross-culturally comparative studies of rationalism embedded in the religious traditions of China, India, and ancient Judaism. From these studies, Weber draws the conclusion that the West has undergone a unique kind and direction of rationalization, which has affected not only its economic system and its principles of bureaucratic organization but also its culture – especially its science, music, art – and even its attitudes towards sexuality.

Weber certainly agrees with the Marxian insight that people make their own history but do not control it. Weber's sociology is full of examples of unintended and often paradoxical historical outcomes of meaningful social action and interaction. *The Protestant Ethic and the 'Spirit' of Capitalism* is a prime example; in this essay, Weber argues that the religious ethos of inner-worldly asceticism became a motivational force contributing to the emergence of a bourgeois, modern Western type of capitalism. This ethos is characterized by self-control, methodical life conduct directed towards work in a calling, and acquisition through a regularly and rationally pursued business. Weber shows how this originally religious ethos has been transformed in the course of capitalist development into our modern, religiously empty work habits and utilitarian attitudes. Although himself religiously 'unmusical', Weber saw a certain dignity in these religious attempts to transcend the narrow boundaries of utilitarian interests through the dramatization of ultimate values and the principled shaping of one's life according to them. It is here that religions have played a major part in the formation of religious elites, which in turn, through their high status and roles as counselors of the laity, have had a significant impact on the shaping of different civilizations.

While 'primitive' religions were hardly differentiated from the pursuit of 'this-worldly' interests, the rise of 'salvation' religions formulated by religious intellectuals and *virtuosi* defined religion as a separable sphere of interests. The very idea of salvation and the different paths to salvation defined the world in relation to an ultimate value, and restructured the attitudes and life conduct of social actors towards worldly spheres of interest. Of course, this did not take place independent of political and economic structures and developments, but it added a dimension of interests, which in turn could exert influence upon economic and political institutions and actors. According to Weber, religious ideas and interests are mediated by institutions, which develop their own dynamics in conjunction with the everyday needs of their followers.

In the West, a very unique type of rationalism of 'world mastery' developed out of the confluence of the rationalism of Judaic ethical prophecy, Greek philosophy, Roman law, Christian monasticism and the emerging bourgeois economy of independent cities. This rationalism was taken up by parts of the Protestant Reformation and systematized into an attitude of inner-worldly asceticism. The rationalization processes set in motion by this religiously motivated ethos contributed to the disenchantment of the world by rejecting all irrational means of attaining salvation, and promoted the emergence of rationally organized institutional orders and ethics. According to Weber, this process of disenchantment and secularization removed the religious ethic from central economic, political, and cultural institutions, freeing them from religious control.

Whoever chooses to live a life based on religious principles can do so only against the institutionalized logic of 'unbrotherly' bureaucratic regimes that no longer recognize religious morality but instead value efficiency, performance, and utility. Therefore, in Western modernity, religion can only survive in more central social institutions if it adapts to their logics and more-or-less sanctifies them. It is only in small voluntary associations at the social margins that religion can preserve an ethos of universal brotherhood. According to Weber, there exists the possibility of new charismatic upheavals, changing people's inner attitudes – but given the rigidity and efficiency of bureaucratic systems, these revolutionary possibilities are rather unlikely to succeed in the modern West.

Secularization, privatization, and civil religion

All three classical paradigms did not expect religion to disappear, but certainly expected it to be more or less radically transformed in the modern world. The next generations of scholars elaborated these arguments in more detail, usually fusing the traditions of Durkheim and Weber as they understood them. Generally speaking, they tended to conceptualize religion as a central cultural institution and focused on its interaction with other institutions. Some placed emphasis upon the ways in which religions have an effect on social norms and life conduct, while others focused on the ways religion was affected by socioeconomic transformations and processes of social differentiation.

One school of thought developed out of Parsonian structural-functionalism and was most influential in the US. This approach considers the process of economic development in the West, driven by a religious, inner-worldly ascetic spirit, to be the paradigmatic form of modernization. Scholars working in this tradition claim that, as societies have modernized, generalized religious values have been increasingly subsumed into their broader cultures. The second major school of thought, often seen as more European in its orientation, built on the phenomenological tradition of Alfred Schutz and focused on religion's capacity to provide a meaningful framework for the interpretation of human experience. Others, including Thomas Luckmann, David Martin, and Bryan Wilson, also built on the classical traditions and explored different aspects of secularization processes.

Modernization and generalized values

As translator of Max Weber's *Protestant Ethic*, Talcott Parsons (1902–1979) encouraged his students to look for its analogs all over the world. The idea was to identify carriers of inner-worldly asceticism, which would promote the passage of 'underdeveloped' societies into a Western type of modernity. From our perspective, this agenda of the Parsons School is based on a rather peculiar reading of Weber. It not only ignores Weber's very ambiguous judgment on Western modernity and transforms it into a happy-go-lucky theory of modernization and progress; it also leaves aside Weber's analysis of the affinity between certain classes and status groups with particular types of religious plausibility structures. Accordingly, scholars using this approach identified such diverse classes as reform bureaucrats and the military as potential carriers of modernization. Nevertheless, the Parsons School has produced some impressive studies, most importantly Robert Bellah's (1957) *Tokugawa Religion* and Shmuel Eisenstadt's (1968) reader on the *Protestant Ethic and Modernization*, both of which have shed new light on the relationship between religion and social change.

Parsons (1963) and his students also further elaborated the Durkheimian perspective and inquired into the integration of modern societies through generalized religious values and civil religions. Parsons focused on the interpenetration of Christian (specifically sectarian Protestant) values into the very fabric of modern industrial (specifically American) society. According to Parsons, the generalization of voluntarism and individualism made the modern US the most Christian society ever.

Bellah's work typifies this view, especially in his evolutionary theory of religion (Bellah 1970). According to Bellah, humanity's need for religious symbols is a constant factor in social life – but as human societies have evolved over time, so have the content and dynamics of religious symbol systems. Historically, religion has developed alongside of social and self-development, and as societies have acquired greater knowledge and have achieved greater capacity for social and self-transformation, religious belief has concurrently become characterized by individual choice. Bellah argues for a five-stage schema of the evolution of religion, ranging from primitive to modern. This schema views religion in the modern West – paradigmatically the Protestant US – as more highly developed and normatively better than other less rationalized and more magical forms. Bellah claims that the doctrinal diversity of Protestantism and the freedom of individuals to choose belief are not evidence of secularization, but rather evidence of human progress.

Following ideas of civil religion earlier explored by Rousseau, Durkheim, and Parsons, Bellah sought institutional settings where essential American values such as civic activism and individualism were interpreted, dramatized, and ritually enacted. Focusing on Presidential addresses at certain decisive moments in American history, he identified expressions of nationally shared ultimate values and a vision of the nation's calling, and claimed civil religion's continuing if fragile existence in America. According to Bellah, the particulars of American civil religion have incorporated Protestant Christian themes of covenant, death, and resurrection or rebirth, and its ritual calendar emphasizes the central importance of family and local community in American democracy. Civil religion, through narrative and collective ritual experience, creates a moral and affective consensus for democratic participation.

In later works, Bellah expresses concern that the actual practice of civil religion in the US has diminished to the point where it no longer provides moral cohesion, and worries that individualism threatens to undermine the moral consensus for participation upon which American democracy is built (Bellah 1975). In *Habits of the Heart*, Bellah concludes that an individualistic ethos cannot supply the moral cohesion needed for democracy, and relocates the affective and cognitive resources necessary for democratic participation back within institutional churches, especially liberal Protestant ones (Bellah *et al.* 1985).

Building on Bellah's approach, Robert Wuthnow (1988) presents an alternative characterization of religion in the contemporary US. Wuthnow argues that, in contrast to the early twentieth-century US when religion was primarily allied with and supportive of the state, religion since the Second World War is increasingly politically polarized and often mobilized against government and other political actors. Brought about by post-war economic expansion and a strong and active state, and catalyzed by special purpose groups, the religious landscape in the contemporary US has been restructured: a cleavage between liberal and conservative religionists has replaced denominationalism as the primary source of identification and religio-political engagement.

Collapsed canopies

Peter Berger's articulation of a theory of secularization represents an alternative school of thought. Berger claims that religion's power to shape social life has largely diminished in Western modernity because of institutional differentiation, the pluralization of worldviews, and a loss of plausibility structures. Berger grounds his theory in a phenomenological perspective, according to which religious worldviews provide shields from the chaotic, uncontrollable aspects of the world which humans inhabit. A religious worldview is reproduced through socialization; since it dominates the social contexts individuals are born into, they take it for granted and learn to interpret their experiences according to this cognitive structure. But religion can remain strong in societies only where it is supported by a dialectical, mutually sustaining, and mutually determining relationship with a social base or plausibility structure. Further, religion is at its strongest when it has a monopoly in a relatively stable society – when it comprises a 'sacred canopy' within which individuals understand and interpret their social existence, and where there is an absence of competing interpretations.

It follows from this characterization that secularization is an inevitable result of change within the economic and social contexts upon which religious worldviews depend. Secularization occurs when a religious worldview and the social reality no longer coincide, because its plausibility structures erode, and a formerly monopolistic religious worldview becomes open to revision and a plurality of interpretations. Once the sacred canopy collapses, religion progressively loses its power to shape social life.

Following in the tradition of Max Weber, Berger historically identifies the seeds of secularization in the rationalizing elements of Christian doctrine and institutional life, reaching back as far as the beginnings of Christianity. This rationalizing process, he argues, was a prerequisite for the development of industrial capitalism, which, through the creation of the bourgeoisie, definitively catalyzed the process of secularization in the Western world. Berger narrates the historical secularization process as one of progressive differentiation. Initially, religion is differentiated from the political sphere as the state becomes more autonomous from the church. As the social base upon which Christianity depends is further eroded, religion becomes increasingly relegated to the private sphere. Finally, religion itself is secularized, taking on market characteristics of pluralism, choice, and privatization. Organized in a denominational system, religious diversity has replaced the monopolistic sacred canopy; now individuals are exposed to many religious worldviews, and can choose among them according to individual preferences. In response, churches must increasingly act as competitors in a religious market situation.

Berger's approach to religion and secularization has had a major impact on authors like Nancy Ammerman and James D. Hunter. Hunter (1983) examines the belief and practice of US evangelicals, accounting for the religious vitality of this group explicitly within the framework of secularization theory. And Ammerman (1987), while assuming a general secularization of modern life, looks to fundamentalists to explore an American religious phenomenon that is neither differentiated nor individualized and privatized.

Whereas Berger sees secularization as a necessary consequence of modernization on a very abstract and general level, David Martin (1978) has focused on secularization from a concrete and historical, comparative institutional perspective. Rather skeptical about the concept of secularization, Martin shows in an admirable comparative study how secularization was conditioned by the character of religious institutions and their relationships to the state. Martin locates the occurrence of secularization at three different social levels of analysis: at the level of social institutions, at the level of belief, and at the level of a people's ethos. He then proposes an ideal-typical schema that classifies the characteristics of nation states along several dimensions, and uses this schema to show how variation in the historical position of religion during state formation, the level of pluralism, and the logics embedded within religions practiced in particular settings, together produce different patterns of secularization. Martin's work did not simply assume secularization as a fact, but showed how different historical conditions produce secularization at different levels of society. For example, historically France's religious monopoly was politically challenged by secular institutions, which lead to a comprehensive victory of secularism. In contrast, the separation of church and state and the pluralistic organization of religion in the US prevented conflict at the political level – and therefore, secularization primarily occurred on the level of the religious ethos. Martin's work remains among the most sophisticated of empirical and theoretical studies of secularization.

Invisible religions

Toward the end of the 1960s and through the 1970s, secularization theories such as Berger's further crystallized and affirmed the view that religious decline in the modern West would inevitably progress. Empirical evidence of secularization was abundant in religion's increasing loss of power within political and cultural institutions, as well as in declining church attendance and aging congregations in many of the countries of Europe. Religion no longer occupied a place at modern societies' centers, and scholars took for granted that this state of affairs was a necessary consequence of modernization. Even where churches were filled, as they were in the US, it seemed clear that much of this practice, especially within liberal churches, was not so much religiously as socially motivated, reflecting the internal secularization of religious institutions. For some scholars, however, this clear evidence of the decline of religion at the center of modern society propelled them to look for authentic religious expression in more hidden and less public arenas.

Thomas Luckmann's (1967) work was a harbinger of this turn: he proposed a theory of secularization as privatization which claimed that religion was not disappearing in modernity, but that its locus had shifted from the public sphere to the inner personal experience of individuals. Like Berger, Luckmann's approach is phenomenological and interpretive, but his conceptualization of religion and his narrative of secularization depart from Berger's in important ways.

In Luckmann's view, religion arises as a necessary part of the social-psychological, meaning-making process in which humans are individuated and selves created. Although religious institutions are historically common, it is not necessary that religion be institutionalized for it to endure. Rather, religion endures in human history because it is a constitutive element of the formation of selves; it is the anthropological conditions giving rise to religion that are indeed universal.

Luckmann describes the historical process of secularization in the West as a consequence of the endurance, growth, and internal workings of religious institutions. As churches grew, they developed secular interests and did not remain exclusively determined by their religious functions. Specialization within these institutions required that religious norms become differentiated from secular norms, and the disjuncture between the two generated inconsistencies between doctrine and its institutional expression. Therefore, where previously religion was merely taken for granted, people were given cause to reflect upon it. Human reflection thereby transformed religion into an increasingly subjective reality.

In this process, institutional religion became progressively emptied of meaning, and the erosion of public religion was replaced by its increased importance in the private sphere. In modern societies, then, religions exist in ever more privatized forms in modern societies and their meanings become properties of individual selves, and thus 'invisible.' In this view, secularization is the process of religious institutions' decline, but religion still endures as its social locations shift. Therefore, the new locus of religion in modernity is individuals' inner lives, even if this inner experience is largely unavailable to empirical scrutiny.

Lively margins

While Luckmann theoretically located modern religion in the inner lives of individuals, other scholars examined the margins of society for the locus of religious beliefs and practices. Bryan R. Wilson's (1982) studies of sectarianism, executed mostly in the interpretive tradition of Weber, typify this approach. Wilson understood the central institutions of modern Western societies to be thoroughly secularized, but demonstrated that religious belief and practice endure among socially marginalized groups. He theorized the distinctiveness of these sectarian forms of religious practice.

Wilson observes that, whereas many in modern societies neither believe nor practice religion and the behaviors of mainline church members are rarely driven by religiosity, within modern sects one can yet observe the powerful social consequences of religion in individual lives. Sects shape in their adherents undifferentiated religious identities, which spill over and suffuse the whole of their lives. For the socially marginalized – for example, for temporal or generational groups such as adolescents and young adults – sects offer reassurance and comfort in the form of salvation beliefs. And with strong ethical norms and distinctive styles of life, sects bring their converts into a social world in which they can perceive themselves as integral to a social group, and in which they are aided in reinterpreting painful experiences of marginality.

Consistent with secularization theory, sectarian religion is withdrawn from the public sphere; sectarians do not engage in public discourse and have little effect on society as a whole. While incorporating aspects of modernity's rational procedures in their organization and practices, they distinguish themselves from modern society by constituting themselves in opposition to it in their creation of undifferentiated identities and distinctive ways of life. It is Wilson's view that social conditions for sectarian adherence include not only social marginality in its modern forms, but also the prerequisite of the lack of previous religious socialization.

Secularism, pluralism, and religious resurgence

By the 1970s the old paradigm of the classics and their revisionist readings and new syntheses came under scrutiny, especially in the US. It certainly helped that simultaneously the empirical-historical evidence had changed. A resurgence of religion had begun in the US: new religious movements spread all over the Bay area in California and conservative religious forces – Protestant, Catholic, Jewish, Mormon – got organized in order to be saved from the 1960s (Tipton 1982). At the same time, a revival of religion was taking place on a global scale: Islam returned as a public force in the Middle East and beyond; religion played a forceful role in the shaping of ethnic identities and the fueling of ethnic conflicts from India and Sri Lanka (Tambiah 1992, 1996) to the Sudan and Ireland; and religious movements had began to challenge the secular state (Juergensmeyer 1993). These historical developments called into question common sense assumptions among social scientists, and stimulated further developments in several areas – in secularization theory, in the application of alternative theoretical frameworks to the study of religion, in empirical work investigating religious resurgence, and in emerging bodies of work examining the relationship of religion to issues of ethnicity, nationalism, gender, and class.

Structural conditions of secularization

In the wake of empirical evidence of religious revitalization, the problematic aspects of older secularization theories became the subject of increasing criticism, revision, and reformulation, resulting in a clearer definition of the conditions of secularization and an extended elaboration of secularization as a theory of social differentiation. Recognizing the empirical reality of religious resurgence, those working within secularization theory strove to theorize secularization in ways that did not entail its inevitability and irreversibility, and moved towards conceptualizations of secularization as an historical process to be located and explored.

Following upon Martin's groundbreaking study, scholars sought to elaborate and distinguish secularization at different levels of analysis and to systematize characteristics of secularization within a larger conceptual framework. Among those taking this synthetic approach, Karel Dobbelaere's (1981) work is perhaps the most comprehensive. Dobbelaere's argument for a multidimensional concept of secularization proposes that secularization be studied through the examination of interrelated processes at three different levels of analysis. Secularization can occur through laicization – the societal differentiation of religion from other social formations and institutions – through organizational religious change, such as may occur within denominations, and in the religious involvement of individuals. Dobbelaere suggests that the relations between secularizing tendencies at each of these three levels do not have determinate outcomes and should be empirically investigated in order to more clearly theorize them. Although Dobbelaere believes that secularization is a contingent process, not a necessary or irreversible one, his canvas of empirical studies led him to conclude that secularization is empirically, if not theoretically, linearly progressive in the modern West.

Dobbelaere's theory has been influential in recent years, especially among those interested in analyzing organizational religious change. His formulation has been used successfully to elaborate the occurrence of organization-level secularization in the US through analyses of denominational leadership (Chaves 1993). Unlike the earlier comprehensive narratives, the newer frameworks have allowed scholars to explore the structural conditions of secularization at various levels of analysis, and have the capacity to provide explanations for empirically specific instances of secularization in modern societies.

Homo religionomicus

Concurrent with work advancing secularization theory in the 1970s and 1980s, other scholars began a move towards its wholesale rejection, and reinterpreted evidence of varying levels of religious participation among nation states and across religious denominations under a utilitarian rubric. These mostly North American scholars have been led by Rodney Stark and William S. Bainbridge (1979), who first used rational choice principles to construct a theory of religion. Stark and Bainbridge begin with the utilitarian assumption that individuals act to attain preferred ends while minimizing costs in an environment of opportunities and constraints. But the benefits desired by individuals are sometimes unattainable, either because of their social structural contexts, or because of the physical human limitations imposed by illness, disability, and the inevitability of death. In these life situations, religious rewards – such as doctrines promising salvation and eternal life, or religious experiences providing comfort and emotional benefits – can be sought as substitutes. In this view then, religion is conceptualized as a system of compensators for benefits unattainable to individuals. And since the human condition is such that the need for compensators – especially as a substitute for the avoidance of death – does not change, demand for religion is understood as relatively constant.

Since individual preferences are left unproblematized and demand for religious goods are assumed to be constant, the behavior of religious institutions – frequently theorized as following the laws of market dynamics – becomes a primary locus of investigation for those working within this school of thought. Some studies, such as Iannaccone's (1994) work on the vitality of strict churches, offer explanations for why particular religious organizations are especially attractive to seekers on the religious market. Others, like the historical study of church membership in the US by Finke and Stark (1992), focus on the market behavior of religious organizations, claiming that variations in religious practice should be understood primarily as a supply side phenomenon. In their view, the amount of freedom allowed in the market, the degree of regulation, and the resulting level of competition among religious organizations determine levels of religious vitality in a given society.

Rational choice theories of religion have gained broad currency among sociologists of religion in recent years. At the same time, this approach has provoked heated criticisms (Bruce 1999; Chaves 1995; Ammerman 1998; Neitz and Mueser 1998), especially for its use of a utilitarian psychology – long ago demonstrated to be an inadequate theory of human motivations – and its general disinterest in problematizing religious preferences, whose social constructedness is obviously of critical interest in explaining religiously motivated behavior.

A related recent development within sociology of religion in the US is the appropriation of the economic metaphor, combined with a functionalist perspective, as the ground of a 'new paradigm' for the study of religion (Warner 1993). Scholars working within this perspective reject the idea that the US has undergone secularization over time, claiming instead that the disestablishment of religion in the US is causally related to high rates of church attendance and other forms of religious vitality. This new approach has fueled a lively debate around the hypothesis that religious pluralism causes higher levels of religious practice than monopolistic situations – a debate that has rested in large part upon the technical evaluation of statistical evidence supporting the hypothesis (Voas, Olson, and Crocket 2002; Olson 1999; Land et al. 1991). Moreover, empirical evidence from countries like Ireland, Poland, and Iran suggests that accounting for religious vitality requires a more complex explanation than internal religious pluralism.

Deprivatization and the resurgence of religion

Global evidence of religious resurgence has also been studied with particular attention to politics, ethnicity and nationalism, and the construction of gendered identities. This strand of research has yielded some interesting empirical studies and promising theoretical developments.

Jose Casanova (1994) interprets the re-emergence of religion in the public sphere as a reverse movement, or deprivatization, of the historical pattern of secularization in the modern West. Like Martin and Dobbelaere, Casanova problematizes the concept of secularization, but moves beyond other theories by rearticulating secularization in such a way as to account for the re-emergence of religion in the public sphere.

In his critical review of secularization theories, Casanova distinguishes between a central thesis – secularization as one instance of differentiation processes defining and driving modernization – and two subtheses – the decline of religion, and its privatization. He argues that, while secularization as differentiation is structurally bound to modernization, religious decline and privatization are historically contingent processes. Religious privatization is historically common because of religion's internal workings, the influence of liberalism, and external constraints upon religion brought about through the process of differentiation. But religion can also be deprivatized, as he shows in case studies including the liberation theology movement in Brazil, Catholicism in Poland during the rise of Solidarity, the public pronouncements of American Catholic bishops in the 1980s, and US Protestant fundamentalist activities in the political sphere. Interrogating the public-private distinction through these cases, Casanova theorizes the deprivatization of modern religion and convincingly shows that secularization is not only *not* a structurally inevitable consequence of modernity, but also one whose reversibility can be theoretically understood.

James Beckford has likewise directed attention to the re-emergence of religion in the public sphere. Rather than examining the public behaviors of institutional churches, however, he studies the endurance of sects (Beckford 1975) and the emergence new religious movements (Beckford 1985). His work is characterized by a careful evaluation of the limits of theories of religion. Beckford (1989) argues that the categories and distinctions used, the questions asked and the conclusions reached by Durkheim, Marx, and Weber, as well as their descendants were profoundly shaped by the context of emergent industrial capitalism. The progression of industrial capitalism and the diminution of power and influence of old religious institutions are linked empirically in this historical period, and also linked philosophically in the tradition of liberal thought. And while the present context of late industrial capitalism is both continuous with and distinguishable from that earlier variant, its discontinuous characteristics are critical for understanding religion in the present historical period. The analysis of religion in late industrial societies, therefore, must decisively move beyond conceptualizations of religion that emphasize its capacity to create values and socialize individuals and focus upon secularization and religion's marginality.

Beckford pays particular attention to the social structural features of advanced industrial capitalism that differ from its earlier historical form, and to emergent forms of religion in the modern West. The new sociological significance of religion, according to Beckford, includes its capacity to present the perception of new social realities in symbolic forms, and the potential of religion as a tool of mobilization against political establishments. He predicts that, in late industrial societies, the use of religious symbols is likely to be contested and controversial, since religion is no longer exclusively the domain of long enduring social institutions. Religion, then, will often be put to work outside the framework of religious organizations and state relations. He argues that the analysis of religion in contemporary societies will be most fruitful when religion is conceptualized not as a social institution, but as a cultural form or resource.

Beckford's studies of new religious movements support and inform this perspective. Though new religious movements are very small in terms of the numbers of people who are shaped by them, and their ability to influence political actors is negligible, they have yet created a disproportionate amount of public controversy. Analysis of this public controversy draws attention to the way in which new religious forms in late industrial societies can serve as a barometer of issues of value and concern to broader segments of these societies.

Steve Bruce has also produced a rich sequence of studies of religious resurgence, directing his attention mostly at conservative and fundamentalist forms of religious revival, and at the insertion of religious-political agendas into the public sphere – from anti-Catholicism in Scotland and the role of evangelicalism in the politics of Northern Ireland to the political mobilization of conservative Protestants by the New Christian Right.

In studies of Ulster Protestantism (Bruce 1992, 1994), Bruce shows how religion was historically important in the creation of politically mobilized ethnic identities, and how religion continues to play a vigorous role in shaping the ways in which Protestants and Catholics perceive their positions within society. He elaborates the attraction of evangelical Protestantism and its agenda among non-evangelicals as an aspect of ethnic identity, and shows how these religio-ethnic identities are sustained through continued conflict in Northern Ireland.

Bruce's studies of the New Christian Right and tele-evangelism in the US (Bruce 1988, 1990) present a contrasting case in which conservative religion, though gaining in importance relative to the liberal mainline, has been much less successful politically. Bruce argues that televangelism is a result – not a cause – of the growth of conservative Protestantism, and that its 'mass' characteristics entail a lessening of the distinctiveness of conservative religious agendas as the medium reaches for a wide audience. The successful fundraising strategies of these preachers have led to the creation of alternative social institutions, especially fundamentalist colleges and universities, which can sustain fundamentalist Protestantism into the future. But Bruce argues that, while conservative Protestants continue to press their political struggle against secular humanism, the New Christian Right is much less influential in American politics than it is commonly perceived to be.

In his cross-culturally comparative study of the emergence of Protestant fundamentalism in the US and Shi'ite fundamentalism in Iran, Martin Riesebrodt (1993a) has attempted to conceptualize fundamentalism as a specific type of social movement. He argues that a central feature of fundamentalist movements across traditions consist in their emphasis on patriarchal structures of authority and social morality, with the strict control of the female body often perceived to be the solution to the problems of modernity. Riesebrodt claims that since the transformation of patriarchal family structures and gender relations represent a central experience of the emergence of Western modernity, issues of patriarchal authority and morality are not just symbolizations of other, 'real' problems, but of central concern. However, because of their centrality, they also often come to symbolize the general protest against dramatic social change, marginalization, disappointed expectations of upward social mobility, and fears and experiences of downward mobility.

Explorations of religious resurgence have included a number of studies of the success of mostly charismatic forms of Christianity in non-Western countries. It is again

David Martin who set the example, with his groundbreaking comparative study of the global spread of charismatic Protestantism (Martin 1990). In this work he also draws an interesting historical parallel to the rise of Methodism in England during the Industrial Revolution.

Recent work on the re-emergence of religion as a social force has also included a new emphasis on religion and gender. This body of work includes work both by sociologists and anthropologists and traverses a broad range of topics from women's religious participation and the construction of gendered identities (Stacey 1990; Davidman 1991) to the study of organizational processes surrounding denominations' ordination of women ministers (Chaves 1997; Nesbitt 1997). Perhaps the most promising studies executed under this broad rubric investigate modern women's adherence to conservative, evangelical, and fundamentalist religious groups articulating patriarchal gender ideologies (Kaufman 1991; Neitz 1987; Riesebrodt 1993b; Griffith 1997; Gallagher 2003). Moving beyond explanations that view these women as passive victims of either male domination or false consciousness, these studies explore women's active roles in the appropriation and transformation of traditionalist forms of religion that, from a progressive Western point of view, are contrary to their real interests. They argue that participation in traditionalist religious associations often enables women to restructure and remoralize domestic social relations. These studies also make it clear that these women live under conditions in which gender equality does not present itself as a realistic option. However, not all studies agree with this rather benign view of religious traditionalism's effect on women and argue that, in cases where patriarchal structures of authority have not yet broken down, they tend to reinforce female submission under patriarchal authority (Riesebrodt and Chong 1999; Chong 2002).

Sociology of religion's future

As we have seen, sociology's founding fathers have written some of their most important studies on religion, and several generations of scholars have made their living off the classics' theoretical capital. At the same time, the sociology of religion has become a rather marginal field within sociology. Since it predicted the decline of its object of study, scholars understandably doubted its significance. With the global resurgence of religion, however, the sociology of religion seems to have a future again. Since this future is not predetermined, but produced by sociologists themselves, we conclude by speculating on how the sociological study of religion can reclaim some of its original importance.

First of all, a thorough revision of its theoretical perspectives is urgently needed. On the one hand, the resurgence of religious movements and personal piety on a global scale has shed serious doubt on the secularization thesis, which has strongly shaped most previous sociological theories of religion. On the other hand, it would be ludicrous to deny that secularization in terms of processes of institutional differentiation has actually taken place. Modern states are widely secular, and neither capitalism and bureaucracy, nor modern science and modern culture, are based on or even compatible with most religious principles. And since much of resurgent religion is directed against modern secularism, one would actually misunderstand these movements unless one acknowledges secularization as a fact. Therefore, the sociology of religion must come to grips with these seemingly contradictory trends and must revise its theoretical frame in order to better explain how these processes are interrelated (Riesebrodt 2003).

In order to achieve this goal, religion should be analyzed sociologically as a relatively autonomous system of meaningful actions and interactions – a system interconnected with other systems of practices, but not a reflection of them. The sociology of religion, moreover, should attempt to account for the subjective side of religion as well as its objective side, analyzing and theorizing the individual religious actor as well as the institutional order. With regard to the subjective side, sociology should resist utilitarian simplifications in the explanation of social action. In their intentions and effects, religious practices – like those in other spheres – are neither exclusively rational and instrumental nor exclusively irrational. Therefore, the rational choice model, which assumes a rarely existing ideal market situation where individuals act consistently according to the results of cost-benefit analyses, turns out to be either tautological or empirically false. Moreover, since rational calculation is usually not a pleasurable task – but often a rather painful one – people should not be expected to rationally calculate unless the stakes are relatively high. Ultimately, the rational choice model might be useful for religious market research, but for an understanding and explanation of religious practices it lacks sociological depth, since it widely ignores culture as well as social structure.

As a second step in reclaiming lost relevance, the sociology of religion must overcome its rampant parochialism. To develop theoretical paradigms which work just for one country cannot be an option for a social science that wants to be taken seriously. Also the pervasive tendency for scholars to limit their studies either to their country of citizenship or to the religious tradition of their own affiliation attests to the provincialism of the discipline. Moreover, the sociology of religion would be well advised to leave the tiring debate on secularization behind, and turn instead to contemporary issues of real concern. Religion and gender has been studied empirically, but there is still plenty of theoretical work to do. In addition, new topics of study have emerged and re-emerged, such as religion and the legitimation of violence against oneself and others (Juergensmeyer 2000; Hall 2000), the impact of new technologies on the forms and spread of religion, and the globalization of religion (Beyer 1994).

While the great majority of sociologists of religion have studied their own backyard, they have widely left the study of religion in non-Western countries to anthropologists and historians of religion. With few exceptions, cross-culturally comparative work is absent from the sociology of religion. The roles played by religion in colonial and post-colonial situations and in processes of globalization have widely become the domain of anthropologists. In order to reclaim its legitimate place, the sociology of religion must eschew parochialism, broaden its perspective and revisit its theories in light of these global historical processes and contemporary events. The sociology of religion needs to become again a universal social science.

Bibliography

Ammerman, Nancy T. 1987. *Bible Believers: Fundamentalists in the Modern World.* New Brunswick, NJ: Rutgers University Press.
—— 1998. 'Religious Choice and Religious Vitality: The Market and Beyond.' in Lawrence A. Young, (ed.) 1998: 119–32.

Beckford, James. 1975. *The Trumpet of Prophecy: A Sociological Study of Jehovah's Witnesses.* New York: John Wiley & Sons.

—— 1985. *Cult Controversies: The Societal Response to New Religious Movements.* London and New York: Tavistock.

—— 1989. *Religion and Advanced Industrial Society.* London: Unwin Hyman.

Bellah, Robert N. 1957. *Tokugawa Religion.* New York: Free Press.

—— 1970. *Beyond Belief.* New York: Harper & Row.

—— 1975. *The Broken Covenant.* New York: Seabury Press.

—— Richard Madsen, William M. Sullivan, Ann Swidler and Steven M. Tipton. 1985. *Habits of the Heart: Individualism and Commitment in American Life.* Berkeley: University of California Press.

Berger, Peter. 1967. *The Sacred Canopy: Elements of a Sociological Theory of Religion.* Garden City, NY: Doubleday.

Beyer, Peter. 1994. *Religion and Globalization.* London: Sage.

Bruce, Steve. 1988. *The Rise and Fall of the New Christian Right: Conservative Protestant Politics in America 1978–1988.* Oxford: Clarendon Press.

—— 1990. *Pray TV: Televangelism in America.* London and New York: Routledge.

—— 1992. *The Red Hand: Protestant Paramilitaries in Northern Ireland.* Oxford and New York: Oxford University Press.

—— 1994. *The Edge of the Union: The Ulster Loyalist Political Vision.* Oxford: Oxford University Press.

—— 1999. *Choice and Religion: A Critique of Rational Choice Theory.* Oxford and New York: Oxford University Press.

Casanova, Jose. 1994. *Public Religions in the Modern World.* Chicago: University of Chicago Press.

Chaves, Mark. 1993. 'Intraorganizational Power and Internal Secularization in Protestant Denominations.' *American Journal of Sociology* 99(1): 1–48.

—— 1995. 'On the Rational Choice Approach to Religion.' *Journal for the Scientific Study of Religion* 34(1): 98–104.

—— 1997. *Ordaining Women. Culture and Conflict in Religious Organizations.* London: Harvard University Press.

Chong, Kelly H. 2002. 'Agony in Prosperity: Evangelicalism, Women, and the Politics of Gender in South Korea.' Ph.D. Thesis. Department of Sociology. University of Chicago.

Comaroff, Jean and John. 1991. *Of Revelation and Revolution: Christianity, Colonialism and Consciousness in South Africa.* Chicago: University of Chicago Press.

Comaroff, John and Jean. 1995. *Of Revelation and Revolution: The Dialectics of Modernity on a South African Frontier.* Chicago: University of Chicago Press.

Davidman, Lynn. 1991. *Tradition in a Rootless World.* Berkeley and Los Angeles: University of California Press.

Dobbelaere, Karel. 1981. 'Secularization: A Multidimensional Concept.' *Current Sociology* 29: 1–216.

Durkheim, Émile. 1912/1995. *The Elementary Forms of the Religious Life.* Translated by Karen Fields. New York: Free Press.

—— 1914/1960. 'The Dualism of Human Nature.' In Kurt H. Wolff ed., *Émile Durkheim, 1858–1917: A Collection of Essays.* Columbus: Ohio State University 1960: 325–40.

Eisenstadt, Shmuel N. ed. 1968. *The Protestant Ethic and Modernization. A Comparative View.* New York: Basic Books.

Finke, Roger and Rodney Stark. 1992. *The Churching of America, 1776–1990: Winners and Losers in Our Religious Economy.* New Brunswick, NJ: Rutgers University Press.

Gallagher, Sally. 2003. *Evangelical Identity and Gendered Family Life.* New Brunswick, NJ: Rutgers University Press.

Griffith, R. M. 1997. *God's Daughters: Evangelical Women and the Power of Submission*. Berkeley and London: University of California Press.

Hall, John R. 2000. *Apocalypse Observed*. London and New York: Routledge.

Hunter, James D. 1983. *American Evangelicalism: Conservative Religion and the Quandary of Modernity*. New Brunswick, NJ: Rutgers University Press.

Iannaccone, Laurence. 1994. 'Why Strict Churches are Strong.' *American Journal of Sociology* 99(5): 1180–211.

Juergensmeyer, Mark. 1993. *The New Cold War? Religious Nationalism Confronts the Secular State*. Berkeley: University of California Press.

Juergensmeyer, Mark. 2000. *Terror in the Mind of God*. University of California Press.

Kaufman, D.R. 1991. *Rachel's Daughters: Newly Orthodox Jewish Women*. New Brunswick, NJ: Rutgers University Press.

Land, Kenneth C., Glenn Deane and Judith Blau. 1991. 'Religious Pluralism and Church Membership: A Spatial Diffusion Model.' *American Sociological Review* 56(April): 237–49.

Luckmann, Thomas. 1967. *The Invisible Religion*. New York: Macmillan.

Martin, David. 1978. *A General Theory of Secularization*. Oxford: Blackwell.

—— 1990. *Tongues of Fire: The Explosion of Protestantism in Latin America*. London: Blackwell.

Neitz, Mary Jo. 1987. *Charisma and Community*. New Brunswick, NJ: Transaction Press.

—— and Peter R. Mueser. 1998. 'Economic Man and the Sociology of Religion: A Critique of the Rational Choice Approach.' In Lawrence A. Young, (ed.) 1998: 105–18.

Nesbitt, Paula. 1997. *Feminization of the Clergy in America*. New York and Oxford: Oxford University Press.

Olson, Daniel V. 1999. 'Religious Pluralism and US Church Membership: A Reassessment.' *Sociology of Religion* 60: 149–74.

Parsons, Talcott. 1963. 'Christianity and Modern Industrial Society.' In E. Tiryakian, (ed.), *Sociological Theory, Values, and Sociocultural Change*. New York: The Free Press, pp. 13–70.

Riesebrodt, Martin. 1993a. *Pious Passion*. Berkeley: University of California Press.

—— 1993b. 'Fundamentalism and the Political Mobilization of Women'. In Said Arjomand (ed.), *The Political Dimensions of Religion*. Albany: SUNY Press.

—— 2003. 'Religion in Global Perspective'. In Mark Juergensmeyer (ed.), *Global Religions: A Handbook*. Oxford: Oxford University Press.

—— and Kelly H. Chong. 1999. 'Fundamentalisms and Patriarchal Gender Politics.' *Journal of Women's History*, Vol. 10, No. 4 (Winter): 55–77.

Stacey, Judith. 1990. *Brave New Families: Stories of Domestic Upheaval in Late Twentieth Century America*. New York: Basic Books.

Stark, Rodney and William Sims Bainbridge. 1979. *A Theory of Religion*. New York: P. Lang.

Swatos, William H., Jr (ed.) 1999. 'The Secularization Debate'. Special Issue of *Sociology of Religion*, Vol. 60, No. 3, Fall 1999.

Tambiah, Stanley J. 1992. *Buddhism Betrayed? Religion, Politics and Violence in Sri Lanka*. Chicago: University of Chicago Press.

—— 1996. *Leveling Crowds: Ethnonationalist Conflicts and Collective Violence in South Asia*. Berkeley: University of California Press.

Tipton, Steven. 1982. *Getting Saved from the Sixties: Moral Meaning in Conversion and Cultural Change*. Berkeley: University of California Press.

Tucker, Robert C. (ed.) 1978. *Marx-Engels Reader*. London: W.W. Norton.

Voas, David, Daniel V.A. Olson, and Alasdair Crockett. 2002. 'Religious Pluralism and Participation: Why Previous Research is Wrong.' *American Sociological Review* 67: 212–30.

Warner, R. Stephen. 1993. 'Work in Progress Toward a New Paradigm of the Sociological Study of Religion in the United States.' *American Journal of Sociology* 98(5): 1044–93.

Weber, Max. 1904/1958. *The Protestant Ethic and the Spirit of Capitalism*. Tr. Talcott Parsons. London: Allen and Unwin.

——— 1922/1993. *The Sociology of Religion*. Boston: Beacon Press.

——— 1946. *From Max Weber: Essays in Sociology*, ed. by Hans H. Gerth and C. Wright Mills, New York: Oxford University Press.

Wilson, Bryan R. 1982. *Religion in Sociological Perspective*. New York: Oxford University Press.

——— 1990. *The Social Dimensions of Sectarianism: Sects and New Religious Movements in Contemporary Society*. Oxford: Clarendon Press.

Wuthnow, Robert. 1988. *The Restructuring of American Religion*. Princeton, NJ: Princeton University Press.

Young, Lawrence A. (ed.) 1998. *Rational Choice Theory and Religion: Summary and Assessment*. New York: Routledge.

Chapter 8

Anthropology of religion

Rosalind I. J. Hackett

The (sub-)field of enquiry known as anthropology of religion has been enjoying some long overdue renewal and recognition over the last decade, with the development of new texts and research areas, and new communities of scholars.[1] This renewal of interest is related in part to the growing salience of religion on the world stage, not least as a marker of identity and source of resistance at the local, translocal, and transnational levels. This in turn has generated a greater need for those with special-ized knowledge of religious actors and formations in diverse and changing contexts.

The scholarship of today, whether conducted by anthropologists who specialize in religion (e.g. Glazier 1999; Lambek 1993; Coleman 2000), or scholars of religion who employ anthropological theory and method (e.g. Brown 1991; Johnson 2002b; Geertz 2003), has come a long way from those early landmark texts of E. E. Evans-Pritchard on *Witchcraft, Magic and Oracles among the Azande* (1937) and *Nuer Religion* (1974 [1956]), and Émile Durkheim's *The Elementary Forms of the Religious Life* (1912). The new look anthropology of religion can be traced to three general factors: first, the changing nature and location of the subject matter (e.g. movement of peoples, influence of mass-mediated religion, and market forces); second, greater inter-disciplinarity among academic disciplines, and third, the critical insights derived from post-colonialism, post-structuralism, and postmodernism.[2] In particular, the once discernible distinction between ethnography (empirical research on particular cultures/peoples/regions conducted through fieldwork and participant observation), and more generalized, theoretical reflection (anthropology or ethnology), is now blurred. Some would attribute this merging of the empirical, and cross-cultural, comparative approaches to the work of Clifford Geertz whose body of writings has been influential far beyond the bounds of traditional anthropology.

As a way of offsetting the current difficulties of delineating academic boundaries due to the shared body of social and cultural theory, and the growing diversification of 'topics' or 'sub-fields,' Henrietta Moore argues that it is to the history of a disci-pline that we should look for its defining characteristics, rather than specific objects of inquiry (1999: 2). Similarly, many scholars consider that it is now more appro-priate to treat 'religion,' 'politics,' and 'economics' as pervasive rather than bounded categories (see, e.g. Herzfeld 2001: xi). Thus, it will behove us to trace briefly some of the roads traveled by anthropologists since the nineteenth century, in their quest to identify and interpret religious ideas, symbols, and practice. This will provide the backdrop needed to consider some of the more promising current and future devel-opments in anthropological approaches to religion. A comprehensive, representative synthesis of what Henrietta Moore calls the 'master narratives,' (1999: 10) as well as the conceptual basics of the anthropology of religion is not feasible in the present context, so the emphasis here is more on salient highlights, updates, and productive areas of debate. More extensive overviews and resources are available in the various texts/textbooks, and readers on the subject.[3]

Pioneering the discipline

Anthropology enjoys an ongoing dialectical tension between its scientific and humanistic sides. This is well characterized by James Peacock in his valuable introductory text on the anthropological enterprise: 'Emphasis on culture and recognition of the subjective aspect of interpretation link anthropology to the humanities, yet its striving for systematization, generalization, and precise observation reflects the inspiration of the sciences' (1986: 92). When Sir Edward Tylor (1832–1917) was appointed to the first chair in anthropology in Britain (in the United States, Franz Boas (1858–1942) is regarded as the founding father of cultural anthropology), the field was then described as the 'science of man.' Influenced by the rationalist and evolutionist views of the nineteenth century, Tylor speculated that humans developed the idea of a soul, and from that, spirits, who might also inhabit natural phenomena, in their attempt to rationalize mysterious experiences such as dreams, trances, and hallucinations (1970 [1871]). He postulated that this early human belief, which he termed animism, eventually gave way to polytheism and monotheism, although traces of spiritualism persisted in beliefs such as reincarnation and immortality of the soul.

French sociologist Émile Durkheim saw religious beliefs and concepts as the product of particular social conditions, rather than in intellectualist terms. In his classic work, *Les Formes Élémentaires de la Vie Religieuse* (Durkheim 1965 [1912]), he argued that religion, predicated on a distinction between the sacred and the profane, was an essentially social phenomenon. Like many of the pioneering functionalist and evolutionist scholars, he turned to what he perceived to be some of the earliest and most elemental forms of religion, namely the totemic beliefs of the hunting and gathering Australian Aborigines. He argued that totemic symbols were mystically charged emblems of group loyalties, and that ritual expressed and strengthened the social organism. In fact, the 'collective effervescence' experienced at these ritual events was, he proposed, at the heart of the religious impulse. I. M. Lewis critiques Durkheim's insistence on the holistic approach, which was a type of 'social determinism,' trumping any 'historical determinism' or questions about the origins of social institutions (1976: 52). It did, however, constitute a significant advance over the decontextualized, comparative approach of Sir James Frazer, in his landmark study of ritual and magic from classic texts around the world, *The Golden Bough* (1996 [1890]). Frazer believed there was an evolution in the ways in which people made sense of, and tried to control, their worlds, from magic, through religion, to science.

Frazer's lack of recognition of the scientific knowledge of 'primitive humanity' was roundly criticized by subsequent scholars. For example, Mary Douglas argued that the primitive worldview was not compartmentalized, but far more integrated and holistic than modern thought (Douglas 1975). Moreover, Bronislaw Malinowski (1884–1942) challenged the 'armchair anthropology' of Frazer and other scholars of the time and became, in I. M. Lewis' words, 'the pioneer, bush-whacking anthropologist' who turned fieldwork in exotic cultures into a doctrine and tenet of professionalism (Lewis 1976: 55–56). Based on the two years that he spent among the Trobriand Islanders in the Pacific, Malinowski explained religion and science in light of his function-alist theory of human needs (1954 [1925]). Magical rituals were performed when the situation was dangerous and unpredictable, such as fishing at sea, while religious rituals offered psychological assurance in the face of death.

Malinowski's contemporary A. R. Radcliffe-Brown (1881–1955) was more theor-etically inclined and he developed the idea of 'structural-functionalism' (1952). From his viewpoint, social life was predicated on an orderly, organized foundation, and social organizations functioned in order to sustain social solidarity. His work spawned a whole generation of scholars. Drawing more on structural linguistics, French scholar Claude Lévi-Strauss (1963) promoted the idea of structures or patterns of culture existing at various levels of consciousness. These structures have functional signifi-cance, serving to resolve contradictions and binary oppositions in human life (Lewis 1976: 65–66). Later scholars, such as Luc de Heusch, have adapted structuralist principles to the complexities of religion elsewhere in the world (Heusch 1982).

With E. E. Evans-Pritchard's still influential work on the thought of the Azande people of central Africa came a shift in focus from that of 'structure' to that of 'meaning' (Evans-Pritchard 1937). He was particularly interested in how their beliefs in witchcraft, oracles, and magic translated into the actions of their everyday lives and social relations. His study raised important questions about rationality and cultural translation, subsequently generating a body of literature on the similarities or differences between unfalsifiable, so-called primitive belief systems and supposedly rational scientific worldviews (see Gellner 1999: 29). Some of this discussion centered on the rationality of millenarian movements such as the 'cargo cults' of the Pacific region, in achieving political ends (Worsley 1968; Lattas 1998). Rodney Needham questioned the use of the term 'belief' in many non-Western cultures (Needham 1972). He preferred the notion of 'idea,' since it conveyed the embedded aspect of cosmologies, and did not connote distance between 'observers' and 'informants.'

The intellectualist interpretation was given a new lease of life with Robin Horton's classic, and much debated, article, 'African traditional thought and Western science' (Horton 1993). In it he demonstrates the ways in which traditional African cultures and Western cultures both seek to explain, predict and control events. In addition to the continuities, he argues that the former thought-system is more closed than the latter. Both Horton's intellectualist view and Malinowski's functionalist perspec-tive were in fact more positive about the role of religion than French philosopher Lucien Lévy-Bruhl's position that primitive people's thought was pre-logical, in that it did not separate cause from effect (Bennett 1996: 66).

From modes of thought to modes of practice

Viewing cosmologies as resources for, rather than determinants of, action can help lessen the persistence of evolutionist or binary thinking, argues Michael Herzfeld (2001: 192f.). It may also undermine the tendency to treat cosmologies in isolation, along with 'religion.' He advocates greater recognition of the role of choice and agency in how people (whether 'primitives,' ethnographers, or scientists) organize their ideas about the universe. Addressing the question of myth, Herzfeld is troubled by the ongoing distinction between mythical and historical narratives, as held by Mircea Eliade and Claude Lévi-Strauss among others, as it leads to larger social distinctions between primitive or archaic and modern, and literate and non-literate societies. It also fails to recognize the ideological manipulation in both, as in nationalist myths of origin. So, while drawing on the insights of some of the early functionalist accounts of myth as providing models for human behavior, explaining disorder and failure (theodicy), and creating 'timeless temporalities,' anthropology must be true to its comparativism, and turn its lens onto the cosmology of the West itself, revealing its own cultural specificities (Herzfeld 2001: 206).

In his remarks on ritual, Herzfeld again underscores the need to not get too predicated on rites as reordering and instrumental (ibid.: 257f.). He states that all rituals are about time and the passage of existence. This is well illustrated by Arnold van Gennep's (1960) three-stage model of rituals (separation, marginality or liminality, and aggregation) which Victor Turner (1974) then gave more of a social interpretation. The latter argued that ritual could generate 'communitas' (the realm of anti-structure and the leveling of differences), allowing people to overcome uncertainty and ambiguity at the key transitional moments in their lives. Turner's work remains very popular with religion scholars because of its attention to indigenous cultural notions, notably Ndembu symbolism and ritual, and broader humanist concerns (Gellner 1999: 30).

Current scholarship on ritual evidences the shift in focus from structure to agency, and the influence of practice theory. Catherine Bell prefers the term 'ritualization' over a more objectified notion of ritual, viewing it as 'a matter of variously culturally specific strategies for setting some activities off from others, for creating and privileging a qualitative distinction between the 'sacred' and the 'profane,' and for ascribing such distinctions to realities thought to transcend the powers of human actors' (Bell 1992: 74). Thomas Csordas' analysis of the Catholic Charismatic Renewal movement serves as a fine example of the imaginative and complex ways in which ritual life can be interpreted (Csordas 1997).

From meaning to power

The emphasis on religion as a social institution by earlier anthropologists, notably of the British school, was given a new orientation in the 1970s by the American anthropologist, Clifford Geertz, in an influential essay entitled, 'Religion as a Cultural System' (Geertz 1973). Michael Lambek characterizes Geertz as 'the major exponent of a Weber-inspired interpretive anthropology which attempts to understand religion within a broadly cultural/symbolic domain, but also with reference to public circumstances in all their messiness' (Lambek 2002: 61). Geertz is well known for his advocacy of the need for 'thick description,' that is, interpretation of 'natives'' own interpretations of events, based on the anthropologist's empirical knowledge. As noted by David Gellner (1999: 20), this change marked the move from 'etic' (looking at cultures from the outside and in the light of broader principles) to 'emic' (viewing cultures from the inside and in terms of their own categories) approaches.

An important counterpoint to Geertz's interpretivist approach is the work of Talal Asad, notably in his piece, 'The Construction of Religion as an Anthropological Category' (1993: 27–54). In this trenchant critique of essentialist definitions of religion, he claims that 'there cannot be a universal definition of religion, not only because its constituent elements and relationships are historically specific, but because that definition is itself the historical product of discursive processes' (ibid.: 29). To insist that religion has an autonomous essence, and is conceptually separate from the domain of power, is, he argues, a modern Western norm generated by post-Reformation history. This account, Lambek states, is 'indicative of a shift away from a symbolic anthropology toward a poststructuralist one that is more centrally concerned with power and discipline and with the way that religious subjects (i.e. practitioners) are formed' (Lambek 2002: 114). It also reflects efforts to contextualize ethnographic knowledge, notably in terms of the various colonial settings in which such knowledge was generated.

Historicizing and problematizing

Similar concerns to problematize and locate dominant anthropological concepts are found in the historical anthropology of Jean Comaroff and John Comaroff. For example, in their edited volume on *Modernity and its Malcontents*, they state decisively at the outset that the concept of modernity 'is profoundly ideological and profoundly historical' (Comaroff and Comaroff 1993: xi). As with much of their influential output, they tie their theoretical strengths into exciting empirical explorations that relate to the subject matter of 'religion' – generally situated in colonial and/or post-colonial Africa (Comaroff and Comaroff 1991, 1992). The authors in the volume on modernity, all former students of the Comaroffs, share a common orientation,

> that tries to dissolve the division between synchrony and diachrony, ethnography and historiography; that refuses to separate culture from political economy, insisting instead on the simultaneity of the meaningful and the material in all things; that acknowledges – no, stresses – the brute realities of colonialism and its aftermath, without assuming that they have robbed African peoples of their capacity to act on the world.
>
> (ibid.: xiv)

Their 'analytic gaze' is turned upon the role of ritual in African modernity/modernities. It yields some excellent studies of the persistence, even efflorescence, of occultism, magic, and witchcraft in late twentieth-century African communities, as paradoxical consequences of 'modernity' and 'development' (ibid.). For example, based on her field studies of reports about witchcraft and other supernatural activities in the popular press in Onitsha, a large Igbo-speaking market town in south-eastern Nigeria, Misty Bastian argues that witchcraft is not seen as solely associated with the 'traditional' or the 'village' (Bastian 1993). In fact, it may even gain new power and meanings from the urban context, as it constitutes a useful medium for making sense of the complexity of West African life experiences (cf. Meyer 1999 on Ghana). Anthropologists have long believed that one of the most distinguishing characteristics of a society is the way that it deals with affliction and suffering. Witchcraft beliefs and practices offer a particularly illuminating window onto such existential questions. Building on, as well as contesting, the earlier analytical foundations laid by Evans-Pritchard (1937), and I. M. Lewis (1986), recent scholarship has generated some insightful analyses of the ways in which ideas about occult practice inform contemporary African social, political, and religious life (for example, Geschiere 1997; Bongmba 2001; Niehaus 2001; Ciekawy 1998; Hackett 2003).

The rethinking of the traditional/modern dichotomy in anthropological research is linked to the renewed appreciation for the historical dimension. Johannes Fabian argues that suppressing temporality allows investigators to ignore the fact that the people they study are actually living in the same time period as they are (1983). Contemporary anthropologists tend to be more interested in how various populations and interest groups *use* their images of the past to constitute or strengthen present interests, and also how far those who study such groups are themselves implicated in such processes. Herzfeld reminds us, in no uncertain terms, that '[t]he idea that we somehow stand outside our object of study is *preposterous*' (Herzfeld 2001: 55, emphasis added). The adjudication of the accuracy of historical accounts is controlled by the powerful, whose own 'literal' records need also to be read as 'interpretational devices' (ibid., 62).

The reproduction of the past, or its suppression, through social and ritual performance, allows people to come to terms with 'a discomfiting present' (Herzfeld 2001: 58). In her illuminating and multi-layered work on West African slavery (which Herzfeld alludes to), Rosalind Shaw describes how ritual practices, namely divination, and images of pernicious occult powers, may be understood as 'memories of temporally removed processes created by an Atlantic commercial system that spanned three continents' (2002: 3). Interestingly, Shaw notes that, while divinatory skills lost favor in the light of the hegemony of a twentieth-century Western education, they enjoyed renewed salience with the catastrophic failure of Sierra Leone's economy and infrastructure during the 1980s and 1990s, and the emergence and entrenchment of the rebel war. She shows how mnemonic stories of European cannibalism under colonialism and present-day popular stories of 'big persons,' namely national politicians and top civil servants, rumored to have gained their prestige through evil ritual practices prescribed by diviners, serve as social critiques. These stories draw on colonial and pre-colonial memories of power and its abuses. It is noteworthy that the memories of suffering and exploitation detailed in her study are condensed and expressed via ritual means, as well as highly charged sacred objects and locations. Stephan Palmié's riveting study of Afro-Cuban religious culture also discloses how local forms of moral imagination constitute a response to the violent slave-trading past, rivaling Western understandings of modernity and rationality (2002).

Experience and experiencing

As with many other disciplines in the human sciences, anthropology experienced a 'crisis of representation' and the 'postmodern turn' in the 1980s and 1990s. In the wake of this critique, authors tend to be more transparent about their field experiences, even life trajectories. This is more than understanding positionality – frequently theoretical exploration is involved in trying to factor in the voices, or better still, knowledge, of women and indigenous peoples, or negotiate a balance between subjectivism and objectivism, for instance.[4] Research on religion appears to compound these ethical and epistemological issues, yet such methodological reflection by scholars of religion has been less forthcoming (see, however, Spickard, Landres, and McGuire 2002; Dempsey 2000).

As an anthropologist with comparative religion and philosophy strings to his bow, Michael Jackson has been exemplary on this question of reflexivity. In his much-praised book *Paths Toward a Clearing* (1989), he reflects on 'the presumed coevalness that permits an ethnographer to have an understanding of the people he or she lives with and the images of radical otherness that pervade much anthropological writing' (ibid.: x). Drawing on his skills as novelist and poet, and on theoretical ideas from the existentialist and pragmatist traditions, Jackson focuses on experiences which are shared by both ethnographers and the people they study. He sets out to probe the dialectic at the heart of the anthropological project, namely the tensions between the search for universal cultural patterns and the empirical diversity of social life. He does this in the context of his experiences both among the Kuranko of Sierra Leone, and the Walpiri of Central Australia (Jackson 1995).

In the course of twelve years of intensive research and collaboration with a Haitian Vodou priestess and her family in Brooklyn, Karen McCarthy Brown felt the need for more integrity, honesty, as well as imagination in her work (Brown 1991). Coming to the conclusion that fieldwork was more of a 'social art' than a social science, she wove fictional and autobiographical threads into the overall ethnographical analysis.[5] Similarly, Sam Gill, a professor of religious studies known for his work on the religions of indigenous peoples, develops 'storytracking' as an approach which allows him to trace the 'colonialist underbelly' of academic accounts of the Arrente, a Central Australian people, as well as to examine critically his own life and the challenge of living 'responsibly and decisively in a postmodern world' (Gill 1998).[6]

The anthropological study of experience and its inter-subjective expressions was seen by Victor W. Turner as a way of revitalizing a field that had become stultified by structural-functional orthodoxy. He drew inspiration for this new hermeneutical and humanistic direction from the German philosopher Wilhelm Dilthey. In *The Anthropology of Experience*, edited by Turner and Edward M. Bruner (but which appeared after Turner's death in 1983), several leading scholars discuss the intersections and disjunctures between life as lived, life as experienced, and life as told (V. W. Turner and Bruner 1986; see, also, E. Turner 1985). Drawing on their own ethnographic experiences, they document and analyze the symbolic manifestations and processual activities that are the 'structured units of experience,' such as the enactment of rituals, manipulation of images, performance of drama, or recitation of texts.

Experience is arguably central to the rich body of literature on spirit possession and shamanism. These staple topics of the field have generated a variety of cross-cultural and multi-perspectival accounts.[7] Paul Stoller's own experiences of sorcery and possession among the Songhay of Niger inform his body of writings (Stoller 1995, 1997). He is particularly attentive to the neglected senses (smell, taste, and touch) in Western anthropology (Stoller 1989, 1997), as is Constance Classen, who calls for a 'sensory anthropology' (Classen 1993). In fact, it could be argued that all issues of importance to a culture, including religious beliefs and practices, are infused with sensory values, while not forgetting that these same values may be used to express and reinforce divisions and hierarchies pertaining to race, gender and religion (Herzfeld 2001: 252–253). Dutch anthropologists Rijk van Dijk and Peter Pels underscore the need to deconstruct the 'politics of perception' at play in the relationship between anthropologist and interlocutor(s) (Dijk and Pels 1996). This lies behind the Western privileging of natural over supernatural, or observation over occultism or secrecy, rather than any given 'objectivity.' In fact, they provocatively, yet persuasively, claim that 'the anthropological study of religion tends to reflect, more than any other anthropological topic, the preconceptions of the Western observer' (ibid.: 247). This is probably the reason, they suggest, why so little has been written (except autobiographically) about fieldwork on religion.

Focusing more on the experiences of those who are petitioners and practitioners, Adeline Masquelier explores the 'ritual economy' of *bori* spirit possession cults (albeit a small minority) in the town of Dogondoutchi in south-western Niger, as they contest the rapidly growing Muslim community which has taken control of the trade networks and village affairs (Masquelier 2001). She demonstrates how *bori* allows people to remember an idealized past as to articulate and negotiate the problems of contemporary life: 'to transform the experience of novel, ambiguous, or threatening realities into symbols of a shared consciousness' (ibid., 10–11). Masquelier, in searching for the appropriate interpretive lens for her case study, provides a helpful overview of the rich literature on spirit possession (Masquelier 2001: 11–31; see, also, Boddy 1994). She rejects those approaches which explain possession in pathological, biological, or functionalist terms, as in I. M. Lewis's well-known claim that both spirit possession and shamanism must be studied as social phenomena primarily to do with power and marginality (Lewis 1989). Masquelier opts instead for an approach which does justice to the therapeutic and performative aspects of possession, and which analyzes both its 'cultural logic' and wider historical and political contexts.

Engendering and embodying the field

At the outset of her much-cited work *Feminism and Anthropology*, Henrietta Moore stresses that '[t]he basis for the feminist critique is not the study of women, but the analysis of gender relations, and of gender as a structuring principle in all human societies' (1988: vii). For example, she looks at the relation between pollution beliefs and sexual antagonism in Melanesian societies (ibid.: 16–21). Susan Sered articulates well why anthropologists cannot ignore the role of religion in this and other areas of social life, '[t]he 'natural' and the 'supernatural' serve as complementary tools for naturalizing and sanctifying difference, prestige, and hierarchy' notably in regard to questions of gender (1999: 9). In some societies, the ritual context provides for much greater fluidity and reversal of gender roles (Sered 1999: 231–245).

'Mutually toxic' is the way Rosalind Shaw described the relationship between feminism and mainstream religious studies (in the early 1990s) (Shaw 1995). She saw a collision between the 'view from below,' contextual approach of feminist anthropology, and the 'view from above,' *sui generis* tradition of religious studies, with its privileging of texts and beliefs. However, Fiona Bowie argues that it is both possible and productive to accommodate the contested (Western origins, pro-women) and contesting (critical, deconstructive) nature of feminism in the study of religion (Bowie 2000: 91–118).

One of the positive offshoots of the feminist impulse in anthropological scholarship has been a heightened attention to the social and cultural significance of the body (Lock 1997). Earlier social scientists, such as Durkheim, were interested in the relationship between the physical, social, and psycho-social domains. Mary Douglas stimulated an appreciation of the body for its symbolic properties (Douglas 1970). Michael Lambek and Andrew Stathern, in their inter-regional study of the relations between persons and bodies in Africa and Melanesia, attribute the heightened interest in the body to its 'increased visibility and objectification within late capitalist consumer society,' as well to shifts in academic focus to the domain of lived experience and the effects of the social realm on the body, to the body as signifier, and to mind/body holistic issues (Lambek and Strathern 1998: 5). So, as they rightly suggest, the body constitutes a type of centripetal concept around which current academic interests can be organized. They underscore the significance of embodiment as the model (supported by current scientific findings in brain/body studies) for discussing the interactions of body and mind, notably in the context of illness and health.

Michael Jackson is critical of prevailing tendencies in anthropology to interpret embodied experience in terms of belief and language, and to treat the body as inert and passive (1989: 122). Reviewing his earlier analysis of Kuranko rituals of initiation, which was unduly abstract and intellectualist, he now holds that 'what is done with the body is the ground of what is thought and said' (1989: 131; cf. Moore 1996: 3–12, 79–97). He also maintains that this focus on bodily praxis is more empathic and in line with indigenous interpretations, rather than being dependent on external experts in symbolic analysis. Jackson also shows how the use of bodily imagery enables the Kuranko (and others) 'to place self and world on the same scale,' and to act in the belief that 'mastery of the universe is reciprocally linked to mastery of self' (ibid., 155).

Some studies highlight the intersections between the body, religious symbols, and political and economic power. Jean Comaroff shows how Zionist Christians in South Africa appropriated symbols of power from the dress of colonialists and missionaries, transforming these into messages of dissent and self-empowerment (Comaroff 1985). Two new edited collections (Arthur 1999; Arthur 2000) provide a fascinating range of examples of how religious dress may be used, especially in the case of women, to negotiate new social environments, or to control sexuality and social behavior.

Closely tied to studies of the body are studies of illness and healing from a range of different perspectives (see Csordas 2002). René Devisch's detailed analysis of a healing cult, *mbwoolu*, among the Yaka of Congo (formerly Zaire) demonstrates how, through the use of liturgy and figurines, an ill person is ritually induced to die in his former condition and be reborn into a new one (Devisch 1998). The imaginary, transgressive, and intimate qualities of this esoteric trance-possession cult differ from the more public, daytime ceremonies of initiation. Bruce Kapferer's impressive study of Sinhalese exorcism rituals in Sri Lanka stresses the critical importance of performance and ceremony (Kapferer 1991 [1983]). Some studies address the impact of exogenous forces. For example, Stacey Pigg's original, multi-level analysis of local theories of sickness and healing practices in Nepal weaves in the role of the state and international development agencies (Pigg 1996).

In a lucid theoretical piece, 'Body and Mind in Mind, Body and Mind in Body' (1998), Michael Lambek stresses that it is important not to view the mind–body relationship reductively or incommensurably, but as a 'central dialectic in the ongoing constitution of human culture, society, and experience (and hence of anthropological theory)' (ibid., 120). The celebration of the body, and the turn to practice theory, as useful as they have been in transcending problematic dichotomies, should not, he insists, lead us to forget that 'contemplative reason' is a fundamental characteristic of the human condition, regardless of time and place (ibid., p. 119). This assertion seems especially pertinent to the study of religious worlds, still haunted as they are by the specters of essentialism, reductionism, and Orientalism (unintended or otherwise).

New moves and movements

Because of the quest for holistic analysis, anthropologists have been drawn over the years to the study of small-scale societies. This is where they find what Peacock calls 'the interrelatedness of meaning and life, culture and existence' (1986: 18). However, to downplay the exoticism and primitivism commonly associated with the work of Western anthropologists, and to address new social and cultural flows, many younger anthropologists have shifted their focus to new locations and phenomena. Some may still retain an interest in qualitative research on smaller, popular groups of other societies (as opposed to sociology's more traditional emphasis on the quantitative analysis of [our own] large-scale societies), but they are increasingly attuned to the national and global forces which shape communal identity and survival. Diaspora, travel, tourism, and transnationalism are now on the agenda, reflecting the fluid, multi-sited nature of contemporary anthropology (Vertovec 2000; Johnson 2002a; Tsing 1993). Syncretism and fetishism have also been experiencing a revival of interest in the post-colonial world of hybridized and creolized cultures (Shaw and Stewart 1994; Apter and Pietz 1993).

The rich body of work now emerging on global Pentecostalism and its local manifestations, for example, illustrates these new trends exceptionally well (Corten and Marshall-Fratani 2001; Harding 2000; Coleman 2000; Meyer 1999), building on earlier work on religious change and innovation (e.g. MacGaffey 1983). Evangelicalism and (Christian) fundamentalism have also been subject to anthropological analysis (DeBernardi 1999; Nagata 2001), and there is ongoing interest in missionary activities, and the problematic of conversion and cultural translation (Veer 1996). Joel Robbins has been instrumental in formulating an anthropology of Christianity (Robbins 2003). There is no shortage of works on Islam in a host of different contexts, whether in the public spheres of the Middle East (Eickelman and Salvatore 2002), Indonesia (Hefner 2000; Bowen 2003), Egypt (Starrett 2003), or Mali (Soares 2004). Anthropologists have also ventured into the worlds of neo-pagan/Wicca (Luhrmann 1989) and new age religions (Brown 1997), while Talal Asad has recently called for an anthropology of the secular (2003). Some have turned to cognitive anthropology for naturalistic explanations about religion (see, e.g. Whitehouse and Laidlaw 2004).

Material and media cultures

One of the most significant new areas in the anthropological study of religion is that of the visual and performing arts (Hackett 1996; Coote and Shelton 1994).[8] Theorists in this field have done much to problematize the concept of 'primitive.' An early land-mark text, linking ritual and cosmology to art and architectonics, was James Fernandez's dense study of a Central African religious movement, *Bwiti* (Fernandez 1982). This has been followed by other scholars who have explored the relationship between the materiality and spirituality of place (see, e.g. Low and Lawrence-Zuniga 2003).

The French anthropologists who conducted extensive research on the Dogon of Mali were also attentive to the intersections of their elaborate masking and cosmo-logical traditions (Griaule 1938). Greater attention to material and performance culture elucidates hidden cosmological and philosophical meanings (see, e.g. Abiodun 1994), although much more needs to be done on music and dance. Studies on secrecy (Nooter 1993) and on divination (Pemberton III 2000) illustrate this well. In fact, the findings have served to challenge prevailing Western understandings of power and aesthetics, for in some African art forms the least visible and least attractive art works may be the most spiritually charged. The magnificent study, *A Saint in the City* (and museum exhibition), of the urban arts associated with Sheikh Amadou Bamba, the Senegalese Sufi mystic, illustrates the devotional power of his sacred images for members of the Mouride order the world over (Roberts *et al.* 2003).[9] *Ways of the Rivers* is a stunning example of the intersections of art, religion, and the environment in the Niger Delta (Anderson and Peek 2002).[10]

Analyzing the growing interest in Australian Aboriginal visual culture, Fred Myers and Howard Morphy reveal how contemporary Australian Aboriginal spirituality is (re)constructed in the commodification of contemporary Aboriginal paintings (Myers 2002; Morphy 1992). These and other studies consider the how indigenous art works circulate transculturally due to the art and tourist trades, and museum exhibitions, and how this affects their (original) ritual meanings and use, and present-day artistic production.

An exciting new area of investigation for anthropologists in general, and espe-cially for those who focus on religion – notably the newer and/or minority movements seeking recognition and expansion – is the burgeoning mass media sector. Long absent from the purview of mainstream anthropology because of their perceived hegemonic and homogenizing tendencies, the media, particularly local and indigenous forms, are now the subject of conferences and publications (Ginsberg, Abu-Lughod, and Larkin 2002; Herzfeld 2001: 294–315). An important new volume assembles the work of several scholars who are engaged on the intersections of religion and media in a variety of locations (Meyer and Moors 2005).[11] It is in the area of audience recep-tion, practice, and agency that anthropologists, with their professed interest in everyday experience, can make their contribution to media studies (Herzfeld 2001: 17, 302f.). Comparative scholarship on Islam and the media is particularly well developed both substantively and theoretically (Anderson 2003).

Perduring and maturing debates

The changes in focus and content, adumbrated above, serve to raise old and new questions about the conscience of present-day anthropologists, and their purpose in a world plagued by conflict and injustice. The first of these perduring concerns is *epistemological*, in that it problematizes the relations of power and authority (both at the empirical and representational level) between anthropologist and the 'other'

(Moore 1999: 5) Herzfeld opts for a methodological stance of 'principled modesty' (2001: 67) and 'reflexive comparativism' (ibid.: 65), both of which keep the core issue of sameness and difference in creative tension, obviating any lapse into reductive or hegemonic interpretations. Armin Geertz believes that ethnographically oriented scholars of religion should not capitulate to those voices who privilege insider authority, knowledge, and cultural competence. He opts for a dialogical relationship between scholar and consultant, which he terms 'ethnohermeneutics' (2003).

The critical insights of cultural anthropologists on these ethical and methodological questions should give pause for reflection, and perhaps, encouragement, to all those who engage in ethnographic work on religion. In his appropriately titled *Anthropology with an Attitude* (2001), Johannes Fabian expresses his frustration that his anthropologist colleagues seem more preoccupied with how they represent their data than with how they obtain it. He acknowledges that the application of hermeneutics and literary criticism to anthropology has produced valuable critical insights, but finds that texts, as produced by the ethnographer as records of verbal interaction in the field, have generated false assurances of objectivity. He would like to see more emphasis on how cultural knowledge is imparted through performance and action, rather than as discursive information. He is critical of the privileging of concepts and images derived from vision, namely, participant *observation*, in the production of 'objective' ethnographic knowledge. A more materialist, and inter-subjective approach in fieldwork can, in his estimation, erase the hierarchy between knower and known.

In his inimitably provocative way, Fabian also asks why 'ecstasis,' should not be included in our theories of knowledge. By this he means (and this links to the section on experience above) ecstatic initiation rituals, hallucinogens, alcohol, exhausting dances, and all-night vigils and wakes.[12] For that matter, he adds, there should be room for 'passion,' or referring to Michael Taussig's work on shamanism and colonialism in Bolivia (1987), 'terror' or 'torture.' For how, Fabian asks, 'can we hope to deal objectively with peoples and cultures whom Western imperialism made the subjects of brutal domination as well as of ethnographic inquiry?' (Fabian 2001: 32). Kirsten Hastrup, who is equally concerned with issues of discrimination and toleration (Hastrup and Ulrich 2001), argues in favor of the use of the 'ethnographic present' to go beyond the dichotomy of subjectivism and objectivism (Hastrup 1995: 9–25). She believes that it can convey both the creativity and inter-subjectivity of the fieldwork *process* and the written, more theoretical *presenting* of the ethnography, and their mutual imbrications.

The second ongoing area of debate is more *teleological* in that it addresses the purpose and outcomes of anthropological research. This is more than just applied anthropology, argues Henrietta Moore, it relates to the 'reconfiguration of the boundaries between academic and non-academic practice' and the recognition that anthropology is a disciplinary project which is part of 'the practice of governmentality' (1999: 3). In other words, there can be no more retreating into cultural relativism. Anthropologists still have to engage with theories that treat the *commonalities*, and not just the *differences*, between all human beings (ibid.: 17).

Michael Jackson is concerned to find 'ways of opening up dialogue between people from different cultures or traditions, ways of *bringing into being* modes of understanding which effectively go beyond the intellectual conventions and political ideologies that circumscribe us all' (1989: x [author's emphasis]; cf. van Binsbergen 2003). Similarly, Michael Herzfeld believes that 'history from below,' i.e. detailed ethnography or thick description, can offer 'daily challenges to the dominance of certain political structures' (and, we should add, religious structures) (2001: 75). Faye Harrison and her contributors to *Decolonizing Anthropology* are even more proactive in exploring how, as 'organic intellectuals,' they can contribute toward 'social transformation and human liberation' (Harrison 1991).

Some scholars are translating their concerns regarding ethics and pragmatics into new arenas or objects of interrogation, such as development, discrimination, or violence and conflict. It is well known that anthropologists have served in an advisory capacity to governments, and development and humanitarian organizations. Some are now reviewing this practice, and analyzing these institutions, occasionally with a focus on religious agencies (see, e.g. Bornstein 2002). However, only two of these emergent areas can be highlighted here, namely violence and conflict, and human rights.

There is no shortage of texts these days on the ethnography and theory of violence and suffering (Das *et al.* 2001; Herzfeld 2001: 217–239; Tambiah 1996). In Cynthia Mahmood's estimation, the new interest of anthropologists in war and peace is generating 'a much richer understanding of how human beings experience violence' (Mahmood 2003). The area of conflict resolution has been particularly open to insights on culture. Clearly, the context of war and conflict compels the fieldworker to consider most carefully methods of communication, knowledge production, and representation. Such extreme contexts also tend to subvert conventional concepts and categories. For example, Swedish anthropologist Sverker Finnstrom, seeking to investigate the cultural practices whereby people in Northern Uganda both engage and try to comprehend existentially the realities of war and violence, and also struggle continuously to build hope for the future, opted for 'participant reflection' over 'participant observation' to reflect his more engaged relationship with his informants (Finnstrom 2003). Carolyn Nordstrom's groundbreaking work on war-torn regions and the strategies people adopt to (re)generate meaning and community in situations of extreme suffering is apposite here (Nordstrom 1997). Marc Sommers, an anthropologist who works on Rwandan and Burundian refugee communities in Tanzania, states revealingly, '[p]erhaps no aspect of African refugee society and culture is as overlooked by researchers and most humanitarian relief agencies as their religious lives' (Sommers 2000: 18). Indeed, this aspect is often under-analyzed in otherwise praiseworthy works on social suffering (Das *et al.* 2001). However, in studies of indigenous peoples the religious or spiritual dimension may be more apparent (Adelson 2001).

Now that human rights constitute the new global *lingua franca* for victims of injustice and oppression the world over, anthropologists are having to overcome their relativist leanings and respond to the call to 'anthropologize' and 'historicize' human rights (Booth 1999). This may invoke, wittingly or unwittingly, religious uses and interpretations of the human rights idea. Several European scholars have indeed set out in a recent volume, *Culture and Rights: Anthropological Perspectives*, to develop more 'empirical, contextual analyses of specific rights struggles' (Cowan, Dembour, and Wilson 2001: 21). They rightly argue that such an intellectual strategy permits them 'to follow how individuals, groups, communities and states use a discourse of rights in the pursuit of particular ends, and how they become enmeshed in its logic.' Empirical studies also raise important questions about who subscribes to and who benefits from this or that version of culture, community, or tradition – all of which can have significant ethical and legal consequences. Minority religious and ethnic groups continue to serve as the interface for the increasingly legalized and politicized battles over cultural identity and survival (Barry 2001; Nye 2001; see, Hussain and Ghosh 2002 on postcolonial situations in South Asia). More research is needed to understand the ways in which the human rights concept is generating new discourses of sameness and difference among religious groups. In other words, against the backdrop of rights culture, identity politics, and the logic of the market, religious formations are more differentiated, yet in another vein, also more standardized, in ever more competitive public spheres (Hackett 2005).[13] Moreover, the current anthropological emphasis on practice is needed to compensate for the Western propensity for 'belief' in interpreting religious freedom issues, and to mediate rights conflict, such as between women's rights and religious rights.

Conclusion

Current scholarship in the anthropology of religion is undoubtedly still indebted to those early monographs and frameworks developed by the likes of Sir Edward Evans-Pritchard, Émile Durkheim, Mary Douglas, and Clifford Geertz. However, the postmodern and postcolonial turns, compressions of time and space with globalization, and rise of 'multiculturalist' issues, have occasioned some significant rethinking and realignment. Determining the general provenance or parameters of religion in 'exotic' small-scale societies has ceased to preoccupy contemporary anthropologists. Some now see their contribution as being rather to reconsider modern, secular society as symbolically and culturally constituted, and as much based on the religious impulse as on reason.

Arguably, then, the increasingly composite nature of anthropological theorizing bodes well for more creative and critical explorations of religious expression, practice, and transformation in a variety of contemporary locations. Current notions of (anthropological) theory as emphasizing the salience of holism, context, practice, and relations of power, and incorporating 'a critique of its own locations, positions and interests' (Moore 1999: 9–10), are clearly invaluable for the academic study of religion more generally. This 'critically productive discomfort' at the heart of the anthropological enterprise – to end with another wonderful turn of phrase from Michael Herzfeld – 'removes anthropology from the role of referee in a game of truth in which there are no winners' (2001: 88). In sum, as stated at the outset, anthropological theory and method appear increasingly well positioned to respond to such pressing social and cultural issues as identity, difference, conflict, and livelihood as they are mediated by religion(s) in our globalizing world.

Notes

1 The Society for the Anthropology of Religion was formally created in the American Anthropological Association in 2000 (http://www.uwgb.edu/sar/). Shortly after that, an Anthropology of Religion Consultation was inaugurated in the American Academy of Religion.

2   It may also derive from personal 'stock-taking' by individual authors at the conclusion of their careers, and their concern to transcend latent interpretations of religion as irrational, as Sarah Caldwell indicates in her insightful review of five major publications in the 1990s (Caldwell 1999).

3   For historical surveys of the field, see Bennett 1996; Morris 1987, and for accessible recent textbooks, see Bowie 2000; Klass 1995; Klass and Weisgrau 1999, and for readers, see Glazier 1999; Glazier and Flowerday 2003; Lambek 2002; Hackett 2001.

✓ 4   See, also, the various essays on their field experiences by religion scholars in a special issue of *Method and Theory in the Study of Religion* 13,1 (2001).

5   Cf. my own reflections on the limitations of my early training in the academic study of religion for conducting field-based research on religion in Nigeria (Hackett 2001).

6   Cf. Robert M. Baum's piece on the ethical considerations of doing fieldwork on a secessionist religious movement in the context of a religiously intolerant state (Baum 2001).

7   For helpful overviews of shamanism and neo-shamanism, see (Vitebsky 1995; Johnson 1995) and (van Binsbergen 1991).

8   *African Arts*, published quarterly for academics and the market, is a rich indication of the current vitality and diversity of the field.

9   http://www.fmch.ucla.edu/passporttoparadise.htm (accessed June 23, 2004).

10   The cross-cultural study of religion and nature will receive a major boost from Bron Taylor's and Jeffrey Kaplan's *Encyclopedia of Religion and Nature* project (New York: Cassell, 2005) http://www.religionandnature.com/ (accessed June 23, 2004).

11   The *Journal of Religion in Africa* has two thematic issues on media (26,4: 1998) (33,2: 2003).

12   See, in this regard, the work of anthropologist/*sangoma* (diviner-healer), Wim van Binsbergen (van Binsbergen 1991) http://www.shikanda.net/index.htm.

13   See the guest edited issue of *Culture and Religion* on 'Law and Human Rights,' edited by Rosalind I. J. Hackett and Winnifred F. Sullivan (6,1: 2005).

References

Abiodun, Rowland. 1994. 'Ase: Verbalizing and Visualizing Creative Power through Art.' *Journal of Religion in Africa* 24 (4): 294–322.

Adelson, Naomi. 2001. 'Reimagining Aboriginality: An Indigenous People's Response to Social Suffering.' In *Remaking a World: Violence, Social Suffering, and Recovery*, edited by V. Das, A. Kleinman, M. Lock, M. Ramphele, and P. Reynolds. Berkeley and Los Angeles: University of California Press.

Anderson, Jon W. 2003. 'New Media, New Publics: Reconfiguring the Public Sphere of Islam.' *Social Research* 70 (3): 887–906.

Anderson, Martha G., and Philip M. Peek, eds. 2002. *Ways of the Rivers: Arts and Environment of the Niger Delta*. Los Angeles: UCLA Fowler Museum of Cultural History.

Apter, Emily, and William Pietz. 1993. *Fetishism as Cultural Discourse*. Ithaca, NY: Cornell University Press.

Arthur, Linda Boynton, ed. 1999. *Religion, Dress and the Body*. Oxford: Berg.

—— 2000. *Undressing Religion: Commitment and Conversion from a Cross-Cultural Perspective*. Oxford: Berg.

✓ Asad, Talal. 1993. *Genealogies of Religion: Discipline and Reasons of Power in Christianity and Islam*. Baltimore: John Hopkins University Press.

—— 2003. *Formations of the Secular: Christianity, Islam, Modernity*. Stanford: Stanford University Press.

Barry, Brian. 2001. *Culture and Equality: An Egalitarian Critique of Multiculturalism*. Cambridge, MA: Harvard University Press.

Bastian, Misty. 1993. '"Bloodhounds Who Have No Friends": Witchcraft and Locality in the Nigerian Popular Press.' In *Modernity and its Malcontents: Ritual and Power in Postcolonial Africa*, edited by J. Comaroff and J. Comaroff. Chicago: University of Chicago Press.

Baum, Robert M. 2001. 'The Ethics of Religious Studies Research in the Context of the Religious Intolerance of the State: An Africanist Perspective.' *Method and Theory in the Study of Religion* 13 (1): 12–23.

Bell, Catherine. 1992. *Ritual Theory, Ritual Practice*. New York: Oxford University Press.

Bennett, Clinton. 1996. *In Search of the Sacred: Anthropology and the Study of Religions*. London: Cassell.

Boddy, Janice. 1994. 'Spirit Possession Revisited: Beyond Instrumentality.' *Annual Review of Anthropology* 24: 407–434.

Bongmba, Elias Kifon. 2001. *African Witchcraft and Otherness: A Philosophical and Theological Critique of Intersubjective Relations*. Albany, NY: State University of New York Press.

Booth, Ken. 1999. 'Three Tyrannies.' In *Human Rights in Global Politics*, edited by T. Dunne and N. J. Wheeler. New York: Cambridge University Press.

Bornstein, Erica. 2002. 'Developing Faith: Theologies of Economic Development in Zimbabwe.' *Journal of Religion in Africa* 32 (1): 4–31.

Bowen, John Richard. 2003. *Islam, Law, and Equality in Indonesia: An Anthropology of Public Reasoning*. New York: Cambridge University Press.

Bowie, Fiona. 2000. *The Anthropology of Religion*. Oxford: Blackwell.

Brown, Karen McCarthy. 1991. *Mama Lola: A Vodou Priestess in Brooklyn*. Berkeley: University of California Press.

Brown, Michael F. 1997. *The Channeling Zone: American Spirituality in an Anxious Age*. Cambridge, MA: Harvard University Press.

Caldwell, Sarah. 1999. 'Transcendence and Culture: Anthropologists Theorize Religion.' *Religious Studies Review* 25 (3): 227–232.

Ciekawy, Diane. 1998. 'Witchcraft in Statecraft: Five Technologies of Power in Coastal Kenya.' *African Studies Review* 41:119–141.

Classen, Constance. 1993. *Worlds of Sense: Exploring the Senses in History and Across Cultures*. New York: Routledge.

Coleman, Simon. 2000. *The Globalization of Charismatic Christianity*. Cambridge: Cambridge University Press.

Comaroff, Jean. 1985. *Body of Power, Spirit of Resistance*. Chicago: University of Chicago Press.

——, and John L. Comaroff. 1991. *Of Revelation and Revolution*. Vol. 1. *Christianity, Colonialism, and Consciousness in South Africa*. Chicago: University of Chicago Press.

—— 1992. *Ethnography and the Historical Imagination*. Boulder, CO: Westview.

—— eds. 1993. *Modernity and Its Malcontents: Ritual and Power in Postcolonial Africa*. Chicago: University of Chicago Press.

Coote, Jeremy and Anthony Shelton, eds. 1994. *Anthropology Art and Aesthetics, (Oxford Studies in the Anthropology of Cultural Forms)*. New York: Oxford University Press.

Corten, André, and Ruth Marshall-Fratani, eds. 2001. *Between Babel and Pentecost: Transnational Pentecostalism in Africa and Latin America*. Bloomington, IN: Indiana University Press.

Cowan, Jane K, Marie-Benedicte Dembour, and Richard A. Wilson, eds. 2001. *Culture and Rights: Anthropological Perspectives*. New York: Cambridge University Press.

Csordas, Thomas J. 1997. *Language, Charisma, and Creativity: The Ritual Life of a Religious Movement*. Berkeley and Los Angeles: University of California Press.

—— 2002. *Body/Meaning/Healing (Contemporary Anthropology of Religion)*. New York: Palgrave Macmillan.

Das, Veena, Arthur Kleinman, Margaret Lock, Mamphela Ramphele, and Pamela Reynolds, eds. 2001. *Remaking a World: Violence, Social Suffering, and Recovery*. Berkeley and Los Angeles: University of California Press.

DeBernardi, Jean. 1999. 'Spiritual Warfare and Territorial Spirits: The Globalization and Localization of a Practical Theology.' *Religious Studies and Theology* 18 (2): 66–96.

✓ Dempsey, Corinne. 2000. 'Religion and Representation in Recent Ethnographies.' *Religious Studies Review* 26 (1):37–42.

Devisch, René. 1998. 'Treating the Affect by Remodelling the Body in a Yaka Healing Cult.' In *Bodies and Persons: Comparative Perspectives from Africa and Melanesia*, edited by M. Lambek, and A. Strathern. New York: Cambridge University Press.

Dijk, Rijk van, and Peter Pels. 1996. 'Contested Authorities and the Politics of Perception: Deconstructing the Study of Religion in Africa.' In *Postcolonial Identities in Africa*, edited by R. Werbner and T. Ranger. London and New Jersey: Zed Books.

Douglas, Mary. 1970. *Natural Symbols: Explorations in Cosmology*. New York: Pantheon Books (Random House).

—— 1975. *Implicit Meanings*. London: Routledge.

Durkheim, Émile. 1965 [1912]. *The Elementary Forms of the Religious Life*. New York: The Free Press.

Eickelman, Dale F., and Armando Salvatore. 2002. 'The Public Sphere and Muslim Identities.' *European Journal of Sociology* 43: 92–115.

Evans-Pritchard, E. E. 1937. *Witchcraft, Oracles and Magic Among the Azande*. Oxford: Clarendon Press.

—— 1974 [1956]. *Nue-Religion*. New York: Oxford University Press.

Fabian, Johannes. 1983. *Time and the Other: How Anthropology Makes its Object*. New York: Columbia University Press.

—— 2001. *Anthropology with an Attitude: Critical Essays*. Stanford: Stanford University Press.

Fernandez, James W. 1982. *Bwiti: An Ethnography of the Religious Imagination in Africa*. Princeton, NJ: Princeton University Press.

Finnstrom, Sverker. 2003. *Living with Bad Surroundings: War and Existential Uncertainty in Acholiland, Northern Uganda*. Vol. 35, *Uppsala Studies in Cultural Anthropology*. Uppsala: Acta Universitatis Upsaliensis.

Frazer, James. 1996 [1890]. *The Golden Bough*. New York: Touchstone Books.

Geertz, Armin. 2003. 'Ethnohermeneutics and Worldview Analysis in the Study of Hopi Indian Religion.' *Numen* 50 (3):308–348.

Geertz, Clifford. 1973. 'Religion as a Cultural System.' In *The Interpretation of Cultures*, edited by C. Geertz. New York: Basic Books.

Gellner, David N. 1999. 'Anthropological Approaches.' In *Approaches to the Study of Religion*, edited by P. Connolly. London: Cassell.

Geschiere, Peter. 1997. *The Modernity of Witchcraft: Politics and the Occult in Postcolonial Africa*. Charlottesville: University Press of Virginia.

Gill, Sam D. 1998. *Storytracking: Texts, Stories, and Histories of Central Australia*. New York: Oxford University Press.

Ginsberg, Faye, Lila Abu-Lughod, and Brian Larkin, eds. 2002. *Media Worlds: Anthropology on New Terrain*. Los Angeles and Berkeley: University of California Press.

Glazier, Stephen D., ed. 1999. *Anthropology of Religion: A Handbook*. New York: Praeger.

——, and Charles A. Flowerday, eds. 2003. *Selected Readings in the Anthropology of Religion: Theoretical and Methodological Essays*. New York: Praeger.

Griaule, Marcel. 1938. *Masques Dogons*. Vol. 33. Paris: Université de Paris, Travaux et Mémoires de l'Institut d'Ethnologie.

Hackett, Rosalind I. J. 1996. *Art and Religion in Africa*. London: Cassell.

—— 2001. 'Field Envy: Or, the Perils and Pleasures of Doing Fieldwork.' *Method and Theory in the Study of Religion* 13 (1): 98–109.

—— 2003. 'Discourses of Demonisation in Africa.' *Diogenes* 50 (3): 61–75.

✓ —— 2005. 'Mediated Religion in South Africa: Balancing Air-time and Rights Claims.' In *Media, Religion and the Public Sphere*, edited by B. Meyer, and A. Moors. Bloomington, IN: Indiana University Press.

Harding, Susan. 2000. *The Book of Jerry Fallwell*. Princeton, NJ: Princeton University Press.

Harrison, Faye V., ed. 1991. *Decolonizing Anthropology: Moving Further Toward an Anthropology for Liberation*. Washington, DC: Association of Black Anthropologists/American Anthropological Association.

Hastrup, Kirsten. 1995. *A Passage to Anthropology*. New York: Routledge.

——, and George Ulrich, eds. 2001. *Discrimination and Toleration: New Perspectives, International Studies in Human Rights*. The Hague: Martinus Nijhoff.

Hefner, Robert W. 2000. *Civil Islam: Muslims and Democratization in Indonesia*. Princeton, NJ: Princeton University Press.

Herzfeld, Michael. 2001. *Anthropology: Theoretical Practice in Culture and Society*. Oxford: Blackwell.

Heusch, Luc de. 1982. *The Drunken King Or, the Origin of the State*. Bloomington, IN: Indiana University Press.

Horton, Robin. 1993. 'African Traditional Thought and Western Science.' In *Patterns of Thought in Africa and the West: Essays on Magic, Religion and Science*, edited by R. Horton. New York: Cambridge University Press.

Hussain, Monirul, and Lipi Ghosh, eds. 2002. *Religious Minorities in South Asia: Selected Essays on Post-Colonial Situations*. New Delhi: Manak.

Jackson, Michael. 1989. *Paths Toward a Clearing: Radical Empiricism and Ethnographic Inquiry*. Bloomington, IN: Indiana University Press.

—— 1995. *At Home in the World*. Raleigh, NC: Duke University Press.

Johnson, Paul C. 1995. 'Shamanism from Ecuador to Chicago: A Case Study in New Age Ritual Appropriation.' *Religion* 25: 163–178.

—— 2002a. 'Migrating Bodies, Circulating Signs: Brazilian Candomblé, the Garifuna of the Caribbean, and the Category of Indigenous Religions.' *History of Religions* 41 (4): 301–327.

—— 2002b. *Secrets, Gossip, and Gods: The Transformation of Brazilian Candomblé*. New York: Oxford University Press.

Kapferer, Bruce. 1991 [1983]. *A Celebration of Demons: Exorcism and the Aesthetics of Healing in Sri Lanka*. 2nd edn. Providence, RI/ Washington, DC: Berg/Smithsonian Institution Press.

Klass, Morton. 1995. *Ordered Universes: Approaches to the Anthropology of Religion*. Boulder, CO: Westview Press.

——, and Maxine K. Weisgrau, eds. 1999. *Across the Boundaries of Belief*. Boulder, CO: Westview Press.

Lambek, Michael. 1993. *Knowledge and Practice in Mayotte: Local Discourses of Islam, Sorcery, and Spirit Possession*. Toronto: University of Toronto Press.

—— 1998. 'Body and Mind in Mind, Body and Mind in Body: Some Anthropological Interventions in a Long Conversation.' In *Bodies and Persons: Comparative Perspectives from Africa and Melanesia*, edited by M. Lambek and A. Strathern. New York: Cambridge University Prss.

—— ed. 2002. *A Reader in the Anthropology of Religion*. Malden, MA: Blackwell.

——, and Andrew Strathern, eds. 1998. *Bodies and Persons: Comparative Perspectives from Africa and Melanesia*. New York: Cambridge University Press.

Lattas, Andrew. 1998. *Cultures of Secrecy: Reinventing Race in Bush Kaliai Cargo Cults*. Madison, WI: University of Wisconsin Press.

Lévi-Strauss, Claude. 1963. *Structural Anthropology*. New York: Basic Books.

Lewis, I. M. 1976. *Social Anthropology in Perspective*. Harmondsworth, Middlesex, UK: Penguin.

—— 1986. *Religion in Context*. Cambridge: Cambridge University Press.

—— 1989. *Ecstatic Religion*. 2nd ed. New York: Routledge.

Lock, Margaret. 1997. 'Cultivating the Body: Anthropology and Epistemologies of Bodily Practice and Knowledge.' *Annual Review of Anthropology* 22: 133–155.

Low, Setha M., and Denise Lawrence-Zuniga, eds. 2003. *The Anthropology of Space and Place: Locating Culture*. New York: Blackwell.

Luhrmann, Teresa M. 1989. *Persuasions of the Witch's Craft: Ritual Magic in Contemporary England.* Cambridge, MA: Harvard University Press.

MacGaffey, Wyatt. 1983. *Modern Kongo Prophets: Religion in a Plural Society.* Bloomington, IN: Indiana University Press.

Mahmood, Cynthia Kepley. 2003. 'Agenda for an Anthropology of Peace.' *Anthropology News*: 8.

Malinowski, Bronislaw. 1954 [1925]. *Magic, Science and Religion and Other Essays.* Garden City, NY: Doubleday.

Masquelier, Adeline. 2001. *'Prayer Has Spoiled Everything': Possession, Power, and Identity in an Islamic Town of Niger.* Durham, NC: Duke University Press.

Meyer, Birgit. 1999. *Translating the Devil: Religion and Modernity among the Ewe in Ghana.* Edinburgh: Edinburgh University Press.

——, and Annelies Moors, eds. 2005. *Religion, Media, and the Public Sphere.* Indiana: Indiana University Press.

Moore, Henrietta. 1988. *Feminism and Anthropology.* London: Polity Press.

—— 1996. *Space, Text, and Gender: An Anthropological Study of the Marakwet of Kenya.* New York: The Guildford Press.

—— ed. 1999. *Anthropological Theory Today.* Cambridge: Polity Press.

Morphy, Howard. 1992. *Ancestral Connections.* Chicago: University of Chicago Press.

Morris, Brian. 1987. *Anthropological Studies of Religion: An Introductory Text.* New York: Cambridge University Press.

Myers, Fred. 2002. *Painting Culture: The Making of an Aboriginal High Art.* Durham, NC: Duke University Press.

Nagata, Judith. 2001. 'Beyond Theology: Toward an Anthropology of "Fundamentalism".' *American Anthropologist* 102 (2): 481–498.

Needham, Rodney. 1972. *Belief, Language and Experience.* Oxford: Blackwell.

Niehaus, Isak. 2001. 'Witchcraft in the New South Africa.' In *Witchcraft, Power and Politics: Exploring the Occult in the South African Lowveld*, edited by I. Niehaus, E. Mohlala and K. Shokane. Sterling, VA: Pluto Press.

Nooter, Mary (Polly) H., ed. 1993. *Secrecy: African Art that Conceal and Reveals.* New York: The Museum for African Art.

Nordstrom, Carolyn. 1997. 'The Eye of the Storm: From War to Peace-Examples from Sri Lanka and Mozambique.' In *Cultural Variation in Conflict Resolution: Alternatives to Violence*, edited by D. P. Fry and K. Bjorkqvistm. Mahway, NJ: Lawrence Erlbaum Associates.

Nye, Malory. 2001. *Multiculturalism and Minority Religions in Britain: Krishna Consciousness, Religious Freedom, and the Politics of Location.* London: Curzon.

Palmié, Stephan. 2002. *Wizards and Scientists: Explorations in Modernity and Afro-Cuban Tradition.* Durham, NC: Duke University Press.

Peacock, James L. 1986. *The Anthropological Lens: Harsh Light, Soft Focus.* New York: Cambridge University Press.

Pemberton III, John, ed. 2000. *Insight and Artistry in African Divination.* Washington, DC: Smithsonian Institution.

Pigg, Stacy Leigh. 1996. 'The Credible and the Credulous: the Question of "Villagers' Beliefs" in Nepal.' *Cultural Anthropology* 11 (2): 160–201.

Radcliffe-Brown, Arthur Reginald. 1952. *Structure and Function in Primitive Society.* Glencoe, IL: The Free Press.

Robbins, Joel. 2003. 'What is a Christian? Notes Toward an Anthropology of Christianity.' *Religion* 33 (3): 191–291.

Roberts, Allen F., Mary Nooter Roberts, Gassia Armenian, and Ousmane Gueye. 2003. *A Saint in the City: Sufi Arts of Urban Senegal.* Los Angeles: Fowler Museum of Cultural History, University of California Los Angeles.

Sered, Susan. 1999. *Women of the Sacred Groves: Divine Priestesses of Okinawa.* New York: Oxford University Press.

Shaw, Rosalind. 1995. 'Feminist Anthropology and the Gendering of Religious Studies.' In *Religion and Gender*, edited by U. King. Cambridge, USA: Blackwell.

—— 2002. *Memories of the Slave Trade: Ritual and the Historical Imagination in Sierra Leone.* Chicago: The University of Chicago Press.

——, and Charles Stewart, eds. 1994. *Syncretism/Anti-Syncretism: The Politics of Religious Synthesis.* New York: Routledge.

Soares, Benjamin F. 2004. 'Islam and Public Piety in Mali.' In *Public Islam and the Common Good*, edited by A. Salvatore and D. F. Eickelman. Leiden: Brill.

Sommers, Marc. 2000. 'Urbanization, Pentecostalism, and Urban Refugee Youth in Africa.' Boston: Boston University African Studies Center.

Spickard, James V., S. Shawn Landres, and Meredith B. McGuire, eds. 2002. *Personal Knowledge and Beyond: Reshaping the Ethnography of Religion.* New York: New York University Press.

Starrett, Gregory. 2003. 'Violence and the Rhetoric of Images.' *Cultural Anthropology* 18 (3): 398–428.

Stoller, Paul. 1989. *The Taste of Ethnographic Things.* Philadelphia: University of Pennsylvania Press.

—— 1995. *Embodying Colonial Memories: Spirit Possession, Power and the Hauka in West Africa.* New York: Routledge.

—— 1997. *Sensuous Scholarship.* Philadelphia: University of Pennsylvania Press.

Tambiah, Stanley J. 1996. *Leveling Crowds: Ethnonationalist Conflicts and Collective Violence in South Asia.* Berkeley and Los Angeles: University of California.

Taussig, Michael. 1987. *Shamanism, Colonialism and the Wild Man.* Chicago: Chicago University Press.

Tsing, Anna Lowenhaupt. 1993. *In the Realm of the Diamond Queen.* Princeton, NJ: Princeton University Press.

Turner, Edith, ed. 1985. *On the Edge of the Bush: Anthropology as Experience.* Tucson, AZ: University of Arizona Press.

Turner, Victor W. 1974. *Dramas, Fields and Metaphors: Symbolic Action in Human Society.* Ithaca, NY: Cornell University Press.

——, and Edward M. Bruner, eds. 1986. *The Anthropology of Experience.* Urbana, IL: University of Illinois Press.

Tylor, Edward B. 1970 [1871]. *Religion in Primitive Society.* Gloucester, MA: Peter Smith.

van Binsbergen, Wim. 1991. 'Becoming a Sangoma: Religious Anthropological Field-Work in Francistown, Botswana.' *Journal of Religion in Africa* 21 (4): 309–344.

—— 2003. *Intercultural Encounters: African and Anthropological Lessons towards a Philosophy of Interculturality.* Berlin/Muenster: LIT.

Van Gennep, Arnold. 1960. *The Rites of Passage.* Translated by M. B. Vizedom and G. L. Caffee. Chicago: University of Chicago Press.

Veer, van der Peter, ed. 1996. *Conversion to Modernities: the Globalization of Christianity.* New York: Routledge.

Vertovec, Steve. 2000. *The Hindu Diaspora: Comparative Patterns.* New York: Routledge.

Vitebsky, Piers. 1995. *The Shaman: Voyages of the Soul, Trance, Ecstasy and Healing from Siberia to the Amazon.* London and Basingstoke: Macmillan in association with Duncan Baird Publishers.

Whitehouse, Harvey, and James Laidlaw. 2004. *Ritual and Memory: Toward a Cognitive Anthropology of Religion.* Walnut Creek, CA: AltaMira.

Worsley, Peter. 1968. *The Trumpet Shall Sound: A Study of 'Cargo' Cults in Melanesia.* New York: Schocken Books.

Chapter 9

Psychology of religion

Dan Merkur

The psychology of religion studies the phenomena of religion in so far as they may be understood psychologically. Religions and their denominations differ regarding the extent of the psychologizing that they each embrace, tolerate, and reject. For many religious devotées, psychological understanding is inherently antagonistic to religion because it ascribes to the human mind what those devotées credit to more-than-human agencies. They view the psychology of religion as a program that reduces religion to psychology. Other devotées are instead sympathetic to the psychology of religion. They value critical research as an irreplaceable means for the purification of religion from idolatry of the merely human.

Like psychology in general, the psychology of religion is an umbrella term for the findings of several, mutually exclusive schools of thought, each with its own research agenda and methodology. The major disciplinary affiliations include: the academic study of religion; academic psychology; psychoanalysis; analytic psychology; and transpersonal psychology. These several approaches to the psychological study of religion tend to be pursued in isolation from each other, as non-communicating and mutually disdainful subdisciplines. A useful way to comprehend both their strengths and their differences is to attend to the questions that they seek to answer. The overall project of each school of thought determines both what data it addresses and what methodologies it considers appropriate.

Psychology in the service of the history of religion

Psychologically oriented studies by historians of religion adhere to the methodological phenomenology of the history of religion in general. The manifest contents of religious experience are discussed, but no mention is ever made of the unconscious. The question of primary interest for this school of research has been whether psychology can explain otherwise inexplicable features of the historical record of the world's many and diverse religions. The psychology of religion, so conceived, subserves the writing of the history of religion, addresses the religious past more frequently than the religious present, and has been minutely attentive to cross-cultural findings in world religions.

Rejecting theories of cultural evolution that contrasted 'magic' and 'religion', Rudolf Otto (1932) suggested that experiences of the holy or 'numinous' were the defining characteristics of religion. For Otto (1950 [1917]), the numinous was a *sui generis* category of human experience. The quality of numinosity is sometimes experienced as awe and urgency at the mystery and immanent majesty of the Wholly Other; it may alternatively be known as a fascination at an august and transcendent 'Something More'. Otto's student and colleague, Nathan Söderblom (1933), argued that experiences of the numinous explained the veneration of sacred books. The world's scriptures are not held to be holy merely because of the ideas that they contain. Rather, the texts are sacred because their ideas concern living powers. Scriptures pertain to spirits, gods, or God that people encounter in personal religious experiences. When the numina cease to be experienced, interest in the books fails.

Many historians of religion pursued similar lines of inquiry with increasing detail. Söderblom's student Ernst Arbman (1939) argued that myths are venerated because the gods that they portray are credited with invisible responsibility for the fortuitous events of everyday life. Should belief in providential miracles fail, however, the myths decline into folktales. Biblical scholars noted that some Israelite prophets were described in fashions consistent with physically active trance states. Other ancient prophets were clearly not in trances. Some biblical data pointed to hypnagogic states, which occur between waking and falling asleep. Other prophets may have experienced inspirations during dream-like states of deep trance. Attention was also called to the ecstatic, experiential side of classical Greek religion; and the distinctive features of shamanism were noted in a variety of contexts. Zoroaster, the prophet who reformed ancient Iranian religion, was alleged to have been a shaman; and the legend of the opening of Muhammad's breast was treated as a folklore motif that described a shamanic initiation. The character of Vainamoinen in the Finnish national epic, *The Kalevala* was identified as a shaman; and detailed studies were made of Siberian, Lapp, Native American, and other cultural variations of shamanism, past and present.

Underlying these psychologically oriented studies in the history of religion is the axiomatic assumption that most people are religious because they personally have religious experiences. Good and bad fortune may be attributed to demons, spirits, gods, God, karma, or what you will. Both conversions and subsequent encounters with numinous beings and numinous states of existence may proceed through dreams, visions, voices, or mystical unions. Notice needs also to be taken of occasional, highly emotionally charged rites. These orders of religious experience are, for those who have them, the very core of religion itself. In this approach to religion, people believe in myths, they subscribe to theologies, they engage in rites, precisely because they have religious experiences. For devotees, religious experiences confirm, prove, modify, extend – in short, motivate – the balance of what religion entails.

Two Swedish scholars who were trained by Söderblom formalized the axiomatic assumption with detailed psychological theories. Ernst Arbman argued that religious trance states, which he documented on a worldwide basis, varied in their contents in accord with the religious beliefs and expectations of the devotée. The religious belief complex was converted by the trance state from a series of ideas into a vivid, dream-like experience. Differences among visions, voices, automatic behaviour, stigmata, solipsistic mystical unions, and all other trance phenomena, reflected differences in the pre-trance beliefs and expectations.

Hjalmar Sundén instead adapted the notion of a 'social role' from its original context in reference to interpersonal behavior as observed by social psychologists. The term had greater application in the study of religion, he maintained, than in explaining the roles of shaman, prophet, priest, lay person, mystic, and so forth. Sundén applied the concept to the apparent behavior of a greater-than-human personality, such as a spirit, angel, or God, as it manifests in a religious experience. Sundén proposed that people may learn a variety of roles that may manifest in the course of their religious experiences.

The theories of Arbman and Sundén both imply that religious experiences are learned behaviour, whose differences are to be sought in the contents of the learning. It then follows that whether discussion is to be made of belief complexes or religious roles, analysis of the learned materials can be pursued competently by historians, without need for special training in psychology. This conclusion is a product of historians' methods, however. Only when the psychology of religion is limited to the identification of patterns in historical religious data does psychological expertise become unnecessary.

Religion as group pathology

Sigmund Freud (1856–1939), the founder of psychoanalysis, once privately remarked, 'Mankind has always known that it possesses spirit: I had to show it that there are also instincts'. A few sentences later, he went on to reject the validity of religion. 'Religion originates in the helplessness and anxiety of childhood and early manhood. It cannot be otherwise'. The apparent contradiction is to be explained by the special senses in which Freud referred to spirit and religion. For Freud, spirit (in German, Geist) was an objectively existing intellectual power abroad in the cosmos that is responsible for life, consciousness, and telepathy. Religion, by contrast, was defined, in conformance with liberal nineteenth-century Christian and Jewish theologies, as a 'system of doctrines and promises' concerning 'a careful Providence' that is imagined 'in the figure of an enormously exalted father'. Freud saw both magic and religion as misunderstandings of the nature of spirit that substituted infantile hopes and wishes for a scientifically valid parapsychology.

Freud wrote very little about spirit, but extensively about magic and religion. His writings regularly addressed the questions: What is religion? And why are people religious? His answer was always that religion was an error, a cultural neurosis that a rational and realistic person ought to abandon.

Freud expressed his basic view of religion in a dense paragraph in 'Leonardo da Vinci and a Memory of His Childhood' (1957 [1910]):

> Psycho-analysis has made us familiar with the intimate connection between the father-complex and belief in God; it has shown us that a personal God is, psychologically, nothing other than an exalted father, and it brings us evidence every day of how young people lose their religious beliefs as soon as their father's authority breaks down. Thus we recognize that the roots of the need for religion are in the parental complex; the almighty and just God, and kindly Nature, appear to us as grand sublimations of father and mother, or rather as revivals and restorations of the young child's ideas of them. Biologically speaking, religiousness is to be traced to the small human child's long-drawn-out helplessness and need of help; and when at a later date he perceives how truly forlorn and weak he is when confronted with the great forces of life, he feels his condition as he did in childhood, and attempts to deny his own despondency by a regressive revival of the forces which protected his infancy.

With very few changes, Freud maintained the same position for the remainder of his life. Religion functions primarily to offer consolation for human helplessness. The consolation is fictional. God is a fantasy that is based on infantile memories of father and mother and motivated by human helplessness.

In an essay entitled 'Obsessive Actions and Religious Practices' (1959 [1907]), Freud noted several parallels between personal rites that occur as symptoms of neurosis and the public rites of religions. He suggested that both arise as symbolic substitutes for unconscious guilt. In neurotic rites, the unconscious guilt is sexual; in religious rites, it is a response to egoism.

In *Totem and Taboo* (1958 [1913]), Freud expanded his argument to book length. He began by summarizing the anthropological evidence that incest is prohibited in aboriginal Australian cultures. Noting the widespread practice of avoiding mothers-in-law, Freud commented that extreme forms of avoidance had been added in these cases to a core prohibition of incest, in much the same irrational manner that obsessional neurotics multiply inhibitions. Because no one bothers to prohibit anything that is not desired, the two basic taboos of aboriginal Australian religions – not to kill the totem animal, and not to marry within the clan – indicate the content of the oldest and most powerful human desires. These desires are to kill the ancestral totem animal and to commit incest. Freud also connected guilt over the desire for patricide with the widespread belief in, fear of, and devotion toward ancestral spirits. Working with the assumption, widely shared at the time, that aboriginal Australian religion was a surviving instance of the most primitive form of religion, Freud located the Oedipus complex – a boy's unconscious wish to kill his father and have sex with his mother – at the core of the evolution of religion.

Like many of his contemporaries, Freud treated magic and religion as categorically separate phenomena. Freud maintained that magic was to be explained by the 'omnipotence of thoughts', a phenomenon that is found in obsessional neurosis in which thoughts are projected onto and substituted for reality. Magic is narcissistic in that it attributes supernatural power to the self, rather than to ancestral ghosts, totem spirits, and so forth. Because magic does not presuppose the existence of personal spirits, as religion does, Freud treated it as an older, pre-Oedipal stage in cultural evolution. In locating spirit outside the self, religion is less incorrect than magic, although still categorically short of a realistic, scientific worldview. Freud considered totem animals to be earlier than anthropomorphic deities, because they are more fantastic. *Totem and Taboo* continued with a demonstration that the chief features of animism and magic occur normally in childhood; and concluded with a speculative reconstruction of how the Oedipus complex may have evolved in the species.

In subsequent presentations, Freud repeatedly revised his theory of conscience. He discarded his notion of 'social instincts', introduced the concept of personally variable 'ego ideals', and settled finally on a partly conscious and partly unconscious process that he termed the 'superego'. In all cases, religion arose through the repression and symbolic displacement of unconscious guilt, where neurosis arose through the repression and symbolic displacement of sexual instincts.

In *Group Psychology and the Analysis of the Ego* (1955 [1921]), Freud created a theoretic bridge between individual and group psychology. He suggested that group members share an ego ideal that consists of or is embodied by the group leader. The devotion to the leader provides cohesion to the group, despite the rivalry that is also inevitably present. To illustrate the processes of group psychology, Freud used the examples of an army and the Roman Catholic Church.

Freud's next major statement on religion, *The Future of an Illusion* (1961 [1927]), was written as an imaginary dialogue with a proponent of religion. To his previous accounts of religion as a consolation, Freud added several new points. Civilization depends on coercion and the renunciation of instinct. Prohibitions are initially external and imposed on the individual, but through the course of a child's development they are internalized as the superego. The superego houses both personal ideals that can be a source of rivalry and group ideals that are the basis for forming cultural units. Religious ideals play an important role in the promotion of civilization through their internalization in the superego.

The valuable socializing function of religion does not mitigate the fallacies of its contents. Religion has its basis in the anthropomorphizing of nature. Religion asserts that external reality is subject to personal spirits and gods, on whom one may safely depend as in childhood, one depended on one's parents. The belief that nature is benign and parental is an illusion. The illusion can be neither verified nor falsified; its treatment as true proceeds out of the wish that it were so, rather than through logical necessity. The illusion is maintained at the cost of denying the corresponding reality. Diagnosing religion as 'the universal obsessional neurosis of humanity' that intimidates the intelligence in order to maintain its illusions, Freud predicted that religion would everywhere be abandoned in response to the advancement of science. At the same time, he acknowledged that the veneration of nature had historically promoted the close observations that led to the rise of natural science.

In *Civilization and Its Discontents* (1961 [1930]), Freud repeated his arguments concerning the regulatory function of religion, but placed greater emphasis on its punitive dimension. Where, in 1927, Freud had written of the superego internalizing civilization, in 1930, he stated that the superego turns aggression against the self. It is this diversion of aggression into guilt that makes civilization possible. Art, religion, and other illusions flourish under the protection, as it were, of the superego. Religion compares badly with art, however, 'since it imposes equally on everyone its own path to the acquisition of happiness and protection from suffering. Its technique consists in depressing the value of life and distorting the picture of the real world in a delusional manner – which presupposes an intimidation of the intelligence'. In keeping with his increased pessimism, Freud now called religion a 'mass-delusion' – a malignancy significantly greater than the merely fanciful error of an 'illusion'.

Freud also acknowledged that religion has a third function, additional to consolation and socialization. Religion permits instinctual wishes to be 'sublimated' through their diversion to social valued and refined ends. Freud viewed religion as second only to art in promoting culture through transformations of sexuality and aggression into civilized behaviour. Freud placed little weight on sublimations, however, saying 'their intensity is mild as compared with that derived from the sating of crude and primary instinctual impulses'. In his private correspondence with Oskar Pfister, Freud nevertheless acknowledged that pastoral psychology makes more efficient use than psychoanalysis of the therapeutic potential of sublimation.

Freud's trivialization of the religious function of sublimation was partly nominalistic. In keeping with his definition of religion as ethical theism, Freud asserted that the 'oceanic feeling' of mystical experience was not religious, but was connected with religion only secondarily. Freud's exclusion of mysticism from his discussions of religion may be contrasted, for example, with the many writers, from William James onward, who place the joys of mystical experience at the very centre of their psychologies of religion.

Unlike *Totem and Taboo* (1958 [1913]), which anthropologists regarded as amateurish but stimulating, Freud's *Moses and Monotheism* (1964 [1939]) made no useful contribution to modern Biblical criticism. Its rejection by academic scholarship has been unequivocal, and its thesis, that Moses was an Egyptian whose impositions on the Jews induced them to murder him, is perhaps best treated as a fantasy requiring psychoanalysis.

The book's addition to Freud's theory of religion consists of its analysis of the Mosaic commandment that prohibits the making of Divine images. Freud took the commandment to imply that Moses conceived of a God who has no form. Proceeding from this premise, Freud suggested that the abstract concept of God is derived from concrete images of God, through a 'triumph of intellectuality over sensuality or, strictly speaking, an instinctual renunciation'. Freud remarked that 'all such advances in intellectuality have as their consequence that the individual's self-esteem is increased' (p. 115).

Freud's view of religion exhibits his lifelong method of shaping a piece of theory to explain a piece of data, and gradually accumulating a great many pieces. There was no overall system. Many pieces cohere, but others do not. The total picture suffers, as is often remarked, from Freud's clinical orientation. He understood religion best in so far as religion resembled phenomena that he encountered among his patients: obsessive ritual behavior, delusional belief-systems, and the like. Freud partly or wholly neglected other features of religion.

Object relations and the revalorization of religion

Freud's questions – what is religion? why are people religious? is religion healthy? – have remained the major concerns of psychoanalytic writings on religion. Psychoanalysts quietly abandoned the most egregious features of Freud's position: his devotion to telepathy, his cultural evolutionism, and his amateurish Bible scholarship. His paradigm was otherwise retained by both classical psychoanalysts and psychoanalytic ego psychologists.

Oskar Pfister, a Lutheran pastor, psychoanalyst, and personal friend of Freud, was the first person to apply psychoanalytic principles to education. Pfister's major contributions (1923, 1948) to the study of religion had a clinical thrust. Where Freud saw religion as intrinsically pathological, Pfister saw psychoanalysis as a means to purify religion by identifying its morbid components. The neurotic aspects of religion could then be abandoned, and only healthy aspects retained.

Pfister's orientation was given powerful support by the clinical studies of Ana-Maria Rizzuto (1979), who noted that psychoanalytic patients' relations with God are complex, nuanced, and in process of continuous development, in a fashion that is consistent with their relations with other people. Rizzuto's finding has been amply confirmed by other psychoanalysts. The finding is inconsistent with Freud's theory that God is the exalted father. Were God a symbol that displaces memories of the father as he was seen by the young child, a person's relation with God would be fixated and unchanging in its infantilism. It would not be in process of continuing growth and development.

There are cases, however, when people's relations with God are fixated, in part or whole. In these cases, the fixations prove isomorphic with the fixations in the same people's relations with other people. They are cognitively and emotionally irrational in the same ways in their relations with God and with other people. Jacob Arlow (1995) has consequently referred to God as a transferential figure. Rather than to analyze a person's relation with the psychoanalyst, a person's relation with God can sometimes be analyzed to therapeutic ends. This clinical psychoanalytic finding is again inconsistent with Freud's diagnosis of morbidity. In at least some cases, religion can be therapeutic.

Because Freud's theories of religion cannot account for these clinical findings of religion's wholesomeness, contemporary psychoanalysts favour a revision of Freud's diagnosis. The preferred position was advanced by Donald W. Winnicott, a major contributor to the British school of psychoanalytic object relations theory. Winnicott began by drawing attention to the infant's special attachment to its 'first not-me possession', a cloth, teddy bear, or doll that the infant cannot bear to be without. Its importance for the infant is accepted by the family, given social validation through tolerant regard, and surrounded with appropriate ritualized behaviors. Winnicott contended that a 'transitional object' is, for the infant, both part of the infant and an external reality. Logically paradoxical, it is experientially coherent, for it belongs to 'an intermediate area of *experiencing* . . . which is not challenged, because no claim is made on its behalf except that it shall exist as a resting-place for the individual'.

Winnicott was primarily concerned with infancy, but in a remarkable intuitive leap he extrapolated from the clinical evidence to a general theory of culture. Alluding to Freud's designation of religion as an illusion, Winnicott revalorized illusion:

> *Illusion* . . . is allowed to the infant, and . . . in adult life is inherent in art and religion, and yet becomes the hallmark of madness when an adult puts too powerful a claim on the credulity of others, forcing them to acknowledge a sharing of illusion that is not their own. We can share a respect for *illusory experience*, and if we wish we may collect together and form a group on the basis of the similarity of our illusory experiences.

Winnicott asserted that illusory experiences range from the transitional objects of infancy through play to creativity and the whole of cultural life. Because illusory experiences are unavoidable, they must be considered normal and healthy. They remain projections that buffer the individual from reality. However, Freud's either/or distinction between inner (psychic) and external (physical) reality is overly simplistic. Illusory experiences form a third class of phenomena.

Paul W. Pruyser (1974), a pastoral psychologist, maintained that an individual's capacity for illusory experience determines 'a disposition or a talent for the numinous', as is also the case for artistic creativity and art appreciation. Not everyone needs or likes to develop the transitional sphere. Among those who do, differences in taste – which are partly constitutional and partly acquired – lead to different preferences among art, literature, drama, music, religious ideas, metaphysical speculation, and ethical propositions. Arguing in the tradition of the historians of religion Otto and van der Leeuw, Pruyser asserted the intrinsically religious character of 'limit situations' because they involve '*transcendence* and *mystery* . . . charged with cognitive, ontological, epistemological, and emotional implications'.

Pruyser emphasized that 'adequate reality-testing is needed to keep the transitional sphere properly bounded, and its content and language consensually validated'. Religions have historically permitted illusions to shade over into hallucination and delusion whenever 'excessive fantasy formation' has led to 'flagrant disregard of the obvious features of outer reality'. In Pruyser's view, the truth claims of religions may be valid if they are maintained as illusions – that is, as matters of faith – but they are definitely and necessarily false if they are presented as theological certainties.

Pfister's concern with the questions, 'What is sick? and what healthy in religion?', remains a major focus of clinical interest. The impact of religion on psychotherapy and the handling of religious issues in psychotherapy are pressing concerns for psychotherapists who work with religious clientele.

The psychological shaping of religion

The term 'applied psychoanalysis' refers to the application of clinical psychoanalytic theories to cultural data. The term implies that art, religion, literature, and other cultural expressions are used to illustrate and popularize theories that have been developed clinically. In keeping with this procedure, most psychoanalytic writings on religion seek to explain which stages of child development are at work in specific rituals and myths. Classical psychoanalysts assumed that rituals and myths were pathological symptoms of psychosexual fixations. Psychoanalytic ego psychologists introduced the view that different myths are of interest to people at different times in their lives, because the myths give symbolic expression to the developmental issues of different stages of life. Myths and other cultural expressions may be either wholesome or morbid. In both cases, they provide models in the use of symbols for the organization of their audiences' emotional lives.

Because these studies use religious data to illustrate developmental theories, they have rarely been of interest to academic students of religion. A notable exception is Erik Erikson's (1958) biography of Martin Luther, whose major contention was that Luther's adolescent rebellion against an abusive and domineering father was prototypical of his rebellion against the Roman Catholic Church. His personality both limited and promoted different aspects of his religion.

Spiritual awakening

A third major trend in the psychology of religion was begun by two founders of academic psychology, Edwin Diller Starbuck (1911 [1899]) and William James (1958 [1902]), but went into eclipse during the heyday of behaviourism. Familiar as Starbuck and James were with the evangelical tradition of American Protestantism, they conceptualized the psychology of religion, above all else, as the study of the process by which a non-religious person becomes religious. Where Freud had asked, 'What religious phenomena become coherent through their resemblance to psychopathology?', Starbuck and James implicitly asked, 'How does religion differ from irreligion? What psychological phenomena are uniquely religious, that is, are unlike any and all non-religious phenomena?'. These questions led them to study religious experiences.

In Starbuck's opinion, the spiritual path begins with conversion but culminates in a further experience termed sanctification. Because sin ceases to be tempting, evil habits are abandoned, altruism increases, and there is a sense of having achieved complete union with one's spiritual ideals.

James expanded Starbuck's model to address Catholicism as well as evangelical Protestantism. According to James, 'healthy-minded religion' develops straightforwardly, without dramatic processes. Because the healthy-minded are at peace with their own imperfections, they feel no need to undergo spiritual development in any meaningful sense of the term. It is only the sick soul that must be twice-born in order to attain its natural inner unity and peace. The divided self gains unity through conversion. Some conversions occur during mystical moments. Others do not. When conversion is not followed by backsliding but is permanent, the individual achieves saintliness – a quality that is characterized by asceticism, strength of soul, purity, and charity.

Following Starbuck and James, many studies were made of conversion, but the treatment of a theological category, 'conversion', as though it were a psychological one has proved unworkable. Discussions of religious conversion address three separate psychological phenomena: (1) a change from irreligiosity to religiosity; (2) a change of existing religiosity from conventional routine to personal and devout; and (3) a change of affiliation from one religion to another. Because studies of conversion often proceeded at cross-purposes with each other, the larger topic of spiritual transformation was neglected until the rise of humanistic and transpersonal psychology in the 1960s and 1970s.

A pioneer of humanistic psychology, Abraham Maslow (1964) suggested that people have a hierarchy of motives, that commence with physiological needs, safety, belongingness and love, and progress to less necessary objects of desire, such as self-esteem, satisfaction striving or growth motivation, the need to know, aesthetic needs, and Being-values. Maslow identified Being-values through an analysis of peak experiences, including mystical. The values included: truth, goodness, beauty, wholeness, dichotomy-transcendence, aliveness, uniqueness, necessity, completion, justice, order, simplicity, richness, effortlessness, playfulness, and self-sufficiency.

Maslow contended that psychological changes conform with progress along the hierarchy of values. The changes that are sought through psychotherapy serve to heal deficiencies in the areas of belongingness, love, and self-esteem. Their function is to end existing psychic pain. Psychotherapy may be considered successful when these motives are satisfied. It is also possible, however, for the personality to move beyond health into excellence, when the further motives for growth, knowledge, aesthetics, and Being-values come to the fore. Maslow adopted the term 'self-actualization' in order to discuss the achievement of these goals.

Maslow argued, and quantitative studies have since confirmed, that traditional religious beliefs and observances are obstacles to self-actualization, particularly if they are conservative. On the other hand, because self-actualized people tend to have mystical peak experiences, Maslow and several other psychologists assumed the converse, that the world's mystical paths are techniques, among other matters, for self-actualization. The term 'transpersonal' denoting progress beyond self, to achieve something more than self alone, was introduced by Roberto Assagioli, who had founded psychosynthesis decades earlier. As it was defined in the 1970s, the project of transpersonal psychology was to place spiritual transformation and spiritual direction, so far as possible, on cross-cultural and scientific footing.

Assagioli (1991) developed a longitudinal, psychodynamic account of a clinically observable process that he termed 'self-realization' or 'spiritual awakening'. The process begins with an existential crisis regarding the meaning of life that is often attended by resistance of all solutions. One or more religious experiences occur next. The experiences are typically euphoric and profoundly meaningful. Their occurrence terminates the existential crisis, but frequently precipitates a crisis of another sort. The newly discovered meaningfulness of spirituality is made the pretext of narcissistic inflation or grandiosity. Once the inflation wanes, depression may set in. The depression often has an ethical content of remorse over past moral failings. If the depression is intolerable, the religious experiences may be denied, much as ideas born of alcoholic intoxication are discounted during subsequent sobriety. Alternatively, the newly appreciated spiritual values may be made the basis of behavioural change to embody the values. The reformation or transformation of character inevitably proceeds gradually, by small increments.

In many and perhaps most cases, spiritual awakenings do not proceed in uncomplicated fashions that would be consistent with Maslow's concept of a growth from mental health toward excellence. Because very few people are completely nonneurotic, most awakenings are complicated by pathological symptoms that arise out of unresolved conflicts within the personality. Christina and Stanislav Grof (1990) introduced the term, 'spiritual emergency', to denote a spiritual awakening that is complicated by psychopathology. The differences between a spiritual emergency and a psychiatric disorder include: absence of physical disease; absence of brain pathology; absence of organic impairment; intact, clear consciousness and coordination; continuing ability to communicate and cooperate; adequate pre-episode functioning; ability to relate and cooperate, often even during religious experiences; awareness of the intrapsychic nature of the process; sufficient trust to accept help and cooperate; ability to honor basic rules of therapy; absence of destructive or self-destructive ideas and tendencies; good cooperation in things related to physical health, basic maintenance, and hygienic rules. Spiritual emergencies are among the syndromes that have been recognized in the *Diagnostic and Statistical Manual IV* of the American Psychiatric Association as 'V62.89 Religious or Spiritual Problem'.

The conceptualization of single religious experiences in terms of creativity, commensurate with scientific and artistic achievement, was suggested by the social psychologists Daniel Batson and Larry Ventis (Batson, Schoenrade, and Ventis 1997). Merkur compared the longitudinal process of spiritual awakening with Wallas's classic model of four phases of creativity: (1) the establishment of a problem, for example, an existential crisis, or a developmental growth in intelligence; (2) the unconscious incubation of the problem's solution; (3) the manifestation of a creative solution as the content of one or more religious experiences, possibly precipitating a spiritual emergency; and (4) the refinement of the solution through its practical, behavioural implementation. In Merkur's (1999) model, religious experiences differ from the creative inspirations of painters, writers, musicians, scientists, and so forth, in having numinous 'limit situations' as their subject matter.

Some writers conceptualize spiritual awakening as spiritual in a metaphysical sense. In other cases, it is psychologized, for example, as self-actualization in Maslow's model or, alternatively, from Merkur's psychoanalytic perspective as a process of positive superego manifestation and integration.

Transpersonal psychotherapy

Because transpersonal psychology was unable to find a home in the academy, many practitioners came to depend for their income on private practices as psychotherapists. These financial constraints motivated a change in many transpersonalists' agendas. Rather than to research spiritual awakening, transpersonalists who were therapists came to promote spiritual practices as adjuncts to psychotherapy. Meditations, visualizations, prayer, and other religious practices were found to be useful in psychotherapy, for example, in learning self-observation, in cultivating self-discipline, and in building self-esteem.

Valuable as the procedures are clinically, the results are inevitably sectarian. Whichever meditations, visualizations, prayers, and so forth that a therapist enjoins on a client inevitably belong to one particular religion or another. The practices never belong to religion in general. Some transpersonal therapists are syncretistic in their borrowings; others confine themselves to the practices of a particular religious tradition.

The slippage of transpersonal psychology from the study into the practice of religion has given rise to a genre of apologetic literature. The writings claim that one or another tradition of religious mysticism (Zen, Sufism, Kabbalah, and so forth) is inherently therapeutic. Although the writings are published as psychology, they are better considered as theology.

Religious development

All authorities agree that religiosity takes different forms at different ages. No consensus has emerged, however, regarding the contents and duration of the stages. William W. Meissner, a Jesuit and a psychoanalyst, has argued that a person's religion reflects whatever may be the person's developmental stage at the time. Working, for example, with Erikson's model of the developmental growth of ego autonomy, Meissner suggested that faith and hope are issues in infancy. Contrition comes to the fore in early childhood. The central issues in later years are: penance and temperance in the kindergarten years; fortitude in grade school; humility in adolescence; the love of neighbors in young adulthood; service, zeal, and self-sacrifice in adulthood; and charity in maturity.

Recognizing that people's experiences are not necessarily limited to their current developmental issues, but may involve reversions to previous concerns, Meissner (1984) later proposed a typology of five modes of religious experience. The first is dominated by an absence of subject–object distinctions. The second reflects the worldview of toddlers. The veneration of idealized religious figures is necessary to sustain and maintain the sense of self. Faith is 'riddled with a sense of utter dependence, a terror of the omnipotence of the godhead, and a superstitious and magical need to placate by ritual and ceremonial'. The third mode reflects the anal stage of psychoanalytic theory. The self is cohesive, but efforts must be made to secure self-esteem.

Concepts tend to be concrete, literal, and one-dimensional. Religious figures are authoritative, and myths tend to be anthropomorphic. Religious concerns address the permitted and the prohibited, the fear of punishment for transgressions, and the dutiful performance of obligations and rituals. The fourth mode presupposes the consolidation of the superego and, with it, the internalization of conscience around age six. Ethics and social concerns are at a premium. Recognition is made of the diversity of authorities. Conflicts are resolved partly through compartmentalization but partly through reliance on one's own judgment. Meissner remarked that 'by far the largest portion of adult religious behavior falls into this modality'.

Meissner's fifth and final mode of religious experience becomes possible when still greater maturity has been attained. In the fifth mode, instinctual drives are managed successfully, so that the ego enjoys considerable autonomy. Anxiety is lessened dramatically and is largely restricted to realistic external concerns. Wisdom, empathy, humor, and creativity come to the fore, and conflicts tend to be resolved through synthesis rather than compartmentalization. 'The religious belief system and its tradition are seen in increasingly realistic terms that affirm their inherent tensions and ambiguities and accept the relativity, partiality, and particularity of the beliefs, symbols, rituals, and ceremonials of the religious community'.

A significantly different developmental scheme was offered by James W. Fowler (1981), who worked with a Piagetian model of cognitive development. Fowler postulated a preverbal stage of undifferentiated faith and counted six further stages through the life span. He attributed a fantasy-filled, imitative 'intuitive-projective' faith to children between 3 and 7 years of age, a 'mythic-literal' faith to grade schoolers, and a 'synthetic-conventional faith' to adolescents. After remarking that many adults never progress beyond synthetic-conventional faith, Fowler listed 'individuative-reflective' faith in young adulthood when people take responsibility for themselves, 'conjunctive faith' in mid-life when exceptions and compromises seem most realistic, and a 'universalizing' faith in rare individuals, martyrs among them.

Whether psychoanalytic or cognitive in the stages that they discern in the life span, existing accounts of religious development have regularly treated liberal, church-going Christianity as normative. Their descriptions of optimal development are inconsistent with the literalism of Christian fundamentalism; they are equally inconsistent with a personal practice of mystical experiences. Given the bias of the developmental models, it is relevant to note that spiritual awakenings typically lead to beliefs in clairvoyance, precognition, and providential miracles. James seems to have been correct in suggesting that the religion of the healthy-minded does not achieve the immediacy and intensity of the religion of the twice-born.

Religion as psychotherapy

Analytic psychology, which Carl G. Jung developed following his break with Freud in 1912, is the approach to the psychology of religion that has been most favored by religious devotées, both in the academy and in the public at large. It was the first of the modern systems of psychology to be premised on the question, 'Is religiosity not inherently therapeutic?'.

Jung (1969) premised analytic psychology on the assumption that the 'collective unconscious' or 'objective psyche' is universal in compass. The objective psyche is responsible, among other phenomena, for astrology, telepathy, prophecy, and fortuitous physical events – all of which Jung summarized under the term 'synchronicity'. The objective psyche is cosmic, yet it is simultaneously a component of the personal psyche of each human individual. Dreams manifest materials that originate from both the personal and the collective unconscious.

The objective psyche is composed of archetypes. Archetypes exist in the personal psyche as inborn clusters of form and motivation that constitute 'mentally expressed instincts'. However, the forms and behavioural urges have their source in the objective psyche and not in human genetics alone. Archetypes are personal entities that exist independently of human beings. Jung described them as 'autonomous *animalia* gifted with a sort of consciousness and psychic life of their own'.

Archetypes are always unconscious. They are unable to become conscious. What manifests is not an archetype but a mental image that expresses an archetype. The major archetypal images are three: the anima, which represents the feminine; the animus, which represents the masculine; and the shadow, which represents all that is rejected as evil and projected as other. Jung counted the sage, the father, the mother, the child, the hero, and the trickster as archetypal images of lesser importance.

Jung held that the unconscious manifests to consciousness in a compensatory manner. Should an archetype's manifestations be undervalued or repressed, or its opposite be overemphasized in consciousness, the psyche's need for equilibrium causes the archetype to manifest a compensatory quantity of appropriate archetypal images. Because every spontaneous manifestation of an archetypal image is compensatory, archetypal manifestation is intrinsically therapeutic. Although the design of the objective psyche is intelligent and purposive, the process of compensatory manifestation is itself regulated automatically in a quantitative manner.

In Jung's view, both dreams and religious experiences are instances of direct and unmediated manifestations of archetypal images. Although they are compensatory, dreams are irrational, while religious experiences consist of 'passionate conflicts, panics of madness, desperate confusions and depressions which were grotesque and terrible at the same time'. Jung provided no criteria for distinguishing acute psychosis from a spiritual emergency; he seems to have made no such distinction.

For Jung, myths were to be seen in parallel, as culturally shared manifestations of the archetypes that give expression to the instinctual structures of the objective psyche. Like dreams, myths are compensatory. Although the archetypes that they manifest are eternal, myths are historical phenomena that provide correction for 'the inadequacy and one-sidedness of the present' in fashions appropriate to their eras and cultures.

Therapy consists of 'individuating' or achieving psychic distance from archetypal images. One may then be able to experience the images, without being compelled to act on their basis. Organized religion is semi-therapeutic. Through 'a solidly organized dogma and ritual', Jung wrote, 'people are effectively defended and shielded against immediate religious experience'. A complete therapy moves beyond dogma and ritual into innovative, creative manipulations of archetypal images.

Jung also explained the individuation process in developmental terms. A child's worldview consists of a naive realism, an unreflecting and uncritical assumption that the habitual has the objective status of truth and law. This stage is succeeded by a maturing worldview whose rational and critical character liberates consciousness to a measure of autonomy. In its autonomy, however, critical consciousness suffers from the relativism of its own subjectivity. With a variety of differing subjectivities equally tenable, the psyche is driven into illness. The third and final developmental stage consists of the compensatory intervention of the unconscious. The pathogenic isolation of consciousness is interrupted by the manifestation of archetypal images. The images collectively alert consciousness to its grounding in the unconscious. Stability is regained, but with the naive ontological assumptions of the first stage replaced by the self-consciously psychological considerations of the third. In the process, consciousness becomes aware of, and makes its adjustment to, the unconscious. Because the unconscious is both personal and collective, the individuation process is inherently religious. Psychological health is not possible without religiosity.

Jung considered God and the Self to be archetypes. In some passages, he acknowledged that the two were indistinguishable. His concept of Self was adapted from the Hindu *atman*, which is one with God (*Brahman*) and equivalent to the mind and substance that are the cosmos. For Jung, the Self was an archetype that represents the unity of consciousness and the unconscious, and individuation was not complete until the Self was realized and psychic integration achieved.

Because Jung insisted that the 'God within' was a psychological phenomenon that was not to be confused with an external spiritual being intended by theologians, the case has sometimes been made that Jung psychologized religion and was ultimately concerned only with psychology. If so, Jung psychologized not only God, but the entire process of spiritual emergency. Analytic psychology may alternatively be seen as a psychologically informed practice of religion, whose rejection of theologians' God in favor of human self-deification is consistent with its roots in Romanticism and Western esotericism.

Social psychology

Academics' concern in the 1920s for a scientific psychology, engaged in quantification and independently duplicable results, led the discipline of psychology to replace mental experience with behaviour as its primary datum. Mental experience is accessible only through introspection and self-reports, both of which are unavoidably subjective. Behaviour can instead be measured, as it were objectively, by external observers.

Due to its methodological concerns, the discipline of psychology largely abandoned the study of religion upon the rise of behaviourism. Behaviourism was incapable of discussing any of the aspects of religion that were of keenest interest to other schools of research. Behaviourism could not ask: what are the subjective phenomena of religion? why are people religious? what are the processes of becoming religious? what in religion is morbid, wholesome, and therapeutic?

Academic psychologists were unable to engage in the study of religion until the monopoly of behaviourism was broken in the 1950s and the methods of social psychology gained prominence. Even today, however, the methodological self-limitations of academic psychologists makes their findings of limited interest to academic students of religion – and vice versa. Like academic psychology in general, social psychology uses its research methods to determine which data will and will not be examined. It is not prepared to adapt its research methods to whatever the data may happen to be. Methodological purity, rather than practicality, remains the scientific standard. Social psychology addresses data that it alone generates (via questionnaires, experiments, and so forth) and it fails to address data generated by academic students of religion. For these reasons, the social psychology of religion has not contributed significantly to the academic study of religion. Social psychologists nevertheless claim exclusive title to the name of 'science' and dismiss as unscientific all other approaches to the psychology of religion.

The major question that academic psychologists ask of religion is: 'What aspects of religion can be quantified statistically and correlated with other religious statistics?' This preoccupation with measurable variations means that social psychologists end up addressing the implicit question, 'When, or under what circumstances, are people more and less religious?'.

Because questions concerning measurable variations take for granted the definitions of whatever is being measured, the research program conceals two methodological flaws. As Benjamin Beit-Hallahmi has remarked, the social psychology of religion is a historical psychology. It is a historically and culturally limited body of findings concerning social behavior in the twentieth century, and almost entirely in the various societies of Western culture. Its findings cannot responsibly be considered universal. Nor are the findings reliable so far as they go. Most have been skewed by amateurism as well as by ethnocentricity. When social psychologists circulate a survey questionnaire, the responses are limited both by the questions asked, and by the respondents' understanding of the questions. The scoring of experimental behaviour is similarly constrained by the experimenters' subjectivity. Although several social psychologists are competent in the study of religion, the majority are not. Accordingly, many of the questions that social psychologists have asked, together with almost all of the answers that they have received on questionnaires, have been naive as well as ethnocentric. When, for example, the frequency of church attendance is used as a measurable index of religiosity, the findings are not merely limited to Christianity. They are skewed, in that they have to do with church attendance and not necessarily with religiosity.

With the warning, then, that academic psychologists' findings on religion are as subjective, speculative, and as little 'scientific' as anyone else's, let us review some of the more interesting results. People are religious because they have been taught to be so. Parental religiosity is the most important influence. Most studies show a positive correlation between religiosity and self-esteem. Religiosity is associated with life satisfaction and subjective well-being. Religiosity can increase optimism and a sense of control. There is also a correlation with self-ideal conflicts and guilt feelings. Religiosity does not affect suicidal behaviours. In general, religiosity correlates positively with both subjective or self-rated health, and objective measures of physical health. In some cases, however, religions cause physical harm, for example, through physical punishment, asceticism, and the denial of medical help. The findings regarding religion and mental health are inconclusive.

Religion is socially cohesive. Religious people divorce less frequently, commit fewer crimes, work harder, and are more socially integrated than non-religious people. Religious people are more likely to be women, over the age of 50, and lower class. The greater religiosity of women may correlate with women's greater ease with being dependent, or with men's aversion to loving a masculine deity. Women report more religious experiences than men do. Parapsychological experiences are more frequent for people who are or have been unhappy and socially marginal; whereas mystical experiences correlate with positive affect and life satisfaction. Contact with the dead correlates with being widowed. On the other hand, there is a 99 percent probability that psychedelic drugs use will induce a religious experience in anyone, if the setting is engineered to promote one. Music, prayer and meditation, group worship, experiences of nature, emotional distress, and sensory deprivation are all less effective.

Freud's claim that God is the exalted father has been examined repeatedly. Some studies have found that God is described as more similar to father, but others noted a similarity to mother. Still others noted a similarity to whichever was the preferred parent. Cultures that favour accepting, loving, and nurturing parenting styles tend to favor benevolent deities, while rejecting parenting styles correlate with malevolent deities. Catholics find God more maternal than Protestants do.

There is a decline in religiosity during adolescence. Conversion experiences are nevertheless most frequent at 15 years of age. Conversion experiences correlate with socially isolated individuals and also with a strong emotional attraction to the proselytizer whose ideas and practices are accepted. Loss of religious faith or conversion from one religion to another is frequently associated with a rejection of parents. Conversion through coercion or 'mind control' is a fiction.

Unmarried people are more active religiously than married people. Religious involvement declines in the third decade of life. Religious involvement increases after age 30 and continues into old age.

Religious orientations

The social psychologist Gordon Allport (1959) introduced a distinction between 'extrinsic' and 'intrinsic' attitudes to religion. People for whom religion is a means to a social or other end regard it as extrinsic; whereas people for whom religion is an end in itself value it for its intrinsic character. Allport introduced the distinction to refine the statistical correlation of religiosity with prejudice, authoritarianism, dogmatism, and suggestibility. Allport argued that prejudice correlates with extrinsic religiosity, which prioritized the social functions of religion. Intrinsically religious people, by contrast, are not markedly prejudiced, because they treat seriously the commandment to love one's fellow as oneself.

The modern liberal Protestant bias of Allport's analysis should be self-evident. The love commandment is not a universal teaching. Neither is its application to humanity in general, rather than to members of one's denomination or sect alone. In most eras, devout Jews and Christians have been intolerant of outsiders. Further, there is no such thing as religion for its own sake. Every religion promises a supernatural good, whether physical providence of health, wealth, and progeny, or advantageous metaphysical existence in the hereafter. Due to the ethnocentricity in Allport's argument, a debate surrounds the question whether extrinsic and intrinsic are useful categories for the psychology of religion. Intrinsics enjoy better mental health, have less fear of death, and are more altruistic than other religious people; but it is unclear whether 'intrinsic' is the quality being measured.

Batson and Ventis proposed a third basic orientation to religion that is additional to extrinsic and intrinsic. For many people, the contents of religious belief and practice are not settled. Religion is instead a quest that involves uncertainty and on-going discovery. The reality of a quest orientation has been questioned, however, because the data from which it was inferred may instead reflect the skepticism and consumerism of the university student population.

Concluding reflections

The humanistic psychologist David Bakan (1996) noted that psychology, in all of its major schools, has conceptualized human beings on the model of machines that are regulated exclusively by causal determinism. The psychological models abolished such older categories as origination, causativity, will, virtue and vice, heroism, cowardice, and so forth. As a consequence, what is currently being presented as psychology is inconsistent with our experience of ourselves.

We today possess a variety of psychologies of people imagined as machines. They are not psychologies of people as we are, nor are they what psychology must someday become. All of our current psychologies are arbitrarily and artificially truncated. The portions omitted may very well be the most significant of all. Need we be surprised that a bridge to theology has yet to be found?

Bibliography

Allport, Gordon W. 'Religion and prejudice'. *Crane Review* 2:1–1–10, 1959. Reprinted in *Personality and Social Encounter: Selected Essays*. Boston: Beacon Press, 1960, pp. 257–67.

Arbman, Ernst. 'Mythic and religious thought'. *Dragma: Martin P. Nilsson . . . Dedicatum*. Lund, 1939.

Assagioli, R. *Transpersonal Development: The Dimension Beyond Psychosynthesis*. London: HarperCollins, 1991.

Bakan, David. 'Origination, self-determination, and psychology'. *Journal of Humanistic Psychology* 36(1): 9–20, 1996.

Batson, C. D., Schoenrade, P. and Ventis, W. L. *Religion and the Individual: A Social Psychological Perspective*. London: Oxford University Press, 1997.

Beit-Hallahmi, B. and Argyle, M. *The Psychology of Religious Behaviour, Belief and Experience*. London and New York: Routledge, 1997.

Erikson, E. H. *Young Man Luther: A Study in Psychoanalysis and History*. New York: W. W. Norton, 1958.

Fowler, III, James W. *Stages of Faith: The Psychology of Human Development and the Quest for Meaning*. San Francisco: Harper & Row, 1981.

Freud, S. 'Group psychology and the analysis of the ego'. *Standard Edition*, 18: 69–143. London: Hogarth Press, 1955 [1921].

—— 'Leonardo da Vinci and a memory of his childhood'. *Standard Edition*, 11: 63–137. London: Hogarth Press, 1957 [1910].

—— 'Totem and taboo: Some points of agreement between the mental life of savages and neurotics'. *Standard Edition*, 13: 1–161. London: Hogarth Press, 1958 [1913].

—— 'Obsessive acts and religious practices'. *Standard Edition*, 9: 117–27. London: Hogarth Press, 1959 [1907].

—— 'The future of an illusion'. *Standard Edition*, 21: 5–56. London: Hogarth Press, 1961 [1927].

—— 'Civilization and its discontents'. *Standard Edition*, 21: 64–145. London: Hogarth Press, 1961 [1930].

—— 'Moses and monotheism: three essays'. *Standard Edition*, 23: 6–137. London: Hogarth Press, 1964 [1939].

—— *The Standard Edition of the Complete Psychological Works of Sigmund Freud*, 24 vols. Ed. James Strachey, with Anna Freud, Alix Strachey, and Alan Tyson. London: Hogarth Press, 1966. (Cited elsewhere as *Standard Edition*.)

Grof, C. and Grof, S. *The Stormy Search for the Self: A Guide to Personal Growth through Transformational Crisis*. Los Angeles: Jeremy P. Tarcher, 1990.

James, William. *The Varieties of Religious Experience: A Study in Human Nature*. Reprinted New York: New American Library, 1958 [1902].

Jung, C. G. *Psychology and Religion: West and East*, 2nd edn. Trans. R. F. C. Hull. Princeton: Princeton University Press, 1969.

Maslow, A. H. *Religions, Values, and Peak Experiences*. 1964; rpt. Harmondsworth: Penguin Books Ltd., 1976.

Meissner, W. W. *Psychoanalysis and Religious Experience*. New Haven: Yale University Press, 1984.

Merkur, D. *Mystical Moments and Unitive Thinking*. New York: State University of New York Press, 1999.

Otto, Rudolf. *The Idea of the Holy: An Inquiry into the Non-rational Factor in the Idea of the Divine and its Relation to the Rational*, 2nd edn. Trans. John W. Harvey. London: Oxford University Press, 1950 [1917].

—— 'The sensus numinis as the historical basis of religion'. *Hibbert Journal* 30: 283–97, 415–30, 1932.

Pfister, Oscar. *Some Applications of Psycho-Analysis*. London: George Alen & Unwin Ltd, 1923.

—— *Christianity and Fear: A Study in History and in the Psychology and Hygiene of Religion*. Trans. W. H. Johnston. London: George Allen & Unwin Ltd, 1948.

Pruyser, P. W. *Between Belief and Unbelief*. New York: Harper & Row, 1974.

Rizzuto, A.-M. *The Birth of the Living God: A Psychoanalytic Study*. Chicago: University of Chicago Press, 1979.

Söderblom, Nathan. *The Living God: Basal Forms of Personal Religion*. Gifford Lectures 1931. London: Oxford University Press, 1933.

Starbuck, Edwin Diller. *The Psychology of Religion: An Empirical Study of the Growth of Religious Consciousness*, 3rd edn. London, New York and Melbourne: Walter Scott Publishing Co., Ltd., 1911 [1899].

Chapter 10

Phenomenology of religion

Douglas Allen

Scholars of religion often describe 'the phenomenology of religion' as one of the major twentieth-century disciplines and approaches to religion. Many readers probably have some idea of what is involved in other disciplines and approaches to religion, such as 'the history of religion,' 'the anthropology of religion,' 'the psychology of religion,' 'the sociology of religion,' or 'the philosophy of religion,' even if some initial ideas may not be accurate. However, few readers will have any clue as to what the term 'phenomenology of religion' means or what this discipline and approach describe.

An introductory exercise

The following exercise will help to illustrate the rationale for phenomenology of religion and several of its major characteristics. This rationale and the leading characteristics will then be described later in the chapter.

Most societies and cultures have been described as 'religious.' Several billion human beings today describe themselves as 'religious.' Some of our most common language – emphasizing such terms as 'God,' 'soul,' 'heaven,' 'salvation,' 'sin,' and 'evil' – is 'religious.' Even human beings who claim that they are not religious usually think that they know what it is to be 'religious' and hence they know what they reject.

All scholarly approaches to religion, including phenomenology of religion, involve critical reflection. When we reflect critically on such common terms as 'religion' and 'religious,' it becomes apparent that we usually use these terms in vague ways and that it is not precisely clear what we mean. This exercise is an attempt to begin such critical reflection as key to understanding phenomenology of religion.

The exercise

This exercise will work best for a class or other group of participants. If the group has more than 20 participants, divide it into smaller groups allowing for more individual participation. This exercise will also work well through an internet group communication. If you are alone, you can do the exercise by yourself, but it will work much better if you ask others for their responses. Each class or group should ask for one person to record the responses and summarize the results.

Phenomenology of religion starts with the view that religion is based on religious experience. Human beings have experiences that they describe as religious. These may be traditional or nontraditional. They may focus on inner feelings or outward forms and relations. They may be institutional and involve organized religion, or they may be highly personal and outside of any institutional framework. They may involve prayer, worship, rituals, nature, or cosmic experiences. Human beings who reject any personal identification with religion claim that they do not have such religious experiences.

In this exercise, many or most of the participants will state that they are religious and that they have had religious experiences. Religious participants should be encouraged to describe their religious experiences. What kind of an experience was it? What did it mean to the person who had such an experience? This should not be rushed. It may take time for participants to feel comfortable or sufficiently confident to share orally or in writing the nature of their religious experiences. It is important to be nonjudgmental and to emphasize that there is no right or wrong answer. It is important to maintain an atmosphere in which others, even when they personally disagree, are respectful and attempt to empathize with and understand what religious participants are expressing.

As a variation, after all religious participants have had the opportunity to describe their religious experiences, the group may focus on respondents whose descriptions involve more traditional expressions involving 'God.' These religious participants may be asked to describe at greater length the nature of such an experience of God and what is intended by their use of the term God. As another variation, the group may focus on others who have not responded because they are not religious and have never had a religious experience. What are the characteristics that make all of their experiences secular or nonreligious and prevent them from describing their experiences as religious?

After eliciting as many responses as possible, compile the results. Do not include or exclude responses based on agreement or disagreement. Summarize the major ways of describing religious experience, possibly the more restrictive descriptions in terms of experiences of God, and possibly the descriptions of the contrasting non-religious experiences. Do this before going on to the next section on results.

Results of the exercise

After compiling the results, reflect critically on them and analyze the data. Phenomenology of religion involves certain kinds of critical reflection and analysis.

When considering the major features expressed by religious participants, are there common characteristics in all or most of the descriptions of religious experience? What are they? Or are the descriptions so individualistic or subjective that there are no common characteristics, structures, or patterns? Do the descriptions allow us to detect certain defining or essential characteristics present in religious experiences and not present in nonreligious experiences? In reflecting on the tremendous variety of expressions of religious experiences, phenomenologists of religion claim that there are common general characteristics, structures, and patterns revealed only in religious experiences.

Religious people do not believe that their religious experiences are nothing more than subjective psychological feelings. They believe that they have experienced some religious reality: the experience of X. Based on your descriptions of religious experiences, what is the content or nature of X? How have participants described X? As God? In other terms?

In this regard, phenomenology and phenomenology of religion embrace a doctrine of 'intentionality.' Intentionality emphasizes that all experience is experience of something; experience points beyond itself to some intended referential meaning. Is there a common religious referent expressing the experienced religious meaning in your descriptions? If there is not one, essential, universal intended structure or meaning, are there several essential patterns and variations?

Phenomenologists of religion focus on language. Although we start with religious experience, we never have direct access to the religious experiences of others. Instead we always have expressions of others as they try to describe their experiences and religious realities. When religious participants described their experiences, how were they using language? Is there a specific or unique religious language? If the intended religious referent or reality transcends human attempts at definition and conceptual analysis, does this mean that religion and religious experience cannot be studied in a critical, reflective, scholarly way? Phenomenology of religion analyzes both the limits and the power of language in revealing religious experience.

In reflecting on the assembled data, here are several likely questions and concerns. On the one hand, are many of the descriptions of 'religion,' 'religious,' and 'religious experience' too narrow? This is not a criticism of highly personal, individual formulations. However, when we attempt to generalize and look for common features, we may find that formulations are too restrictive. It is likely that many religious participants will be uncomfortable with some descriptions and will conclude that their religious experience is something very different. For example, a Buddhist may not be comfortable identifying with certain God expressions. Even participants using God expressions usually feel that other God formulations have little to do with their experiences. A believer in God may be uncomfortable with certain personal anthropomorphic descriptions or with various traditional exclusivistic formulations. To the extent that participants reflect religious, ethnic, class, and other differences, there will be a great plurality and diversity in responses. From the perspective of phenomenology of religion, which attempts to uncover universal or general structures and meanings, think about whether various expressions are too narrow and how they might be broadened.

On the other hand, are some of the descriptions too broad? Are some of the descriptions true, but they are also true of experiences and beliefs that are not religious? For example, some may describe religion as consisting of whatever is true or real for the experiencer. But don't nonreligious people also experience what they consider true or real? From the perspective of phenomenology of religion, our general descriptions must allow us to distinguish religious phenomena from nonreligious phenomena and analyze the religious as a specific kind of experience.

Reflecting on the assembled data, do some of the descriptions reveal a clear ethnocentrism, expressing one's own background, socialization, and beliefs but not adequate to describe the religious experiences and phenomena of others? Do some of the descriptions reflect clear normative positions, based on specific value judgments, that do not do justice to religious others who do not accept such religious positions?

This is not meant to criticize such ethnocentric and normative formulations. They are inadequate on phenomenological grounds. On theological, philosophical, or some faith-based grounds, Christian fundamentalists may describe religious experience as consisting only in the experience of Jesus Christ, and they may argue that those who do not experience and accept this reality are doomed to Hell. Many Muslims may describe religious experience as submitting to Allah and recognizing Muhammad as the true Messenger, and they may argue that others are nonbelievers whose experiential referents are unreal or demonic.

Phenomenology of religion, by way of contrast, attempts to avoid such narrow, overly broad, ethnocentric, and normative approaches. It attempts to describe religious experiences with their religious phenomena as accurately as possible. In its descriptions, analysis, and interpretation of meaning, it attempts to suspend value judgments about what is real or unreal in experiences of others. It attempts to describe, understand, and do justice to the religious phenomena as they appear in religious experiences of others.

The term 'phenomenology of religion'

Although 'phenomenology' and 'phenomenology of religion' are not part of ordinary language, they are popular terms in various scholarly disciplines. Starting in the early twentieth century with its origins mainly in Germany, philosophical phenomenology became one of the major philosophical approaches. Phenomenology of religion emerged as one of the most influential modern disciplines and approaches to religion. Scholars sometimes identify phenomenology of religion as a discipline and approach within the general modern field of *Religionswissenschaft*, usually identified as the scientific or scholarly study of religion. We shall use the more common term 'religious studies' to identify modern scholarly approaches to religion that include phenomenology as well as other approaches to religion grounded in history, sociology, anthropology, sociology, psychology, linguistics, cognitive science, and other modern disciplines.

It is possible to differentiate four groups of scholars who use the term *phenomenology of religion*. First, there are works in which the term means nothing more than an investigation of the phenomena or observable objects, facts, and events of religion. Second, from the Dutch scholar P. D. Chantepie de la Saussaye to such contemporary scholars as the Scandinavian historians of religions Geo Widengren and Åke Hultkrantz, phenomenology of religion means the comparative study and the classification of different types of religious phenomena.

Third, numerous scholars, such as W. Brede Kristensen, Gerardus van der Leeuw, Joachim Wach, C. Jouco Bleeker, Mircea Eliade, and Jacques Waardenburg, identify phenomenology of religion as a specific branch, discipline, or method within *Religionswissenschaft* or religious studies. This is where the most significant contributions of phenomenology of religion to the study of religion have been made.

Fourth, there are scholars whose phenomenology of religion is influenced by philosophical phenomenology. A few scholars, such as Max Scheler and Paul Ricoeur, explicitly identify much of their work with philosophical phenomenology. Others, such as Rudolf Otto, van der Leeuw, and Eliade, use a phenomenological method and are influenced, at least partially, by phenomenological philosophy. There are also influential theological approaches, as seen in the works of Friedrich Schleiermacher, Paul Tillich, and Jean-Luc Marion, that utilize phenomenology of religion as a stage in the formulation of theology.

The terms *phenomenon* and *phenomenology* are derived from the Greek word *phainomenon* (that which shows itself, or that which appears). The term phenomenology has both philosophical and nonphilosophical roots.

One finds nonphilosophical phenomenologies in the natural sciences in which scientists want to emphasize the descriptive, as contrasted with the explanatory, conception of their science. A second nonphilosophical use of phenomenology appears in the descriptive, systematic, comparative study of religions in which scholars assemble groups of religious phenomena in order to disclose their major aspects and to formulate their typologies.

In the late eighteenth century, the German philosopher Immanuel Kant devoted considerable analysis to 'phenomena' as the data of experience, things that appear to and are constructed by human minds. Such phenomena, which Kant distinguishes from 'noumena,' or 'things-in-themselves' independent of our knowing minds, can be studied rationally, scientifically, and objectively. For example, I can give a causal explanation of why the frisbee was thrown at a certain direction, velocity, and distance. However, I cannot give the same kind of spatial, temporal, causal analysis to explain noumena such as 'God.' A similar distinction between religious phenomena as appearances and religious reality-in-itself, which is beyond phenomenology, is found in the descriptive phenomenologies of many phenomenologists of religion.

Of all the uses of phenomenology by philosophers before the twentieth-century phenomenological movement, the term is most frequently identified with the German philosopher G. W. F. Hegel and his *Phenomenology of Spirit*. Hegel was determined to overcome Kant's phenomena-noumena bifurcation. Phenomena are actual stages of knowledge – manifestations in the development of Spirit – evolving from undeveloped consciousness of mere sense experience and culminating in forms of absolute knowledge. Phenomenology is the science by which the mind becomes aware of the development of Spirit and comes to know its essence – that is, Spirit as it is in itself – through a study of its appearances and manifestations.

This background led to two distinct senses of phenomenology that have shaped phenomenology of religion. On the one hand, there is the older, wider sense of the term as any descriptive study of a given subject matter of observable phenomena. On the other hand, there is also a narrower twentieth-century sense of the term as a philosophical approach utilizing a phenomenological method.

Some background to the phenomenology of religion

Before turning to philosophical phenomenology and then a more detailed examination of the phenomenology of religion, it may be helpful to examine some of the context within which they originated and developed. By having a sense of other approaches to religion and what phenomenology was reacting against, the rationale for the phenomenology of religion becomes more evident.

Phenomenologists of religion, with their emphasis on the religious experience, recognize that being religious is not identical with studying religion. There is a first, primary, or foundational level of religious experience for the religious believer. Phenomenology and other scholarly approaches always involve some distance between the scholar and the subject matter necessary for critical reflection, analysis, interpretation, and attempts at verifying one's findings. Scholars disagree on possible relations between being religious and studying religion. However, all agree that scholarly study is not identical with being religious or having religious experience.

Scholars have attempted to accumulate religious data and interpret the meaning of religious phenomena for thousands of years. Much of this arose from exposure to new religious phenomena from expeditions of explorers, military and political conquests, religious missionary work, and economic exploitation. Earlier studies were usually shaped by self-serving, apologetic, religious, political, and economic assumptions and judgments. Comparative religion often became competitive religion in which scholars studied others in order to demonstrate the superiority of their own religion or culture. Rarely did scholars attempt to understand religion through the eyes of the other. From the perspective of phenomenology of religion, these earlier scholarly studies did not do justice to the religious phenomena of the religious other.

The origin of the modern scholarly study of religion is usually traced to the nineteenth century and especially to the influences of the Enlightenment. These modern scholars of religion were determined to free their approaches and disciplines from pre-modern investigations with their subjective and normative assumptions and judgments, their dependence on supernatural and other external authority, and their lack of concern for rigorous standards of objective knowledge. By insisting on unbiased impartial investigations, the careful accumulation of data or facts, and the authority of human reason to analyze and interpret the meaning of phenomena, modern scholars had confidence in the human capacity to make progress and arrive at objective, intersubjectively verifiable knowledge.

From the perspective of phenomenology of religion, these modern scholarly studies also were limited and did not do justice to the religious phenomena of the religious other. Built into their scientific or scholarly studies were all kinds of unacknowledged normative assumptions and judgments. For example, most of these philologists, ethnologists, and other modern scholars of religion adopted a positivistic view of empirical observable 'facts' and 'objective' knowledge. Phenomenologists of religion assert that the scale or method makes the difference and our approach must be commensurate with the nature of our subject matter. An approach yielding factual, objective knowledge when dissecting a worm in a laboratory may not provide objective knowledge about religious experience. To dismiss religious experience as subjective and not factual is not very helpful if we are trying to gain a greater understanding of religious phenomena.

To provide a second illustration, most nineteenth-century scholars of religion adopted from Darwin a notion of evolution and then applied it to language, culture, religion, and other subject matter. Typically, they arranged their religious data in an assumed, predetermined, unilinear framework, starting with the lowest and most undeveloped stage of 'primitive' religions and evolving to the evolutionary apex of Western monotheism and especially Christianity. In some scholarly frameworks, human beings evolved beyond all religion to a higher rational, scientific stage of human development. From the perspective of the phenomenology of religion, imposing such an outside, normative evolutionary scheme on the religious phenomena prevents us from accurately describing and understanding the meaning of the phenomena for the religious other.

Scholarly approaches have been highly normative, applying their standards to make disciplinary value judgments. The following illustration will make this point and the contrasting phenomenological approach.

Human beings repeatedly claim that they have 'experiences of God.' Psychologists of religion attempt to analyze and explain such experiences and their religious phenomena in terms of some psychological account. Sociologists of religion analyze and explain such phenomena in terms of social needs, functions, and structures. From the perspective of phenomenology of religion, these approaches provide psychological and sociological explanations, but questions still remain involving the interpretation of religious meaning.

Philosophers of religion also ask normative philosophical questions. What are the meaning, truth, and reality in propositions claiming to experience God? Can we use reason to prove the existence of such a God? Can we reconcile the existence of such a God with so much evil in the world?

Phenomenologists of religion react against such normative approaches to religion. Human beings claim to have experiences of God. What does it mean to live such a religious existence? What are the meaning and significance of such experienced phenomena? Other approaches, with their assumed norms and methodological framework, do not do justice to the religious phenomena of others. How can we suspend our own assumptions and value judgments, enter into the religious world of the religious believer, describe the religious phenomena and interpret their religious meaning as accurately as possible?

Philosophical phenomenology

As one of the major schools, movements, or approaches in twentieth-century philosophy, phenomenology takes many forms. One can distinguish, for example, the 'transcendental phenomenology' of Edmund Husserl, the 'existential phenomenology' of Jean-Paul Sartre and Maurice Merleau-Ponty, and the 'hermeneutic phenomenology' of Martin Heidegger and Paul Ricoeur.

The phenomenological movement

The primary aim of philosophical phenomenology is to investigate and become directly aware of phenomena that appear in immediate experience, and thereby to allow the phenomenologist to describe the essential structures of these phenomena. In doing so, phenomenology attempts to free itself from unexamined presuppositions, to avoid causal and other explanations, to utilize a method that allows it to describe that which appears, and to intuit or decipher essential meanings.

Husserl is usually identified as the founder and most influential philosopher of the phenomenological movement. The earliest phenomenologists worked at several German universities, especially at Göttingen and Munich. Outside of Husserl's predominant influence, other significant German phenomenologists include Scheler and Heidegger. Phenomenology remained an overwhelmingly German philosophy until the 1930s when the center of the movement began to shift to France. Leading French phenomenologists include Sartre, Merleau-Ponty, Gabriel Marcel, and Ricoeur.

Characteristics of philosophical phenomenology

One may delineate five characteristics of philosophical phenomenology that have particular relevance for the phenomenology for religion.

Descriptive nature   Phenomenology aims to be a rigorous, descriptive science, discipline, or approach. The phenomenological slogan 'Zu den Sachen!' ('To the things themselves!') expresses the determination to turn away from philosophical theories and concepts toward the direct intuition and description of phenomena as they appear in immediate experience. Phenomenology attempts to describe the nature of phenomena, the way appearances manifest themselves, and the essential structures at the foundation of human experience. As contrasted with most schools of philosophy, which have assumed that the rational alone is real and which have a philosophical preoccupation with the rational faculties and with conceptual analysis, phenomenology focuses on accurately describing the totality of phenomenal manifestations in human experience. A descriptive phenomenology, attempting to avoid reductionism and often insisting on the phenomenological *epoché* (see pp. 189–90, 198–9), describes the diversity, complexity, and richness of experience.

Antireductionism   Phenomenological antireductionism is concerned with freeing people from uncritical preconceptions that prevent them from becoming aware of the specificity and diversity of phenomena, thus allowing them to broaden and deepen immediate experience and provide more accurate descriptions of this experience. Husserl attacked various forms of reductionism, such as 'psychologism,' which attempts to derive the laws of logic from psychological laws and, more broadly, to reduce all phenomena to psychological phenomena. In opposing the oversimplifications of traditional empiricism and other forms of reductionism, phenomenologists aim to deal faithfully with phenomena as phenomena and to become aware of what phenomena reveal in their full intentionality.

Intentionality   A subject always 'intends' an object, and intentionality refers to the property of all consciousness as consciousness of something. All acts of consciousness are directed toward the experience of something, the intentional object. For Husserl, who took the term from his teacher Franz Brentano, intentionality was a way of describing how consciousness constitutes phenomena. In order to identify, describe, and interpret the meaning of phenomena, phenomenologists must be attentive to the intentional structures of their data; to the intentional structures of consciousness with their intended referents and meanings.

Bracketing   For many phenomenologists, the antireductionist insistence on the irreducibility of the intentional immediate experience entails the adoption of a 'phenomenological *epoché*.' This Greek term literally means 'abstention' or 'suspension of judgment' and is often defined as a method of 'bracketing.' It is only by bracketing the uncritically accepted 'natural world,' by suspending beliefs and judgments based on an unexamined 'natural standpoint,' that the phenomenologist can become aware of the phenomena of immediate experience and can gain insight into their essential structures. Sometimes the *epoché* is formulated in terms of the goal of a completely presuppositionless science or philosophy, but most phenomenologists have interpreted such bracketing as the goal of freeing the phenomenologist from unexamined presuppositions, or of rendering explicit and clarifying such presuppositions, rather than completely denying their existence. The phenomenological *epoché* is not simply 'performed' by phenomenologists; it must involve some method of self-criticism and intersubjective testing allowing insight into structures and meanings.

Eidetic vision   The intuition of essences, often described as 'eidetic vision' or 'eidetic reduction,' is related to the Greek term *eidos*, which Husserl adopted from its Platonic meaning to designate 'universal essences.' Such essences express the 'whatness' of things, the necessary and invariant features of phenomena that allow us to recognize phenomena as phenomena of a certain kind.

For all of their differences, the overwhelming majority of phenomenologists have upheld a descriptive phenomenology that is antireductionist, involves phenomenological bracketing, focuses on intentionality, and aims at insight into essential structures and meanings. The following is a brief formulation of a general phenomenological procedure for gaining insight into such essential structures and meanings.

In the 'intuition of essences' (*Wesensschau*), the phenomenologist begins with particular data: specific phenomena as expressions of intentional experiences. The central aim of the phenomenological method is to disclose the essential structure embodied in the particular data.

One gains insight into meaning by the method of 'free variation.' After assembling a variety of particular phenomena, the phenomenologist searches for the invariant core that constitutes the essential meaning of the phenomena. The phenomena, subjected to a process of free variation, assume certain forms that are considered to be accidental or inessential in the sense that the phenomenologist can go beyond the limits imposed by such forms without destroying the basic character or intentionality of one's data. For example, the variation of a great variety of religious phenomena may disclose that the unique structures of monotheism do not constitute the essential core or universal structure of all religious experience.

The phenomenologist gradually sees that phenomena assume forms that are regarded as essential in the sense that one cannot go beyond or remove such structures without destroying the basic 'whatness' or intentionality of the data. For example, free variation might reveal that certain intentional structures of 'transcendence' constitute an invariant core of religious experience. When the universal essence is grasped, the phenomenologist achieves the eidetic intuition or the fulfilled *Wesensschau*.

Most phenomenologists who use a method of *Wesensschau* propose that historical phenomena have a kind of priority, that one must substitute for Husserl's purely imaginary variation an actual variation of historical data, and that particular phenomena are not constituted by an individual but are the source of one's constitution and judgment.

The majority of philosophical phenomenologists have not focused on religious phenomena, but the vocabulary of philosophical phenomenology and, in some cases, its methodology have greatly influenced the phenomenology of religion.

The phenomenology of religion

The modern scholarly study of religion arose largely as a product of the rational and scientific attitude of the Enlightenment. The first major figure in this discipline was F. Max Müller (1823–1900), who intended *Religionswissenschaft* to be a descriptive, objective science free from the normative theological and philosophical studies of religion.

P. D. Chantepie de la Saussaye (1848–1920) is sometimes considered the founder of phenomenology of religion as a special discipline of classification. Phenomenology of religion occupied an intermediary position for him between history and philosophy and is a descriptive, comparative approach collecting and grouping religious phenomena. The Dutch historian C. P. Tiele considered phenomenology the first stage of the philosophical part of the science of religion.

Many scholars of religion point to the phenomenology of religion's sense of generality, with its approach invariably characterized as systematic. For Widengren, the phenomenology of religion aims at a coherent account and provides the systematic synthesis of the historical phenomena of religion.

Scholars, such as the Italian historian of religions Raffaele Pettazzoni, view phenomenology and history as two complementary aspects of the integral science of religion. Phenomenology provides a deeper understanding of the religious meaning of the historical data.

Major phenomenologists of religion

What follows are brief formulations of the approaches and contributions of seven influential phenomenologists of religion: Max Scheler, W. Brede Kristensen, Rudolf Otto, Gerardus van der Leeuw, C. Jouco Bleeker, Mircea Eliade, and Ninian Smart. Included are criticisms of three influential phenomenologists of religion: Otto, van der Leeuw, and Eliade.

Max Scheler Of the major philosophers who founded and developed philosophical phenomenology, Scheler (1874–1928) had the greatest focus on religion. In many ways, he can be considered the most significant early phenomenologist of religion. Influenced by Brentano, Husserl, Kant, Nietzsche, Dilthey, and Bergson, Scheler developed his own original phenomenological approach. His books *On the Eternal in Man* and *Formalism in Ethics and Non-Formal Ethics of Values* bring out his phenomenological method, his description and analysis of sympathy, love, and other values, and key characteristics of his phenomenology of religion.

Reminiscent of Schleiermacher and Otto, Scheler focused on a phenomenological description and analysis of the unique religious human mode of experience and feeling; the being of the human being for whom structures and essences of religious values are presented to consciousness. Phenomenological disclosure, focusing on what is 'given' to consciousness as the Absolute, the Divine Person, or God, is not achieved through reason but only through the love of God orienting one toward experiential realization of the Holy.

Philosophical phenomenologists of religion are greatly indebted to Scheler. The turn to religion in some of philosophical phenomenology and other forms of continental philosophy at the end of the twentieth century often exhibit characteristics similar to Scheler's phenomenological orientation.

W. Brede Kristensen   Much of the field has been dominated by a Dutch tradition of phenomenology of religion. Kristensen (1867–1953) illustrates an extreme formulation of the descriptive approach within phenomenology. Phenomenology is a systematic and comparative approach that is descriptive and not normative. In opposing the widespread positivist and evolutionist approaches to religion, Kristensen attempted to integrate historical knowledge of the facts with phenomenological 'empathy' and 'feeling' for the data in order to grasp the 'inner meaning' and religious values in various texts.

The phenomenologist must accept the faith of the believers as the sole 'religious reality.' In order to achieve phenomenological understanding, scholars must avoid imposing their own value judgments on the experiences of believers and must assume that the believers are completely right. In other words, the primary focus of phenomenology is the description of how believers understand their own faith. One must respect the absolute value that believers ascribe to their faith. An understanding of this religious reality is always approximate or relative, since one can never experience the religion of others exactly as the believers experience it. After describing the belief of believers, scholars may classify phenomena according to essential types and make comparative evaluations. But all investigations into essence and evaluations of phenomena entail value judgments by the interpreter and are beyond the limits of descriptive phenomenology.

Rudolf Otto   Two interdependent methodological contributions made by Rudolf Otto (1869–1937) deserve emphasis: his experiential approach, which involves the phenomenological description of the universal, essential structure of religious experience, and his antireductionism, which respects the unique, irreducible, 'numinous' quality of all religious experience.

In *Das Heilige* (translated as *The Idea of the Holy*), Otto presents what is probably the best-known phenomenological account of religious experience. Otto describes the universal 'numinous' element as a unique a priori category of meaning and value. By *numen* and *numinous*, Otto means the concept of 'the holy' minus its moral and rational aspects. By emphasizing this nonmoral, nonrational aspect of religion, he isolates the 'overplus of meaning' beyond the rational and conceptual. This constitutes the universal essence of religious experience. Since such a unique nonrational experience cannot be defined or conceptualized, symbolic and analogical descriptions are meant to evoke within the reader the experience of the holy. The religious experience of the numinous, as an a priori structure of consciousness, can be reawakened or recognized by means of our innate sense of the numinous.

In this regard, Otto formulates a universal phenomenological structure of religious experience in which the phenomenologist can distinguish autonomous religious phenomena by their numinous aspect and can organize and analyze specific religious manifestations. He points to our 'creature feeling' of absolute dependence in the experiential presence of the holy. This *sui generis* religious experience is described as the experience of the 'wholly other' that is qualitatively unique and transcendent.

This insistence on the unique a priori quality of religious experience points to Otto's antireductionism. Otto rejects the one-sidedly intellectualistic and rationalistic bias of most interpretations and the reduction of religious phenomena to the interpretive schema of linguistic analysis, anthropology, sociology, psychology, and various historicist approaches. This emphasis on the autonomy of religion, with the need for a unique, autonomous approach that is commensurate with interpreting the meaning of irreducibly religious phenomena, is generally accepted by major phenomenologists of religion.

Various interpreters have criticized Otto's phenomenological approach for being too narrowly conceived. According to these critics, Otto's approach focuses on nonrational aspects of certain mystical and other 'extreme' experiences, but it is not sufficiently comprehensive to interpret the diversity and complexity of religious data, nor is it sufficiently concerned with the specific historical and cultural forms of religious phenomena. Critics also object to the a priori nature of Otto's project and influences of personal, Christian, theological, and apologetic intentions on his phenomenology.

Gerardus van der Leeuw   In his *Comparative Religion*, Eric J. Sharpe writes that 'between 1925 and 1950, the phenomenology of religion was associated almost exclusively with the name of the Dutch scholar Gerardus van der Leeuw (1890–1950), and with his book *Phänomenologie der Religion*.' Van der Leeuw acknowledges that his phenomenology is strongly influenced by Wilhelm Dilthey's formulations on hermeneutics and 'understanding' (*Verstehen*).

In *Phänomenologie der Religion* (translated as *Religion in Essence and Manifestation*), van der Leeuw defines the assumptions, concepts, and stages of his phenomenological approach. The phenomenologist must respect the specific intentionality of religious phenomena and simply describe the phenomenon as 'what appears into view.' The phenomenon is given in the mutual relations between subject and object; that is, its 'entire essence' is given in its appearance to someone.

Van der Leeuw proposed a subtle and complex phenomenological-psychological method of systematic introspection, going far beyond a descriptive phenomenology. This involves 'the interpolation of the phenomenon into our lives' as necessary for understanding religious phenomena. Phenomenology must be combined with historical research, which precedes phenomenological understanding and provides the phenomenologist with sufficient data. Special note may be taken of van der Leeuw's emphasis on the religious aspect of 'power' as the basis of every religious form and as defining what is religious. Phenomenology describes how humans have religious experiences in relating to such extraordinary power.

Influences from van der Leeuw's own Christian point of view are often central to his analysis of the phenomenological method for gaining understanding of religious structures and meanings. For example, he submits that 'all understanding rests upon self-surrendering love.' Van der Leeuw considered himself a theologian and asserted that phenomenology of religion leads to both anthropology and theology. Numerous scholars have concluded that much of his phenomenology of religion must be interpreted in theological terms.

Critics, while often expressing admiration for *Religion in Essence and Manifestation* as an extraordinary collection of religious data, offer many objections to van der Leeuw's phenomenology of religion: his phenomenological approach is based on numerous theological and metaphysical assumptions and value judgments; it is often too subjective and highly speculative; and it neglects the historical and cultural context of religious phenomena and is of little value for empirically based research.

C. Jouco Bleeker Bleeker (1898–1983) distinguished three types of phenomenology of religion: the descriptive phenomenology that restricts itself to the systematization of religious phenomena, the typological phenomenology that formulates the different types of religion, and the specific sense of phenomenology that investigates the essential structures and meanings of religious phenomena. In terms of this more specific sense, phenomenology of religion has a double meaning: it is an independent science that creates monographs and handbooks, such as van der Leeuw's *Religion in Essence and Manifestation* and Eliade's *Patterns in Comparative Religion*, but it is also a scholarly method that utilizes such principles as the phenomenological *epoché* and eidetic vision. Although Bleeker frequently used technical terms borrowed from Husserl and philosophical phenomenology, he claimed that they were used by phenomenology of religion in only a figurative sense.

According to Bleeker, phenomenology of religion combines a critical attitude and concern for accurate descriptions with a sense of empathy for phenomena. It is an empirical science without philosophical aspirations, and it should distinguish its activities from those of philosophical phenomenology and of anthropology. Phenomenology of religion systematizes historical facts in order to understand their religious meaning.

Bleeker analyzes phenomenology of religion as inquiry into three dimensions of religious phenomena: *theoria*, *logos*, and *entelecheia*. The *theoria* of phenomena discloses the essence and significance of the empirical facts. The *logos* of phenomena provides a sense of objectivity by showing that hidden structures 'are built up according to strict inner laws' and that religion 'always possesses a certain structure with an inner logic.' The *entelecheia* of phenomena reveals the dynamics and development of religious life as 'an invincible, creative and self-regenerating force.' Phenomenology, it is frequently stated, abstracts from historical change and presents a rather static view of essential structures and meanings. The phenomenologist of religion must also study the dynamics and development of religious phenomena.

Mircea Eliade As one of the major interpreters of religion, symbol, and myth, the Romanian Eliade (1907–1986) submits that religion 'refers to the experience of the sacred.' The phenomenologist works with historical documents expressing *hierophanies*, or manifestations of the sacred, and attempts to decipher the existential situation and religious meaning expressed through the data. The sacred and the profane express 'two modes of being in the world,' and religion always entails the attempt of religious beings to transcend the relative, historical, temporal, 'profane' world by experiencing a 'superhuman' sacred world of transcendent values.

Eliade's phenomenology of religion includes many morphological studies of different kinds of religious symbolism; interpretations of the structure and function of myth, with the cosmogonic myth and other creation myths functioning as exemplary models; treatments of rituals, such as those of initiation, as reenacting sacred mythic models; structural analysis of sacred space, sacred time, and sacred history; and studies of different types of religious experience, such as yoga, shamanism, alchemy, and other 'archaic' phenomena.

Three key methodological principles underlying Eliade's phenomenological approach are his assumption of the 'irreducibility of the sacred,' his emphasis on the 'dialectic of the sacred' as the universal structure of sacralization, and his uncovering of the structural systems of religious symbols that constitute the framework in terms of which he interprets religious meaning.

The assumption of the irreducibility of the religious is a form of phenomenological *epoché*. In attempting to understand and describe the meaning of religious phenomena, the phenomenologist must utilize an antireductionist method commensurate with the nature of the data. Only a religious frame of reference or 'scale' of interpretation does not distort the specific, irreducible religious intentionality expressed in the data.

The universal structure of the dialectic of the sacred provides essential criteria for distinguishing religious from nonreligious phenomena. There is always a sacred–profane dichotomy and separation of the hierophanic object, such as a particular mountain or tree or person, since this is the medium through which the sacred is manifested; the sacred, which expresses transcendent structures and meanings, paradoxically limits itself by incarnating itself in something ordinarily finite, temporal, and historical; the sacred, in its dialectical movement of disclosure and revelation, always conceals and camouflages itself; and the religious person, in resolving existential crises, evaluates and chooses the sacred as powerful, ultimate, normative, and meaningful.

Among the characteristics of symbols are: (1) their 'logic,' which allows various symbols to fit together to form coherent symbolic systems; (2) their 'multivalence,' through which they express simultaneously a number of structurally coherent meanings not evident on the level of immediate experience; and (3) their 'function of unification,' by which they integrate heterogeneous phenomena into a whole or a system. These autonomous, universal, coherent systems of symbols provide the phenomenological framework for Eliade's interpretation of religious meaning. For example, he interprets the meaning of a religious phenomenon associated with the sun or moon by reintegrating it within its solar or lunar structural system of symbolic associations.

Although Eliade was extremely influential, many scholars ignore or are hostile to his history and phenomenology of religion. The most frequent criticism is that Eliade is methodologically uncritical, often presenting sweeping, arbitrary, subjective generalizations not based upon specific historical and empirical data. Critics also charge that his approach is influenced by various normative judgments and an assumed ontological position that is partial to a religious, antihistorical mode of being and to certain Eastern and archaic phenomena.

Ninian Smart   Born in Cambridge, England to Scottish parents, Smart (1927–2001) had a major impact on religious studies. He was committed to phenomenology as the best way to study religion. His phenomenology of religion avoids what were two dominant approaches to religion: (1) ethnocentric, normative, especially Christian, theological approaches in the study of religion; and (2) normative philosophical approaches with their exclusive focus on belief and conceptual analysis to the exclusion of other dimensions of religious phenomena. Smart was capable of technical scholarly analysis, but he is probably better known as a popularizer in his study of religion, as seen in *The Religious Experience of Mankind*. He believed that profound insights can be presented in simple understandable language and ordinary phenomenological categories.

Smart emphasized many points that became easily recognizable and widely accepted in phenomenology of religion and other approaches to religious phenomena. He emphasized suspension of one's own value judgments and the need for phenomenological empathy in understanding and describing religious phenomena of others. He endorsed a liberal humanistic approach that upholds pluralism and diversity. In Smart's phenomenological approach, one recognizes that religion expresses many dimensions of human experience. Such an approach is 'polymethodic,' multiperspectival, comparative, and cross-cultural. The phenomenologist of religion needs to take seriously the contextual nature of diverse religious phenomena; to ask questions, engage in critical dialogue, and maintain an open-ended investigation of religion; and to recognize that religions express complex, multidimensional, interconnected worldviews. This focus on religions in terms of worldview analysis leads to the contemporary interest in the globalization of religion and global pluralism.

Characteristics of phenomenology of religion

The following features, some of which have already been mentioned, are characteristic of much of phenomenology of religion: a comparative, systematic, empirical, historical, descriptive discipline and approach; antireductionist claims and its autonomous nature; adoption of philosophical phenomenological notions of intentionality and *epoché*; insistence on empathy, sympathetic understanding, and religious commitment; and claim to provide insight into essential structures and meanings.

Comparative and systematic approach   There is widespread agreement that phenomenology of religion is a very general, comparative approach concerned with classifying and systematizing religious phenomena. Phenomenologists are able to gain insight into essential structures and meanings only after comparing a large number of documents expressing a great diversity of religious phenomena.

Empirical approach   Bleeker, Eliade, and most phenomenologists of religion insist that they use an empirical approach that is free from a priori assumptions and judgments. Such an empirical approach, often described as 'scientific' and 'objective,' begins by collecting religious documents and then goes on to describe just what the empirical data reveal.

One of the most frequent attacks on phenomenology of religion is that it is not empirically based and that it is therefore arbitrary, subjective, and unscientific. Critics charge that the universal structures and meanings are not found in the empirical data and that the phenomenological discoveries are not subject to empirical tests of verification.

Historical approach   Phenomenologists of religion usually maintain not only that their approach must cooperate with and complement historical research but also that phenomenology of religion is profoundly historical. All religious data are historical; no phenomena may be understood outside their history. The phenomenologist must be aware of the specific historical, cultural, and socioeconomic contexts within which religious phenomena appear.

Critics charge that phenomenology of religion is not historical, both in terms of a phenomenological method that neglects the specific historical and cultural context and with regard to the primacy – methodologically and even ontologically – it grants to nonhistorical and nontemporal universal structures.

Descriptive approach   Almost all phenomenologists of religion today do not restrict themselves to mere description of religious phenomena. While cognizant of Kristensen's concerns about the subjective nature of much past scholarship in which interpreters filtered data through their own assumptions and value judgments, phenomenologists go far beyond the severe methodological restrictions of his descriptive phenomenology.

And yet these same phenomenologists invariably classify their discipline and approach as a descriptive phenomenology of religion. They claim to utilize a descriptive approach and see their classifications, typologies, and structures as descriptive. Sometimes phenomenologists of religion distinguish the collection and description of religious data, which is objective and scientific, from the interpretation of meaning, which is at least partially subjective and normative.

Antireductionism   Phenomenologists oppose reductionism, which imposes uncritical preconceptions and unexamined judgments on phenomena, in order to deal with phenomena simply as phenomena and to provide more accurate descriptions of just what the phenomena reveal.

More than any other approach within the modern study of religion, phenomenology of religion insists that investigators approach religious data as phenomena that are fundamentally and irreducibly religious. Otto, Eliade, and others defend their strong antireductionism by criticizing past reductionist approaches. Phenomenologists criticize the reductions of religious data to fit nonreligious perspectives, such as those of sociology, psychology, or economics. Such reductionisms, it is argued, destroy the specificity, complexity, and irreducible intentionality of religious phenomena. In attempting sympathetically to understand the experience of the other, the phenomenologist must respect the 'original' religious intentionality expressed in the data.

Autonomy   Directly related to the antireductionist claim of the irreducibility of the religious is the identification of phenomenology of religion as an autonomous discipline and approach. If there are certain irreducible modes by which religious phenomena are given, then one must utilize a specific method of understanding that is commensurate with the religious nature of the subject matter. One must provide irreducibly religious interpretations of religious phenomena.

Phenomenology of religion is autonomous but not self-sufficient. It depends heavily on historical research and on data supplied by philology, ethnology, psychology, sociology, and other approaches. But it must always integrate the contributions of other approaches within its own unique phenomenological perspective.

Intentionality   Phenomenology analyzes acts of consciousness as consciousness of something and claims that meaning is given in the intentionality of the structure. In order to identify, describe, and interpret the meaning of religious phenomena, scholars must be attentive to the intentional structure of their data. For Otto, the a priori structure of religious consciousness is consciousness of its intended 'numinous object.' Van der Leeuw's phenomenological-psychological technique and Eliade's dialectic of the sacred are methods for capturing the intentional characteristics of religious manifestations. The major criticism made by phenomenologists of religion of reductionist approaches involves the latter's negation of the unique intentionality of religious phenomena.

Religious experiences reveal structures of transcendence in which human beings intend a transcendent referent, a supernatural meta-empirical sacred meaning. Religious language points beyond itself to intended sacred structures and meanings that transcend normal spatial, temporal, historical, and conceptual categories and analysis. That is why religious expressions are highly symbolic, analogical, metaphorical, mythic, and allegorical.

At the same time, no intentional referent and meaning is unmediated. Such intentionality is always historically, culturally, and linguistically situated. For meaningful religious experience and communication, the intended transcendent referent must be mediated and brought into an integral human relation with our limited spatial, temporal, historical, cultural world with its intended objects and meanings. This is why symbolism, in its complex and diverse structures and functions, is essential for revealing, constituting, and communicating religious intentional meaning. Religious symbolic expressions serve as indispensable mediating bridges. On the one hand, they always point beyond themselves to intended transcendent meanings. On the other hand, by necessarily using symbolic language drawn from the spatial, temporal, natural, historical world of experience, they mediate the transcendent referent, limit and incarnate the sacred, allow the disclosure of the transcendent as imminent, and render sacred meanings humanly accessible and relevant to particular existential situations.

This specific religious intentionality ensures that the structures of religious experience, as well as interpretations and understandings, will remain open-ended. The necessary structural conditions for religious experience, the construction of religious texts, and the formulation of scholarly interpretations ensure that meaningful human understandings necessarily reveal limited intentional perspectives. And such relative, situated, intentional, religious perspectives always point beyond themselves to structures of transcendence; to inexhaustible possibilities for revalorizing symbolic expressions, for bursting open self-imposed perspectival closures, and for new, creative, self-transcending experiences, interpretations, and understandings.

Epoché, empathy, and sympathetic understanding   By bracketing and suspending our unexamined assumptions and ordinary preconceptions and judgments, we become attentive to a much fuller disclosure of what manifests itself and how it manifests itself in experience. This allows for greater awareness of phenomena experienced on prereflective, emotive, imaginative, nonconceptual levels of intentional experience, thus leading to new insights into the specific intentionality and concrete richness of experience.

The phenomenological *epoché*, with an emphasis on empathy and sympathetic understanding, is related to methodological antireductionism. By suspending all personal preconceptions as to what is real and insisting on the irreducibility of the religious, phenomenologists attempt sympathetically to place themselves within the religious 'life-world' of others and to grasp the religious meaning of the experienced phenomena. Critics charge that phenomenologists often give little more than vague appeals to abstain from value judgments and to exercise a personal capacity for empathetic participation, but without scholarly criteria for verifying whether such sympathetic understanding has been achieved.

There are limitations to this personal participation, since the other always remains to some extent the 'other.' This phenomenological orientation may be contrasted with the ideal of detached, impersonal scientific objectivity that characterizes almost all nineteenth-century approaches within the scholarly study of religion and that continues to define many approaches today.

In assuming a sympathetic attitude, the phenomenologist is not claiming that religious phenomena are not 'illusory' and that the intentional object is 'real.' (As a matter of fact, many phenomenologists make such theological and metaphysical assumptions and judgments, but these usually violate the self-defined limits of their phenomenological perspectives.) The phenomenological bracketing entails the suspension of all such value judgments regarding whether or not the holy or sacred is actually an experience of ultimate reality.

Many phenomenologists argue for the necessity of religious commitment, a personal religious faith, or at least personal religious experience in order for a scholar to be capable of empathy, participation, and sympathetic understanding. Other phenomenologists argue that such personal religious commitments generally produce biased descriptions. It seems that a particular faith or theological commitment is not a precondition for accurate phenomenological descriptions. Rather it is a commitment to religious phenomena, manifested in terms of intellectual curiosity, sensitivity, and respect, that is indispensable for participation and understanding. Such a commitment may be shared by believers and nonbelievers alike.

Insight into essential structures and meanings   No subject matter is more central to philosophical phenomenology than analyses of the eidetic reduction and eidetic vision, the intuition of essences, the method of free variation, and other techniques for gaining insight into the essential structures and meanings of phenomena. By contrast, phenomenology of religion, even in the specific sense of an approach concerned with describing essential structures and meanings, has usually avoided such methodological formulations.

One generally finds that most phenomenologists of religion accept both Bleeker's qualification that such terms as 'eidetic vision' are used only in a figurative sense and his warning that phenomenology of religion should not meddle in difficult philosophical questions of methodology. The result is that one is frequently presented with phenomenological typologies, 'universal structures,' and 'essential meanings' that lack a rigorous analysis of just how the phenomenologist arrived at or verified these discoveries.

Phenomenologists aim at intuiting, interpreting, and describing the essence of religious phenomena, but there is considerable disagreement as to what constitutes an essential structure. For some phenomenologists, an 'essential structure' is the result of an empirical inductive generalization expressing a property that different phenomena have in common. In the sense closest to philosophical phenomenology, essence refers to deep or hidden structures, which are not apparent on the level of immediate experience and must be uncovered and interpreted through the phenomenological method. These structures express the necessary invariant features allowing us to distinguish religious phenomena and to grasp religious phenomena as phenomena of a certain kind.

Controversial issues

The examination of major characteristics of phenomenology of religion raises many controversial issues.

Descriptive versus normative claims   There are controversial issues regarding the claim that phenomenology of religion is a descriptive discipline with a descriptive method, especially since almost all phenomenologists go far beyond a mere description of the data, offering comparisons and evaluations of phenomena, universal structures, and essential meanings.

Many of these issues arise from the acceptance of a rather traditional descriptive–normative distinction. The adoption by many phenomenologists of religion of a radical, at times absolute, descriptive–normative dichotomy has been consistent with the classical empiricism of such philosophers as David Hume, with the Kantian philosophical framework, and with most nineteenth- and twentieth-century approaches to religions.

Even those phenomenologists of religion who go beyond Kristensen's descriptive restrictions frequently adopt a clear distinction between the collection and description of religious data, which is seen as objective and scientific, and the interpretation of meaning, which is at least partially subjective and normative. Despite its rejection of earlier models of positivism, it may be that phenomenology of religion has unintentionally retained some of the positivistic assumptions regarding the description of unconstructed, uninterpreted, objective 'facts.'

Recent scholarship often challenges this absolute dichotomy. What is taken as objective and scientific is historically, culturally, and socially situated, based on presuppositions, and constructed in terms of implicit and explicit value judgments. For example, how does one even begin the investigation? What facts should be collected as religious facts? One's very principles of selectivity are never completely value-free. Indeed, philosophical phenomenologists have never accepted this sharp dichotomy, since the entire phenomenological project is founded on the possibilities of describing meanings. The challenge to phenomenology of religion is to formulate a phenomenological method and framework for interpretation that allows the description of essential structures and meanings with some sense of objectivity.

Understanding versus explanation claims   Many controversial issues involve a sharp understanding–explanation dichotomy. Phenomenology often claims that it aims at understanding, which involves describing meanings, and avoids explanation, which involves uncovering historical, psychological, and other causal relationships. Phenomenologists describe what appears and how it appears, and they interpret the meaning of such phenomena, but they do not provide causal explanations. This 'understanding' often has the sense of *Verstehen* as formulated by Dilthey and others as the method and goal of hermeneutics. Phenomenologists aim at interpreting meaning and understanding the nature of religious and other 'human' phenomena, as opposed to scientific, reductionistic approaches that give causal and other explanations and do not grasp the irreducibly human and irreducibly religious dimension of the phenomena they investigate.

Critics challenge such methods and goals as unscholarly and unscientific, and many scholars question whether phenomenological understanding and nonphenomenological explaining can be so completely separated. Explanatory approaches always involve understanding, and understanding is not possible without critical explanatory reflection. For example, even in terms of phenomenological understanding, the expressions of the religious other are not the final word, absolute and inviolable. The other may have a limited understanding of phenomena shaping her or his religious life-world, provide false explanations, talk nonsense, and engage in blatantly unethical behavior. Phenomenology of religion necessarily involves critical reflection, including contextual awareness and scholarly interpretations, understandings, and explanations that go beyond describing the expressed position of the religious other.

This in no way denies the value of phenomenological approaches that are self-critical in rendering explicit one's own presuppositions, suspend one's own value judgments, empathize and hear the voices of the religious other, and describe as accurately as possible the religious phenomena and intended meanings of the religious other. Such phenomenology of religion aims at finding ways to allow other voices to be heard and is informed by a history of dominant, critical, normative approaches and reductionistic explanations that ignore, silence, and misinterpret the religious phenomena of others.

Antireductionist claims Many critics attack phenomenology of religion's antireductionism, arguing that it is methodologically confused and unjustified and that it arises from the theological intention of defending religion against secular analysis. Critics argue that all methodological approaches are perspectival, limiting, and necessarily reductionistic. The assumption of the irreducibility of the religious is itself reductionistic, since it limits what phenomena will be investigated, what aspects of the phenomena will be described, and what meanings will be interpreted. Phenomenologists of religion cannot argue that other reductionistic approaches are necessarily false and that their approach does justice to all dimensions of religious phenomena.

Phenomenology of religion must show that its religious antireductionism is not methodologically confused, does not beg serious scholarly questions, and does not simply avoid serious scholarly challenges. It can argue for an antireductionist methodological primacy on the basis of such key notions as intentionality and insight into essential structures and meanings. It must show, in terms of a rigorous method with procedures for verification, that its particular perspective is essential in shedding light on such religious structures and meanings.

Empirical and historical claims Much of philosophical phenomenology, even when described as a radical empiricism, is conceived in opposition to traditional empiricism adopted by many approaches to religion. Husserl called for a 'phenomenological reduction' in which the phenomenologist 'suspends' the 'natural standpoint' and its empirical world in order to become more attentive to phenomena and to intuit the deeper phenomenological essences.

Critics often claim that phenomenology of religion starts with a priori nonempirical assumptions, utilizes a method that is not empirically based, and detaches religious structures and meanings from their specific historical and cultural contexts. Such critics often assume a clear-cut dichotomy between an empirical, inductive, historical approach and a nonempirical, often rationalist, deductive, antihistorical approach. They identify their approaches with the former and phenomenology of religion with versions of the latter. They conclude that the phenomenology of religion cannot meet minimal empirical, historical, inductive criteria for a scientific approach, such as rigorous criteria for verification and falsification.

Controversies arise from criticisms that phenomenology of religion is highly norma-tive and subjective because it makes nonempirical, nonhistorical, a priori, theological, and other normative assumptions, and because it grants an ontologically privileged status to religious phenomena and to specific kinds of religious experience. Critics charge that Kristensen, Otto, van der Leeuw, Eliade, and others have nonempirical and nonhistorical, extraphenomenological, theological, and other normative assump-tions, intentions, and goals that define much of their phenomenological projects, taking them beyond the domain of a descriptive phenomenology and any rigorous scientific approach.

The status granted to essential religious structures and meanings is also contro-versial insofar as they exhibit the peculiarity of being empirical – that is, based on investigating a limited sample of historical data – and, at the same time, universal. These structures are therefore empirically contingent and yet also the essential neces-sary features of religious phenomena.

Finally, there is controversy regarding the insistence by many phenomenologists of religion that they proceed by some kind of empirical inductive inference that is not unlike the classical formulations of induction developed by John Stuart Mill and others. Critics charge that they cannot repeat this inductive inference, that the phenomenological structures do not appear in the empirical data, and that phenom-enologists read into their data all kinds of essential meanings. Some, such as Douglas Allen in *Structure and Creativity in Religion*, respond by formulating a method of 'phenomenological induction' different from classical empirical induction, in which essential structures and meaning are based on, but not found fully in, the empirical data.

Questions of verification Many criticisms that phenomenology of religion is method-ologically uncritical involve questions of verification. Phenomenological 'intuition' does not free one from the responsibility of ascertaining which interpretation of a given phenomenon is most adequate nor of substantiating why this is so. Fueling this controversy is the observation that different phenomenologists, while investi-gating the same phenomena and claiming to utilize the phenomenological method, continually present different eidetic intuitions. How does one resolve this contin-gency introduced into phenomenological insights? How does one verify specific interpretations and decide between different interpretations?

Such questions pose specific difficulties for a phenomenological method of *epoché* and intuition of essences. A phenomenological method often suspends the usual cri-teria of 'objectivity' that allow scholars to verify interpretations and choose between alternative accounts. Does this leave phenomenology of religion with a large number of very personal, extremely subjective, hopelessly fragmented interpretations of uni-versal structures and meanings, each relativistic interpretation determined by the par-ticular temperament, situation, and orientation of the individual phenomenologist?

The phenomenologist of religion can argue that past criteria for verification are inadequate and result in a false sense of objectivity, but phenomenology of religion must also overcome the charges of subjectivity and relativism by struggling with ques-tions of verification. It must formulate procedures for testing its claims of essential structures and meanings that involve criteria for intersubjective verification.

Response to controversial issues   Many writers describe phenomenology of religion as in a state of crisis. They usually minimize the invaluable contributions made by phenomenology to the study of religion, such as the impressive systematization of so much religious data and the raising of fundamental questions of meaning often ignored by other approaches.

If phenomenology of religion is to deal adequately with its controversial issues, the following are several of its future tasks. First, it must become more aware of historical, philological, and other specialized approaches to, and different aspects of, its religious data. Second, it must critique various approaches of its critics, thus showing that its phenomenological method is not obliged to meet such inadequate criteria for objectivity. And most importantly, it must reflect more critically on questions of methodology so that phenomenology of religion can formulate a more rigorous method, allowing for description of phenomena, interpretation of their structures and meanings, and verification of its findings.

Recent developments in phenomenology of religion

Developments within phenomenology of religion during the last decades of the twentieth century and the early years of the twenty-first century convey a very mixed and confusing picture about the present status and future prospects for the field.

Within religious studies

Phenomenology of religion continues as a major discipline and approach within the general scholarly study of religion. Phenomenologists of religion are influenced by earlier phenomenologists, and they share the general phenomenological orientation defined by the major characteristics previously delineated. Phenomenology of religion has also been successful to the extent that many other scholars, who do not consider themselves phenomenologists, adopt a phenomenological approach during early stages of their scholarly investigations because it has great value in allowing them to assemble data and do justice to the religious perspectives of religious persons.

At the same time, phenomenology of religion is sometimes described as being in a state of crisis. There are no contemporary phenomenologists of religion who enjoy the status and influence once enjoyed by a van der Leeuw or an Eliade. Some scholars, doing phenomenology of religion, are uncomfortable with the term since it carries so much past baggage from Husserlian philosophical foundations and from Eliadean and other phenomenology of religion they consider outdated. In general, contemporary phenomenologists of religion attempt to be more contextually sensitive and more modest in their phenomenological claims.

Recent challenges

Most scholarly challenges to phenomenology of religion continue major criticisms previously described. Robert Segal and other leading scholars of religion, usually identified with social scientific and reductionist approaches, repeatedly criticize phenomenology of religion for being unscientific, highly subjective, and lacking scholarly rigor. Scholars identifying with reductionistic cognitive science and claiming that this is the only rigorous method and model for gaining objective knowledge provide a recent illustration of such challenges.

There are also challenges to phenomenology of religion that offer opposite criticisms from the social scientific reductionist approaches. They criticize the phenomenology of religion's claim to uncover universal structures and essences as being too reductionistic in denying the diversity and plurality of religious phenomena. Included here are a variety of approaches often described as postmodernist, deconstructionist, post-structuralist, narrativist, pragmatist, feminist, and relativist.

For example, in *Beyond Phenomenology: Rethinking the Study of Religion*, Gavin Flood argues that the inadequate presuppositions, central concepts, and models of Husserl's philosophical phenomenology have dominated the study of religion. Influenced primarily by Mikhail Bakhtin's dialogical analysis and Ricoeur's hermeneutical analysis, Flood proposes a dialogical, narrativist, interactional, dynamic model for rethinking the study of religion. This model includes: recognition of signs and language as a starting point; rejection of essentializing hegemonic approaches with universalizing claims to objectivity; recognition that self is always embodied and embedded, relational and interactive, contextualized, constituted and constituting subject; recognition of complex narrativist situatedness of both investigator and subject matter with dialogical, mutually interactive relations between the two perspectives; and affirmation of open-ended, perspectival nature of all knowledge with emphasis on nonclosure of interpretations and explanations.

In response, one can submit that Flood greatly exaggerates the impact of Husserlian transcendental phenomenology on the study of religion, and that most critiques of phenomenology and the anti-phenomenological features he formulates can be found within later developments of philosophical phenomenology and phenomenology of religion.

Philosophical phenomenology of religion

The emphasis in this chapter has been on phenomenology of religion as a discipline and method within *Religionswissenschaft* (general history of religions or religious studies). The emphasis has not been on philosophical phenomenology with its limited focus on religion.

Special mention may be made of two influential European philosophers. Emmanuel Levinas, a student of Husserl with deep roots in phenomenology, became one of the dominant continental philosophers in the late twentieth century. With his major focus on ethics, spirituality, and Jewish philosophy, Levinas emphasized radical alterity and the primacy of the 'other,' thus reversing earlier phenomenological self–other emphasis on the privileged status of the constituting self or ego. Ricoeur, also with deep roots in Husserl and phenomenology, has made invaluable contributions to our understanding of religious phenomena with his analysis of philosophy as the hermeneutical interpretation of meaning and with his focus on religious language, symbolism, and narrative.

Beginning in the last part of the twentieth century, continental philosophy often takes a religious turn. It is not always clear whether to classify such developments under 'the phenomenology of religion,' although scholars such as Michel Henry and especially Jean-Luc Marion are often discussed as part of the renewed interest in philosophical phenomenology of religion and under the 'new phenomenology.' Most of these key philosophers are deeply influenced by Husserl's phenomenology, but they often seem to transgress phenomenology's boundaries and express ambiguous relations to phenomenology.

While significant developments in continental philosophy, usually influenced by Husserl and philosophical phenomenology, increasingly focus on religion, it is not yet clear whether such philosophical developments will have a significant influence on phenomenology of religion within religious studies.

Several recent contributions

Finally, there are three, recent, interrelated contributions to phenomenology of religion that often contrast with earlier dominant characteristics: focus on the 'other,' givenness, and contextualization.

Philosophical phenomenology and phenomenology of religion emphasize the need to become aware of one's presuppositions, suspend one's value judgments, and accurately describe and interpret the meaning of phenomena as phenomena. Past philosophy, theology, and other normative approaches have been critiqued for ignoring or distorting the intentional structures and meanings of the religious phenomena of the 'other.' More recent phenomenologists recognize that earlier phenomenology, with its essentializing projects and universalizing claims, often did not pay sufficient attention to the diverse experiences and meanings of the other. One sometimes learns more about the scholar's phenomenological theory of religion than about the particular religious phenomena of others. Recent phenomenology has been more sensitive to providing a methodological framework for becoming attentive to the tremendous diversity of the religious voices of others.

Related to this is the focus on givenness. Philosophical phenomenology and phenomenology of religion emphasize the need to become attentive to what is given in experience. Phenomenological reflection involves an active openness and deeper kind of attentiveness to how religious phenomena appear or are given to us in experience. Over the decades, phenomenology of religion has become much broader, more self-critical, and more sophisticated in recognizing the complexity, ambiguity, and depth of our diverse modes of givenness. For example, in their very dynamic of givenness, religious phenomena both reveal and conceal structures and meanings; are multidimensional and given meaning through pre-understandings, the prereflective, the emotive, and the imaginative, as well as rational and conceptual analysis; are not disclosed as bare givens but as highly complex, inexhaustible, constituted, self-transcending givens; and are given in ways that affirm the open-ended perspectival nature of all knowledge and the nonclosure of descriptions, interpretations, and explanations.

Phenomenologists of religion are much more sensitive to the complex, mediated, interactive, contextual situatedness of their phenomenological tasks. Philosophical phenomenology and phenomenology of religion are continually criticized for claiming to uncover nonhistorical, nontemporal, essential structures and meanings largely detached from specific contexts within which religious phenomena have been expressed. Recent phenomenologists of religion tend to be more sensitive to the perspectival and contextual constraints of their approach and more modest in their claims. There is value in uncovering religious essences and structures, but as embodied and contextualized, not as fixed, absolute, ahistorical, eternal truths and meanings.

By now, it may be clear to many readers that phenomenology of religion has had a profound impact on diverse branches of religious studies, sometimes overtly and sometimes almost imperceptibly. Many scholars within religious studies, who would never call themselves phenomenologists, have had their teaching and research shaped by the contributions of phenomenology of religion. Their concerns about uncritical presuppositions and reductionism, empathy and essential structures, and other characteristics of phenomenology, as well as the phenomenological focus on such topics as sacred space and time, myth and ritual, have been influenced by their exposure to the phenomenology of religion.

Within the specific discipline and approaches of the phenomenology of religion, a more self-critical and modest phenomenology of religion may have much to contribute to the study of religion. It will include awareness of its presuppositions, its historical and contextualized situatedness, and its limited perspectival knowledge claims. But it will not completely abandon concerns about the commonality of human beings and the value of unity, as well as differences. Such a self-critical and modest phenomenology of religion will attempt to formulate essential structures and meanings through rigorous phenomenological methods, including intersubjective confirmation of knowledge claims, while also attempting to formulate new, dynamic, contextually sensitive projects involving creative encounter, contradiction, and synthesis.

Bibliography

Allen, Douglas. *Structure and Creativity in Religion: Hermeneutics in Mircea Eliade's Phenomenology and New Directions* (The Hague: Mouton, 1978). Modern approaches to religion with focus on Eliade's phenomenology.

Bleeker, C. Jouco. *The Sacred Bridge: Researches into the Nature and Structure of Religion* (Leiden: Brill, 1963). Essays on Bleeker's phenomenology of religion.

Eliade, Mircea. *Patterns in Comparative Religion*, translated by Rosemary Sheed (New York: World, 1963). Systematic morphological work illustrating Eliade's phenomenological framework for interpreting religious meaning.

——— *The Quest: History and Meaning in Religion* (Chicago: University of Chicago Press, 1969). Essays on Eliade's phenomenological method and discipline.

Flood, Gavin. *Beyond Phenomenology: Rethinking the Study of Religion* (London and New York: Cassell, 1999). Narrativist, dialogical, postmodernist challenge to phenomenology of religion.

Honko, Lauri, ed. *Science of Religion: Studies in Methodology* (The Hague: Mouton, 1979). Essays under the title 'The Future of the Phenomenology of Religion.'

Idinopulos, Thomas A. and Edward A. Yonan, eds. *Religion and Reductionism: Essays on Eliade, Segal, and the Challenge of the Social Sciences for the Study of Religion* (Leiden, New York: Brill, 1994). Includes Robert Segal's 'In Defense of Reductionism.'

Janicaud, Dominique. *Phenomenology and the 'Theological Turn': The French Debate* (New York: Fordham University Press, 2000). Essays by Janicaud, Courtine, Ricoeur, Chrétien, Marion, and Henry illustrating a turn toward religion in French philosophy influenced by phenomenology.

Kristensen, William Brede. *The Meaning of Religion: Lectures in the Phenomenology of Religion*, translated by John B. Carman (The Hague: Nijhoff, 1960). Restricted descriptive phenomenology.

Leeuw, Gerardus van der. *Religion in Essence and Manifestation: A Study in Phenomenology*, 2 vols, 2nd edn., translated by J. E. Turner (New York: Harper & Row, 1963). Classic work in phenomenology of religion.

Marion, Jean-Luc. *Being Given: Toward a Phenomenology of Givenness*, translated by Jeffrey Kosky (Stanford, Calif.: Stanford University Press, 2002). Leading philosopher in 'new phenomenology' focusing on religious phenomena.

Otto, Rudolf. *The Idea of the Holy: An Inquiry into the Non-Rational Factor in the Idea of the Divine and its Relation to the Rational*, translated by John W. Harvey (New York and London: Oxford University Press, 1950). Best-known phenomenological account of religious experience.

Ricoeur, Paul. *The Symbolism of Evil*, translated by Emerson Buchanan (New York: Harper & Row, 1967). One of Ricoeur's many philosophical works focusing on religious phenomena.

Scheler, Max. *On the Eternal in Man*, translated by Bernard Noble (London: SCM, New York: Harper, 1960). First major philosophical phenomenologist with focus on religion.

Sharpe, Eric J. *Comparative Religion: A History*, 2nd edn. (La Salle, Ill.: Open Court, 1986). Includes survey of phenomenology of religion.

Smart, Ninian. *The Science of Religion and the Sociology of Knowledge: Some Methodological Questions* (Princeton, N.J.: Princeton University Press, 1973). Background on his phenomenological approach.

Spiegelberg, Herbert, *The Phenomenological Movement: A Historical Introduction*, 2 vols., 3rd edn. (The Hague: Nijhoff, 1982). Most comprehensive general introduction to philosophical phenomenology.

Waardenburg, Jacques. *Classical Approaches to the Study of Religion: Aims, Methods, and Theories of Research*, 2 vols. (The Hague: Mouton, 1973–1974). General introduction to scholars identified with modern study of religion including phenomenologists of religion.

Chapter 11

Comparative religion

William E. Paden

Comparative religion originated as an academic movement in the late nineteenth century. It signified then, as today, the cross-cultural study of all forms and traditions of religious life, as distinguished from the study or exposition of just one. As such, it entails the disciplined, historically informed consideration of any commonalities and differences that appear among religions.

Seeing similarities and differences is a basic activity of the human mind. The perception of relationships and patterns is the way individuals and cultures organize their experience of the world. It is a process without which there would be undifferentiated chaos, or at best only isolated facts. Likewise, specialized knowledge in any field advances by finding or constructing concepts and categories that give order and intelligibility to otherwise unrelated data. Comparison, among other things, is the process by which generalizations and classifications are produced, and is the basis of scientific and interpretive enterprises of every kind. The very concept 'religion,' as an academic definition of a certain area of culture, is such a cross-cultural, comparative category.

There can be no systematic study of religion as a subject matter without cross-cultural perspective. Lacking this, studies of religion would amount either to separate collections of unrelated historical data, or to speculative generalizations based only on the perspective of one culture. Modern generations of scholars have therefore tried to build an objective, or at least transcultural, vocabulary for describing a subject matter that is found in very different times, places and languages. For one cannot generalize about religion on the basis of the language and norms of just a single case, just as geologists do not construct a geology on the basis of the rocks that merely happen to be in one's neighborhood. The neighborhood rocks, analogues to one's own local religion, are themselves instances of certain common, universal properties of geological formations, chemical structures, and evolutionary development. Accordingly, without knowing these 'comparative' elements, one cannot know what is common and what is different about any particular religious phenomenon. Without them, one might not be able to see certain transcultural structures and functions in a given religious system.

Comparative analysis, then, both builds and applies the perspectives, reference points, and materials for any cumulative, interpretive study of religion. Moreover, these resources must necessarily be the collective, synthetic result of the contributions of many specialists, as no single person will have first-hand and technical knowledge of all of the world's religious cultures. While comparison is a tool that can be applied locally or among restricted historical and regional data, this essay focuses on its cross-cultural, generalizing functions.

Comparison: the factor of selectivity

The process of comparison has a basic structure. First, there must be a point of commonality that allows for the comparison of two or more objects. Notably, the very term 'comparison' contains this idea, deriving from the Latin elements *com*, 'with,' and *par*, 'equal.' But comparison does not have to be limited to seeing commonalities. It can also perceive difference with respect to some aspect of what is otherwise in common. In everyday terms, for example, one can compare new houses (= the common factor) with regard to price (= the chosen criterion or aspect of difference). Likewise, one could compare religions (= the broad common factor) with regard to their population size, or their types of authority, or their views on gender; or compare purification rites with regard to their specific methods of removing impurity.

The history of the comparative study of religion is the history and application of what its scholars have taken these common factors and these criteria of difference to be. Comparison in itself is an activity, and not a theory or ideology, but it has been a tool of many different theories and hence employed for either scientific or religious purposes. For example, it has been a means for:

- demonstrating the superiority of one's own religion;
- showing that all religion is based on the same spiritual reality;
- undercutting the absolutist claims of any one religion by showing that it is not unique;
- giving idealized interpretation to religions that might otherwise be considered inferior, marginal, or foreign;
- demonstrating the ability to show 'understanding' of other religions from their own point of view;
- demonstrating or testing any theory (about religion) by giving 'evidence' for it in different cultures.

To take but one example: How might the biblical story of creation appear in the light of some very different 'comparative' approaches? For the believer, to whom the account presents itself as the unique, authoritative Word of God, any comparison with other 'origins' accounts might be to show the superiority of Genesis. In that case, the ancient Babylonian account of creation, the *Enuma Elish*, could be shown to represent a more primitive 'polytheistic' idea of the world, compared to the Bible's ostensibly 'pure' monotheism. The scenarios in the *Enuma Elish* that describe many gods and goddesses generating offspring and having to fend off chaos, would be picked out to contrast unfavorably with the Genesis version of one supreme god who is in charge of creation from the beginning and has no equals.

But for those interested in goddess mythologies, the Genesis story has been presented quite differently. Here the biblical account has been viewed as a latter-day, patriarchal version of mythologies that once honored a primal goddess with her sacred tree and companion serpent. In this comparative sequence, the Hebrew account would be construed as a story that demoted the power of the goddess – who in Genesis becomes the very human Eve, the source of man's fall, and the prototype of female subservience to males.

For those interested in the unity of all religions, and the unity of the human and the divine, the relevant 'comparative' aspect of the Genesis story might be the part about humans being made in God's own image in a time before 'the Fall.' Mythologies depicting an original oneness, for example in Hindu traditions, would then be juxtaposed with this to indicate the universality of the theme.

While the present article focuses mainly on academic, secular comparativism, the traditional role of religious approaches has been so pervasive that it does require some preliminary attention, too.

Religious forms of comparison

For those approaching comparison with religious motivation, their own beliefs are understandably used as a standard of comparison. Historical Christian versions of comparative endeavors provide a range of examples of this.

Examples of Christian 'comparative religion'

Christian theologians needed to account for the existence of other religions and their gods, and traditional strategies included a whole spectrum of negative and positive interpretations that may be summarized briefly.

Demonic origins   Who or what were these 'pagan' gods that received so much devotion? Perhaps they were not really gods at all but demons seeking their own worshippers? How were missionaries to explain the presence of sculpted 'crosses' in Mayan temples that pre-dated the arrival of Christianity? Such overt parallels could easily be seen as the mocking work of Satan, understood to be aping or imitating the true religion.

Historical diffusion   A second Christian strategy of explanation was the idea of 'historical' diffusion. Insofar as nonbiblical religions appeared to have anything truly religious about them, like the belief in a creator god, this could be explained as having been ultimately derived from the original pure monotheism of the biblical patriarchs. Likewise, where there was 'idolatrous' religion, such as the worship of forces of nature, this could be interpreted as a historical 'degeneration' from that same once pure source. Thus, any religious expression could be seen in terms of a unified theory of historical diffusion which assumed that all religions, as all cultures, could be traced to and from the survivors of the Great Flood. Sometimes etymologies were relied on to explain the transmission of these 'survivals' or 'remnants' of the patriarchal times. For example, the Hindu god Brahma was understood as a latter-day historical transformation of the biblical name, 'Abraham.' On other occasions, the idea of travel contact was used to explain how religions like those of the native American Indians were able to obtain their ideas about a creator god. Could knowledge of God have been brought to them across the ocean by one of the lost tribes of Israel?

Allegorical truths   A third mode of Christian comparison was to view other religions as containing *symbols* of Christian truths. Christians were already used to the idea that the Hebrew Bible contained images and events that allegorically prefigured the coming of the Christian messiah. Ancient Hebraic sacrifices, for example, were interpreted as symbolizing the sacrifice of Christ. Likewise, deities of other religions could be seen as representing attributes of the true God – for example, the goddess Athena was interpreted as pointing to God's 'wisdom.'

Natural vs. revealed religion   Christians also developed the idea of natural vs. revealed religion. This is the notion that all humans, by being made in the divine image, have a natural potential to know God. Such endowment could therefore account for the presence of other religions. Yet, while all humans have access to a basic knowledge of God, 'revealed' knowledge was God's *full* revelation through Christ to the biblical communities. In comparison, Christ could naturally be seen as the fulfillment of the innate yearnings of other religious peoples, and Christianity would be understood as religion in its highest, most complete, and universal form.

Dialogue   From modern theology has come the idea of 'dialogue' between religions. This means adopting a 'listening' stance toward others, and not merely a dogmatic, prejudging position that stereotypes others. For example, a statement of the Roman Catholic Church (from the Second Vatican Council, 1962–1965), urged its members to appreciate the presence of 'the holy' in other traditions, and also established a permanent commission to study the other faiths and explore their meaning through open dialogue. Wilfrid Cantwell Smith (1916–2000), an influential comparativist and specialist in Islam, emphasized that the comparative study of religion needs to responsibly describe the living qualities of other peoples' faiths in a way that those other persons themselves would be able to recognize as their own position.

Universalism

In contrast to Christian comparisons, there is another religious approach that may be termed universalism. This affirms that all religions refer to the *same* underlying spiritual reality, but do so through different cultural forms and languages. Just as water is water, regardless of what it is called, so, in universalistic thinking, God is God, regardless of name. Even in the world of ancient Greece, there was a well-known doctrine of 'the equivalence of the gods.' Thus, the fifth-century BC Greek historian Herodotus reported that the gods of Egypt were basically Egyptian names for Greek divinities: Ammon was but another name for Zeus, Horus was the same as Apollo, and Isis was taken as equivalent to the goddess Demeter.

Universalism became highly developed in classical Stoicism and during the European Renaissance, and was later fostered by the Romantic, Transcendentalist, and New Age movements. It has been a basic premise of many Asian and mystical traditions. In the Far East, Buddhists commonly interpreted native Chinese and Japanese gods as 'manifestations' of cosmic buddhas. Buddhas were the 'originals,' and the local gods were their 'appearances.'

Universalism has variants. For some, it is motivated by a sense that all humans are basically alike. Many find a common set of precepts undergirding the world's religions, such as the need to honor a divine being and assume ethical responsibility. Some look for common affirmations about peace or nonviolence. Still others understand the universal basis of religion in terms of a core spiritual experience or revelation of the divine. In that outlook, institutional and doctrinal differences are merely seen as the secondary, outward elaborations of a shared, intuitive sense of the 'wholly other' mystery that grounds all life.

The rise of comparative religion as an academic field

Interpreting and comparing religions evolves along with expanding knowledge of other cultures. One can only compare what lies within one's horizon of information. One can only study 'others' on the basis of the *kind* of knowledge of other cultures that is available at the time. In the Hebrew Bible, for example, references to other religions are always citations of other Near Eastern religions, not of Chinese, Japanese, or Indian religion. As recently as the early nineteenth century, Western Christendom still basically classified all religion into only four kinds, namely the three biblical monotheisms (Judaism, Christianity, Islam) and all others, lumped together as 'idolatry,' or 'paganism,' a derogatory term referring to those who supposedly worshipped false gods. Accounts brought back by missionaries and travelers continued to support the stereotype of the benighted state of non-Western or non-biblical peoples.

By the mid to late nineteenth century, however, the comparative study of religion, by that name, was being put forth as a modern academic field of knowledge. Several developments made this possible. One was the expanding knowledge of Asian religions, particularly through access to translations of their scriptures. A second was the emerging knowledge of pre-literate cultures, produced partly by the new field of anthropology. A third was a new idea of history, namely that the whole of human culture had undergone a long evolution from primitive origins (in contrast to the biblical account of human origins). And a fourth was the general trend toward classifying and mapping the data of the world's various subject matters. Together, these factors created a broad, new canvas for the study of religion.

The most influential nineteenth-century advocate of comparative religion was F. Max Müller (1823–1900). A native of Germany and then scholar at Oxford University from age 23, Müller was an authority on Sanskrit, the classical religious language of India. He edited an important 50-volume translation series termed *The Sacred Books of the East*. He urged that the study of religion should no longer be limited to the religions of the Mediterranean and that the great civilizational religions of the East, and their scriptures, should be taken seriously. Asian religions were to be brought into a horizon of respectful comparability with biblical religions. Here the older, parochial Western view of religious history as a simple contest of biblical vs. pagan traditions was to become obsolete.

Along these lines, more accurate histories of religion were produced. These replaced the previous provincial notions that all human languages derive from Hebrew, that all cultures and religions were traceable to the family of Noah, and that the dating of scriptures – whether biblical or nonbiblical – should be taken at face value.

Müller and others held that comparative religion is to any one religion as comparative philology is to the study of any particular language, and as comparative anatomy is to the anatomy of any one species. As the life sciences made progress through application of this method, so too would religious inquiry. The study of one religion would throw light on the study of another. Müller liked to apply to religion what the poet Goethe said of language: 'he who knows one . . . knows none.' In addition, Müller also outlined a broad program and methodology of comparative study. This included principles like gaining knowledge of others through their own writings, grouping religions according to their regional, linguistic contexts, and avoiding the common distortion of comparing the positive aspects of one religion with the negative aspects of another (Müller 1872).

Toward an academic comparativism

In principle, though not always in practice, academic comparativism does not presuppose the value or truth of any one religion, but sets out to investigate religion as a patterned phenomenon of human culture and behavior. The rise of comparativism as a concern of the human sciences required in the first place that all religion would be studied by the same criteria. No religion would be privileged. No religious version of history would be used as normative. While all religions professed their own ancestral accounts of the past, the new, panhuman, naturalistic worldview now showed quite a different story of origins – a long, complex evolution of culture that did not coincide with the self-interested accounts of the various world scriptures. Religion – once the norm in terms of which all history and culture was perceived – now itself became an object to be interpreted in terms of wider patterns of human history.

Again, one source of this new knowledge was so-called primitive cultures, and anthropologists looked to these to find the origin of the fundamental structures of religious belief and practice and to identify universal laws about their evolution. The English scholar Edward B. Tylor (1832–1917) found 'belief in spiritual beings' (which he worked into a theory he called 'animism') to originate in the experience of dreams and of deceased relatives, and thence to evolve into forms of polytheism and monotheism. Others focused on the universal role of 'power' or *mana* (Melanesian term for supernatural force) in religions. The influential French sociologist Émile Durkheim (1858–1917) advocated that the source and structuring principle of religious life was 'the totemic principle.' In this theory, sacred objects were maintained as sacred because they symbolized each group's own social identity and tradition. Arnold van Gennep's classic, *Rites of Passage* (original French edition, 1908), showed the universality of ritual patterns by which social and life-cycle transitions were performed, and became part of the currency of comparative thinking. An influential application of comparativism to biblical religion was W. Robertson Smith's *The Religion of the Semites* (1889). Smith located ancient Hebrew practices in terms of common 'primitive' categories of totemic communion, sacrificial rites, sacred places, and taboos. The suggestion that biblical religion could be seen in such contexts was a scandal to many in his day.

The best known of these pre-modern comparativists was James G. Frazer (1854–1941), particularly through his book, *The Golden Bough*, first published in two volumes in 1890, and later to grow to twelve volumes. *The Golden Bough* was a vast compendium of examples of ritual, myth, and religion, organized by patterns and themes, and presented as an instance of comparative method. Frazer made extensive use of sources from primitive and folk cultures. The work began by citing an obscure Roman rite about the practice of succession to the priesthood of the goddess Diana, an institution that appeared to involve a ritual killing of the old priest by a new priest who would then assume the office. As a way of throwing comparative light on this, Frazer marshaled extensive illustrations from around the world that addressed the theme and subthemes of the ritual renewal of life, thus providing a universal context to the original Italian example. *The Golden Bough* became a study of the transcultural themes of sacred kingship, rites of succession, seasonal renewal festivals, mythologies of dying and rising gods, rites of scapegoating and expulsion, various forms of sympathetic and 'contagious' magic, and substitutionary ritual deaths, among other topics. Frazer thought that these showed the patterned way that the premodern human mind worked – a kind of archaeology of mentality. He held that once these universal patternings were understood, then particular cultural practices and beliefs, otherwise obscure or foreign, might become more intelligible.

Psychologists Sigmund Freud (1856–1939) and C.G. Jung (1875–1961) also began to interpret religious patternings as expressions of the way the human psyche works. In particular, Jung correlated stages of the development of the human ego/self with what he took to be the equivalence of those stages expressed in the projection and history of mythological symbols. Hence certain psychological patterns or 'archetypes' could be found in religion – expressed, for example, in images of a primal paradise, a Great Mother, the journey of the 'hero,' or the reconciling 'union of opposites.' 'God-images' were understood to represent various features of the 'archetype of the self,' in all its stages. The writings of Joseph Campbell (1904–1987) – including the classic, *The Hero with a Thousand Faces* – would bring much of this approach into the public domain.

If recurring religious representations and practices appear independently in different cultures, with no explanation for their resemblances in terms of historical influence, then that might suggest that the parallels express something common to the human condition. But what? What is it that the patternings of religious life ultimately express? What are they patterns *of*? The human psyche? Social bonding? Political power? Gender empowerments? Varying environments? Social class? Are there stages of development that religious history goes through, and do the stages of the development of society and consciousness explain the varieties of religion? All of these trajectories of explanation utilized, indeed, required, comparative data. All have served as frameworks for pursuing and organizing the cross-cultural study of religion. Here, then, comparison ultimately involves more than description. It is guided by issues of explanation, too, and becomes a testing ground for theories of human behavior.

Inventories, taxonomies, phenomenologies

In late-nineteenth-century Europe, the general 'science of religion' included two principle components: historical and phenomenological. The latter referred mainly to a description of *types* and *forms* of religious experience. Its task was to collate and organize all the data of religious history into groupings or classes of religious expressions – that is, to identify an overall taxonomy or anatomy of religious life. This was an inventorial enterprise that resulted in encyclopedic catalogues illustrating all the common forms of religion. An example was the influential work of P.D. Chantepie de la Saussaye published in 1887 (in German) and translated as *Manual of the Science of Religion*. Chantepie classed kinds of religious 'phenomena' together, along with subclasses. For example, the class, 'objects of veneration,' included stones, trees, animals, sky, earth, sun, moon, fire, ancestors, saints, heroes, and gods. He grouped together 'practices' under rubrics like divination, sacrifice, prayer, sacred dance and music, processions, rites of purification, sacred times and places, and described categories such as priests (and other religious specialists), scriptures, types of religious communities, myths, and theologies. Chantepie illustrated each category with examples from different cultures, and summarized the research that had been done on it. What naturalists like Linnaeus had done for the botanical world was now to be done for religion. The religious world had to be mapped, and its many species, here its 'classes of phenomena,' named and typed.

The phenomenology of religion tradition also went beyond just mapping. It began to look for an understanding of how religious forms function in the worlds of the adherents. Two major figures that developed this were Gerardus van der Leeuw in his *Religion in Essence and Manifestation* (German original, 1933), and Mircea Eliade. Van der Leeuw's book, which described religion as a relationship to an 'other power,' focused on some 106 patterns of religious life. For each one he tried to bring out the essential religious values, structure, and meanings connected with it.

Mircea Eliade's comparative patterns

The best-known comparative religion scholar of the last generation was the Rumanian-born Mircea Eliade (1907–1986), who came to the University of Chicago in 1956. Eliade's interest was in the recurring patterns and symbolisms by which religious cultures construct and inhabit their particular kinds of 'worlds,' through the language of myth and ritual. Such systems are structured by the factor of 'the sacred,' which makes them different from the nonreligious worlds which lack that dimension. Eliade used the term *hierophany*, which literally means 'a manifestation of the sacred,' to refer to any object or form believed to convey spiritual power and value. Examples include trees, places, hunting, eating, one's country, personal gods, cosmic gods, or yogic techniques that aim at liberation from the human condition. Moreover, 'To many a mystic,' Eliade writes, 'the integrated quality of the cosmos is itself a hierophany' (Eliade 1958: 459). Some particularly distinctive comparative 'modalities of the sacred' as interpreted by Eliade include:

Sacred space   All humans have the experience of space, but religious cultures endow special places as gateways or connectors to the world of the sacred. Religious systems orient life around certain fixed points that form a site of communication with the gods. The sites may be natural, provided by the environment, like certain rivers or mountains, or they may be human constructions like shrines and temples. Sometimes these linkages are explicitly understood to connect heaven and earth, the above and the below. Around such an axis, or 'Centre of the World,' the rest of the world, the ordinary world, rises up and receives its value. A grand-scale example would be the great shrine at Mecca, the Ka'ba, the spiritual point on earth that Muslims believe God ordained as a bond with humanity. But local altars may also comprise an *axis mundi* (world axis), too.

The history of religion will show innumerable 'centres of the world,' each of which is absolute for the respective believers. Eliade's point is that this kind of language should not be judged literally or geographically, but as illustrative of a common religious way of structuring one's world through concentrative, centripetal points of focus (objects, places, mountains, shrines). That is, because a 'world' is relative to a people, these centres are not superstitious beliefs, but examples of a way the mind orients itself in space. Traditional Christian beliefs that placed Jerusalem's Church of the Holy Sepulchre (the traditional site of the tomb of Christ) at the centre of the world and world maps, or the equivalent claims in other traditions, may be then understood in this wider comparative context. In Eliadean usage, such comparative perspective on sacred space gives context, dimensionality and universal humanity to any particular version of religious places and orientations.

Mythic time   A related religious pattern featured in Eliade's work is 'sacred time.' These are ritual or festival occasions when believers step into the revered 'Great Time' of the founders and gods. Religious cultures see themselves in terms of their own foundational sacred histories – accounts of primal, originary times when the world was created by the actions of the great beings of the past. However, it is not just past, chronological time. It is time that always underlies present time, and can be accessed periodically and reenacted through ritual time. In this way, one's world is renewed and reempowered.

Sacrality of nature   Eliade held that for *homo religiosus* ('religious man') sacrality is often revealed through the very structures of nature. These include patterns connected with the infinity and transcendence of the sky, the fecundity of the earth, the power of the sun, the waxing and waning cycle of the moon and of life and death, the durability of stones, and the solubility and creativity of water. As such, these 'systems of symbolism' form connections with various religious motifs. Examples are the association of creator deities with the sky, goddesses with earth and moon, and baptismal rebirth with water. These and other complexes are described at length in Eliade's *Patterns in Comparative Religion* (first French edition 1949).

Eliade's approach, which he referred to as the 'History of Religions,' provided a set of comparative categories that cut across the particular religious traditions. At the same time, for Eliade the study of religion was a study in human creativity, on the analogy that religions are complex symbolic universes like great works of art. Studying these 'creations,' he thought, would have a culturally de-provincializing and rejuvenating effect.

In most respects Eliade's work is representative of both the strengths and weaknesses of traditional academic comparative religion. Many of the contemporary critiques of comparativism are critiques of Eliadeanism, and typically include the charge that cross-cultural categories illegitimately override significant cultural contexts and differences. This and other issues will be addressed next.

Issues and critiques

Comparativism is not without its problems and critics. It can make superficial parallels, false analogies, misleading associations. Many historians believe that the best way to study religion is to avoid the application of abstract, generic concepts, with their preestablished meanings, and to build a knowledge of a particular religious tradition on its own terms, through its own primary sources. Critics of comparativism therefore often claim that it is always the specific, not the general, that is 'the real,' and that religious phenomena are indelibly embedded in unique sociocultural settings and hence are incomparable. As well, the 'same' theme – such as water or sacred space – may have different meanings and functions in different historical contexts. The distinctiveness of religious cultures, in this sense, would seem to remain elusively off the comparative grid. Briefly, here is a summary of these critical issues:

Comparativism as suppressing difference   Perhaps the most common criticism of cross-cultural categorizations is that they suppress or conceal significant difference, giving the illusion of homogeneity by making the expressions of other cultures conform to the concepts used by the scholar. The comparativist's concepts, the critic maintains, are themselves cultural, for example, European or Christian. Other societies are then reduced to instances of Euro-Christian classifications. Vague and dubious resemblances are abstracted from rich diversity, and the representation of others is limited to only those points which illustrate the scholar's own vocabulary. If a Westerner sets out to compare different ideas of 'God' around the world, he already has a standard of what to look for and it may be inadequate to describing non-Western representations of the superhuman.

A major advocate of the need for more rigorous contextual analysis in the comparative enterprise is the University of Chicago scholar, Jonathan Z. Smith. Many of his essays (Smith 1982, 1987, 1990) challenge traditional categories and methods of comparison. To take one instance, Smith critiques Eliade's interpretation of the sacred 'pole' of a certain aboriginal Australian tribe. Eliade had maintained that the pole represented a kind of world axis that could nevertheless be carried from place to place. This portable link with the world above would allow the tribe to remain 'in its universe.' Smith's careful examination of the evidence showed that Eliade had superimposed the notion of a 'World Center' onto a culture which had very different notions of space and no notions of ritual linkages with a world above. The world axis idea, Smith pointed out, belonged to other kinds of cultures, like those of ancient Near Eastern city states, where political power was highly centralized and manifest in temples linking the human and the gods. But the Australian notion of space and environment lacked these elements. Smith concluded that 'The "Center" is not a secure pattern to which data may be brought as illustrative; it is a dubious notion that will have to be established anew on the basis of detailed comparative endeavors' (Smith 1987: 17).

Comparativism not only has been accused of inaccuracy of representation, but has been charged with political arrogance: appropriating 'others' to one's worldview and depriving them of their own voices. So-called cross-cultural thought can thus become a form of colonialist ideology – a means of extending one's own values over all and at the same time suppressing the 'subjectivity' of those who differ. According to this criticism, comparativism amounts to a kind of conceptual imperialism exercised by one culture, class, or gender over others.

So-called postmodern thinking challenges the notion of objectivity and maintains that comparative accounts are grounded in ideologies and used for the scholar's own theoretical purposes. Thus, what the comparativist takes as patterns 'out there,' should really be seen as strategies for manipulating data for subjective or cultural goals.

Comparativism as theological/ontological   Many comparative religion scholars have strong religious interests. Even if those interests are not narrowly sectarian, scholars often assume that religion is based on a general divine reality of some kind, which they sometimes generically call 'the Sacred' or 'the Holy.' This gives a hierarchic tone to religion, whereby 'the Sacred' is understood to be that which 'manifests' itself in so many different experiential, ritual, or conceptual domains. Eliade's comparativism, too, was interwoven with a vocabulary about 'the sacred' that many critics think insinuated a theological reality, and thus an unwarranted, unscientific reference to a metaphysical foundation to all religion.

Comparativism as untheoretical   There is also the charge that comparative religion lacks scientific value. The argument is that the practice of just grouping together examples of a topic does not get at the factor of explanation. In order to contribute to scientific knowledge, one would need to show how the presence of religious ideas and practices – for example, monotheism, sacrifice, or a certain idea of salvation – occur in and vary in relation to specific social or historical conditions. What *explains* difference and commonality? Anthropologists, for their part, have a long scholarly tradition of comparative analysis – including statistical analysis – of cross-cultural topics (like kinship), with attention to complex variables and co-variables (cf. Naroll and Cohen 1970: 581–1008); and sociologists of religion have comparable analyses of new religious movements. But, it is charged, comparative religion scholarship has yet to incorporate and apply the canons of empirical and analytical methods (Martin 2000).

Some elements of contemporary comparativism

The critiques have meant that the methods and process of cross-cultural concept formation have had to be qualified and defined in more careful ways. Hence, the post-Eliadean phase of comparativism has seen emergent articulations and emphases that in some ways address and remediate the problems just listed (Smith 1982, 1987, 1990; Poole 1986; Martin *et al.* 1996; Martin 2000; Patton and Ray 2000; *Numen*, 2001). The following summarizes some of the elements and affirmations found in contemporary comparativism:

1 The first, as mentioned above and as will be shown in the next sections, is that comparison is *not* just a matter of describing commonality, but a tool that may be used either to find similarity or difference. Insofar as comparison can be used to highlight particulars, it is less subject to the above criticisms (cf. the essay by Robert Segal, 'In Defense of the Comparative Method' in *Numen* 2001: 339–373).

2 'Common factors' or patterns can be understood as matters to be *tested* rather than assumed or taken for granted. As such, a comparative pattern would be like a hypothesis to be explored or a question to be asked in relation to each of its cultural examples (cf. Neville 2001). Counter-evidence would be examined, complexity acknowledged. The cultural bias of the pattern would be taken into account. Thematic inquiry – like the use of any concept that might guide an historian's work – would then amount to a starting point for the complexities of research, leading toward areas of unforeseen possibilities, rather than an ideological gridwork imposed on history once and for all. Certainly comparative analysis is not a substitute for historical analysis. They go together.

3 Comparison should be clearly based on defined *aspects* of that which is compared. By focusing on and controlling the exact point of analogy, the comparativist understands that the objects may be quite incomparable in other respects and for other purposes. Because two or more things do not appear 'the same' on the surface, or as wholes, does not mean that they are not comparable in *some* ways (cf. Poole 1986). There is folk wisdom to the phrase, 'You can't compare apples and oranges,' because on the surface and as a whole, they are not 'the same,' yet they *are* comparable *in some aspects*: both belong to the class 'fruit,' both are edible, both are round and similar in size, and so forth.

4 Another qualifier is that 'cross-cultural' does not necessarily mean universal. A comparative pattern can be widespread, general, a 'near-universal' (a familiar anthropological concept), or applicable to a certain type of culture, without being universal. A cross-cultural pattern does not need to appear in *all* cultures, but only needs to *recur* in relation to certain types or conditions of culture and religious systems. For example, not all religions have shamans, priests, savior figures, animal sacrifices, or scriptures. But the ones that do have certain recurrent social patterns in common.

5 Comparison may legitimately proceed by the use of clear cultural norms or prototypes, as long as the terms and purpose of comparison are understood. For example, one could take something like the Hebrew sacrificial system of the biblical period, and without assuming that it is an adequate basis for understanding all other sacrificial cults, one could investigate other systems that have some resemblances or likeness to it. The resemblance could be a matter of degree, not identity. In fact, if one examines any comparative pattern carefully, one can often find that it is implicitly based on a particular cultural version or prototype *of* that pattern. This is typically the case with the concept 'religion' itself. When Westerners use the term, what they often have in mind is a version of the Christian religion, so that, for example, religion signifies a system with a scripture, a creator god, and a concept of salvation. While this would be too narrow a way by which to describe everything religious, it is not in itself a faulty or uncontrolled comparative enterprise. The problem would be if there was no awareness that one was in fact limiting the analysis to the use of a particular historical norm or prototype (on the prototype issue see Saler 1993).

6 Academic comparativism should recognize a distinction between the perspectives, purposes and language of the comparativist and those of the insider. This is not to assert that the comparativist approach is better or more genuine in some absolute sense. Rather, the committed insider and the observing comparativist have different purposes. The object of the student of comparative religion is not simply to reiterate, replicate or 'understand' what particular religions say or do, though she must also be able to do that, but to find relationships and differences among religious traditions and to hold these up to view with a more wide-angled lens. These would be linkages that the insider, as insider, may neither see, be able to see, or be interested in.

To use the famous example of the philosopher William James, a crab does not see itself as a crustacean (the latter being an 'outsider's' concept). But the biologist does. The scientist sees all the crustacean features (and against a broad evolutionary background) that the crab shares with over 40,000 other subspecies. The comparative anatomy scholar therefore sees continuities and differences unobservable to the single organism, and builds a new vocabulary to describe them. Likewise, comparativists in religion generate a terminology about 'types' of religious behaviors and representations.

7 If religion should be studied from all angles, then comparative themes should not be limited to religious patterns only. Comparison needs to be versatile – as complex as its subject matter. Religion can be analyzed in terms of any concept or topic. The 'common factor' in comparison can even be a complex combination of factors. For example, the relation of sacrifice to patterns of male authority; or the relation of ideas of deity to changes in technology in developing countries; or the cross-culturally patterned ways fundamentalist movements respond to modernist governments.

Comparative religion thereby extends its repertory of concepts and patterns, the better to do justice to the subject's intimate connection with complex social realities, and to connect with some of the same theoretical concerns found in other human and social sciences.

8 In the face of the criticism that religion is always unique to culture and incomparable, there is a recent counter trend to reach behind culture in order to ground cross-cultural thinking in the shared behavioral and cognitive patterns of the human species per se. The next section illustrates that approach.

Human behavior and human universals

Behind all cultures are human beings. One could therefore look for continuities in the kinds of things people *do* as humans and in the processes by which humans organize experience, rather than in the specific content of what they *believe* as insiders to their respective cultures.

Commonality among humans is not merely physical. All humans engage in common activities not only by their shared bodily make-up but also by their mental, social, and linguistic nature (cf. Brown 1991). They not only sleep, eat, reproduce, and react to pain, but they also create societies that form relationships and bonds, maintain moral order and codes of behavior, socialize the young, pass on examples of ancestral tradition, distinguish between insiders and outsiders, set and defend boundaries, perform periodic rites, endow objects and persons with special prestige and authority, punish transgressions, experiment with alternative forms of consciousness, recite sacred histories and genealogies, interpret events and objects, form communicative systems with culturally postulated immaterial beings, classify the universe, and fashion their own worlds of time, space, language, and obligation. In these and many other ways, all human societies build and maintain world-environments (Brown 1991: 130–141; cf. also the W. Paden essay in *Numen* 2001: 276–289).

Behaviors such as those just cited form building blocks for the construction of kinds of religious life. In turn, the religious systems, like the cultures of which they are manifestations, fill in these behavioral infrastructures with their local languages and meanings. Some scholars, in the context of evolutionary perspective, have even begun to compare religious behaviors – like submission, guilt, and reciprocity – with their analogues among other natural species (Burkert 1996).

An example of one of the noticeable features of religious worldmaking is the activity of making certain objects sacred. A point of comparability here is the authoritative function these sacred objects are given and the strategic absoluteness they convey within their respective systems. Thus, within the horizon of the history of religions, there appear *many* such religious worlds, each revolving around its own sacred objects – objects that function like the nuclei of a cell – and thus each constructing and inhabiting its own maps and domains. The comparativist finds innumerable accounts of the 'origin of the world,' of 'the center of the world,' and of 'the one supreme god' – all existing variously and independently, side by side, within the larger human tapestry. He finds that each religious system has its own past, its own absolute authorities, its own calendar, and its own accounts of miraculous events surrounding its founders and sacred objects. Each of these maps, for the insider, constitutes the way the world 'is.' To the comparativist, however, these are world *versions*.

The fact of the plurality of cultural worlds does not mean that there is nothing in common and that therefore comparison is hopeless. Rather, paradoxically, it is a universal feature of human life to build specific worlds for specific, different environments. Such a notion of world formation supplies a basis for comparative analysis because it constitutes a universal human activity against which cultural differences may be recognized and in terms of which variants may be contrasted (Paden 1994: 51–65).

Common form, different content

The distinction of common, transcultural *forms* of behavior and different cultural *content* (including meanings to the insider) then becomes important. Consider three illustrations:

Sacred histories Each religion forms its own history of the world. The comparativist observes that there are as many of these 'origins' – with their prestigious founders and special founding events – as there are cultures. For insiders to these traditions, such 'historical' origins are absolute. Every past rises up around key events and figures, not because it is objectively true by standards of modern historiography, but because it represents the given, operating tradition and memory of a particular community. Even within the large Christian and Buddhist traditions, each denomination has its own special lineages of authority and models of history, just as villages, neighborhoods and families will have their own patron saints, salient memories, and ancestral icons.

These histories share common functions. They account for that on which the life of the group depends and the self-identity of the society; they create lines of transmission and authorization of power from the founders and exemplars; and they provide exemplary, idealized models for how to live.

But difference comes into the picture insofar as each group sees the past in terms of its own idea of what life is based on or its own idea of what is sacred. Navaho myths link the origin of humans with the origin of corn; Masai myths address the origin of the gift of cattle; ancient Babylonian myths deal with the founding deeds of their god-king Marduk; mystical sects describe their versions of the fall and redemption of the soul.

Sacred histories also showcase different social structures. They give superhuman authorization to particular social boundaries and roles, imperial descent, ethnic identity, or collective destinies. Many, such as the Judeo-Christian scriptures, include detailed genealogies. A well-known Hindu myth describes the origin of the four main castes from the body of a primal being, the brahmans emerging from the head, and the manual labor caste from the feet. The miraculous appearance of the 'Virgin of Guadalupe' to an indigenous Indian in 1531 is at once a national, ethnic, and religious 'foundation account' for Mexican identity.

Thus, 'myths of the past,' or 'sacred histories,' encoded either in scripture, oral tradition or ritual reenactments, not only have the common functions of indexing memory and guiding or inspiring behavior, but may also be read as representations of different social values and meanings to be investigated in contextual detail.

Periodic renewal rites   Cultures not only represent pasts, they also recollect them in periodic rituals. Here, the values and venerated objects of the culture are celebrated and are imprinted on the life of the group's members through the participatory media of the festival – such as unusual forms of fasting, feasting, music, dance, or other impressive collective performances.

Again, while the function of these celebrative actions is similar, the content is not. In fact, only when the common factor is identified can the differences become appreciated. One of the important areas of difference is that of the social values that are meshed with the rites. For example, in traditional China the New Year festival highlighted the foundational role of family tradition and relationships. But in traditional South Asian Buddhist communities, major annual observances feature the mutually supportive relationship of the monks and laity. Annual rites in Pygmy culture feature the sanctity of the forest, but in Eskimo cultures the focus of honor is the sea mammals, and in ancient Athens the festivities celebrated the patron of the city, Athena. The Passover tradition for Jews focuses on the distinctive history of that people; and for Christians, Easter celebrates the transformative power of their founder.

As renewal rites are not just expressions of religion, but of the broad activity by which humans 'build' time, they naturally appear in nonreligious versions, too, such as in national celebrations which honor the founders and accomplishments of one's country.

Each version of renewal rites adds a context to the comparativist's perception of the others. And just as the versions bring out differences, by juxtaposition, with each other, they also add resonance to the common theme.

Again, any one of these festivals can be read for the way it reveals different meanings to different social classes within the society. Festivals often show patterns of status, social inclusion and exclusion, kinship, gender roles, local traditions, and other forms of social identity. Rites may be experienced with quite different cultural messages according to gender, age, or degree of marginalization.

Sacred order   A third example of a general human universal form that serves comparative study while highlighting 'difference' is the notion of sacred order. All cultures draw lines, identify boundary transgression, and punish violations. All establish categories that require defense and monitoring. All maintain and defend a system of allowable and unallowable behavior; all have some version of authority, law and tradition. If order is violated, all exercise techniques for addressing the infraction.

But no two orders are the same. The content of what constitutes order and disorder is relative to the sociocultural system. Boundaries and their negotiation are mingled with complex social norms related to ideas of honor, obligation, kinship, sexuality, selfhood and any number of value configurations peculiar to any society. While there are some specific, recurring patterns of restrictive behavior among diverse cultures, such as the prohibition against incest, murder, and theft, it remains that much that is obligatory or violative pertains to each culture's own norms. These might include notions of purity about food, social status, ritual, or protocols of the hunt. Classical Confucianism identified some 3,000 forms of 'proper' observance for as many different occasions in life.

Summation   Thus, comparative perspective allows for a move 'downward' toward shared, panhuman features of behavior, and at the same time 'upward' to cultural specifics and differences, with all their particular inflections of texture and significa-tion. Either or both directions may serve the comparativist's purposes. The upward revelation of specificity means that historical particularities are not just insignificant, homogeneous versions of given structures – as so much dough to be rolled out and merely replicated by a given, patterned mold. Rather, history is the constant recre-ation of new versions of world and therefore new definitions and versions *of* history, time and space, identity, community, and the general 'order of things.'

There is some contrast here, then, to Eliadean comparativism. The latter cited examples of 'sacred space' (for example) in order to show how they embodied patterns like 'the Center,' or the 'world axis.' But the examples typically illustrated what one already knew about the spatial archetypes. Hence, Eliade mentions a New Guinea shrine to illustrate how its roof 'represents the celestial vault,' and how its four walls 'correspond to the four directions of space,' thus making the shrine an example of how space is made to mirror the totality of the cosmos (Eliade 1959: 46). But in Eliadean (and before that, Frazerian) comparativism, the many listed examples of a theme tend to be essentially replicas of the same thing. By contrast, a sociologically sensitive comparativism looks also for why spaces are different and for the ways they show nuances of social, ethnic and political identities. Hopi kivas, Quaker meetinghouses, modern suburban megachurches, Mormon Temples, Buddhist relic shrines, and Australian aboriginal 'markings' reflect very *specific* cultural values and worldviews.

Religious patterns in secular life

From the above, it would follow that comparative religion has implications for the general understanding and explanation of human behavior; and also the other way around, because religious patterns are in many ways 'natural' human behaviors writ large and given a sacred basis. All cultures, not just religious ones, have special histo-ries, places and times; all have renewal rites, sacred order and boundary marking. Even more specific 'forms' like pilgrimage, sacrifice, rites of passage, rites of purifica-tion, states of trance, ethical precepts, are not limited to religious domains. The notion of sacredness itself is a broader concept than religion: modern arenas where the factor of sacredness can be found include social justice, individual rights, and national sovereignty.

In these ways, the comparative religion endeavor invites reflection about any cultural system and its continuities with human worldmaking generally. The anthropologist Colin Turnbull thus discovered revealing aspects of adolescent 'passage' customs of British school boys *after* he had lived in the Pygmy culture and observed its puberty rites. Studying other cultures can thus have the reflexive effect of noticing the myths and rituals of one's own for the first time.

Traditionally, American college religion departments offered just one course on the 'Non-Christian Religions,' while all the other offerings would be on theological and historical facets of the ruling Judeo-Christian tradition. Today, in many academic settings, and particularly in secular, public universities, this disproportion is being redressed. Indeed, one of the challenges of the comparative study of religion now is to be able to evenhandedly apply its perspectives to the study of biblical traditions.

The comparative study of religion is evolving. It develops along with a culture's knowledge of the world. As such, comparative perspective is not a static entity, with lists of patterns and parallels pinned down for all time, but an ongoing process of thought and discovery.

Bibliography

Brown, Donald E., 1991, *Human Universals*, McGraw-Hill, New York. A useful history and analysis of the concept of cultural universals, with extensive annotated bibliography.

Burkert, Walter, 1996, *Creation of the Sacred: Tracks of Biology in Early Religions*, Harvard University Press, Cambridge, MA.

Eliade, Mircea, 1958, *Patterns in Comparative Religion*, trans. Rosemary Sheed. World Publishing Company, Cleveland. Eliade's classic, encyclopedic account of recurrent types of religious symbolism.

—— 1959, *The Sacred and the Profane: The Nature of Religion*, trans. Willard R. Trask. Harcourt, Brace, Jovanovich, New York. Widely-read summary statement by the leading comparativist of the last generation.

Frazer, James G., 1963, *The Golden Bough*, abridged edn, Macmillan, New York. Condensed version of Frazer's landmark work, first published in 1890, for those interested in the history of comparative religion.

Jones, Lindsay, ed. 2004, *Encyclopedia of Religion*, 2nd edn, 15 vols, Macmillan, Detroit, MI. Major source of articles, with bibliographies, on comparative topics, and a thorough updating of the original 1987 edition (ed. by Mircea Eliade).

Martin, Luther H., 2000, 'Comparison,' in Willi Braun and Russell T. McCutcheon, eds, *Guide to the Study of Religion*, 45–56. Cassell, London. Statement about the need to link comparison with scientific generalization.

——, M. Hewitt, E.T. Lawson, W. Paden and D. Wiebe, 1996, 'The New Comparativism in the Study of Religion: A Symposium,' in *Method and Theory in the Study of Religion*, VIII/1: 1–49. Debate on the prospects of a post-Eliadean comparativism.

Müller, F. Max, 1872, *Lectures on the Science of Religion*, Charles Scribner Co., New York. Seminal lectures on the importance of comparative perspective by a founder of the discipline.

Naroll, Raoul and Ronald Cohen, eds, 1970, *A Handbook of Method in Cultural Anthropology*, The Natural History Press, New York. Includes valuable essays by anthropologists on issues of comparative method, pp. 581–1008.

Neville, Robert Cummings, ed. 2001, *Ultimate Realities: A Volume in the Comparative Religious Ideas Project*. The State University of New York Press, Albany, NY. A major, collaborative study of the process of adjudicating comparative concepts with historical data.

Numen: International Review for the History of Religions 2001, vol. 48, no. 3. Brill, Leiden. An issue wholly dedicated to contemporary perspectives on comparison.

Paden, William E., 1994, *Religious Worlds: The Comparative Study of Religion*, 2nd edn, Beacon Press, Boston. General study of key patterns and variations in religious 'worldmaking.'

Patton, Kimberley C. and Benjamin C. Ray, eds, 2000, *A Magic Still Dwells: Comparative Religion in the Postmodern Age*, The University of California Press, Berkeley. Essays by fourteen contemporary scholars on the importance of comparative perspective in relation to the challenge of postmodernism.

Poole, Fitz John Porter, 1986, 'Metaphors and Maps: Towards Comparison in the Anthropology of Religion,' *Journal of the American Academy of Religion* 54: 411–457. A perceptive, sophisticated analysis of comparative method by an anthropologist of religion.

Saler, Benson, 1993, *Conceptualizing Religion: Immanent Anthropologists, Transcendent Natives, and Unbounded Categories*, Leiden, Brill. Extensive review of resources for conceptualizing comparative categories.

Sharpe, Eric C., 1986, *Comparative Religion: A History*, 2nd edn, Open Court, La Salle, Ill. A useful, informative overview of the development of comparative religion as a modern field.

Smart, Ninian, 1996, *Dimensions of the Sacred: An Anatomy of the World's Beliefs*, University of California Press, Berkeley. An accessible text demonstrating seven key categories by which religions can be studied (ritual, mythic, experiential, doctrinal, ethical, social, and material).

Smith, Jonathan Z., 1982, *Imagining Religion: From Babylon to Jonestown*, University of Chicago Press, Chicago. Chapters 1 and 2 review and pose critical issues about comparative method.

—— 1987, *To Take Place: Toward Theory in Ritual*, University of Chicago Press, Chicago.

—— 1990, *Drudgery Divine: On the Comparison of Early Christianities and the Religions of Late Antiquity*, University of Chicago Press, Chicago. Issues of method in comparison by way of a critique of Christian interpretations of Hellenistic-period religions.

Part 2

Key issues in the study of religions

Chapter 12

Gender

Darlene M. Juschka

What is gender? What is sex? What is gender/sex?

Historical prelude

Gender as a category of analysis has operated in a variety of ways depending on pedagogical location or historical period. For example, in sociological studies gender consists of the study of sex roles in pre-industrial and industrial societies. Or, historically in Europe, gender has simply been the natural designation of the sexes as opposite since the eighteenth century. However, in the 1960s gender became a central category of feminist studies. So for example, in feminist language studies gender becomes the means by which to look at the erasure of women by the generic term 'man' and the thingification of women as the object of the male gaze.

The development of gender as a category of analysis can be seen in the work of Margaret Mead and Catherine Berndt, for example, as a slow transformation of the belief in natural sex-roles and sex-role assignments to an analysis of the social construction of these roles. In other words, people like Mead and Berndt began to think about how the labor and roles given to men and women may have less to do with biological certainties and more to do with societal demands. These anthropologists examined women's ritual activities and beliefs among pre-industrial peoples, a focus that had been hitherto overlooked by their more androcentric colleagues. They found that the women they investigated tended to operate in a separate female sphere with rituals, symbols, and myths centered on such concerns as fertility and birth, economics, healing, or the well-being of the society, e.g. tending ancestors, the land, or myth cycles. They also became aware of two significant issues in the study of human society: one, the erasure of women and their activities from all fields of knowledge; and two, that women and men's gendered practices, e.g. work, parenting, status, were in fact social roles that were secondarily assigned as sex roles. Under the influence of first- and second-wave feminism,[1] then, the analysis of women as gendered, gender relating to both the oppression of women and creating a new subject of study based upon women, was established.

What is gender?

Gender is something we all know, or think we know. We immediately categorize people (or most everything, e.g. language, animals, planets, or inanimate objects) on the basis of their gender. We categorize ourselves repeatedly by ticking the appropriate box on a form to indicate our gender. We are careful to enter the proper washroom, and we choose particular apparel appropriate to our gender. We presuppose gender as it is manifested in all aspects of our lives. As such, we do not question gender. However, under the influence of second-wave feminism gender as a category of analysis emerged. Gender, in this formulation, was seen to be a way to understand the oppression of women by men. The category of gender, then, was developed in order to think about how social systems, cultures, and religions, for example, were gender coded and how these codes impacted upon women and men. This coding was seen to define, regulate, and circumscribe the group named/marked women. Equally the coding was seen to define and regulate the group called men, but as man and human were synonymous, it afforded this group privileges it did not afford women, e.g. men as priests in Catholicism.

From here, then, gender ideology, which was seen to construct and mystify (locate in nature) inequalities between men and women, became an operative analytical tool in feminist theorizing. It was used to examine religious, social, national formations and operations, and further, under the sign of postcolonialism and/or international feminisms, to examine political, social, cultural relations between nations and countries. For example, in feminist postcolonial theorizing it became apparent that often countries and their populations colonized by the West were feminized and, as such, were understood as irrational and highly sexual in comparison to the masculinized West. A good example of this is Rudyard Kipling's poem 'The White Man's Burden' published in 1897. In response to this feminization, the elite men of colonialized locations often demanded the subjugation of the women of their nation via a strict gender differentiation. A good example of this is the discourse around the veil in twentieth-century Middle Eastern identity politics. Gender ideology was also used to examine economic, historical, medical, and ethical discourses, to name but a few, and their contribution to the production of knowledge. This knowledge, then, that seeks to explain human social, political, cultural organization, and production was determined to be gender coded.

In the development of gender as a category of analysis, gender was separated from sex. Sex, male and female, or the two-sex model, was seen to be a natural fact or the biological reality that gender overlays. What is assumed in such a formulation of gender is that sex is real and gender is artificial, or sex is an ahistorical (outside of history) natural fact of human nature, while gender is a social and historical construction built upon that natural fact. Linda Nicholson (1994) comments that when gender and sex are thus formulated sex is not dealt with as a conceptual category, but a biological truth. As such, then, gender becomes the conceptual category that is hung upon the 'coat-rack' of sex. Formulated as such, sex is fixed and immutable while gender is social, historical, and mutable.

In this perspective, then, an assumption resides: that sex is neutral or carries no inherent value. Gender, however, carries value and this value is subsequently placed on 'normatively' sexed bodies. Indeed, these sexed bodies are not just human bodies, but can include all plants and animals. When such proofs as plants and animals are used, they are then called upon secondarily to uphold the truth of the naturalness of the category of sex. However, in due time, the mid- to late-1980s, this kind of understanding of sex and gender, or what is call the gender/sex dimorphism was called into question (see Gilbert Herdt 1994).

Complicating the category of gender

Judith Butler (1990) and Christine Delphy (1996) also argued that treating sex as a fixed and immutable truth of human existence not only confuses the analysis, but also expresses a necessity to adhere to a closely organized system of beliefs, values and ideas without question or thought. In Delphy's effort to make apparent how taxonomies are products of the social and therefore equally socially encoded, she pushed the analysis to include sex, male and female and the variations therein, as a social construct. She argues that sex, like gender, is a social and historical category and not a natural category. Sex is not a natural category because we already understand it in accordance with gender. We read sex through the lens of gender. As such, sex is a social and historical category. She further argued, as we read sex through a gender lens, gender precedes sex and not the reverse (1996: 30). Therefore, our understanding of men as physically strong and women as physically weak is a socially created truth enforced by, for example, girls being discouraged from developing muscles and boys being encouraged to develop muscles.

Such an argument would appear to be counterintuitive. But following the development of the category of gender in academic discourses, Delphy suggested that gender as a concept was founded upon 'sex roles' – a line of analysis that looks at the division of labor and the differing statuses of men and women. This line of thinking, developed primarily in sociology and anthropology, was picked up and used by feminists. The category of sex, then, in this reasoning, consisted of biological differences between the male and female while gender was the cultural manifestation of these differences or, as she states, 'a social dichotomy determined by a natural dichotomy' (1996: 33). Delphy asked; why it is assumed that sex would give rise to any sort of classification? Her argument proceeded from the position that:

> sex itself simply marks a social division: that it serves to allow social recognition and identification of those who are dominants and those who are dominated. That is that sex is a sign, but that since it does not distinguish just any old thing from anything else, and does not distinguish equivalent things but rather important and unequal things, it has historically acquired a symbolic value.
>
> (1996: 35)

Delphy's position was clear: both gender and sex are social constructions.

Speaking of sex and its history

In 1978 the first volume of Michel Foucault's *Histoire de la Sexualité* (Paris: Gallimard) in French and English *The History of Sexuality* (New York: Pantheon) was released. The series in the end would consist of three volumes, and as the title promises, the category of sexuality would itself be historicized. To historicize sex and sexuality was to recognize that different periods of time produced different conceptualizations of sex and sexuality. Foucault's work has implications for all those who think about the categories of gender and sex. Following Foucault have been many writers who continue to think about changes and breaks in the discourses of sex, sexuality, and gender.

Thomas Laqueur (1990), influenced by Foucault, examines the social and historical nature of the category of sex. He argued that a one-sex Aristotelian-Galenic model of human sexuality was operative prior to the 1800s in Europe. In this model of sexuality female was misbegotten and genitally inverted and male properly begotten and genitally extroverted. A one-sex model, then, was used to define the natural state of the female and male of the human species. Subsequent to this the two-sex model emerged wherein female and male sexes are understood to be opposite:

> By around 1800, writers of all sorts were determined to base what they insisted were fundamental differences between the male and female sexes, and thus between man and woman, on discoverable biological distinctions and to express these in a radically different rhetoric . . . Thus the old model, in which men and women were arrayed according to their degree of metaphysical perfection, their vital heat, along an axis whose telos was male, gave way by the late eighteenth century to a new model of radical dimorphism, of biological divergence.
>
> (1990: 5–6)

The implication of Foucault and Laqueur's (see also Blackwood 1999, Brown 1988) historicizing of sex and sexuality was the dislodging of sex from the realm of nature to locate it in the realm of the social, at least for those who were convinced. Foucault made apparent that sexuality, and sex therein, as much as gender, was a politically charged category that was intimately related to power. Foucault (and Laqueur), in his historical–political foray into sex, wished to discover or rather uncover how sex and sexuality were discursively formed: 'What is at issue, briefly, is the over-all "discursive fact," the way in which sex is "put into discourse"' (Vol. 1, 1990: 11). Sex, then, like gender is a discursive construction with implications of power. Although Foucault does not read sex through the sign of gender as Delphy does, he equally recognizes that sex is a category that is central to 'the order of things' and as such is a way that we organize ourselves. Like gender, then, sex has intimate relations to the dissemination of power in discourses, and religions have often been powerful and authoritative disseminators of the 'truth' of gender and sex. For example, in Christianity during the witch-craze or witch-hunt in Europe (1450–1700) women were understood to be more inclined toward evil because of their 'normative' femaleness. Signed as inclined toward evil and in league with the devil, all ages of females were tortured and murdered in numbers estimated conservatively to be 200,000. Or during the same period in India, women who outlived their spouses were encouraged or forced to commit Sati. Sati is the act of a widow being burned alive with the body of her dead husband.

Elaborating a model of gender and sex

Gender, as an academic category of analysis, has been greatly debated since the 1980s. The majority of analyses focused on two categories, gender and sex, as indicated above. In this kind of analysis, gender is examined as a social category and sex as a biological category. Although this split rendered gender very useful as a category of analysis for purposes of the study of religions, the theoretical difficulties this split raised began to be discussed in studies of sexuality, under the influence of Foucault, and in feminist theorizing. With theorists like Foucault it became apparent that sex was itself socially constructed and demonstrated a historicity of its own. The work produced by feminist academics in religious studies called into question the biological givenness of sex (e.g. the female as inherently evil and weak and the male as inherently good and strong), as a category of analysis and, furthermore, sought to theorize gender and sex as produced in and by the social (e.g. male as inherently good meant he was closer to deity and therefore naturally in positions of power such as a religious leader). But, by grounding gender/sex in the social and material two significant problems have emerged.

The first difficulty encountered, notably discussed in the 1970s, was that gender and sex were dealt with as separate formative elements of human identity so that sex was seen to establish kinds of bodies, while gender was thought to subsequently shape those bodies. In this understanding sex marked bodies as differentiated (fixed) while gender invested such marking with meaning (mutable). Here gender is seen to follow naturally from sex, or gender and sex are seen as superficially connected in a consecutive fashion, e.g. male is to man and female is to woman. What is not clearly theorized, then, is how gender and sex are interrelated and dependent upon each other for definition. Understanding that gender and sex are interrelated and dependent means they need to be understood as related to each other by the tension and interaction (dialectics) between the two categories. In this kind of understanding, gender and sex are related in a formative and primary fashion, e.g. man is to male as woman is to female.

The second problem that emerged in the 1980s was the lack of theorizing the interdependence of the categories of gender and sex. Instead gender and sex were presented as if they were interchangeable categories or simply synonyms. In this kind of analysis the dialectical (tension and interaction) mechanisms of gender and sex are erased. This theoretical position meant that gender ideology, or the power operations of social inequalities based on gender and sex, could not be adequately analyzed.

Understanding gender and sex as oppositional categories, the layering of gender and sex, or the blurring of gender and sex are all equally problematic. Without a clear theorizing of the dialectical relationship between gender and sex, studies continue to produce work wherein one or both the categories are reified (understood as things rather than concepts) and therefore resistant to a thoroughgoing analysis.

The difficulties encountered in the theorizing of gender as a category of analysis can be related to two basic issues: (1) essentialism (the sexed body remains fixed according to evolutionary requirements, e.g. man the hunter, female the gatherer) versus constructionism (the sexed body is mutable reflecting the social roles and lives situated in particular social and historical surroundings); and (2) the lack of a theory of gender and sex.

Some of the most successful studies of gender/sex have emerged from two areas of study: feminist cultural studies (the study of cultural productions from a feminist deconstructive perspective, e.g. film, media, and written text) and queer theory (deconstruction of the discursive production of sexuality and gender, e.g. challenge to heterosexuality as normative sexuality as presented in Genesis 1:27). In both of these locations there has been the recognition that the categories of gender and sex each require careful delineation and intersection. Feminist theorists in the study of religion have directed their attention toward this challenge and the analysis of gender and sex, as ideology (gender/sex), should prove a fruitful trajectory for the continued development of the categories of gender and sex.

The importance of gender/sex in the study of religion

If, in the study of religion, the scholar is to understand the structural development of the system under study, and is to understand the means by which that system is communicated, if s/he is to grasp why deity in the *Tanakh* (Hebrew Bible), for example, takes on both masculine and feminine attributes, then certainly how gender and sex are understood and used to express belief about existence in ancient Hebrew systems of religious belief is necessary to know. Examining the complexities of gender/sex, as produced in the social (e.g. myth) and signed on the level of the metaphysical (e.g. symbol) and enacted on the level of the biological (e.g. ritual), means engaging the study of religion as a human signing system. A human signing system refers to language, art, stories, and traditional practices and the like used to express beliefs about existence, the world, the human, male and female, or deity.

To engage religions as human signing systems requires paying attention to such things as who is speaking, in other words, the person, the group or institution that is generating the discourse, and to whom the discourse is directed. By tracking the who and the whom in the communicative event, by paying attention to what is at stake, and investigating what kinds of persuasions proliferate one is better able to elucidate their understanding of social systems. Toward this end, then, one will want to examine gender/sex as they are delineated through religious discourses. An example of this kind of analysis is Helen Hardacre's study of a Japanese new religious movement Buddhist *Risshōkoōseikai*.

In her study Hardacre relates how Buddhist *Risshōkōseikai* had been co-founded by a woman, Naganuma Myōkō, but after her death in 1957 there was an internal power struggle. Out of this struggle emerged a new myth of origin, one that erased Myōkō as a co-founder of the group. Instead her male co-founder was given sole recognition. At one particular gathering of the women of the *Risshōkōseikai*, who had come together in order to celebrate the anniversary of their female founder's death, the importance of Myōkō within the movement was undercut directly by reference to her gender/sex. At this gathering a male elder, in support of the new male genealogy of *Risshōkōseikai*, spoke to these women about gender/sex and to do so drew on gender ideology to validate the new male genealogy. This was done, of course, in order to assert the legitimacy of masculine domination. To do this he naturalized men's domination over women via reference to femaleness and maleness in the 'state of nature':

> You women know that in the animal world, it is the males who are the most powerful. Take the gorilla for example – did you ever hear of a female gorilla leading the pack? . . . And it is the males who are prettiest. Whoever paid any attention to a drab female duck? . . . Being the stronger and most powerful, naturally the males are the most attractive as well. What I'm trying to tell you today is that it's the same way with human beings. It's the men who are superior, and the women who are behind all the trouble in the world.
>
> (Hardacre 1994: 111)

Delineated in a specific gender-based narrative, there is a necessity to understand how gender/sex operate on the sociopolitical level in order to know what is at stake for the speaker and the listeners. Clearly the male elder was attempting, via his use of biology, to locate men over women. But equally that the women of the group had come together to celebrate their female founder's death anniversary indicates that they were resisting the new myth of origin that located the founding of *Risshōkōseikai* with only its male co-founder.

Equally, when doing a gender/sex analysis another aspect that requires attention is awareness that the discourse of the hegemonic elite (those limited few who have control and power over the social, economic, political, cultural, and religious domains) is not the sole or only representation of the religion or culture. Often the views, perspectives, religious activities, and so forth of a small elite group of men have been, and continue to be, used as representative of the entire group. In this formulation any contestation and differences within the group related to class, race, or gender/sex are erased. To ignore such social categories as status, gender/sex, sexuality, race, or class that speak about power and that point to the particulars of social formations is to ignore the social and historical parameters of the system of belief under study. Engaging gender and sex as interrelated categories of analysis in the study of religion clarifies the object of one's study.

In the past, under the influence of enlightenment epistemology, wherein the category of the human was the origin and basis for much theorizing done in the study of religion, complexity and diversity within an analysis were erased in order to ensure the subject of European philosophy, man. This man haunted, and in some measure continues to haunt, theorizing in religious studies, anthropology, sociology, philosophy, history, or science. At the same time, those studies that have shifted from this perspective continue to remain marginal in the university. Focusing solely on this man not only misses the social complexity and the structures that hold the religious edifices in place, but also distorts the analysis. Paying attention to gender/sex, sexuality, race, and class allows us to theorize the structures and understand better the multifaceted complexity of human social bodies.

The gendering of religions

The intersection of gender/sex and religions has been of interest to a number of theorists who study religions. Over the last five decades excellent work that looks at the ideological implications of gender/sex in the study of religion, or how gender and sex effect and affect the practice of religion, has been produced. These kinds of studies share a common interest in examining how religion has been one method to ensure the subordination of women in a variety of social and cultural locations, and the absence of women as living persons within the development and dissemination of religions. Such studies have sought to reveal the power imperatives and to bring women as subjects back into the various religions under study. From here those interested in the intertwining of gender/sex and religion have developed analyses that examine historical and social shifts in a variety of cultures as registered by gender/sex, the political efficaciousness of gender/sex, and linked to this, the intersection of gender/sex with colonization. The interrelated categories of gender and sex provide a means and a way to understand not only the how and why of religions, but equally the how and why of social organization and the manufacturing of culture in and of itself.

Gender/sex and religious ideologies

The work of gendering religions has been taken up by a variety of feminists studying religions and theology. In the late 1960s and into the 1970s the work of Mary Daly, Rosemary Radford Reuther, and Elisabeth Schüssler Fiorenza presented some of the earlier gender interventions into the study of religion. Each of these feminists did triple duty in terms of their work in the study of religion. First, they brought tools of analysis to the study of religion in order to think about how these systems of belief were used to legitimate and shape the social body. Second, each then focused on women in the religious system under analysis in order to make apparent women's activities and contributions. Third, each then furthered their analyses by interrelating patriarchal imperatives with women's contributions and activities in order to think about religion.

Daly's approach, after her rejection of Christianity, was to propose a two-world system located in most if not all societies. One part of this two-world system she named the foreground, which was a patriarchal construction operating in terms of patriarchal relations. The foreground was the site of women's exploitation and oppression, and detrimental to women's well-being. The second aspect of this two-world system was the Background, which was the real world that was obscured by the patriarchal world of the foreground. It is, Daly argued, in the Background that women can find their true being. This dualist world system, in large measure, reflects aspects of what is called feminist standpoint epistemology.

Feminist standpoint epistemology developed by Nancy Hartsock, Dorothy Smith, Patricia Hill-Collins (black feminist standpoint), and Mary Daly, among others, takes the position that women, as an oppressed group, are in a position to have a clearer and less distorted picture of reality as they are outside of, or marginal to, the dominant system of power relations and therefore considerably less invested in maintaining it. According to standpoint theory, the picture of reality developed in patriarchy (and all oppressive systems) is an inversion of reality and those who are marginal to the system are able to see this inversion. Further to this, as patriarchy is invested in maintaining its vision of the world, which empowers it, it is unable to see beneath the surface. Only the oppressed can clearly determine the operations of this inversion, based upon their experiences, and envision a means to move beyond it. Institutionalized religion, understood as patriarchal religion, Daly argues, is one of the pillars that support the foreground. God the father is merely an inversion of the reality of the Goddess and a means and a way to ensure that the patriarchal reality of the foreground continues to endure.

Schüssler Fiorenza's contribution to the gendering of religion came in the form of uncovering patriarchal imperatives found in the New Testament and other texts related to the study of early Christianities. This method she called a feminist hermeneutics of suspicion, which exposes the intention to locate in the heavens and in nature the gender ideologies produced by the group. So for example, Paul's letter to the Corinthians (I Corinthians 11: 1–16), when discussing men's and women's hair related to normative male and female being, makes apparent Paul's operative gender ideology, which is his own and is one that emerges from his social location and has little to do with either deity or nature. Certainly Paul supports his understanding of normative male and female being by making recourse to deity and nature. Much as in the Buddhist *Risshōkōseikai* example, Paul's understanding of normative male and female appearance and behavior calls on nature to legitimate his view. In this passage Paul understands that it is a disgrace for women to have short hair and dishonorable for men to have long hair. Working within the honor–shame oriented culture, the maintenance of social standing is intimately linked to honor and for women to attempt to appear masculine (short hair) and therefore elevate their status is a disgrace, while for men to appear feminine (long hair) means a loss of social status and therefore dishonor. Male and female hairstyles, then, are culturally coded and reflect a gender ideology.

Second, she sought to make apparent women's activities in the early Christian communities through a feminist hermeneutics of remembrance. In this gender-sensitive methodology she would examine not only the actions and contributions of men, but also those of women in these communities. Finally, by combining the hermeneutics of suspicion and remembrance, she developed what she termed a feminist critical hermeneutics of liberation. Through this model she hoped to be able to reclaim Christian history for concerned women and men of all nations, colors, and sexual orientation without engaging in Christian apologetics.

Rosemary Radford Ruether's gendering of religion also challenged patriarchal imperative of religions, particularly Judaism and Christianity. She too noted the absence of women and set upon a project of reclaiming and reconstructing women's Christian histories. She too developed a project of rereading and rewriting in order to reconceptualize a new Catholic Christianity as a system of belief that creates a positive space for concerned women and men of all nations, colors, and sexual orientation. By gendering religion she, like Daly and Schüssler-Fiorenza, sought not only to understand the ideological impact of religion on women, and construct histories of women and religion, but also to move the study of religion toward developing analyses that reflected more honestly the social and historical realities of human systems of meaning.

Gender/sex and religious practices

The kinds of analyses indicated above represent some of the work of feminists in the study of religion through the 1970s and 1980s. Feminists, having learned the need to reread and rethink religious and historical texts, went on to think about how the interrelated categories of gender/sex shaped the knowledge and the systems of belief that women produced. A particularly influential thinker working in this frame is Susan Starr Sered and her comparative text *Priestess, Mother, Sacred Sister: Religions Dominated by Women* published in 1994. There were of course other texts published in a similar vein, for example, Diane Bell's text *Daughters of the Dreaming* published in 1983. In such texts, theorists took gender/sex as their cue and began to examine the religious orientations, creations, and inclinations of women. At the center of their studies was an interest in women's symbolic discourses and how women's symbolic discourses might differ from men's.

Sered's introductory chapter in *Priestess, Mother, Sacred Sister* briefly relates how the author engages the category of gender specifically in order to think about what might be central to women's religiosity and how this might be different from men's religiosity. This question, circling around the category of gender/sex assumes from the outset that if indeed there is a difference between men's and women's religious beliefs and actions, that this difference could be related to their differing social lives. She notes that cross-culturally women of differing social groups share concerns such as childbearing and motherhood, which of course intersect with economic, social, physiological, and psychological concerns. Connected to this explicitly is child rearing and related to child rearing is healing. These appear to be issues that are often at the center of women's religiosity and as such suggest a gender/sex difference.

However, as Sered notes, men and women's religiosity are more alike than they are unalike. Although concerns may demonstrate gender/sex differences, both women and men make recourse to superordinate beings (singular or plural), both use ritual to imaginatively interact with these beings, and both have central myths that organize the system of belief. As female and male are not opposite in sex, so women's and men's religions are not opposite in religion. Sered (1994: 8–9) suggests that when women and men's religiosity do differ, it is related to how superordinate beings are imagined, e.g. Jesus as feminine as among the Shakers of the American Colonies; the how and why of engagement with superordinate beings, e.g. through possession to heal the afflicted as with the *Zar* cult in the northern Sudan; the shaping and understanding of ritual actions, e.g. women as ritual leaders; and the way that they engage such issues as existence, e.g. women's ritual power as social power as with the *Sande* secret society in Sierra Leone and Liberia. But equally important to women and men's religiosity is the issue of power. Religiosity can and does confer power, whether on the basis of gender/sex, status, race, prestige, or age and is a means by which power is delineated or contested. Because of the propensity of gender/sex to be related to power, it is necessary to analytically engage gender/sex head-on when studying religion.

Gender/sex and performance

Judith Butler in her formative text *Gender Trouble*, first published in 1990 (10th anniversary edition 1999), equally suggests that it is gender that supports the category of sex and not the reverse. Following up on this, she makes an extended and complex argument demonstrating what is at stake politically when the category of sex is left as fixed and immutable beneath the category of gender, heterosexism. Linked to heterosexism, she argues, is the idea that individuals are trapped, not by biological imperatives as feminism had challenged this by socializing the category of gender, but now by cultural imperatives, since feminists had left the category of sex untheorized. She states that '[t]he institution of a compulsory and naturalized heterosexuality requires and regulates gender as a binary relation in which the masculine term is differentiated from a feminine term, and this differentiation is accomplished through the practices of heterosexual desire' (30). Butler clearly and succinctly demonstrated how gender in feminist theorizing continued to uphold 'normative' ideas concerning sex and gender to the peril of a feminist analysis and its claims to be liberating.

Added to this keen observation, Butler made another equally important observation that gender/sex is performed. Butler, a feminist poststructuralist, underscored in her text the political imperative affiliated with the categories of gender/sex, and asked what might be the effects of such an imperative. This question allowed her to conjecture how identity itself was a political category with gender/sex central to this identity. Linked to this, then, was the necessity to perform gender/sex, so that those who ascribe to (are ascribed to) the category of female must perform as feminine or those who ascribe to (are ascribed to) the category male must perform as masculine. Furthermore, those ascribed as male, but desiring to the female, could perform as feminine and those ascribed as female, but desiring to the male, could perform as masculine; although this was done at their peril, as they would be disciplined for transgressing gender boundaries. Butler argued '[t]here is no gender identity behind the expressions of gender; that identity is performatively constituted by the very "expressions" that are said to be its results' (33).

In the field of religious studies, particularly ritual, the instability and performativity of gender/sex are immanently apparent. Most visible in rites such as female and male circumcision, one sees the instability of sex as a natural category since the cutting of the body's genitals, the primary site of gender/sex, is used to properly fix the sex of the initiate. Furthermore, one notes the necessity to perform as woman or man in the acceptance of the cut that moves the child who would shriek, to the adult who would capture it between clenched teeth.

Gender/sex and historicity

In the text *Spirited Women: Gender, Religion and Cultural Identity in the Nepal Himalaya* (1996) Joanne C. Watkins, an anthropologist, is concerned with the 'interplay between changing trade patterns, gender meanings, and cultural identity in *Nyeshang* society' (4). Her concern, among other things, is to chart the changing gender ideology under the pressure of trade with the larger world. The interrelated categories of gender and sex, formulated in relation to religious beliefs, cultural systems and imperatives of kinship relations, are shifting and that these shifts register change in the social body and in the smaller social identity of the group (Buddhist). In this kind of formulation, gender/sex, then, provides a window not only into understanding a cultural system, but provides a way to chart changes within a cultural system. It is this latter function, a window for understanding social and cultural change, for example, that has led some to assume that gender/sex was a means by which to determine religious fundamentalism, rather than a means by which to chart change. In other words, rather than assume a change toward more austere gender relations marks a shift toward fundamentalism, one should recognize that gender/sex actually becomes a means and a way to mark change in itself. Gender and sex, then, as they are both social categories are historical categories that reflect changes in the belief system over time (see also Laura L. Vance, *Seventh-day Adventism in Crisis: Gender and Sectarian Change in an Emerging Religion* (1999) who also registers changes in the social body by using the category of gender/sex).

Gender/sex and politics

The categories of gender/sex are a central concern in Patricia Jeffery and Amrita Basu's edited text *Appropriating Gender: Women's Activism and Politicized Religion in South Asia* (1998). In this text, as the title suggests, gender ideology acts as a category to register political activism. Basu states that 'in the past decade or so, religion and gender have become increasingly intertwined in the political turmoil that envelops South Asia' (3). Women, the gendered category, have, in some locations, become the repository of 'religious beliefs, and the keepers of the purity and integrity of the community' (3) felt to be under attack by the increasing globalization gener-ated by such institutions as the World Bank, the World Trade Organization, the International Monetary Fund, and the United Nations. As noted above, gender and sex are not static categories and indeed register shifts and change in social bodies and, as the authors note, can become the means by which to initiate or resist social change. For example, the state, which can take on the masculine in relation to the feminized social body, can act as a paternalistic force that oversees the social body ensuring its proper functioning. It can be the state, as evinced in the United States in the early twenty-first century, that calls upon a particular gender ideology, hetero-sexual and masculine in this instance, to shore up and protect a social body it perceives to be under attack. The twin towers, symbols of American masculinity, attacked and felled in September of 2001, initiated a hypermasculine response of excessive militarism that was launched against the feminized Middle Eastern 'other.' 'Gender provides,' as Basu rightly comments, 'an extremely fruitful lens through which to interpret the actions of the state and of ethnic and religious communities' (5–6).

Gender/sex: where to from here?

As I hope I have made clear in the above, the interrelated categories of gender and sex are infinitely useful categories by which to interrogate and understand religions. In many ways gender/sex is a signing system that acts as a window that allows the viewer to see the complexities of human existence. Gender/sex, although still not a central category of analysis in the study of religions for many theorists, must be further sounded to push our understanding of human social and cultural systems.

For example, in my own work I have sought to make apparent the mythological ground of gender ideology. This has been a process of revealing or bringing to con-sciousness the binarism that continues to fuel the ways in which we understand gender/sex. To first uncover the logic of binarism, noting that a significant root binary in most cultural systems is the male/female binary, and then to underscore the linguisticality of binarism allow for the socialization and historicization of binaries and subsequently, gender/sex. Yet this does not fully reveal just what is at stake in gender ideology.

First, gender ideology includes sex as a mythologized discourse. The foundational quality of myth – its apparent rootedness in nature – means that the social, histor-ical, and political aspects of gender *and* sex are elided. As I have indicated, *both* gender and sex, as dialectically related categories, must be submitted to a thorough-going social and historical analysis. Second, what is at stake in gender ideology is power. Although this would seem evident, evidently it is not. 'I am a man' or 'I am a woman' seem not to be political statements that mark power. But indeed they do; such terms mark social power. Therefore to analytically engage gender/sex is to under-stand a significant aspect of the complexity of human signing systems mapped through that which we call religion.

Note

1   First-wave feminism refers to women's political and social action to provide women with both political and civil rights in the west activities in the mid-1800s and early 1900s. Second-wave feminism refers to women's political, social, cultural, and legal activities and analyses, beginning in the late 1950s and continuing to the present, toward addressing the

oppression on women. Both first- and second-wave feminisms are terms used to designate the rise and resurgence of western feminism and do not refer to the rise and resurgence of feminisms of the nineteenth and twentieth centuries in, for example, India, the Middle East, or Latin and South America. Third-wave feminism is a current term that is used to reflect a shift toward technology, globalization, and international feminisms that began in the mid-1990s.

References

Bell, Diane (1993 [1983]). *Daughters of the Dreaming*. 2nd edn. Minnesota: University of Minnesota Press.
Bell's comprehensive and thoughtful text is an ethnographic study of Australian Aboriginal women's rites, symbols, and myths. What Bell makes apparent is the importance of Australian Aboriginal women's ritual work toward the development and maintenance of the Dreamtime.

Blackwood, Evelyn and Saskia E. Wieringa (eds) (1999). *Same Sex Relations and Female Desires: Transgender Practices Across Cultures*. New York: Columbia University Press.
This text is a fine collection of historical, sociological and ethnographic studies of transgendered practices. Focused upon women's same-sex desire, the category of gender is shown to be intimately connected with and foundational for the category of sex, while sexuality intersects with both sex and gender in a definitive fashion.

Brown, Peter (1988). *The Body and Society: Men, Women and Sexual Renunciation in Early Christian Society*. New York: Columbia University Press.
Brown's text is a wonderful engagement with the category of gender/sex in the formative years of Christianity. Under the influence of theorists such as John Winkler, Brown makes apparent the historicity of the categories of gender and sex, and how these categories, understood differently in the ancient world, were central to the ideological formation of a 'normative' Christianity.

Butler, Judith (1999 [1990]). *Gender Trouble: Feminism and the Subversion of Identity*. New York and London: Routledge.
This is a formative and pivotal text that is understood to be one of the founding texts of queer theory. This text engages the feminist category of gender, pointing to the shortcomings of the theorizing of the category of gender and underscoring the heterosexism that is prevalent in this theorizing.

Delphy, Christine (1996 [1993]). 'Rethinking Sex and Gender.' In Diana Leonard and Lisa Adkins (eds), *Sex in Question: French Materialist Feminism*, 30–41. London: Taylor & Francis.
Delphy's article is a logical and coherent analysis of the category of gender as it has operated in feminist theorizing from 1970 until 1990. She engages the concept of gender and demonstrates the limited nature of ignoring sex as a social and historical category.

Foucault, Michel (1990 [1978–1984]). *The History of Sexuality*. 3 vols. Robert Hurley (trans.). New York: Vintage.
Foucault's trilogy intersects with the category of sexuality toward historicizing and politicizing it. Beginning with seventeenth-century Europe in volume one, he then interrogates sexuality and erotic literature in volume two and ends by interrogating sexuality in relation to Greco-Roman philosophy in his third volume.

Hardacre, Helen (1994). 'Japanese New Religions: Profiles in Gender.' In John Stratton Hawley (ed.), *Fundamentalism and Gender*, 111–133. New York: Oxford University Press.
This article is an interesting and well-documented discussion of the category of gender/sex and how it is used in religions to limit the political and social power of women in Buddhist *Risshōkōseikai*.

Herdt, Gilbert (ed.) (1994). *Third Sex, Third Gender: Beyond Sexual Dimorphism in Culture and History*. New York: Zone Books.
This anthology of articles is a marvellous delineation of the multiplicity of the categories of gender, sex, and sexuality. Linking all three categories in an effort to make apparent how each is reliant upon the other, this anthology is a cross-cultural and multi-historical analysis of human systems of meaning and social organization.

Jeffrey, Patricia and Amrita Basu (eds) (1998). *Appropriating Gender: Women's Activism and Politicized Religion in South Asia*. New York and London: Routledge.
This is a nicely developed anthology of articles that examine the political aspects of both gender/sex and religion. In these articles authors note, for example, how the state and women's groups employ the categories of gender/sex, linked to religious beliefs, for political purposes.

Laqueur, Thomas L. (1990). *Making Sex: Body and Gender from the Greeks to Freud*. Cambridge, Mass. and London: Harvard University Press.
Laqueur's text engages the categories of gender and sex and examines how their understanding shifted in the period of the 1800s in medical discourses. He links this shift to political change in Europe during this time period and changes in the conceptualization of the human under the influence of enlightenment philosophy.

Lincoln, Bruce (1989). *Discourse and the Construction of Society: Comparative Studies of Myth, Ritual and Classification*. New York: Oxford University Press.
A pivotal text that engages ritual, myth, and classification demonstrating their historicity, their political potency, and their importance toward constructing social bodies that subsequently impact on individual bodies.

Nicholson, Linda (1994). Interpreting Gender. *Signs*, 20, 1: 79–105.
A well-developed analysis of the use of the category of gender in the work of second-wave feminists. Nicholson makes apparent the unexamined idea of the immutability of sex as a biological category which resides beneath the concept of gender as a socialized category.

Sered, Susan Starr (1994). *Priestess, Mother, Sacred Sister: Religions Dominated by Women*. New York and Oxford: Oxford University Press.
Sered's cross-cultural examination through ethnographic literature of women's religiosity is a well-informed and thoughtful text. Her clear description of the multiplicity of women's religions and the rituals, symbols, and myths developed and utilized by women, allows her to speculate on common threads that link these variegate practices toward answering the question of how gender/sex intersects with and shapes religious beliefs.

Vance, Laura L. (1999). *Seventh-day Adventism in Crisis: Gender and Sectarian Change in an Emerging Religion*. Urbana and Chicago: University of Illinois Press.
This study, based on official and unofficial publications and interviews, examines gender, sex, and sexuality and their relations to the worldview of Seventh-day Adventists. In line with this, the author examines concepts of femininity, masculinity, and sexuality and their relation to social practices.

Watkins, Joan (1996). *Spirited Women: Gender, Religion and Cultural Identity in the Nepal Himalaya*. New York: Columbia University Press.
This interesting ethnographic study examines the changing gender ideology among the Nyeshangte, a Tibetan Buddhism group found in the Himalayan Highlands. The author theorizes upon the intersection of modernism and capitalism with the cultural of the Nyeshangte and the subsequent changes in their understanding of gender and sex.

Chapter 13

Insider/outsider perspectives

Kim Knott

Many students who have come to study religions at the university where I work have been introduced to the subject through a course called 'Religious Lives'. The purpose of the course is to develop an understanding of religions and their study by means of an examination of the autobiographies and biographies of a variety of religious people – what we might here call 'religious insiders'.[1] The students come as 'outsiders' to these stories; but they also have their own stories, their own subjective experiences which they are asked to reflect on and write about during the course. They are the 'insiders' in these accounts. The process of thinking about other people's religious lives as well as their own raises many critical questions and issues for discussion during the course. Can we ever fully understand someone else's experience? What is the difference between an account of a religion by an insider and one by an outsider? Does translation from one language to another bridge a gap or create a barrier between the person telling the story and the one reading it? Additionally, we find ourselves considering the nature and limits of objectivity and subjectivity, 'emic' and 'etic' positions, 'experience-near' and 'experience-distant' concepts, empathy and critical analysis, the effect of personal standpoint, and the process of reflexivity. We even find that some of the lives we read about make us ask whether it is actually helpful to distinguish between insider and outsider perspectives. We will come to these matters in more detail shortly, but my purpose in listing them here is to show the range of concerns that are related to the insider/outsider debate, many of which have been at the heart of the study of religions since its inception as a discipline distinct from theology. The debate challenges us by raising questions about the extent and limits of our knowledge and understanding. It invites us to consider whether or not our field of study is scientific. It is central to our methodology. It has an ethical dimension, and a political one.

Insider/outsider perspectives in the history of the study of religions

These questions came to the fore from the mid-1980s in a highly charged debate about the nature of Sikh studies and the contribution and motivation of particular scholars writing on Sikh religion.[2] Who could understand and represent Sikh traditions? What were the personal motivations, epistemological standpoints and ideological interests of those who studied Sikh history and theology?[3] As we shall see towards the end of this chapter, the issues in this debate eventually extended beyond the problem of the insider/outsider, but the problem was certainly of central importance early on. For example, in 1986, a collection of papers entitled *Perspectives on the Sikh Tradition* was published. Several of its authors strongly criticised Western scholarship on Sikhism, focusing particularly on the work of W. H. McLeod, who was held to have undermined the Sikh faith as a result of his historical and critical-textual approach to Sikh tradions (Singh 1986: 10; Grewal 1998: 126–31). Then, in 1991, in a review of the work of several Western scholars, including McLeod, Darshan Singh raised a key issue:

> The Western writers' attempt to interpret and understand Sikhism is an outsider's or non-participant's endeavour ... Primarily, religion is an area which is not easily accessible to the outsider, foreigner or non-participant. The inner meaning of a religion unfolds only through participation; by following the prescribed path and discipline.
>
> (1991: 3)

As we see from this case, the question of who can reliably understand and present a religion is contested. Darshan Singh and the authors of *Perspectives*, while accepting that Western outsiders have played a significant role in the development of Sikh studies, are suspicious of their motives (whether Christian or secular in origin), critical of their academic methods, and favour – by extension – the contribution of insiders to such studies. The strengths and weaknesses of participation and non-participation by scholars in the religions they study is a subject I shall return to shortly, but first I shall consider how, from the mid-nineteenth century onwards, Western scholars of the kind criticised above tackled the question of studying religions – both their own and those of others.

Emerging in the West as a field of enquiry with different objectives and methods to theology, the proponents of the early study of religions[4] drew attention to its scientific, objective and comparative character. They stressed the value of impartial scholarly accounts, and the development of appropriate conceptual tools, theories and methods. Writing in 1873, Max Müller stated that, as the object of study, religion should be shown reverence, but that it should also be subjected to critical scholarship.[5] Twenty years later Cornelius Tiele, stressing the need among scientists of religion for objectivity but not judgement about the forms of religion, considered whether such scholarship was best done by believers or non-believers, concluding that, 'It is an error to suppose that one cannot take up such an impartial scientific position without being a sceptic; that one is disqualified for an impartial investigation if one possesses fixed and earnest religious convictions of one's own' (Tiele from *Elements of the Science of Religion* (1897–9), in Waardenburg 1973: 99). He distinguished between the private religious subjectivity of the individual and his or her outward impartiality as a scholar of religion. Tiele was not asserting that only sceptical non-believers or outsiders could study religions; rather, he was suggesting that those who were themselves religious were fully able to be impartial in their studies. This view, that those studying religion should set to one side their subjective experience and cultural baggage, and take an objective position with regard to the other, prevailed for nearly a century.

These issues were given consideration by other scholars, especially those associated with the phenomenology of religion, particularly Kristensen, van der Leeuw and

Otto in Northern Europe, and later Eliade and Cantwell Smith in North America and Ninian Smart in Britain. They held the view, to quote Kristensen, that all religious phenomena were 'unique, autonomous and incomparable', yet capable of understanding by means of empathy, that is, by reliving in one's own experience that which appears to be alien (Kristensen from *The Meaning of Religion* in Waardenburg 1973: 391). While it was impossible to apprehend religion or the sacred in and of itself, it was possible to understand its manifestations or appearances (van der Leeuw 1963).[6] The underlying aim of the phenomenological approach was to understand – by empathetic and imaginative re-experience – the insider position while refraining from forming a judgement about its truth or falsity (that being the domain of the theologian or philosopher).

The contemporary form of the insider/outsider debate, which has focused on the limits and desirability of such an approach, has raised different issues. A number of critics have argued that the phenomenology of religion has been implicitly theological (Segal 1983; Wiebe 1985), even a spiritual technique in its own right (McCutcheon 1997). Its assumptions about the essential, fundamental and totalising nature of the sacred, and its frequent adoption of Christian categories and types for the theorisation of religion have been deemed to be problematic (Fitzgerald 2000).[7] Critics have questioned the rhetoric of impartiality and critical distance associated with phenomenology (Flood 1999).

Two rather different approaches to the study of religions have emerged in the West in recent decades. One is avowedly secular and scientific.[8] It values an objective, outsider stance. It starts from the view that we cannot assume a common human nature across which categories such as religion and experiences of the sacred are shared. Instead, the social nature of religion and its capacity to be studied like other ideologies and institutions must be acknowledged. The aim of the scholar of religion should not be to get inside the experience and meaning of religious phenomena, but to build upon the benefits of critical distance to explain religion from the outside. The second approach focuses upon reflexivity.[9] Rather than requiring greater objectivity, as the previous approach does, it requires greater awareness on the part of the scholar about the dialogical nature of scholarship. While not being necessarily opposed to phenomenology, its criticism of that approach has been that the exponents of the latter were insufficiently aware of their intellectual and personal standpoint vis-à-vis others. They failed to take sufficient account of the effect of their position – either as individuals, often themselves religious, or as members of privileged groups of scholars, often Western and male – on their understanding of religion. Critics of this take a reflexive stance which requires that, as scholars, they research and write consciously from within their context and standpoint, whether as insiders or outsiders. Some couch this criticism in terms of post-colonialism, stressing the importance of a scholarly engagement with issues of identity, power and status (Shaw 1995; Flood 1999; King 1999; Donaldson and Pui-Lan 2002).

McCutcheon (1999) sought to categorise these responses to the insider/outsider problem as follows: (i) the autonomy of religious experience, which he associated with the phenomenological approach; (ii) reductionism, exemplified by those taking a scientific, objective outsider stance; (iii) neutrality and methodological agnosticism, as adopted by those such as Ninian Smart who relied on insider accounts without evaluating their truth or falsity; and (iv) reflexivity.[10] McCutcheon's presentation and discussion of these responses was introduced with reference to two terms which derive from the work of the linguist, Kenneth Pike. The *emic* perspective arises 'from studying behaviour as from inside the system' (Pike 1967: 37); the *etic* perspective, as from the outside. The former, then, is an attempt,

> to produce as faithfully as possible – in a word, to describe – the informant's own descriptions ... The etic perspective is the observer's subsequent attempt to take the descriptive information they have already gathered and to organize, systematize, compare – in a word redescribe – that information in terms of a system of their own making ...
>
> (McCutcheon 1999: 17)

These terms are of central importance for understanding the perspectives of insiders and outsiders.

Researching religious groups: insider/outsider perspectives and participant observation

Having dealt briefly with how some of the issues relating to the insider/outsider debate have been theorised, I shall turn now to a range of examples in order to investigate how these issues have been dealt with in practice. Our focus moves, then, from the theoretical to the methodological. For this purpose, I have developed a diagram to portray insider and outsider positions based on a model of participant/ observer roles from the social sciences. The term 'participant observation' has commonly been used in anthropology to refer to the process of conducting research by living within a community over a period of time, participating in its life and observing its activities and use of symbols in order to develop an understanding of its meaning and structures (Davies 1999). This anthropological strategy need not detain us here. Rather, it is the four role conceptions of complete participant, participant-as-observer, observer-as-participant, and complete observer – first identified by two sociologists called Junker and Gold in the 1950s – that we shall consider here with reference to insider and outsider perspectives (Gold 1958: 217). They may be plotted on a continuum as follows:

OUTSIDER			INSIDER
Complete	Observer-as-	Participant-	Complete
observer----------------participant----------------------as-observer------------------participant			

If we take this diagram as illustrating the roles of those involved in researching religious groups, we can see that a number of positions are possible. I shall take the polar opposites first, followed by the two mid-way positions. At one end are those who are fully involved in religious activity as participants.[11] They write about religion as insiders. Objectivity is not their purpose; critical distance is not their aim. They are scholars who write about their religion, with the benefit of an insider's knowledge, as engaged participants. They are unapologetic about this position, often believing that insiders like themselves provide the most informed and reliable accounts of their religion. I will look to the work of Fatima Mernissi, a Muslim scholar, for an example of this. Mernissi (1991) does not make a general case for the value of participant insider accounts, but rather shows how such accounts arise from particular standpoints and motivations. There is no single, uncontested view of what constitutes a religion like Islam; there are many differing participant accounts.

Moving to the far left of the diagram, we will turn to the role of the complete observer. Here we might expect to find a scholar who researches and writes about religion from the outside, eschewing any kind of participation. This is a position often associated with the psychology and sociology of religion, particularly with studies in which the researcher observes by means of the scientific use and analysis of questionnaires or structured interviews. My example is the fascinating study by Festinger, Riecken and Schachter carried out in the mid-1950s that revealed what happened to a religious group when its prophecy failed. We shall see how the researchers attempted to reproduce the complete observer stance in a situation where participation turned out to be unavoidable.

The role of the observer-as-participant will be examined in relation to Eileen Barker's stance in *The Making of a Moonie* (1984). From this we will discern a line of continuity with the phenomenological approach outlined earlier, particularly with the strategy of 'methodological agnosticism' commonly associated with the work of Ninian Smart (1973).

We will turn finally to those scholarly participants who adopt the role of observer in the midst of their own religious communities. They generally adopt a more critical stance than those who are complete participants, while remaining of the faith and sharing in the benefits of an insider's knowledge of the beliefs and practices of the community. For an understanding of this role we will examine the reflections of Samuel Heilman, a modernist Jew and sociologist writing in the 1980s before turning to those scholarly participants who have developed a reflexive and postmodernist critique of the insider/outsider problem (Pearson 2002; Collins 2002; Mandair 2001).

(a) Fatima Mernissi: a complete but contentious participant?

---Complete

participant

The majority of books written about religions are written by those who participate in them. There are numerous publishing houses associated with religious institutions; many groups have in-house newsletters and journals. In all of these, people of faith share with their co-religionists accounts of religious experience, religious ideas, responses to scripture, and thoughts about religious behaviour, ethics and the public demonstration of their faith. In addition, most religions have a class of scholars who reflect on, speak and write about their doctrinal, philosophical, legal or textual traditions, and may interpret them according to the needs of the time, or codify them so that they may be remembered and used in the future. Those who comprise such classes of scholars (theologians, rabbis, muftis, pandits and so on), often men, are by definition participants and insiders.

I have chosen Fatima Mernissi to illustrate the complete participant role, notably the stance she takes in *Women and Islam: An Historical and Theological Enquiry* (1991). As a Muslim feminist sociologist, she is hardly the obvious choice. Mernissi herself cites a case where she was denounced, by the editor of an Islamic journal, as a liar and misrepresentative of Islamic tradition. She is certainly not an authorised Islamic leader nor a trained theologian, but, as one who writes as a Muslim with the deliberate intention of recovering the Islamic past in order to understand women's rights, she evidently counts herself as an insider. What is more, she has a clear sense that this is not just a matter of private belief, but of legal requirement and communal identity:

> It is time to define what I mean when I say 'we Muslims'. The expression does not refer to Islam in terms of an individual choice, a personal option. I define being Muslim as belonging to a theocratic state . . . Being Muslim is a civil matter, a national identity, a passport, a family code of laws, a code of public rights.
>
> (20–1)

It is the denial of such rights to women in Muslim states that is of concern to Mernissi and that passionately engages her as a Muslim, a feminist and a scholar, as a result of which she turns her intellectual powers and scholarly training to the Hadith, the collections by later scholars of the sayings of the Prophet Muhammad. She is a critical religious insider tackling an issue of significance to contemporary Muslim women by recovering the foundational stories of the women around Muhammad and interrogating the misogynism of later interpretative accounts. In the preface to the English edition to her book, she writes:

> We Muslim women can walk into the modern world with pride, knowing that the quest for dignity, democracy, and human rights, for full participation in the political and social affairs of our country, stems from no imported Western values, but is a true part of the Muslim tradition.
>
> (viii)

Mernissi's is an emic, but not uncritical perspective. Rather than using the 'experience-distant' language of either comparative religion or sociology, she uses the 'experience-near' language of Islam, stressing, in particular, the centrality of the concept of *hijab* for an understanding of Muslim civilisation.[12] Although she has not received the training associated with the *ulama*, she draws on the same sources of authority, though emphasising different stories and offering variant readings.

Although her book is not directed explicitly at a non-Muslim audience, Mernissi is clearly aware of the dominant Western critique, which has tended to see Islam as undemocratic and oppressive of women, and is keen to show that, in its foundational stories, there are 'matters dangerous to the establishment, of human dignity and equal rights' (ix). She wishes to make clear to other Muslims that taking up the cause of women's rights does not place her outside Islamic tradition or Muslim society. She eschews the role of the secular feminist outsider and embraces that of participant in the narration of Islamic memory (10).

Can a single example, like that of Mernissi, point to a plurality of cases? I believe so. In choosing Mernissi – an insider who cites and disputes the views of many other Muslim insiders – I have indicated the complexity of insider perspectives. Choosing a feminist insider as an example has raised the issue of contestation between different insider-scholars within a single religion.

(b) The struggle to be the complete observer

Complete---

observer

From an emic account in which experience-near concepts are to the fore, we now move to an etic one in which the language of social science is used to explain psychological behaviour resulting from religious belief. In the final part of their study of what happens to a messianic group when prophecy fails, Festinger, Riecken and Schachter (1956) examined the methodological difficulties that arose when trying to sustain the stance of the complete observer in a qualitative study of a dynamic religious community.[13] At the time when they conducted their study, the key principles of social scientific research were objectivity, neutrality, the ability to repeat experiments, to demonstrate the validity of their results and to generalise from them. Many sociologists and psychologists used a quantitative approach, for example, by developing and administering a questionnaire.[14] Festinger and his co-researchers decided that such an approach was inappropriate for examining the cognitive and behavioural responses of a group of believers to 'undeniable disconfirmatory evidence' (4). Rather, it was essential to observe a group closely during such a process. Had it been possible to set up an experiment of this kind in a laboratory, behind glass, the researchers would no doubt have done so.

In fact, what they did was to await signs (in the media) of prophetic group activity, gain covert admittance to a group, and then observe the behaviour of its members from the inside. They adopted insider roles, as seekers who were 'non-directive, sympathetic listeners, passive participants who were inquisitive and eager to learn whatever others might want to tell us' (234). Such undercover work was deemed necessary to avoid alerting the group to the fact that it was being researched, and thus to avoid influencing the very beliefs, attitudes and responses they wished to observe.

Although the researchers were scientific outsiders, to the prophet, Mrs Keech, and her followers, they appeared to be complete participants. They were, however, students and staff from a variety of university psychology and sociology departments trained in observational methods. As such, they were conscious of the need to satisfy social scientific conditions, though they found themselves departing from 'the orthodoxy of social science in a number of respects', notably, in being unable 'to subject the members of the group to any standardized measuring instrument, such as a questionnaire or structured interview' (249). Further, they unintentionally reinforced members' beliefs, e.g. by seeming to confirm the view that they had been sent to join the group for a special purpose. They found it impossible to avoid discussing the belief system with members, answering calls from enquirers, and being seen as messengers (from the Guardians) by the movement's leaders.[15] All of these put them in a position of influencing those people they were supposed to be observing.

Despite these difficulties, *When Prophecy Fails* is an etic account as its purpose, hypothesis, methods, analysis, reporting and audience are evidently social scientific and not religious. While the researchers took seriously members' beliefs and responses, they did so only in so far as these were data to be collected and evaluated. The issue of their truth or falsity was not mentioned. Neither did the authors formally reflect on whether they accepted any of the beliefs of the group.[16] Rather, they pretended 'to be merely interested individuals who had been persuaded of the correctness of the belief system' (249). Their pretence as insiders raises ethical questions about whether and in what ways the subjects of research should be informed and involved in decisions about the research process. The use in the book of terms such as 'covert', 'detective' and 'surveillance' heightens the distinction between the outsider-observer on the one side (in control, invisible, investigating), and the insider-observed on the other (passive, highly visible, exposed to detailed investigation), thereby raising the issue of power in the scholarly study and presentation of religious groups.

Arguably, this case fails to do full justice to the observer role because the demands of the research required the scholars involved to compromise their position as outsiders (by necessitating that they pretend to be participants). Nevertheless, we have been able to see how difficult it is for even the most determined observers to remain uninvolved, impartial and scientific when examining the subject of religious belief at close quarters. In the next section, we will consider whether an observer-as-participant who is known to and accepted by insiders encounters fewer problems. What are the characteristics of this stance? What difference does it make to the research if the participating observer owns up to being an outsider?

(c) In neutral: the observer-as-participant

```
-------------------------------Observer---------------------------------------------------

                              as-participant
```

From the start of her investigation, Eileen Barker rejected the possibility of undertaking covert research on the Unification Church on both practical and ethical grounds. 'It was known that I was not a Moonie. I never pretended that I was, or that I was likely to become one' (1984: 20).

> I usually found my time with the movement interesting, and I grew genuinely fond of several individual Moonies, but at no time could I believe in the Unification version of reality. On the other hand, I could not accept the picture of the movement that outsiders kept telling me I ought to be finding.
>
> (21)

Barker's purpose in investigating the Unification Church, or 'Moonies' as they were frequently called, was to answer the question, 'Why should – how could – anyone become a Moonie?' (1). Little was known about them in the mid-1970s (despite the fact that the movement had been founded in 1954, in Korea), except for what was gleaned from negative media coverage about the leader and the conversion strategies of the movement which tended to stimulate fear and fascination rather than a desire to learn or to be informed. Sceptical of both the movement's self-image and the media account, Barker became an authorised observer whose research method was one of engaged participation. She lived in Unification centres, attended workshops, listened to members, engaged in conversations and asked questions.[17] Her stance, by her own admittance, had its strengths and weaknesses.

> Being known to be a non-member had its disadvantages, but by talking to people who had left the movement I was able to check that I was not missing any of the internal information which was available to rank-and-file members. At the same time, being an outsider who was 'inside' had enormous advantages. I was allowed (even, on certain occasions, expected) to ask questions that no member would have presumed to ask either his leaders or his peers.
>
> (21)

Barker borrowed a term from the work of Max Weber to identify her approach to understanding why people became Moonies: 'Verstehen is a process of inquiry during which the researcher tries to put himself in other people's shoes or . . . to see the world through their glasses' (20). Although she contextualised this with reference to the social sciences, it had much in common with the empathetic approach favoured by the phenomenologists of religion reviewed earlier in this account: Kristensen, van der Leeuw and, latterly, Ninian Smart. It was Smart who first used the term 'methodological agnosticism' to signal the need for neutrality and the bracketing out of truth claims and judgements in research on religion. Barker shared this view, believing that 'passing value judgements should be an enterprise that is separate from social science' (36). Rather, she hoped to bring together what she saw as 'an objective factual account of the history and beliefs of the movement' (10) with diverse voices from within and outside it.

Barker's etic account, interspersed with the experiences of Moonies, ex-Moonies, non-Moonies and anti-Moonies, represented a conscious attempt to *translate* Moonie reality and values for those unfamiliar with them. She found that she was able to stay in touch with outsiders' often unsympathetic and quizzical attitudes while becoming engrossed in Moonie reality by regularly re-reading her research diary. She was reminded of her own journey from ignorance to knowledge about the movement. She believed in the attempt to bridge the divergent perpectives of insiders and outsiders, and saw this as an appropriate scholarly task. Furthermore, she held that it was 'perfectly possible to see things from other people's points of view without necessarily agreeing that they are right' (35). At the same time, she recognised that there were those on both sides who believed that neutrality was impossible, even immoral.

The methodological agnosticism identified by Smart – and pursued by Barker – dominated the study of religion in the 1970s and 1980s. It upheld the dichotomy between inside and outside, positing the need for a value-free translator who would bridge the two perspectives. Barker exemplified the role of observer-as-participating translator. But could an outsider ever fulfil this role?[18] Could such a scholar really be agnostic, or would his or her act of observation necessarily call such a stance into question?

(d) The participant-as-observer comes of age

--Participant-----------------------------------

as-observer

As we saw in the 1890s with Tiele and in the 1980s with Barker, many scholars of religion – with personal religious convictions or with none – have held that an impartial stance is possible. Indeed, many religious people have sought to research and write about their own religion *as if* they were observers, with objectivity and critical distance. It has often been the aim of such participants-as-observers to provide an entrée into their religion, its beliefs and practices, for outsiders; to make comprehensible, often through the use of 'experience-distant' concepts and commonly accepted scientific methods, the esoteric world from which they come. They have often shared this aim with observers-as-participants (like Barker), and have sought to exercise a bridge-building role with the purpose of communicating what is thought or practised within the religion to those outside it.

Many participants-as-observers have commented sensitively on their own position and purpose in writing as believers and practitioners. This has been especially true since the 1990s, with the impact of a critical postmodernist and reflexive stance. Several examples which exemplify this will be considered later in the section. First, we will look at an example from the 1980s in which orthodox religiosity and modernist sociology met in an autobiographical account by Samuel Heilman, *The Gate Behind the Wall* (1984, partially reproduced in Comstock 1995).

> I live in two worlds . . . In one, I am attached to an eternal yesterday – a timeless faith and ritual, an ancient system of behavior. In that world, I am an Orthodox Jew. In my other world, there is little if any attachment to the enchantment of religion or sacred practice, and what is happening today or tomorrow matters far more than the verities embedded in the past. In that domain, I am a university professor of sociology.
>
> (Comstock 1995: 214)

Heilman describes this as 'a double life' in which the two aspects are compartmentalised, and which is generally maintained by forgetting one aspect while living out the other. He proceeds, though, to describe the attempt he made 'to collapse the boundaries between these two worlds and find a way to make myself whole' (214).

Starting out as a modern Orthodox Jewish sociologist, Heilman undertook a sociological study of his own synagogue community, believing that as an insider I could supply, through both introspection and a sense of the relevant questions to ask, information about dimensions of inner life not readily available to other researchers . . . I would be able to give a fuller picture of the synagogue than could any outsider, however well prepared and trained he might be.

(218)

Reflecting back on this exercise, he discovered that he had 'found my way back into the traditional synagogue from my new home in the University via the tools of my social science' (218). However, he harboured a further ambition, to fulfil his sacred duty to engage in *lernen*, the Yiddish term for the Orthodox Jewish practice of reviewing the sacred texts with devotion and awe (216). On the advice of his rabbi, he further utilised his professional skills as a participant observer in seeking out and participating in a traditional study circle or *chavruse* in Jerusalem. We see in this a desire both to fulfil personal religious commitments and to describe and explain the world of the *chavruse* to outsiders. What is of interest in Heilman's powerful account is, first, the way in which his position as participant-as-observer is demonstrated through the use of spatial imagery and specialist concepts, and, second, the way in which he reflects upon that position.

Heilman's title, *The Gate Behind the Wall*, in addition to situating us in Jewish Jerusalem at or near the Wailing Wall, promises us entry into a traditional and esoteric world from which, as outsiders, we are normally excluded, but to which, as an insider/outsider Jew, he was powerfully attracted. Further, he uses the imagery of walls, gates, rooms and doors to describe his modernist journey: 'Old walls made new through a process of uncovering seemed the right metaphor for my own quest' (221). In distinguishing between the compartmentalisation from which he was trying to escape and the wholeness he sought, he used the metaphor of rooms: in the former, 'one simply learns to dim the lights in one room while passing into the other'; in the *chavruse*, 'compartments collapse, and rooms open into one another' (229). Despite his most fervent efforts, though, as a modernist Jew, he felt unable to transcend his sense of distance; unable to escape 'the barriers of biography' (230).

Heilman's two purposes (and two worlds) are mirrored in his use of both 'experience-near' and 'experience-distant' concepts. He does not shy away from using Yiddish and Hebrew terms, but he also uses the language of religious studies and the social sciences in order to move his account beyond the descriptive and ethnographic to the analytical and theoretical. Repeatedly, he uses terms such as tradition, culture, liturgy and sacred text (rather than equivalent terms from Orthodox Judaism), and also introduces social scientific concepts such as liminality (227), authenticity (225) and organising principle (228). As autobiographical scholarship, Heilman's account is subjective in character. However, it goes beyond description of the participant's experience by offering an examination of the limits of Heilman's role as a modernist Orthodox Jewish sociologist. He suggests that the process of observation – of others and the self – by one who is an insider produces a feeling of separation. His repeated references to walls, borders, gates, barriers, doors and limits demonstrate this seemingly unalterable affliction: 'As if by some sort of biological rejection process, the strangeness in me was forcing me out (of the *chavruse*)' (230).

How have participants-as-observers since Heilman found this role? Have their purposes in writing from the inside out been comparable to his? Have their experiences of observation and the practice of writing about it been similar? Two authors, writing in a recent book on the insider/outsider problem, reveal the way in which the understanding of this role is changing. Both authors are critical of the juxtaposition of insiders and outsiders, and see the value of the critical insider stance. However, the first asserts the benefits of the both/and principle; the second commends the dissolution of the distinction between the two positions.

Jo Pearson (2002), whose study of British Wicca is entitled 'Going native in reverse', notes that there are some religions, requiring initiation, which are largely inaccessible to outsiders. For an understanding of these, we are dependent upon insiders who act as a bridge between the inside and outside, and facilitate the two aspects of involvement and distance. Such an insider-researcher acts as both insider and outsider, and the movement back and forth opens him or her up to a range of types of information: that which is available to outsiders, that which is only available to those within the researched community (insiders), and that which becomes available to the researcher through his or her reflexive participation in the research process.

At the end of an ethnographic account of his own Quaker meeting, Peter Collins (2002) disputes the notions of self and society which underlie the dualism of insider and outsider. He uses imagery similar to Heilman's to invoke the modernist perspective which sees society 'as a series of buildings each with a single door which serves both as entrance and exit: either one is in or one is out, and if one is in one building then one cannot at the same time be in another' (93). Collins's view, of a more processual society and a more dynamic self, in which worlds are overlapping and interactive rather than isolated and separate, makes the distinction between insider and outsider largely redundant. All participants create social meaning through the common practice of story telling, and this, in turn, dissolves the boundaries between inside and out.

Heilman writes of the unresolved tension of being between two worlds as a Jew who is also a sociologist. Pearson suggests that, whatever its difficulties, the both/and position of the insider-scholar is productive, the reflexive nature of its stance giving it the edge over outsider scholarship. Collins concludes that the distinction between insider and outsider becomes irrelevant when we recognise that all those who participate, whether of the faith or not, contribute to the co-construction of the story. The insider/outsider dichotomy is an unhelpful consequence of a modernist view of self and society.

Where does the problem lie, and what is the way forward?

This last view is similar to one expressed by Mandair, a recent participant in the Sikh studies debate with which I began. In an attempt to understand its ideological contours, Mandair (2001) locates the problem in 'the current intellectual and methodological crisis or rupture in the human and social sciences' (49) in which 'secular reason has been placed in a position of supervision in respect of any possible inquiry into religion' (50). As he sees it, the Sikh studies debate is not so much a function of the insider/outsider problem (as suggested by Darshan Singh) as of the modernist turn from religious to secular thinking. In the case of Sikh studies, this has had the effect of making insider critiques of Western scholarship look like traditionalist, even fundamentalist, attacks.

Mandair is not merely being defensive here; there is a case to answer. Most twentieth-century studies of religions – whether they be historical, in the case of Sikh studies, phenomenological or sociological, in the case of our other examples – were rooted in the discourse of secular reason and scientific enquiry. Their authors spoke the language of neutrality, impartiality, objectivity, observation, reductionism, methodological agnosticism and atheism. Both outsiders and scholarly insiders sought to articulate their positions in these terms. With the latter, as we saw with Heilman, this led to a sense of tension, the result of being an insider subjectively caught up in an experience while endeavouring to maintain the appropriate level of critical distance required by the scholarly establishment.

Both Collins and Mandair invite us to step away from the imprisonment of this modernist position, but their diagnoses are different. Collins offers a postmodern response: the abandonment of dichotomous views of insider/outsider in favour of a more dynamic view in which everyone is a co-participant in the formulation of a narrative about religion. Mandair favours the move to a study of religion (Sikhism) that 'is at once a form of self-discovery, no less spiritual than political, no less therapeutic than classificatory' (68–9), in short, an antidote to the dominant objectivist, secularist approach.[19]

The scholars discussed in this chapter have not only shown us the centrality of the insider/outsider problem in the study of religions, they have also highlighted the complex issues of subjectivity and objectivity, emic and etic perspectives, the politics and ethics of researching and writing about religion (whether as an outsider or an insider), the epistemological and methodological implications of the problem, and its ideological location within Western secular modernism. These are profound matters for anyone studying religions. Collins and Mandair invite us in different ways to reconceptualise the terms of our discipline in such a way that we are no longer compelled to compartmentalise the world of faith and the world of scholarship. For some other scholars this is a step too far, one which undermines the distinction between those doing religion and those observing it, between theology and the study of religions, indeed the very *raison d'être* of the latter as a field of study with its own terms of reference.[20] In an attempt to rethink the direction and terms of the study of religions, Flood offers us an alternative, a strategy for reconfiguring critical distance, 'outsideness' and situated observation which depends not upon modernist notions of objectivity and the phenomenological assertion of non-confessionalism, but rather upon a dialogical and reflexive engagement between scholars and the religious people they study.[21]

What these new perspectives show is that the problem of the insider and outsider is as vital now for understanding the theory and method of religious studies as it was when the latter first emerged as a discipline separate from theology more than a century ago.

Notes

1   Among other autobiographies and biographies used in connection with this course is the collection edited by Gary Comstock entitled *Religious Autobiographies* (1995) that includes accounts by men and women from a wide variety of religious backgrounds.

2   A full account of this debate can be found in Grewal (1998). See also McLeod (2000: 267–79), and articles by Oberoi and Mandair in Shackle, Singh and Mandair (2001). Insider/outsider approaches to Islam have been discussed by Goddard (1995), and by Knott in relation to Hindu movements (1998a, 1998b).

3   Westerners' approaches to non-Western 'others' have been unmasked by anthropologists and cultural critics from the late-1970s, the pre-eminent work being Edward Said's *Orientalism* (1978), see also King (1999).

4   The study of religions at the end of the nineteenth century and in the early twentieth century was referred to variously as 'the scientific study of religion', '*Religionswissenschaft*', 'comparative religion', 'the history of religions' and, later, 'the phenomenology of religions'. These terms had differing meanings though they were all used to signal an area of study distinct from theology (see Waardenburg 1973; Sharpe 1975; Whaling 1995).

5   Müller acknowledged that some people believed religion too sacred to be treated scientifically while a number of scientists thought it erroneous and beneath their professional consideration.

6   The activities involved in bringing this about were (a) the assigning of names to what becomes manifest, (b) the interpolation of the phenomenon into the scholar's own life, (c) the observance of bracketing or *epoché*, (d) the clarification of what has been observed and (e) the achievement of understanding (van der Leeuw 1963, pp. 671–9).

7   This is one of the points made by Darshan Singh in his critique of Western scholars of Sikhism.

8   See Segal (1983), Wiebe (1985), McCutcheon (1997). This approach takes several disciplinary forms, e.g. social scientific and cognitivist.

9   See Hufford (1995), Flood (1999) and feminist contributors to King (1995). For a practical demonstration of this approach, see Brown (1991).

10 McCutcheon's reader may be consulted in association with this chapter. Several of the articles cited in this chapter may be found in his collection (Geertz, Hufford, Pike, Segal, Shaw, Wiebe), and relevant articles by other scholars I have mentioned (Eliade, Smart, Brown) are also included.

11 Gold had a different view of the complete participant to the one I have adopted here. To him, all roles were outsider positions, with the complete participant being the sociologist who *pretended* for the purposes of the research to be a full and active participant. The example I have given on p. 245 of Festinger, Riecken and Schachter might best exemplify this position. Unlike Gold, I have used these role conceptions to distinguish between the insider and outsider positions of researchers.

12 The notion of 'experience-near' and 'experience-distant' concepts comes through the anthropological work of Clifford Geertz from the psychologist Hans Kohut. 'Experience-near concepts' are those which subjects use naturally to describe things with which they are familiar, and the latter are those which specialists, such as anthropologists, use for scientific and other academic purposes when discussing the practices of the people they are studying (Geertz 1974).

13 Social scientific research methods are commonly divided into quantitative and qualitative methods, the former being those which use statistical measures for analysing attitudes and behaviour (particularly questionnaires), the latter being those which focus on personal testimony and behaviour in interviews and other ethnographic practices.

14 See Beit-Hallahmi and Argyle (1996) for examples.

15 The 'Guardians' were supernatural beings thought by members to be guiding the movement.

16 This is not surprising given that the book was written some thirty years before the rise in popularity of self-reflexive accounting among social anthropologists and sociologists.

17 Schooled in social science methodology, Barker also administered questionnaires to members and to those who had expressed an initial interest but had not joined. It is likely that Barker's study is the most extensive ever conducted of a new religious movement.

18 This was the question asked by Darshan Singh (1991) and other Sikh critics (Grewal 1998).

19 For an example of such scholarly self-discovery I would suggest the compelling work of Karen McCarthy Brown (1991) in which she presents the biography of Mama Lola, a

Brooklyn Vodou priestess, through a dynamic and increasingly personal engagement resulting in an intimate and sometimes self-revelatory account.

20 See Flood (1999), Fitzgerald (2000) and McCutcheon (2003) for a full discussion of these issues.

21 Flood's perspective (1999: Chapter 6) is indebted to the ideas of Bakhtin in particular.

References

Barker, Eileen, 1984, *The Making of a Moonie: Brainwashing or Choice?*, Oxford, Blackwell.

Beit-Hallahmi, B. and Argyle, Michael, 1996, *The Social Psychology of Religion*, London, Routledge.

Brown, Karen McCarthy, 1991, *Mama Lola: A Vodou Priestess in Brooklyn*, Berkeley CA, University of California Press.

Collins, Peter J., 2002, 'Connecting anthropology and Quakerism', in Elisabeth Arweck and Martin Stringer, eds, *Theorising Faith: The Insider/Outsider Problem in the Study of Ritual*, Birmingham, Birmingham University Press, pp. 77–95.

Comstock, Gary L., 1995, *Religious Autobiographies*, Belmont CA, Wadsworth.

Davies, Charlotte Aull, 1999, *Reflexive Ethnography: A Guide to Researching Selves and Others*, London, Routledge.

Donaldson, Laura E. and Pui-lan, Kwok, eds, 2002, *Postcolonialism, Feminism, and Religious Discourse*, New York and London, Routledge.

Festinger, Leon, Riecken, Henry W. and Schachter, Stanley, 1956, *When Prophecy Fails: A Social and Psychological Study of a Modern Group that Predicted the Destruction of the World*, New York, Harper & Row (reprinted 1964).

Fitzgerald, Timothy, 2000, *The Ideology of Religious Studies*, New York, Oxford University Press.

Flood, Gavin, 1999, *Beyond Phenomenology: Rethinking the Study of Religion*, London, Cassell.

Geertz, Clifford, 1974, '"From the native's point of view": on the nature of anthropological understanding', *Bulletin of the American Academy of Arts and Sciences*, 28: 1.

Goddard, Hugh, 1995, *From Double Standards to Mutual Understanding*, London, Curzon.

Gold, Raymond L., 1958, 'Roles in sociological field observations', *Social Forces*, 36, 217–23.

Grewal, J. S., 1998, *Contesting Interpretations of the Sikh Tradition*, New Delhi, Manohar.

Heilman, Samuel, 1984, *The Gate Behind the Wall*, Georges Bourchardt.

Hufford, David J., 1995, 'The scholarly voice and the personal voice: reflexivity in belief studies', *Western Folklore*, 54, 57–76.

King, Richard, 1999, *Orientalism and Religion: Postcolonial Theory, India and the Mystic East*, London, Routledge.

King, Ursula, ed., 1995, *Religion and Gender*, Oxford, Blackwell.

Knott, Kim, 1998a, *Hinduism: A Very Short Introduction*, Oxford, Oxford University Press.

——— 1998b, 'Insider and outsider perceptions of Prabhupada', *Journal of Vaisnava Studies*, 6: 2, 73–91.

Kristensen, William Brede, 1960, *The Meaning of Religion*, The Hague, Martinus Nijhoff.

McCutcheon, Russell T., 1997, *Manufacturing Religion: The Discourse of Sui Generis Religion and the Politics of Nostalgia*, New York and Oxford, Oxford University Press.

——— ed., 1999, *The Insider/Outsider Problem in the Study of Religion: A Reader*, London and New York, Cassell.

——— 2003, *The Discipline of Religion*, London and New York, Routledge.

McLeod, W. H., 2000, *Exploring Sikhism: Aspects of Sikh Identity, Culture and Thought*, Oxford, Oxford University Press.

Mandair, Arvind-Pal Singh, 2001, 'Thinking differently about religion and history: issues for Sikh Studies', in Christopher Shackle, Gurharpal Singh and Arvind-Pal Mandair, eds, *Sikh Religion, Culture and Ethnicity*, Richmond, Curzon, pp. 47–71.

Mernissi, Fatima, 1991, *Women and Islam: An Historical and Theological Enquiry*, Oxford, Blackwell [1987].

Müller, Max F., 1873, *Introduction to the Science of Religion*, London, Longmans, Green & Co.

O'Connor, June, 1995, 'The epistemological significance of feminist research in religion' in Ursula King, ed., *Religion and Gender*, Oxford, Blackwell, pp. 45–64.

Pearson, Jo, 2002, '"Going native in reverse": the insider as researcher in British Wicca', in Elisabeth Arweck and Martin Stringer, eds, *Theorising Faith: The Insider/Outsider Problem in the Study of Ritual*, Birmingham, Birmingham University Press, pp. 97–113.

Pike, Kenneth, 1967, *Language in Relation to a Unified Theory of the Structure of Human Behaviour*, 2nd edn, The Hague, Mouton.

Said, Edward, 1978, *Orientalism*, London, Routledge and Kegan Paul.

Segal, Robert A., 1983, 'In defense of reductionism', *Journal of the American Academy of Religion*, 51, 97–124.

Shackle, Christopher, Singh, Gurharpal and Mandair, Arvind-Pal, eds, 2001, *Sikh Religion, Culture and Ethnicity*, Richmond, Curzon.

Sharpe, Eric, 1975, *Comparative Religion: A History*, London, Duckworth.

Shaw, Rosalind, 1995, 'Feminist anthropology and the gendering of religious studies', in Ursula King, ed., *Religion and Gender*, Oxford, Blackwell, pp. 65–76.

Singh, Darshan, 1991, *Western Perspective on the Sikh Religion*, New Delhi, Sehgal Publishers Service.

Singh, Gurdev, ed., 1986, *Perspectives on the Sikh Tradition*, Patiala, Siddharth Publications.

Smart, Ninian, 1973, *The Science of Religion and the Sociology of Knowledge: Some Methodological Questions*, Princeton, Princeton University Press.

Tiele, Cornelius P., 1897–9, *Elements of the Science of Religion*, 2 vols, Edinburgh/London, Blackwood and Sons.

van der Leeuw, Gerardus, 1963, *Religion in Essence and Manifestation*, 2 vols, New York, Harper Torchbooks [1938].

Waardenburg, Jacques, 1973, *Classical Approaches to the Study of Religion*, The Hague, Mouton.

Whaling, Frank, ed., 1995, *Theory and Methods in Religious Studies: Contemporary Approaches to the Study of Religions*, Berlin, Mouton de Gruyter.

Wiebe, Donald, 1985, 'Does understanding religion require religious understanding?', in Witold Tyloch, ed., *Current Progress in the Methodology of the Science of Religions*, Warsaw, Polish Scientific Publishers.

Chapter 14

Postmodernism

Paul Heelas

Introduction

The term 'postmodernism' can mean many things. Here, with the term being deployed in connection with the *study* of religion, it is primarily taken to refer to a mode/s of inquiry whereby religion (or, for that matter, anything else) is investigated. The key theme in what follows is that postmodernism, reacting to Enlightenment thought, questions – even disgards – the possibility of arriving at the truth, the essential, the clear-cut definition or interpretation, the explanation. Regarding the most extreme forms of postmodernism, this means that the study of religion comes to a close. However, it will be seen that in less radical forms postmodern thought can enrich debates about what is involved in studying religion.

To place this essay in context, by and large the application of postmodern thinking to the study of religion has lagged behind this kind of application in fields like cultural studies, women's studies, cultural anthropology and media studies. Most investigations of religion still take place in terms of those canons of inquiry developed by the modernist Enlightenment 'project': the quest for clear definitions, rigorous analysis, convincing interpretation, recurrent correlations or patterns as revealed by comparison, logically coherent propositions and explanations based on the best available evidence, in sum something at least approaching the goal of *the* definitive account. However, there has been a shift away from some of the canons of inquiry of the Enlightenment. Most obviously, this is seen in the reluctance of the great majority of modernist scholars today to explain religion away by reducing it to socio-cultural or psychological states of affairs, to establish the origins and evolution of religion and thereby predict the future, or to find universal laws of a causal/functional nature. And it can be argued that this modification of Enlightenment aspirations owes a considerable amount to that 'climate' of postmodern thought which has become widely in evidence within the academy. Furthermore, as we shall see, postmodern thought is beginning to be directly applied to the study of religion.

This essay is organized in terms of six main sections. The first – 'The Enlightenment project' – provides a summary of this pivotal feature of modernity. It might seem strange to begin in such a fashion, given that so much postmodern thought is so opposed to the project. However, given that much postmodernism has been fuelled by rebellion against the Enlightenment, it has to be understood by reference to what is being rejected. The second section – 'Radical postmodernism and the assault on the Enlightenment project' – summarizes some of the more philosophically informed ways in which postmodern thought has generated a clear break with what has proceeded it. The emphasis here is very much on loss of faith in the Enlightenment project. The third section – 'Postmodernism as the radicalization of difference' – draws attention to a rather different (although in some ways interlinked) dynamic, where values and politics would appear to be as important as philosophy (if not more so) in fuelling postmodern thought. Paradoxically, it will be seen, as well as opposing a very great deal indeed of Enlightened modernity, perhaps the key feature of much postmodern thought – the radicalization of 'difference' – also owes a very great deal to such key values of Enlightened modernity as equality, 'respecting the other' and 'the freedom of the other'.

As well as serving to 'ground' postmodern thought by showing how it relates to Enlightened modernity, implications for the study of religion are also discussed in the second and third sections. The theme of what *kinds* of study (if study is possible at all) are associated with varieties of postmodern thought is taken further in the next two sections. These are entitled 'Critical reflections: on the wild side and the death of the *study* of religion' and 'Critical reflections: the "middle way"'. The former summarizes the negative consequences of radical postmodernism (of whatever variety: philosophical, value-driven or both) for the study of religion. The latter explores what postmodernism, especially in its more value- and politically-driven dynamic, might have to offer to religious studies. As for the last main section of this essay – 'A note on postmodern religion' – attention is paid to whether the postmodern (and modern) study of religion serves to reveal the existence of postmodern religion.

Finally, by way of introduction, a note on how this chapter has been written. Postmodernism is not so easy to characterize. A major theme running through this way of thinking is opposition to 'metanarratives' (that is, systematized, universalized and forceful modes of knowledge). As a modernist, however, I have to accept that I have quite naturally written this essay *on* postmodernism and the study of religion in terms of a particular metanarrative – that of intellectual inquiry as spelt out by ways of thinking articulated by the Enlightenment. No doubt this means that I do violence to postmodern thought, most obviously over-systematizing or 'over-metanarrativizing' it. My justification for writing as a modernist, though, is that an entry written (seriously) in the spirit of postmodernist suspicion or rejection of meta-narratives would not be able to lay out, analyse, compare and critically discuss postmodern (and other) ways of studying religion. Furthermore, it could well be the case that my approach is justified by the fact that postmodernism, itself, is in fact a metanarrative/s.

The Enlightenment project

As has already been indicated, postmodern thought has largely – although by no means entirely – grown up in opposition to that of the Enlightenment project. Accordingly, it is helpful to begin with a summary of this project: a summary which will be drawn upon later when we explore the ways and extent to which postmodern thought has broken with the canons of the Enlightenment.

The Enlightenment project has provided a, if not the, central dynamic with regard to the construction of modernity. Enlightenment thought has by no means been limited to the realm of philosophy (where Kant has been the most influential figure). For it has also had a crucial role to play in the development of the other academic disciplines of modernity (including various ways of studying religion). Furthermore, by way of science, Enlightenment thought has been highly influential in the development of the great institutional developments of modernity, including the industrial 'revolution', the capitalist 'revolution', and political change (the democratic 'revolution', the development of the nation state and the development of the ethic of humanity).

Four key value-laden assumptions lie at the heart of the Enlightenment project. The first concerns faith in the exercise of reason. In the words of Thomas Paine (1998, orig. 1792), 'Reason obeys itself; and Ignorance submits to whatever is dictated to it' (p. 190). Rationality, it has been widely assumed, operates according to its own, *sui generis*, objective if not infallible laws. And applied to empirical evidence, the exercise of reason enables claims to be tested; claims which, if verified, can be counted upon as being firmly grounded.

This leads on to the second (and intimately related) great assumption of the project, namely that it is possible to arrive at 'the truth'. Whether it be the fields of science, technology, politics or ethics, it has been widely maintained that it is possible to arrive at the correct answer or solution; the accurate definition or classification; the correct explanation; the true ethicality.

Furthermore, and turning to the third great assumption, Enlightened thinkers have great faith in 'the same'. The quest has been to determine the unitary, the universal, that essence which lies behind superficial differences. Thus the quest has been to demonstrate that there is such a thing as 'humanity', lying behind or within the difference made by tradition, ethnicity or race. Again, the quest has been to determine universally applicable laws to explain, for example, human progress.

Mention of progress leads on to the fourth cardinal assumption: that the successful application of reason ensures that humankind moves into an ever better-perfected future. As the matter is put by Kant, in what is perhaps the most famous of all the rallying cries of the Enlightenment,

> *Enlightenment is man's emergence from his self-incurred immaturity.*
> *Immaturity* is the inability to use one's own understanding without the guidance of another. This immaturity is *self-incurred* if its cause is not lack of understanding, but lack of resolution and courage to use it without the guidance of another. The motto of enlightenment is therefore: *Sapere aude!* Have courage to use your *own* understanding!
>
> (1970: 54; original emphasis)

Having introduced the Enlightenment project, we can now briefly turn to some of the (exemplificatory) ways in which it has born fruit with regard to the study of religion. Going back to the nineteenth century, 'progress' translated into widespread evolutionary theorizing of religion, essentialized notions of 'magic', 'religion' and 'science' (or cognates) serving to chart development. Moving into the twentieth century, attention turned to correlatory studies. Deploying (supposedly) precise definitions (of, say, ancestor worship), the aim was to seek out causally significant (as recurrent if not universal) connections (between, say, ancestor worship and a particular socio-cultural formation). Or again, and now thinking of the structuralist approach of the 1960s and 1970s, Lévi-Strauss (1966, orig. 1962) sought 'the same' – particularly with reference to apparently disparate mythologies – at the level of fundamental structures of the human mind.

To conclude this introduction to the Enlightenment project and its application to the study of religion, it remains to draw attention to two more (interrelated) points. First, although in recent decades many scholars have lost faith in the 'grander' ambitions of Enlightened study (such as establishing the origins of religion), there certainly has for long been a strongly reductionistic thrust to much social scientific investigation. To put it simply, Enlightenment thought has supposed that reason can only be applied to arrive at verifiable, determinate truths when it can work with publicly available – or empirically sustainable – evidence. Since the putatively *sui generis* religious realm is not empirically accessible, religion must be reduced to that which belongs to the public domain (psychological or sociological states of affairs, for example) in order to be explained. And second, this means that Enlightenment (social scientific, etc.) theorizing has typically involved moving beyond the participant's frame of reference. Participants might believe in their religions, but since such beliefs – for the reason just given – are not of explanatory value, the investigator has to go 'deeper' to find empirical referents. Explanations are 'extra-religious'. Thus for Durkheim religion is 'really' about society; and for Lévi-Strauss myths are 'really' about meanings operating more or less entirely beyond the ken of participants. In short, much Enlightenment theorizing about religion has traditionally involved the assumption that the 'enlightened' investigator can arrive at knowledge which is superior to – as truer than – the knowledge of those being studied.

Radical postmodernism and the assault on the Enlightenment project

The extent to which postmodern thought can on *occasion* – although by no means always – run counter to the Enlightenment project can be gleaned from this excellent characterization provided by Judith Squires:

> The postmodern condition may be characterised ... as involving three key features: the death of Man, History and Metaphysics. This involves the rejection of all essentialist and transcendental conceptions of human nature; the rejection of unity, homogeneity, totality, closure and identity; the rejection of the pursuit of the real and the true. In the place of these illusory ideals we find the assertion that man is a social, historical or linguistic artefact; the celebration of fragmentation, particularity and difference; the acceptance of the contingent and apparent. Such a postmodern celebration of relativism and rejection of absolutism (or particularism over universalism) has led ... to a relativism of the vocabulary of 'judgement', 'worth', and merit in aesthetics; 'rights', 'freedom' and 'duty' in ethics; and 'truth', verification' and 'objectivity' in epistemology; all are seen as discourse dependent. There is, we are often told, nothing outside the text.
>
> (1993: 2)

The sacred projects of 'Enlightened' modernity – not least the pursuit of truth – are put to waste.

The kind of radical postmodernism portrayed by Squires (radical because, as we shall see later, there are more qualified renderings) is very much informed by the idea that it is not possible to acquire knowledge of what might exist beyond the text. Indeed, in the classic statement of Jacques Derrida's *Of Grammatology*, it is maintained that *'Il n'y a pas d'hors texte'* ('There is *nothing* outside of the text') (1976, orig. 1967; my emphasis). With nothing lying beyond the text (or, for some postmodernists, the idea that it is not possible to acquire knowledge of what lies beyond the text), the objective and essentialized states of affairs discerned by the Enlightenment project are no longer in evidence. Hence, as in Squires' summary, the talk of 'death'.

What are the implications for the study of religion? Religion can be added to Squires' list of 'Man, History and Metaphysics'. As envisaged in terms of Enlightenment thought, that is to say, 'Religion' too has died. It does not exist – or it cannot be studied as existing – as something 'out there' with its 'own', definable reality, whether to do with naturalistic or sacred realms of existence. It only exists as text. And it follows from all these 'deaths' that many of the ways of studying religion informed by the Enlightenment project have to be disbanded. It is no longer possible, for example, to explain the generation of religious beliefs – in the fashion of Freud – by reference to independently existing emotional processes; it is no longer possible to decode mythological symbols – in the fashion of Lévi-Strauss – by reference to fundamental structures of the human mind; and neither is it possible to explain religion by reference to the social, in the fashion of Durkheim.

But what of religion *as* 'text'? What are the implications of this claim for the study of religion? In order to pursue this question, it is first necessary to say a few words about how (many) postmodernists approach text, that is, by way of 'deconstruction'. In contrast to what can be thought of as the classic theory of meaning associated with the Enlightenment project, namely the (semiological) idea that the meaning of a sign is to be sought by way of what it refers to (its referent), deconstruction only involves the text. For as we have seen, the assumption is that there are no independently existing referents (indeed signifieds) to appeal to. So what happens when meanings are sought within the text? To put the matter graphically, you look up the meaning of a word in the dictionary; you find more words; you look them up; and you find yet more; ad infinitum. Meanings are interconnected; meanings interplay; words have different meanings depending on how they are used; that is, in connection with what other words they are used with. Of particular note, as Kate Currie (1996) makes the point, 'Within Derrida's conceptual apparatus there are no instances of absolute truth [or meaning] only "difference" in which everything *is* only as it differs from something else' (p. 114). The meaning of a word is what the word is *not*, for the meaning only operates by virtue of how the word links up with other words – and since this can take place in countless ways, there is no one determinate meaning.

Overall, the shift to deconstruction means that *connotation*, not *denotation*, is what matters. Implications, mutual entailments, hybridizations, prevail over/resist/abolish those determinate meanings (supposedly) established by way of concrete referents or the exercise of analysis. As for the implications of this for the study of religion, the indeterminacy of meaning thesis obviously means (!) that it is no longer possible to arrive at those clear-cut definitions which are required for much – if not all – social scientific study of religion. One cannot make correlations, for example, in order to discern causes, unless one can clearly define what one is correlating; one cannot say that a particular kind of religion functions in a particular kind of way unless one clearly defines the kind of religion (and the function, for that matter). But the implications of Derridian deconstructuralism are worse than this for the study of religion. For it is not only 'harder' social science which comes out badly; it is also 'softer' interpretative studies. Those (many) such studies relying on binary oppositions (sacred vs profane, for example) do not fare well, deconstructors arguing that supposedly opposing binaries actually inhere in one another. And more generally, any *interpretation* so to speak becomes 'infected' by the indeterminancies of whatever texts are being interpreted. Indeterminancies of meaning with regard to the text, that is to say, ensure that any interpretation is equally indeterminate (and all the more so because interpretations are themselves texts).

Religion as text is 'out of control'. Indeed, with the death of 'the author' – or the individual human subject – those 'scholars' carrying out the interpretations are only texts, and are themselves unable to control where the meanings which they write might lead. In short, the radical endpoint of deconstruction is a world in which any one interpretation (or scholarly monograph), of any particular religious text, would appear to be as 'good' – or as 'bad' – as any other. The future for the study of religion would not appear to be promising.

Postmodernism as the radicalization of difference

The argument thus far has concentrated on postmodern thought as a powerful counter-current to the Enlightenment project. But this is by no means the whole of the story. For it can *also* be argued that a key dynamic running through much of postmodern thought concerns the extension or radicalization of central *values* of enlightened modernity.

Seyla Benhabib alerts us to this possibility:

> Postmodernism presupposes a *super-liberalism*, more pluralistic, more tolerant, more open to the right of difference and otherness than the rather staid and sober versions presented by John Rawls, Ronald Dworkin and Thomas Nagel. As far as I am concerned this is not troublesome. What is baffling though is the lightheartedness with which postmodernists simply assume or even posit those *hyper-universalist* and *superliberal* values of diversity, heterogeneity, eccentricity and otherness.
>
> (1992: 16; my emphases)

Leaving to one side her observation concerning 'lightheartedness', the important thing for present purposes concerns her references to 'super-liberalism' and the 'hyper-universalist'. As we will see shortly, Benhabib would appear to be absolutely correct to point to these features within postmodern thought. And if indeed this is the case, then this aspect of postmodern thought can be treated as being a radicalization of the 'ethic of humanity' (as it can be called) of the Enlightenment project.

To develop this argument, we have to begin with the ethic of humanity. Drawing on Durkheim's analysis, the logic of this ethic runs as follows. Since we are all humans, and since the 'human personality' is of 'incomparable value', we are called upon to: 'respect' all those who share humanity as much as we respect ourselves; treat everyone with 'dignity'; treat all humans 'as though we were equal'; exercise 'sympathy', 'pity', our 'thirst for justice', our responsibilities; avoid killing ('except in cases allowed by law'); and avoid 'unlawful attack' 'on the property of the human person'. In addition, the ethic valorizes 'freedom'. By virtue of being human we are entitled to rights, most generally the right (or freedom) to live 'out' what it is to be human. We have the right to live; the right to be treated with dignity; the right to be treated as equal; indeed, all those rights which (supposedly) serve to protect us from those outside forces which threaten our freedom to live as human beings. Furthermore, people also have *the right (or freedom) to be different*: the importance attached to 'respect' is bound up with the importance attached to people having the freedom to live – at least within limits – different forms of life.

Despite the role played by freedom, however, this is a 'strong' form of liberalism. The contrast is with 'weak' (relativistic, laissez-faire) liberalism: emphasizing freedom (people being free to hold different values), weak liberalism attaches equal importance to equality, respect and toleration, and this means that one cannot judge the freedom of others as wrong (for to do so would mean that they were no longer being treated as equals). The ethic of humanity, on the other hand, places 'freedom' under scrutiny. Some forms of life (and their associated exercise of freedom) are *wrong*, namely those forms of life which attack other of the values bound up with the universal ethic of 'being human'. Thus one cannot respect those who exercise their freedom to take away human dignity; who destroy human life in an unlawful fashion; and so on. In short, far from uncritically propounding that all forms of life, all freedoms, are equal, the ethic has a powerful cutting edge.

What, then, has this ethicality to do with postmodern thought and the study of religion? Postmodern radicalization, we can now see, allows 'freedom', the right (freedom) to be different, (together with associated values of the ethic), to run riot.

Recalling Benhabib's observation that 'postmodernists simply assume or even posit those *hyper-universalist* and *superliberal* values of diversity, heterogeneity, eccentricity and otherness', to value difference in this kind of way – one can then go on to argue – is *ipso facto* to value 'respect' (for otherwise differences could not be positively evaluated), 'equality' (in that positive evaluations of differences mean that they must at least approximate to being equal) and 'freedom'. And the last – I think – is the key to the matter. From (at least) Nietzsche, the reason why *difference* matters, is evaluated as it is, is that it is bound up with that great priority – the freedom to live as one wills.

Postmodern ethicality here involves the radicalization – or valorization – of the key 'freedom/difference' component of the ethic of humanity. However, whereas the traditional ethic of humanity of modernity serves to restrain the operation of 'freedom' (as we have seen, one should not exercise one's freedom to engage in acts which run counter to what it is to be human by failing to treat people with dignity, for example), postmodern freedom tends to run riot. The reason is simple: recalling Judith Squires earlier in this essay, postmodernity 'involves the rejection of all essentialist and transcendental conceptions of human nature'. The exercise of postmodern freedom or difference, in other words, can no longer be tested – that is evaluated – by reference to the (essentialized) virtues taken to be bound up with what it is to *be* human: equality, dignity, responsibility for the welfare of others, and so on. Difference is simply 'difference'. And hence – of course – the criticism so often levelled against (much) postmodern ethicality, namely its political and moral inability to identify and deal with 'real' or 'really significant' differences – like the exercise of racism – by judging them to involve the wrong exercise of freedom. Respect for the freedoms of others results in political paralysis.

This said, however, the fact remains that many (somewhat modified) postmodernists *have* developed a politics of freedom and liberation, and one which – we will shortly see – has very considerable significance for the study of religion. Although this politics is grounded in Enlightenment values (freedom, equality, liberation), precisely because of this it involves expunging those domineering metanarratives so characteristic of Enlightenment or modernist thought. The idea 'of respecting the other', that is to say, by no means extends to respecting all 'the others' of Enlightenment/modernist metanarratives. And the reason is simple. Systematized, universalized forms of knowledge are held to disavow, misrepresent, control or repress those who do not belong to the applications of any particular metanarrative. The cry, instead, is for freedom, expression, articulation, voice, for *all*. And hence the *value-driven* attack on the totalizing 'Big Other/s'.

Thinking of the highly influential work of Jean-Francois Lyotard, in key passages of *The Postmodern Condition. A Report on Knowledge* (1984) he writes that 'consensus does violence to the heterogeneity of language games'; that we need to 'tolerate the incommensurable'; that we should 'wage a war on totality' and 'activate the differences' (pp. xxv, 82). 'Metanarratives', namely those discourses which use the language of sameness, identity, totality, unity and consensus, must be deconstructed – that is dismantled – to reveal the discourses of 'micronarratives', namely those discourses which emphasize heterogeneity, multiplicity, diversity, difference, incommensurability and dissensus. Totalization must give way to particularization.

Metanarratives, according to this account, dominate and repress; impose the ethnocentric same on the different. Consider, for example, the ethic of humanity, and the Gianni Vattimo (1992) critique: 'ethnic, sexual, religious, cultural, or aesthetic minorities' have been 'repressed and cowed into silence by the idea of a single true form of humanity that must be realized irrespective of particularity and individual finitude, transience, and contingency' (p. 9). Or consider postmodern feminists, who have severely criticized the ethic for taking away the freedom of women to be women. The ethic is seen as a Western, white, male construction, serving (in the fashion of Foucauldian analysis) to articulate male concerns and values at the expense – for example – of genuine women's rights. Furthermore, the ethic is seen as serving to define women as human, when what really matters is their womanness. And this is where deconstruction comes back into the picture. To put it graphically, deconstruction here serves as another word for liberation. Demolition of the metanarrative, that essential truth which – by virtue of presenting one truth/set of truths – necessarily excludes other truth claims, is taken to be a vital ingredient in the quest for freedom.

We are now in the position to turn to what the valorization of 'freedom', and therefore of 'difference', together with the critique of 'Enlightened' metanarration has to do with the study of religion. Writing on postmodernism and the study of Zorostrianism (2000), John Hinnells notes that 'The Modernist conviction that western (all male), unbiased scholars could write "scientific", objective accounts of a clearly definable, homogeneous, unitary phenomenon, Zorastrianism, whose essence is characterized by formal theological doctrines in "classical" texts, has under-pinned Zorastrian studies until the 1980s' (p. 2). (And much the same can surely be said for scholarship on other (all?) 'major' (and not-so-'major'?) religious tradi-tions.) In the same article, Hinnells also provides an excellent summary of that approach to the study of religious tradition which attends to the micronarrative, the liberating, the importance of letting the repressed tell their stories:

> at the risk of appearing simplistic and of reducing postmodernism to a list of defined rules, which it is not, some of the characteristic features of many post-modern studies of religion may be listed as: (i) the rejection of grand meta-narratives; (ii) each scholar's awareness of their own 'situated' position; (iii) the move away from the exclusive dependence on the official textual traditions [macronarration] to the practices associated with the home and daily life [micronarration]; (iv) the conviction that there is no such thing as 'true', objective, scientific History, there are only discourses about history ...
>
> (p. 1)

And as he continues, 'A different, but not unrelated branch of postmodernism has been a concern to deconstruct many received notions, or reifications, such as the notion of Buddhism, Hinduism, etc' (pp. 1–2).

By no means all of the literature that Hinnells has in mind is of a radically decon-structive nature, let alone with many scholars committing themselves to the view that 'There is nothing outside of the text'. This said, however, there are distinct signs of the study of religion entering those 'wilder' domains of postmodern thought entailed by some of the points made in Hinnells' summary. For instance, one can think of Mark C. Taylor's recent edited volume, *Critical Terms for Religious Studies* (1998). In his Introduction, Taylor cites Wendy Doniger:

> [T]he academic world ... now suffers from a post-colonial backlash: in this age of multiculturalism, to assume that two texts from different cultures are 'the same' in any significant way is regarded as demeaning to the individualism of each, a reflection of the old racist attitude that 'all wogs look alike' – in the dark, all cats are gray. And in the climate of anti-Orientalism, it is regarded as imperialist of a scholar to stand outside (presumably above) two different cultures.
>
> (p. 14)

Taylor himself then continues to write:

> it is necessary to develop comparative analyses that do not presuppose universal principles or reinscribe ahistorical essences. Whether or not it is possible to realize such a comparativist program, many critics schooled in poststructuralism insist that the very effort to establish similarities where there appear to be differ-ences is, in the final analysis, intellectually misleading and politically misguided. When reason is obsessed with unity, they argue, it tends to become as hege-monic as political and economic orders constructed to regulate whatever does

not fit into or agree with governing structures. In this situation, critical theory becomes a strategy for resisting dominant power by soliciting the return of the repressed.

(p. 15)

In the volume as a whole, 'critical theory' is applied by a number of scholars to a whole range of (largely) 'standard' terms deployed by Enlightenment religious studies. Such critical theory involves varying degrees of deconstruction, this being bound up with arguments purporting to show that terms such as 'belief', 'experience' and 'sacrifice' are the 'invention' of particular sociocultural circumstances (specifically Christianity and Western modernity): thereby serving in intellectually misleading and politically misguided ways when applied cross-culturally. Although there is surely much to be said for standing for freedom by deconstructing terms which have served repressive ends, which have eroded significant differences by imposing 'the same' (that is Enlightenment/modernist defined terms), and which have thereby silenced/muted the voices and power of other 'religions', there is cause for concern. Namely that with this quite radical postmodern approach to 'religion', comparative, globalized language gets lost. Deconstruction, together with strong hints – if not more – that authors of the articles in the volume would agree, if pressed, with Derrida's 'There is nothing outside of the text', means that the language of religious studies itself is under some considerable threat.

Most fundamentally on this front, and citing Taylor's summary of recent argumentation, if indeed 'Far from existing prior to and independent of any inquiry, the very phenomenon of religion is constituted by local discursive practices', if indeed 'Investigators create – sometimes unknowingly – the objects they profess to discover', and if indeed 'that appearances to the contrary notwithstanding, religion is a *modern Western invention*' (pp. 6–7), religious studies loses its global 'hold'; that comparative, analytical, explanatory purchase *via* the term and substance 'religion'. 'It' ['religion'] does not 'exist' elsewhere, that is beyond where it was 'invented'. Other Enlightenment-designated 'religions' might become liberated from an inaccurate – and therefore supposedly repressive – label, but – we might add – how are *these* erstwhile 'religions' to be characterized in ways that make sense across cultures without lapsing into the kinds of pitfalls which, it has been argued, befall the category 'religion'? In short, what language are we left with to discuss and explore religions across cultures?

At the end of the day, the valorization of 'freedom' or 'the right to be different', clearly operative in Taylor's edited volume, means that the right, the freedom, of 'religions' to '*be*' whatever they 'are' would appear to place severe restraints on the study of religion per se. There might be good political and academic reasons for allowing 'religions' the right to 'speak' for, or 'represent' themselves, but taken too far such courses of action undermine cross-cultural investigation, leaving the Other simply as the Other.

Critical reflections: on the wild side and the death of the *study of* religion

It would be absurd, in the present context, to engage in systematic critical assessment of what 'wilder' postmodernism has to offer to the study of religion. So what now follows is modest reflection, expanding upon – as well as drawing on – a number of points raised earlier.

The reader might have thought that he or she had reached the wildest reaches of postmodern thought – to recall Squires, 'the death of Man, History and Metaphysics'. Or recall what has been said about the death of 'Religion' as a reality which can be explored/explained by reference to other psychological or sociocultural realities. But far from it. Reason itself, that critical tool for any (conventionally defined) academic study of religion (or anything else) is undermined. Reason – other, perhaps, than when mathematical and other technical tools are deployed – utilizes words. And more radical – Derridian – postmodernists claim that words by no means have determinate, and therefore logically deployable, meanings.

To the extent that the exercise of reason is undermined (or deconstructed), so too is research as that activity has traditionally been understood. Combine this with the idea that with the radical deconstructionist perspective any interpretation is as good as any other, and traditionally envisaged research takes another blow. Then there is the consideration that (some) radical postmodernists take the value of respecting the Other to mean (!) that the Other should not be explained, decoded, classified, defined, compared, translated – by way of supposedly superior transcultural terminology, knowledge or theory – or even studied at all. (It is impossible, for an obvious reason, to provide an illustration of the last.) The logical end result of 'freedom to be different', that is to say, is to leave the 'Other' entirely alone; entirely liberated from external adjudication or interference. (For additional and specific points whereby postmodern thought has impacted upon, and curtailed, social scientific theorizing of religion see Rosenau (1992) and Masuzawa (1993).)

All this rules out too much: arguably on the grounds of academic research per se, but perhaps even more significantly on the grounds of politics. It is surely the case that we need to arrive at the best *possible* understanding of the 'religions' of 'Others' in order not to misrepresent them; to know how to live with them; to learn how to respond to them in an increasingly interfused world (albeit an increasingly divisive one in many regards). Whatever the case on this front (and the matter is returned to shortly), there remains the consideration that radical postmodern thought has to be questioned by virtue of the (apparent) fact that it undermines itself. Considering this by reference to the notion of 'religion', to follow those who deny that religion has some supra-historical/textual essence or substance is in fact to make an ontological claim. Furthermore, this is a claim informed by another claim of equally ontological stature: that (to recall Derrida) 'There is nothing outside of the text'. And, it should go without saying, it is difficult if not impossible to see how ontological judgements of this kind can be made within the deconstructed realms of the Derridian postmodernist.

One suspects that the 'ontologizing' of many of the more radical postmodernists has a great deal to do with the 1960s. What fuels deconstruction and the denial of anything beyond the text is not so much the exercise of reason (for that itself is deconstructed) and appeal to evidence (for that is not *in* evidence) but the faith in freedom, liberation, respecting the other, the right to be different: all key 1960s values. Derrida's *Of Grammatology* is perhaps better called *Politics Through Grammar*: deconstruction meaning liberation from metanarratives and the tyranny of reason; deconstruction aimed at providing a powerful politics of freedom, liberation, emancipation. The 'logical' end result of the value attached to the freedom to *be* different has thus been driven by the revolutionary changes – in certain circles – of the 1960s. It is this which explains that radical shift, which took place during the 1960s and earlier 1970s, from the structuralism of Lévi-Strauss – epitomizing high Enlightenment thought in critical regards – to the wilder side.

Critical reflections: the 'middle way'

An increasing number of scholars (including Benhabib and Squires), in a range of disciplines including religious studies, are attempting to extract what they take to be the lessons of postmodern thought while avoiding what they consider to be counter-productive excesses. These scholars also attempt to marry what is taken to be of value in the realm of the postmodern with what they take to be of value from Enlightenment thought. Regarding the latter, the aim is to avoid what is considered to be the limitations of (in particular) 'hard' social science.

Looking at the development of the 'middle way', we can begin with the fact that much of the study of religion has now moved a long way from the blunt instruments and grand – if not imperialistic, totalizing – theories of the earlier days of the application of Enlightenment thought and knowledge to religion. Few today have much faith in the quest for origins; in predictable evolutionary sequences; in universal laws; in universally applicable essentialized definitions. What has happened, in fact, is that research – broadly within the modernist or Enlightenment frame of reference – has increasingly moved in the direction of what is now spelt out – in more radical fashion – by those within the postmodernist camp. One might consider, for example, Peter Winch's highly influential *The Idea of a Social Science* (1994, orig. 1958). Arguing that meanings are constitutive of the sociocultural – that is that forms of life such as marriage or religion only exist by virtue of their being meaningful – Winch claims that supposedly causal explanations are in fact tautological (for meanings are interconnected). Furthermore, since meanings are 'vague' ('How many grains of wheat does one have to add together before one has a heap?' (p. 73)), strict definitions of the kind required by 'hard' social science are not on the cards. Or one might consider Rodney Needham's *Belief, Language, and Experience* (1972). The argument, in this regard, is that it is mistaken to suppose that 'belief' is a universally applicable category with universally applicable descriptive, let alone explanatory, value.

Attending to the 'middle way' from the point of view of postmodern thought, there is no doubting the fact that – for many scholars – more radical postmodern claims have come to inform ideas and practices which merge with those that have developed out of the Enlightenment project. The radical claims of the postmodern might continue to provide the 'climate' which fuels the middle way – and on both sides of the Enlightenment/postmodern 'divide' – but they no longer operate 'on the wild side'.

Turning to some examples of the middle way, consider first Hinnells' point (cited earlier in his characterization of postmodernism) concerning 'the move away from the exclusive dependence on the offical textual traditions to the practices associated with the home and daily life'. Which (thoughtful) scholar could possibly object to this widening of the frame of (increasingly politically significant) inquiry? Or, second, take Hinnells' point concerning 'each scholar's awareness of their own "situated" position'. Again, who could possibly object to scholars reflecting on – and then attempting to change – prejudices which they bring to their studies? Or, third, consider the objection that 'situated scholars', as they might be called, engage in theoretical-cum-methodological-cum-conceptual imperialism, arrogantly asserting that they know the true meaning (of, say, myth) while more or less ignoring how participants themselves understand matters. Again, not many today would want to deny that participant interpretation – itself open to diverse interpretation – is important, whatever 'objective' analysis might reveal; indeed, that 'objective' analysis might well benefit from close attention being paid to the participant frame of reference. Or, fourth, there is the 'postmodernist' objection that situated scholars, in particular those of the 'harder' social science variety, work with crude, universalized, definitions which distort the very nature of that which is supposedly under scientific scrutiny. Yet again, who would want to deny that this is profoundly problematic, not just because the religious realm is misrepresented but because the social scientific approach can undermine itself by redefining/conceptualizing its subject matter to suit itself.

The middle way owes a great deal to *both* Enlightenment and postmodern thought. The former is in evidence, for example, in that religion – or something akin to it – is taken to be active in the world 'out there', beyond the texts of the scholar. The latter is in evidence in that there is a profound awareness that Enlightenment meta-narratives and definitional formations can only too readily serve the cause of cultural, political, conceptual, explanatory, imperialism. A zone of inquiry has developed, between the 'wilder' shores of Enlightenment *and* postmodern thought – although ultimately informed by both – in which these modes of thought have come into creative and constitutive interplay. This is a new(ish) interplay given that post-modern thought – in connection with religion – is a recent development. And rather than worrying about whether this interplay is best seen as being informed by *either* Enlightenment *or* postmodern thought, it is surely best to rest content with the formulation 'the middle way in the study of religion': having *emerged* from two (main) sources, it now operates with its own dynamics.

The work of Edward Said provides a 'classic' illustration of the middle way in action. Without question, the intellectual 'climate' of postmodern thought percolates through his work. His concern in *Orientalism. Western Conceptions of the Orient* (1995) is to dismantle imperializing/totalizing metanarratives of the Orient, showing in Foucauldian fashion how power interests, on the side of the West, have generated false and oppressive power relations. But at the same time, Enlightenment thought is well in evidence. Said describes himself as a 'humanist' (p. 9). He is able to argue his case that 'Orientalism' is 'a Western style for dominating, restructuring, and having authority over the Orient' (p. 3) by virtue of the fact that he assumes that it is possible to test metanarrative against 'the case', the truly existing 'Other'. He is able to argue that the *Cambridge History of Islam* serves to 'radically misconceive and misrepresent Islam as a religion' (p. 302) on the grounds of evidence to do with history and power relations. He 'deconstructs' (and the word is used) cultural imperialism, the repressive, by reference to the referent, the real world; the events of a world beyond text in that it involves the facts of the historical record – those deaths, sufferings, disempowerments which have actually taken place and which are therefore not to be treated as simply matters of language. And, it can be added, this is a crucial factor in explaining why so many regard his work to be so politically effective.

Conclusion

In sum, in the fashion of liberal inquiry and with an eye on the valorization of freedom found in many postmodern quarters, perhaps the only conclusion to be drawn is that it is *good* to find that the study of religion today is informed by 'wilder' post-modern thought, (some) 'harder' Enlightenment studies, and, increasingly, the middle way. All of these approaches have their virtues in that they are good to think with. The variety generates vitality. Perhaps the only drawback to this scenario is that the two extremes are not especially well represented in the study of religion today. 'Hard' social scientists have become relatively few and far between. 'Wilder' postmodernists have not yet made much direct impact on the study of religion (although this is not the case for theology).

This is a pity, for the emergent middle way is perhaps best kept in dynamic and creative tension when the poles – High Enlightenment and Wild Postmodernity – are forcefully argued. Indeed, I am inclined to conclude that what is most urgently required to vitalize the study of religion – a study which is nowhere near as exciting as it was when the Enlightenment project had its heyday – is an injection from the 'wilder side'.

A note on postmodern religion

The reader might be wondering: but what has all this to do with what is *studied*? Surely discussion of the study of religion cannot ignore the ways in which study comes to bear on its subject matter? Accordingly, although this essay is primarily concerned with ways of studying religion, we now turn – all too briefly – to what different forms of study (modernist and postmodernist) have to say about the nature of religion in everyday practice. Specifically, do they reveal the operation of postmodern religion?

Before listing the possibilities, the meaning of the term 'postmodern religion' has to be introduced. The best characterization that I know – summarizing as it does much of the literature (both modernist and postmodernist) – is provided by James Beckford. He writes:

> It seems to me that the following are most commonly associated with post-modernity [and therefore postmodern religion]:
>
> 1 A refusal to regard positivistic, rationalistic, instrumental criteria as the sole or exclusive standard of worthwhile knowledge.
> 2 A willingness to combine symbols from disparate codes or frameworks of meaning, even at the cost of disjunctions and eclecticism.
> 3 A celebration of spontaneity, fragmentation, superficiality, irony and playfulness.
> 4 A willingness to abandon the search for over-arching or triumphalist myths, narratives or frameworks of knowledge.
>
> If these characteristics are the hallmarks of the post-modern sensibility in general, then one might expect, on the analogy with post-modern fine arts, architecture and literature, that it would receive a distinctive expression in religion. My expectation would be that putatively post-modern forms of religion would embrace

diversity of discourse and the abandonment of unitary meaning systems; cross-referencing between, and pastiches of, different religious traditions; and an accent on playfulness or cynicism.

(1992: 19–20)

With this formulation in mind, it is now possible to turn to the possibilities: that is to say, the relationship between different forms of study and claims concerning whether or not postmodern religion is operative in the everyday world.

The first possibility is that postmodern thought of the radical variety reveals the existence of postmodern religion. Given what has been said earlier about the fact that this kind of thought finds it difficult if not impossible to engage in the study of what is taking place in the real, 'objective' world, this possibility is highly unlikely.

The second is that those pursuing what we are calling the middle way are able to show that religions partake of the postmodern to a (much) greater extent than has been acknowledged by those working in terms of (radical) Enlightenment thought. This possibility has to be taken very seriously indeed. Those, like Said, who aim to deconstruct what they take to be the essentialized, totalizing characterizations of, say, what has come to be called 'Islam', do so by pointing to the fact that the term 'Islam' actually refers to much more fluid, unstable, shifting, contestable discourses; to what Beckford describes as 'diversity of discourse and the abandonment of unitary meaning systems' (ibid.).

As for the third possibility, could it be the case that 'hard' social scientists are able to find postmodern religion? I wonder. Their commitment to that which is modern, their attention to the determinate or precise 'Religion' as traditionally defined, means that they might well not be attuned to recognizing postmodern religion – even if it exists.

That leaves the possibility as explored by 'softer' social scientists like Beckford. Unlike the 'hard' social scientist, Beckford can indeed identify postmodern religion. Unlike practitioners of the middle way, however, he does not do this by deconstructing metanarratives. He finds postmodern religion simply by observing what is 'the case'. Quite probably complementing the deconstructive approach, this joins it in being another possibility which has to be taken very seriously.

To end on a rather different note, there is also the consideration that postmodern thought is actively contributing to the construction of postmodern religion. This is undoubtedly happening. It has to do with the theological-cum-postmodern assault on those metanarratives (specifically that of the Enlightenment) which have (supposedly) undermined religion. It has to do with the development of religion beyond the criticisms, restaints and excesses of modernity and its thinking. But since this has to do with 'doing religion' – theology rather than 'the study of religion' – the topic is best explored on another occasion.

References

Beckford, James A. 1992 Religion, Modernity and Post-modernity. In B. R. Wilson (ed.) *Religion: Contemporary Issues*. London: Bellew (pp. 11–23). A concise account of religion in connection with modernity and postmodernity.

Benhabib, Seyla 1992 *Situating the Self. Gender, Community and Postmodernism in Contemporary Ethics*. Cambridge: Polity Press. An exploration of what modern and postmodern thought have to offer.

Currie, Kate 1996 *Beyond Orientalism. An Exploration of Some Recent Themes in Indian History and Society*. Calcutta: K P Bagchi & Company. A good summary of the Orientalism debate.

Derrida, Jacques 1976 (orig. 1967) *Of Grammatology*. Baltimore and London: The John Hopkins University Press. One of the great 'classics' of radical postmodern thought.

Hinnells, John R. (2000) Postmodernism and the Study of Zorastrianism in *Zoroastrian and Parsi Studies: Selected Works of John R. Hinnells*. Aldershot: Ashgate Publishing, pp. 7–25. A succient account of how studies of a religious tradition can be looked at in terms of a modern-postmodern spectrum.

Kant, Immanuel, 1970 An Answer to the Question: What is Enlightenment? In Hans Reiss (ed.) *Kant's Political Writings*. Cambridge: Cambridge University Press. (pp. 54–60) *The* statement of the Enlightenment.

Lévi-Strauss, Claude 1966 (orig. 1992) *The Savage Mind*. London: Weidenfeld and Nicolson. *The* book which best exemplifies the structuralism of 'high' Enlightenment thought.

Lyotard, Jean-Francois 1984 *The Postmodern Condition: A Report on Knowledge*. Minneapolis: University of Minnesota Press. A classic, if disappointing statement of the postmodern condition seen as involving the rejection of metanarratives.

Masuzawa, Tomoko 1993 *In Search of Dreamtime. The Quest for the Origin of Religion*. Chicago and London: The University of Chicago Press. A thoughtful work, of a postmodernist variety, deconstructing theories of the High Enlightenment.

Needham, Rodney 1972 *Belief, Language, and Experience*. Oxford: Basil Blackwell. An under-appreciated, but brilliantly performed, argument to deconstruct 'belief' as a univerally applicable category.

Paine, Thomas 1998 *Rights of Man. Common Sense. And other Political Writings*. Oxford and New York: Oxford University Press. Arguably the classic work concerning Enlightenment politics.

Rosenau, Pauline 1992 *Post-Modernism and the Social Sciences. Insights, Inroads, and Intrusions*. Princeton: Princeton University Press. A presentation, not evaluation, of the implications for the social sciences of the chief tenets of postmodernism.

Said, Edward, E. 1995 (orig. 1978) *Orientalism. Western Concepts of the Orient*. London: Penguin. Certainly the classic text regarding the deconstruction of Enlightenment thought and the appropriation of the Orient.

Squires, Judith 1993 Introduction. In Judith Squires (ed.) *Principled Positions. Postmodernism and the Rediscovery of Value*. London: Lawrence & Wishart (pp. 1–13). A lucid account of what can be salvaged from both Enlightenment and postmodern thought.

Taylor, Mark C. 1998 Introduction. *Critical Terms for Religious Studies*. Chicago: The University of Chicago Press (pp. 1–19). By far and away the most impressive attempt, to date, to decon-struct the familiar – as Enlightenment inspired – terms central to religious studies.

Vattimo, Gianni 1992 *The Transparent Society*. Baltimore: The Johns Hopkins University Press. A powerful rendering of the sociocultural in terms of postmodern thought on the 'wild side'.

Winch, Peter 1994 (orig. 1958) *The Idea of a Social Science and Its Relation to Philosophy*. London: Routledge. One of the most influential works to argue that 'hard' social science must be replaced by investigations which fully take on board the fact that meanings – with their complexities – are critically constitutive of human affairs.

Chapter 15

Orientalism and the study of religions

Richard King

Introduction

How often have you watched a news report on television, read a newspaper article or been exposed to an advertisement conveying some image of 'Eastern' culture? Whether it is a scene of crowds of angry Muslims burning an American flag, a shaven-headed Buddhist monk clothed in a saffron robe and quietly meditating, militant Hindus attacking a Muslim mosque or a billboard promoting a perfume that evokes the 'mystic sensuality' of India, what all of these images have in common is their involvement in a long history of Western representations and stereotypes of Asia as an 'other' – that is as essentially different from the West. One consequence of such images, whether positive or negative in their connotations, is that 'we' (the West) become clearly separated from 'them' (the East). The acceptance of a basic opposition between Eastern and Western cultures characterizes what has been called 'Orientalism.'

Indeed images of the East have often functioned as a means of defining the cultural identity of the West, however differently that has been conceived throughout history. The Christian identity of medieval Europe was bolstered by concerns about the incursion of Turkish Muslims. In the eighteenth and nineteenth centuries, Asia represented both a mysterious and timeless realm of wisdom and spirituality, but also the site of unspeakable social depravities and primitive religious practices. In this regard the West was able to comfort itself that it was progressive, civilized and thoroughly modern in contrast to an ahistorical and unchanging Orient. Widespread beliefs about the indolent and despotic nature of Oriental societies also justified a Western sense of superiority and the belief that it was the duty of the West to civilize the savage and aid the Oriental in their progression away from tradition and dogmatism and towards modernity and civilization. In the modern era, whether it is the threat of the 'yellow peril' (Chinese communism) in the 1970s, or the militant Islamic fundamentalist of the 1980s and 1990s, the West has always maintained its own sense of cultural identity by contrasting itself with a radically different 'Orient'.

The latter part of the twentieth century has seen the demise of Western political rule of Asia and the emergence of countries such as India, Pakistan and Sri Lanka as independent nation-states. The British Empire, for instance, has become the British Commonwealth. However, many still question whether the world has really entered a 'post-colonial' era, arguing that Western political, economic and cultural dominance represents continuity rather than a fundamental break with the colonial past.

Are we living today in a *post*-colonial or a *neo*-colonial age? Although the influence of Britain and the rest of Europe has receded to a significant degree since the end of the Second World War, it is clear that with the demise of Eastern European communism, the United States of America is the new global power in the West. Capitalism, consumerism and multi-national corporations continue to influence an increasingly global marketplace. Western dominance is apparent not only on an economic and political level, but on a cultural one also, having an inevitable impact upon traditional beliefs and practices in non-Western societies. What are we to make of the cultural impact of the 'new technologies'? When American television soap operas are beamed into middle-class Asian homes via satellite, punctuated by adver-tisements for Coca-Cola and McDonalds, where does one draw the line between the modernization of Asia and its Westernization? Is the 'global network' of cyberspace a realm in which Asian and Western cultures can meet as equal participants in a worldwide celebration of human diversity or does the rhetoric of 'globalization' mask the continued dominance of 'the rest' by the West?

What is Orientalism?

Orientalism refers to the long-standing Western fascination with the East and the tendency to divide the world up into East and West, with the East acting as a kind of mirror or foil by which Western culture defines itself. The question of the complicity between Western scholarly study of Asia – the discipline of Orientalism, and the imperialistic aspirations of Western nations became a subject of consider-able attention in Western academic circles after the publication of Edward Said's work, *Orientalism* (1978). In this book, Said offered a stinging indictment of Western conceptions of and attitudes towards the Orient. According to Said 'Orientalism' refers to three inter-related phenomena (1978: 2–3):

1   the academic study of the Orient;
2   a mind-set or 'style of thought' founded upon a rigid dichotomy of 'East' and 'West';
3   the corporate institution authorized to dominate, control and subjugate the peoples and cultures of the East.

For Said the mutual intersection of these three dimensions of Orientalism demon-strates the complicity between Western discourses about the Orient and Western colonialism. Orientalism then is primarily a 'Western style for dominating, restruc-turing, and having authority over the Orient' (Said 1978: 3). Although credit has usually been given to Said for highlighting this dimension of the Orientalist enter-prise his work was certainly not the first to suggest complicity between scholarly analysis of the East and Western imperialist aspirations. Said's work is also clearly indebted to earlier studies (Schwab 1950; Pannikar 1959; Abdel-Malek 1963; Steadman 1970).

    The study of religion, both in the concern to explore comparative and cross-cultural issues and themes, and in the more specific attempt to understand and examine the religions and cultures of Asia, has had a seminal role to play in the development of Western conceptions of and attitudes towards the Orient, particularly from the nineteenth century onwards. Western intellectual interest in the religions of the East developed in a context of Western political dominance and colonial expansionism. It is perhaps surprising then to discover that it is only in recent years that the discipline of religious studies has begun to take seriously the political implications and issues involved when Western scholars and institutions claim the authority to represent and speak about the religions and cultures of others. Recent collections of scholarly articles such as *Orientalism and the Post-colonial Predicament* (1993) and *Curators of the Buddha* (1995), explore the impact of Western colonialism upon South Asia and the study of Buddhism respectively. Such developments have occurred in response to the growing post-colonial agenda to be found in other academic disciplines such as literary studies, anthropology and history. Specific studies such as Philip Almond's *The British Discovery of Buddhism* (1988), Talal Asad's *Genealogies of Religion* (1993) and Richard King's *Orientalism and Religion* (1999) have taken up the mantle left by Edward Said and applied it to the disciplines of Buddhist Studies (Almond), anthropology (Asad) and religious studies/Indology (King). It is likely that the trend toward post-colonial approaches to the study of religion will continue, if only because the issues highlighted by such an orientation remain central to international politics and debates about globalization, modernity and the future of cross-cultural analysis in a post-colonial world.

Knowledge and power

Edward Said (1935–2003) was a diaspora Palestinian educated according to Western conventions and standards. He was a professor of English and Comparative Literature at the University of Columbia from 1963 until his death in 2003. This background in Western literary studies is reflected in Said's work, which displays the influence of a number of Western theorists and writers, most notably the French poststructuralist Michel Foucault (1926–84). The importance of Foucault in this context resides in his comprehensive analysis of the relationship between power and knowledge. In a number of critical studies on the history of madness, the birth of the clinic and the history of sexuality in the west, Foucault argued that all claims to knowledge involve an attempt to establish a particular set of power relations. Foucault described his method as a 'genealogy of knowledge' (supplementing what he describes in his earlier works as an 'archaeology of knowledge'). This involves an examination of the socio-historical roots of an ideology or institution in order to highlight the ways in which certain groups within society have constructed discourses which have promoted their own authority (Carrette 1999).

The impact of Foucault's work has grown as postmodernist and poststructuralist approaches have gained support in contemporary academic circles. Critics of Foucault's approach have questioned his apparently relativistic stance towards all knowledge and truth claims. Foucault seems to be arguing not just that knowledge is always associated with power, but that knowledge *is* power, i.e. that what we call knowledge is merely a manifestation or reflection of the will-to-power within any given society. It is this aspect of his approach, clearly influenced by the German philosopher Friedrich Nietzsche (1844–1900), which has drawn the fiercest criticism of his work, with the suggestion that Foucault's approach makes it impossible to establish any definitive truth about the nature of reality. From Foucault's perspective the concern is to overturn the modern ideal of an objective and value-free knowledge of universally applicable truths. But as other critics have argued there are many notions of truth at work in Foucault's writings (Prado 1995: 119). Nevertheless, in place of the notion of absolute and universal 'truths', Foucault advocates an approach that focuses upon a diversity of localized 'truths' and a concern to explore their complicity with power structures within that specific locality. Thus, for Foucault:

> Truth is a thing of this world: it is produced only by virtue of multiple forms of constraint. And it induces regular effects of power. Each society has its own régime of truth, its 'general politics' of truth: that is, the types of discourse which it accepts and makes function as true.
>
> (Foucault 1977, translation in Gordon 1980: 131)

Said found Foucault's analysis and his equation of power and knowledge useful conceptual tools for articulating his own conception of Orientalism as the West's exercising of its will-to-power over the East. He remained unwilling, however, to adopt Foucault's general stance since it seemed to allow no room for ethical judgements based upon universal truths and humanistic principles. Moreover, if there is no truth 'out there' one can offer no basis for a critique of Western representations of the Orient on the basis of their *unrepresentative* nature. Thus, Said argued that:

> It would be wrong to conclude that the Orient was *essentially* an idea, or a creation with no corresponding reality ... But the phenomenon of Orientalism as I study it here deals principally, not with a correspondence between Orientalism and Orient, but with the internal consistency of Orientalism and its ideas about the Orient (the East as career) despite or beyond any correspondence, or lack thereof, with a 'real' Orient.
>
> (Said 1978: 5)

The truth is out there or is it?

The ambiguities of Said's analysis and methodology have been a central theme of many of the responses to his work. Some critics have argued that *Orientalism* reflects theoretical inconsistencies in Said's account (al-'Azm 1981; Lewis 1982; Clifford 1988; Ahmed 1992), with the author arguing on the one hand that 'the Orient' is constructed in Western imaginations and yet attacking Western characterizations of the East as misrepresentations of a real Orient 'out there'. Other reviewers have celebrated such ambiguities as deliberately disruptive and anti-theoretical (Behdad 1994; Prakash 1995), a position that Said himself came to endorse when reflecting, some years later, upon his own work (Said 1995: 340). Indeed, Said's reluctance to offer an alternative representation of 'the Orient' is grounded in his firmly held belief that the division between 'East' and 'West' is an act of the imagination, and a pernicious one at that. This, however, does not mean that the social and human realities that these images of 'the Orient' are meant to refer to are also imaginary. Far from it, it is precisely because representations of the Orient are essentially imaginary that they can be said to be unrepresentative of the diversity of Asian peoples and cultures (King 1999: 209). Said's challenge to his successors, therefore, is to find alternative and ever more nuanced ways of representing cultural diversity to replace those founded upon a simplistic and oppositional logic of 'Occident vs. Orient' – of 'us' and 'them':

> Can one divide human reality, as indeed human reality seems to be genuinely divided, into clearly different cultures, histories, traditions, societies, even races, and survive the consequences humanly? By surviving the consequences humanly, I mean to ask whether there is any way of avoiding the hostility expressed by the division, say of men into 'us' (Westerners) and 'they' (Orientals).
>
> (Said 1978: 45)

Other scholars, however, have been more willing to embrace a postmodernist or poststructuralist view of knowledge, with its rejection of any unproblematic appeal to a reality 'out there' beyond the play of representations. Anthropologist Ronald Inden, for instance, agrees with Foucault in rejecting a representational view of knowledge. There is no privileged or unmediated access to reality.

> [K]nowledge of the knower is not a disinterested mental representation of an external, natural reality. It is a construct that is always situated in a world apprehended through specific knowledges and motivated by practices in it. What is more, the process of knowing actively participates in producing and transforming the world that it constructs intellectually.
>
> (Inden 1990: 33)

Inden maintains that the study of South Asia has been based upon a misleading search for essences such as 'the Hindu mind,' 'the Indian village,' 'caste' and 'divine kingship' – as if entire cultures could be represented by such basic categories. These approaches also imply that the Western scholar has some special ability to discern the central features of Asian cultures in a way that is unavailable to Asians themselves. Inden advocates the abandonment of approaches that search for cultural essences and 'fundamental natures' because they ignore historical change and cultural diversity and therefore provide stereotypes of Asian culture. In their place Inden proposes an emphasis upon the historical agency of indigenous Asians. This approach, he suggests, would avoid the tendency to conceive of the Orient as an unchanging and timeless realm – as if Asian cultures and peoples were *subject to* rather than *agents of* historical change. The critical response to Inden's work has been varied. Some scholars have questioned his universal indictment of Western scholarship on the East as an example of the very essentialism that he attacks: 'If, as Inden says, India and the Indians were "essentialized" by the Indologists, it is certainly no less true and obvious that Indology and Indologists are being essentialized by his own sweeping statements' (Halbfass 1997: 19).

Other critics such as the Marxist literary theorist Aijaz Ahmad (1991) worry that Inden's appeal to indigenous agency lends itself too easily to appropriation by right wing Hindu groups in contemporary India. Indeed, the work of scholars such as Robert Sharf (1994; 1995) and King (1999) demonstrate that indigenous spokesmen for Asian religious traditions, such as D. T. Suzuki (Zen Buddhism) and Swami Vivekananda (Hinduism) were implicated in their own forms of 'internal colonialism' in the manner in which they represented their respective religious traditions at home and abroad. Moreover, many scholars have highlighted Western colonial influences upon contemporary forms of Hindu nationalism and communalism (Pandey 1990; Thapar 1992; Chatterjee 1986; van der Veer 1994).

Questions have also been raised about the poststructuralist theory of knowledge expounded by Inden. Is it possible, following Inden, to make any sort of appeal to a 'real India' underlying the various representations of it? In a similar fashion David Ludden criticizes Edward Said for believing that 'there is to be found in the East a real truth' (1993: 271). What we are dealing with are more or less powerful images of the Orient and not a 'real Orient' out there. Indologists such as Wilhelm Halbfass (1997: 16–17) have been quick to reject this approach on the grounds that it is self-refuting. Such a claim, he argues, prevents any critique of Orientalism based upon the misleading and *unrepresentative* nature of Orientalist accounts. How can one offer a critique of representations if there is no way of appealing to a real Orient or India 'out there'?

Orientalism in South Asia: the Asiatic Society of Bengal

Such has been the influence of Said's work in the decades succeeding the publication of his study that 'Orientalism' has now become a pejorative term, suggesting academic complicity with Western colonialism, rather than a neutral designation for the Western study of the East. For critics such as Bernard Lewis and David Kopf, Said's work has meant that the term 'Orientalist' is now 'polluted beyond salvation' (Lewis 1982: 50), representing 'a sewer category for all the intellectual rubbish Westerners have exercised in the global marketplace of ideas' (Kopf 1980: 498). Indeed before the publication of Said's study, the term 'Orientalism' had a specific meaning in a South Asian context, referring to the academic discipline which came into being as a result of the work of Sir William Jones, judge of the East India Company. Orientalism began with the formal establishment of the Asiatic Society of Bengal in Calcutta in 1784. The administrative and academic work of the Asiatic Society has been credited as the prime instigator for the Bengali Renaissance, a resurgence of intellectual interest in Hindu culture and reform among the Hindu intelligentsia of Bengal in the nineteenth century.

William Jones, the first President of the Asiatic Society of Bengal, is best known for his early work on Sanskrit – the ancient sacred language of the Hindus. Jones was a founding father of comparative linguistics and established links between Sanskrit and the European family of languages. In this sense he was an important catalyst for the explosion of interest in the cultural splendor of India's past, and also in the Romanticist tendency to conceive of India as the cradle of European civilization. Indeed under the influence of Romanticism India increasingly functioned as the canvas upon which a number of idealized representations and images were painted in the eighteenth and nineteenth centuries. India represented 'the childhood of humanity', an image which had positive as well as negative connotations. For the German writer Schlegel, India was 'the real source of all tongues, of all thoughts and utterances of the human mind. Everything – yes, everything without exception has its origin in India' (cited in Iyer 1965: 194). For his contemporary the German philosopher G. W. F. Hegel, however, the infantile nature of Indian culture meant that it had nothing to teach Europeans about modernity. India remained lost in an ancient fog of unprogressive mythologies and superstitions.

The Anglicists and the Orientalists

Assessment of the role, impact and motivations of Western Orientalists in India has become a subject of considerable debate in South Asian studies in response to Said's indictment of the Orientalist project. Historian David Kopf suggests that Said has missed his target with reference to the South Asian context. The Asiatic Society of Bengal, far from being a handmaiden to European colonialism, 'helped Indians to find an indigenous identity in the modern world' (Kopf 1980: 498). Early Orientalist scholarship on India, Kopf argues, was overwhelmingly attracted to and fascinated by its object, and defended the study of the indigenous traditions and languages of Asia when criticized by anti-Orientalist groups such as the Anglicists. This latter group, best exemplified by Lord Thomas Babington Macauley (1800–59), argued that the most expedient means of educating Indians was to introduce them to Western ideas and literature and to teach these through the medium of the English language. Babington believed that 'a single shelf of a good European library was worth the whole native literature of India and Arabia', a view that he claimed would not be refuted by the Orientalists themselves. In his famous 'Minute on Indian Education' (1835) Macauley declared his vision for the transformation of India under British imperial rule:

> We must at present do our best to form a class who may be interpreters between us and the millions whom we govern; a class of persons, Indian in blood and colour, but English in taste, in opinions, in morals, and in intellect.
>
> (Harlow and Carter 1999: 59)

Affirmative Orientalism

Kopf contrasts the attitude of Anglicists such as Macauley with the more enthusiastic and positive attitude towards India to be found in the writings of Orientalists such as Sir William Jones, Max Müller and Henry Thomas Colebrooke. The ensuing debate between these two positions, he argues, demonstrates the diversity of motivations and attitudes towards India at this time. Said's sweeping generalizations about the complicity of Orientalist scholarship with a Western colonial agenda wildly overstep the mark. Many Western Orientalists were often deeply sympathetic towards the object of their study (Clifford 1988; Fox 1992). Richard G. Fox argues, for instance, that Said's own analysis ignores the fact that 'resistance to Orientalist domination proceeds from within it.' (Fox 1992: 153). A similar point is made by Bernard Lewis when he argues that 'The most rigorous and penetrating critique of Orientalist scholarship has always been and will remain that of the Orientalists themselves' (Lewis 1982: 56). However, as Ulrike Freitag notes, this response by Lewis reiterates 'the exclusivist Orientalist stance'. This only serves to reconfirm 'the idea that only outsiders – that is, Orientalists – could really represent 'the Orient' and [are] the only ones competent to review their own scholarship' (Freitag 1997: 630).

Despite its obvious fascination and affirmation of Oriental culture, Ronald Inden (1990) describes examples of 'affirmative Orientalism' as 'the Loyal Opposition' precisely because they do not question the basic opposition between Eastern and Western cultures that underlies the Orientalist enterprise. Many of the stereotypical presuppositions of the Orientalist project remain intact, even if treated sympathetically. What this demonstrates is that it is misleading to see the critique of Orientalism initiated by scholars such as Said and Inden as a simple rejection of the negativity of Western attitudes towards the East. The love affair that Western Romanticism has had with the Orient (and which persists to this day in New Age conceptions of 'eastern mysticism and philosophy') is equally problematic because it continues to represent the diversity of Oriental cultures in terms of homogenized stereotypes.

Furthermore, in India the nationalist struggle for home rule (*swaraj*) and independence from British rule often built upon the legacy of colonial stereotypes rather than uprooting them. This has led some (mainly diaspora) Indian historians to advocate the writing of a 'history from below' that focuses upon the meanings and actions of 'subaltern' (non-elite) groups within Indian society. The subalternist movement has similarities with Marxist approaches but rejects the universalism of the Marxist theory of 'class consciousness'. Instead the subalternist historians examine the localized context and aims of oppressed groups rather than reduce their history to the grand narrative of Marxism. According to subalternists such as Ranajit Guha (1988) and Partha Chatterjee (1986), Indian nationalist (and Marxist) accounts, like those written by the European colonialist, represent an elitist approach to history because they ignore or suppress the specific agency of non-elite groups within Indian society. The subalternist approach therefore offers a potential 'third way' beyond the options of Orientalism and Occidentalism ('Orientalism-in reverse'). This is achieved by rejecting the elitism of both Western colonial histories and indigenous nationalist histories. The latter, although usually anti-colonial in nature, exercises its own form of domestic or internal colonialism by replacing colonial rulership with a new elite – that of indigenous elite groups.

Hybridity and the diversity of Orientalist discourses

Recent scholarship has also emphasized the diversity of Orientalist accounts. Lisa Lowe (1991) rejects Said's portrayal of Orientalism as a monolithic project. She argues that there are a number of factors impinging upon Western representations of the East, including race, nation, gender and sexuality. Similarly, Homi Bhabha (1996: 42) questions Said's one-sided emphasis upon the power of the colonizer. This, he argues, gives too much power to the Western Orientalist and ignores the role played by the colonized subject in the production and interpretation of Orientalist discourses (see also Hallisey 1995: 32–3). For Bhabha the encounter between the Western colonizer and the colonized Asian subject is complex, producing a hybrid representation that is always beyond the control of both the colonialist and the native. Influenced by the French poststructuralist Jacques Derrida, Bhabha's point is that the authors of texts cannot hope to control the meaning attributed to their writings once they enter the public domain. Once an author provides an account of the Orient it can be interpreted in a variety of ways and pressed into the service of a number of different agendas. Bhabha makes much of the example of the English educated Indian. For Angliclists such as Lord Macauley (see p. 281) this figure represented the ideal for the future of India – civilized according to British cultural standards. However, in his mimicry of the English colonizer the Anglo-Indian represents a hybrid form of 'Englishness' that confronts the colonizer in unexpected ways. Frankenstein has created a monster that he can no longer control!

A good example to illustrate Bhabha's point is the 'discovery' of the *Ezourvedam*. This text, circulated in the form of a French 'translation', was said to be an ancient Hindu scripture and caught the attention of a number of eighteenth-century European intellectuals. The *Ezourvedam* proclaims the superiority of monotheism and rejects the polytheism and ritualism of the uneducated Hindu masses. Voltaire vigorously promoted the text as a testament to the superiority of ancient Hindu culture in comparison to the decadence of Christianity. However, the *Ezourvedam* was a 'fake', produced by French Jesuits in Pondicherry with the probable aim of discrediting Hindu beliefs and practices and convincing Hindus of the superiority of the Christian message. Thus, a text that was initially produced by missionary Christians to spread the 'good news' of the Gospel, was adopted by French intellectuals such as Voltaire and used to demonstrate the inferiority and decadence of Christianity. How ironic! Similarly, Western notions of India as 'backward' and undeveloped in comparison to the material and technological might of the modern West were adopted and transformed by Hindu intellectuals such as Swami Vivekananda in the anti-colonial struggle for Indian independence. The West may be materially prosperous, Vivekananda argued, but this only serves to highlight that it lacks the spirituality of India. In one simple move Vivekananda took a standard Western stereotype about India and used it to counteract Western claims to superiority. What examples like the *Ezourvedam* and Vivekananda illustrate rather well is the multiple meanings and directions that can be attributed to Orientalist discourses.

Problems with the notion of 'religion'

The colonial domination of the West over 'the rest' in recent centuries has caused many Western categories and ideas to appear more universal than they might otherwise have seemed. An important feature of recent scholarship, therefore, has been to cast doubt upon the universal application of Western ideas and theories. Even the appropriateness of the notion of 'religion' in a non-Western context has been questioned on the grounds that it is the product of the cultural and political history of the West. For Talal Asad (1993), the modern Western tendency to conceive of religion in terms of belief – that is as something located in the private state of mind of a believer, leads Westerners to think of religion as something that is essentially private and separate from the public realm of politics. When Islamic or Hindu leaders in Asia express political views this is often seen in the West as a dangerous mixture of two separate realms of human life. Next time you watch a television news report about politics in the Middle East or India notice the style, presentation and reporting of events. How does the media portray foreign religious leaders in positions of political authority? Often news reports contain implicit assumptions about the 'normality' of the separation of religion from politics. However, as ex-BBC journalist Mark Tully suggests in his discussion of religion and politics in modern India:

> If we are really serious about coping with India's poverty we too have to show far greater respect for India's past and perhaps even learn from it ourselves . . .

Many will say I am trying to drag India backwards – to deny it the fruits of modern science and technology and to rob it of the freedom of democracy. Such critics are, I believe, in effect accepting the claim that there is now only one way: that Western liberal democracy has really triumphed.

(Tully 1991: 12)

We should bear in mind then that the separation of religion from politics is a feature of modern Western societies, reflecting eighteenth-century northern European disputes and the eventual separation of Church and State in modern Western nations. It is problematic therefore to impose this model of religion onto Asian cultures. Indeed for Asad all attempts to find a universal definition or 'essence' of religion are to be avoided because they imply that religion is somehow able to operate in isolation from other spheres of human cultural activity such as politics, law and science (1993: 28). Moreover, the sheer diversity of human cultures mean that the search for universal definitions of terms like 'religion' is fruitless. In its place, Asad advocates an approach to the study of cultures that focus upon embodied practices and the specific power-relations in which they operate.

King (1999) has also questioned the usefulness of the category of religion in the study of non-Western cultures. Modern notions of religion reflect Christian theological assumptions, in particular the preoccupation with orthodoxy and truth (rather than practice and forms of life) and with a canon of authorized scriptures as the location of the true essence of religion (King 1999: Chapters 2 and 3). As a consequence of colonial influence, world religions such as 'Hinduism' and 'Buddhism' have come to the fore in the colonial and modern periods, reflecting Western (Protestant and secular) assumptions about the nature of religion (see also Almond 1988; Fitzgerald 1990). It is not that these religions were simply 'imagined' by Westerners without the input of indigenous elite groups, but rather that their representation and subsequent developments within South Asian culture continue to reflect Western Orientalist concerns and assumptions. King argues that academic disciplines such as religious studies and Indology (the study of India) should work to extricate themselves from the Christian categories and secular assumptions, which continue to influence representations of the Orient, particularly the emphasis that is placed upon the so-called 'world religions'.

Orientalism and the study of Islam

Given that Said's work in this area focused almost exclusively upon the Middle Eastern and Islamic dimensions of Western Orientalist writings it is not surprising to find that his work has had a great deal of influence upon modern debates about the role and impact of Western Orientalism upon modern representations of Islam and Muslims. The debate has generally focused upon the legacy of Western colonialism in the Middle East and the continued existence of a number of negative stereotypes of Islam in the West. What is the relationship between modernity and Western culture? In Western culture modernity and traditionalism are usually seen as opposed to one another. Can one be modern and still align oneself with Islamic traditions? How is Islam to respond to the economic and political dominance of the West and the legacy of Western colonial rule in the Middle East?

Broadly speaking, there have been two main responses to these issues and the challenge laid down by the work of Edward Said. Some Arabic intellectuals and scholars of Islam have argued that Western scholarship should be abandoned in favor of an Islamicization of knowledge. Why, such proponents argue, should Muslims feel obliged to conform to the intellectual conventions and secular presuppositions of Western scholarship? This strand of Islamic scholarship has increasingly described itself as 'Islamism' as an indigenous alternative to the negative connotations of the Western term 'fundamentalism'. The Islamists tend to reject Western scholarship as a cultural attack upon Islam. In its place they advocate continuity with older traditions of Islamic scholarship, the use of Arabic as the primary linguistic mode of expression and an ongoing exploration of the truth expressed in the holy words of the Qur'an. Critics of this approach argue that Islamism represents the development of Occidentalism – a reversal of the Orientalist approach and a denigration of the West as inferior. Edward Said made it clear, however, that this was not the intention of his own analysis, concerned as he was to overturn and reject the dichotomy between Occident and Orient rather than reverse it. Nevertheless, for writers such as Akbar Ahmed this has been the result of Said's analysis:

> One inevitable consequence is the rejection of Western scholarship by Muslims. Muslim scholars in the West, whether Arab or Pakistani, are deeply suspicious of Western Orientalism. They are thus pushed into the hole, Said has unwittingly dug for them. For Muslims in Africa and Asia, imperfectly grasped bits of Marxist dogma, nationalism, and religious chauvinism create incorrect images of the West . . . Said has left us with what he sets out to denounce: stereotypes and large blocks – Orientalist, Oriental, Orient.
>
> (Ahmed and Donnan 1994: 5)

Islamism represents a contemporary response to what has been called 'westoxification' (the pollution of Islamic culture by Western influences) and a reassertion of Islamic values and beliefs in a context of Western economic, political and cultural dominance. Scholars such as Mahmûd Hamdî Zaqzûq (1983) for instance, have called for a scientific response to Western Orientalism founded upon the truth of Islam. Others, such as Hasan Hanafi (1991), call for the creation of Occidentalism, that is the academic study of the West, as a post-colonial response to the cultural and intellectual dominance of Western scholarship.

In contrast to the Islamists, there are also a number of Arabic intellectuals engaging with the concerns and issues of Western scholarship. In most cases such scholars are migrants, often educated *by* and now working *in* Western universities. The main concern for such writers remains the mutual proliferation of stereotypes about Arabs and Westerners and the question of the impact of globalization, cultural interaction and politics upon representations of Islam. Clearly these two strands of contemporary Arabic scholarship do not sit easily with each other. The Islamists direct much of their criticism towards those Arab intellectuals who have adopted or utilized Western methodologies in their analysis. This is seen as a rejection of Islam and complicity with the secularism of the Western colonial aggressor. Similarly, Western influenced Arabic scholars tend to reject Islamist approaches as 'Orientalism in reverse', questioning the privileged insulation of Arabic culture from wider international debates concerning modernism, postmodernism and globalization.

Orientalism, gender and religion

In the concern to highlight politics and the marginalization of the Other, the post-colonial agenda in scholarship has much in common with the development of feminist approaches to the study of religion (King 1999: 111–16). It is not surprising then to find that recent works have shown an increasing awareness of gender as a factor relevant to the Orientalist debate (Miller 1990). Lata Mani (1987) argues that nineteenth-century debates about the legality of *sati* (the ritual burning of a Hindu widow on her deceased husband's funeral pyre) – a practice abolished by the British in 1829, did not allow the women concerned to emerge as either 'subjects' or 'objects'. Instead the Hindu widow became the 'site of contestation' in a debate which centered instead upon the question of whether or not the burning of widows was sanctioned by ancient Hindu sacred texts. All participants in this debate, whether abolitionists or preservationists, accepted without question the authority of Hindu brahmanical scriptures as the definitive source for 'the Hindu position'. The location of the 'essence' of Hinduism in ancient texts clearly reflects the Protestant presuppositions of the early Orientalists and gained further support from their reliance upon the scholarly community of brahmanical pandits as the authorized spokesmen for Hinduism (King 1999: Chapters 5 and 6).

Similarly, recent work has also paid attention to the images of the 'sexualized Orient' found in Western fantasies about the Oriental 'harem' and 'the veil' (Lewis 1996; Mabro 1996; Yegenoglu 1998). Notions of the seductive and sensual nature of the Orient and of the Oriental woman in particular also continue to this day in media advertising and popular culture. Whether this involves popularized accounts of the 'secrets of the *Kama Sutra*' (which is thereby transformed from an ancient Hindu text on the etiquette of courtship and lovemaking into an exotic manual of sexual positions), or the commodification and sexualization of Thai therapeutic massage, modern Western consumer culture continues to build upon much older colonial legacies and Orientalist stereotypes.

Attention has also turned to the role played by women in the Orientalist and imperial enterprises. Reina Lewis (1996), taking her lead from the work of Lisa Lowe (1991), argues that an examination of the location of female Orientalists in a complicated and sometimes contradictory network of power-relations demonstrates the diversity of the Orientalist project. Female Orientalists took up a variety of stances with regard to Western imperial superiority over the East at the same time as being involved in a complex series of domestic debates about the status and role of women in Western society. Her analysis suggests that an adequate critique of Orientalism should avoid the tendency to focus upon the expressed intentions and motivations of individual Orientalists and consider instead the broader structural relations of power that Orientalist discourses maintain: 'When we look at European women's representation of and participation in processes of othering, we are looking at representations made by agents who are themselves partially othered (as the symbolic feminized other of men in Europe)' (Lewis 1996: 238).

The most recent work within the field of post-colonial studies has focused upon the mutual involvement of a variety of factors (including race, class, gender and sexuality), in the study of the cultures, histories and religions of Asia. Anne McClintock (1995: 6–7) argues for instance that 'imperialism cannot be understood without a theory of gender power'. Similarly, Mrinalini Sinha (1995) has examined the ways in which nineteenth-century British notions of 'masculinity' developed in opposition to the perceived 'effeminacy' of the Bengali male. Sinha's work demonstrates rather well the complex interaction of Hindu and British notions of gender, race and sexuality in the colonial period. Attention has also turned in recent works to the existence of manipulative strategies and representations in pre-colonial Asian societies (Pollock 1993: 96–111; Killingley 1997; King 1999). These works suggest that the Orientalist tendency to stereotype and diminish the 'Other' is by no means an exclusively Western practice.

Concluding remarks

One of the most important insights to be drawn from the Orientalist debate is an awareness of the political nature of knowledge itself. Fundamentally, what post-colonial approaches teach us is to be more aware of the ongoing influence of colonialism upon the representation of others, and also of ourselves. Like feminist scholarship, post-colonialism is diverse but remains grounded in an awareness of the politics of knowledge, that is the involvement of scholarship in issues of power, authority and justice. This is especially relevant when dealing with the cultures and traditions of others, but 'indigenous' accounts by cultural 'insiders' are no less implicated by issues of authority and representation. Moreover, such has been the impact of Western domination over the last few centuries that indigenous traditions have themselves been transformed by the material and cultural violence of Western colonialism. Rejecting the separation of religion and its study from political concerns, post-colonial analysis opens up the possibility, indeed for such theorists the *necessity*, of exploring alternative ways of understanding and representing human diversity. How are we to make sense of differences between people in a *pluralistic* rather than an *oppositional* way? How might we try to understand the diverse ways of living that represent our common global heritage? This is perhaps the central issue confronting humanity today and no doubt will continue to influence debates within the study of religion. In this regard the comparative study of religion has a key role to play in the quest for greater understanding of the various cultures, peoples and forms of life that make up the world in which we live.

References

Abdel-Malek, Anouar (1963), 'Orientalism in Crisis' in *Diogenes*, 44: 103–40.
Ahmad, Aijaz (1991), 'Between Orientalism and Historicism: anthropological knowledge of India' in *Studies in History*, 7.1: 135–63.
—— (1992), *In Theory: Classes, Nations, Literature*, London: Verso.
Ahmed, Akbar S. and Hastings Donnan (eds) (1994), *Islam, Globalization and Postmodernity*, London: Routledge.
al-ʿAzm, Sadiq Jalal (1981), 'Orientalism and Orientalism in Reverse' in *Khamsin*, 8: 5–26.
Almond, Philip (1988), *The British Discovery of Buddhism*, Cambridge: Cambridge University Press.
Behdad, Ali (1994), *Belated Travelers: Orientalism in the Age of Colonial Dissolution*, Durham and London: Duke University Press.

Bhabha, Homi (1996), 'The Other Question,' in Padmini Mongia (ed.), *Contemporary Postcolonial Theory. A Reader*, London, New York, Sydney and Auckland: Arnold (Hodder Headline Group), 37–54. This article was first published in *Screen*, 24.6 (1983).

Carrette, J. R. (ed.) (1999), *Religion and Culture by Michel Foucault*, Manchester: Manchester University Press.

Chatterjee, Partha (1986), *Nationalist Thought and the Colonial World – A Derivative Discourse*, London: Zed Books.

Clifford, James (1988), *The Predicament of Culture: Twentieth Century Ethnography, Literature and Art*, Cambridge: Cambridge University Press.

Fitzgerald, Timothy (1990), 'Hinduism and the "World Religion" Fallacy' in *Religion*, 20: 101–18.

Foucault, Michel (1977), 'Truth and Power,' in Gordon, Colin (ed.) (1980), *Michel Foucault, Power/Knowledge. Selected Writings and Interviews 1972–1977, by Michel Foucault*, New York, London, Toronto: Harvester Wheatsheaf: 109–33.

Fox, Richard G. (1992), 'East of Said' in Michael Sprinker (ed.), *Edward Said. A Critical Reader*, Cambridge, MA and Oxford, England: Blackwell.

Freitag, Ulrike (1997), 'The Critique of Orientalism' in Michael Bentley (ed.), *Routledge Companion to Historiography*, London and New York: Routledge, 620–38.

Guha, Ranajit (1988), 'On Some Aspects of the Historiography of Colonial India' in *Subaltern Studies*, vol. 1, Delhi: Oxford University Press.

Halbfass, Wilhelm (1997), 'Beyond Orientalism? Reflections on a Current Theme' in Eli Franco and Karin Preisendanz (eds), *Beyond Orientalism. The Work of Wilhelm Halbfass and its Impact on Indian and Cross-Cultural Studies*, Amsterdam and Atlanta, GA: Rodopi, Poznan: *Studies in the Philosophies of the Sciences and the Humanities*, vol. 59: 1–28.

Hallisey, Charles (1995). 'Roads Taken and Not Taken in the Study of Theravada Buddhism' in Donald Lopez Jr (ed.) *Curators of the Buddha*, Chicago: University of Chicago Press, 31–62.

Hanafi, Hasan (1991), *Prolegomena to the Science of Orientalism*, Cairo (in Arabic).

Harlow, Barbara and Mia Carter, Mia (eds) (1999), *Imperialism and Orientalism. A Documentary Sourcebook*, Oxford: Blackwell.

Iyer, R. (ed.) (1965), *The Glass Curtain between Asia and Europe. A Symposium on the Historical Encounters and Changing Attitudes of the Peoples of East and West*, London: Oxford University Press.

Killingley, Dermot (1997), 'Mlecchas, Yavanas and Heathens: Interacting Xenologies in Early Nineteenth Century Calcutta' in Eli Franco and Karin Preisendanz (eds), *Beyond Orientalism. The Work of Wilhelm Halbfass and its Impact on Indian and Cross-Cultural Studies*, Amsterdam and Atlanta GA: Rodopi, Poznan: *Studies in the Philosophies of the Sciences and the Humanities*, vol. 59: 123–40.

Kopf, David (1980), 'Hermeneutics versus History' in *Journal of Asian Studies*, vol. 39, no. 3.

Lewis, Bernard (1982), 'The Attack on Orientalism' in *New York Review of Books*, 24 June 1982: 49–56.

Lewis, Reina (1996), *Gendering Orientalism. Race, Femininity and Representation*, London and New York: Routledge.

Lowe, Lisa (1991), *Critical Terrains: French and British Orientalism*, Ithaca and London: Cornell University Press.

Ludden, David (1993), 'Orientalist Empiricism: transformations of colonial knowledge' in Carol Breckenridge and Peter van der Veer (eds), *Orientalism and the Postcolonial Predicament*, Philadelphia: University of Pennsylvania Press, 250–78.

Macauley, Thomas Babington (1835), 'A Minute on Indian Education' in Baubara Harlow and Mia Carter (eds) (1999), 56–62.

McClintock, Anne (1995), *Imperial Leather: Race, Gender and Sexuality in the Colonial Context*, London and New York: Routledge.

Mabro, Judy (1996), *Veiled Half-Truths. Western Traveller's Perception of Middle Eastern Women*, New York: New York University Press.

Mani, Lata (1987), 'Contentious Traditions. The Debate on Sati in Early Nineteenth Century Bengal' in *Cultural Critique*, 7: 119–56.

Miller, Jane (1990), *Seductions: Studies in Reading and Culture*, London: Virago.

Pandey, Gyanendra (1990), *The Construction of Communalism in Colonial North India*, Delhi and Oxford: Oxford University Press.

Panikkar, K. M. (1959), *Asia and Western Dominance*, London: George Allen & Unwin.

Pollock, Sheldon (1993), 'Deep Orientalism? Notes on Sanskrit and Power beyond the Raj' in Carol Breckenridge and Peter van der Veer (eds), *Orientalism and the Postcolonial Predicament*, Philadelphia: University of Pennsylvania Press, 73–133.

Prado, C. G. (1995), *Starting with Foucault. An Introduction to Genealogy*, Boulder, CO and Oxford, England: Westview Press Inc.

Sardar, Ziauddin (1998), *Postmodernism and the Other. The New Imperialism of Western Culture*, London: Pluto Press.

Schwab, Raymond (1950), *The Oriental Renaissance: Europe's Discovery of India and the East, 1680–1880*, English translation, New York: Columbia University Press, 1984.

Sharf, Robert (1994), 'Whose Zen? Zen Nationalism Revisited' in James S. Heisig and John C. Maraldo (eds), *Rude Awakenings: Zen, the Kyoto School, and the Question of Nationalism*, Honolulu: University of Hawaii Press, 40–51.

—— (1995), 'The Zen of Japanese Nationalism' in Donald Lopez Jr (ed.), *Curators of the Buddha*, Chicago: University of Chicago Press, 107–60.

Sinha, Mrinalini (1995), *Colonial Masculinity. The 'Manly Englishman' and the 'Effeminate Bengali;' in the Late Nineteenth Century*, Manchester: Manchester University Press.

Steadman, John M. (1970), *The Myth of Asia*, London: Macmillan.

Thapar, Romila (1992), *Interpreting Early India*, Oxford: Oxford University Press.

Tully, Mark (1991), *No Full Stops in India*, London: Penguin.

van der Veer, Peter (1994), *Religious Nationalism: Hindus and Muslims in India*, Berkeley: University of California Press.

Yegenoglu, Meyda (1998), *Colonial Fantasies. Towards a Feminist Reading of Orientalism*, Cambridge: Cambridge University Press.

Zaqzûq, Mahmûd Hamdî (1983), *Orientalism and the Intellectual in the Cultural Struggle*, Doha (in Arabic).

Further reading

Talal Asad (1993), *Genealogies of Religion. Discipline and Reasons of Power in Christianity and Islam*, Baltimore, MD: John Hopkins University Press.
A scholarly examination of Christian monastic discipline, the history of anthropological concepts of religion, and the Salman Rushdie affair from a post-colonial perspective. Not for the general reader.

Stephen Batchelor (1994), *The Awakening the West. The Encounter of Buddhism and Western Culture*, London: Aquarian Press.
A readable account of the interaction and reception of Buddhism in Western culture. Highly recommended.

Ronald Inden (1990), *Imagining India*, Cambridge, MA and Oxford, England: Blackwell.
Inden is an anthropologist specializing in South Asia. This book offers a wide-ranging critique of the study of South Asian religion and society, and is strongly influenced by Edward Said and poststructuralist theory. An important work.

Richard King (1999), *Orientalism and Religion. Post-colonial Theory, India and 'the Mystic East'*, London and New York: Routledge.
An exploration of 'the Orientalist debate', postcolonial theory and their implications for the comparative study of religion. Chapters explore the nature of religious studies, Orientalism, the study of Hinduism and Buddhism and the comparative study of mysticism.

Donald Lopez Jr (ed.) (1995), *Curators of the Buddha. The Study of Buddhism Under Colonialism*, Chicago: University of Chicago Press.
A collection of six scholarly articles examining the Orientalism question in relation to various aspects of the study of Buddhism. The work presupposes a great deal of knowledge of Buddhism and its study and is aimed at the academic scholar rather than the student or general reader.

Padmini Mongia (ed.) (1996), *Contemporary Postcolonial Theory: A Reader*, London, New York, Sydney and Auckland: Arnold (Hodder Headline Group).
A collection of important contributions to contemporary postcolonial theory, though with no specific reference to religion.

Edward Said (1981), *Covering Islam. How the Media and the Experts Determine How We See the Rest of the World*, London: Routledge.
A readable discussion of Western media portrayals of Islam.

Edward Said (1978, 2nd edn 1995), *Orientalism. Western Conceptions of the Orient*, London and New York: Penguin.
The classic text examining the link between Western colonialism and representations of the Orient.

Bryan Turner (1994), *Orientalism, Postmodernism and Globalism*, London and New York: Routledge.
An examination of the impact of postmodernism and globalism on Western sociological studies of Islam.

Chapter 16

Secularization

Judith Fox

> The Sea of Faith
> Was once, too, at the full, and round earth's shore
> Lay like the folds of a bright girdle furl'd.
> But now I only hear
> Its melancholy, long, withdrawing roar,
> Retreating, to the breath
> Of the night-wind, down the vast edges drear
> And naked shingles of the world.
>
> From *Dover Beach*
> by Matthew Arnold, 1867.

Many sociologists of religion in the 1970s believed that the world was becoming increasingly secular, and that fewer people were religious than before. This view was consistent with the predictions of some theologians. Western cultural commentators often talked of the 'death of God'. And this seemed to fit with a growing indifference to established religion in Western Europe. Those making the argument explained that social forces associated with 'modernity' were responsible for the progressive secularization occurring. Since then, however, increasing numbers have questioned the validity of the thesis. Today, only a minority support the view that progressive secularization is taking place. Yet the whole issue of secularization has by no means been settled, and still manages to generate considerable debate.

There are a number of reasons for the continuing disagreement between scholars on the subject of secularization. One is that there has been considerable confusion over the definition of terms. Another is that the arguments have been founded on rather different ideological assumptions. So this account begins by introducing the different ways in which the terms 'secular', 'secularization' and 'secularism' have been used. Subsequently, I draw attention to the historical antecedents of the arguments put forward today, and to some presuppositions inherent in the notion of secularization. Finally, after sketching out the key elements of the various arguments, and summarizing some critiques of the thesis, I conclude with a reconsideration of its more problematic aspects.

A question of definitions

A useful starting point is to review the proposition contained in the first sentence of this chapter. It appears to be saying, in rather general terms, that during the 1970s

sociologists believed that religiosity was in decline. But appearances can be deceptive. In fact, the statement is, intentionally, somewhat less than straightforward. For
the interpretation I have just suggested to be the case, one would have to equate
the proposition that 'far fewer people were religious than before' with the idea that
'the world was becoming increasingly secular'. And, unfortunately, these two phrases
are not necessarily synonymous. This is due, in part, to the disparity between the
meanings attributed to the term 'secular' and its derivatives.

According to the *Oxford English Dictionary* (*OED*), the term 'secular' is derived
from the same etymological root (L. *sæculum*) as the French word *siecle*, meaning
'century', or 'age'. Interestingly, this derivation is evident in the astronomical use of
the word secular to talk about processes of change over long periods of time, such
as changes in planetary orbits. However, most people are perhaps more familiar with
the usage that originated in early ecclesiastical texts, in which the term 'secular' was
commonly opposed to 'regular'. 'Regular', in this context, was a term applied to those
persons subject to the rule of a monastic order. Thus, its opposite – 'secular' – was
used to denote worldly affairs. Today, this is the most commonly understood meaning
of 'secular'.

The principal definition of the term 'secularization' given by the *OED* emphasizes
its institutional character. There, secularization is described as: 'the conversion of an
ecclesiastical or religious institution or its property to secular possession and use'. In
contrast secularism, some sociologists of religion have argued, has a more personal
orientation. It is the belief that morality should only take into account human and
visible considerations. Secularists do not consider that moral codes should take into
account, for instance, the existence of God, or of an afterlife. So, these scholars have
maintained, secularization takes place in the 'public' arena, and secularism is a
'private' affair. Secularization, they have said, refers only to the diminishing of the
public significance of religion. It does not refer to private levels of religiosity. It is,
therefore, not synonymous with secularism. In fact, they have argued that the withdrawal of religion from the public domain might well imply an increase in personal
forms of religiosity.

But, to complicate matters, this distinction between private religiosity and public
religion has not been held universally by sociologists of religion. Peter Berger made
the suggestion early on that: 'As there is a secularization of society and culture, so
is there a secularization of consciousness' (Berger 1969: 107–08). He felt that secularization could have a private as well as a public component. A number of his
colleagues agreed with him. It should also be noted that some who have argued for
secularization have not defined it as an irrevocable and irreversible trend. Instead,
they have asserted that secularization ebbs and flows. Old religious forms die out,
but they are replaced. Yet others have used the term secularization to describe a shift
from 'other-worldly' to 'this-worldly' concerns within religious organizations, rather
than in society at large.

Secularization theory, in other words, is one of those topics where the same word
has been used very differently in the debates. However, as already noted, this confusion over meaning has not been the only reason for the disagreements over
secularization. So, to complete our preparations for an examination of these debates,
we should become conversant with the ideological antecedents of the different views
being argued. To do so, we will look briefly at the work of the two men widely

regarded as the founding fathers of the sociology of religion, Max Weber (1864–1920) and Émile Durkheim (1858–1917), and at the goals of 'the Enlightenment project'.

The antecedents of contemporary theories of secularization

The Enlightenment project that matured in the eighteenth century represented a revolutionary intellectual movement. Enlightenment thinkers believed that there was an underlying order to the world that could be progressively understood through the use of the rational faculties of men. Intellectual progress would be achieved by abandoning articles of faith, by rising above instinctual drives and by renouncing irrationality. They assumed that men could lift themselves out of the mire of received wisdom and become autonomous human subjects. Men were capable of discovering foundational truths about the nature of reality by relying on intelligence rather than on divine revelation. These discoveries would come about by focusing on the objective facts of the world, and so discerning the laws governing life. Everything could ultimately be understood through science and rational thought. Then, once this understanding had been achieved, man would be able to control both Nature and his own destiny.

These assumptions permeated the intellectual milieu in which Max Weber lived. Marx and Nietzsche, both whom he regarded as brilliant, also represented major influences in his work. Weber did not uncritically accept all of the tenets of Enlightenment thinking. He believed, for example, that there are some spheres in which science has no role to play. Nevertheless, Enlightenment assumptions are clearly visible in a number of his key ideas. Weber assumed that the foremost trend in Western society was towards increasing rationalization. He felt that social progress involved a move away from traditional, localized and sentimental ways of life and towards ordered bureaucracies and centralized control. Weber found this modern trend profoundly disturbing, but also inevitable. He saw it as the logical outcome of the rise of the nation state, and of capitalism. In particular, he believed, modernizing forces such as urbanization, the specialization of labour and industrialization would have a profound impact on religion.

Weber argued – nostalgically, it has been said – that traditional life was permeated with a magical enchantment. Rationalization, he predicted, would lead to a progressive 'disenchantment' and, ultimately, to a world in which religion would no longer play a role in public life. This was not to say that religion would necessarily disappear altogether. However, it would increasingly become a matter of private choice. Weber believed this secularization would gradually occur because religion would no longer be able to exist in a state of unquestioned authority. Weber also suggested that Protestantism carried within itself the seeds of secularization. First, this was because it encouraged the idea that brotherly love could be manifested through 'a peculiarly objective and impersonal character, that of service in the interest of the rational organization of our social environment' (Weber 1930: 109). Thus, it promoted rationalization and, therefore, disenchantment. Second, he argued, Protestantism encouraged scientists to reflect upon the natural laws of divine creation as a way of knowing God. Since it allowed scientific explanations to undermine religious ones, its own internal logic would eventually undercut itself.

Weber has been described by a number of biographers as a brilliant scholar and a troubled soul. Unlike some contemporaries, he did not see the decline of religious influence as a liberating outcome of modernity. He simply saw it as unavoidable, given the social forces at play. Durkheim's position was very different. He was an atheist, and as influenced by Enlightenment thinking as Weber. But his assessment of the future of religion was far more optimistic. His view was that religious sentiment was essential to society, whether traditional or modern. Religion, he argued, enhances feelings of social solidarity. He, therefore, did not see it as something that could ever be outgrown by mankind, or as something that could be fully separated from society.

So Durkheim believed that religion would never lose its social significance. Instead, he maintained that: 'there is something eternal in religion that is destined to outlive the succession of particular symbols in which religious thought has clothed itself' (Durkheim 1912: 429). Religion would persist, not because it was necessarily true but because it had a public function to perform. Society required religion in order to maintain social cohesion and to strengthen collective feelings and ideas. He believed that forms of religion could be expected to change as society changes. But, Durkheim concluded, religion itself could never be extinguished or pushed to the margins, even when disputed by science. Science had the capability to challenge outmoded religious dogmas. But new religious forms, more in keeping with the times, would inevitably arise to take their place. Durkheim acknowledged that religion was apparently in decline during his lifetime. But he felt that a resurrection was imminent:

> In short, the former gods are growing old or dying, and others have not been born . . . [but] A day will come when our societies once again will know hours of creative effervescence during which new ideals will again spring forth and new formulas emerge to guide humanity.
>
> (ibid.: 429)

The ideas of these two men, have at least implicitly, dominated more recent debates over secularization. Part of their legacy is evident in the type of grand theorizing involved. Weber explicitly rejected the notion that religion is generalizable in an ahistorical sense. But both men sought to understand the underlying laws governing religion, and offered large-scale explanatory models based on the trends they observed. Contemporary theories of secularization fit neatly into this genre. Their influence is also visible in the assumptions underpinning contemporary arguments. All presume that social conditions have an impact on religion. But some, including Bryan Wilson and Roy Wallis, are explicitly Weberian in orientation. Others, such as Rodney Stark and William Sims Bainbridge, and Grace Davie, exhibit elements of Durkheimian thought in their challenges to the views of the former. To review the later perpetuation of the ideas of Weber and Durkheim, I shall turn first to the classic secularization thesis outlined by the Oxford academic Bryan Wilson. I will then examine the reactions of other scholars, before making some more general observations on the debate.

The great secularization debate

Bryan Wilson was seen by many to be the foremost British sociologist of religion of his day. His book *Religion in Secular Society*, published in 1966, laid out the principles of his secularization thesis and became a founding document of the contemporary debate. In it, Wilson defined secularization as 'the process whereby religious thinking, practice and institutions lose social significance' (Wilson 1966: 14). His argument was that religion had formerly occupied a central position in society but, by the twentieth century, this was no longer the case. Wilson largely confined his analysis to Western society and, especially, to the position of religion in Britain and the United States. He agreed with Weber's view on the secularizing character of the Protestant ethos. He also maintained, like his august intellectual predecessor, that religion must be examined in terms of its historico-social context. Wilson allowed that in countries like Japan, concomitant with industrialization, secularizing processes were discernable. However, following Weber, he asserted that secularization was more markedly evident in Christianity than in other religions around the world. The effects of secularization were, therefore, also more in evidence in Christian, and especially Protestant, countries.

Wilson's adoption of a Weberian conceptual framework was unambiguously evident in his view that the onset of modernizing processes in the West were linked to the emergence of Protestantism. Before the advent of Protestantism, he believed, religious understandings were adopted as axiomatic. After it, they began to be seen as matters of faith rather than universals. The Church could no longer claim to hold sway over the hearts, minds and lives of the general populace, as it had in simpler times. Institutions that had previously been ecclesiastically governed, such as hospitals, schools and universities, began to be transferred to secular authorities. By the twentieth century, Western man was increasingly more rational than before:

> It seems to me difficult to maintain that man in western society is not more rational than ever he was, within the normal usage of the term 'rational'. So much more of his ordinary behaviour is controlled by cause-and-effect thinking, even if only because he knows more about the workings of the physical and social worlds ... The dominance of economic costing over spiritual aspiration in modern society, is the evidence of the growth of rationality in our social affairs, and consequently, at least in some measure, in our own habits of thought.
>
> (Ibid.: 17)

Like Weber, Wilson regarded rationalizing processes as consequences of modernity that were both inevitable and inexorable. Due to their onslaught, religion would become increasingly marginalized and lacking in social significance. This had already happened in many parts of Europe, he said, where religion had been relegated from public life. It existed mainly on the periphery of society, where it continued to flourish mainly in the form of socially insignificant sectarian religious organizations. Indeed, sects were evidence for secularization:

> It is in conditions in which the sacred order has been suborned to the secular – usually the religious institution to the political – as in the Roman Empire or Europe from the sixteenth to the nineteenth century, or in twentieth-century Japan, that sectarianism becomes most manifest and institutionalized.
>
> (Ibid.: 207)

Wilson conceded that religious organizations had managed to remain in mainstream public life in the United States. However, he believed they were doomed to become increasingly bureaucratic and rationalized.

In this early book, Wilson included empirical evidence of processes of secularization. Although these processes were present in both countries, he argued, they followed different paths in Britain and the United States. In Britain, he used statistics published by a range of Protestant churches in England. The figures appeared to support his theme of a decline in religious membership and 'the general standing of the Church in society'. Wilson chose infant baptism, confirmation, church weddings, and attendance at Sunday school and Easter communion, as indices of levels of religious participation. His conclusion was that a decline was statistically evident. Turning his attention to America, he was not convinced that the statistics he was given were fully accurate. But he allowed that religion appeared far more resilient in the United States, and that the numbers indicated that religious membership was increasing rapidly. The main thrust of his argument for secularization taking place in America, therefore, differed from that which he used for Britain. Instead, he began by querying the authenticity and depth of religious commitment in America:

> The travellers of the past who commented on the apparent extensiveness of Church membership, rarely omitted to say that they found religion in America to be very superficial. Sociologists generally hold that the dominant values of American society are not religious.
>
> (Ibid.: 112)

Religious affiliation in the United States, he argued, was part and parcel of 'being an American'. Public American religiosity, therefore, signified a social commitment rather than a sacred one. He theorized that the United States had needed to forge a common identity during the formative years of the Union, despite the plurality of its religious organizations. This need had led to the downplaying of religious difference. Religious values had thereby been eroded. Wilson suggested: 'though religious practice has increased, the vacuousness of popular religious ideas has also increased: the content and meaning of religious commitment has been acculturated' (ibid.: 122).

Wilson did not see the secularization he observed in both countries as being entirely dissimilar in kind. He linked secularization, wherever it occurred, to the increasingly mobile, urban and impersonal society he associated with the modern world. Comparing Britain and the United States, he also identified two other secularizing tendencies they had in common: denominationalism and ecumenicalism. Each new denomination, he said, eroded the notion of a unitary religious authority and so fuelled further secularization. Increasing numbers of denominations meant more competing views and an increase in doctrinal tension that undermined the basis of religious control. Some scholars saw ecumenicalism as a sign of a vigorous Church ready to engage with the doctrines and practices of others. For Wilson, however, ecumenicalism was a symptom of weakness rather than a sign of strength. This was because, he argued, organizations are most likely to amalgamate when they are weak. The desire for alliance leads to compromise and the amendment of commitment.

Some scholars saw the new religious movements that appeared in the West in the 1970s and 1980s as heralding the kind of religious regeneration envisaged by

Durkheim. During this period, however, Wilson continued to affirm the view that, in common with sects in general, these movements were of little social consequence. In the 1990s, in a more conciliatory tone, he commented that new religions might indeed have positive benefits for individuals, and had significance on that basis. However, he saw no indication that any of them would or could transform the structure of society. They were, therefore, private forms of religion, and not to be taken as signs of the revival of public religion.

Wilson did not particularly distinguish between religious thinking and religious institutional presence in his earlier work on secularization. He believed that both, at different rates and in different ways, were under attrition in Western society. In his later work, however, he consistently reaffirmed the public character of the religious decline he was describing. In response to reactions to his earlier work, he emphasized that his own model of secularization did not necessarily imply the growth of a secular consciousness. It did not even necessarily entail the idea that most individuals living in secular societies have relinquished their interest in religion. Secularization simply meant that religion had ceased to be significant in public life.

Responses to Bryan Wilson's theory of secularization

Wilson was far from the first to argue that secularization was taking place in the modern world. It is, however, his work that is most often referred to by other sociologists as 'the classic thesis'. Also, it is his writings that are seen to have initiated the contemporary debate. In a moment, I shall turn to some alternative models that have been put forward in response. However, it is worth briefly reviewing a few of the criticisms made about the specific content of his argument.

In an early rebuttal of the thesis, David Martin called for the concept of secularization to be abandoned, on the grounds that it was: 'less a scientific concept than a tool of counter-religious ideologies' (Martin 1969: 9). Martin went on to produce an important later comparative contribution to the debate, *A General Theory of Secularization*, but in this early work he objected to Wilson's position on a number of counts. One was that the notion of secularization implied a definition of religion, but religion is notoriously difficult to define. Another was that the thesis appeared to suggest that there once existed a 'Golden Age' of religion from whose norms we have subsequently diverged. This 'Golden Age', in his view, was an ideal based on representations of eleventh- to thirteenth-century Catholicism. However, said Martin, no such utopian period ever existed. A third objection he raised was that the view of 'modern man' put forward by Wilson was 'over-secularized'. Instead, Martin argued that contemporary society 'remains deeply imbued with every type of superstition and metaphysic' (ibid.: 113).

Other commentators, including Andrew Greeley, questioned the validity of the empirical evidence Wilson had marshalled (Greeley 1972). Greeley, an American priest and scholar, argued that statistics about church membership were not necessarily accurate indicators of levels of religious practice. He pointed out that many parishes did not keep records, and noted that the concept of membership is open to a number of interpretations. Different figures can be arrived at depending upon which interpretation is used. Greeley was also one of the scholars who objected to Wilson's view of ecumenicalism as a sign of weakness. He commented that engaging in dialogue with other Churches could equally well be seen as a response to plurality, and as a sign of strength. Generally, he rejected Wilson's suggestion that America was increasingly secular, along with the notion that modernity has a deleterious effect on religion. Agreeing with the misgivings raised by Greeley, other scholars described Wilson's attitude towards American religiosity and, indeed, towards sectarian religion, as unduly dismissive. They took exception to his assumption that a localized European model of religious 'authenticity' could be taken as a universal norm. It is worth noting, however, that Wilson was not alone in this. A number of the early sociologists who supported his thesis assumed the European model of secularization as the norm, and evidence to the contrary as merely exceptions to the rule (Casanova 1994: 22).

The 'religious economies' model

It was two other American scholars, Rodney Stark and William Sims Bainbridge, who began the formulation of an alternative to Wilson's thesis. Their model was predicated on the existence of 'religious economies'. Notably, unlike Wilson, they defined secularization as both a public and private matter. For them, it was not only as a process affecting societies, but also one to which individual religious organizations were susceptible. Stark and Bainbridge suggested that religion arises through basic social exchanges. Within social exchanges, which are economic in nature, people attempt to gain rewards and avoid costs. Religion offers rewards in the form of 'compensators', these being rewards that are accepted as a matter of faith. Stark's and Bainbridge's view was that science alone does not offer sufficient rewards to individuals. This is because, they said, science is incapable of solving the central problems of human existence. For this reason, they argued, humans have continued to postulate supernatural entities able to meet their demands.

Stark and Bainbridge believed that religious revival and innovation is stimulated by supply and demand. Because of secularizing forces within organizations, they argued, religious entities that can offer powerful enough compensators are sometimes in short supply. This is because, over time, religious organizations tend to become more rational and secular. In so doing, they lose supernatural credibility. Human beings, however, have a fairly constant need for powerful religious compensators. When these compensators are in short supply, new forms of religion emerge that can meet the demand by offering the rewards necessary. In other words, the two American scholars agreed with Wilson that there was evidence of secularization. But they suggested that the history of religion exhibited patterns of cyclic decline and regeneration rather than a linear decline:

> Viewed in this way, secularization is not something new under the sun. It did not begin with the rise of science. . . . [and] secularization *does not bring the end of religion*. Rather, secularization is self-limiting in that it stimulates significant processes of reaction in other sectors of any religious economy.
>
> (Stark 1985: 302, his italics)

Stark and Bainbridge also challenged Wilson's claim that new religious movements are proof of the withdrawal of religion from public life. The two pointed to European data that showed that cults – groups inspired from somewhere besides the primary religion of the culture in which they were located – were more numerous and stronger in those regions where conventional churches were weak. The data also indicated that sects – breakaway Christian groups – abounded in areas where the Church was stronger. In Stark and Bainbridge's view, these facts undermined Wilson's thesis that there was a declining interest in religion in Europe. In fact, Europe, according to them, was not secular at all in the way envisaged by Wilson.

Stark and Bainbridge, in other words, were following a far more Durkheimian theoretical trajectory. They assumed that religion had an enduring function and that it would therefore always be needed. Disagreeing with Wilson, they saw religion as a universal that was more or less constant, and rejected the notion that it would be inexorably removed from the public sphere over time. Instead, like Durkheim, they believed that religious innovation and renewal are inevitable. They did, however, part company from Durkheim, in that the latter held that society requires religion. For Stark and Bainbridge, religion was an enduring phenomenon because of individuals' need for compensators. Nevertheless, they still clearly owed him a substantial intellectual debt.

Perhaps at least partly because of their theoretical divergence with Weber's vision, their thesis met with friendly ridicule on the other side of the Atlantic. Their most vocal adversary was the sociologist Roy Wallis, a former student of Wilson's. He accepted their premise that sectarian religious organizations become more rational with the passage of time. But Wallis argued that the figures offered by Stark to substantiate the view that revival and innovation was taking place in Europe were founded on too few cases. He also cast doubt on the accuracy of Stark's statistics, and suggested they were skewed. Wallis said that Stark should not have used numbers of cult movements in Europe as a basis for his claims that the continent was still religious. His objection was that just because someone opens an office 'does not mean that he has any customers' (Wallis 1986: 497). In so doing, he managed to convey the impression that the Americans had no idea about the religious situation in Europe. Therefore, their views on secularization were not to be accorded any degree of seriousness.

The 'rational choice' model

Stark, however, had only just begun his amicable assault on the bastions of European sociological expertise. Following other collaborative work, he reformulated his model along more sophisticated lines with Laurence Iannaccone (Stark and Iannaccone 1994). Like that of Stark and Bainbridge before, the framework of the revamped model was economic. It assumed a fairly constant need for religion since, they said, there is always human suffering that cannot be satisfactorily addressed by other means. It also assumed religious change to be a cyclic rather than a linear process. It differed from the earlier model, however, in that it focused on supply rather than demand.

Stark and Iannaccone attributed variations in devotion to discrepancies in the supply of religious services rather than to different levels of demand, or indeed to secularizing tendencies. In fact, the model dispensed with the need to posit processes of secularization entirely. Instead, it incorporated elements of rational choice theory. Consequently, it was predicated on the assumption that a free market is always more active and efficient than one dominated by a monopoly. The two presumed that this assumption holds good when applied to the religious as well as the commercial arena.

Stark and Iannaccone predicted that in those countries where there is a monopoly on religion, there is little interest in religion on the part of the population, and demand is low. Conversely, in those countries where religious organizations must compete for members, such as America, a higher degree of religious enthusiasm could be expected.

Like David Martin before them, but for different reasons, Stark and Iannaccone disagreed with the notion that there had been 'a golden age of faith'. They rejected the received wisdom that medieval Europe was an era in which religiosity was high, because it went against what their own model predicted should have been the case. As the Church had a monopoly during that period, their theory suggested that religious enthusiasm should have been correspondingly low. The two scholars also pressed the case, as Stark and Bainbridge had before, that modern Europe was more religious than British sociologists were prepared to admit. In other words, they turned the Wilsonian version of events on its head. Their view was that a more religious Europe had not given way to an increasingly secular one. Instead, they argued that Europeans had been less interested in religion in the past. This was because Europe had been dominated by a religious monopoly. More recently, they said, this situation had given way to a more devout contemporary Europe, as it was supplied by a plurality of religious organizations. And they presented historical as well as contemporary data to support their argument.

Their critics were not slow to respond. Some took exception to the model because of its economic orientation. It was suggested that models of behaviour linked to commercial monopolies and the free market could not, and should not, be applied unproblematically to religion. Others poured scorn on the idea that religious affiliation could ever be the result of 'rational choice'. Seeing the two as a contradiction in terms was perhaps because of the way in which religion has been associated with irrationality in dominant European discourses. The most vociferous critic of the new model in Britain, however, was Steve Bruce, a former student of Roy Wallis. A professor at the University of Aberdeen, Scotland, he, too, presented historical and contemporary data in support of his argument. Describing their 'iconoclasm' as 'misplaced', he, in by now time-honoured tradition, suggested that it was unfortunate that Stark and Iannaccone

> are not better acquainted with the work of British historians or with recent survey data. Only by making unreasonably light of the many signs of religiosity in pre-modern British culture and making unreasonably much of the very slight evidence of religious sentiment beyond the churches in contemporary Britain are they able to claim that Britain's religious climate has not changed drastically. Britain was once religious, it is now secular.
>
> (Bruce 1995: 428)

The dismissal, once more, conveyed the distinct impression that the Americans had got 'the Brits', and so by implication the whole of Europe, all wrong.

Secularization and confusion

A year later, Sharon Hanson, then engaged in postgraduate work at Kings College, London, conducted an examination of the arguments over secularization. Her analysis exposed weaknesses in both camps (Hanson 1996). First, she drew attention to the fact that Bruce, Stark and Iannaccone were often talking at cross purposes, and for this reason were not always so opposed as they appeared. One camp, she said, would often critically evaluate the claims of the other without taking into account that they were using different definitions of both secularization and religion. The result was confusion. Second, she noted that at times they seemed to use evidence to support their own view that could be more readily used to support the opposing side.

Third, said Hanson, the work she examined often relied heavily on historical data to legitimate claims. However, the data tended to be used without much circumspection:

> Historical data is presented as unproblematic, often juxtaposed to contemporary data, without any attempt to note the difficulty of comparing contemporary and historical data. Using historical data in this way lacks rigour, sources are not properly investigated and generalisations are hastily reached.
>
> (Ibid.: 164)

Hanson, additionally, pointed out that data appearing to suggest religion has lost social significance does not tell us *why* this might be so. Nevertheless, she said:

> Both Stark and Iannaccone (1994) and Bruce (1995, 1996) use their purported statistical proofs and historical narrative to speak of the why. They then use this rationale as proof that religion has, indeed, lost its significance or has not done so. Thus, a cyclical self-supporting argument is set up on weak proofs and propositions, gaining artificial credibility by mere repetition.
>
> (Ibid.: 164)

Notwithstanding these observations, Hanson was by no means entirely condemnatory of the positions of Bruce, Stark and Iannaccone. And all three have maintained their original allegiances thereafter (Bruce 2002; Swatos and Olson 2000). However, during the course of her critique she made a further point deserving of mention. This is, first, because she was not the first to make it. It therefore warrants inclusion on the grounds that it is a common criticism made of most secularization theories. Second, it has some bearing on a third formulation of religious change about to be, very briefly, outlined. Hanson, as others have done, noted that both critics and proponents of secularization have had a markedly 'christo-centric' understanding of 'religion'. The equation of Christianity with religion means that if the former appears to be in decline then so does the latter. However, religious affiliation has become increasingly plural throughout the world. In some areas, it might be the case that Christianity is undergoing a decline in influence in the public sphere. Given the multitude of faiths and beliefs, however, this fact does not necessarily signal the disappearance of religion altogether.

Religious pluralism

Pursuing this line of reasoning, a third group of scholars, albeit working independently of each other, have recently focused on our increasingly pluralistic religious 'landscape' rather than processes of secularization. Advocates of this approach, including Peter Berger and Grace Davie, have incorporated this pluralism into their own diagnoses of the state of religion. Rather than continuing the debate in terms of decline or persistence, they have identified diversity and fragmentation as more fruitful ways of thinking about religion today. Wilson used the contemporary proliferation of new religious movements to argue that religion was becoming an increasingly private, and often less 'authentic', affair. Stark and his associates used them to argue for continuing religious innovation. Grace Davie cites them simply as multiple religious constituencies in her argument that, while more people may believe rather than belong these days, religion still has an important, if less visible, function as a source of identity in multi-faith Britain (Davie 1994).

Some closing thoughts

What, then, is the status of secularization theory today? Lately, many scholars have come to agree with Thomas Luckmann's early comment that the secularization thesis is best described as a mythological account of the emergence of the modern world. However, it is not easy to dispense with the theory, on account of its Enlightenment presuppositions. As Casanova has noted, it:

> Is so intrinsically interwoven with all the theories of the modern world and with the self-understanding of modernity that one cannot simply discard the theory of secularization without putting into question the entire web, including much of the self-understanding of the social sciences.
>
> (Casanova 1994: 18)

It cannot be rejected without implicitly calling into question a host of other theories and assumptions commonly taken for granted. For instance, the idea that progress, brought about by intellectual means rather than by articles of faith, will eventually lead to a complete and rational understanding of the laws underpinning nature and society.

Because it is such an all-encompassing theory, it is also practically impossible to refute empirically, in whatever form it takes. For example, Wilson and others have suggested that the inexorable process they envisage might not be entirely linear. It could hypothetically occur at very different rates in different locations, depending on local conditions. At times, it might even seem to be reversed in the short term. So it is possible to challenge specific elements of their argument, for instance the unreflective adoption of a Christian idea of religion. But it is difficult to know what evidence could be brought to bear that would convincingly refute the argument in its entirety. A confirmed believer could always dismiss contrary evidence as a temporary setback, an insignificant exception to the rule, or as evidence of something other than 'religion' being at work: 'superstition', 'nationalism' or 'ethnic identity'.

It is also the case that, even if one accepts that religion has generally been removed from the public sphere, other scenarios than its decline can equally well explain this trend. For instance, a gender sensitive account might be that there has been a shift away from public, 'male-centred' religion. Individuals have moved towards private religious activity that is more 'female' in character, reflecting the increased value attached to 'the feminine' in the West. Or, as some have argued, it could be said that public Christianity has retreated because of immigration and competition resulting from increased global communication, rather than through secularization. Such an argument would be that it has been replaced by less traditional religious forms, reflecting the increasingly multicultural and option-ridden world in which we live. It is hard to see how either explanation is any less plausible than that of the Weberian sociologist.

As Karl Popper pointed out, millions of people believe in astrology because it is possible to assemble a wealth of evidence indicating that it 'really works' (1989). He reflected that believers believe in astrology, and many other theories, because of the propensity of human beings to see confirming instances all around them once they have adopted a particular perspective. But confirming instances cannot be used as proofs, since any particular situation can be interpreted in light of a particular theory. So Popper concluded that only a theory couched in such a way as to be open to indisputable refutation can be properly tested, and be said to be scientific. It is not possible to prove that astrology definitively works, said Popper, since its statements cannot be unequivocally falsified. The same can be said of secularization. Both have explanatory power, but cannot be subjected to rigorous scrutiny and refutation. Following Popper's argument, neither astrology nor secularization may be properly considered a scientific theory.

Steve Bruce, in particular, might protest at what I have just said. Indeed, in a 1996 article, Bruce put forward a number of statements in opposition to his own view. These included such hypotheses as: 'Insofar as it can be measured or gauged, compared with 1800, 1850, 1900, or 1950, there is now greater competition to join the clergy'. He then set about dispatching each one in order to show that secularization was occurring (Bruce 1996). But each of his arguments can be disputed, and in no case is his refutation unequivocal. For example, regarding the question of numbers joining the clergy, Bruce discounted the recent ordination of women in the United Kingdom and elsewhere as irrelevant. Instead, he focused on the fact that the younger sons of British gentry, who often chose to join the Church in centuries past, do not become ordained today in the same numbers as before. It is, however, equally possible to conclude that economic changes have meant that other career options have opened up to such individuals rather than to assume that this is evidence of secularization. Further, just because the constituencies of the would-be ordained have shifted is not proof of secularization either. Arguably, it is merely evidence of changing class structures and of women's increasing public participation. In other words, despite his hypotheses and testing, Bruce did not produce conclusive evidence for secularization over some other explanation. Yet those who have championed a more Durkheimian view of secularization, suggesting that religious innovation works in cyclic fashion, have not always been persuasive in making their case either. Their arguments have often rested on highlighting of instances of religion flourishing in contemporary society. On occasion, this has involved overlooking, or explaining away, apparent examples of religion in decline.

However, as in the case of astrology, this does not necessarily mean that any of the theories of secularization that have been considered are wrong. It simply means that they are impossible to test rigorously. We can take a persuasive and informed view in relation to secularization. We can try to think about religion without invoking it. But we cannot know beyond doubt whether the theory is correct or not, in any of its forms. And as with astrology, the view that we do adopt is likely to be coloured by our ideological and personal loyalties and prejudices. My own view of secularization is a case in point. For myself, I would like to think that what I mean by the term 'religion' would be enduring. Like many others, I can see plenty of evidence to support that view. On the other hand, I know that such evidence does not prove conclusively that 'religion' will survive. And it is always possible to argue over what is meant by 'religion'. So I am caught on the proverbial fence, and usually attempt to think about religious change in other terms. But while the utility of secularization theory may be in doubt, one thing is certain: if anyone in the future asks for your view on whether secularization is occurring, you should require him or her to first explain exactly what is meant by the question.

Bibliography

Berger, P. (1969) *The Sacred Canopy: Elements of a Sociological Theory of Religion*. Garden City, NY: Anchor Books.
  Berger examined the phenomenon of secularization in the second half of this classic work. In more recent works, Berger has rejected the notion of secularization.

Bruce, S. (1995) 'The Truth About Religion in Britain' in *Journal for the Scientific Study of Religion* 34: 417–430.
  The article comprised a succinct example of Bruce's argument.

Bruce, S. (1996) 'Religion in Britain at the Close of the 20th Century: a Challenge to the Silver Lining Perspective' in *Journal for Contemporary Religion* 11 (3): 261–275.
  Further arguments making the case for secularization.

Bruce, S. (2002) *God Is Dead: Secularization in the West*. Oxford: Blackwell.
  The book covered the arguments of major contributors to the secularization debate and includes a restatement of Bruce's position.

Casanova, J. (1994) *Public Religions in the Modern World*. Chicago: University of Chicago Press.
  An informative and well-researched book in which Casanova looked at what he termed the 'deprivatization' of religion in the modern world.

Davie, G. (1994) *Religion in Britain since 1945: Believing Without Belonging*. Oxford: Blackwell.
  Davie argued that religious belief persists, but not necessarily in traditional forms, hence her use of the phrase 'believing without belonging'.

Durkheim, É. (1912) *The Elementary Forms of Religious Life* (trans. Karen Fields 1995). New York: Free Press.
  Durkheim's classic work on religion, in which he concluded that, because it is essential to society, religion will not disappear.

Greeley, A. (1972) *Unsecular Man: The Persistence of Religion*. New York: Schocken.
  The book was an early rebuttal of Wilson's thesis, and especially its applicability to the United States.

Hanson, S. (1997) 'The Secularization Thesis: Talking at Cross Purposes' in *Journal of Contemporary Religion* 12(2): 159–180.
  A concise account of problems arising from the way terms and data are deployed in the secularization debate.

Martin, D. (1969) *The Religious and the Secular*. London: Routledge & Kegan Paul.
David Martin has produced a number of important works on secularization. This early work comprised another rebuttal to Wilson's thesis.

Popper, K. (1989) *Conjectures and Refutations: The Growth of Scientific Knowledge*. London: Routledge. 5th edn (revised).
In which Popper sets out the conditions under which a theory is properly scientific.

Stark, R. (1985) 'Europe's Receptivity to Religious Movements' in R. Stark (ed.) *Religious Movements: Genesis, Exodus and Numbers*. New York: Paragon.
A classic account of Stark and Bainbridge's thesis, in which Stark argued that Europe was far more religious than proponents of secularization suggested.

Stark, R. and L. R. Iannaccone (1994) 'A Supply-side Re-interpretation of the 'Secularization' of Europe' in *Journal for the Scientific Study of Religion* 33: 230–252.
The article outlines rational choice theory and their understanding of its contribution to the secularization debate.

Swatos, W. H. and Olson, D. V. (eds) (2000) *The Secularization Debate*. Lanham, MD: Rowman & Littlefield.
A collection of essays from critics and supporters of the secularization thesis.

Weber, M. (1930) *The Protestant Ethic and the Spirit of Capitalism* (trans. by Talcot Parsons). London: Allen & Unwin.
Weber's classic work on Protestantism and its secularizing impact.

Wallis, R. (1986) 'Figuring Out Cult Receptivity' in *Journal for the Scientific Study of Religion* 25: 494–503.
Roy Wallis's reply to Rodney Stark's 1985 article that argued that Europe was not as secular as had been suggested.

Wilson, B. (1966) *Religion in Secular Society*. Harmondsworth: Penguin.
Wilson's classic account of the removal of religion from the public sphere.

Chapter 17

Mysticism and spirituality

Richard King

What do we mean by mysticism and spirituality?

'Mysticism' and 'spirituality' have proven particularly difficult concepts to define for a number of reasons. First, such terms tend to be used in a rather woolly and ill-defined manner in everyday language. The adjective 'mystical', for instance, is commonly used to describe any object, person, event or belief, which has a vaguely mysterious aspect to it. It is also applied to extraordinary experiences of union, whether religious or not, and to the supernatural, the magical and the occult in general. 'Spiritual' is similarly vague in its popular usage. The term 'mysticism' as a specific category is of more recent origin, reflecting the modern love of '-isms,' and did not come into use until the end of the nineteenth century when it was used to denote that aspect of the Christian tradition which emphasised the indescribable (ineffable) nature of God and the importance of attaining an experiential union with the divine. Both terms are related to the term 'la mystique', which, as Michel de Certeau (1992) has demonstrated, first came to the fore in seventeenth-century France.

In the modern era mysticism has also been closely associated with the notion of spirituality and with the religions of the East. Today it is not uncommon for people to say that they are spiritual or that they have spiritual beliefs but that they are not religious, meaning of course that they do not affiliate with a particular religious institution or movement but still have some experience of the sacred. This association reflects modern shifts in Western understandings of religion since the Enlightenment and a tendency for many to distinguish between an inward and personal experience of the sacred (spirituality or mysticism) and allegiance to a particular form of organised religion (Carrette and King 2005). In a comparative context mysticism has come to denote those aspects of the various religious traditions which emphasise unmediated experience of oneness with the ultimate reality, however differently conceived. However, in the late twentieth century, the term of choice for those wishing to emphasise a more individualistic and less tradition-bound approach to the mystical, has been the notion of 'spirituality'. This reflects cultural trends related to secularization and the 'de-traditionalization' of contemporary religious forms (as in much of 'the New Age') in the West. However, for the sake of understanding the trajectory of twentieth-century scholarship within this field of study, this chapter will generally refer to the phenomenon under discussion as 'mysticism' rather than 'spirituality' since this was the preferred term within scholarship until fairly recently. The contemporary preference for the language of 'spirituality' will be briefly addressed at the end of this chapter.

Within Christian theological circles mysticism has often been viewed with great suspicion being seen as a potential source of heresy and schism. If left unchecked, it has been argued, the unitive aspects of the mystical experience can lead to the adoption of heretical doctrines such as monism (everything is one), pantheism (everything is divine) and antinomianism (the claim to have transcended conventional moral guidelines). The mystic's claim to have experienced an unmediated experience of the divine has also been seen by many theologians as a direct threat to the authority of the Church as the sole mediator between the divine and human realms. Nevertheless, many of the most revered figures in the Christian tradition have been described as mystics, representing a vibrant tradition of orthodox spiritual teachings. In the twentieth century, interest in the cross-cultural dimensions of mysticism has also been seen by many as evidence of a spiritual common core at the centre of all world religions, providing a basis for inter-faith dialogue between religious traditions for some, and the hope of a truly globalised spirituality for others.

Origins of the term 'mystical'

Although the category of mysticism is relatively modern, its adjectival form – 'the mystical' has a much longer history. In the pre-Christian era the Greek term *mystikos* was used by the various mystery religions of the early Roman Empire. These movements usually focused upon specific deities, such as the Goddess Isis, or the God Mithras. In this context, the mystical seems primarily to have been concerned with the secrecy of ritual practices performed by initiates of these movements. The secrecy of *mystikos* functioned to exclude outsiders. Etymologically, both 'mysticism' and 'mystical' seem to derive from the Greek *muo*, meaning to close. This derivation reflects the esoteric nature of the Graeco-Roman mystery religions. The mystical therefore denotes the practice of closing one's eyes or of closing one's lips (i.e. remaining silent). In the modern study of mysticism both relate to different ways of understanding the nature of mysticism. On the one hand the mystical is often taken to be an experience which goes beyond the range and scope of everyday sensory experiences (such as visions). On the other hand, mysticism is often associated with the ineffable – that about which one should not, or perhaps cannot, speak.

As Louis Bouyer (1990) has demonstrated there are three aspects to the early Christian understanding of 'the mystical' – all of which remain intertwined in their usage:

1   *Hermeneutics* – the mystical as the allegorical, spiritual or hidden meaning of scripture.
2   *Liturgy* – the mystical as a description of the mysterious power of Christian liturgy, in particular the Eucharist as the act of communion with the Body and Blood of Christ.
3   *Experience* – the mystical as an experiential knowledge of the divine.

Medieval conceptions of the mystical

In the sixth century CE we also find the development of the notion of a mystical theology in the works of Pseudo-Dionysius (so named because of the false attribution of his works to Dionysius the Areopagite, a disciple of St Paul mentioned in Acts 17: 34). For Dionysius there are two fundamental ways of speaking about the divine: kataphatic or affirmative theology, which speaks of God in terms of positive attributes ('God is good', God is love', etc.) and apophatic or negative theology, which takes seriously the mysterious, and indescribable nature of the divine. Negative theology, therefore, involves rejecting all affirmative statements about God and for Dionysius is also to be known as 'mystical theology'.

The path of negation involves an ascent of the hierarchy of reality, until one reaches the ineffable and divine Oneness that is the source of all things. One can speak positively about the things that God creates but not about the transcendent Cause Himself. Indeed it is Dionysius who first coined the term 'hierarchy' to denote a graduated conception of creation with God at the summit and various angelic beings acting as mediators between the divine and human realms. However, for Dionysius positive and negative theologies are intrinsically related and cannot occur in isolation from each other. Negation cannot occur unless one first makes an affirmation. Similarly, affirmative statements about God must be negated at a higher level if one is to avoid making a false image out of one's own limited conception of God. Negative theology is necessary therefore if we are to take seriously the transcendent nature of the divine. Moreover, as one ascends the celestial hierarchy towards God, words fall away, whilst at lower levels words become more and more effective in their representation of reality. The goal, argued Dionysius, was for the Christian to aspire to the highest realm and achieve a knowledge of God which left all conventional knowledge behind in a mystical 'darkness of unknowing':

> We would be like sculptors who set out to carve a statue. They remove every obstacle to the pure view of the hidden image, and simply by this act of clearing aside (*aphairesis*, denial) they show up the beauty which is hidden.
> (*Mystical Theology* Ch. 2, Pseudo-Dionysius, 1987: 138)

Negative theology, that is the idea that the divine being is too magnificent to be approached or described in any form, has come to be regarded as one of the defining features of mysticism and displays the unmistakable influence of Greek Neoplatonic philosophy. Medieval works such as the anonymously authored English text *The Cloud of Unknowing*, and the writings of figures such as the German Dominican Meister Eckhart (1260–1328) and the highly intellectual path of negation involves the renunciation of all images of God as inadequate. God must always transcend the limitation of our human conception of the divine if He (She/It) is truly the supreme Creator of everything. As Eckhart explains:

> Unsophisticated teachers say that God is pure being. He is as far above being as the highest angel is above a gnat. I would be speaking incorrectly in calling God a being as if I called the sun pale or black. God is neither this nor that. A master says 'Whoever imagines that he has understood God, if he knows anything, it is not God that he knows.' However, in saying that God is not a being and is above being, I have not denied being to God, rather I have elevated it in him.
>
> (German Sermon 9 in McGinn, 1986: 256)

Although ultimately rejecting all intellectual attempts to represent the divine, the popularity and practice of negative (apophatic) theology tended to presume significant theological training and a knowledge of Christian and neoplatonic philosophical arguments. To identify mysticism in general and Christian mysticism in particular exclusively with these apophatic trends would be to ignore the diversity of trends encompassed by this term. As well as the highly intellectual path of negation there were also more affective strands of Christian mysticism represented by figures like Bernard of Clairvaux (1090–1153), Hildegard of Bingen (1098–1179) and Julian of Norwich (b. 1342). This trend placed a much greater emphasis upon love and the emotions as a means of encountering God rather than a highly abstract and intellectual path to the divine.

The scriptural basis for these more affective types of mysticism was the Song of Songs (*Song of Solomon*), a romantic poem that forms part of the Hebrew Bible/ Old Testament. Although originally a composition outlining the loving relationship between God and Israel, early Christian writers tended to interpret the Song of Songs as a poetic exploration of the relationship between God (the Bridegroom) and the Church (the Bride). However, from the time of Origen (*c.* 185–254 CE), the Song of Songs has also been given a 'mystical interpretation' as an exposition of the loving intimacy that characterises God's relationship with the soul. Bernard of Clairvaux composed an extensive commentary upon the Song of Songs, outlining a three-fold path of pilgrimage in the soul's path to God. This began with the kiss on the feet and culminating in a union with the divine which he describes, following the Song of Songs, as 'the kiss on the mouth' (*Song of Solomon* 1: 2). The apparent eroticism of much of this literature has caused some controversy in Christian theological circles, with scholars such as Dean Inge (1899) and Anders Nygren (1953) criticising what they see as a confusion of the carnality of *eros* with the spiritual love of *agape*.

The medieval period in particular, however, also saw an explosion of activity by female mystics. Mostly excluded from formal theological training and therefore uninitiated in the abstract intellectualism of the mysticism of negation, many of these women placed a great deal of emphasis upon visions as a source of spiritual knowledge and authority, and in some cases were persecuted and even executed for their claims. Modern feminist scholarship has become increasingly interested in the resurgence of female spirituality during this period and the historical task of recapturing some of the silenced voices of these remarkable women has only just begun (Bynum 1982; Petroff 1986; Beer 1992; Jantzen 1995).

William James and the modern study of mysticism

In the modern era the hermeneutic and liturgical dimensions of the mystical have been largely forgotten, as have the complex network of social forces and power-relations that constituted all claims to mystical insight. As a result the experiential dimensions of the category have come to the fore, often to the exclusion of broader understandings of the subject matter. An excellent example of this is the influential work of the philosopher, psychologist and early scholar of the mystical, William James (1842–1910). In his 1901–2 Gifford Lectures (subsequently published as *The Varieties of Religious Experience*), James provides the classic exposition of mysticism in terms of mystical experience.

James was interested in establishing an intellectual framework for the comparative study of mysticism and religious experience in general. For him this framework was provided by the emerging discipline of psychology, though James remained critical of reductionist approaches which interpreted religious experiences either in terms of neurological functions of the brain or as repressed sexual desires projected in the form of an erotic encounter with the divine. An important dimension of James' approach was his sensitivity to the mystical impulse within humans. For James, however, institutional and organised religion was 'second hand' in the sense that the true core of religion resided in individual religious experiences. Accounts of such experiences therefore provided the basic data for James' psychological analysis.

While the emphasis upon the study of private and extraordinary experiences has come to dominate the modern study of mysticism since James it is important to realise the influence of the European Enlightenment in the development of this approach to the subject matter. In the modern era the separation of the Church and State and the process of secularisation has precipitated a movement away from traditional patterns of organised religion. Migration of ethnic groups as a result of colonial expansion, the rise of individualism and modern capitalism have also resulted in a much greater awareness of the multi-cultural nature of society and an emphasis upon personal choice with regard to issues of religious affiliation. One consequence of these trends within the Western world has been the tendency to conceive of religion as essentially a *private* rather than a public matter. We can see the emergence of this orientation for instance in James' understanding of the mystical, which is now almost exclusively related to the extraordinary and private experiences of individuals, thereby ignoring or at least underplaying the social, communal and, some might argue, political dimensions of the mystical in the history of Christianity (see Jantzen 1995; King 1999; Carrette and King 2005).

The study of mysticism since James has taken a peculiarly psychological turn and has often been seen as the study of 'altered states of consciousness' and the phenomena associated with their attainment. James suggests that although such states are inaccessible to the ordinary rational mind (as it is often called), but such experiences may impart exceptional meaning and truth-giving quality to the agent: '[O]ur normal waking consciousness, rational consciousness as we call it, is but one special type of consciousness, whilst all about it, parted from it by the filmiest of screens, there lie potential forms of consciousness entirely different' (James 1977: 374).

James' characterisation of mysticism continues to have a powerful influence upon contemporary conceptions of the subject matter. Mystical experiences, he argued exhibit four basic attributes: ineffability, noetic quality, transiency and passivity. In offering this account James was not arguing for some trans-cultural common core that might be thought to underlie the different forms of mystical experience, rather he was interested providing a theoretical framework for exploring the rich diversity of mystical texts and traditions throughout the world. The first quality, ineffability refers to the indescribable nature of the mystical experience. Such experiences, James felt, were so extraordinary in nature that ordinary language struggles to express their innermost nature. The first attribute, ineffability, has clearly been an important dimension of the mystical throughout history and in this regard James is following in the tradition of figures such as Pseudo-Dionysius and Eckhart in the association of the mystical with negative theology. Nevertheless, as recent scholarly work has suggested (Turner 1995; Jantzen 1995) when pre-modern Christian mystics made claims of ineffability they were invariably referring to the transcendent nature of the Creator and not to a transient and extraordinary state of consciousness.

Second, noetic quality refers to the impact mystical experiences have upon the mystic. Such experiences strike one as undeniably true, as the acquisition of some insight or knowledge of reality – the way things really are. James stresses this dimension of the mystical to distinguish such experiences from hallucinations and delusions. There is something about mystical experiences that provide their own self-validation for the experiencer. However, James is quick to point out, the cognitive authority of such experiences is only applicable to the individual concerned. One cannot expect those who have not had such an experience to take such insights on faith alone. This reflects James' own interest in the role of philosophical analysis as a publicly accountable arbiter of such experience. This issue of course brings up a number of interesting questions. What authority should one ascribe to mystical experiences per se? How might one distinguish between authentic and inspirational experiences and delusional or demonic ones? Traditionally, the Church adopted a variety of criteria for assessing the validity of mystical experiences ranging from conformity to orthodoxy and scripture to an examination of the effects of such experiences on the conduct of the individual. The proof of the pudding is in the eating, and an authentic mystical experience, it was argued, should at least result in moral behaviour and actions in accordance with the Church. Such criteria, of course, will not satisfy those who do not feel bound by traditional ecclesiastical authority, especially those living in a modern secular era where the Church no longer holds sway. Hence James' interest in the role of philosophy as a rational arbiter for such truth claims.

The third quality of mystical experiences in James's account is transiency. Such experiences are limited in duration. Of course one is entitled to point out that all states of consciousness (including everyday 'waking' consciousness) are also transient if only in the rather trivial sense that we regularly enter dream and deep sleep states throughout our lives. Moreover, it would seem that we enter a number of different states of consciousness even whilst awake, reflecting mood changes, levels of concentration, daydreaming, etc. James has made the assumption here that so-called 'normative' states of mind predominate throughout our lives and that they should be regarded as normative. Interesting work has been pursued in this regard by transpersonal psychologists such as Charles Tart (1969) and Arthur Deikman (1980, 1982) in an attempt to take seriously the insights to be gained from an analysis of so-called 'altered states of consciousness'.

The fourth and final feature of mystical experiences, according to James, is their passivity. Such experiences tend to render the subject immobile in the face of an overwhelming presence or sense of the unity of all things. Part of James's point here is to acknowledge the sense in which such episodes are experienced as 'given' rather than the result of an overly active imagination. However, passivity implies that the experience is given by some external power rather than being a consequence of the agency of the mystic. In theistic traditions such as Christianity it is often believed that such raptures are a gift from God, but this ignores traditions such as Buddhism and some forms of Hinduism where the highest states of meditative concentration (samadhi) are the result of sustained yogic practice and the cultivation of a receptive mind. Such traditions advocate the explicit cultivation of meditative states as a prerequisite on the path to enlightenment and need not imply passivity on the part of the mystic. Moreover, although James does not wish to imply this in his own analysis, the association of mysticism with passivity, otherworldliness and quietism is flagrantly contradicted by the countless examples of figures such as Teresa of Avila, Francis of Assisi, Hildegard of Bingen and Mahatma Gandhi, all of whom were inspired to social activism by their mystical experiences and not in spite of them.

The mystical and the numinous

Another important figure in the early study of mysticism was Rudolf Otto (1869–1937). In 1917 Otto published *Das Heilige* (translated into English as *The Idea of the Holy* in 1923), an attempt to outline the central features of mystical and religious experiences. Otto was heavily influenced by the German theologian Friedrich Schleiermacher for whom religion was best characterised by the 'feeling of creatureliness' when confronted with the awesome power of the Wholly Other. Otto, like Schleiermacher and James before him, believed that the core of religion resided in experience; more specifically, the experience of the holy or the sacred (Latin: *numen*). Otto characterised this 'numinous feeling' using the Latin terms *mysterium tremendum et fascinans*. Religious experiences involve a sense of being overpowered by a wholly other or transcendental presence. They induce in the subject a sense of mystery, awe, dread and fearfulness and yet at the same time are strangely attractive and fascinating. These features of the religious impulse are neither rational nor irrational, Otto argued, but constitute the non-rational feeling that provides the basis for all subsequent religious expression.

Otto believed that the non-rational dimensions of religion were too easily overlooked in theological discussions about the notion of God. Indeed, it is this non-rational aspect which constitutes the essential core of all religious experiences. Otto then was something of an apologist for the mystical within Protestant circles, arguing explicitly against the association of the mystical with the irrational (as opposed to the non-rational). Otto accepted that religion requires rationalism, which for him means theological orthodoxy, but it also requires the *mysterium* element in religion, that is the non-rational or supra-rational. It is this which orthodoxy attempts to express in rational terms. The problem with mysticism (and for many Protestant theologians, mysticism has often been seen as a problem!), is that it often results either in the identification of oneself with the transcendent creator (pantheism) or a complete negation of the reality of the self when compared to the magnificence of the wholly other. Both positions are indeed erroneous, Otto argued, because they over-emphasise the non-rational dimension of the experience and therefore do not take seriously enough the role of reason (and orthodoxy) in the interpretation and framing of the numinous experience: '[E]ssentially mysticism is the stressing to a very high degree, indeed the overstressing, of the non-rational or supra-rational elements in religion; and it is only intelligible when so understood' (Otto 1959: 22).

Mysticism then is fundamentally grounded in something akin to Schleiermacher's feeling of creatureliness – described by Otto as *mysterium tremendum et fascinans* – and involves either an explicit *identification with* or an *obliteration of* the subject in relation to God – the wholly other. This means of course that mystical experiences are not *essentially* different from the broader range of religious experiences available to humanity, being little more than an over-emphasised sense of the numinous.

Two of the best illustrations of the numinous feeling in religious literature are Arjuna's vision of Krishna in the Hindu text the *Bhagavad Gita* and Isaiah's vision of the throne of God from the Old Testament:

> I see you everywhere, many-armed, many-stomached, many-mouthed, many-eyed, infinite in form; I cannot find out your end, your middle or your beginning – Lord of the universe form of everything . . . This space between heaven and earth is filled by you alone, as is every direction. Having seen this, your marvellous terrible form – the three worlds totter -great Self! . . . Vishnu, seeing you touching the sky, shining, rainbow-hued, cavern-mouthed, with luminous distended eyes, I am shaken to the core; I can find neither resolution nor rest . . . Seeing your mouths dancing with tusks, like the flames of universal dissolution, I am disorientated and without shelter. Have mercy, lord of gods, home of the world!
>
> (*Bhagavad Gita* Ch. 11: 16, 20, 24, 25, Johnson 1994: 50–1)

> I saw the Lord sitting upon a throne, high and lifted up; and his train filled the temple. Above him stood the seraphim; each had six wings: with two he covered his face, and with two he covered his feet, and with two he flew. And one called to another and said:
>
> 'Holy, holy, holy is the Lord of hosts; the whole earth is full of his glory.'
>
> And the foundations of the thresholds shook at the voice of him who called, and the house was filled with smoke.
>
> (The Book of Isaiah, 6: 1–4, *Revised Standard Version of the Bible*, 1973: 604)

For Otto, the numinous feeling is present to varying degrees in a variety of religious experiences, from the sense of awe when gazing at the stars at night, a sense of the presence of God when taking part in a religious act (e.g. the Eucharist), to the sense of wonder and majesty when 'communing with nature'. Otto, however, was clear that the numinous is a category in its own right and should not be reduced to or explained in terms of profane terms or categories. This clearly is one reason why Otto describes the numinous using Latin terminology in order to distinguish it from everyday feelings of fear, mystery, fascination and awe. The numinous is an irreducible category. In other words, religious experience cannot simply be explained in terms of 'profane' and everyday emotions. In this sense Otto is putting forward a phenomenological account of the numinous experience – that is one which purports to describe the phenomena of religious experience without attempting to reduce it into non-religious categories (i.e. in terms of everyday feelings and emotions). This is important aspect of Otto's approach since as a Protestant theologian he believes in the Christian God. Consequently, he is at pains to avoid any form of reductionism – that is any attempt to explain religion and religious impulses in terms of non-religious categories. Otto explains the similarities between numinous and profane feelings as an analogy of associated feelings, but he warns readers that if you cannot direct your mind to a moment of deeply-felt religious experience then you should not bother to read his book since you will not be able to understand its significance (Otto 1959: 8)!

Scholars have drawn attention to a number of problems with Otto's account of the numinous. Although Otto describes the mystical as an overstressing of the non-rational he nowhere questions this neo-Kantian assumption and its explicit polarisation of the mystical and the rational. Many of the world's great mystics have also been great systematisers and philosophers. Furthermore, despite Otto's great interest in the mystical systems of the East (e.g. Otto 1932), his work remains fundamentally framed by his own liberal Protestantism. Consequently, Otto's account of the numinous experience fits rather well with the theistic experiences of the Judaeo-Christian and Islamic traditions (and also one might argue with theistic elements within other religions such as Hinduism), but does not work so well when applied to non-theistic traditions such as Buddhism, Jainism and Taoism where experiences are not seen as an encounter between a creature and an overpoweringly majestic wholly other. Indeed, even within the Christian tradition, Otto's account is problematic when applied to figures such as Eckhart where theism appears to shade into monism. Otto's response of course would be that here the overpowering nature of the numinous can indeed fool the mystic into thinking that the duality between Creator and Created has been completely obliterated. Such theological pronouncements, however, will not satisfy those who do not feel bound by Otto's allegiance to traditional notions of Christian orthodoxy. It has also been suggested that Otto's account is patriarchal and gender exclusive, insofar as it ignores experiences of the divine which emphasise not an overpowering Father but an intimate and loving mother-goddess (Raphael 1994).

Concern about the universal applicability of Otto's conception of the numinous has led others to construct typologies for the different types of mysticism. Ninian Smart (1965) for instance, has argued that the numinous and the mystical actually represent radically different types of religious experience. The numinous is an experience of a transcendent otherness and tends to be dualistic, theistic and prophetic in nature. In stark contrast mystical experiences involve an overwhelming appreciation of the underlying unity of existence and an overcoming of dualistic boundaries between self and other. Smart argues that recognition of the difference between these two types of religious experience allows us to appreciate the relative role and significance of such experiences within the various world religions. Traditions which privilege the numinous such as mainstream Judaism, Islam (except Sufism) and mainstream Protestantism tend to devalue, or at least accord far less value, to mystical experiences. On the other hand some traditions explicit favour mystical experiences of union according them more authority than numinous experiences of a wholly other. For Smart this category is represented by Theravada Buddhism, Jainism and Samkhya-Yoga.

However, there are a number of religions that accept the validity of both the numinous and the mystical, though usually with one placed above the other according to the dominant doctrinal stance of the tradition. Thus, for the Advaita Vedanta, the Hindu school or radical monism, a theistic appreciation of the divine is accorded provisional status but only for as long as one has not achieved a direct realisation of the identity of oneself with Brahman – the absolute ground of all being. Similarly, in some Mahayana forms of Buddhism there is an acceptance of devotional beliefs and practices, though these are ultimately to be relinquished once one realises that everything is empty of inherent existence (*shunya-svabhava*). On the other hand,

Roman Catholicism generally values the numinous (as Christianity in general has done throughout its history), but does accord some validity to the mystical path, so long as it remains within the boundaries of orthodoxy. As Smart's analysis suggests then, the problem for the Christian mystic historically has been explaining how an experience of union with the divine remains within the boundaries of an orthodoxy founded upon the truth of the numinous experience. This has led most Christian mystics to provide analogies and descriptions of their experiences which safeguard the numinous regard for dualism, whilst at the same time emphasising the unity of God and the soul. Thus, the predominant Christian analogy for such experiences has been of a loving communion between a bridegroom (God) and his bride (the soul). Those mystics who have offered a more straightforward monistic interpretation of their experiences (such as the Muslim al-Ghazali and the Dominican theologian Meister Eckhart) have incurred the wrath of their respective religious authorities and been branded heretics by their critics. Similarly, in Theravada Buddhism, faith (*shraddha*) and devotion to the Buddha is accorded less authority than an experience of one of the higher jhanas, where distinctions between subject and object are relinquished.

How many types of mysticism are there?

Much of the literature on the study of mysticism, particularly in the 1970s and 1980s, has been concerned with questions of classification. How many different types of mysticism are there? Some writers, most notably Aldous Huxley, have argued that mysticism represents a common core or thread that is present in all of the major world religions. As that which unites all religions, mysticism therefore constitutes a perennial philosophy which occurs in a variety of different cultural and religious contexts throughout human history. In his book, *The Perennial Philosophy* (1944), Huxley provides selections from the writings of a variety of mystics the world over (in English translation) as a means of demonstrating their fundamental unanimity. Other scholars, such as R. C. Zaehner, have rejected this view arguing that the doctrinal differences between these figures are too profound to be ignored or pushed under the carpet. Zaehner suggests that there are three fundamental types of mysticism: theistic, monistic and panenhenic ('all-in-one') or nature mysticism. The theistic category includes most forms of Jewish, Christian and Islamic mysticism and occasional Hindu examples such as Ramanuja and the *Bhagavad Gita*. Theistic mysticism is considered by Zaehner to be superior to the other two categories not only in its appreciation of God and His creation but also in the strong moral imperative that it provides. The monistic type, which Zaehner argues is based upon an experience of the unity of one's own soul, includes Buddhism and Hindu schools such as Samkhya and Advaita Vedanta. Finally, panenhenic or nature mysticism seems to refer to those examples that do not fit easily into his theistic or monistic categories. For Zaehner any experience of unity or fusion with the outside world, whether induced by drugs, the animistic experiences of (so-called) 'primitive' religions, or the writings of poets such as Wordsworth and Blake can be placed in this category. A number of scholars, notably Ninian Smart (see Woods, 1980: 78–91) and Frits Staal (1975: 73–5), have criticised Zaehner for the theological violence his approach does to non-theistic traditions, forcing them into a framework which privileges Zaehner's own liberal Catholicism. Buddhism, for instance, rejects monism as a philosophical position along with any notions of a permanent soul and the Hindu school of Samkhya is avowedly dualistic in nature.

Zaehner is also criticised by Walter T. Stace in his book *Mysticism and Philosophy* (1960) on similar grounds. Stace argues that doctrinal differences between religious traditions are inappropriate criteria when making cross-cultural comparisons of mystical experiences. Mystics of course are predisposed to describe their experiences according to their own cultural and doctrinal background. These differences in interpretation do not necessarily represent differences in the nature of the experiences themselves. Nevertheless, for Stace mystical experiences can be classified into two basic types: introvertive and extrovertive. Introvertive experiences constitute the mystical core of religion, being an introspective and non-sensory awareness of the unity of all things. The extrovertive experience is only a partial realisation of this union, being an outwardly focused and sensory apprehension of the harmony of the universe.

Mystical experience and interpretation

The question of the relationship between mystical experiences and their interpretation has become one of the central concerns of the contemporary study of mysticism. For scholars such as Stace and Smart mystical experiences are phenomenologically the same cross-culturally but differ as a result of the specific interpretations or doctrinal ramifications that are subsequently applied to them by mystics. However, scholars such as Steven Katz reject any attempt to drive a wedge between experiences and their interpretations. Katz argues that it is not just the interpretation but the *experience itself* which is conditioned by the cultural and religious background of the mystic. Christian mystics have Christian mystical experiences and Buddhists have Buddhist ones. This should not surprise us, Katz argues, since this is precisely what the culture and traditions of these mystics condition them to experience (1978: 26–7).

According to Katz – it is not possible to have a pure or unmediated experience. There is no such thing, he argues, as an experience that is free from interpretation or any recognisable content. Katz describes his work as a 'plea for recognition of differences'. There is no perennial philosophy or cross-cultural unanimity between mystics of different religious traditions. Contrary to perennialists such as Huxley and Stace, Katz argues that when a Buddhist speaks of emptiness and Meister Eckhart discusses the nothingness of the Godhead they are not saying the same thing at all. Buddhists reject the idea of an all-powerful creator deity, while Eckhart as a Dominican theologian takes this presupposition for granted. Whereas Buddhists believe that there are no absolute beings or entities (since everything is empty of independent or inherent existence), Christians like Eckhart believe that the world is such only because God – the absolute first cause of everything, creates it. Even the claim that the experience or underlying reality is ineffable does not necessarily imply a common core since if one cannot truly speak about the ultimate reality, how can one be sure one is speaking about the same ultimate reality?

It is probably fair to say that Katz's position has become the dominant orientation amongst scholarship in the field of the comparative study of mysticism since the 1980s. However, more recently there have been a number of critical responses to Katz's position, focusing particularly upon his claim that it is not possible to have an unmediated experience, devoid of conceptual or cultural baggage. It is clear for instance that Katz's stance leaves no room for the unconditioned awareness of reality that is presumed in Buddhist notions of enlightenment (*bodhi*), the Taoist ideal of uncultivated spontaneity (*tzu-jan*) and the non-conceptual state of meditation (*nirvikalpa samadhi*) advocated by many Hindu schools of thought, such as Yoga and Advaita Vedanta. Many scholars of mysticism have been understandably reluctant to rule out the fundamental goals of these traditions, effectively undermining the object of one's analysis before one has even begun. Donald Evans, for instance, asks rhetorically who is Steven Katz to say that such unmediated experiences are impossible? (Evans 1989: 54). Similarly, Robert Forman offers his own autobiographical account of such an experience as an empirical refutation of Katz's thesis (1990: 28). Sallie King has also argued that the experience of drinking coffee, whilst clearly mediated by cultural factors and expectations cannot be reduced to those factors alone. There is simply something about drinking coffee for the first time (whether one likes it or not) that can never be conveyed by descriptions or preparations for such an experience. The mediated aspect of the coffee drinking experience then is a factor but not the most significant aspect of the experience. As an alternative to Katz's (neo-Kantian) model of experience King advocates the adoption of a more open-ended or agnostic approach which allows for the possibility of unmediated experiences, without necessarily implying that they provide insights into the nature of reality (King 1988: 277).

The question of drug induced mysticism

Since time immemorial naturally occurring hallucinogens have been utilised in religious contexts to induce altered states of consciousness. The ancient Vedic hymns, dating from at least 1500 BCE, contain many hymns to the god Soma, a psychotropic plant (possibly fly agaric) utilised in Vedic sacrificial rituals as a means of communing with the gods (*deva*) and intuiting the sacred meanings of the ritual act. Peyote has been used for millennia as a sacramental herb by native Americans as an aid on vision quests. In China, Taoist practitioners have utilised a variety of herbs to induce visions of the gods, as have shamans, in general, the world over.

The question of the status of drug-induced mystical experiences has been the subject of considerable discussion among contemporary scholars of mysticism. Broadly speaking, writers are separated into three camps. Some argue that drugs can expand the horizons of the mind allowing the subject to gain greater insight into the nature of reality. Classic exponents of this position have been Aldous Huxley and Timothy Leary, the so-called 'LSD guru' of the 1960s. Others reject this position, most notably the scholar R. C. Zaehner, who argue that drug-induced experiences are delusory, distorting our perception of reality. A third group, represented by scholars such as Frits Staal, remain open minded on this issue and call for further research.

In 1954 Aldous Huxley published *The Doors of Perception*, an account of his experiments with the drug mescaline. Huxley described a mystical experience of the 'unfathomable mystery of pure being' where sensations became greatly enhanced and where he became aware of 'being my Not-Self in the Not-Self which was the chair' (Huxley 1954: 19). He also drew comparisons (without directly equating) his experiences with those found in the literature of the various world religions. Huxley's account has been criticised by R. C. Zaehner, then Spalding Professor of Comparative Religion and Ethics at the University of Oxford, in his book *Mysticism, Sacred and Profane* (1957). Zaehner rejects Huxley's claim that drug-induced mystical experiences offer greater insight into the nature of reality and also questions the belief that they resemble the mystical experiences of the major world religions. Zaehner's own experiment with mescaline led to a trivial and uncomfortable experience and an upset stomach. Zaehner argued that while it may be possible to induce an experience of oneness with the natural world (a sensory or extrovertive experience of the world as a unity), it is not possible to induce an authentic experience of God through drugs since this would conflict with the Catholic doctrine of grace. One might respond by suggesting that the Creator has merely provided access to an appreciation of the divine by the creation of mind-altering substances in the natural world. Zaehner's theological approach and the privileging of theistic forms of mysticism as superior will do little to convince those whom do not share his particular religious beliefs and affiliation.

Clearly the expectations and the mindset of the individual subject have an important role to play in the evaluation of drug-induced experiences. Huxley was clearly influenced by Buddhism and Hindu Vedanta in his account of his experiences. Indeed, in a manner reminiscent of the neo-Hindu position of Swami Vivekananda, Huxley believed that his experiments with mescaline provided further evidence of the enduring validity of monistic experiences as well as the underlying unity of mysticism in the various world religions. Similarly, we can see the influence of Zaehner's Roman Catholic affiliation in his own discussion of this question. One's attitude and mind-set clearly influences the impact of the experience and the decision as to whether it is a case of *mysterium tremendum* or *delirium tremens*.

Nevertheless, even if one accepts that it is difficult to distinguish between drug-induced experiences and those achieved by other means (e.g. fasting, meditation, the grace of God, etc.), one might still reject the use of drugs for reasons other than the nature of the experience itself. As Frits Staal suggests one of the traditional reasons for censuring the use of drugs to induce religious experiences is the potential threat this brings to institutionalised religion. Staal in fact suggests that the religious criticism of drugs is rather similar to the Church's censure of Galileo's telescope as an instrument of the Devil (Staal 1975: 176–7). As Alan Watts has argued 'Mystical insight is no more in the chemical itself than biological knowledge is in the microscope.' (1965: 20, cited in Staal 1975: 176). Indeed for Watts, as for Huxley, mind-altering drugs are useful starters on the mystical path but can hardly function as a substitute for it. This is an important point to acknowledge since the nature and impact of an experience is clearly influenced by the context, length of preparation, motivations and expectations of the subject. One would expect greater significance to be attributed to experiences gained through the sacramental use of peyote than one would find in the case of a purely recreational use of drugs to achieve a temporary high. As the Hindu text, *Yoga Sutra* 1.12 suggests, states of higher awareness require the cultivation of detachment and vigilant practice to have any lasting impact. Staal (1975: 157) makes a similar point by drawing attention to the impact modern modes of transport can have on religious pilgrimages:

In many religions, pilgrimages are considered meritorious, partly because they require a certain amount of sacrifice or at least discomfort. But they also lead to a certain place, generally an inaccessible spot where a temple or other sacred structure or object exists. With the improvement of modern transportation most inaccessible places have become rather accessible ... The difficult way has become the easy way ... Of course, the physical result, viz. the presence of the worshipper-cum-traveller at a certain place, is just the same ... But expectations grow and the subjective experience is generally not the same. This analogy indicates that we cannot eliminate the possibility that the physical and brain states of a college-kid who has taken a drug are in relevant respects the same as those of a Buddha. Yet their mental states (which might have physical correlates too) need not for that reason be identical.

Expectation and the duration of the path, therefore, can be instrumental factors in the depth of impact, long-term effects and nature of the final experience. Staal, however, remains critical of arguments based upon the immorality or dangerous nature of drug use. Many drugs have no chemically habitual aspect and although some may have long-term side effects if overused, so does staring through a telescope if done too often. Should we give up astronomy? Why, Staal asks, are activities such as the exploration of outer space or climbing Mt Everest to be admired, but the exploration of inner space through the careful and structured use of drugs to be rejected as dangerous and life threatening?

It is not surprising that the religious use of drugs has not met with the approval of the religious establishments. Institutionalised religions are not so much concerned with religious or mystical experience as with ethics, morality and the continuation of the *status quo*.

(Staal 1975: 176)

Nevertheless, Staal remains non-committal on the question of whether drugs clarify or distort our perception of reality. He argues, however, that mysticism should be investigated scientifically and critically, under controlled conditions. Such work must take seriously the mystical traditions and techniques being examined rather than subsuming them under a secular and reductionistic framework. 'If mysticism is to be studied seriously', Staal argues, 'it should not merely be studied indirectly and from without, but also directly and from within' (Staal 1975: 125). This requires an initial suspension of doubt concerning the truthfulness of the mystical system or technique being explored, but should also be followed at some stage by analysis and critical evaluation (1975: 135).

Questioning modern notions of mysticism and spirituality

Although it is often difficult to distinguish between accounts of drug-induced and non-drug-induced mystical experiences, the debate about the role of drugs in the cultivation of mystical states suggests that the phenomena of the mystical is more than a matter of simply inducing an altered state of consciousness. As we have seen, the explicit identification of mysticism with extraordinary and transient states of consciousness is an approach that began in earnest with the work of William James at the beginning of the twentieth century and continues to the present day in debates concerning the relationship between mystical experiences and their interpretation and the question of the possibility (or not) of an unmediated or 'pure' experience of reality.

However, the modern privatisation of 'the mystical' has come under increasing criticism in some of the most recent scholarship in this field. The privatization of the phenomenon of mysticism is most obviously demonstrated in the emergence of 'spirituality' in the late twentieth century to denote some kind of interiorised experience or apprehension of reality. Such approaches are increasingly oriented towards the individual self rather than religious traditions as the source of their authority. Such contemporary shifts have affected the way in which we as 'moderns' understand the spiritual traditions of the past, in both the East and the West. Deny Turner (1994), Grace Jantzen (1995) and Richard King (1999) have all questioned the modern tendency to approach classical and medieval mystical texts as if they were offering psychological accounts of extraordinary experiences. Ineffability in the modern study of mysticism and spirituality has become a question of the indescribable nature of intense and private experiences rather than a reflection of the traditional exploration of the transcendental majesty of God or the ultimate reality. This reflects the tendency to read such historical material in terms of modern psychological theories of the self. This 'psychologisation' of the religious has been an important step in, the unhinging of 'the mystical' from its roots in the world's religious traditions, and its reformulation in terms of privatised and 'custom-made' spiritualities oriented towards the concerns of modern individual consumers searching for meaning in a marketplace of religions (Hanegraaff 1996; see also Carrette and King (2005) for a critical discussion of this trend).

In her feminist analysis of Christian mysticism, Jantzen points to the shifting meanings of 'the mystical' throughout history, highlighting both the power struggles involved in all attempts to define the category and the ways in which women have been excluded by men from positions of authority in this process. Similarly, King (1999), offers an analysis of the colonial origins of the notion of 'the mystic East,' arguing that the representation of Hinduism and Buddhism as mystical religions has functioned to reinforce Western Orientalist stereotypes of eastern religion and culture as world denying, amoral and lacking an impulse to improve society. This has allowed the West to define itself as progressive, scientific and liberal in contrast to the superstitious, tradition-bound and 'underdeveloped' Third World nations of Asia. In this regard the stability of the categories of 'spirituality' and 'the mystical' and the way in which they have been adopted has itself become subject to critical analysis as emphasis has shifted towards the power relations involved in attempts to classify particular religious figures, movements or traditions as mystical or spiritual in nature.

Bibliography

Beer, Frances (1992), *Women and Mystical Experience in the Middle Ages*, Rochester, New York and Woodbridge, Suffolk: Boydell.

Bouyer, Louis (1990), *The Christian Mystery: From Pagan Myth to Christian Mysticism*, Edinburgh: T. & T. Clark.

Bynum, Caroline Walker (1982), *Jesus as Mother: Studies in the Spirituality of the High Middle Ages*, Berkeley: University of California Press.

Carrette, Jeremy and Richard King (2005), *Selling Spirituality. The Silent Takeover of Religion*, London and New York: Routledge.

Certeau, Michel de (1992), *The Mystic Fable Volume 1. The Sixteenth and Seventeenth Centuries*, trans. by Michael B. Smith, Chicago: University of Chicago Press.

Deikman, Arthur J. (1980), 'Deautomatization and the Mystic Experience,' in R. Woods (ed.), *Understanding Mysticism*, London: Athlone Press; Garden City, NY: Image Books.

—— (1982), *The Observing Self: Mysticism and Psychotherapy*, Boston: Beacon Press.

Evans, Donald (1989), 'Can Philosophers Limit What Mystics Can Do? A Critique of Steven Katz' in *Religious Studies* 25: 53–60.

Hanegraaff, Wouter J. (1996), *New Age Religion and Western Culture: Esotericism in the Mirror of Secular Thought*, Numen Book Series, Leiden, New York, Köln: E. J. Brill.

Huxley, Aldous (1954), *The Doors of Perception*, London: Grafton Books (Collins).

Inge, Dean (1899), *Christian Mysticism*, London: Methuen.

James, William (1977), *The Varieties of Religious Experience*, The Gifford Lectures 1901–2, Glasgow: Collins.

Jantzen, Grace (1995), *Power, Gender and Christian Mysticism*, Cambridge: Cambridge University Press.

Johnson, W. J. (1994), *The Bhagavad Gita*, Oxford and New York: Oxford University Press.

Katz, Steven (1978), 'Language, Epistemology and Mysticism,' in Katz (ed.) *Mysticism and Philosophical Analysis*, Oxford: Oxford University Press.

King, Richard (1999), *Orientalism and Religion. Postcolonial Theory, India and 'the Mystic East'*, London and New York: Routledge.

King, Sallie B. (1988), 'Two Epistemological Models for the Interpretation of Mysticism,' in *Journal of the American Academy of Religion* 61(2): 275–9.

McGinn, Bernard (ed.) (1986), *Meister Eckhart. Teacher and Preacher*, London: SPCK and New York: Paulist Press.

Nygren, Anders (1953), *Agape and Eros*, Philadelphia: Westminster.

Otto, Rudolf (1932), *Mysticism East and West. A Comparative Analysis of the Nature of Mysticism*, New York: MacMillan, 1970, London: Quest Edition, 1987.

—— (1959), *The Idea of the Holy* (original, 1917, *Das Heilige*), 2nd edn, London: Penguin.

Petroff, Elizabeth (ed.) (1986), *Medieval Women's Visionary Literature*, Oxford: Oxford University Press.

Pseudo-Dionysius (1987), *The Complete Works*, trans. by Colm Luibheid, *et al.*, New York: Paulist Press.

Raphael, Melissa (1994), 'Feminism, Constructivism and Numinous Experience' in *Religious Studies* 30: 511–26.

Revised Standard Version of the Bible (1973), London/New York/Toronto: Collins.

Smart, Ninian (1965), *Reasons and Faiths. An Investigation of Religious Discourse, Christian and Non-Christian*, London: Routledge & Kegan Paul.

Stace, Walter (1960), *Mysticism and Philosophy*, London: Jeremy P. Tarcher Inc.

Tart, Charles (1969), *Altered States of Consciousness*, New York: Wiley.

Turner, Denys (1995), *The Darkness of God: Negativity in Christian Mysticism*, Cambridge: Cambridge University Press.

Watts, Alan (1965), *The Joyous Cosmology*, New York: Vintage Books.

Zaehner, R. C. (1957), *Mysticism Sacred and Profane*, Oxford: Clarendon Press.

Further reading

Robert Forman (ed.) (1990), *The Problem of Pure Consciousness*.
    Scholarly articles responding critically to the constructivist position of Katz and others.

Aldous Huxley, *The Perennial Philosophy*.
  Wide range of mystical quotations (in English translation) from the major religious traditions, with commentarial remarks by Huxley. A classic anthology and example of the perennialist position.

Steven Katz (ed.) (1983), *Mysticism and Religious Traditions*.
  Scholarly articles on various mystical traditions, mostly espousing the constructivist position.

Frits Staal (1975), *Exploring Mysticism* (Harmondsworth: Penguin).
  Quality study, though rather difficult when dealing with Staal's own specialist area of Hindu and Buddhist mysticism.

Richard Woods (ed.) (1980), *Understanding Mysticism*, London: Athlone Press; Garden City, NY: Image Books.

Chapter 18

New religious movements

Judith Fox

> So many people, so many opinions; his own a law to each.
> Terence 190–159 BCE

Popular representations of new religious movements – or, as they are more often called, 'cults' – are fairly consistent. Newspapers, television and other media usually portray such groups as suspect and subversive, and run by power-crazed leaders intent on exploiting the vulnerable. We are often told that those under their sway can be persuaded to do things that no thinking person would do voluntarily. Hapless followers who naively become involved with new religious movements (commonly abbreviated as NRMs) are considered at risk of sexual and psychological abuse, coercion, financial destitution and the break up of their families. Some, we are often reminded, even lose their lives. New religious movements are, in short, often characterised as 'pseudo-religions', moneymaking schemes or criminal 'rackets' operating under the guise of religion. At best, they are seen as creations of deluded narcissists who believe erroneously that they have a special connection with the divine.

It is important to understand that there is little consensus on several key issues among scholars who study these movements. This is in part because it is almost impossible to discuss NRMs without touching on subjects that tend to provoke heated debate, such as the nature of 'free will', 'authenticity' and even 'religion' itself. Some of these debates have focused on methodological concerns. There have been emotionally charged exchanges, for instance, over the kinds of relationships that researchers should adopt with the groups with which they work; and allegations have been made that some academics have either been duped by or have become complicit with NRMs, and that their research has consequently lacked 'objectivity'. Other important arguments have centred on whether members of NRMs are 'freethinking' members of society, and so entitled to practice their religion as they see fit, or, alternatively, whether they are victims in need of rescue.

A second reason for the lack of consensus on the issue of NRMs is that the scholars involved in the debates have different disciplinary backgrounds, often giving rise to different presuppositions, approaches, experiences and conclusions. But there are also substantial dissimilarities between the many groups that have been labelled as NRMs, yet another factor contributing to the differences in scholarly opinion. Given these differences between the groups themselves, the overview that follows should be read with an awareness that there are always exceptions to any general statement. For example, new religious movements are typically characterised as small, the majority of them having no more than a few hundred members. But in some countries, especially but not exclusively in South-east Asia, groups with millions of members have been classified as NRMs. Most new religious movements teach that it is wrong to injure either oneself or others. Several groups, however, mostly apoc-alyptic in tone, have been responsible for violence against both followers and outsiders, resulting in injury and death. The vast majority of people in new religions are not interested in indulging in any type of criminal activity. Nevertheless, there have also been a small number who have engaged in thoroughly reprehensible and illegal activities. Almost all new religious movements disappear after a short period, often seemingly due to the death of a leader, persecution or the failure of prophecy. But not all end in this way. Indeed, it is salutary, in the face of the stereotypes char-acteristically associated with NRMs, to remember that several of the world's major religions tell of having started from such humble beginnings.

Before addressing the specifics of NRMs, however, it is useful to begin with a dis-cussion of the phrase 'new religious movement' itself. This is important, among other reasons, because it has been the subject of controversy. An examination of the debate also provides a helpful introduction to some of the different positions scholars and others have held in relation to such movements. After this, there will be a brief out-line of some of the most salient characteristics of NRMs, followed by explanations scholars have offered for their emergence and features. The relationships of scholars with NRMs and the impact of the prevailing cultural milieu on their research will be reviewed. Finally, we will look at the rather different public perceptions of NRMs around the world. By introducing some of the problems and issues of the field in this manner, the aim is to increase awareness of the intricacies of the topic and of the diverse ways in which new religious movements are represented in scholarly discourse.

Labelling 'new religious movements'

'New religious movements' is the label generally used by scholars in Europe and America to designate religious groups that have either arrived in the West after 1950, and so are new to Westerners, or that have originated in the West since that time. By contrast, in Africa as well as in South and South-east Asia, most scholars tend to use the end of the nineteenth century as the cut-off point between 'new' and 'older' religious movements. In Japan, which has seen successive waves of new reli-gions since that time, there has been a further differentiation made, between the 'new religions' and the 'new new religions' that emerged since 1970 or so. In other words, there is no single understanding of which groups come under this umbrella designation. Moreover, the confusion over dating is only the first of a number of difficulties encountered in the use of the phrase.

The phrase 'new religious movement' was coined in part to address a lack of con-sensus about other terms more traditionally applied by academics to such movements. It also served as a counter-measure to the pejorative associations that, in particular, became associated with the term 'cult'. Until the introduction of the name NRM, soci-ologists of religion had been accustomed to using the terms 'sects' and 'cults' to talk about small religious movements. Even between sociologists, however, there were dif-fering opinions as to how these terms should be defined (Dawson 2003). For example, the American scholars Rodney Stark and William Sims Bainbridge, on the basis of doctrinal distinctiveness, classified sects as breakaways from older religious groups. Cults, they said, were movements that drew their inspiration from somewhere besides the primary religion of the culture in which they were located, and so they were deemed culturally innovative. The Oxford sociologist Bryan Wilson, by contrast, defined cults and sects on the basis of their social organisation. He characterised sects as exclusive and elitist groups offering salvation through membership, with lifestyles and concerns that were markedly different from those of mainstream society (Wilson 1992). His student Roy Wallis, likewise, redefined cults as loosely organised groups seen by their members to be just one of a variety of paths to salvation, rather than as the only path. According to Wallis, sects were usually authoritarian and run by a single leader. Cults, he argued, characteristically had no clear organisational boundaries and the locus of authority was vested in the members rather than in the leadership. Some cults eventually coalesced into sects, as, for instance, in the case of the self-help oriented Dianetics courses, which eventually transformed into the Church of Scientology. However, many other cults simply dissolved after a short period of time.

Psychologists of religion have used the term 'cult' quite differently. They have applied it to designate authoritarian religious groups that combine group processes with hypnotic techniques, resulting in what is often called 'mind control'. It was this usage that found its way into popular discourse in the 1970s. The word 'cult' gradually took on more sinister connotations, no longer indicating just an enthusiastic and relatively unorganised following. An active coalition of small groups in America and Europe, working against what they perceived as the exploitation of NRM members, became known as 'the anti-cult movement'. These 'anti-cultists' adopted the definition that was in use among psychologists and, with the help of the media, disseminated their understanding – and suspicions – to the public. The menacing associations that they linked to the term 'cult' were legitimated and reinforced by the catastrophic events surrounding groups as diverse as the People's Temple at Jonestown in Guyana, the Branch Davidians at Waco, members of the Solar Temple and Heaven's Gate in North America and Europe, and Aum Shinrikyo in Japan.

Most psychologists are still happy to retain the label, and continue to see it as analytically useful. By the 1980s, however, a feeling grew among other scholars in the field that the term 'cult' had become politicised and unusable, and that the time had come for a new name for the groups they studied. Scholars of religion often look to how the people they study represent themselves when attempting to choose an appropriate label. But, with groups from all major (and minor) religious, spiritual and alternative traditions being included in this category, there was consensus only in one important respect: by now, nobody – perhaps for obvious reasons – wanted to be called a member of a 'cult', or saw themselves as such. In the absence of a commonly agreed upon definition from the movements themselves, the term 'new religious movement' – chosen for its apparent neutrality – became widely used in the academic community.

Some 'pros' and 'cons' of the new label

The phrase 'new religious movement', however, has generated its own issues, the first of which hangs on the word 'new'. As well as the confusion that has been experienced over dating, it is not always obvious at what point in the development of a religion something 'new' has evolved. For instance, when a church splinters, and new break-away groups are formed, are the latter 'new religious movements'? Should the term still be used even if the 'new' splinter group retains much of the original doctrine and prac-tice? Similarly, it is often also unclear at what point a 'new religious movement' becomes a 'not so new religious movement'. Is it when the founder dies, when records start to be kept and a complex organisation emerges? Is it when a newer wave of reli-gious movements becomes apparent in that region? Or is it when a second and third generation is established, or when a movement is no longer associated with contro-versy? Protests over the use of the word 'new' have also been made by a number of the groups usually put into this category. The International Society for Krishna Consciousness (ISKCON), for example, argues that it is only new in the West, and that it can trace its origins back to sixteenth-century Bengal, and even earlier. Like the members of many other groups, ISKCON followers do not accept that they are 'new', and complain that the label is misleading.

Others have objected to the description 'religious' being applied to some of the movements placed in this category, as they do not normally describe themselves in those terms. For example, South Asian groups such as the Brahma Kumaris, and followers of gurus such as Sathya Sai Baba, Mother Meera and Amritanandamayi, think of themselves as belonging to 'spiritual' movements. For a short while in the 1980s, followers of Osho Rajneesh presented themselves as members of a religion, Rajneeshism. The religion was probably deliberately created to assist wide-scale entry into the United States. But for most of the history of his movement, his followers have not articulated their affiliation in religious terms. Osho, after all, spent a good deal of his life denouncing 'religion'. Falun Gong, a movement that has recently gained a high profile in China for publicly protesting against the government, has identified itself on its official web page as an organisation whose members 'simply seek to maintain a strong and healthy body, improve their Xinxing (heart-mind-moral nature) and be good people'. Despite being denounced as a cult by the authorities, the organisation has rejected the claim that it is either a cult or a religion.

More recently, scholars have also noted that the phrase 'new religious movements' has begun to accumulate many of the negative connotations previously ascribed to 'cults'. Opponents of the phrase have charged that academics introduced it in order to deflect what they consider to be legitimate criticism about these movements. In the face of such considerations, one suggestion has been that scholars of religion abandon the label and return to using the technical terms 'sect' and 'cult', having first agreed on their definition. However, most believe that it would be impossible to turn back the clock in this manner. Another proposal has been to extend the phrase 'religious minority' to cover new religious movements as well as diaspora communities (Introvigne 1997). But, though this might have legal advantages, the suggestion has drawbacks of its own. Some groups now described as 'religious minori-ties' in Europe – especially Islamic communities – experience themselves as threatened, marginalized and vulnerable. Hence, being called a 'religious minority' might not necessarily place those previously designated as 'cults' and 'new religious movements' in a more comfortable position in relation to the mainstream. Further, since the meanings of terms are never definitively fixed, pejorative connotations may be taken from the term 'new religious movement' and applied to 'religious minority', just as has happened between the terms 'cult' and 'new religious movement' in the past. There are also groups who, despite being comparatively small, would not recognise themselves as a 'minority'. Instead, they believe that the truths that they have discovered will affect the majority of humankind in the longer term.

Advocates for the scholarly retention, and critical use, of the phrase 'new religious movement' have pointed out that the label is still not as negatively charged as 'cult'. The phrase, they have said, speaks to the fact that, although many groups defined in this way have their roots in older traditions, almost all do see themselves as new in some way. Indeed, it is this experience of newness that allows them to offer their own unique message to humanity. Sociologically speaking, many of these movements, whether they see themselves as 'religious' or not, also exhibit characteristics that are usually associated with 'new religion'. These characteristics include communal ownership of property, charismatic leadership, relationships based on personal trust rather than on institutional regulation, a message of salvation, liberation or transformation, and a high turnover of members. The phrase, therefore, does have some analytical merit. In the face of all these considerations, and despite its methodological problems, 'new religious movement' has prevailed as the label most commonly employed by scholars of religion.

Characteristics of new religious movements

If there has been considerable debate over the labelling of NRMs, there has been less disagreement over the characteristics scholars commonly ascribe to such groups. Some new religious movements, as we have already seen, have millions of adherents. However, most are understood to be relatively small. Typically, sociologists say, new religious movements have less than 300 committed members, with the larger ones usually being able to claim memberships only in the tens of thousands. Those converted are attracted for disparate reasons, depending on the particular movement. Some speak of the sense of purpose and community their membership gives them, and the opportunity to develop spiritually that they have not found elsewhere. Others say they are attracted by the promise of healing or prosperity, or stronger religious experiences than they have had before. Members talk of the feeling that they had of 'coming home' when they first made contact with the NRM, and of the trust they have in the claims of their leader.

Leaders of new religious movements are usually either considered divine or enlightened by their followers or, at the very least, much closer to such a state than they are themselves. They are often thought to possess the ability to work miracles and heal the sick. Many being skilled orators, they are seen as having a singular capability to articulate the will of the divine, and have a charismatic and convincing allure for their followers. These charismatic leaders often seem capricious in behaviour, and contradictory in teaching. Many appear to revel in flouting rules and in inconsistency, or in pushing their followers beyond what is considered normal. Paradoxically and simultaneously, nevertheless, their word is usually final. Although they may change the rules they impose without warning, they can be accorded tremendous control over aspects of their followers' lives. Leaders can be given the power to regulate matters of dress, diet, hygiene, finances, friendships and family relationships, sexual relations and marriage, procreation and even – in rare instances – to decide whether it is time for their followers to end their lives.

The coupling of stringent regulation and effervescent spontaneity in NRMs has been seen to come about through the relationship between the members and the leader. The devotee trusts that the leader is able to deliver the promised spiritual rewards. It is this sense of trust that encourages them to offer their wholehearted commitment. As a result, relations with leaders are often experienced as personal and intimate by members, even if they have never met the head of their movement in person. Members' commitment may be reinforced if the religion offers them ways of looking at the world that are radically different from the mainstream. These new perspectives undercut commitment to concerns other than those of the movement and promote rupture between new and old.

Scholars say that this rupture may be reinforced by other attributes commonly found in new religious movements. One is that these groups are rarely just about accepting scriptures. Instead, they usually offer powerful new experiences to followers. These experiences convince members of the truthfulness of the teaching and the significance of the path. Following the example of the leadership, converts often adopt a vocabulary only used in their movement, allowing them to share the unique experiences of membership with each other. Their sexual norms are also likely to be different from those of the mainstream, whether they advocate celibacy, arranged marriages for Westerners, polygamy in a monogamous society or complete sexual 'freedom'.

This emphasis on difference from the mainstream does not mean that all NRMs that have been studied have been found to be new in all senses. Many 'breakaway' NRMs continue with at least some of the practices of the groups from which they have split. Others combine elements from multiple traditions in order to highlight the way they see themselves as embracing, and thereby transcending, all other religions. The theme of rupture, however, is often continued in teachings relating to the rapidly approaching emergence of a new social order, with which the group in question is associated in some significant way. A number also develop political agendas that explicitly challenge social norms, and are public and active in their pursuit. NRMs usually hope to enjoy a reputation based on their spiritual contribution to humanity. At least some, however, are more likely to have one founded unwittingly on whether their behaviour can be tolerated by the society in which it is located.

The academic study of new religious movements

A recent and useful overview of research on new religious movements is *Cults and New Religious Movements: A Reader* (Dawson 2003), a compilation of some of the most influential articles written by contemporary scholars in the field. But the voice that scholars of new religious movements have, perhaps, drawn on most heavily is that of the early sociologist Max Weber (Weber 1968). His writings have been brought to bear on the question of why the number of NRMs in the West appeared to increase substantially in the 1960s and beyond; on the dynamics involved in conversion to NRMs; and with regard to how commitment is maintained. Most studies of charismatic leadership, the most common form of leadership found in NRMs, have used Weber's portrayal of charismatic leaders as revolutionary and set apart by what are seen as exceptional qualities as their starting point. Bryan Wilson relied heavily on Weber's portrayal of modernity and its rationalizing momentum for his own argument that new religious movements are examples of private forms of religion. Wilson argued that privatised forms of religion appear when religion disappears from the public sphere, this disappearance being due to processes of modernization. Following Weber, he also said that such groups tend to emerge during times of social and political unrest, or when a country is subjected to foreign invasion. Other scholars have utilised Weber's notion of 'routinisation', the premise that practices tend to become routine and fixed over time, to try to understand how and why groups become increasingly institutionalised.

The most popular typology of new religious movements so far devised is that of Roy Wallis (Dawson 2003). Here Weber's influence is discernible as well, especially in Wallis's assumption that groups tend to become increasingly more accommodating towards the mainstream over time. Wallis also divided his typology into three 'ideal types', another Weberian strategy. Earlier typologies were primarily descriptive, concentrating on the classification of groups in terms of doctrine. By contrast, Wallis sought to put together a predictive typology that could be used to forecast what kinds of features, such as recruitment patterns, different NRMs would be likely to display.

The first type he proposed was that of *world-rejecting* groups, and it perhaps most closely conforms to popular images of new religions. World-rejecting groups, according to Wallis, typically take the form of closed communities of followers who believe that the outside world is impure, degenerate and sometimes dangerous, and that contact with it should be minimised. These communities tend to be run along authoritarian lines, and the needs of the group take precedence over those of the individual member. Income and property are often shared. Such movements usually anticipate an imminent transformation of the world, followed by a 'new world order' in which they will play a significant role. Wallis included ISKCON and the Children of God as examples.

Wallis's second type was that of *world-affirming* groups. These are not so recognisably religious, and are more individualistic than the first category. These groups may have reservations about the existing social order. However, unlike their world-rejecting counterparts, they do not tend to view themselves as a refuge of purity in an impure world. Groups located in this category are oriented towards the attainment of 'human potential' through the release of the innate divinity or creativity of the person. They include seminar-oriented organisations such as The Forum and Insight.

The last category identified by Wallis contains *world-accommodating* groups. These are movements who do not necessarily see themselves as an all-encompassing or unique path. Instead, they offer highly experiential techniques that can be utilised by people in order to revitalise their spirituality more generally. Wallis included organisations such as the charismatic churches and Subud in this category.

Wallis's typology has been critiqued on numerous grounds. For instance, its detractors have pointed to its elevation of social orientation over doctrine as a serious shortcoming. Ignoring doctrine, they have contended, unhelpfully allows groups from entirely different traditions, with entirely different histories, to be put together. Critics have also argued that the Wallis typology does not allow for diversity within a particular movement, diversity that would place it in more than one category simultaneously. Sahaja Yoga, for example, appears, on casual contact, to be *world-affirming*. However, the group has also displayed *world-rejecting* characteristics in certain circumstances. Despite such criticisms, the typology remains the most cited in the field, even today.

NRMs and rapid social change

Another sociologist frequently referred to by scholars of religion has been Weber's contemporary, Émile Durkheim. According to Durkheim, social norms and values, especially those of religion, function as a kind of 'glue' to hold society together. In times of rapid social change, existing rules, habits, and beliefs no longer hold. New religious alternatives are, therefore, likely to be sought in order to provide new stability. Scholars have used this idea to explain, at least in part, the emergence of an estimated five new religions per day in different parts of the world. More broadly, a shared assumption of all the explanations put forward is that social change brings about religious change.

In Africa, scholars have noted that most new religions are based in urban areas, those typically populated with displaced families from rural villages, having to cope with new challenges and uncertainties. Over 6,000 independent churches have been counted, almost all of West African origin, the majority of which are said to have begun with a dream, a vision or sickness. Their focus is on prophecy, prayer and the Holy Spirit. Additionally, there are many new evangelical and charismatic churches that have recently been established by missionaries from North America. Africa has also imported some controversial new movements from other regions, including the Unification Church and the Children of God. But whether a movement is indigenous or imported, commentators have attributed their popularity to the need for stability experienced by members. The new groups have been seen as functioning to provide cohesion and a new sense of purpose after the throwing off of years of colonial repression, or following rapid urbanisation (Jules-Rosette 1979).

Similarly, scholars of South-east Asia have written of numerous new religious movements emerging since the turn of the last century; a few of these groups have millions of followers, such as Cao Dai in Vietnam. Japanese scholars have pointed to diverse new religious movements flourishing in urban areas in their country as well. Again, rapid urbanisation has been put forward as a significant factor in their rise. Most of these movements are Buddhist, and it has been estimated that between 10 per cent and 30 per cent of the population belong to one or more of these groups. It is worth remembering that having multiple religious affiliations is not unusual in this region. In South Asia, new religions have been described as coming into being all the time, coalescing around *avatars*, incarnations of the divine, and *self-realised* human beings, *gurus* and *swamis*, *sants* and Sufi *pirs*. Most of these groups are small, but some, such as the Sai Baba movement, are substantial in size and have a considerable international following. The rapid social changes that came about following the end of colonial – or in the case of Japan, feudal – government have regularly been invoked in explanations for the emergence of new religious movements in all these regions. The concurrent increase in communications and other forms of infrastructure has also been seen as a contributing factor in the proliferation of new forms of religion.

In the West as well, rapid social change has been put forward, either implicitly or explicitly, as the most significant factor behind the rise in the number of new religious movements from the 1950s onwards. Increasing globalisation, scholars have argued, has led to an increased access to knowledge about religions, the net result being an increase in religious choice. Europe saw waves of immigration from South Asia, the Middle East and East Africa. Due to the lifting of prohibitive legislation, there was also a marked increase in immigration from South Asia to the United States in the mid-1960s. Scholars have additionally pointed to an increase in the number of travellers abroad, and to increased information from television and, more recently, the Internet. Some have argued that because this increase of information has taken place within a capitalist system, it has given rise to a situation in which a plethora of new and older religious movements now sell their wares in a 'spiritual supermarket'.

A different group of scholars has emphasised the psychological and emotional effects of the rapid economic and cultural changes the West has undergone. Some early studies, in a move reminiscent of the psychologist Abraham Maslow's theory of a 'hierarchy of needs', pointed to the increase in economic growth and leisure time in the 1960s. They explained that the 'baby boomers' of that era could afford, and had the time, to indulge in the often 'narcissistic' pursuit of the spiritual. This pursuit was possible because their other, material, needs had already been satisfied. Such narcissism included far more widespread use of narcotics than before. The ingestion of psychedelic substances during the 1970s added to an already existing climate of questioning and 'seekership'. Against this backdrop, some individuals were motivated to join NRMs that offered them clear-cut messages, be they about gender, morality or purpose about the world.

Studies conducted by psychologists from the 1960s onwards have tended to find that such conversions resulted in damage. By contrast, a few sociologists speculated that NRMs at times acted as a means by which people actually resolved personal and emotional confusion and were rehabilitated. They pointed out that a number of groups in the 1960s emphasised that meditation could offer a better 'trip' with more 'highs' for those searching for Truth. The groups, they said, enabled 'dropouts' to reintegrate with mainstream society. Members were re-inculcated with respect for community values and were supported in breaking their addictive patterns of behaviour. Nevertheless, most scholarly explanations for the emergence of NRMs during that period tended to assume that young people join NRMs because they were deprived in some way. Individuals who could not cope with the stresses and strains of modern life converted to them as a retreat from the 'real world'.

More recent sociological commentators have tended to resist opting for a single easy explanation. They usually acknowledge that a complex of factors led to the increase in numbers from the 1950s onwards. But they affirm that new religion is hardly anything really new, or even particularly unusual. There are now well over 2,000 new religious movements in North America, at least 2,000 in Europe, and over 700 in Britain alone. These NRMs have almost all been inspired by earlier religious forms (Melton 1994). Some are global organisations and are represented in most major countries. Others have remained small and geographically limited. The new movements imported in the 1960s and 1970s tended to attract a predominantly white, middle class and youthful constituency. However, memberships have diversified over time and with the changing social make-up of the West. Most recently, the largest numbers have been attracted to new Buddhist and Islamic movements, as well as to a home-grown, thriving pagan tradition.

Researchers and new religious movements

There has been a substantial amount of scholarly writing on the rise of NRMs, on their characteristics and on individual movements. Another literature has arisen as a response to what has been characterized as the over-involvement of some scholars with particular groups.

Inspired by the desire to 'set the record straight' and to promote religious tolerance, some scholars have been drawn into the role of public defenders of NRMs. They have attempted to counter publicly the depiction of NRMs as 'brainwashing cults'. These scholars have argued their case in the press and on television, as well as in academic circles. Some have advised new religious movements on how to improve their public profile, and have supported them as expert witnesses in court cases. As a result, outraged critics of NRMs have branded these scholars as 'apologists'. They have accused them of being insufficiently aware that they have been used unscrupulously by cults for public relations purposes, and of unfairly using their academic credentials to invalidate opposing views from other expert witnesses. Some have also been denounced on the basis that they have gained financially from their association with groups to which they gave their support. This issue is one to which scholars on all sides of the debate periodically return, in an attempt either to defend themselves, air grievances or re-affirm the need for careful and well-thought-out research not driven by unacknowledged agendas (*Sociological Analysis* 1983; *Nova Religio Symposium* 1998; Zablocki and Robbins 2001).

One of the most well-known critics of academic-NRM relations was Professor Margaret Singer, an American psychologist, who concluded that academics should have no prolonged contact with new religious movements for fear of undue influence. She was publicly highly critical of the close relations other scholars have sometimes established with those they study. Rejecting the view that most people do not feel the attraction of cults, Singer argued that everyone is potentially susceptible, including those she termed 'co-opted academics' (Dawson 2003). Those who disagreed with Singer and her supporters have pointed out that NRMs are often distrustful of outsiders. For this reason, participant observation is the best – and sometimes the only – way of gaining access. This method requires that scholars spend considerable time with members, in order to get behind the public relations façade that may exist, and to gain their trust. Those in favour of this kind of research have cast doubt on the assumption that all academics are at risk of becoming converts or uncritical advocates. They have protested that scholars who have engaged in participant observation have mostly found the agendas of the movements they have studied, as Professor Eileen Barker has put it, 'eminently resistible'.

Cultural assumptions and new religious movements

It seems pertinent to say a few words about the milieu in which such debates have occurred. Trends in popular areas of new religious scholarship – for example, the increased study of gender and violence – reflect the recent increase of interest in these topics outside the study of religions rather than any change in NRMs themselves. Arguably, too, both scholarly consensus and controversy about these movements has been influenced at least as much by outside factors as by the NRMs themselves. Broader cultural narratives and debates have had an impact on what kinds of questions are asked of NRMs. To examine the consequences of certain cultural assumptions is not to belittle the findings and conclusions of scholars. The point is that perceptions of new religions held by the interest groups involved in debating them arise out of wider social contexts and concerns. These need to be included in any analysis.

For example, the hostility that has been generated towards new religious movements cannot be divorced from Western cultural associations applied to the word 'new'. This is especially when it is used in a religious context. Partly because the Western monotheistic religions uphold the notion of having one faith to the exclusion of all others, traditional religion is often upheld as both 'authentic' and 'orthodox'. As non-traditional movements, NRMs are therefore assumed to be 'inauthentic' and 'unorthodox', regardless of their merits or failings. Arguably, the upshot of this has been that similarities between the activities of new, and so 'inauthentic', religious movements, and older, 'authentic' traditions have largely gone unnoticed. Christian monks and nuns have often risen at dawn to chant or say prayers without fear of reproof. Members of new religious movements rising at the same time for the same purpose have been vulnerable to the charge of 'mind control' resulting from sleep deprivation and sensory overload. It is seen as acceptable, and sometimes praiseworthy, that monks and nuns in most of the world's religious traditions should give all their worldly goods to their respective organisations. Members of new religions are likely to be described as having been swindled for doing the same.

The concept of the 'free individual', upheld in both secular and religious narratives in the West, has given rise to another arena of disagreement. Supporters of embattled NRMs have fought to ensure that the 'religious liberty' of members is protected. Critics have accused new religious movements of removing freedom from individuals and so have concluded that they are patently dangerous and subversive. The practice of 'deprogramming', common in the 1980s, was a by-product of this rhetoric of subversion and danger. It involved anti-cultists in Europe and the United States being paid by anxious families and friends to 'liberate' converted loved ones. Deprogramming typically meant the kidnap and forcible holding of a cult member until they had renounced their allegiance to their movement.

These antagonisms have spilled over into the research arena. The most vexed debates between scholars have been on the issue of 'brainwashing' and on the related question of whether those who join new religions are victims of 'mind-control'. Probably the best-known work on the subject is the study of the Unification Church produced by Eileen Barker. In *The Making of a Moonie*, Barker concluded that the Unification Church members she studied were not simply the victims of insidious techniques of persuasion. However, there have been hundreds of other books and journal articles devoted to the issue. Some have taken a firm stand against the possibility of brainwashing occurring in religious movements, while others have argued strongly that the concept of brainwashing is a useful analytic tool of investigation (Zablocki and Robbins 2001; Dawson 2003).

Moving away from monoliths

Reference has already been made to the tendency to portray NRMs in oppositional terms. There have been recent and welcome indications of some rapprochement.

Often, however, members have been seen as *either* passive receptacles of pseudo-religious teachings *or* as genuine spiritual seekers. Critics have been depicted as *either* champions against damaging and fascistic religious regimes *or* unreasonable bigots. Scholars who study them have been represented as *either* objective arbiters *or* complicit dupes. Such depictions have served as rhetorical devices for deployment in order to legitimate or sanction. On the back of such rhetoric, new religions are not always treated in the same way by civil governments, regardless of their location. Their treatment, instead, has depended on which country they are in, the relationship that religion enjoys with the state, the information networks between that country and others, and the degree of rupture the groups manifest with prevailing norms.

New religions, then, may be seen very differently, depending on where they are located. They may be viewed as co-contributors to a healthy, pluralistic society. They may be seen as groups intent on subverting the very fabric of society or as eccentric. Or they may be largely ignored as peripheral – but not necessarily dangerous – organisations. ISKCON, for example, has been viewed as a very controversial movement in Russia. The country has only a small South Asian population and a cautious attitude in its post-communist years to religions other than the Orthodox Church. In continental Europe, it is commonly viewed as a somewhat suspicious cult. In Britain and America, by contrast, it has recently successfully distanced itself from its earlier more controversial reputation. Instead it has developed a public image as an authentic upholder of traditional Indian religion in the West, as well as widespread support from South Asian communities.

Similarly, by the year 2000 in the United States, the Church of Scientology had a number of Hollywood celebrities among its followers. It was being seen as just one more acceptable spiritual path among many. In Britain, Scientology was allowed to promote its message on television. By contrast, it was identified as a dangerous and subversive movement in a number of countries in continental Europe. In 1996, the German Social Democrat Party passed the measure that applicants for public service had to declare in writing that they were not Scientologists. They also decided that local politicians should not award contracts to companies owned or operated by members of the movement, and that companies applying for such contracts had to give written assurances that they were not associated with Scientology. Switzerland's Supreme Court threw out an appeal in 1999 by the Church of Scientology. They upheld a Basel edict aimed at punishing 'anyone who recruits or tries to recruit passers-by in a public place using deceptive or dishonest methods'. And tribunals in both Belgium and France included the movement on their lists of disreputable cult organisations.

The discrepancies in the treatment of NRMs by national governments are partly due to political and cultural differences that exist between countries. But they are also due to the diversity that, scholars have noted, exist within the movements themselves, especially those with an international following. Belying the uniformity of their popular image, this diversity is often visible at national and sometimes even local levels. Differences in emphasis and outlook are apparent due to particular local leaders, the closeness of the relationship with the international leadership and the societies from which followers have come. Additionally, variety is apparent when one takes a closer look at the quite radical changes in course that can occur within movements, and at the degree of commitment an individual has to the norms of the movement to which he or she belongs. So some degree of divergence is usually evident. This is so even in the face of common teachings, shared vocabularies and, sometimes, considerable social pressure to conform. In the 1980s Rajneeshism went through a period in which its communes were ordered to abide by strict codes of conduct issued by the main commune in Oregon. Consequently, the breakfast bowls at the main commune in England were required to be set out in the exact manner in which they were arranged at all the other communes. Similarly, toilets were cleaned according to a rigidly prescribed directive. Despite such enforced consistency, commune members saw themselves as 'the British' manifestation of Rajneeshism, and distinct from their German, Italian or American counterparts. Many followers, more-over, did not live in the communes and had a more relaxed approach to their allegiance to the guru.

Scholars have noted a further reason for differences between the ways new reli-gious movements are viewed in different countries. This is the decision some take to accommodate their message to new environments when they expand. Dada Lekraj, the leader of the Brahma Kumaris, taught initially that the world would soon be devastated by nuclear holocaust. He believed that his followers had a spiritual mission to prepare humanity for its aftermath. Over time, and with the expansion of his movement into Europe, however, this message has been downplayed. The group now emphasises its association with the United Nations. It encourages newcomers to try its meditations in order to bring peace and wholeness into their lives, aiming to foster love and peace on a global level. Another example is Mahikari, a Japanese movement. Mahikari tends to emphasise its links with Christianity to its Western converts far more strongly than to its Japanese ones. The popular image of new reli-gious movements is that they are homogeneous entities peopled with followers who indiscriminately adopt the norms of the international leadership. However, everyday practices usually reveal a degree of differentiation once a movement has expanded abroad, or even within national borders. The differences that can occur are often then fed back into the variety of ways in which they are regarded across the world.

Concluding remarks

Despite the different conclusions that scholars have come to over whether NRMs are dangerous or not, most would agree that they share basic characteristics. New religious movements are usually led by charismatic leaders whose teachings are often at odds with established religious practices or cultural norms. They are generally peopled by enthusiastic converts, and have a high turnover of members. These char-acteristics, it has been argued, generate similarities between them that allow them to be grouped together. Nevertheless, there is also considerable diversity between the kinds of groups to which the label 'new religious movement' is applied, and within them. Furthermore, a religious group can be constituted in the public arena very differently across the globe, depending on where it is and on the agendas of those involved. Such complexity appears, at least to this writer, to underline the need for further sensitive and thorough research by scholars, despite the misgivings of some about the close contact this necessitates.

Bibliography

Barker, E. (1984) *The Making of a Moonie: Choice or Brainwashing?* New York: Basil Blackwell. A fascinating and widely cited study of conversion to the Unification Church by a leading scholar in the field.

Dawson, L.L. ed. (2003) *Cults and New Religious Movements: A Reader.* Second edition. Oxford and Boston: Blackwell. An excellent and readable compilation of some of the most influential scholarly work on new religious movements, including articles by Wallis, Beckford, Stark and Bainbridge, Barker, Singer and Wuthnow, among others.

Introvigne, M. (1997) 'Religious Liberty in Europe' in *ISKCON Communications Journal* 5, 2: 37–48. An argument by the Director of CESNUR, a centre for the academic study of new religions, for such movements to be seen as religious minorities and studied in those terms.

Jules-Rosette, B. ed. (1979) *The New Religions of Africa.* Norwood, NJ: Ablex Publishing Company. An edited volume offering a good overview of the diversity of new religions in Africa.

Melton, J.G. ed. (1994) *Encyclopedia of American Religions.* 4th edn. Detroit, MI: Gale Research Inc. A formidable reference work currently being updated to offer detailed profiles of over 2000 new religious movements.

Nova Religio Symposium (1998) 'Academic Integrity and the Study of New Religious Movements', 2,1: 8–54. The symposium comprised a debate between scholars with close relationships with new religions and their critics.

Sociological Analysis (1983), 44, 3. The issue was devoted to articles on the relationships academics have with the groups they study.

Weber, M. (1968) *Economy and Society: An Outline of Interpretive Sociology. Volumes One and Two.* G. Roth and C. Wittich eds. New York: Bedminster Press. The volumes include Weber's classic writings on charismatic authority.

Wilson, B. (1992) *The Social Dimensions of Sectarianism.* New York: Oxford University Press. The book is a characteristically careful and wide-ranging example of the work of this major proponent of the 'secularization thesis'.

Zablocki, B.D. and Robbins, T. (2001) *Misunderstanding Cults: Searching for Objectivity in a Controversial Field.* Toronto: University of Toronto Press. An edited volume presenting different scholarly opinions on objectivity and 'brainwashing'.

Websites

The Religious Movements Homepage Project @ the University of Virginia. Available at: http://religiousmovements.lib.virginia.edu/

CESNUR. Available at: http://www.cesnur.org/default.htm

These two websites comprise the most permanent and extensive web-based collections of texts on new religion and their scholarly study.

Chapter 19

Fundamentalism

Henry Munson

On May 24, 2001, the *Jerusalem Post* printed an article entitled 'THINK AGAIN: God didn't say "You might want to ...."'. In this article, 'ultra-Orthodox' columnist Jonathan Rosenblum castigates a prominent Conservative rabbi for asserting that the exodus from Egypt did not in fact occur. 'No plagues, no splitting of the sea – all a fairy tale', as Rosenblum puts it. He suggests that what the Conservative rabbi is actually saying is that 'It doesn't really matter that the Torah's claim to be the word of God to man is false', because the Torah is nevertheless 'divinely inspired' and embodies important 'spiritual values'. Rosenblum asks why should Jews look to the Torah (the first five books of the Hebrew Bible) for moral guidance if it consists of 'some really huge whoppers – the Exodus from Egypt, the giving of the Torah at Sinai, the stories of the alleged Patriarchs'. Rosenblum notes that the president of the Jewish Theological Seminary, the principal seminary of Conservative Judaism, which is in fact less conservative than Orthodox Judaism, has dismissed the book of Leviticus as having being superseded by our 'modern sensibility'. Rosenblum observes that if the Torah is simply the product of human authors, and if Jews can discard those parts of it they regard as incompatible with their 'modern sensibility', they can pick and choose those aspects of religious law they want to follow much as shoppers pick and choose in a supermarket. The result is moral chaos. This critique of Conservative Judaism would be qualified by many as 'fundamentalist' insofar as it insists on strict conformity to a sacred text believed to be in some sense the word of God.

Some scholars argue that the term *fundamentalism* should be used only to refer to those conservative Protestants who refer to themselves as fundamentalists. To speak of fundamentalism in other contexts, they argue, is to confuse analysis and attack, scholarship and polemic. This argument is made by people on both the theological and political right and left. From the right, scholars argue that religious liberals (those who pick and choose the commandments they will obey) use the term *fundamentalist* to denigrate those who insist on adhering to and upholding the traditional doctrines of a religion. From the left, scholars often argue that Westerners speak of 'Islamic fundamentalism' in order to undermine the legitimacy of Islamic movements that seek to overcome Western domination of the Islamic world. From both perspectives, the term 'fundamentalist' is seen as illegitimate because it serves to delegitimize.

Conservative Lutheran sociologist Peter Berger suggests that what needs to be explained is not that many people insist on defending their traditional religious beliefs, but that many liberal academics find this strange (Berger 1997). Sociologist Steve Bruce (who may not share Berger's conservatism) elaborates on this theme as follows:

> In the broad sweep of human history, fundamentalists are normal. What we now regard as religious 'extremism' was commonplace 200 years ago in the Western world and is still commonplace in most parts of the globe. It is not the dogmatic believer who insists that the sacred texts are divinely inspired and true, who tries to model his life on the ethical requirements of those texts, and who seeks to impose these requirements on the entire society who is unusual. The liberal who supposes that his sacred texts are actually human constructions of differing moral worth, whose religion makes little difference in his life, and who is quite happy to accept that what his God requires of him is not binding on other members of his society: this is the strange and remarkable creature.
>
> (Bruce 2000: 116–17)

Bruce goes on to say that 'Fundamentalism is a rational response of traditionally religious peoples to social, political and economic changes that downgrade and constrain the role of religion in the public world' (Bruce 2000: 117).

Edward Said approaches the subject of fundamentalism from a different perspective to Berger or Bruce. He has argued that the terms *terrorism* and *fundamentalism* are both 'derived entirely from the concerns and intellectual factories in metropolitan centers like Washington and London':

> They are fearful images that lack discriminate contents or definition, but they signify moral power and approval for whoever uses them, moral defensiveness and criminalization for whomever they designate . . . By such means the governability of large numbers of people is assured . . .
>
> (Said 1993: 310)

Despite this condemnation of fundamentalism as an artifact of the Western imperial imagination, Said has himself used the term. In discussing Karen Armstrong's *Islam: A Short History* in a review essay published in 1992, he writes:

> Her book's most valuable section is that in which she discusses the varieties of modern fundamentalism without the usual invidious focus on Islam. And rather than seeing it only as a negative phenomenon, she has an admirable gift for understanding fundamentalism from within, as adherence to a faith that is threatened by a strong secular authoritarianism. As an almost doctrinaire secularist myself, I nevertheless found myself swayed by her sympathetic and persuasive argument in this section . . .
>
> (Said 1992: 74)

So here we find Said using the very term and concept he has often condemned as an egregious example of Western 'Orientalism'. Yet in this same essay, and on the same page, he reverts to his more usual position regarding 'Islamic fundamentalism' in particular:

> above all, look with the deepest suspicion on anyone who wants to tell you the real truth about Islam and terrorism, fundamentalism, militancy, fanaticism, etc . . . leave those great non-subjects to the experts, their think tanks, government depart-

ments, and policy intellectuals, who get us into one unsuccessful and wasteful war after the other.

(Said 1992)

So here we have one of the most influential intellectuals of the late twentieth century insisting that fundamentalism, like terrorism, is a 'non-subject' conjured up by Western imperialists to discredit Middle Eastern resistance to foreign domination. Yet this same intellectual speaks of 'varieties of fundamentalism', thus suggesting that he believes that fundamentalism really does exist outside the intellectual factories of the West. This contradiction illustrates a basic problem: Most scholars are intensely uncomfortable with the concept of fundamentalism when used outside its original Protestant context, but they often find themselves falling back on it for lack of a better alternative – when describing religious movements of which they disapprove.

In addition to the common criticism that the term *fundamentalist*, when used outside its original Protestant context, denigrates those who adhere to and defend the orthodox tenets of their religion, another common criticism is that the imposition of the originally Christian term *fundamentalist* on other religious traditions tends to force a wide variety of movements into a Procrustean model that ignores many of their distinctive features. This is in turn related to the argument that the very fact of using an originally Christian term in other religious contexts entails some degree of Christocentric distortion.

Despite such criticisms, some scholars defend the use of the term *fundamentalism* as a useful tool for comparative purposes. Martin E. Marty and R. Scott Appleby argue that the use of the term outside the Protestant context has become so common, in the West at least, that it would be impossible to eradicate this usage. They argue that no alternative term has been found for comparative purposes, and that comparison is essential if we wish to transcend the description of specific cases. Moreover, they argue, 'all words have to come from somewhere', therefore the Christian origin of the term *fundamentalism* is not an insurmountable obstacle so long as the comparative use of the term does not involve forcing all movements called fundamentalist to resemble Protestant fundamentalism (Marty and Appleby 1991a: viii). They insist that they do not want to force all movements into a Procrustean bed. They define fundamentalism as follows:

> In these pages, then, fundamentalism has appeared as a tendency, a habit of mind, found within religious communities and movements, which manifests itself as a strategy, or set of strategies, by which beleaguered believers attempt to preserve their distinctive identity as a people or group. Feeling this identity to be at risk in the contemporary era, they fortify it by a selective retrieval of doctrines, beliefs, and practices from a sacred past. These retrieved 'fundamentals' are refined, modified, and sanctioned in a spirit of shrewd pragmatism: they are to serve as a bulwark against the encroachment of outsiders who threaten to draw the believers into a syncretistic, areligious, or irreligious cultural milieu . . .
>
> (Marty and Appleby 1991a: 835)

We shall see that this very broad conception of fundamentalism ignores many important distinctions among the movements Marty and Appleby describe as fundamentalist.

In this essay, we shall speak of movements having a fundamentalist dimension only if they insist on strict conformity to sacred scripture and a moral code ostensibly based on it. These movements articulate moral outrage provoked by the violation of traditional religious values. This is true of many politicized forms of religious conservatism, notably Catholic conservatism, that do not insist on strict conformity to sacred scripture *per se*.

Moreover, and this is crucial, some movements that have a fundamentalist dimension also articulate secular grievances. To focus only on their fundamentalist dimension is to ignore some of the principal sources of their political significance. We should not reduce moral outrage provoked by the violation of traditional religious values to a mere epiphenomenon of ethnic, nationalistic or other social grievances, but we should also avoid ignoring such grievances when the available evidence suggests that they are in fact important sources of the appeal of some movements commonly called 'fundamentalist'.

Perhaps the most obvious problem with the Marty-Appleby conception of fundamentalism is their view that it is a reaction to 'modernity', a vague term that is best avoided. In *Strong Religion: The Rise of Fundamentalisms around the World*, Almond *et al.* argue that 'fundamentalist movements form in reaction to, and in defense against, the processes and consequences of secularization and modernization' (2003: 93). If the rejection of the marginalization of religion is not a movement's 'original impulse and a recurring reference', they argue, it is not in fact a fundamentalist movement (2003: 94). They muddy the definitional waters, however, by declaring:

> In short, the threat to the religious tradition may come from the general processes of modernization and secularization, from other religious groups and/or ethnic groups, from a secular state (imperial or indigenous) seeking to secularize and delimit the domain of the sacred, or from various combinations of these.
>
> (Almond *et al.*)

This passage blurs the fundamental distinction between a conservative religious movement that rejects innovations that violate its traditional beliefs and a movement in which religion serves primarily as a marker of identity. In the first case, moral outrage provoked by the violation of traditional religious values is of central importance. In the second case, it is not.

Identity trumps belief: Protestant Unionism in Northern Ireland and Sikh militancy in India

If we take the case of Northern Ireland, for example, religion serves primarily as a marker of collective identity for both Catholic and Protestant, rather than as a set of beliefs to be defended in the face of secularization. This point is illustrated by the following joke. One night, a distinguished gentleman was walking down a dark alley in Belfast. Suddenly a masked man jumped out in front of him, waved a gun in his face, and asked, 'Are you a Catholic or a Protestant?' The terrified gentleman stammered, 'W-w-w-well, I-I-I am actually an atheist.' 'Well now', responded the gunman, with what appeared to be a twinkle in his eye, 'would you be a Catholic atheist or a Protestant atheist?' Similarly, when rioting Hindus pull men's pants down to see if they are circumcised, they are not interested in whether or not circumcised men are believing or practicing Muslims. A circumcised penis marks a man as the killable 'Other' regardless of what he actually believes or does. Religion serves as a distinctive marker of identity, and notably of national identity, even in the absence of belief.

There are movements in which religion serves primarily as a marker of ethnic or national identity, but which nonetheless have a clear fundamentalist dimension, in the sense that some of their most prominent adherents insist on strict conformity to sacred scripture and a moral code ostensibly based on it. Protestant Unionism (or 'Loyalism') in Northern Ireland is basically an expression of the fears of Protestants who are afraid of losing their identity and their rights in a predominantly Catholic Ireland. Many Unionists are in fact quite secular and only about a quarter, or at most a third, are fundamentalists (Bruce 1998: 68). Yet the fundamentalist Reverend Ian Paisley's Democratic Unionist Party (DUP) won more votes than any other party in Northern Ireland's legislative elections of November 26, 2003. Since 1979, Paisley has also consistently won more votes than any other candidate in Northern Ireland's elections to the parliament of the European Union – despite the fact that Paisley sees the European Union as a Catholic plot to undermine Protestantism (Bruce 1998: 63–4, 67). It is clear that many non-fundamentalist Protestants in Northern Ireland regularly vote for Paisley. Steve Bruce has argued that this is because of the basic role conservative evangelicalism has played in shaping Ulster Protestant identity (1998: 73). It may also reflect Paisley's ability to articulate Protestant concerns in an earthy, populist language everyone can understand. For present purposes, the key point is that Protestantism Unionism is primarily about identity rather than about conformity to scripture even though its most famous leader is a fundamentalist.

The case of Protestant Unionism is strikingly similar to Sikh militancy in India insofar as its fundamentalist dimension is subordinate to its nationalist dimension. The militant Sikh movement first attracted attention in 1978, when the fiery preacher Sant Jarnail Singh Bhindranwale led a march to break up a gathering of the Sant Nirankari sect considered heretical by orthodox Sikhs (Oberoi 1993: 273). Bhindranwale's movement definitely had a fundamentalist dimension to it insofar as it stressed the need for conformity to a sacred text. But Sikh militancy was primarily an ethnic and nationalist movement, with religion serving as the principal marker of Sikh identity. That is, the Sikh militants of the late twentieth century fought primarily for an independent Sikh state in the Indian province of Punjab. While Bhindranwale and his followers did condemn Sikhs who violated the traditional Sikh moral code, the primary enemy of all the Sikh militants, some of whom were more religious than others, was the state of India rather than secularism *per se*. The militants condemned the government of India not for being secular, but for being biased in favor of Hindus (Mahmood 1996).

We shall now consider the principal modern movements often called 'fundamentalist'. We shall focus on the following questions: To what extent are these movements reactions to secular 'modernity'? To what extent do these movements articulate social and nationalistic grievances as well as moral outrage provoked by the violation of traditional religious values? Do these movements have a messianic and apocalyptic dimension? Can these movements be considered totalitarian insofar as they seek to force all aspects of society to conform to religious law or do they withdraw from society to maintain their way of life in secluded enclaves? And are these movements violent?

Christian fundamentalism in the United States

Fundamentalism the thing existed long before the word did. One could speak of the Maccabean revolt of the second century BCE as having a fundamentalist impulse insofar as it insisted on strict conformity to the Torah and Jewish religious law (Munson 2003b). Similarly, Calvin's sixteenth-century Genevan polity and seventeenth-century Puritanism could be called fundamentalist insofar as they insisted on strict conformity to the Bible and a moral code ostensibly based on it. But the term *Fundamentalist* (traditionally written with an upper-case F) was only coined in 1920 by Curtis Lee Laws, the conservative editor of the Baptist newspaper *The Watchman-Examiner*. Laws created the word to refer to militantly conservative evangelical Protestants ready 'to do battle royal for the fundamentals' of Christianity (Beale 1986: 195). Fundamentalists do not simply believe; they fight to defend their beliefs against those who seek to dilute them.

Modern Christian fundamentalism emerged as a revolt against the tendency to rationalize and demythologize Protestant Christianity in the late nineteenth and early twentieth centuries. In response to Protestant liberalism that watered down the basic tenets of Christianity, conservative evangelicals published a series of pamphlets entitled *The Fundamentals* from 1910 to 1915. The central theme of *The Fundamentals* is that the Bible is the inerrant word of God. That it is to say that it is without error. Associated with this idea is the belief that believers should live their lives according to a strict Biblically based moral code.

Evangelical Christians believe that the Bible is the word of God, that one can only be saved from eternal damnation by accepting Jesus Christ as one's savior, and that the Christian is obliged to 'evangelize', that is, to spread the 'good news' of Christ's death and resurrection for the sake of humanity. The acceptance of Jesus as one's savior is linked to the idea of being 'born again' through an experience of the Holy Spirit. George Marsden has described Christian fundamentalists as evangelicals who are 'angry about something' (Marsden 1991: 1).

In the nineteenth century, Christian evangelicals of a fundamentalist orientation (again, the thing preceded the word) had been politically active on both sides of the slavery issue, in anti-Catholic nativism, in the fight to maintain Sunday as a day of rest, and in the temperance movement. This political activism continued in the early twentieth century, with evolution becoming a major issue in the 1920s. Christian fundamentalism also often had a strongly nationalistic dimension. During the First World War, the evangelist Billy Sunday argued that 'Christianity and Patriotism are synonymous terms' (Marsden 1991: 51).

Christian fundamentalists have, however, been torn by an inherent tension regarding political activism. Most Christian fundamentalists have been 'premillennialists'. That is, they believe that Jesus Christ will return before the millennium, a thousand-year period of perfect peace, and that it is pointless to try to reform the world because it is doomed until Jesus returns. This attitude is expressed in the common expression 'Why polish the brass on a sinking ship?' Postmillennialist fundamentalists argue that spiritual and moral reform will lead to the millennium, after which Christ will return. Thus whereas premillennialism logically implies political passivity, postmillennialism implies political activism. But belief and practice do not always coincide. Many premillennialist fundamentalists have embraced political activism while nonetheless anticipating the imminent return of Jesus.

Classical premillennialist eschatology meshed well with another distinctive feature of Christian fundamentalism, the doctrine of separatism. True Christians should separate themselves from the broader society in which they are immersed rather than try to reform it. Yet Christian fundamentalists have nonetheless periodically entered the political arena. The conventional wisdom is that after the Scopes trial of 1925, most Christian fundamentalists avoided the political arena until the late 1970s. This is to some extent true, but not entirely so. Some Christian fundamentalists ran for public office in the 1930s and 1940s on platforms that combined anti-Semitism, anti-communism, populism, and Christian revivalism (see Ribuffo 1983). From the 1950s through the 1970s, fundamentalist preachers like Billy James Hargis combined similar themes, minus the explicit anti-Semitism, with opposition to racial integration.

Although Christian fundamentalist ministers were active in opposing the civil rights movement and communism in the 1960s, they remained politically marginal. No president would have invited a man like Billy James Hargis to the White House. In 1979, however, the Reverend Jerry Falwell formed the Moral Majority in collaboration with important mainstream conservatives in the Republican party to defend religious Christian values. He was often invited to the White House by Ronald Reagan. Falwell, like most fundamentalists and some other Americans, felt that the feminist movement, the prohibition of school-sponsored prayer in public schools, the teaching of sex education, the gay rights movement, and the legalization of abortion all represented a process of moral decay that had to be halted. While most liberal intellectuals would see opposition to these developments as a rejection of secular 'modernity', most religious conservatives would see them as a fight to save their nation's moral integrity.

The federal government's attempt to deny the tax-exempt status of many Christian schools founded to circumvent the federally mandated racial integration of public schools was also one of the reasons for the formation of the Moral Majority, but in the 1980s many southern Christian fundamentalists disavowed their earlier opposition to civil rights. The Christian Right nevertheless remained an overwhelmingly white movement that was viewed with suspicion by most African Americans.

Marty and Appleby, among others, have argued that 'fundamentalism contains within it a totalitarian impulse' because fundamentalists seek to structure all aspects of state and society on the basis of religious law. (Marty and Appleby 1991b: 824). This was not true of most activists in the Christian Right of the late twentieth and early twenty-first centuries. Most of the Christian fundamentalists (and conservative Catholics and Mormons) who were active in this movement focused on moral issues such as abortion, prayer in schools, homosexuality, and the teaching of 'creationism', rather than on restructuring all aspects of society on the basis of scripture. They saw themselves as defending their values in the face of the onslaught of liberal and secular values in American society rather than as trying to impose their values on others.

Some late-twentieth-century Christian fundamentalists in the United States did advocate the creation of a state and society based on strict conformity to Biblical law. They were known as Christian Reconstructionists (Martin 1996: 353–5). But they constituted a small minority of the activists in the Christian Right, and they have been criticized by more moderate evangelical Christians such as Ralph Reed. Some critics of the Christian Right argue that the apparent moderation of evangelicals such as Ralph Reed (who would reject the label *fundamentalist*) was just a tactical maneuver and if they were ever able to establish a totalitarian state based on Biblical law, they would do so. This is a difficult claim to test. All we can say with certainty is that there was nothing explicitly totalitarian about the goals of the mainstream Christian Right in the late twentieth and early twenty-first centuries.

Politicized Jewish Orthodoxy in Israel

Three politicized forms of Orthodox Judaism in Israel (and elsewhere) have often been called 'fundamentalist': militant religious Zionism, Ashkenazi ultra-Orthodoxy, and the Shas party, which represents Jews of Middle Eastern origin. These groups are called 'fundamentalist' by their critics, not their supporters (Heilman and Friedman 1991; Hirschberg 1999; Sprinzak 1999).

Since the fall of Jerusalem's second temple in CE 70, most Jews have lived in the diaspora, that is, dispersed far from the Land of Israel promised by God to the Jewish people according to the Hebrew Bible. During their prolonged 'exile' (*galut*) from the Land of Israel, Jews all over the world prayed daily for the coming of the Messiah who would bring the Jews back to the Land of Israel and deliver them from their gentile oppressors. Zionism secularized this traditional messianic theme. Instead of waiting for God and the Messiah to bring the Jews back to the Land of Israel, Zionists argued that Jews should take it upon themselves to return to this land.

Most Orthodox rabbis opposed Zionism on the grounds that it involved humans doing what only God and the Messiah could do. In traditional Judaism, the return to the Land of Israel was inseparable from the messianic redemption of the people of Israel. For humans to return to this land and create a state there was to defy God's will and postpone the real redemption and the real ingathering of the exiles. Another reason for Orthodox hostility to Zionism was that most of the early Zionist leaders were clearly not interested in a state based on strict conformity to Jewish religious law.

In speaking of Orthodox Judaism, we should distinguish between the 'modern Orthodox' and the 'ultra-Orthodox'. (The ultra-Orthodox themselves generally object to the latter term.) The modern Orthodox insist on strict conformity to Jewish law, but they have nonetheless devised ways to participate in modern society in both the diaspora and Israel. The ultra-Orthodox are more traditional and insist on strict separation from gentile society as well as separation from Jews who do not follow Jewish law as strictly as they do. Hostility toward Zionism prevailed among both modern Orthodox and ultra-Orthodox rabbis in the late nineteenth and early twentieth centuries, though it virtually disappeared among the former when the Holocaust appeared to confirm the Zionist argument that Jews could only be safe in their own state.

Some modern Orthodox rabbis sought to legitimate Orthodox participation in the Zionist movement by severing it from the idea of the Messiah. Rabbi Isaac Jacob Reines (1839–1915), who founded the Mizrahi religious Zionist movement in 1902, agreed with the ultra-Orthodox that Jews should not try to 'force the End' on their own initiative. He embraced the traditional belief that Jews should passively await the coming of the Messiah, but, unlike the ultra-Orthodox, he argued that the Zionist settlement of the Land of Israel had nothing to do with the future messianic redemption of the Jews and thus did not constitute a heretical defiance of God's will. This form of religious Zionism was soon displaced by a radically different view, namely that Zionism was itself part of the gradual messianic redemption of the Jewish people and the Land of Israel. The secular Zionists were doing the work of God and the Messiah but they did not yet know it. This argument was made by Rabbi Avraham Kook (1865–1935), and it has remained a basic theme in religious Zionism (Ravitzky 1996).

Religious Zionists are usually referred to as the 'national religious' (*datim le'umim*) in Hebrew. This term captures the fusion of modern Orthodoxy and nationalism that has always characterized religious Zionism. Unlike the ultra-Orthodox, the religious Zionists have always been willing to cooperate with the far more numerous secular Zionists who were primarily responsible for creating the modern state of Israel. Traditionally, the religious Zionist National Religious Party and its predecessors concerned themselves with domestic religious issues, such as the observance of Shabbat and who is a Jew, and left foreign affairs to the Labor party. They were certainly not a 'totalitarian' party.

Many religious Zionists saw the Six-Day War of 1967 as a miracle and as a major step forward on the way toward the messianic redemption of the Jewish people. East Jerusalem, the Temple Mount, Judea, the very heart of ancient Israel, were now once again in Jewish hands. To return any of this land to the Arabs would be to defy God. The religious Zionists who felt this way began to settle in the territories occupied, or as they saw it, liberated, in the Six-Day War. It should be stressed that there is also a religious Zionist peace movement, known as Meimad, which advocates giving up much of the territory won in 1967 in return for peace.

For the militant religious Zionists in the settler movement, settling the land won in 1967 and preventing the government from withdrawing from it took priority over anything else. These militant religious Zionists did advocate the creation of a state based on strict conformity to what they consider the laws of God and they did conform strictly to these laws in their everyday lives. But their political activities focused primarily on settling and retaining the land won in 1967 rather than on creating a state and society based on strict conformity to religious law. Thus, while militant religious Zionism has a 'fundamentalist' dimension, it is also important to remember its nationalist dimension and its roots in the Revisionist Zionist idea that force must be used to fight the inherently anti-Semitic gentile. Indeed, the religious Zionists tap some basic themes in mainstream Zionism, notably the idea that the goal of Zionism is to create a new Jew who will never submit to oppression. For militant religious Zionists, this involves a return to the Judaism of the Maccabees who fought Hellenism in the second century BCE much as religious Zionists fight decadent secularism today (Munson 2003b).

The ultra-Orthodox are often referred to in Hebrew as *Haredim*, or 'those who tremble' in the presence of God because they are 'God-fearing'. Unlike the modern Orthodox, who are virtually all religious Zionists, the ultra-Orthodox continue to reject Zionism, in principle at least, as a blasphemous attempt to bring about the return of the Jews to the Land of Israel by human means when God intended this to be effected by the Messiah. In practice, this rejection of Zionism results in a variety of different political positions ranging from that of the politically insignificant Neturei Karta to Haredi political parties that sometimes determine which of

Israel's major parties gets to govern. (Israel's major parties often have to make conces-
sions to small religious parties to win the support of a majority of the members of
the Israeli parliament, the Knesset, and thereby form a government.)

The Ashkenazi Haredim, that is, the ultra-Orthodox of eastern European origin,
differ from the ultra-Orthodox of Middle Eastern origin, who will be discussed below.
Unlike the religious Zionists, whose political activities since 1967 have focused
primarily on settling and preventing withdrawal from the territories occupied in the
Six-Day War, the Haredi (ultra-Orthodox) political parties have continued to
concentrate primarily on obtaining funding for their community and on enforcing
strict conformity to their interpretation of Jewish religious law with respect to issues
like observance of the Sabbath, conversion, Kosher dietary laws, and the desecra-
tion of the dead by archaeologists. Since the Six-Day War, however, most Ashkenazi
Haredim have tended to support the hard-line position of the militant religious
Zionists regarding 'land-for-peace' despite their continued theoretical opposition to
Zionism and the state it produced. This is a striking example of how changing social
and political contexts can affect religious beliefs.

The Ashkenazi Haredim traditionally withdrew from surrounding gentile society
in the diaspora and continue to separate themselves from mainstream Israeli society.
Yet in the last few decades of the twentieth century, they became increasingly aggressive in trying to incorporate their moral code into Israeli law. Like Christian
fundamentalists in the United States, they have been torn between the desire to
withdraw from society and the desire to reform it. Because of their high birth rate,
their numbers have grown, and this has meant greater electoral power. This has been
especially evident in Jerusalem, which elected its first Haredi mayor in 2003.

The third major form of Jewish militant Orthodoxy in Israel often called fundamentalist is represented by the Shas party, Shas being an acronym for 'Sephardim
Guardians of the Torah' in Hebrew. Although the term *Sephardim* originally referred
to Jews of Spanish origin, it has come to be used to refer to Jews of Middle Eastern
origin. The Sephardim are, by and large, less well educated and less well paid
than the Ashkenazim, and many of them feel that Israelis of European origin discriminate against them. In addition to celebrating Sephardic identity and advocating
strict conformity to God's laws, Shas provides schools and other social services
for poor Sephardim. Shas is similar to some Islamic movements in this respect
(Hirschberg 1999).

One can speak of a fundamentalist dimension to Shas insofar as it consistently
supports legislation to enforce strict conformity to Jewish religious law. But much of
its popular support is rooted in the frustration, resentment, and even rage of those
Jews of Middle Eastern origin who feel they have been discriminated against by the
Ashkenazi elite of European origin. Most Sephardim who vote for Shas do not themselves conform to the strict moral code advocated by the party. Like the strongly
nationalistic religious Zionist settlers, Shas demonstrates that movements often called
fundamentalist often owe their political success to secular grievances as well as strictly
religious ones.

Many secular Israelis do perceive the Ashkenazi and Sephardi ultra-Orthodox and
the militant religious Zionists as seeking to create a totalitarian state in which aspects
of Israeli life would be structured according to Jewish religious law. And many
Haredim and militant religious Zionists would in fact favor such a state. But as a

practical matter, such a state is out of the question until the Orthodox outnumber the secular. In the mean time, the parties representing these movements generally operate within the framework of Israel's parliamentary democracy. (They generally receive less than 25 percent of the total vote in national elections.) It is true, however, that militant religious Zionists have sometimes resorted to violence.

Islamic militancy in the Middle East

The term *Islamic fundamentalism* tends to conjure up images of fanaticism and terrorism. This is one reason most scholars of Islam prefer the more anodyne term *Islamist*. Islamist movements, like their Christian and Jewish counterparts, come in various forms. There are moderate Islamist movements that seek to create Islamic states and societies by nonviolent means and there are others, like al-Qa'ida (al Qaeda), that do use violence to achieve their goals. Militant Islamic movements clearly resort to violence far more often than do the Christian and Jewish movements commonly called fundamentalist. It is true that Christian fundamentalists were actively involved in the terrorism of the Ku Klux Klan and similar groups. It is also true that Christian fundamentalists have been involved in attacking abortion clinics and killing doctors who perform abortions (Juergensmeyer 2000). Similarly, it is true that militant religious Zionists have engaged in some violence, notably Baruch Goldstein's massacre of 29 Palestinians praying in Hebron and Yigal Amir's assassination of Prime Minister Yitzhak Rabin in 1995. But Christian and Jewish fundamentalists have not engaged in the same scale of violence as militant Islamic groups like Hizb Allah (Hezbollah), Hamas, and al-Qa'ida.

This does not mean that Islam is inherently more violent than Christianity. One can find many verses extolling the slaughter of the enemy in the name of God in the sacred scriptures of Judaism and Christianity (see Deuteronomy 7: 1–2, 7: 16 and 20: 10–18). The history of Christianity is full of holy wars and massacres of Jews condemned as 'Christ-killers'. If violence is more commonly used by militant Islamic movements than by militantly conservative Christian and Jewish movements, this is because of the prevailing social and political situation in the Islamic world, and not because of some immutable feature of Islam.

Whereas messianic and apocalyptic themes are of considerable importance for the conservative Protestants and Jews often called fundamentalists, this is much less true of 'Muslim fundamentalists'. Islam certainly has a messianic dimension, which is especially conspicuous in Shi'ite Islam. But while some militant Islamic revivalists do invoke messianic and apocalyptic themes, such notions are generally of little or no political significance (Gorenberg 2000; Almond *et al.* 2003: 64–69).

Another feature that distinguishes Islamism from conservative Christian and Jewish militancy is its anti-imperial dimension. When the European empires subjugated the Islamic world in the nineteenth and early twentieth centuries, Muslims perceived their wars against European imperialism as forms of *jihad*, or holy war. The distinction between Muslim and infidel became intertwined with the distinctions between the colonized and the colonizer and the oppressed and the oppressor. Thus traditional hostility toward the unbeliever as an unbeliever was now infused with new meaning. This had unfortunate consequences for religious minorities in the Islamic world (much as Irish Protestants suffered from sharing the religion of England).

This anti-imperial dimension persisted in the Islamist movements of the late twentieth century. On February 19, 1978, on the fortieth day of mourning for the 'martyrs' who had died in the first protests that eventually mushroomed into Iran's Islamic revolution, the revolution's leader the Ayatollah Khomeini declared, 'As for America, a signatory to the Declaration of Human Rights, it imposed this shah upon us, a worthy successor to his father. During the period he has ruled, this creature has transformed Iran into an official colony of America' (Khomeini 1981: 215). When Khomeini landed at the Tehran airport on February 1, 1979, after fourteen and a half years of exile, he declared: 'Our triumph will come when all forms of foreign control have been brought to an end and all roots of the monarchy have been plucked out of the soil of our land' (1981: 252). On September 12, 1980, Khomeini told the Iranian pilgrims to Mecca, 'For more than fifty years, the Pahlavi puppet [the shah] has dragged our country down, filling the pockets of foreigners – particularly Britain and America – with the abundant wealth of our land . . .' (1981: 303).

All these fiery denunciations of the Western domination of 'our land' demonstrate that there was a nationalist dimension to Khomeini's militancy. We see this also in many of the slogans chanted during the marches that eventually coalesced into Iran's Islamic Revolution of 1978–9: 'We will destroy Yankee power in Iran! Death to the American dog! Shah held on a leash by the Americans! Hang this American king!' (Munson 1988: 63, 123). Iran's Islamic revolution was, among other things, a nationalist revolution against American domination.

For Khomeini, the goal of creating a strictly Islamic state and society based exclusively on Islamic law was inextricably intertwined with the goal of overcoming foreign domination. In 1972, he declared:

> If the Muslim states and peoples had relied on Islam and its inherent capabilities and powers instead of depending on the East (the Soviet Union) and the West, and if they had placed the enlightened and liberating precepts of the Quran before their eyes and put them into practice, then they would not today be captive slaves of the Zionist aggressors, terrified victims of the American Phantoms, and toys in the hands of the accommodating policies of the satanic Soviet Union. It is the disregard of the noble Quran by the Islamic countries that has brought the Islamic community to this difficult situation full of misfortunes and reversals and placed its fate in the hands of the imperialism of the left and the right.
>
> (Khomeini 1977: 156–7; Khomeini 1981: 210)

Passages like this are commonplace in the Islamist literature, though we do find some variation in this respect from country to country and group to group. In many cases, the resentment of foreign domination articulated in such passages is expressed in terms of preposterous theories that attempt to blame 'crusader' and Jewish plots for all the problems of the Islamic world. As nonsensical as such conspiracy explanations may be, the nationalistic and anti-imperial resentment that spawns them is real. And it is a major source of the appeal of Islamism.

For Islamists like Khomeini, the idea of a 'return to Islam' is linked to the goal of overcoming foreign domination as follows: The believers are suffering because they have deviated from the laws of God. To end their suffering, they have to conform to

God's laws. God has allowed the infidels to dominate the believers because they have deviated from His laws. Once they conform, He will grant them victory. Such reasoning is often meshed with more subtle themes, notably that of cultural authenticity. The return to Islam becomes a means of regaining one's true cultural identity – as opposed to mimicry of the dominant West. Thus, Khomeini's fundamentalism has an anti-imperial dimension lacking in Christian fundamentalism in the United States.

The anti-imperial dimension of Islamic militancy can also be seen in the rhetoric of Osama bin Laden. Given the common assertion, in the United States at any rate, that Bin Laden 'hates us because of our freedoms', it is important to note that he became politically active as a result of his resentment of Western domination. From 1979 to 1989, he actively supported armed resistance to the Soviet occupation of Afghanistan. He inevitably saw this struggle as a *jihad*. He felt it was his duty to help the oppressed believers of Afghanistan to fight the Russian infidels who were oppressing them. Once again, the distinction between believer and infidel was fused with the dichotomies of oppressed and oppressor and colonized and colonizer.

Resentment of the presence of American troops in Saudi Arabia and what bin Laden viewed as the subjugation of Saudi Arabia pervaded his early statements (see Munson 2004). Indeed, bin Laden has condemned the Saudi regime as heretical because of its subordination to the United States. This is significant. Saudi Arabia is viewed by most outsiders, including many Muslims, as a thoroughly fundamentalist state in which all aspects of society are governed by Islamic law. Yet bin Laden condemns the Saudi government for serving the interests of American imperialism!

As he became more famous, bin Laden downplayed the specifically Saudi grievances that dominated his early statements and focused more on the Palestinians and the deaths of Iraqi children because of sanctions. Thus in his videotaped message of October 7, 2001, after the attacks of September 11, he declared:

> What America is tasting now is nothing compared to what we have been tasting for decades. For over eighty years our umma [the Islamic world] has been tasting this humiliation and this degradation. Its sons are killed, its blood is shed, its holy places are violated, and it is ruled by other than that which God has revealed. Yet no one hears. No one responds . . .
>
> A million innocent children are being killed as I speak. They are being killed in Iraq yet they have done nothing wrong. Yet we hear no condemnation, no fatwa from the reigning sultans. And these days, Israeli tanks wreak havoc in Palestine, in Jenin, Ramallah, Rafah, Beit Jalah and elsewhere in the land of Islam, and we do not hear anyone raising his voice or moving.
>
> (bin Laden 2001)

Bin Laden's statements invariably focus on what he sees as oppression of Muslims by the United States and Israel, rather than on moral issues like the status of women or homosexuality. He would of course take very conservative, if not reactionary, positions on such issues, but he rarely mentions them in his public statements. His emphasis on the suffering of the Palestinians and Iraqis has made him a hero even in the eyes of many Muslims who might be unsympathetic to his goal of a totalitarian Islamic state. Gilles Kepel found that even Arab girls in tight jeans saw bin Laden as an anti-imperialist hero. A young Iraqi woman and her Palestinian friends told Kepel in the fall of 2001, 'He stood up to defend us. He is the only one' (Kepel 2002: 65–6). Bin Laden's heroic stature in the eyes of many Muslims is illustrated by the following joke often told after September 11, 2001. A woman is walking toward the men's room in a restaurant. Several employees of the restaurant try to stop her. She then asks, 'Is Bin Laden in this restroom?' They say no, and she responds, 'Then I can go in because there is only one man left in the Arab and Muslim world: him' (Kepel 2002: 41). This joke reflects the sense of impotence and the rage that pervade much of the Islamic world. Many Muslims feel that the United States and Israel can do whatever they wish to Muslims, and their governments are incapable of fighting back. In this context, bin Laden is widely seen as a heroic Osama Maccabeus coming down from his mountain cave to fight the infidel oppressors to whom the decadent rulers of the Islamic world bow and scrape (Munson 2003b).

Hindu nationalism

At first glance, and even second and third, the notion of 'Hindu fundamentalism' seems preposterous. Hinduism does not have a specific sacred text to which conformity can be demanded. Another important objection to the characterization of Hindu groups such as the Bharatiya Janata Party (BJP) as 'Hindu fundamentalists' is that conformity to a religious code of conduct is not of particular importance to them. They do speak of establishing a truly Hindu state and society, but for these people, Hinduism is above all a symbol of national identity rather than a set of rules to be obeyed (Raychaudhuri 1995).

The primarily nationalistic orientation of the Bharatiya Janata Party is reflected in its name, which means 'the Party of the Indian People'. Similarly, the name of a related group, the Rashtriya Swayamsevak Sangh (RSS) means 'the Association of National Volunteers'. In the Hindu fundamentalist literature, the emphasis is always on the threat posed by Muslims and, more recently, converts to Christianity. The Hindu nationalist obsession with Muslims is reflected in the slogan 'For Muslims, there are only two places, Pakistan or the grave' (*Musulmanan ke do-hi shtan, pakistan aur kabristan* (Halliday 1995: 47).

Hindu nationalists do not stress strict conformity to sacred scripture or to a moral code based on it. It is true that members of the militant Hindu nationalist party Shiv Sena have attacked billboards for a film about a lesbian relationship between two Hindu women. They have also vandalized stores selling Valentine's Day greeting cards (Sengupta 2002). But by and large, puritanical insistence on conformity to a strict moral code has not been a distinctive feature of Hindu nationalism.

The activism of the people Marty and Appleby call 'Hindu fundamentalists' was triggered by the conversion to Islam of thousands of untouchables in southern India in the early 1980s. Coupled with the emergence of militant Sikh separatism, the resurgence of Muslim separatism in Kashmir, and the increasingly vocal demands of untouchables and lower-caste Hindus, some high-caste Hindus began to feel that their status in Indian society, and indeed the very survival of Hindu India, was at risk. This sense of vulnerability rather than a sense that divine law was being violated led to the increased political significance of the BJP and related groups in the late 1980s and early 1990s. In short, the basic impulse of groups like the RSS and the BJP is unquestionably nationalistic rather than 'fundamentalist'.

Given the close relationship between religious and national identity in much of the world, it is not surprising that we do find a nationalist dimension in some of the Christian, Jewish, and Muslim movements often called 'fundamentalist'. But the Hindu case differs radically from Christian fundamentalism, for example. Christian fundamentalists do tend to see the United States as God's chosen land, a 'city on a hill', and we have seen that in the early twentieth century Billy Sunday declared that 'Christianity and Patriotism are synonymous terms'.

However, late-twentieth-century Christian fundamentalism in the United States was fueled primarily by the moral outrage provoked by abortion, the banning of school prayer, feminism, gay rights, the teaching of evolution, and similar issues. Such moral issues have been largely absent from the rhetoric of Hindu nationalism.

Among the most salient issues associated with Hindu nationalism is that of the destruction of the Babri Mosque in Ayodhya and the rebuilding of the Hindu temple said to have existed on this site before its destruction by the Muslim Mughal dynasty. While there was undoubtedly some real religious fervor associated with the belief that Ayodhya was the birthplace of Ram (avatar of Vishnu and hero of the *Ramayana*), the impact of the conflict at Ayodhya was above all a reflection of the Hindu nationalists' emphasis on the essentially Hindu character of India and their view of Muslims as inherently alien enemies of Hindu India. The destruction of the mosque at Ayodhya on December 6, 1992 led to widespread rioting in which Hindus killed several thousand Muslims.

Rather than insist on strict doctrinal purity, Hindu nationalists try to encourage Sikhs and Jains to think of themselves as Hindus despite the distinctiveness of many of their beliefs. Some Hindu militants have admittedly tried to systematize Hinduism in the manner of the Western monotheisms. One group has proposed, for example, a uniform code of conduct for all Hindus, with the *Bhagavad Gita* serving as the sacred text of all Hindus. But the fact remains that the defense of the Hindu community, seen as synonymous with the Indian nation, has been the main theme of Hindu militancy rather than the goal of creating a Hindu state and society based on strict conformity to Hindu religious law. Referring to Hindu nationalism as 'fundamentalism' is thus misleading. (There is no messianic or apocalyptic dimension to Hindu nationalism.)

Conclusion

The use of 'fundamentalism' as an analytical category for comparative purposes remains controversial. In fact, one good reason to avoid the term is to avoid having to waste time defending it. That said, we can discern a fundamentalist impulse in the Christian, Jewish, Muslim, and Sikh movements commonly called fundamentalist insofar as they insist on strict conformity to holy writ and to a moral code ostensibly based on it. (The actual links between moral codes and sacred scriptures are sometimes more tenuous than religious conservatives recognize.) Such an impulse is lacking in Hindu nationalism and it is not of equal significance in all Christian, Jewish, and Muslim movements.

We have seen that militant religious Zionism has a very strong nationalist dimension, with the Maccabees seen as models of the Jew who refuses to submit to the gentile. It is very hard to draw the line between the religious and national dimensions

of religious Zionist militancy. This makes it possible for secular Zionists firmly committed to the retention of the territories Israel won in 1967 to cooperate with militant religious Zionist settlers despite their lack of interest in a Jewish state based on
strict conformity to religious law. Militant religious Zionists would agree with most
religious conservatives on issues like homosexuality and abortion, but their political
activities have focused primarily on settling and retaining the land Israel won in 1967
rather than on moral issues involving the regulation of personal conduct.

There is also a nationalist and anti-imperial dimension to most Islamic militancy.
Hamas is a fundamentalist movement in the sense that it advocates a state based on
strict conformity to Islamic law and the followers of Hamas are expected to follow
a strictly Islamic code of conduct. At the same time, however, Hamas is clearly a
Palestinian nationalist movement that echoes most of the traditional demands of the
Palestinian Liberation Organization before it accepted the idea of the partition of
pre-1948 Palestine into a Jewish state on 78 percent of the land and a Palestinian
state on the remaining 22 percent (Munson 2003a). To speak of Hamas only in
terms of its fundamentalist dimension while ignoring its nationalist dimension would
be to distort the nature of the movement. There is also a social dimension to Hamas.
Like Shas in Israel, and like Hizb Allah in Lebanon, Hamas provides an extensive
network of social services that serves to attract supporters (Roy 2003).

The case of Shas illustrates the fusion of politicized religious conservatism with
demands on behalf of an ethnic group that believes it has been discriminated against.
To speak of Shas only as a fundamentalist movement without reference to the sense
of ethnic grievance that fuels it would be, once again, to ignore the social and political context that produced it. Just as religion often serves as a badge of national
identity, so too does it often serve as a badge of ethnic identity within nations.

To speak of all groups that have a fundamentalist dimension simply as 'revolts
against modernity' is inadequate insofar as it tends to downplay or ignore the nationalist and social grievances that often fuel such movements. This is not to suggest
that religious outrage provoked by the violation of traditional religious values cannot
induce people to undertake political action. If someone believes that abortion is
murder, then it is perfectly natural that such a person would engage in political
action to prevent abortion. And it is a mistake to attempt to ignore what people
say when they explain their political acts in terms of their religious beliefs and assert
that they really do what they do because of some sort of alleged disorientation caused
by 'rapid modernization'. But while we should avoid reducing all apparently religious
motivation to underlying secular causes, we should also recognize that moral outrage
provoked by the violation of traditional religious values is sometimes meshed with
outrage provoked by nationalistic and social grievances. (This too may be a form of
moral outrage.)

Comparing the various politicized forms of religious conservatism and religiously
tinged nationalism is useful. But this must be done with careful attention to the
distinctive features of the movements in question and the specific historical contexts
that have shaped them. The neglect of such features and contexts can transform
comparison into caricature.

Bibliography

Almond, G. A., R. S. Appleby, and E. Sivan (2003) *Strong Religion: the Rise of Fundamentalisms around the World*. Chicago: University of Chicago Press.

Appleby, R. S. (1995) But All Crabs are Crabby: Valid and Less Valid Criticisms of the Fundamentalism Project. *Contention* 4 (3): 195–202.

Beale, D. O. (1986) *In Pursuit of Purity: American Fundamentalism since 1850*. Greenville, S.C.: Unusual Publications.

Berger, P. (1997) Secularism in Retreat. *The National Interest* (Winter 1996/97): 3–12.

bin Laden, O. (2001) *Al-Nass al-harfi al-kamil li-kalimat Usama bin Ladin*. The Arabic original is accessible at (April 16, 2003). I have used my own translation. The BBC translation is in Rubin, B. M., and J. C. Rubin, eds. 2002. *Anti-American Terrorism and the Middle East: a Documentary Reader*. New York: Oxford University Press. The Arabic original is accessible at http://www.alitijahalakhar.com/archive/35/here35.htm (last accessed April 9, 2005).

Bruce, S. (1998) *Conservative Protestant Politics*. New York: Oxford University Press.

—— (2000) *Fundamentalism*. Cambridge: Polity.

Gorenberg, G. (2000) *The End of Days: Fundamentalism and the Struggle for the Temple Mount*. New York: Free Press.

Halliday, F. (1995) Fundamentalism and the Contemporary World. *Contention* 4 (2): 41–58.

Heilman, S. C., and M. Friedman. (1991) Religious Fundamentalism and Religious Jews: The Case of the Haredim. In *Fundamentalisms Observed*, edited by M. M. E. and R. S. Appleby. Chicago: University of Chicago Press.

Hirschberg, P. (1999) *The World of Shas*. New York: The Institute on American Jewish–Israeli Relations of the American Jewish Committee.

Juergensmeyer, M. (2000) *Terror in the Mind of God: The Global Rise of Religious Violence*. Berkeley CA: University of California Press.

Kepel, G. (2002) *Chronique d'une guerre d'Orient*. Paris: Gallimard.

Khomeini, R. (1977) *Durus Fi Al-Jihad Wa-Al-Rafd: Yusatiruha Al-Imam Al-Khumayni Khilal Harakatihi Al-Nidaliyah Al-Ra'idah*. S.l.: s.n.

—— (1981) *Islam and Revolution in the Middle East: Writings and Declarations of Imam Khomeini*. Translated by H. Algar. Berkeley CA: Mizan Press.

Mahmood, C. K. (1996) *Fighting for Faith and Nation: Dialogues with Sikh Militants*. Philadelphia PA: University of Pennsylvania Press.

Marsden, G. M. (1991) *Understanding Fundamentalism and Evangelicalism*. Grand Rapids MT: W. B. Eerdmans.

Martin, W. C. (1996) *With God on our Side: the Rise of the Religious Right in America*. 1st edn. New York: Broadway Books.

Marty, M. E., and R. S. Appleby (1991a) The Fundamentalism Project: A User's Guide. In *Fundamentalisms Observed*, edited by M. E. Marty and R. S. Appleby. Chicago: University of Chicago Press.

—— and —— (1991b) Conclusion: An Interim Report on a Hypothetical Family. In *Fundamentalisms Observed*, edited by M. E. Marty and R. S. Appleby. Chicago: University of Chicago Press.

Munson, H. (1988) *Islam and Revolution in the Middle East*. New Haven CT: Yale University Press.

—— (2003a) Islam, Nationalism, and Resentment of Foreign Domination. *Middle East Policy* 10 (2): 40–53.

—— (2003b) 'Fundamentalism' Ancient and Modern. *Daedalus* 132 (3): 31–41.

—— (2004) Lifting the Veil: Understanding the Roots of Islamic Militancy. *Harvard International Review* 25 (4): 20–23.

Oberoi, H. (1993) Sikh Fundamentalism: Translating History into Theory. In *Fundamentalisms and the State*, edited by M. E. Marty and R. S. Appleby. Chicago: University of Chicago Press.

Ravitzky, A. (1996) *Messianism, Zionism, and Jewish Religious Radicalism*. Chicago: University of Chicago Press.

Raychaudhuri, T. (1995) Shadows of the Swastika: Historical Reflections on the Politics of Hindu Communalism. *Contention* 4 (2): 141–62.

Ribuffo, L. P. (1983) *The Old Christian Reight: The Protestant Far Right from the Great Depression to the Cold War*. Philadelphia: Temple University Press.

Roy, S. (2003) Hamas and the Transformation(s) of Political Islam in Palestine. *Current History*, January, 13–20.

Said, E. W. (1992) Impossible Histories: Why the Mary Islans Cannot be Simplified. *Harper's Magazine*, July. Accessed through Academic Search Premier.

—— (1993) *Culture and Imperialism*. 1st edn. New York: Knopf.

Sengupta, S. (2002) Oh, the Heartache! They Want Cupid Banished. *New York Times*, February 12, 2002.

Sprinzak, E. (1999) *Brother Against Brother: Violence and Extremish in Israeli Politics from Altalena to the Rabin Assassination*. New York: The Free Press.

Chapter 20

Myth and ritual

Robert A. Segal

SECTION ONE: MYTH

Whether or not myths are as old as humanity, challenges to myth are as old, or almost as old, as myths themselves. In the West the challenge to myth goes back at least to Plato (*c.* 428–348 or 347 BCE), who rejected Homeric myth on, especially, moral grounds. It was above all the Stoics who defended myth against this charge by reinterpreting myth allegorically. The chief modern challenge to myth has come not from ethics but from science. Here myth is assumed to explain how gods control the physical world rather than, as for Plato, how they behave among themselves. Where Plato bemoans myths for presenting the gods as models of immoral behavior, modern critics dismiss myths for explaining the world religiously rather than scientifically.

Myth as true science

One form of the modern challenge to myth has been to the scientific credibility of myth. Did creation really occur in a mere six days, as the first of two creation stories in Genesis (1:1–2:4a) claims? Was there really a worldwide flood? Is the earth truly but six or seven thousand years old? Could the ten plagues on the Egyptians actually have happened? The most unrepentant defense against this challenge has been to claim that the biblical account is correct, for, after all, the Pentateuch was revealed to Moses by God. This position, known as 'creationism,' assumes varying forms, ranging, for example, from taking the days of creation to mean exactly six days to taking them to mean 'ages.'

At the same time creationists vaunt their views as scientific. 'Creationism' is shorthand for 'creation science,' which appropriates scientific evidence of any kind both to bolster its own claims and to refute those of secular rivals such as evolution. Doubtless 'creation scientists' would object to the term 'myth' to characterize the view they defend, but only because the term has come to connote false belief. If the term is used neutrally for a firmly held conviction, creationism is a myth that claims to be scientific. For creation scientists, it is evolution that is untenable scientifically. In any clash between the Bible and modern science, modern science must give way to biblical science, not vice versa. Creationism, which may have its counterparts in other religions, thus goes beyond other versions of fundamentalism in claiming to be both religious *and* science, not religious *rather than* scientific.

Myth as modern science

A much tamer defense against the challenge of modern science has been to reconcile myth with modern science. Here elements at odds with modern science are either
removed or, more cleverly, reinterpreted as in fact scientific. Myth is credible scientifically because it *is* science. There might not have been a Noah able single-handedly
to gather up all living species and to keep them alive in a wooden boat sturdy enough
to withstand the strongest seas that ever arose, but a worldwide flood did occur.
What thus remains in myth is true because it is scientific. This approach is the opposite of that called 'demythologizing,' which separates myth from science.

In their comment on the first plague, the turning of the waters of the Nile into
blood (Exodus 7:14–24), the editors of the *Oxford Annotated Bible* epitomize this
rationalizing approach: 'The plague of blood apparently reflects a natural phenomenon of Egypt: namely, the reddish color of the Nile at its height in the summer
owing to red particles of earth or perhaps minute organisms' (May and Metzger 1977:
75). Of the second plague, that of frogs (Exodus 8:1–15), the editors declare similarly: 'The mud of the Nile, after the seasonal overflowing, was a natural place for
frogs to generate. Egypt has been spared more frequent occurrence of this pestilence
by the frog-eating bird, the ibis' (May and Metzger 1977: 75). How fortuitous that
the ibis must have been away on holiday when Aaron stretched out his hand to
produce the plague and must have just returned when Moses wanted the plague to
cease![1] Instead of setting myth *against* science, this tactic turns myth *into* science –
and not, as is fashionable today, science into myth.

For the American Near Eastern scholar Samuel Noah Kramer (1897–1990),
Sumerian creation myths thus evince observations about the physical world and scientific-like hypotheses drawn to account for them:

> It cannot be sufficiently stressed that the Sumerian cosmogonic concepts, early
> as they are, are by no means *primitive*. They reflect the mature thought and reason
> of the thinking Sumerian as he contemplated the forces of nature and the
> character of his own existence. When these concepts are analyzed; when the
> theological cloak and polytheistic trappings are removed, ... the Sumerian
> creation concepts indicate a keenly observing mentality as well as an ability to
> draw and formulate pertinent conclusions from the data observed.
>
> (Kramer 1961: 73)

Gods are mere personifications of natural phenomena, and their actions are mere
metaphors for natural processes. The mythic pronouncement that 'The union of
[the male heaven-god] *An* and [the earth-goddess] *Ki* produced the air-god
Enlil, who proceeded to separate the heaven-father *An* from the earth-mother *Ki*' is
to be translated as follows: 'Heaven and earth were conceived as *solid* elements.
Between them, however, and *from them*, came the gaseous element *air*, whose main
characteristic is that of expansion. Heaven and earth were thus separated by the
expanding element *air*' (Kramer 1961: 74, 73). Again, myth is science – modern
science.[2]

Myth as primitive science

By far the most common response to the challenge of science has been to abandon myth for science. Here myth, while still an explanation of the world, is now taken as an explanation of its own kind, not a scientific explanation in mythic guise. The issue is therefore not the scientific *credibility* of myth but the *compatibility* of myth with science. Myth is considered to be 'primitive' science – or, more precisely, the pre-scientific counterpart to science, which is assumed to be exclusively modern. Myth is here part of religion. Where religion apart from myth provides the belief in gods, myth fills in the details of how gods cause events. Because myth is part of religion, the rise of science as the reigning modern explanation of physical events has consequently spelled the fall of not only religion but also myth. Because moderns by definition accept science, they cannot also have myth, and the phrase 'modern myth' is self-contradictory. Myth is a victim of the process of secularization that constitutes modernity.

The key exponents of this challenge to myth have been the pioneering English anthropologist E. B. Tylor (1832–1917) and the Scottish classicist and fellow pioneering anthropologist J. G. Frazer (1854–1941). For Tylor, myth provides knowledge of the world: 'When the attention of a man in the myth-making stage of intellect is drawn to any phenomenon or custom which has to him no obvious reason, he invents and tells a story to account for it . . .' (Tylor 1871: I, 392). For Frazer, the knowledge that myth provides is a means to the control of the world, especially of crops. For both Tylor and Frazer, the events explained or effected by myth are those in the external world such as rainfall, not social phenomena such as customs, laws, and institutions. Myth is the primitive counterpart to natural, not social, science.

For Tylor and Frazer, science renders myth not merely redundant but incompatible. Why? Because the explanations they give are. It is not simply that the mythic explanation is personalistic and the scientific one impersonal. It is that both are *direct* explanations of the *same* events. Gods operate not behind or through impersonal forces but in place of them. According to myth, the rain god, let us say, collects rain in buckets and then chooses to empty the buckets on some spot below. According to science, meteorological processes cause rain. One cannot stack the mythic account atop the scientific one, for the rain god, rather than utilizing meteorological processes, acts in place of them.

Strictly, causation in myth is never entirely personalistic. The decision of the rain god to dump rain on a chosen spot below presupposes physical laws that account for the accumulation of rain in heaven, the capacity of the buckets to retain the rain, and the direction of the dumped rain. But to maintain their rigid hiatus between myth and science, Tylor and Frazer would doubtless reply that myths themselves ignore physical processes and focus instead on divine decisions.

Because Tylor and Frazer assume that myth and science are incompatible, they take for granted not merely that primitives have only myth but, even more, that moderns have only science. Rather than an eternal phenomenon, as the theorists Mircea Eliade, C. G. Jung, and Joseph Campbell grandly proclaim, myth for Tylor and Frazer is merely a passing, if slowly passing, one. Myth has admirably served its function, but its time is over. Moderns who still cling to myth have simply failed either to recognize or to concede the incompatibility of it with science. While Tylor and Frazer do not date the beginning of the scientific stage, it is identical with the beginning of modernity and is therefore only a few centuries old. Dying in the first half of the twentieth century, Tylor and Frazer never quite envisioned a stage past the modern one.

In setting myth against science, Tylor and Frazer epitomize the nineteenth-century view of myth. In the twentieth century the trend has been to reconcile myth with science, so that moderns, who by definition espouse science, can still retain myth. Tylor's and Frazer's theories have been spurned by twentieth-century theorists on many grounds: for precluding modern myths, for subsuming myth under religion and thereby precluding secular myths, for deeming the function of myth scientific-like, and for deeming myth false. Nevertheless, Tylor's and Frazer's theories remain central to the study of myth, and twentieth-century theories can be seen as rejoinders to them. One rejoinder has been to take the function of myth as other than explanatory, in which case myth does not overlap with natural science and can therefore coexist with it. Another rejoinder has been to read myth other than literally, in which case myth does not even refer to the physical world and can therefore likewise coexist with natural science.[3] The most radical rejoinder has been to alter both the explanatory function and the literal reading of myth.

Myth as other than explanatory in function

The most important reinterpreters of the function of myth have been Bronislaw Malinowski, Lucien Lévy-Bruhl, Claude Lévi-Strauss, and Mircea Eliade. It is not clear whether for Malinowski (1884–1942), the Polish-born anthropologist, moderns as well as primitives have myth. What is clear is that for him primitives have science as well as myth, so that myth cannot be the primitive counterpart to modern science, theoretical or applied. Primitives use science both to explain and to control the physical world. They use myth to do the opposite: to reconcile themselves to aspects of the world that cannot be controlled.

Myth reconciles humans to the travails of life by rooting those travails in the primordial actions of gods or humans. Humans age because long ago a god or human did something that brought old age irremediably into the world: 'The longed-for power of eternal youth and the faculty of rejuvenation which gives immunity from decay and age, have been lost by a small accident which it would have been in the power of a child and a woman to prevent' (Malinowski 1926: 104). Myth pronounces the world not the best possible one but, in the wake of irreversible events, the only possible one.

Where for Tylor and Frazer myth deals primarily with physical phenomena, for Malinowski it deals equally with social phenomena. Myth still serves to reconcile humans to the unpleasantries of life, but now to unpleasantries that, far from unalterable, can be cast off by members of society. Myth spurs members to accept the impositions of society by tracing them, too, back to a hoary past, thereby conferring on them the clout of tradition: 'The myth comes into play when rite, ceremony, or a social or moral rule demands justification, warrant of antiquity, reality, and sanctity' (Malinowski 1926: 36). Myths say, 'Do this because this has always been done.' A myth about the British monarchy would make the institution as ancient as possible, so that to tamper with it would be to tamper with tradition. In England today fox hunting is defended on the grounds that it has long been part of country life. In the case of physical phenomena the beneficiary of myth is the individual. In the case of social phenomena the beneficiary is society itself. The modern counterpart to myths of social phenomena, if moderns do not have myth, is ideology.[4]

To say that myth traces back the origin of phenomena is equivalent to saying that myth explains those phenomena. When, then, Malinowski denies strenuously that myths are explanations – primitives 'do not want to "explain," to make "intelligible" anything which happens in their myths' (Malinowski 1926: 41) – he is denying that they are, as for Tylor, explanations for their own sake. He cannot be denying that they are explanations at all, for it is exactly by explaining phenomena that myths serve their conciliatory function.

The French philosopher Lucien Lévy-Bruhl (1857–1939) does not contest Tylor's and Frazer's restriction of myth to primitives. Like Malinowski, he contests less Frazer's than Tylor's characterization of primitives and thus of myth. Where for Malinowski primitives are too overwhelmed by the world to have the luxury of reflecting on it, for Lévy-Bruhl primitives are too emotionally involved in the world to be capable of accounting for it. Their feelings shape the way they perceive as well as conceive the world. Rather than, as for Tylor, first experiencing a natural world of animals and plants and then postulating gods to account for their behavior, primitives project their 'collective representations' onto the world and thereby experience all things in the world as filled with a sacred, or 'mystic,' reality pervading the natural one:

> Primitive man, therefore, lives and acts in an environment of beings and objects, all of which, in addition to the properties that we recognize them to possess, are endued with mystic properties. He perceives their objective reality mingled with another reality.
>
> (Lévy-Bruhl 1926: 65)

All phenomena, including humans, are mystically identical with one another.

Myth functions not to explain this mystical world view but to preserve it. As long as members experience oneness with the group, they experience oneness with the world, and myth is barely needed. But once members begin to experience themselves as individuals, they turn to myth to restore the feeling of oneness with society and the world:

> Where the participation of the individual in the social group is still directly felt, where the participation of the group with surrounding groups is actually lived – that is, as long as the period of mystic symbiosis lasts – myths are meagre in number and of poor quality ... Where the aggregates are of a more advanced type, ... there is, on the contrary, an increasingly luxuriant outgrowth of mythology. Can myths then likewise be the products of primitive mentality which appear when this mentality is endeavouring to realize a participation no longer directly felt – when it has recourse to intermediaries, and vehicles designed to secure a communion which has ceased to be a living reality?
>
> (Lévy-Bruhl 1926: 368–69)

For Lévy-Bruhl, myth is part of a mythic mentality, and from him comes the notion of a distinctively mythic, or 'mythopoetic,' way of thinking. Where for Tylor myth is as logical as science, for Lévy-Bruhl it is conspicuously illogical, or 'pre-logical.' For primitives, despite their yearning to re-experience the oneness of all things, simultaneously and inconsistently deem all things distinct. Theorists of myth influenced by Lévy-Bruhl include the German philosopher Ernst Cassirer (1955).

At first glance the French structural anthropologist Claude Lévi-Strauss (b. 1908) seems a throwback to Tylor. For Lévi-Strauss, myth is not only an exclusively primitive enterprise but, more, a rigorously intellectual one. Lévi-Strauss denounces nonintellectualists like Malinowski and Lévy-Bruhl as vigorously as they denounce intellectualists like Tylor. Indeed, in declaring that primitives, 'moved by a need or a desire to understand the world around them, . . . proceed by intellectual means, exactly as a philosopher, or even to some extent a scientist, can and would do' (Lévi-Strauss 1978: 16), Lévi-Strauss seems indistinguishable from Tylor. Yet he is in fact severely critical of Tylor. For Lévi-Strauss, primitives think differently from moderns, rather than fail to think as well as moderns.

Primitive, or mythic, thinking is concrete. Modern thinking is abstract. Primitive thinking focuses on the observable, sensory, qualitative aspects of phenomena rather than, like modern thinking, on the unobservable, nonsensory, quantitative ones. Yet myth for Lévi-Strauss is no less scientific than modern science. It is simply part of the 'science of the concrete' rather than the science of the abstract. For Lévi-Strauss, myth *is* primitive science and not just the primitive counterpart to exclusively modern science. But because primitive and modern science concentrate on different aspects of the physical world, they are compatible rather than, like myth and science for Tylor, incompatible. And primitive science is not inferior to modern science, the way myth is to science for Tylor.

If myth is an instance of mythic thinking because it deals with concrete, tangible phenomena, it is an instance of thinking *per se*, modern and primitive alike, because it classifies phenomena. According to Lévi-Strauss, all humans think in the form of classifications, specifically pairs of oppositions, and project them onto the world. Many cultural phenomena express these oppositions, which Lévi-Strauss calls 'binary oppositions.' Myth is distinctive in resolving the oppositions it expresses: 'the purpose of myth is to provide a logical model capable of overcoming a contradiction' (Lévi-Strauss 1958: 105). Myth resolves a contradiction by providing either a mediating middle term or an analogous, but more easily resolved, contradiction. Either tactic narrows and thereby alleviates the contradiction, but, strictly, neither fully resolves it.

Like the contradictions expressed in other phenomena, those expressed in myth are for Lévi-Strauss apparently reducible to the fundamental contradiction between 'nature' and 'culture.' That contradiction stems from the conflict that humans experience between themselves as at once animal-like, hence a part of nature, and civilized, hence a part of culture. This conflict arises from the projection onto the world of the oppositional character of the mind. Humans not only think 'oppositionally' but, through projection, experience the world 'oppositionally' as well. By showing a way of diminishing that opposition, myth makes life more bearable and, even more, solves a logical conundrum.

In calling his approach to myth 'structuralist,' Lévi-Strauss distinguishes it from a 'narrative' approach, which adheres to the plot of myth. All other theories take for granted that the meaning of myth lies in its plot. Lévi-Strauss dismisses the plot and locates the meaning of myth in the structure. The plot is that element – say, event – A leads to event B, which leads to event C. The structure, which is identical with the expression and diminutim of contradictions, is either that events A and B constitute an opposition mediated by event C or that events A and B are as opposed to each other as events C and D, an analogous opposition, are opposed.

Lévi-Strauss confines himself to, primarily, Native American myths, but other structuralists analyze modern myths. In *Mythologies* (1972) the French semiotician Roland Barthes (1915–80) takes as myths various cultural artifacts and shows how they serve to justify the bourgeois outlook of postwar France. The function of myth here is not intellectual but ideological. Myth has nothing to do with natural science. Where Lévi-Strauss largely analyzes myths independent of their social context – the grand exception is his analysis of the myth of Asdiwal – others inspired by him have, like Barthes, tied myths to their contexts. For the classicists Jean-Pierre Vernant (1983), Marcel Detienne (1977), Pierre Vidal-Naquet, and Nicole Loraux, the relationship between myth and society is much more malleable, subtle, and ironic than it is for Malinowski or even Barthes. Myth can as readily challenge as bolster existing ideology.

Unlike Malinowski and Lévy-Bruhl, the Romanian-born historian of religions Mircea Eliade (1907–86) has no hesitation in making one function of myth explanatory. For him, myth explains less how the gods presently control the world, as for Tylor and Frazer, than how they created it. Like Malinowski, Eliade includes myths of social phenomena as well as of physical ones. Explanation for Eliade is both an end in itself and, even more, a means to another end. To hear, to read, and above all to reenact a myth is magically to return to the time of the myth, the time of the origin of whatever phenomenon it explains. It is when the world is fresh that gods, the creators in myth, are believed to be closest at hand, as in the biblical case of 'the Lord God['s] walking in the garden of the cool of the day' (Genesis 3:8). The return to this 'primordial time' reverses the subsequent separation from gods, a separation that is equivalent to the fall, and is regenerative spiritually: 'What is involved is, in short, a return to the original time, the therapeutic purpose of which is to begin life once again, a symbolic rebirth' (Eliade 1968: 8). The ultimate benefit of myth is proximity to the gods, one or more.

Eliade ventures beyond the other respondents to Tylor and Frazer in proclaiming myth panhuman rather than merely primitive. Instead of showing how myth is logically compatible with science, he circumvents the issue by citing modern plays, novels, and movies with the mythic theme of yearning to escape from the everyday world into another, often earlier one:

> A whole volume could well be written on the myths of modern man, on the mythologies camouflaged in the plays that he enjoys, in the books that he reads … Even reading includes a mythological function … particularly because, through reading, the modern man succeeds in obtaining an 'escape from time' comparable to the 'emergence from time' effected by myths. Whether modern man 'kills' time with a detective story or enters such a foreign temporal universe as is represented by any novel, reading projects him out of his personal duration and incorporates him into other rhythms, makes him live in another 'history.'
>
> (Eliade 1968: 205)

If moderns, who by definition have science, also have myth, then for Eliade myth simply must be compatible with science – not quite the conclusion that Tylor and Frazer would draw. If even professedly atheistic moderns have myths, then myth must be universal. How modern myths, which do not involve gods, can still provide access to gods, Eliade never reveals. Likely for him, the agents in modern myths are merely human heroes, but heroes so elevated above ordinary mortals as to be virtual gods.

Myth as other than literal in meaning

The most prominent reinterpreters of not the function but the meaning of myth have been the German New Testament scholar Rudolf Bultmann (1884–1976) and the German-born philosopher Hans Jonas (1903–93). Both were students of the philosopher Martin Heidegger (1889–1976) in his earlier period and consequently offer existentialist readings of myth. While they limit themselves to their specialties, Christianity and Gnosticism, they apply a theory of myth *per se*.

Bultmann acknowledges that, read literally, myth is about the physical world and is incompatible with science. But unlike Malinowski and Eliade as well as Tylor, he reads myth symbolically. In Bultmann's exasperatingly confusing phrase, one must 'demythologize' myth, by which he means not eliminating, or 'demythicizing,' myth, the way Kramer does, but on the contrary extricating its true, symbolic subject matter. Once demythologized, myth is no longer about the external world but is instead about the place of human beings in that world. Myth no longer explains but instead describes, and it describes not the external world but humans' experience of that world: 'The real purpose of myth is not to present an objective picture of the world as it is, but to express man's understanding of himself in the world in which he lives. Myth should be interpreted not cosmologically, but anthropologically, or better still, existentially' (Bultmann 1953: 10). Myth depicts the human condition.

Read literally, the New Testament for Bultmann describes a cosmic battle between good and evil anthropomorphic gods for control of the physical world. These gods intervene miraculously not only in the operation of nature, as for Tylor and Frazer, but also in the lives of human beings. The beneficent beings direct humans to do good; the malevolent ones compel them to do evil. Taken literally, the New Testament presents a prescientific outlook:

> The world is viewed as a three-storied structure, with the earth in the centre, the heaven above, and the underworld beneath. Heaven is the abode of God and of celestial beings – the angels. The underworld is hell, the place of torment. Even the earth is more than the scene of natural, everyday events, of the trivial round and common task. It is the scene of the supernatural activity of God and his angels on the one hand, and of Satan and his daemons on the other. These supernatural forces intervene in the course of nature and in all that men think and will and do. Miracles are by no means rare. Man is not in control of his own life. Evil spirits may take possession of him. Satan may inspire him with evil thoughts. Alternatively, God may inspire his thought and guide his purposes.
>
> (Bultmann 1953: 1)

Demythologized, the New Testament still refers in part to the physical world, but now to a world ruled by a single, nonanthropomorphic, transcendent God. Satan does not even still exist. He becomes a symbol of one's own evil inclinations:

> Mythology expresses a certain understanding of human existence. It [rightly] believes that the world and human life have their ground and their limits in a power which is beyond all that we can calculate or control. Mythology speaks about this power inadequately and insufficiently because it speaks about it as if it were a worldly [i.e., physical] power. It [rightly] speaks of gods who represent the power beyond the visible, comprehensible world. [But] it speaks of gods as if they were men and of their actions as human actions ... Again, the conception of Satan as ruler over the world expresses a deep insight, namely, the insight that evil is not only to be found here and there in the world, but that all particular evils make up one single power which in the last analysis grows from the very actions of men, which form an atmosphere, a spiritual tradition, which overwhelms every man. The consequences and effects of our sins become a power dominating us, and we cannot free ourselves from them.
>
> (Bultmann 1958: 19, 21)

Damnation refers not to a future place but to one's present state of mind, which exists as long as one rejects God. There is no physical hell. Hell symbolizes despair over the absence of God. As John Milton's Satan declares, 'Which way I fly is Hell; myself am Hell.' Similarly, salvation refers to one's state of mind once one accepts God. Heaven refers not to a place in the sky but to joy in the presence of God. The eschatology refers not to the coming end of the physical world but to the personal acceptance or rejection of God in one's everyday life. The Kingdom comes not outwardly, with cosmic upheavals, but inwardly, whenever one embraces God.

Demythologized, myth ceases to be purely primitive, as for Tylor and Frazer, and becomes universal, as for Eliade. Myth ceases to be false, as for Tylor and Frazer, and becomes true. Where Eliade invokes the existence of modern myths as *ipso facto* evidence of the compatibility of myth with science, Bultmann actually labors to reconcile myth with science. Where Eliade claims that moderns have myths of their own, Bultmann claims that moderns can retain biblical myths.

Bultmann's boldest response to Tylor and Frazer is to circumvent the function of myth. In translating the meaning of myth into terms acceptable to moderns, he sidesteps the issue of why moderns, even if they can have myth, need it. Unlike other symbolic interpreters of myth such as the religious philosopher Paul Ricoeur (1967) and the philosopher Philip Wheelwright (1968), Bultmann never asserts that the meaning of myth is untranslatable into nonmythic terms and is therefore indispensable for expressing or even revealing its contents. Since he takes the meaning of myth from Heidegger's philosophy, he can hardly be doing so. He is thereby left with a theory that makes myth palatable to moderns but unnecessary for them. And even the palatibility of myth for moderns is tenuous, for myth still refers to God, albeit of a nonphysical kind. One must still believe in God to accept myth.

Like Bultmann, Jonas seeks to show that ancient myths have a meaning that continues to speak to moderns. For both Bultmann and Jonas, myth describes the alienation of humans from the world as well as from their true selves prior to their acceptance of God. Because Gnosticism, unlike mainstream Christianity, is radically dualistic, humans remain alienated from the physical world and from their bodies even after they have found the true God. And they find the true God only by rejecting the false god of the physical world.

Unlike Bultmann, who strives to bridge the divide between Christianity and modernity, Jonas acknowledges the divide between Gnosticism and modernity. In Gnosticism the state of alienation is temporary; in modern, secular existentialism alienation is permanent. Alienation *is* the human condition, not a fall from it. Jonas does not, then, seek to 'demythologize' either the source of alienation or the solution to it – as if alienation were temporary – but the fact of alienation. He translates Gnostic myths into existentialist terms not to make Gnosticism acceptable to moderns but only to show the similarity between the Gnostic and the existentialist outlooks: 'the essence of existentialism is a certain dualism, an estrangement between man and the world . . . There is only one situation . . . where that condition has been realized and lived out with all the vehemence of a cataclysmic event. That is the gnostic movement' (Jonas 1963: 325).

Like Bultmann, Jonas bypasses the function of myth and confines himself to the meaning. But he, like Bultmann, is thereby still left with finding a use for myth. Since he, too, takes his glossary from Heidegger, modern philosophy unlocks myth and not vice versa. What function, then, does myth serve?

Myth as both other than explanatory and other than literal

The most radical departures from Tylor and Frazer have transformed both the explanatory function and the literal meaning of myth. The most influential theorists here have been the Austrian physician Sigmund Freud (1856–1939) and the Swiss psychiatrist C. G. Jung (1875–1961). For both, the subject matter of myth is the unconscious, and the function of myth is to manifest the unconscious. The two differ sharply over the nature of the unconscious and in turn over the reason myth is needed to manifest it.

Because the Freudian unconscious is composed of repressed sexual and aggressive drives, myth functions to release those drives, but in a disguised way, so that the creator and the user of a myth need never confront its meaning and thereby their own nature. Myth, like other aspects of culture, serves simultaneously to reveal and to hide its unconscious contents. Compared with Jung, Freud wrote little on myth. His key discussion is his analysis of the myth of Oedipus in *The Interpretation of Dreams* (1953). The classical psychoanalytic study of myth is that of his one-time disciple, fellow Austrian Otto Rank (1884–1939). Focusing on myths of male heroes, Rank sees the myths as providing an unconscious, vicarious fulfillment of, above all, Oedipal drives. By identifying oneself with the named hero, whose own saga must be psychologized, one gains a partial fulfillment of lingering childhood desires. Myth serves neurotic adult males fixated at their Oedipal stage: 'Myths are, therefore, created by adults, by means of retrograde childhood fantasies, the hero being credited with the myth-maker's personal infantile history' (Rank 1914: 82).

By no means do Freudians still take myth so negatively. Spurred by ego psychology, contemporary Freudians such as the American Jacob Arlow (b. 1912) take myth positively. For them, myth helps to solve the problems of growing up rather than to perpetuate them, is progressive rather than regressive, and facilitates adjustment to society and the physical world rather than childish flight from both. Myth may still serve to vent repressed drives, but it serves even more to sublimate them and to integrate them. Moreover, myth serves everyone, not just neurotics:

> Psychoanalysis has a greater contribution to make to the study of mythology than [merely] demonstrating, in myths, wishes often encountered in the unconscious thinking of patients. The myth is a particular kind of communal experience. It is a special form of shared fantasy, and it serves to bring the individual into relationship with members of his cultural group on the basis of certain common needs. Accordingly, the myth can be studied from the point of view of its function in psychic integration – how it plays a role in warding off feelings of guilt and anxiety, how it constitutes a form of adaptation to reality and to the group in which the individual lives, and how it influences the crystallization of the individual identity and the formation of the superego.
>
> (Arlow 1961: 375)

Jungians have taken myth positively from the outset. For them, the unconscious expressed in myth is not the Freudian repository of repressed, anti-social drives but a storehouse of innately unconscious 'archetypes,' or sides of the personality, that have simply never had an opportunity at realization: 'Contents of an archetypal character ... do not refer to anything that is or has been conscious, but to something essentially unconscious' (Jung 1968: 156). Myth is one means of encountering this Jungian, or 'collective,' unconscious. The function of myth is less release, as for classical Freudians, than growth, as for contemporary ones. But where even contemporary Freudians see myth as a means of adjusting to the demands of the outer world, Jungians see myth as a means of cultivating the 'inner world.' The payoff is less adjustment than self-realization. Some Jungians and Jungian-oriented theorists such as the American Joseph Campbell (1904–87) (1949) so tout the benefit of myth that it becomes a panacea for humanity's problems. But Jung himself never goes this far. For Jung, myth works best as part of therapy. For Campbell, myth makes therapy unnecessary, and only the absence of myth makes it necessary.

For even contemporary Freudians, myth harks back to childhood. For Jungians, myth points forward. Myth especially serves adults already settled in the outer world but largely severed from the unconscious. Myth is to be read symbolically, as for Freudians, but not because its meaning has intentionally been disguised. Rather, the unconscious speaks a language of its own and simply awaits grasping. Understanding myth is less like breaking the Enigma Code, as for Freudians, and more like deciphering the Rosetta Stone.

'Post,' or 'archetypal,' Jungians such as James Hillman (b. 1926) (1975) and David Miller (b. 1936) (1981) maintain that classical Jungian psychology, by emphasizing the therapeutic message of mythology, reduces myth to psychology and reduces god to a concept. They advocate the reverse: that psychology be viewed as irreducibly mythological. Myth is still to be interpreted psychologically, but psychology itself is to be interpreted mythologically. One grasps the psychological meaning of the myth of Saturn by imagining oneself to be the figure Saturn, not by translating Saturn's plight into clinical terms like depression. Moreover, the depressed Saturn represents a legitimate aspect of one's personality. Each god deserves its due. The psychological ideal should be pluralistic rather than monolithic – in mythological terms, polytheistic rather than monotheistic. Post-Jungians maintain that Jung's psychological ideal of a single, unified self (or 'Self') reflects a Western, specifically monotheistic, more specifically Christian, still more specifically Protestant, outlook. Instead of the Bible, Hillman and Miller take their mythic cues from the Greeks, however simplistic the equation of Greece with polytheism and of the Bible with monotheism may be. The title of Miller's key book says it all: *The New Polytheism*.

Furthermore, the Western emphasis on progress is purportedly reflected in the primacy that Jung accords both hero myths and the ego, even in the ego's encounter with the unconscious. For the encounter is intended to abet development. According to Hillman and Miller, the ego is just one more archetype with its attendant kind of god, and it is the 'soul' rather than the ego that experiences the archetypes through myths. Myth serves to open one up to the soul's own depths. The payoff of mythology is aesthetic rather than moral: one gains a sense of wonder and contemplation rather than, as for classical Jungians, a guide to living. Consequently, the most apposite myths are those of the playful pure archetype and of the receptive anima archetype rather than, as for classical Jungians, those of the striving hero archetype and of the fully united, or integrated, wise old man archetype.

SECTION TWO: MYTH AND RITUAL

Myth is commonly taken to be words, often in the form of a story. A myth is read or heard. It says something. Yet there is an approach to myth that finds this view artificial. According to the myth and ritual, or myth-ritualist, theory, myth does not stand by itself but is tied to ritual. Myth is not just a statement but also an action. The most uncompromising form of the theory maintains that all myths have accompanying rituals and all rituals accompanying myths. In tamer versions some myths may flourish without rituals or some rituals without myths. Alternatively, myths and rituals may originally operate together but subsequently go their separate ways. Or myths and rituals may arise separately but subsequently coalesce. Whatever the tie between myth and ritual, the myth-ritualist theory differs from other theories of myth and from other theories of ritual in focusing on the tie.

The myth and ritual, or myth-ritualist, theory was pioneered by the Scottish biblicist and Arabist William Robertson Smith (1846–94), who argued that ritual came first and that myth arose to explain 'the circumstances under which the rite first came to be established, by the command or by the direct example of the god' (Smith 1889: 19). In Smith's version of myth-ritualism, myth is clearly subordinate to ritual.

The fullest development of the theory came in, especially, the second and third editions (1900, 1911–15) of Frazer's *Golden Bough*, itself dedicated to Smith. Frazer ties myth to magic, specifically to the first of his two laws of magic. The first law, that of homeopathy, is epitomized by voodoo, according to which the imitation of an action causes the action to occur. Ritual puts magic into practice. The aim is to get the crops to grow.

Frazer ties myth not only to ritual but also to kingship. In one version of his myth-ritualist scenario the king, merely human, plays the part of the god of vegetation, the key god of the pantheon, and acts out the myth of the god's death and rebirth. The ritualistic imitation of the death and rebirth of the god is believed to cause the same to happen to the god. And as the god goes, so go the crops. The ritual is performed at the end – the desired end – of winter, presumably when provisions are running low. The myth can be said to explain the ritual, as for Smith, but from the outset and in the form of the script of a play. Without the myth, there would be no ritual. At the same time the subject of myth is, as for Tylor, the world and not, as for Smith, the ritual: myth is about the death and rebirth of vegetation, not about the ritual used to effect that rebirth.

In the other version of Frazer's myth-ritualist scenario the king does not merely play the part of the god of vegetation but *is* the god, whose soul resides in the body of the incumbent. Here the king does not act out the death and rebirth of the god but is himself killed, with the god's soul then being transferred to the body of his successor. This ritualistic regicide occurs as often as annually or as infrequently and as unpredictably as the earliest sign of the king's weakening. Now as the king goes, so goes the god and so in turn goes vegetation.

Strictly speaking, no magic is involved here. The replacement of the king does not imitate the revival of the god but effects it. In fact, no myth is involved either. The killing of the king is not the enactment of the myth of the death of the god of vegetation but the sheer killing of the king. The ritual – the killing – really stands alone, undirected by any mythic script. It is Frazer's disciple Lord Raglan (1936) who provides a mythic script for the ritual: for him, hero myths describe ideal kings whose willingness to die for their community should be emulated by present-day kings. In both of Frazer's scenarios the ritual, whether with or without myth, is the primitive counterpart to *applied* science rather than, as for Tylor, the counterpart to scientific *theory*.

The classicists Gilbert Murray, F. M. Cornford, and A. B. Cook, all English or English-resident, applied the first version of Frazer's myth-ritualist scenario to such ancient Greek phenomena as tragedy, comedy, the Olympic games, science, and philosophy. These seemingly secular, even anti-religious phenomena are interpreted as latent expressions of the myth of the death and rebirth of the god of vegetation.

Among biblicists, the English S. H. Hooke, the Swedish Ivan Engnell, the Welsh Aubrey Johnson, and the Norwegian Sigmund Mowinckel differed over the extent to which ancient Israel in particular adhered to a myth-ritualist pattern based on Frazer's first version. Engnell saw an even stronger adherence than the cautious Hooke. Johnson, and especially Mowinckel, saw a weaker one.

Invoking Frazer, Bronislaw Malinowski applied his own, qualified version of the theory to the myths of native peoples worldwide. Malinowski argues that myth, which for him, as for Smith, explains the origin of ritual, gives rituals a hoary origin and thereby sanctions them. Society depends on myth to spur adherence to rituals. But if all rituals depend on myth, so do many other cultural practices. They have myths of their own. Myth and ritual are therefore not coextensive.

Mircea Eliade applied a similar form of the theory but, going beyond Malinowski, applied the theory to modern as well as 'primitive' cultures. Myth for Eliade, too, sanctions phenomena of all kinds, not just rituals, by giving them a primeval origin.

For him, too, then, myth and ritual are not coextensive. But Eliade again goes beyond Malinowski in stressing the importance of the ritualistic enactment of myth in the fulfillment of the ultimate function of myth: when enacted, myth acts as a time machine, carrying one back to the time of the myth and thereby bringing one closer to God.

The most notable application of the myth-ritualist theory outside of religion has been to the arts, especially literature. Jane Harrison (1913) daringly derived all art from ritual. She speculates that gradually people ceased believing that the imitation of an action caused the action to occur. Yet rather than abandoning ritual, they now practiced it as an end in itself. Ritual for its own sake became art, Harrison's clearest example of which is drama. More modestly than Harrison, Murray and Cornford rooted specifically Greek epic, tragedy, and comedy in myth-ritualism. Murray then extended the theory to Shakespeare.

Other standard-bearers of the theory have included Jessie Weston on the Grail legend, E. M. Butler on the Faust legend, C. L. Barber on Shakespearean comedy, Herbert Weisinger on Shakespearean tragedy and on tragedy *per se*, Francis Fergusson on tragedy, Lord Raglan on hero myths and on literature as a whole, and Northrop Frye and Stanley Edgar Hyman on literature generally. As literary critics, these myth-ritualists have understandably been concerned less with myth itself than with the mythic origin of literature. Works of literature are interpreted as the outgrowth of myths once tied to rituals. For those literary critics indebted to Frazer, as the majority are, literature harks back to Frazer's second, not first, myth-ritualist version. 'The king must die' becomes the familiar summary line.

For literary myth-ritualists, myth becomes literature when myth is severed from ritual. Myth tied to ritual is religious literature; myth cut off from ritual is secular literature, or plain literature. When tied to ritual, myth can serve any of the active functions ascribed to it by myth-ritualists. Myth can even change the world. Bereft of ritual, myth is demoted to mere commentary.

Literary myth-ritualism is a theory not of myth and ritual themselves, both of which are assumed, but of their impact on literature. Yet it is a not a theory of literature either, for it firmly refuses to reduce literature to myth. Literary myth-ritualism is an explanation of the transformation of myth and ritual into literature.

The French-born literary critic René Girard (b. 1923) (1977) offers an ironic twist to the theory of Raglan. Where Raglan's hero is willing to die for the community, Girard's hero is killed or exiled by the community for having caused its present woes. Indeed, the 'hero' is initially considered a criminal who deserves to die. Only subsequently is the villain turned into a hero, who, as for Raglan, is heroic exactly for dying selflessly for the community. Both Raglan and Girard cite Oedipus as their fullest example. (Their doing so makes neither a Freudian. Both spurn Freud.) For Girard, the transformation of Oedipus from reviled exile in Sophocles' *Oedipus the King* to revered benefactor in Sophocles' *Oedipus at Colonus* typifies the transformation from criminal to hero.

Yet this change is for Girard only the second half of the process. The first half is the change from innocent victim to criminal. Originally, violence erupts in the community. The cause is the inclination, innate in human nature, to imitate others and thereby to desire the same objects as those of the imitated. Imitation leads to rivalry, which leads to violence. Desperate to end the violence, the community selects an innocent member to blame for the turmoil. This 'scapegoat' can be anyone and can range from the most helpless member of society to the most elevated, including, as with Oedipus, the king. The victim is usually killed, though, as with Oedipus, sometimes exiled. The killing is the ritualistic sacrifice, as in Frazer's second myth-ritualist scenario. But rather than directing the ritual, as for Frazer, or inspiring it, as for Raglan, myth for Girard is created *after* the killing to *hide* it. Myth comes from ritual, as for Smith, but it comes to mask rather than, as for Smith, to explain the ritual. Myth turns the scapegoat into a criminal who deserved to die and then turns the criminal into a hero, who has died voluntarily for the good of the community. Typical of twentieth-century rather than nineteenth-century approaches to myth, the function of myth and ritual for Girard is social rather than physical: myth serves to affect the community, not the earth.

SECTION THREE: RITUAL

Classical theories

Within the social sciences there have been two main classical views of ritual. One view has considered ritual a matter of feelings, which ritual either implants or releases. This view, by far the more common one, is found above all in Émile Durkheim (1915, esp. Bk. 3), A. R. Radcliffe-Brown (1922, esp. ch. 5), Malinowski (1925), Karl Marx (1957), and Sigmund Freud (1955). For Durkheim and Radcliffe-Brown, ritual *creates* feelings – for Durkheim, feelings of dependence on society and of possession by society; for Radcliffe-Brown, feelings of dependence on society and also of love and hatred toward phenomena which, respectively, help and hurt society. For Malinowski, Marx, and Freud, ritual *discharges* feelings – for Malinowski, feelings of helplessness before nature; for Marx, pent-up economic desires; for Freud, pent-up instinctual ones.

The other main classical view of ritual has deemed it fundamentally a matter of *belief*, which ritual applies. This view is found above all in Tylor and Frazer. For both, ritual controls the world by applying prescientific beliefs about it. Frazer gives far more attention to ritual than Tylor, for whom myth, working by itself as an explanation of the world, is by far the more important component of religion.

Contemporary theories

Ritual as the expression of belief

Among contemporary theorists, the English-born anthropologist Victor Turner (1920–83) (1967, 1968, 1969), the American anthropologist Clifford Geertz (b. 1926) (1973, 1983), and the English anthropologist Mary Douglas (b. 1921) (1970, 1973) follow Tylor and Frazer in taking ritual as belief. Unlike Tylor and Frazer, the three consider ritual the *expression*, not the *application*, of belief. Even more unlike them, the three consider the belief expressed other than the primitive counterpart of science. For Tylor and Frazer, ritual is the primitive equivalent of applied science: for the purpose of controlling the world, ritual puts into practice the primitive belief that personal gods rather than impersonal laws of nature regulate the world. For especially Frazer, not just ritual but religion as a whole gives way to modern technology.

For Turner, Geertz, and Douglas, by contrast, ritual is a modern as well as primitive phenomenon. It can be modern exactly because even as part of religion it does not compete with science and therefore does not get superseded by science. Rather than either explaining or controlling the world, ritual for all three describes the place of human beings in the world. For the three, ritual does what for Bultmann and Jonas myth does. Ritual describes the place of humans in not only the cosmos but also society. It describes the place of humans *vis-à-vis* not only the physical world and god but also other humans. Strikingly, all three credit ritual, not myth, with this function, and myth barely garners any attention in their writings.

For Turner and Geertz, the need for a place is existential: a fixed, certain place makes life secure, fair, and tolerable. For Douglas, the need is intellectual: a fixed, certain place makes life intelligible. Perhaps because Turner and Geertz deal with changing societies, they are more attentive to 'existential' anxiety than Douglas, who, dealing with stable societies, is freer to concentrate on purely intellectual issues.

As concerned as Turner, Geertz, and Douglas are with the function of ritual for the individual, they also are concerned with its function for society. As resolutely as they reject Durkheim and Radcliffe-Brown for the pair's 'emotivist' view of ritual, they accept the view of Durkheim and Radcliffe-Brown that the function served by ritual is social, not merely individual. Turner, Geertz, and Douglas assert that ritual serves at once to uphold society and to give humans places in both it and the cosmos.

As an example, take Turner, the contemporary most celebrated as a theorist of ritual.[5] *The Drums of Affliction* typifies his approach. He begins by defining ritual as a process of communication: it serves 'the highly important functions . . . of storing and transmitting information' (Turner 1968: 1). The function of ritual is thus less instrumental than expressive. Ritual is expressive not because it, like an archaeological find, merely reflects beliefs but because it intentionally discloses them. To say that myth conveys information would be commonplace. To say that ritual does is not. Turner rejects the conventional split into nonverbal and verbal behavior. Physical as well as verbal behavior conveys information.

The information conveyed by ritual concerns both the present and the ideal place of the individual in society and the cosmos alike:

> We are not dealing with information about a new agricultural technique or a better judicial procedure: we are concerned here with the crucial values of the believing community, whether it is a religious community, a nation, a tribe, a secret society, or any other type of group whose ultimate unity resides in its orientation towards transcendental and invisible powers.
>
> (Turner 1968: 2)

The Drums of Affliction focuses on Ndembu rituals of affliction, or rituals performed on behalf of persons whose illnesses or misfortunes are blamed on either ancestors or witches. Symptoms of affliction include backache, fever, boils, and difficulties in childbirth and hunting. The ritual tries to placate the spirits responsible. In the Ndembu village studied by Turner there loomed economic, political, and social decay in the wake of the colonial government's withdrawal of official recognition of the village chieftain. The loss of that recognition cost the village jobs, goods, and most of all clout. The village was also facing problems in hunting and farming.

The consequent frustration stirred previously suppressed tensions among individuals and among clans – tensions rooted ultimately in the clash between matrilineal descent and virilocal marriage. Because of both his particular lineage and his passive, effeminate personality, one villager, Kamahasanyi, became the scapegoat. Overwhelmed by the scorn of his relatives and neighbors, he developed various physical ills. His ancestors, he claimed, were punishing him for the failure of his line to retain the chieftainship, and his relatives and neighbors were bewitching him out of frustration at their own plight. Kamahasanyi demanded and received ritual curing. During the rituals all the personal antagonisms, which had been less unrecognized than ignored, were acknowledged and at least temporarily purged. Kamahasanyi himself was vindicated, and his ailments ceased, though the underlying tensions were scarcely eliminated.

On the one hand ritual for Turner serves to alleviate *social* turmoil: 'Ndembu ritual . . . may be regarded as a magnificent instrument for expressing, maintaining, and periodically cleansing a secular order of society without strong political centralization and all too full of social conflict' (Turner 1968: 21). On the other hand ritual for Turner also serves to alleviate *existential* turmoil:

> In the idiom of the rituals of affliction it is as though the Ndembu said: 'It is only when a person is reduced to misery by misfortune, and repents of the acts that caused him to be afflicted, that ritual expressing an underlying unity in diverse things may fittingly be enacted for him' . . . It is as though he were stripped of all possessions, all status, all social connections, and *then* endowed with all the basic virtues and values of Ndembu society.
>
> (Turner 1968: 22)

Ritual restores order to, at once, society and individuals' lives. Existential turmoil may grow out of social turmoil, but it is more than an expression of social turmoil.

Ritual alleviates both kinds of turmoil by acting out, by literally dramatizing, the situation it remedies. To use one of Turner's pet phrases, ritual is 'social drama.' As drama, ritual is not merely a part of social life but the depiction of it.[6] Where for Harrison drama is the legacy of ritual, for Turner drama is part of ritual.

Ritual for Turner describes not only how things are but also how they should be. It thereby serves as a model for altering society, not merely as a model of existing society:

> Ritual is a periodic restatement of the terms in which men of a particular culture must interact if there is to be any kind of a [sic] coherent social life . . . It has been more than once suggested that religious ritual is mainly 'expressive', that it portrays in symbolic form certain key values and cultural orientations. This is true as far as it goes, but it points to only one of many properties it possesses. More important is its creative function – it actually creates, or re-creates, the categories through which men perceive reality – the axioms underlying the structure of society and the laws of the natural and moral orders. It is not here a case of life being an imitation of art, but of social life being an attempted imitation of models portrayed and animated by ritual.
>
> (Turner 1968: 6–7)

Turner is claiming that ritual actually works, not merely is believed to work, and works by making sense of participants' experiences, not merely, as for Malinowski, Marx, and Freud, by releasing or redirecting their emotions. The individual ills treated by ritual are psychosomatic, and Turner often compares Ndembu rituals with psychoanalysis. But he is not thereby reducing the ills to feelings. On the contrary, he is elevating them to thoughts, or beliefs. Ndembu rituals work precisely because, like psychoanalysis, they make manifest not only repressed or, here, suppressed feelings but also suppressed beliefs.

Ritual as the alleviation of fear and guilt

The German classicist Walter Burkert (b. 1931) (1979, 1985, 1996) has developed a theory of ritual that derives from the ethology of Konrad Lorenz and, more recently, from the sociobiology of Edward O. Wilson. For Burkert, as for Turner, ritual is drama. It is 'as if' behavior. To take his central example, ritual, as he uses the term, is not the customs and formalities involved in hunting but the transformation of actual hunting into dramatized hunting. The function is no longer that of securing food, as for Frazer, since the ritual proper arises only in agricultural times, when farming has supplanted hunting as the prime source of food. Where for Frazer ritual is exactly a pre-scientific means of getting crops to grow, for Burkert ritual serves social and psychological ends – a shift in subject and function that applies as much to twentieth-century theories of ritual as to twentieth-century theories of myth and of myth plus ritual. Rather than rooted in agriculture, as for Frazer, ritual for Burkert is rooted in the prior stage of hunting and is simply preserved in the wake of agriculture:

> Hunting lost its basic function with the emergence of agriculture some ten thousand years ago. But hunting ritual had become so important that it could not be given up. Stability stayed with those groups who managed to make use of the social and psychological appeal of the ritual by transforming, by redirecting, it until the whole action became a ritual.
>
> (Burkert 1979: 55)

Hunting, according to Burkert, stirred feelings of fear and guilt. The fear was not merely of getting killed by the animal hunted but also of killing a fellow hunter and, too, of depleting the food supply:

> Killing to eat was an unalterable commandment, and yet the bloody act must always have been attended with a double danger and a double fear: that the weapon might be turned against a fellow hunter, and that the death of the prey might signal an end with no future, while man must always eat and so must always hunt.
>
> (Burkert 1985: 58)

The even deeper fear was of one's own aggression and one's own mortality. The guilt was over the killing of a fellow living creature. The communal nature of hunting functioned to assuage the individual's fear and guilt, and at the same time functioned to cement a bond among hunters: 'From a psychological and ethological point of view, it is the communally enacted aggression and shared guilt which creates solidarity' (Burkert 1985: 58). The function of ritual for Burkert, as for Turner, Geertz, and Douglas, is social as well as individual.

Like Douglas above all, Burkert sharply contrasts the magical, practical, efficacious, Frazerian view of ritual – ritual intended to secure rain, food, or fertility – to the symbolic, expressive one. Like Douglas as well, he dismisses the efficacious view and espouses the expressive one. For him, as for her, ritual makes a statement rather than carries out action. Where for Harrison ritual carries out an action and drama makes a statement, for Burkert and Douglas alike ritual, *as* drama, makes a statement rather than carries out an action. The shift in the study of ritual mirrors the shift in the study of myth and of myth plus ritual: for twentieth-century theorists, the efficacy of ritual is social, psychological, and existential, not physical.

Ritual as the reconciliation of contradictions

The English anthropologist Edmund Leach (1910–88) was well known for his structuralist analyses of, especially, biblical myths (1969). But unlike Claude Lévi-Strauss, who primarily analyzes myths, Leach analyzes rituals equally (1976). Also unlike Lévi-Strauss, who concentrates mostly on Native American myths – his programmatic structuralist analysis of the myth of Oedipus is an exception – Leach analyses modern rituals as often as 'primitive' ones. Still, as a Lévi-Straussian, he finds in rituals the same kinds of binary oppositions needing mediation that Lévi-Strauss finds in myths. For Leach, rituals are doing physically what myths are doing verbally.

In this later, structuralist phase Leach analyzes myths and rituals identically but separately. In his earlier, social functionalist phase he tightened the tie between myth and ritual beyond that of, so he assumed, even Harrison: 'Myth, in my terminology, is the counterpart of ritual; myth implies ritual, ritual implies myth, they are one and the same . . . As I see it, myth regarded as a statement in words 'says' the same thing as ritual regarded as a statement in action' (Leach 1965: 11–12). He claimed to be carrying myth-ritualism to its limits. In fact, Leach is really drawing the same close tie as Harrison and also Hooke.[7]

Ritual as the instillment of belief

Where Tylor and Frazer view ritual as the *application* of belief, and where Turner, Geertz, and Douglas view ritual as the *expression* or, at best, the *instillment* of belief, American anthropologist Roy Rappaport (1926–97) credits ritual with actually *creating* belief. Where for the others ritual is at most the key part of religion, for Rappaport it is nearly the whole. Rappaport does consider myth, but he subordinates it to ritual.

Rappaport's *Ritual and Religion in the Making of Humanity* (1999) represents an extraordinary venture beyond the approach to ritual in the work that made Rappaport's name, *Pigs for the Ancestors* (1968). There the function of ritual is ecological. The raising of pigs in abandoned gardens by the Tsembaga Maring farmers of New Guinea serves to clear the ground and make planting easier. The ritualistic killing of pigs serves to keep an increasing number from damaging the ground and making planting harder. The eating of pigs, which ordinarily happens only during rituals, provides protein to keep the people healthy. While Rappaport does note the social function of pig sacrifice – for example, the more pigs, the more dispersed the residents and so the less the social contact – he stresses the ecological function.

In *Ecology, Meaning, and Religion* (1979) Rappaport at once continues the ecological analysis of *Pigs* and moves radically beyond it. The key essay in the collection is 'The Obvious Aspects of Ritual.' Where, before, Rappaport had concentrated on the function of ritual, now he tends to the form of ritual. He tries to identify what makes ritual ritual by differentiating it from anything else. For example, ritual must be done precisely, repeatedly, and at set times and places. But an assembly line is equally formal yet scarcely a ritual. Ritual must, in addition, be performed. But so must dance. Ritual is a means to an end, not an end in itself. But so, too, is drama. Where, however, drama involves an audience, ritual requires a 'congregation,' which does not merely witness the action but also participates in it. Rappaport returns to the differentiation of ritual from drama found in Harrison. In *Pigs* Rappaport sees ritual as merely the human means of maintaining the ecosystem we share with animals. From 'Obvious' on, ritual becomes distinctly human.

Ritual and Religion in the Making of Humanity constitutes a grand elaboration of the 'Obvious' essay. Invoking concepts from fields as diverse as speech acts theory and cybernetics, Rappaport constructs one of the fullest and richest theories of ritual to be found. He claims that ritual does almost everything, not least things that others would automatically attribute to belief.

To take an example of which Rappaport would have approved, the biblical Patriarch Isaac, wanting Esau, his firstborn son, to succeed in life, does not merely state his wish but utilizes the ritual of a blessing to ensure it (Genesis 27). Even when the blind Isaac discovers that he has been duped into bestowing his deathbed blessing on Jacob instead, the blessing cannot be undone. The ritual is itself efficacious, no matter what the intent of either party. To take a more positive example, most couples planning to spend their lives together still partake of the ritual of marriage. The ceremony binds the parties even if, let us say, one of them only pretends to be in love with the other.

Against Rappaport, one might note that even if Isaac's blessing, once offered, cannot be rescinded, it still does not transform Jacob into Isaac's firstborn or favorite. A wedding ceremony presupposes that the bride and groom are committed to each other and expresses, not establishes, that commitment. The ritual is hollow if the commitment is missing. And marriage, unlike Isaac's blessing, can be annulled, albeit by another ritual.

Rappaport roots other aspects of religion in ritual. To participate in a ritual is to accept it, so that acceptance spells obligation and therefore morality. Yet one might argue that just as ritual seemingly presupposes belief rather than dispenses with it, so ritual seemingly presupposes morality rather than creates it. When two parties ritually shake hands after agreeing to something, the faith that they have in each other does not stem from the handshake, which merely expresses, not establishes, their mutual trust.

Rappaport argues that not even homicide is always immoral – unless it violates a ritual: 'There are conditions, so common as to require no illustration, under which killing humans is laudable or even mandatory. What is immoral is, of course, killing someone whom there is an obligation, at least tacit, not to kill' (Rappaport 1999: 132).

Having rooted morality in ritual, Rappaport is prepared to conclude that ritual is the center of social life: 'In enunciating, accepting and making conventions moral, ritual contains within itself not simply a symbolic representation of social contract, but tacit social contract itself. As such, ritual . . . is *the* basic social act' (Rappaport 1999: 138). Ritual socializes in other ways, too. Notably, it links what is private to what is public. A rite of passage turns the physiological changes in an adolescent into a change in status.

Ritual ties human beings not only to one another but also to the external world. Ritual orders experience in many ways, with Rappaport emphasizing the experience of time over the experience of space. Most straighforwardly, ritual organizes time into clearcut divisions: the ritual of Christmas divides the year into two seasons. Above all, ritual, specifically religious ritual, connects humans to the cosmos. All rituals for Rappaport communicate, but religious rituals, which for him are the highest kind, convey something other than information since they are the most invariant and therefore the most repetitive. Their repetitiveness makes them ideal communicators of eternal, hence repetitive, 'sacred' truths. 'Sacred' truths are metaphysical. They provide certitude not only because they are unchanging but also because they lie beyond the realm of proof or disproof. Rappaport's originality is his claim that, once again, religious rituals do not merely assume, evince, or inculcate transcendent truths but somehow also establish and validate them.

Ritual as the ordering of the world

Where Burkert draws on ethology and sociobiology, where Leach draws on structuralism, and where Rappaoport draws on cybernetics and other fields, cognitive theorists of ritual draw on cognitive psychology. Led by the French anthropologist Pascal Boyer (1994, 2001), cognitive theorists have become so numerous and so organized as to constitute what the philosopher of science Imre Lakatos would have called a 'research program.' Cognitivists analyze the cognitive constraints that direct thinking, including religious thinking. Strikingly, they focus not on myth, which barely gets considered, but on ritual. Like Leach and others, they see ritual as a cognitive enterprise. In stressing the constraints under which thinking and in turn acting occurs, they really echo Tylor, for whom myth, despite appearances, has an orderliness that reflects the orderliness of the mind. In stressing the centrality of supernatural agents – gods – to religion, they again echo Tylor, for whom the distinctiveness of religion is exactly the postulation of gods rather than, as in science, natural processes (see Chapter 27 on religion and cognition).

In the nineteenth century ritual was assumed to be the 'primitive' counterpart to modern technology, which rendered it superfluous and, worse, impossible. In the twentieth century ritual has been seen as almost anything but the outdated counterpart to technology. Ritual, it has been maintained, is about the human world and not just about the physical world. Consequently, its function is not physical but social, psychological, or existential. Even for cognitive psychologists, the focus is now on how humans think ritually, not on what ritual is intended to do.

Notes

1   The classic attempt not to replace but to reconcile a theological account of the plagues and of succeeding events with a scientific account is that of the Jewish existentialist philosopher Martin Buber, for whom the believer, on the basis of faith, attributes to divine intervention what the believer acknowledges can be fully accounted for scientifically: see Buber 1958, esp. pp. 60–8, 74–9. Buber is the Jewish counterpart to the Protestant Rudolf Bultmann.
2   The classic work on finding science in myth is de Santillana and von Dechend (1969).
3   To be precise, Frazer, while assuming, like Tylor, that adherents read myth literally, himself reads it symbolically. The life – specifically, the death and rebirth – of the god of vegetation is a metaphorical description of the death and rebirth of the crops: '[T]he story that Adonis spent half, or according to others a third, of the year in the lower world and the rest of it in the upper world, is explained most simply and naturally by supposing that he represented vegetation, especially the corn, which lies buried in the earth half the year and reappears above ground the other half' (Frazer 1922: 392). By contrast, Tylor insists that the only proper reading of myth is the literal one.
4   The classical theorist of myth as ideology is Georges Sorel (1961), for whom, to be sure, myth serves not to bolster society, as for Malinowski, but to foment revolution.
5   As Ronald Grimes, the organizer of the field of 'ritual studies,' writes of Turner's status, 'This academic generation's intellectual task seems to be that of getting beyond Victor Turner. His work has exercised considerable formative influence on the initial phases of ritual studies' (Grimes 1995: xvii).
6   Sometimes for Turner ritual is itself social drama. Other times ritual is a response to a social drama, in which case the drama refers to the turmoil itself and the ritual to the depiction of the turmoil. More precisely, ritual is here the last stage within a social drama, which begins with the turmoil and ends with what Turner calls 'redress.' Ritual is only one form of redress. A law suit is another.
7   Leach (1965: 13) lumps Harrison with Durkheim and Malinowski, neither of whom in fact brings myth and ritual so closely together, and is likely unaware of Hooke and other biblical myth-ritualists.

Bibliography

Arlow, Jacob A. 1961 'Ego Psychology and the Study of Mythology.' *Journal of the American Psychoanalytic Association* 9: 371–93.
Barthes, Roland 1972 *Mythologies*, trans. Annette Lavers. New York: Hill & Wang; London: Cape.
Boyer, Pascal 1994 *The Naturalness of Religious Ideas*. Berkeley: University of California Press.
—— 2001 *Religion Explained*. New York: Basic Books.
Buber, Martin 1958 [1946] *Moses*. New York: Harper Torchbooks.
Bultmann, Rudolf 1953 'New Testament and Mythology' (1944), in Hans-Werner Bartsch, ed., *Kerygma and Myth*, vol. 1, trans. Reginald H. Fuller (London: SPCK), 1–44. Reprinted, with revised translation: New York: Harper Torchbooks, 1961.
—— 1958 *Jesus Christ and Mythology*. New York: Scribner's.
Burkert, Walter 1979 *Structure and History in Greek Mythology and Ritual*. Berkeley: University of California Press.
—— 1985 *Greek Religion*, trans. John Raffan. Cambridge MA: Harvard University Press.
—— 1996 *Creation of the Sacred*. Cambridge MA: Harvard University Press.
Campbell, Joseph 1949 *The Hero with a Thousand Faces*. New York: Pantheon Books. 2nd edn 1968.
Cassirer, Ernst 1955 *The Philosophy of Symbolic Forms*, vol. 2. Trans. Ralph Manheim. New Haven CT: Yale University Press.

De Santillana, Giorgio, and Hertha von Dechend 1969 *Hamlet's Mill*. Boston MA: Gambit.

Detienne, Marcel 1977 *The Gardens of Adonis*, trans. Janet Lloyd. Atlantic Highlands NJ: Humanities Press.

Douglas, Mary 1970 *Purity and Danger*. Originally published 1966. Baltimore MD: Penguin Books.

—— 1973 *Natural Symbols*. 2nd edn (1st edn 1970). New York: Vintage Books.

Durkheim, Émile 1915 *The Elementary Forms of the Religious Life*. Trans. Joseph Ward Swain. London: Allen & Unwin.

Eliade, Mircea 1968 [1959] *The Sacred and the Profane*, trans. Willard R. Trask. New York: Harvest Books.

Frazer, J. G. 1922 *The Golden Bough*. Abridged edn. London: Macmillan.

Freud, Sigmund 1953 [1913] *The Interpretation of Dreams*. In Freud, *The Standard Edition of the Complete Psychological Works of Sigmund Freud*, eds and trans. James Strachey *et al.* vols 4 and 5. London: Hogarth Press and Institute of Psycho-Analysis.

—— 1955 [1950] *Toten and Taboo*. In Freud, *The Standard Edition of the Complete Psychological Works of Sigmund Freud*, eds and trans. James Strachey *et al.* vol. 13, ix–161. London: Hogarth Press and Institute of Psycho-Analysis.

Geertz, Clifford 1973 *The Interpretation of Cultures*. New York: Basic Books.

—— 1983 *Local Knowledge*. New York: Basic Books.

Girard, René 1977 *Violence and the Sacred*. Trans. Peter Gregory. London: Athlone Press; Baltimore MD: Johns Hopkins University Press.

Grimes, Ronald L. 1995 *Beginnings in Ritual Studies*. Revised edn (1st edn 1982). Columbia: University of South Carolina Press.

Harrison, Jane Ellen 1913 *Ancient Art and Ritual*. New York: Holt; London: Williams and Norgate.

Hillman, James 1975 *Re-Visioning Psychology*. New York: Harper & Row.

Jonas, Hans 1963 'Gnostic, Existentialism, and Nihilism' (1952), in Jonas *The Gnostic Religion*, 2nd edn. Boston MA: Beacon Press, 320–40.

Jung, C. G. 1968 *The Archetypes and the Collective Unconscious*. 2nd edn (1st edn 1959). In Jung, *The Collected Works of C. G. Jung* eds Sir Herbert Read *et al.*, trans. R. F. C. Hull *et al.* vol. 9, pt 1. Princeton NJ: Princeton University Press.

Kramer, Samuel Noah 1961 *Sumerian Mythology*. Revised edn (1st edn 1944). New York: Harper & Row.

Leach, Edmund 1965 *Political Systems of Highland Burma*. With new introduction. Originally published 1954. Boston MA: Beacon.

—— 1969 *Genesis as Myth and Other Essays*. London: Cape.

—— 1976 *Culture and Communication*. Cambridge: Cambridge University Press.

Lévi-Strauss, Claude 1958 'The Structural Study of Myth' (1955), in Thomas A. Sebeok, ed., *Myth*. Bloomington: Indiana University Press, 81–106. Reprinted in Claude Lévi-Strauss, *Structural Anthropology*, vol. 1, trans. Claire Jacobson and Brooke Grundfest Schoepf. New York: Basic Books, 1963; London: Allen Lane, 1968, ch. 11.

—— 1978 *Myth and Meaning*. Toronto: University of Toronto Press.

Lévy-Bruhl, Lucien 1926 *How Natives Think*, trans. Lilian A. Clare. London: Allen & Unwin. Reprinted: Princeton NJ: Princeton University Press, 1985.

Malinowski, Bronislaw 1925 'Magic, Science and Religion,' in Joseph Needham, ed., *Science, Religion and Reality*, 20–84. New York and London: Macmillan. Reprinted in B. Malinowski *Magic, Science and Religion and Other Essays*, ed. Robert Redfield. Glencoe IL: Free Press, 1948, 1–71.

—— 1926 *Myth in Primitive Psychology*. London: Kegan Paul; New York: Norton. Reprinted in B. Malinowski, *Magic, Science and Religion and Other Essays*, ed. Robert Redfield. Glencoe IL: Free Press, 1948, 72–124.

Marx, Karl, and Friedrich Engels 1957 *On Religion*. Moscow: Foreign Languages Publishing.

May, Herbert G., and Bruce M. Metzger, eds 1977 [1962] *The New Oxford Annotated Bible with the Apocrypha*, Revised Standard Version. New York: Oxford University Press.

Miller, David L. 1981 *The New Polytheism*. 2nd edn (1st edn 1974). Dallas: Spring.

Radcliffe-Brown, A. R. 1922 *The Andaman Islanders*. Cambridge: Cambridge University Press.

Raglan Lord 1936 *The Hero*. London: Methuen. Reprinted in Otto Rank, Lord Raglan and Alan Dundes, *In Quest of the Hero*. Princeton NJ: Princeton University Press, 1990, 89–175.

Rank, Otto 1914 *The Myth of the Birth of the Hero*. 1st edn, trans. F. Robbins and Smith Ely Jelliffe. Nervous and Mental Disease Monograph Series, no. 18. New York: Journal of Nervous and Mental Disease Publishing. Reprinted in Otto Rank, Lord Raglan and Alan Dundes, *In Quest of the Hero*. Princeton NJ: Princeton University Press, 1990, 3–86.

—— 2004 *The Myth of the Birth of the Hero*. 2nd edn. Trans. Gregory C. Richter and E. James Lieberman. Baltimore MD: Johns Hopkins University Press.

Rappaport, Roy A. 1968 *Pigs for the Ancestors*. New Haven CT: Yale University Press.

—— 1979 *Ecology, Meaning, and Religion*. Richmond CA: North Atlantic Books.

—— 1999 *Ritual and Religion in the Making of Humanity*. Cambridge: Cambridge University Press.

Ricoeur, Paul 1967 *The Symbolism of Evil*, trans. Emerson Buchanan. New York: Harper & Row.

Segal, Robert A. 1999 *Theorizing about Myth*. Amherst: University of Massachusetts Press.

—— 2004 *Myth*. Oxford: Oxford University Press.

Smith, William Robertson. 1889 *Lectures on the Religion of the Semites*. 1st edn. Edinburgh: Black.

Sorel, Georges A. 1961 [1950] *Reflections on Violence*, trans. T. E. Hulme and J. Roth. New York: Collier Books; London: Collier-Macmillan.

Turner, Victor W. 1967 *The Forest of Symbols*. Ithaca NY: Cornell University Press.

—— 1968 *The Drums of Affliction*. Oxford: Clarendon Press.

—— 1969 *The Ritual Process*. Chicago: Aldine.

Tylor, E. B. 1871 *Primitive Culture*. 2 vols. London: Murray. 5th edn. 1913.

Vernant, Jean-Pierre 1983 *Myth and Thought among the Greeks*. Trans. not given. London: Routledge & Kegan Paul.

Wheelwright, Philip 1968 *The Burning Fountain*. Revised edn. (1st edn. 1954). Bloomington: Indiana University Press.

Chapter 21

Religious authority

Scripture, tradition, charisma

Paul Gifford

All human groups need some authority, some generally accepted means of resolving at least the major questions, merely to persist without disintegrating. However, authority is not a simple concept. It is not necessarily linked with power in any hard sense, although there are cases where the religious and secular realms may be so intertwined that the religion may take on some form of secular coercive power. Good analogues of religious authority are provided in the medical or academic fields. A doctor, for example, has authority: he is authorised by his training and professional expertise. With true authority he can say 'you must' or 'you must not'. Likewise an academic may have authority: her authority arises from her superior knowledge of the subject, which enables her to say 'this is so' or 'this is not so'. To maintain her credibility, she must continually vindicate this authority by evidence of competence, her ability to formulate new ideas, her capacity to stimulate students to new insights. Before clarifying further the kinds of authority influential in religious communities, some preparatory remarks are in order.

Religions are not all the same; there are distinct categories like 'primal' religions, the archaic religions of Egypt or Mesopotamia or Greece, and the founded ('world') religions like Islam. Furthermore, different religions within a single one of these categories can have surprisingly diverse internal dynamics; the role played by theology in Christianity, for example, is played within Judaism by law. Further, it is a mistake to presume any particular religion is a monolithic entity, to essentialise it. Christianity has its divisions into Catholic, Protestant and Orthodox branches, to name just three, and in each of them authority is exercised significantly differently. Islam embraces Sunni, Shi'ite, Ahmadiyya, Ismaili – these branches all have different understandings of precisely where authority lies. But most importantly, religions are not static; they exist in living communities enduring through time, and thus continually change. Some of these changes can be profound. For example, we now think of Judaism as a religion centred on a book, but it was not always so. Judaism was for centuries centred on a sacrificial cult in the temple; it was the destruction of the first temple (587 BCE) that heightened its emphasis on its scriptures, and the definitive destruction of the third (70 CE) that carried this process to its ultimate conclusion. Other religions have undergone transformations just as profound. Zoroastrianism has been in turn the state religion of the Persian Empire, the religion of an oppressed and marginalised (and largely uneducated) minority under Muslim domination, the religion of a wealthy sector of modern India, and now increasingly the religion of influential professionals of a diaspora scattered throughout the West. The religion – its expression, its embodiment, its self-understanding – has not remained unaffected by these changing contexts. And the elements of authority within a religion, the way they are balanced, perceived, experienced, are among the things that have changed. This may be so, even if formal appearances mask this. Bishops have been authority figures within Christianity from its early years. Now, they would most naturally be perceived as part of the administrative bureaucracy. But they were not always best understood in that way. Medieval Europe was not a bureaucratically governed society; effective authority was exercised through the personal presence of an itinerant ruler, the exercise of patronage, the bonds established with dependents, the power to work miracles, the ceremonial projection of sacrality. In the last resort, a medieval bishop's authority may have more closely approximated the charismatic power of holy men (Mayr-Harting 1990: 124). Thus the office has persisted, but the kind of authority exercised has changed greatly.

These are some of the complications we will have to bear in mind in what follows. These factors will prevent us distinguishing neat categories of religious authority, or making any simple identification of certain forms of authority with particular religions. They will also prevent us from reaching much in the way of hard conclusions. However, even after this disclaimer, we can still raise many questions and shed some light in the general area of religious authority. In this chapter, we will focus on the three significant elements of scripture, tradition and charisma. We will ask in what way they are authoritative, how they are perceived to exert their influence, how their power is experienced and whether they function independently or in combination.

We have already observed that different religions may have different internal dynamics. This is crucially so in the matter of sacred texts. Scripture (with cognates like 'ecriture', 'scrittura', 'escritura') is a western term (etymologically, from the Latin *scribere* 'to write') with its roots in the Christian West, and with its original reference to the Christian Bible. Initially, as 'Holy Scripture', the reference was exclusively to the Christian Bible, carrying connotations of inspiration, revelation, perhaps inerrancy. It is only in the last 150 years that the term has come to be applied in a less metaphysical and more descriptive sense to the sacred books of other religious traditions. (Max Müller's fifty-volume edition (1879–94) of *The Sacred Books of the East* was a milestone in this development.) Sometimes the connotations of the word as traditionally used in the West were much less fitting when applied to other traditions. If the term is not unduly distorting when applied to the other founded religions of the Near East, to Judaism and Islam, its suitability to Eastern religions is less obvious. It is only in recent decades that serious efforts have been made to allow for the subtle distortions likely when a concept taken from one tradition is applied to others.

Nevertheless it is obviously characteristic of many religions to have sacred texts – which we will follow current convention and indiscriminately call 'scripture'. If we ask what it is that constitutes these particular texts scripture or sacred, we quickly see that it is not a matter of form or content. There is no essence, or intrinsic formal quality, or even set of family resemblances, that characterise all these diverse texts. As regards content, the diversity is enormous – from the hymns (*gathas*) of Zoroaster to the letters of Paul, the law codes of Deuteronomy and the sacrificial rituals of the Vedas. Even beauty or profundity is not an essential characteristic. Undoubtedly many have this sublimity – taken to its ultimate in Islam with its doctrine of the inimitability of the Qur'an (*i jaz al-Qur'an*) – but alongside the sublime we can find other parts which may be genealogies, crude hagiography or fairly banal chronicles. It would be hard to list any criteria of form or content that could isolate precisely these texts and not others.

Likewise, authorship does not provide a criterion for elevating a text to the status of scripture, for here too there is enormous diversity. Although some (like the Qur'an) are intimately linked to the founder, others are by subsequent leaders (as is much of the Sikhs' Adi Granth), others have authors who are completely unknown (the case for a large part of the Jewish scriptures). In the case of the Hindu religion, with no individual founder, the scriptures are believed to have no author at all, not even God.

No, to label a text 'scripture' essentially involves none of these things. What makes a text or texts scripture is something of another level altogether, namely the text's relationship to a community. It is this relationship that is constitutive. Scripture is a relational term, like husband or mother; it has meaning only in relation to another. It is the community's persistence in according it an authoritative position in its life that constitutes a text scripture. Hence, as Smith well puts it, scripture is not an attribute of texts, but a 'human activity'. And it is an ongoing activity. 'No doubt, their scripture to a mighty degree makes a people what they are. Yet one must not lose sight of the point that it is the people who make it, keep making it, scripture' (Smith 1993: 18–19).

Thus authority over a community is built into the idea of scripture. Yet the various scriptures may exert their authority in many diverse ways. Scriptures (or parts of them) may provide the main prayers that adherents utilise throughout the day. In some forms of worship, the scriptures may become a sacred object; thus Jews may dance with the Torah in the synagogue. Most traditions have all kinds of significant popular uses – many Muslims use the Qur'an as a protective device against evil, even using a potion made from mixing water with the ink used to write a Qur'anic charm. Some religions regard scripture as the supreme source of their 'doctrine' or 'morals' or 'law'. However, a scripture's influence can be much more subtly pervasive; it is not always conscious or direct. Anyone familiar with medieval Europe will understand the role of the Bible as providing the source material for most European art; in this way the biblical narratives provided the images that fed the imagination and moulded cultural life. Within Islam, although pictorial representation is generally shunned, Qur'anic calligraphy has played a similar role. In such various ways, focused and diffuse, explicit and implicit, hard and soft, scriptures mould and direct their particular communities. The ability to guide and influence is there by definition, from the mere fact of being scripture.

However, for any living community the context changes over time. We have already drawn attention to the changes Zoroastrianism and Judaism have undergone in history, but change is universal. Islam has changed from a desert religion to the religion of the Abbasids and the Umayyads and the Ottomans. Christianity has transformed itself from a Jewish sect to the Byzantine state religion, to the cultural soul of Europe, to the religion of Latin American peasants. Continuity through change is a problem for any religion, and scripture is often one of the key things enabling the community to negotiate major transformations, providing the means of rendering changes explicable and manageable, thus ensuring some experience of identity over time.

The complexity of this process has become obvious only in relatively recent years. What has disclosed the complexity is the rise of a radical new perspective, historical consciousness. At its heart is the awareness that everything is relative, or related to the context in which it arose or in which it exists. Nothing human is supra-temporal, supra-cultural or supra-historical. Everything human is culturally conditioned. Where such a consciousness has taken root (notably in the West, especially Western academia), it has had important effects on the understanding of the past in general, and in particular has affected our attitude to historical texts.

It has altered our attitude to past 'authorities'. By and large, previous ages were incredibly respectful of past authorities. C.S. Lewis says of the European Middle Ages that they were 'ages of authority'.

> If their culture is regarded as a response to environment, then the elements in that environment to which they responded most vigorously were manuscripts. Every writer if he possibly can, bases himself on an earlier writer, follows an *auctour*, preferably a Latin one. This is one of the things that differentiates that period . . . from our modern civilisation.

He remarks later of medieval people: 'They find it hard to believe that anything an old *auctour* has said is simply untrue' (cited in Nineham 1976: 45). The traditional Christian attitude to the Bible must be seen in this light, as part of a cultural disposition. That it is broadly cultural rather than narrowly religious is obvious from the fact that the same attitude was shown to classical authors. Indeed the Roman poet Virgil (Publius Vergilius Maro, 70–19 BCE) is an example of someone in the past whose work became almost mystically revered. It was repeated, commented on, embellished, used as an oracle, put into catenae and all sorts of legends grew up around the author. Virgil's writings, or (more correctly) what Virgil is supposed to have written, became part of the mental furniture of the European Middle Ages. Another example of an *auctour* given unquestioned status is Galen (131–201 CE), one of the founders of the western medical tradition. He had described an organ in the human body called the *rete mirabile*. It is recorded that when medical dissection began, and this organ was not found, it seemed far more probable to those first clinical anatomists that there had occurred an organic change in the human body since his time than that Galen had made a mistake (see Nineham 1976: 268).

In the West, that attitude to the past has now changed radically. We can conveniently date the stirrings of change to about the time of the founding of the Royal Society, which received its charter in 1662 (Newton was to be its president from 1703 to 1727). The Royal Society's motto was: 'Nullius in verba'; in other words, 'We refuse to be bound by the words of any authority, however venerable or sacred' (Nineham 1976: 61). This change in mentality was linked to the rise of science, but came to be accepted far more widely. The newer understanding is succinctly encapsulated in Marx and Engels' reference in the 1848 Communist Manifesto to 'the burden of all the dead generations weighing like a nightmare on the mind of the living', and equally in Thomas Paine's claim that 'the vanity and presumption of governing beyond the grave is the most ridiculous and insolent of all tyrannies' (Paine 1798: 9).

An understanding of this change of mentality is crucial for the modern academic study of religion, and for understanding the role of scripture in particular. The 'clash of science and religion' arose not because Darwin had discovered a truth that 'disproved' some 'biblical' truth. The clash arose because the rise of science depended on a new view of truth; no longer as something revealed *back there* and enshrined in a text to which those coming after must continually refer. Now truth was seen as *out there ahead*, to be discovered by hypothesis, experiment and verification. Another cultural shift was at play here too. One of the reasons for the earlier respect for *auctours* was that most ages have been very aware of their own inferiority in regard to the past. Previous ages almost by definition deferred to their predecessors, sometimes because of the sentiment expressed by Plato: 'The ancients are better than we, for they dwelled nearer to the Gods' (*Philebus* 16c). With this perception, it was well nigh impossible to think of questioning the categories with which those earlier cultures had worked. However, it is much harder for the beneficiaries of the industrial and technological and information revolutions to 'feel' that previous ages were their superiors.

It is worthwhile unpacking some of the consequences of this new attitude to the past. Obviously, it tends to heighten the otherness of the past. Whereas even in relatively recent times people might have seen naturally the connections and similarities with antiquity, historical consciousness tends to flag up the strangeness, the discontinuities, the differences. When the world of a text from the distant past is perceived as so very different from our own, to take such a text as normative becomes much less natural, and the easy submission to a text, no matter how traditionally authoritative, less spontaneous. This is in marked contrast to many epochs that have naturally and spontaneously looked to the past for guidance.

Besides, quite often historical analysis has disclosed that a text was not really saying what it was claimed to say. This is not primarily because modern research shows that a text has been totally misunderstood (although this cannot be ruled out; the Zoroastrian *gathas* are a nightmare to interpret). It is much more likely that historical study shows that the traditionally accepted 'scriptural meaning' is just one among many views extractable from different portions of the scripture. In most cases, this is because although unicity (the presumption of one coherent interlocking whole) is almost invariably attributed to scripture, scripture in the vast majority of cases is in fact a compilation of pieces of quite diverse provenance. A rigorous historical approach often reveals that what has been taken to be *the* meaning has resulted from privileging one segment, and reading the whole through the spectacles provided by this privileged segment. In these cases it is evident that the scripture is far from self-interpreting: it is tradition or the living community that has been influential in ensuring that *this* is the received meaning of scripture. Examples abound, but the point is succinctly captured in this vignette of Africa's response to Christian missions:

> Protestant missionaries introduced the Bible to Africans as the ultimate earthly authority, but were bewildered when their African converts selected their biblical data so differently, highlighting the complex rituals, revelations through dreams and visions, the separation between clean and unclean animals, the practice of polygamy, the descent of God upon prophets, miraculous healings and exorcisms, and so on.
>
> (Hastings 1979: 70)

All these things so peripheral for the missionaries are just as clearly in the Christian Bible as the images, motifs and narratives that the missionaries stressed. It was only when other 'readings' were proffered that it became obvious that the received reading was a highly selective interpretation, even if traditionally authoritative.

Further, historical analysis often reveals that what the text has been traditionally taken to mean is, on closer inspection, found to be a later idea retrojected back into it. Judaism provides a classic example. The Mishnah and Talmud are widely viewed as commentaries on the Tanakh (the Torah, the Prophets, the Writings). They are presented in that guise, in the form of comment on or elaboration of the earlier text. On deeper inspection, however, the secondary or derivative appearance is revealed as just that – an appearance arising from the framework imposed on them. In fact both the Mishnah and the Talmud are deeply original works; in some cases their novelty is quite startling. It is the prior assumption that they must be expounding the 'more authoritative' Tanakh that has obscured this. In fact, rather than seeing it as a commentary on a preceding scripture, 'one might suggest rather that (the Mishnah) presents as it were that preceding scripture, if at all, as a commentary on itself' (Smith 1993: 114).

The Mishnah and Talmud were the creation of so many (the former collated by Judah ha Nasi, the latter produced by the Amoraim) that they might be considered genuinely community products. But gifted or charismatic individuals within the community must often be viewed in the same light; the contribution of individual commentators has often been enormous. Their works, too, are often not best understood as commentaries at all, but more adequately as remarkably creative developments which might well have been celebrated as such except for the overriding assumption of the priority of the scripture, an assumption that functioned to disguise any innovation as a deeper elaboration of the text. Consider Augustine of Hippo (354–430 CE). His influence on subsequent Christianity is unparalleled, even though much of his influence is disguised by the fact that he did much of his theological work in terms of commentaries or homilies on scripture. His influence is so great that what subsequent Christian tradition has often understood as Paul, is really Augustine's reading of Paul. When subsequent Christians thought they were harkening to scripture they were in fact harkening to Augustine's understanding of scripture. Augustine's role or influence is underestimated because in the received understanding of scripture the canonical author Paul should be regarded as authoritative.

In Judaism, this phenomenon is perhaps even more salient. Until well into the twentieth century the Tanakh was hardly ever published without a key commentary, normally by Rashi (1040–1105 CE), Radak (1160–1235) or Ramban (1194–1270). It was through the often highly original lenses provided by these great commentators that the Tanakh was read. One observer perceptively catches the dynamics here: 'The bulk of Jewish literature is in the form of commentary on Scripture, whether this form is always justified or not (often the pretense of commentary disguises a full-fledged original personal viewpoint)' (Greenberg, cited in Smith 1993: 117).

Much the same could be said within Islam of jurists up to the Ayatollah Khomeini (1902–89 CE), countless gurus within the Hindu tradition, and masters within the Zen tradition. Under the rubric of interpreting their respective scriptures they were providing their community with new resources to meet new situations. In many cases they would have positively repudiated any idea that they exercised an authoritative role within a tradition, seeing themselves as simply servants of the text. But they were obviously far more than that, as historical criticism reveals.

The scripturalising of a text, therefore, has in many cases obscured as much as it has revealed the dynamics operative in the life of the religious community. By dint of scripturalising a text, the community has committed itself to presenting novelty in the form of exposition of or commentary on 'what was there already' in the community's scripture. In many cases this commitment has the effect of reducing the scripture almost to a *tabula rasa* on which the community can read what it wants to or has to. Barton has referred to this quality of 'semantic indeterminacy' of sacred texts. 'Sacred texts . . . tend to be semantically indeterminate, for they have to be read as supporting the religious system to which they belong, even at the expense of their natural sense' (Barton 1997: 61). The classic instance of this is in the Christian interpretation of the Jewish scripture as Christian. This was the result of a certain combination of presupposition and need: 'They [the Jewish Scriptures] were ostensibly the absolutely authoritative divine revelation; but in reality they functioned as a *tabula rasa* on which Christians wrote what they took (on quite other grounds) to be the meaning of Christ' (ibid.: 19). That this is more than something uniquely Christian is evident from the fact that the sectaries of the Dead Sea saw the Jewish scripture as referring to their Teacher of Righteousness (see especially their Habbakuk Commentary).

This tendency to find in the scripture whatever the community needs for its continuing development is remarkably widespread. This is in effect the purpose of all forms of figurative or non-literal interpretation, namely to enable the community to find there what it must. In many traditions this approach has been taken to considerable lengths, often through elaborate theories of multiple senses of scripture. In Christianity, there were sometimes as many as seven, but most often four: the literal, the allegorical, the moral and the anagogic (or related to the end times). Judaism had its system of *pardes*, from the different forms of exegesis: *peshat* (literal), *remez* (allusive), *derash* (homiletical) and *sodh* (mystical). Islam has its *ta'wil* to explore symbolic and inner meanings (especially prominent in Shi'i and Sufi or mystical contexts). Once again, it is significant that this whole trajectory (through Judaism, Christianity and Islam) actually has its roots outside religion and in the world of classical literature. The techniques of allegory were introduced into the classics to avoid having to find in Homer and Hesiod meanings (the natural or common sense meanings) that were considered unworthy of them by scholars who looked back to them with awe and reverence. These approaches flourished in Alexandria, whence Philo introduced them into Judaism, Christian Fathers (again most notably of the Alexandrian school) adopted them, and later they found their way into Islamic scholarship. These multiple senses of the text, with the 'literal' not necessarily the most important, persisted right through until the rise of modern historical consciousness, when (at least in the West) the literal tended to become all-important, and the others largely fell away.

The scripturalising of a text has thus obscured much of the activity of the community in creatively addressing new issues and contexts. The theories constructed to explain the elevated role of scripture have most often reflected what was thought should have been happening, rather than what in fact was happening. Historical research has laid bare what was in fact occurring as the community utilised its scriptures. An additional aspect of this phenomenon is that the books that matter (in our sense, have authority) are in many cases not the theoretically acknowledged scripture at all, but others. In some religions there are evident layers of sacred books. The Avesta, Qur'an and the Tanakh are recognised in their respective religions as scripture par excellence, but these religions have other texts (respectively the Pahlavi texts, Hadith and the Mishnah) as a subordinate or supporting layer. Historical criticism may reveal that in some cases it is not the primary but the secondary layer that is more authoritative. Much popular Hinduism is of this kind. In entire swathes of India the Mahabharata (especially the *Bhagavad-Gita*) and the *Ramayana* are far more significant than the Vedas, even though the former are *smrti* ('that which is remembered') the secondary and derivative scriptural category, and the latter *sruti* ('that which is heard', namely by the seers) or scripture par excellence. Indeed, for Hinduism on Mauritius, the really authoritative works are the theoretically very subsidiary Ram-carit-manas of Tulsi Das and the religious poems of Kabir, as remembered by the indentured labourers taken there.

In all these ways, where on the face of it scripture seemed determinative, and frequently enough was claimed to be determinative, it is at least as helpful to see the community determining its own shape in response to new needs, but portraying these responses as derived from the resources of the sacred text. It seems to be an essential element of scripture that it be used in this way.

This radical reappraisal arising from historical criticism does not mean that scripture is no longer of any significance for those religious communities where historical thinking has taken root. After all, the most fastidious historical critic may worship in scriptural forms, and meditate on scriptural texts. For his or her personal religious life (indeed for the spiritual life of the community), all sorts of processes may be fruitful. One can do other things with scriptures than situate them in their context, find their 'original' meaning, analyse them historically (although the historical approach has become so dominant in the West that restricting significant enquiry to these issues is a real danger, particularly for academics). Nevertheless, in the West, it is widely agreed that if it is historical questions that are at issue – and the nature and extent of scripture's impact on a religious community over time is such a historical question – they must be answered with the strictest historical warrants. In such cases, even a believer cannot merely repeat the accepted doctrinal position in the face of historical evidence to the contrary.

No one should be in any doubt about the extent of the rethinking required by the rise of historical consciousness. (I repeat that in discussion here is the narrow historical point of the nature and extent of the influence of scripture on the community; broader questions of the impact of scientific or historical thinking on religion itself are beyond our present scope.) Two important Christian theologians, in an article entitled 'Scripture and Tradition', begin:

> Until recently, almost the entire spectrum of theological opinion would have agreed that the scriptures of the Old and New Testaments, together with their doctrinal interpretations, occupy a unique and indispensable place of authority for Christian faith, practice and reflection. But this consensus now seems to be falling apart.

(Farley and Hodgson 1985: 61)

They then rethink the traditional view, in light of such considerations as have been raised above. Their conclusion is that the accepted theory is 'actually inappropriate' to Christianity 'when properly understood' (ibid.: 62).

It is Christianity and Judaism that are most affected by historical criticism because their centre of gravity has long been in the West, and the dominant strands of both are by and large committed to a general cultural relevance (as opposed to cultural isolation). Other religious traditions have been affected differently. Some have rejected the whole historical approach (Muslims tend to see the attempt to address the Qur'an or Hadith through historical criticism as yet another Western attempt to denigrate Islam). Some other traditions, still cocooned from the 'corrosion' of historical criticism, have been able to carry on relatively unchanged. Yet even in these latter instances, they have not proved totally impregnable; many have sizeable diasporas in the West, and their young, learning at school to approach texts historically, inevitably begin to address their scriptures in the same way.

This last point highlights a further complication hindering a simple correlation between kinds of authority and particular religions. We mentioned above the different attitudes to scripture within a single religion. Protestants have differed from Catholics (usually expressed in the terms of precisely our problematic – 'Scripture versus Tradition'); Mahayana Buddhists differ from Theravada Buddhists; Shi'ites from Sunni Muslims. But in the twentieth century we see a new phenomenon. Now Judaism and Christianity have a totally new division, between those who accept the legitimacy of historical criticism, and those who do not. In the West, most mainstream Christians, whether Catholic or Protestant, have come to accept it (officially as late as 1964 for Catholics). However, most Christians are now found in the Third World, where most are pre-critical and can maintain an unselfconscious attitude to scripture virtually impossible now for their western co-religionists. In a further complication, some in the West positively deny the legitimacy of applying the historical approach to scripture, seeing this as destructive of Christianity itself. This is indeed a third and different stance, for such fundamentalists are not so much either critical or pre-critical as anti-critical. Despite the frequent claim of these fundamentalists to preserve the traditional attitude to scripture, their stance is every bit as modern as the critical approach to which they are reacting. Here then we have a profound three-way split within the one religion in attitudes to scriptural authority (and indirectly tradition).

We should be clear what is being claimed here. We are not arguing that academic historical study of religion has 'destroyed' the authority of scripture in the sense of rendering scripture superfluous. The scriptures remain important, even where they are now understood to exert their influence as an originating repository of the images, myths, symbols, metaphors, narratives, laws, persons and paradigms that have given the community its identity, recalled it to its roots, anchored its legal structures, linked it with its founder, provided its classic access to the divine, created its general cultural ambiance, suggestively guided it through history, and exercised a critical role in facing new challenges. These are, of course, the functions that scripture always played, although so often something rather more was claimed. So, in one sense, this approach has merely brought theory into line with practice. Scripture has always functioned in a way that involved the living community. It never functioned in some absolute, unqualified, mechanical way, even though this was often presumed in theories about scripture (understood as blueprint, charter, constitution, inspired revelation, timeless word of God). You cannot talk of the authority of scripture apart from the religious community on its ongoing historical journey (that is, apart from its tradition). You cannot talk of authority, scripture or tradition in isolation. Graham has well expressed it: 'A text becomes scripture in living, subjective relationship to persons and to historical tradition. No text . . . is sacred or authoritative in isolation from a community' (Graham 1987: 134).

It should be obvious that this historical consciousness has affected the understanding of tradition as much as of scripture. The awareness of inevitable change that constitutes this historical consciousness reveals that tradition persists only as a continual process of reinterpretation. The role of tradition, too, has been discovered to be anything but simple. In 1983 Hobsbawm and Ranger edited a remarkable book showing that so many 'time-honoured' and 'immemorial' traditions have been rather recently invented. They describe the overmastering impulse, beginning about 1870 and peaking around 1900 and spreading right across the world, to invent traditions in every aspect of national life – in politics, education, recreation as well as religion (again we meet a phenomenon broadly cultural rather than narrowly religious). National festivals, stamps and statues, anthems and flags, uniforms, military parades, monuments and jubilees are all quite modern. The creation of national symbolism where none before existed was not unconnected with the changing context. In the West there arose an urgent need to popularise traditional institutions as politics became mass politics. (The ritualism of the British monarchy increased in inverse proportion to the political power of the sovereign.) 'Traditions' were taking hold quite widely; around that time the British began to invent native 'African traditions' such as tribal divisions and customary law. Their book focused on a particular period and Britain primarily, but it made a serious point of wide application; so often, in claims about the past far more is going on than meets the eye. Very often the claim 'this is our tradition' is not a statement about the past at all (just as the claim 'our scripture says' is not necessarily a statement in any strict sense about the meaning of a document); it is a statement about the present – most often a statement of what the present might, or even should, be.

I have spoken above of the living community, without specifying how a community operates. Here, obviously, due allowance must be made for the influence of the gifted individuals within a community, and we naturally move to our third focus of religious authority, charisma (from the Greek *charis*, 'grace' or 'favour', although the word is not widely found in profane Greek, the roots of our concept being in St Paul). The currency of the concept in contemporary study of religion comes from Weber, who treated the phenomenon at length (Weber 1978). Weber's concern was to distinguish types of leader: traditional, rational-legal and charismatic. The third type is based upon the perception of followers that an individual is endowed with exceptional (even divine) qualities. (Thus the concept of 'charisma' is just as much a relational term as 'scripture'.) Weber's ideal-type charismatic leader possesses authority based on his own qualities rather than on tradition or rational considerations. He offers a new revelation and way of life, demands obedience to his mission, and imposes new obligations. Charismatic leadership is unpredictable, personal and unstable, and hence normally must become 'routinised' if the mission of the originator is to persist.

This kind of authority is found most purely in shamanism or primal religions generally. In many religions of Africa, the most obvious religious figures are the healer-diviner, the witch and the medium. Some healer-diviners may be considered to have come by their skills through learning from their predecessors, but usually all three are considered to derive their exceptional gifts from the spirits. Some, particularly the spirit mediums, can even be taken over by their indwelling spirits in ecstatic trances. It is this possession that gives the charismatic religious figure his or her authority. Although charismatic authority is regarded with some suspicion in the increasingly bureaucratised West, it should not be thought that charisma is restricted to 'primal' religions. For one thing, for many scholars of religion it is the founders of the world religions that are the classic examples of this phenomenon. In Jewish tradition, Moses has been considered to have been endowed with the prophetic gifts to such a degree that he was 'the greatest of the prophets'. Jesus taught 'as one having authority, and not as the scribes' (Mk 1,22). Muhammad is understood to have possessed more *barakah* (blessing) than any other man. ('*Barakah*' is an important Islamic concept generally.) The Buddha was said to have had an aura surrounding his body, bringing all he met into submission. For another thing, it is the charismatic leaders of New Religious Movements (NRMs) who constitute a key focus of contemporary religious research.

Frequently charisma links with the other sources of authority considered above. As noted earlier, charisma must become routinised into standardised procedures and structures if the group is to persist beyond the life of the figure who triggered it, but in themselves charisma and tradition tend to tug in different directions; charisma and tradition inevitably enjoy a somewhat conflictual relationship. But with scripture, charisma often has an almost symbiotic relationship. Many charismatic leaders of NRMs ground their authority in texts. Someone like David Koresh of the 1993 Waco tragedy, in which 86 people died in a stand-off with US law enforcement agencies, possessed authority not just because of personal qualities, but because he was able to convince others that he was part of the end-time events supposedly predicted in scriptures. (His Branch Davidians were an offshoot of the millenarian Seventh Day Adventists.) American televangelists, the focus of so many studies of charisma, depend upon their own gifts but at the same time take care to anchor their authority in scripture. Scripture actually functions to reinforce their personal charismatic authority. Gurus of many religions win and hold their following to the extent that they are seen to reveal the 'real' meaning of scripture.

As a concluding illustration of several of the foregoing points, consider Sikhism. The founder of Sikhism was Guru Nanak (1469–1539 CE), who was succeeded by nine other Gurus. The tenth Guru, Gobind Singh (1675–1708 CE) decreed that the line of Gurus would stop with him, ultimate authority being shared thereafter by both the Panth (community) and the Adi Granth (also known as the Guru Granth Sahib, the collection of writings of the Gurus – and some precursors – assembled essentially by the fifth Guru but given final form by the tenth).

Historical criticism shows that Guru Nanak, the undisputed founder of the religion, discounted outward observance, teaching that true religion is interior, and liberation is achieved through inward meditation directed to Akal Purakh (the 'Timeless Being') who reveals himself in the *nam* or divine name, and brings liberating karma, when transmigration comes to an end. This is achieved through *nam simaran*, a regular discipline of inner meditation that focuses on the omnipresence of the divine name.

Such teaching was current among the Sants of North India at the time, thus 'effectively destroying any claims to significant originality' (McLeod 1989: 23). However, over time circumstances transformed Sikhism. The tenth Guru, Gobind Singh, institutionalised the community in the *Khalsa* in 1699, and began the formation of its special code of conduct (*Rahit*), which evolved throughout the eighteenth century. Over this time what had been a religion of interiority assumed an ever more exterior identity, marked particularly by uncut hair and the bearing of arms (militancy had first developed under the fifth, ninth and tenth Gurus especially). Under British occupation, a reform movement begun in the late nineteenth century attempted for the first time to distinguish Sikhs from Hindus. The self-understanding and marks of identity established over the late nineteenth and early twentieth centuries are still determinative today.

The Sikh scripture, the Adi Granth, is given enormous respect. Its mere presence constitutes any room or building a *gurdwara* (temple). No one may sit on a level higher than the lectern on which it is placed. Sikhs marry by circling it four times. Daily prayers are derived from it. Yet paradoxically, 'Within the Panth itself knowledge of the actual contents of the Adi Granth is very limited' (ibid.: 88). A second work, the Dasam Granth, had in the eighteenth century almost the same respect as the Adi Granth; now 'the Dasam Granth as a whole is seldom invoked and little understood' – probably because 'the material which dominates the narrative and anecdotal portion . . . is scarcely consonant with the preferred interpretation of the Sikh tradition' (ibid.: 90–1). On yet a third level of scripture are works by two distinguished Sikhs of the Guru period, Bhai Gurdas and Bhai Nand Lal. Both 'are explicitly approved for recitation in gurdwaras and as such they constitute a part of what we may regard as an authorized Sikh canon' (ibid.: 92). In practice, however, both are 'seldom read or heard' (ibid.: 94), probably because their spirit and content are so different from what the Khalsa came to be. A further class of scripture comprises the *Janam-sakhis*, cycles of narratives of the first Guru, very hagiographical, often miraculous. 'Although they have never been accepted as sacred scripture, their immense popularity has conferred on them a major role in the sustaining and transmission' of the Nanak tradition (ibid.: 97–8) – in our sense, made them enormously authoritative. Still another set of works, known as the Gur-balas, concentrates on tales of the two warrior Gurus, the sixth, Hargobind, and particularly the tenth, Gobind Singh, whose ideals inspired the eighteenth-century Khalsa. There is yet other literature, notably of the Singh Sabha or nineteenth-century reform movement, that offer the traditions reinterpreted in the light of western ideals, but there is no space to elaborate on them here. I have merely outlined this history and this range of texts to illustrate the complex ways in which the community has regulated itself and (something slightly different) claimed it was regulating itself. The community has transformed itself over time. The 'traditional' practices and self-understanding have evolved in accordance with changing conditions. Revered and theoretically decisive scriptures are unstudied and neglected, because of their lack of harmony with later tradition; other books, not part of any canon, are far more influential or authoritative in determining the life of the community, because so compatible with later tradition.

Sikhism is a religion that is quite specific where authority lies: it is virtually undisputed that the mystically present Guru persists equally in the Panth and the Adi Granth. This theoretically precise doctrine, however, leaves much unresolved. Radical ambiguity persists in the translating of mystical authority into actual decisions. The Adi Granth provides 'little specific guidance on issues relating to the Rahit, and differences of opinion quickly emerge whenever the attempt is made to apply its general principles to particular cases' (ibid.: 75). However, in practice, the Panth has learnt to live with 'a radically uncertain theory of ultimate authority' (ibid.: 77). Undoubtedly there are stresses and strains, and certain issues continue to trouble the Panth, but the evolving tradition in most cases offers sufficient guidance to preserve an ongoing identity. We might complete our illustration by noting that it is the historical approach that enables scholars to establish the community's development (we have here followed McLeod, but our point about authority within a community is not narrowly dependent on his reconstruction), and to understand individual books in the light of particular contexts; yet Sikhism itself tends to reject this approach. However, the young Sikhs of the western diaspora increasingly find such a historical approach unavoidable.

Religious authority, in practice, is thus a very complex reality. Understanding its various forms is rendered more difficult because so often the accepted theory does not so much reveal as obscure what is going on. We have drawn attention to three aspects or elements: scripture, or sacred books; tradition, or the living community itself as it survives through time; charisma, or exceptionally gifted individuals. Although it is legitimate to consider these separately, we have discovered so often an extremely complex interplay, not made less complex because so often the religion itself claims that there is in question a simple and transparent process. Here, as frequently elsewhere, theory can be one thing, practice another.

References

Barton, John, 1997, *People of the Book*, London: SPCK. A brief treatment of many of the issues, focusing on the Christian tradition.

Farley, Edward and Hodgson, Peter C., 1985, 'Scripture and Tradition', in Peter C. Hodgson and Robert King (eds), *Christian Theology: an Introduction to its Tradition and Tasks*, Philadelphia PA: Fortress Press.

Graham, W.A., 1987, 'Scripture', in M. Eliade (ed.), *Encyclopedia of Religion*, New York: Macmillan; and London: Collier Macmillan. Succinct summary of the issues.

Hobsbawm, Eric and Ranger, Terence (eds), 1983, *The Invention of Tradition*, Cambridge: Cambridge University Press. Shows the problematic nature of 'tradition'.

McLeod, W.H., 1989, *The Sikhs: History, Religion and Society*, New York and Guildford: Columbia University Press. A superb treatment of the Sikh tradition; profound yet clear.

Mayr-Harting, Henry, 1990, 'The West: The Age of Coversion (700–1050)', in John McManners (ed.), *The Oxford History of Christianity*, Oxford: Oxford University Press.

Müller, Max, 1879–94, *The Sacred Books of the East*, 50 vols, New Delhi: Motilal Banarsidass.

Nineham, Dennis, 1976, *The Use and Abuse of the Bible: A Study of the Bible in an Age of Rapid Cultural Change*, London: Macmillan. A provocative treatment.

Paine, Thomas, 1798, *Rights of Man*, London: Wordsworth Classics.

Plato, 360 BCE, *Philebus*. Trans. Robin Waterfield, 1982, London: Penguin Books.

Smith, Wilfred Cantwell, 1993, *What is Scripture?* Minneapolis MN: Fortress Press. A magisterial treatment of all the issues involved, covering all traditions.

Weber, Max, 1978, *Economy and Society*, Berkeley: University of California Press, especially I, 241–5; II, 1111–56. The classic treatment of charismatic leadership.

Chapter 22

Hermeneutics

Garrett Green

For provisional purposes, one can define hermeneutics quite simply as the *theory of interpretation*. Although this straightforward definition may do as a point of entry into a subject notable for its complexity, controversy, and jargon-ridden discourse, it will need to be qualified in a number of ways before it can do justice to the field of hermeneutics as it impinges on the scholarly study of religion today.

Our provisional definition can be expanded, first of all, by identifying hermeneutics as *theoretical reflection on the principles and rules of interpretation and understanding*. Implicit in this still basic definition is a duality that reflects the disparate origins of modern hermeneutics and helps to account for its complexity. On the one hand are those who would think of hermeneutics primarily in terms of method and practice. Here the emphasis lies on the actual interpretation of texts by scholars, exegetes, or religious teachers. Hermeneutics in this sense articulates and codifies the principles and rules of textual interpretation – an activity that has enjoyed a long history under a variety of names and plays an important role in virtually all of the world's religions. On the other hand are those for whom the object of hermeneutics is not in the first instance the texts being interpreted so much as the human act of understanding that every interpretation presupposes and instantiates. Hermeneutics in this sense is more like a philosophy than a methodology. Indeed, in the influential modern tradition of hermeneutical speculation reaching from Schleiermacher to Gadamer, hermeneutics becomes the name for a comprehensive philosophy of understanding. When one thinks of hermeneutics as something to be 'applied,' one is using the term in the former (methodological) sense; when one uses it to describe a mode of reflection on the nature of human understanding, one is employing it in the latter (philosophical) sense. To make matters more complex, thinkers rarely adopt one or the other of these two types in its 'pure' form, so that the polarity represents not two kinds of hermeneutics but rather two tendencies or emphases within the modern hermeneutical discussion – tendencies that can take on endless variations and can be combined in myriads of ways.

Further clarification of hermeneutics requires that we look at the actual historical traditions that have led to our contemporary situation. The reason for this procedure should be plain from what has already been said: we cannot first establish the meaning of the term and then go on to describe the various ways of doing it, because every attempt at a formal definition already involves us in the controversial issues of the content of hermeneutical theory. The shape of the field today results not from the systematic unfolding of its conceptual meaning but rather from the interplay of concrete human personalities, cultures, and religious and philosophical traditions.

Origins and etymology

No one knows for certain the origins of the Greek verb *hermēneuein* ('to interpret'), from which our modern word derives, but most of the tendencies and controversies of later hermeneutical theory are foreshadowed in the ancient conversation about this term and its cognate noun *hermēneia*, which became a technical term and often appeared in titles – preeminently in Aristotle's treatise 'On Interpretation' (*Peri Hermēneias*). Though the etymological connection is obscure, the most illuminating feature of ancient hermeneutics is its association with Hermes, the messenger of the gods. This connection underscores the fact that hermeneutics, while not a religious term per se, has always had an intrinsic relationship to religion. The archetypal problem of interpretation, one could say, is embodied in the mystery of the divine word that must first be translated (one of the root meanings of *hermēneuein*) into understandable human terms before it can be heard, obeyed, and appropriated. The most important texts calling forth the art of interpretation have long been religious texts, so that scriptural interpretation is not simply one category in a series of hermeneutical tasks but rather the source or model for all the others. Even in the highly secularized world of the modern academy one can find traces of this heritage in the continuing fascination and controversy aroused by issues of canon: how authoritative texts – pre-eminently the Bible in Western civilization – are to be interpreted.

The link between ancient Greek *hermēneia* and modern hermeneutical theory is found in the history of interpretation in the Jewish and Christian communities that were the successors to classical Greek and Roman culture and the forerunners of modern European and global culture. The shape of that history is largely determined by the texts whose interpretation was crucial for those communities. In classical culture the need to interpret Homer was the driving force behind hermeneutical thought, since the *Iliad* and the *Odyssey* functioned as foundational texts in those societies. The two main alternatives that developed were *grammatical* interpretation, which sought meaning in the structure and shape of the language in which the stories were told, and *allegorical* interpretation, in which the meaning of the text was sought in an external symbolic key. The grammatical interpreter looked at the way the text itself is put together, believing that the key to its meaning will be found within the structure of the text itself. Allegorical interpreters, on the other hand, believed that the meaning hidden in the text could only be deciphered with the help of an external key that would unlock its symbolism. First Jewish and then early Christian interpreters adapted and extended these methods for their own use in interpreting the Bible. The most important bridge figure is Philo of Alexandria (roughly a contemporary of Jesus, though the two were surely unaware of one another's existence), a Hellenistic Jewish philosopher who applied allegorical interpretation to the anthropomorphic narratives of the Torah, and whose ideas influenced the Christian thinkers who subsequently flourished in Alexandria. Rabbinic Judaism generally followed a different direction, which included several approaches to scripture, including literalist interpretations, midrashic exegesis, which tried to find meaning beyond the literal sense of the text, and others. Their overarching concern was to fit scripture into a theologically meaningful framework without succumbing to a dead literalism on the one hand or opening the floodgates to spiritualizing excesses on the other – interpretations which, by encouraging subjective or mystical readings, might endanger the identity and integrity of the community.

The Christian church fathers faced similar issues, compounded by the need to integrate the proclamation of Jesus with the Jewish scriptures. In addition to the kinds of interpretation already mentioned, the Christian fathers advocated the use of typological or figural interpretation, an approach often confused with allegory but in fact quite distinct from it. In this kind of interpretation, an earlier event (typically from the Old Testament) is taken as a figure or type for a later (New Testament) event. Unlike allegory, both figures, type and antitype, are real historical persons and events (e.g. Moses as *figura* of Jesus), whose meaning is found in the transcendent link between them. Figural interpretation has recently become the subject of renewed hermeneutical interest through the work of Erich Auerbach, whose book *Mimesis* (1953) describes the ancient practice, and through Hans W. Frei's book *The Eclipse of Biblical Narrative* (1974), which applies it to the modern history of theological hermeneutics.

The most important link between the hermeneutics of the early Christian church and the medieval period in Europe is the thought of Augustine of Hippo (354–430), whose importance for virtually every aspect of later Western thought can scarcely be exaggerated. Inheriting from the earlier church fathers the polarity between 'literal' and 'spiritual' senses of the scriptural text, he attempts to synthesize the legitimate concerns of both methods by investigating the role of signs (thereby becoming the precursor of the modern theory of signs, or semiotics). He sees the scriptures not as identical with the things to which they refer but rather as signifiers pointing to God. The upshot of this approach is a new stress on praxis – the living faith that is the goal of Christian teaching – as the proper context for interpretation of scripture. No mere theory can provide the conditions for right interpretation but only the faithful practice of reading the Bible in the context of the ongoing Christian community. In this way, scripture and tradition are linked in a dialectical relationship.

Of the many thinkers and schools of interpretation that might be mentioned in the long history of medieval interpretation of scripture, perhaps the most important for the later development of hermeneutics is the doctrine of the fourfold meaning of scripture. Earlier thinkers – following St Paul's admonition that 'the letter kills but the spirit gives life' (2 Cor. 3: 6) – had distinguished between two senses of the text, the literal and the spiritual. In medieval hermeneutics the spiritual came to be distinguished into three distinct senses: the allegorical, seen as the key to the content of faith; the tropological, which concerned the moral significance of the text; and the anagogical, which dealt with the relation between the text and the future hope of believers. The effect of this doctrine of the fourfold meaning of scripture was increasingly to separate the various theological disciplines – biblical studies, moral theology, eschatology, etc. – both from one another and from the practical life of faith. A shift in hermeneutical emphasis occurred after the rediscovery of Aristotle in the twelfth century and the founding of the first universities. In the Scholasticism that followed, theology became an academic discipline, and theologians took pains to give their speculations a scientific basis. The greatest of the medieval thinkers, Thomas Aquinas, formally retained the theory of the fourfold meaning of scripture while in fact de-emphasizing allegorical interpretation in favor of increased attention to the literal meaning of the text. The upshot of these developments was that theology (what Thomas called sacred doctrine) became an academic enterprise that concentrated on the literal text, while the spiritual meaning of the text became by default largely the concern of popular piety and spirituality.

Questions about the single or multiple meanings of texts, and about the relationships among the different senses, came to a head in the Protestant Reformation, with its insistence on the sole authority of scripture. It is no accident that the one who first galvanized the discontent of sixteenth-century Christians into the movement we know as the Protestant Reformation – Martin Luther (1483–1546) – was a professor of Bible, whose new theological direction was the direct result of a new interpretation of scripture. Hermeneutical issues thus stand at the heart of the Reformation and have continued to play a major role in Western Christianity ever since. Luther, together with the other leading Reformers – such as Ulrich Zwingli (1484–1531), the early leader of the Swiss Reformation, and John Calvin (1509–1564), who became the defining figure of the Reformed branch of the Protestant movement – all agreed that the church should be reformed in accordance with scripture, understood as the sole authority for faith and practice. Rejecting the claims of the Roman Catholic Church to be the final authority for the interpretation of the Bible, the Protestants insisted that 'scripture interprets itself.' This hermeneutical principal meant that the literal meaning of the words is primary and that obscure passages are to be understood in the light of those that are plain. Both Luther and Calvin rejected allegorical interpretation but supplemented a literal reading with figural interpretation, allowing them to read all of the scripture, Old and New Testaments, as one great text communicating the one Word of God. This hermeneutical approach should not be confused with the doctrine of direct verbal inspiration that has become so important and divisive in more recent Protestant debate. For the Reformers the Bible itself is not the final authority but rather communicates to us the Word of God, Christ himself, and its right interpretation thus requires not only the inspired text but also the internal inspiration of the Christian reader by the Holy Spirit. The issues of interpretation that first came to a head in sixteenth-century Europe have continued to arouse vigorous debate among Christians and Jews – and increasingly among other religious traditions as well – right up to the present day.

Beginning in the latter part of the seventeenth century in Europe, another cultural shift with hermeneutical implications began to take place. The movement that some of its proponents called Enlightenment was both a development with profound religious repercussions and also the beginning of the modern secular movement to shake off the restraints of theology and church. Wearied by a century of strife over religious issues unleashed by the Reformation, some European thinkers began searching for a new common basis, an authority that could unite, rather than divide people as religion seemed to have done. What they discovered was natural reason, understood to be the universal foundation of all truth, to which all human beings have access, and which could therefore adjudicate the many conflicting claims to truth and authority. In particular, Enlightenment thinkers developed the notion of a natural religion, based on the principles of universal reason and thus shared by human beings of all cultures and times. This natural religion was both the foundation and criterion for what they called the 'positive' religions, the existing historical traditions with their particular and arbitrary claims to authority. Immanuel Kant (1724–1804), whose monumental philosophical work represents the culmination of the Enlightenment, drew the hermeneutical implications of the commitment to natural reason in his proposal for a 'religion within the limits of reason alone' (the title of his book of 1794), whose principles and practices could be deduced by philosophical analysis and used to judge the truth of the positive religions. He interprets the narratives and commandments of scripture as mere pictorial representations of universal and rational religious truths.

The rise of modern hermeneutics

As we have seen, the issues that today we call hermeneutical have a long history. The ideas and activities comprising that history, however, only began to be called by the name hermeneutics with the rise of modernity in the West. Theoretical hermeneutics, in other words, is a product of modern culture, and its most distinctive and influential line of development has taken place in the context of Continental European philosophy over the past two centuries.

The thinker generally credited with being the founder of modern hermeneutical theory – Dilthey dubbed him the 'Kant of hermeneutics' – was the German theologian and Plato scholar F. D. E. Schleiermacher (1768–1834). As a major figure in the early Romantic movement, he articulated a hermeneutics in accordance with the notion of creativity, in which the work is understood as an expression of the creative genius of the author. Rejecting the traditional distinction between sacred and profane interpretation, he insisted that scripture can be understood in the same way as other texts. He argued that what is needed in both cases is a hermeneutics defined as the 'art of understanding' (*Kunstlehre des Verstehens*), thereby shifting attention away from the nature of the text itself to the nature of the understanding by which the text is read and interpreted. By focusing on the concept of understanding, Schleiermacher effectively re-conceives hermeneutics as an independent philosophical enterprise (though he insists upon calling it an 'art') rather than the handmaid of theology or literature studies. Though a theologian himself, he sought to minimize the distinction between general rules of textual interpretation and those rules appropriate to scriptural exegesis, insisting that the latter must remain subject to the former. Even the claim that the Bible is divinely inspired, therefore, cannot be invoked on behalf of a special theological hermeneutics. The theologian interprets texts according to the same general principles that apply in all situations of understanding. This move not only has significant consequences for the task of theology but also represents a major step in the direction of a disciplined study of religion distinct from the theology of Christianity or any other of the 'positive' religions. This contribution to the emerging field of religious studies is important in the light of another significant step taken by Schleiermacher: he, a Protestant clergyman and professor, was the first thinker in the European tradition to write a book on religion, understood as a phenomenon distinct from Christianity – his 1799 book *On Religion: Speeches to Its Cultured Despisers*.

Schleiermacher's hermeneutical 'art of understanding' has a bipolar structure, in which he distinguishes a grammatical (objective) dimension from a psychological or technical (subjective) aspect in the act of understanding. The former task requires that the interpreter be grounded in the linguistic and cultural modes of expression in which the author lived, while the technical-psychological aspect requires the interpreter to grasp the unique subjectivity of the author as expressed through the unified whole of the work. This latter task involves what Schleiermacher calls divination, a term that has provoked considerable controversy and misunderstanding. His intent is not to make understanding into a mysterious means of entry into the mind of the author, but he does believe that interpretation – though it entails an intuitive risk – can lead to understanding the mind of the author better than the author knows himself. The goal, like that of his fellow Romantics, is to grasp the universal in the individual, to do justice both to the uniqueness of particular expressions and to the general spirit of which they are incarnations. Schleiermacher's influence on his contemporaries was modest, especially in view of the immense influence his ideas eventually came to have on the development of hermeneutical theory. What made the difference was the subsequent discovery of Schleiermacher's hermeneutics by a man born the year before Schleiermacher's death.

Wilhelm Dilthey (1833–1911) became the main link between the Romantic hermeneutics of Schleiermacher in the early nineteenth century and the leading figures in the remarkable explosion of philosophical hermeneutics in the twentieth. Unlike Schleiermacher, Dilthey was not a theologian but a philosopher, and he had no hesitation about developing Schleiermacher's insights into a full-fledged philosophical hermeneutics. His most important accomplishment was to make hermeneutics into the foundational and definitive method of the human or cultural disciplines (*Geisteswissenschaften*) as distinguished from the natural sciences (*Naturwissenschaften*). Whether one believes this distinction to be a great achievement or a confusion with disastrous consequences, one can hardly deny the importance of Dilthey's conceptual innovations at this point. He argued that the human sciences differ from the natural sciences on the basis of their qualitatively different objects of inquiry. Natural scientists are able to observe their objects from an external perspective, so that the act of observation remains separate from the phenomena observed. The object of the human and cultural sciences, on the other hand, is not the outside world but what Dilthey calls *Erlebnis*, or lived experience, in which knower and known are related internally. Such an object one must understand, as it were, from the inside out, on the basis of one's own lived experience. Dilthey refers to the more objective task of the natural scientist as explanation (*Erklären*), which he contrasts with the hermeneutical task of understanding (*Verstehen*). In the study of religion today, as in other humanistic disciplines, scholars often divide sharply just at this point. Those who follow Dilthey in emphasizing the difference between natural scientific explanation and hermeneutical understanding are typically critical of scholars who seek the objectivity of scientific explanation in religious studies. The latter, on the other hand, often suspect the former of using questionable hermeneutical theories to legitimate apologetic or uncritical accounts of religion 'from the inside.' Most theorists today would acknowledge that in some way both explanation and understanding are required in any adequate approach to the study of religion, though they often disagree fundamentally about the methodological consequences of this hermeneutical situation.

Dilthey's ideas have been most influential in the continuing tradition of European hermeneutical speculation in the twentieth century, whose most important figures are Martin Heidegger, Hans-Georg Gadamer, and Paul Ricoeur. The entire philosophical program of Heidegger (1889–1976) can be characterized as hermeneutical (indeed, he originally did so himself), and his philosophy also lies behind the more specifically hermeneutical theories of Gadamer and Ricoeur. Despite his considerable debt to Dilthey, Heidegger believed that he, along with most of the other modern philosophers since Descartes, had failed to escape from psychologism and subjectivity. Heidegger's alternative is to propose a hermeneutical ontology, a philosophical analysis of Being, starting not from the subjectivity but rather from the existential situation of the interpreter. We humans find ourselves in a unique situation, because unlike other things in the world, which simply 'are,' we understand *that* we are. We *ex-ist*, says Heidegger, 'stand out'; he especially likes the implications of the German word for existence, *Dasein*, since it literally means 'being there.' In other words, only humans can raise the question of Being Itself. In the resulting philosophy, interpretation does not appear merely as one among various human activities but rather takes on a foundational role in which existence itself is characterized as interpretation. In so doing, Heidegger revolutionized the meaning of philosophy, as has long been recognized. For our purposes, however, it is more important to note that he also changed the meaning of hermeneutics. By rejecting the Cartesian concept of the ego as thinking subject, he turns away from the Romantic focus on the creative individuality of the author expressed in the text. Since for Heidegger hermeneutics has become the cornerstone of philosophy, its focus shifts away from texts and their interpreters to ontology. Far from being an isolated methodological inquiry, hermeneutics on this account gives us access to the most universal and fundamental truths about human life in the world. Heidegger's approach has some particular implications that have profoundly influenced subsequent reflection on hermeneutics, even by thinkers who do not follow his philosophy in all its ramifications. Because of the existential situation of the human thinker, Heidegger emphasizes that understanding and interpretation never begin 'in neutral' without presuppositions but are always undertaken by people who are already involved, and who therefore have interests, presuppositions, and pre-understanding of the subject they are interpreting. But this situation implies that understanding is always circular in form; it can never begin in a hermeneutical vacuum. It is especially important to understand that for Heidegger and his successors this *hermeneutical circle* is not something negative; its circularity is not 'vicious.' Rather, it is a warning against any hermeneutical theory that tries to deny or ignore that necessary circularity of interpretation.

Heidegger's hermeneutical legacy

Relatively few students of religion are likely to master the difficult philosophy of Heidegger, but his ideas are nevertheless of major importance in religious studies, largely through the mediation of two thinkers who have appropriated significant aspects of his thought and presented them in works that *are* widely read, not only in philosophy and theology but also in religious studies.

A single book – *Truth and Method*, by Hans-Georg Gadamer (1900–2002), which first appeared in German in 1960 – catapulted hermeneutics into the center of discussion in theology and religious studies in the second half of the twentieth century and has made Gadamer's name synonymous with hermeneutical theory. While hardly an easy book to read, *Truth and Method* nevertheless makes accessible to non-philosophers an approach to hermeneutics that owes much to Heidegger. But Gadamer also returns hermeneutics to the traditional concerns of Schleiermacher and Dilthey: human understanding as it functions in the interpretation of authoritative texts. From Heidegger he takes his starting point within the hermeneutical circle; that is, he recognizes that understanding always and only takes place in the context of prior understandings – which is to say within a specific historic tradition of reading and interpreting texts. Gadamer's controversial way of making this basically Heideggerian point is by attempting to rehabilitate the term 'prejudice,' which the Enlightenment had seen as an entirely negative encumbrance to objective knowledge. Gadamer insists that every act of understanding begins in prejudice, in the original sense of pre-judgment: one is not simply neutral or detached from the object of understanding but rather already stands in some relationship to it. Far from constituting a barrier to be removed, such pre-judgments play an essential role in all acts of understanding. Unlike Schleiermacher, Gadamer does not see hermeneutics as a way of overcoming the historical distance between interpreter and text but rather insists on the historical nature of understanding itself, since interpretation always occurs within a concrete historical tradition and makes no sense when removed from this context. It is this common link with the overarching tradition that allows the modern interpreter to understand an ancient text, for the two are in fact already related to one another through a process that Gadamer calls *Wirkungsgeschichte*, 'effective history' – a history of the effects by which everything later in a tradition has been influenced by all that has gone before. The continuum constituted by this history of effective relationships allows Gadamer to conceive the goal of interpretation as a 'fusion of horizons' (*Horizontverschmelzung*), in which the horizon of the interpreter merges into that of the text. Gadamer believes that this phenomenological account of how understanding takes place is superior to every 'method' by which other theorists seek to arrive at the truth – a conviction alluded to in the title *Truth and Method*.

In an ongoing debate that has attracted widespread attention, Jürgen Habermas has accused Gadamer of failing to do justice to the limits of understanding. On Gadamer's account it would appear that understanding can always take place successfully as long as the interpreter acknowledges the context of tradition in which the text is embedded and is willing to enter into it. Habermas maintains that communication is often distorted in ways that the participants in a conversation do not and cannot recognize without the intervention of someone from the outside. An adequate hermeneutics must therefore be able to take into account the possibility and actuality of distorted communication. Otherwise the interpreter will be vulnerable to ideological bias, especially when he or she shares the bias of the text. The question raised by Habermas is whether or not Gadamer's traditionalist hermeneutics amounts in effect to a conservatism without critical resources for recognizing and combating ideology.

The other important theorist with roots in Heidegger's philosophy, Paul Ricoeur (1913–), is much more attuned to hermeneutical distortion and conflict than is Gadamer. Indeed, one of his major writings is titled *Conflict of Interpretations*. As the first major hermeneutical theorist since Schleiermacher to take a particular interest in religion, his work has been especially influential in theology and religious studies. Ricoeur is a philosopher, not a theologian, but he writes out of an explicit commitment to Reformed Christianity and in recent years has divided his academic career between Paris and the Divinity School of the University of Chicago. He is thus a bridge both between philosophical and religious hermeneutics and also between the Continental and Anglo-American academic worlds. His early work was devoted to an attempt to mediate the traditions of phenomenology and existentialism, which led him to develop a philosophical account of the symbol as the starting point for his hermeneutical theory. A symbol is any sign that contains, in addition to its direct or primary meaning, a secondary or hidden meaning that requires intellectual effort to uncover. In other words, symbol and interpretation become correlative terms. His hermeneutical point of departure is captured in the aphorism that he uses as a title for the conclusion to his 1967 book *The Symbolism of Evil*: 'The Symbol Gives Rise to Thought.' The problematic relationship between symbol and critical thought is epitomized in the hermeneutical circle, which Ricoeur puts this way: 'We must understand in order to believe, but we must believe in order to understand.' The way beyond circularity lies in taking the commitment to the truth of the symbol as a wager (borrowing a notion from his French predecessor Pascal). The interpreter must take the risk of assuming that the symbol offers the best way to human understanding, which means making his presuppositions explicit and then trying to demonstrate the power of the implicit symbolic truth through interpretation in the explicit form of articulate thought. In a schema that has appealed to many, Ricoeur conceives the modern hermeneutical situation in terms of three stages. The first is the pre-critical situation of original or primary naïveté: the world of myth in which symbols are experienced as immediately true. But for the modern interpreter this world has been shattered by criticism, which ushers in the second stage. Now the problem is to find a way to restore the power of the symbols without simply returning to primitive naïveté (something we would be unable to do in any event). Ricoeur calls this third stage a 'second naïveté,' for in one sense it is a return to the first stage. But unlike the original naïveté, this stage has been through the fires of criticism and is no longer simply an unreflective or immediate grasp of the symbols. Ricoeur is not always clear about just what second naïveté would consist of or how one might reach it, but the articulation of the goal itself has found resonance in other modern thinkers, including many who do not follow the specific path recommended by Ricoeur. What is at least clear is that the way to second naïveté is through interpretation, which means not a rejection of critical thought but rather a constructive application of criticism.

Ricoeur's most systematic attempt to work out his hermeneutical ideas in detail is contained in his 1976 book *Interpretation Theory*. Rather than seeking, like Schleiermacher, to go behind the text to find its meaning in the mind of the author, Ricoeur insists that the sense is to be found 'in front of' the text. Rather than seeking, like Gadamer, to fuse the horizons of text and interpreter, Ricoeur stresses the 'distanciation' from the author that first gives the text its autonomy and creates the hermeneutical situation. And rather than seeking, like Dilthey, to separate humanistic understanding from scientific explanation, Ricoeur sets the two in a dialectical relationship that forms the context for interpretation. He also seeks to go beyond Gadamer's uncritical acceptance of tradition by introducing a critical element into hermeneutics itself, so that interpretation includes both a retrieval of tradition and a critique of ideology. Like Heidegger, Ricoeur emphasizes the existential significance of interpretation; it is our primary means for understanding ourselves and our existence in the world. Texts – especially religious texts – disclose possible worlds, so that the interpretation of texts becomes a primary means of reflecting on the meaning of human existence. Once again it becomes apparent that hermeneutics as an enterprise has a special connection with the study of religion.

The hermeneutics of suspicion

Paul Ricoeur's attention to the *conflict* of interpretations has its roots in a historical thesis about the modern hermeneutical situation. He has coined the phrase 'the hermeneutics of suspicion' to designate a change that has taken place in the modern world, a hiatus in our relationship to texts, especially those authoritative texts that include the scriptures of the world's religions. Ricoeur identifies this rupture in our hermeneutical history with three figures from the late nineteenth century whom he dubs the 'masters of suspicion': Marx, Nietzsche, and Freud. Philosophers since Descartes had generally taken the ego, the thinking self, as a given – as the foundation and point of departure for understanding. With the masters of suspicion this assumption is subjected to scrutiny and found wanting. Marx, Freud, and Nietzsche – each in his own way – suggest that subjectivity may indeed be deceived, not from without, but from within: it is self-deceived. Marx's term 'false consciousness' could be extended to include the others as well: for all three of them, the goal of interpretation cannot simply be to establish the ground of an incorrigible self-consciousness; rather, the thinking subject must also be called into question, treated with suspicion. According to Marx, for example, class interest distorts both text and interpreter because both are unaware of its influence. The Marxist therefore engages in a critique of ideology in order to uncover the covert interests lurking behind the apparent meaning of the text. A Freudian is suspicious of received texts for quite different reasons, but the hermeneutical effect is comparable. Here the 'ideological' factor is not economic and social but unconscious and individual: to understand a text rightly the interpreter must take into account the *unconscious* motivations that may be at work behind the façade of rational discourse. With Nietzsche the situation is more complex, as we shall see shortly, but the need to take a kind of false consciousness into account links his position to that of Marx and Freud.

The true father of the hermeneutics of suspicion, the one from who the 'masters' first learned to identify false consciousness, is the philosopher Ludwig Feuerbach (1804–1872). Originally a student of Hegel's philosophy, Feuerbach rejected Hegelian idealism very early in favor of materialism, while nevertheless retaining the dialectical logic of the system. Whereas Hegel had identified thought and being, Feuerbach believed that material nature was the ground of human consciousness and therefore the origin of religion as well. His best-known work, *The Essence of Christianity*, attempts to demonstrate how religion arises out of a dialectic of self-alienation, whereby humans project their own essential worldly attributes onto an illusory heavenly subject or subjects, the gods. In his later work, especially his *Lectures on the Essence of Religion*, Feuerbach abandons even this inverted Hegelianism and argues that religion arises out of a misinterpretation of our experience with nature. In both versions of his critique, however, Feuerbach consistently identifies the imagination as the organ of religion, the source of all illusion. Religious people, he is convinced, 'misimagine' the world by reversing cause and effect, subject and predicate, of their experience. This account of religion entails that one cannot simultaneously understand the essence of religion and continue to be religious. The field of religious studies remains divided to this day between those who study religion as members of religious communities and those who, like Feuerbach, believe that understanding religion is incompatible with its practice. Both sides, however, can agree with Feuerbach that imagination is the organ of religious belief and practice while disagreeing on the question of truth. Feuerbach's hermeneutical legacy is the lingering suspicion that at least some forms of religion falsify reality by their very nature. A more problematic corollary of this legacy is the assumption that religion is false *because* it employs imagination.

The hermeneutics of suspicion has made important inroads into religion in recent decades – into both the religious traditions themselves, insofar as they participate in the intellectual debates of the modern academy, and into the scholarly study of religion. Liberation theologians, for example, have appropriated Marxist suspicion about religion by trying to use it as a critical tool for purifying traditional belief and practice of its unholy alliance with the forces of oppression and exploitation. Their program entails a revision of classical Marxism, of course, insofar as liberation theology assumes that only 'bad' religion is vulnerable to ideological critique. A similar development has taken place among religious feminists, who seek to expose the implicit patriarchy of many or all authoritative religious texts. One finds this approach both within religious traditions themselves – primarily Christianity and Judaism, but increasingly in other traditions as well, including especially Islam – in the form of feminist theology, and also among feminist scholars of religion, who apply a feminist hermeneutics of suspicion to the religious traditions they are investigating. These approaches, of course, have been controversial, not least because in some of their more extreme forms, the practitioners of suspicious hermeneutical theory often succumb to ideology themselves, making implicit historical, philosophical, or theological claims that are immune to criticism. In response, some members of the religious studies community have proposed submitting the hermeneutics of suspicion itself to a suspicious critique. The debate is one more reminder that the 'hermeneutical circle' is unavoidable – and not only within the religious traditions but also in the practice of religious studies. For the same reason it is unlikely that any hermeneutical theory will ever achieve the status of an accepted method to be applied universally by scholars of religion without reference to their own convictions.

Hermeneutics and postmodernism

The most recent and radical development in the hermeneutics of suspicion could be called the postmodern turn. So different is this variety of theory from the nineteenth-century 'masters of suspicion' identified by Ricoeur that it needs to be treated as a significant new departure in hermeneutics. Its historical connection with the older tradition is through Nietzsche, who plays a double role in modern interpretation theory. On the one hand, there is what we can call the 'modernist Nietzsche,' the one whom Ricoeur classifies together with Marx and Freud because he in effect identifies religion as a form of false consciousness. His variation on this theme locates the root of distortion in a Jewish and then Christian 'slave revolt of morality,' in which the weakest elements of society inverted the values of classical Greek nobility. What had been virtues – strength, valor, physical beauty – came to be represented as vices, while their opposites were exalted as virtues – that is, all the sickly values of the weak and diseased elements of society, above all pity. For Nietzsche this 'transvaluation of values' is epitomized in the cross of Christianity. This moralistic disease, Nietzsche believes, is not confined to religion but has its modern secular forms as well, such as socialism. The hermeneutical point is that texts, especially religious ones, cannot be taken at face value but must be subjected to radical critique. It is not only the misunderstanding of texts by interpreters that is the problem, one could say, but also the distortions of reality embodied in the texts themselves.

The other Nietzsche is the source of postmodern hermeneutics – the Nietzsche who declares that 'there are no facts, only interpretations.' (Whether or not the modern and postmodern Nietzsches can be reconciled is a serious question for Nietzsche scholars but one we need not address here, since both impulses flowing from this brilliant and bizarre mind have powerfully influenced hermeneutics in the century since he wrote.) Those recent thinkers who have come to be called 'postmodern' – especially Jacques Derrida (1930–2004) – have developed the 'other Nietzsche,' with help from Heidegger, into a powerful if controversial force in the contemporary intellectual world, one that has important consequences for hermeneutics. Derrida's position depends on a theory of language that emphasizes the instability of signs. Every linguistic sign refers, not to non-linguistic realities lying beyond language, but rather to other signs, which in turn refer to still other signs – and so on, in an endless deferral of meaning. The implication is not that communication is impossible but that it is always incomplete, continually in flux. The attempt to evade this situation, to appeal to some bedrock of certainty and meaning, constitutes the popular but ultimately futile quest for what Derrida calls a 'transcendental signified,' that is, a sign that refers to no further signs but only to itself. The hermeneutical implications of this state of affairs have particular importance for religious studies, since religions would appear to have a significant stake in interpretive stability and certainty – just what postmodernist hermeneutics denies is possible. Instead, interpretation appears endless and incapable of achieving closure. Another contemporary French theorist, Jean-François Lyotard, defines postmodernism as 'incredulity toward metanarratives' – a position that might appear to set all traditional religions in opposition to postmodernity.

The most important idea to emerge from Derrida's philosophy is *deconstruction*. For all its familiarity in the contemporary academic world, it is notoriously difficult to define – and the difficulty is presumably intentional on Derrida's part. Deconstruction is clearly the heart of his hermeneutics, yet he denies that it is a method or a technique for interpreting texts. In the hands of some of his devotees, however, it has in fact become a technique, a critical device (even a blunt instrument) for uncovering the covert ways in which texts try to stabilize meaning and disguise the flux of signs. Derrida intends deconstruction to be an antidote to what he calls 'logocentrism,' the prevalent assumption throughout Western thought that words have a fixed relationship to reality, that they can therefore put us in direct touch with a reality beyond or behind language. He labels the pursuit of such an essential reality the 'metaphysics of presence' and endeavors to show that it is based on the seductive but illusory 'myth of presence.'

The other French postmodernist whose influence on contemporary hermeneutics one can scarcely overlook is Michel Foucault (1926–1984). Mixing writing and lecturing with political activism and sexual experimentation, his life epitomized the Nietzschean postmodernism that he advocated in his writings. Even his academic discipline is difficult to pin down: trained in philosophy, psychology, and psychopathology, he focused much of his attention on the social sciences while calling himself an 'archeologist of knowledge' and devoting much of his writing to historical studies.

Although he did not choose the label postmodern, his passionate rejection of the Enlightenment and the modernism it produced has helped to define postmodernism. Like Derrida, Foucault rejects every attempt to establish a single meaning for a text, and opposes every theory that sees language as representing reality. Especially interested in anthropology, he opposes the typically modern assumption that 'man' has a 'human nature' that somehow persists through change. He prefers to follow Nietzsche by practicing 'genealogy,' the method of uncovering the historical layers underlying the present 'order' (another Enlightenment notion he criticizes). Genealogical analysis destroys the myth that there are laws or principles of development guiding the course of history, and shows the arbitrary and haphazard ways in which the present situation has emerged out of the conflicts of the past. His intent – virtually the opposite of Gadamer's at this point – is to call into question the legitimacy of the established order. But the point at which Foucault has had the greatest impact on hermeneutical thinking – including the study of religion – is his theory of the intimate relationship linking knowledge and power. Because knowledge is always embedded in actual social institutions and practices, it is never neutral but always involved in power relationships. So intimate is the relation between knowledge and power that the two virtually merge into a single concept in Foucault's thought (one of his books bears the title *Power/Knowledge*). The effect on hermeneutics is virtually to collapse the distinction between theory and practice: theorizing *is* the uncovering of the hidden sources of truth in specific power interests. The inevitable bias of this kind of theory is against every established order – a bias that Foucault, for whom the student uprising of 1968 was a defining event, by no means tries to deny. Consequently, his hermeneutic approach has been most eagerly adopted by those who see themselves as victims or outsiders to the established institutions of knowledge, and thus of power. Feminists, for example, in various fields, including theology and religious studies, have found Foucault's ideas useful in their attempt to wrest control of ideas and the institutions in which they are embedded from a patriarchal establishment. If Gadamer's hermeneutics portrays interpretation as a means for reclaiming tradition, Foucault makes the act of interpretation inherently subversive of every established order.

Ad hoc hermeneutics

The duality or ambivalence within contemporary hermeneutics that we noted at the outset can lead to very different overviews of its history and significance. It is perhaps inevitable that in writing about hermeneutics one will emphasize those thinkers who present their task explicitly in terms of hermeneutical theory. But we need to remind ourselves that most of the activity that would today be called hermeneutical – that is, the actual practice of interpreting texts in order to understand and use them in all kinds of social and individual ways – has been (and still is) carried out without the benefit of any theory of hermeneutics. Thus scholars of religion studying the 'hermeneutics' of various religious communities seldom encounter the kind of self-conscious reflection on the meaning of interpretation found in Schleiermacher and his successors right up through Gadamer, Ricoeur, and the postmodern philosophers. Religious studies needs to pay at least as much attention to the implicit hermeneutics of religious communities as to the explicit hermeneutical theories, both religious and secular, that dominate so much academic discussion.

Those who have tried to give theoretical voice to such an ad hoc approach to hermeneutics often appeal to the ideas of Ludwig Wittgenstein (1889–1951) for inspiration and support. Like most recent philosophers, Wittgenstein focused his attention particularly on language, which he believed to be the proper subject matter of philosophy. His posthumously published *Philosophical Investigations* (1953) supplied the original impulse for what came to be known as ordinary language philosophy. Wittgenstein is the champion of language as used non-technically in everyday situations, where communication typically takes place without benefit of formal theorizing. The negative correlate of this emphasis is the thesis that we – especially if we are academic philosophers and theoreticians – allow ourselves to be 'bewitched by language,' and Wittgenstein thought of his own philosophy as a kind of therapy for the linguistic conundrums of modern philosophers. His way of doing philosophy, in keeping with his point of view, is unsystematic and ad hoc – often aphoristic. He is the opponent of every essentialist theory that tries to understand phenomena by reducing them to a shared essence, something they all have in common. Using the example of family resemblances, he demonstrates that our recognition of kinship need not depend on any single shared trait. The notion has had considerable influence in religious studies, making scholars far more cautious about claims concerning the 'essence of religion.' We call phenomena religious for a variety of reasons and should be wary of over-schematizing their interrelationships. The implications of Wittgenstein for hermeneutics might be summed up by invoking one of his best-known aphorisms: 'Look and see!' Taken as a watchword, this non-theoretical advice is a reminder to keep one's eyes open, to look at the bewildering variety of religious phenomena without forcing them too quickly into preconceived theoretical molds. It is not that scholars ought to eschew theory altogether but rather that they should use it heuristically rather than systematically, that is, as a source of suggestion and a goad to new discovery, applying it in ad hoc ways as each situation requires.

An example of ad hoc hermeneutical practice within a religious community is found in the work of Karl Barth (1886–1968), a theologian in the Reformed tradition, and one of the major figures in twentieth-century Christian theology. Barth's chief opponents, including Rudolf Bultmann and Paul Tillich, were heavily influenced by Heidegger's existentialism. Bultmann in particular appeals to the notion of pre-understanding in his theological hermeneutics, a practice that caused Barth to accuse him of importing an alien philosophical criterion into theology instead of taking his hermeneutical bearings from the symbolic world of scripture itself. Their debate is far too complex to deal with here except to note that Barth's insistence on doing theology out of a theological perspective rather than basing it on prior acceptance of a philosophical theory represents a hermeneutical approach that one can find in many religious traditions and which ought to be given its due in religious studies. A classic statement of this approach is the Protestant Reformers' principle that 'scripture interprets itself,' meaning that the way to understand obscure or difficult passages of scripture is not by importing a hermeneutical theory from philosophy but rather by attending to the intratextual relations of the scriptural canon itself. Religious studies should resist the temptation to supply a supertheory, focusing instead on the implicit hermeneutical ideas and practices of the religious traditions themselves. After all, the notion of the hermeneutical circle – according to which one always interprets out of prior immersion in a tradition of reading texts and not as a 'neutral' outsider – has been a mainstay of the major hermeneutical theorists of the modern (and postmodern) age. Applied to religious studies, the hermeneutical circle implies that an ad hoc application of theory, hermeneutical and otherwise, is the wisest course to follow in studying the diverse phenomena of the world's religious traditions and practices, because it respects the unique features of those traditions while seeking to interpret them both sympathetically and critically.

Bibliography

Auerbach, Erich, *Mimesis: The Representation of Reality in Western Literature*. Princeton NJ: Princeton University Press, 1953.

Caputo, John D., *Radical Hermeneutics: Repetition, Deconstruction, and the Hermeneutic Project*. Bloomington and Indianapolis: Indiana University Press, 1987.

Ebeling, Gerhard, 'Hermeneutik.' In *Die Religion in Geschichte und Gegenwart: Handwörterbuch für Theologie und Religionswissenschaft*. 3rd edn. Tübingen: J. C. B. Mohr (Paul Siebeck), 1959, 3: 242–62.

Ferraris, Maurizio, *History of Hermeneutics*. Translated by Luca Somigli. Atlantic Highlands, NJ: Humanities Press International, 1996.

Feuerbach, Ludwig, *The Essence of Christianity*. New York: Harper, 1957.

—— *Lectures on the Essence of Religion*. New York: Harper & Row, 1967.

Foucault, Michel, *Power/Knowledge: Selected Interviews and Other Writings, 1972–1977*. New York: Pantheon Books, 1980.

Fowl, Stephen E., ed., *The Theological Interpretation of Scripture: Classic and Contemporary Readings*. Cambridge, MA: Blackwell, 1997.

Frei, Hans W., *The Eclipse of Biblical Narrative: A Study in Eighteenth and Nineteenth Century Hermeneutics*. New Haven and London: Yale University Press, 1974.

Gadamer, Hans-Georg, *Truth and Method*, 2nd rev. edn. Translation revised by Joel Weinsheimer and Donald G. Marshall. New York: Crossroad, 1991.

Green, Garrett, *Theology, Hermeneutics, and Imagination: The Crisis of Interpretation at the End of Modernity*. Cambridge: Cambridge University Press, 2000.

Grenz, Stanley J., *A Primer on Postmodernism*. Grand Rapids, MI, and Cambridge: William B. Eerdmans Publishing, 1996.

Jeanrond, Werner G., *Theological Hermeneutics: Development and Significance*. London: Macmillan, 1991.

Kant, Immanuel, *Religion within the Limits of Reason Alone*. Translated by Theodore M. Greene and Hoyt H. Hudson. New York: Harper & Bros, 1960 [1974].

Ramm, Bernard L., *Protestant Biblical Interpretation: A Textbook of Hermeneutics*. Grand Rapids, MI: Baker Book House, 1976.

Ricoeur, Paul, *Conflict of Interpretations: Essay in Hermeneutics*. Evanston: Northwestern University Press, 1974.

—— *Interpretation Theory: Discourse and the Surplus of Meaning*. Fort Worth, TX: Texas Christian University Press, 1976.

Schleiermacher, Friedrich, *Hermeneutics: The Handwritten Manuscripts*. Edited by Heinz Kimmerle, translated by James Duke and Jack Forstman. Missoula, MT: Scholars Press, 1977.

—— *On Religion: Speeches to its Cultured Despisers*. Translated by Richard Crouter. Cambridge: Cambridge University Press, 1988 [1799].

Wittgenstein, Ludwig, *Philosophical Investigations: The German Text with a Revised English Translation*. Translated by G. E. M. Anscombe. Oxford: Blackwell, 2001.

Chapter 23

Religious pluralism

Michael Barnes

'Religious pluralism' is implicit in almost every page of this book: the fact that in modern Western societies there is more than one set of religious practices and beliefs. In this descriptive sense, religious pluralism is synonymous with the phenomenon of religious diversity or plurality, what is 'religiously other' within a given social context. As such, religious pluralism touches on a number of complex socio-political questions about the nature of religious freedom, about the limits of toleration and about the place and role of religion in secular society. Many of these questions are dealt with in other chapters of this book. While recognising an inevitable element of overlap, this chapter deals with a different issue: the *meaning* of religious pluralism. How to interpret the sheer unremitting otherness of religious diversity while recognising the claims to objective truth which persons of faith make? How to study and order such phenomena in a way that understands and respects the life of faith from which they arise?

These two inter-related questions, the one hermeneutical, the other more ethical, form the agenda for what follows. The multiple engagements that have formed, and continue to affect, religious communities raise many other questions, especially about truth and reference. And no easy distinction can be drawn between such questions and issues about the meaning and intentionality of religious practice.[1] Nevertheless, there is more to the *religious* significance of religious pluralism – that is to say, its meaning for the faith and practice of religious communities – than the philosophical problematic. Whether or not religions are rooted in a historical relationship which is in some way intrinsic to their self-understanding – Judaism and Christianity, Brahmanical Hinduism and Buddhism, for instance – there is no doubt that in the contemporary world all inter-religious relationships are affected by social, cultural, political – as well as purely historical – factors. When, for example, the Babri Masjid in Ayodhya was demolished, Sikh gurdwaras in London were attacked; when the Pope wrote a book in Rome with slighting reference to Buddhist 'atheism', it caused enormous upset in Śri Lanka. The hideous events of 9/11 and the aftermath of the war in Iraq have left many Muslims in the West nervous and isolated. Religions are neither parochial tribalisms nor isolated totalities. To quote a remark of O'Leary's: 'A religious tradition is not a cathedral which contains everything, but a crossroads which is open to everything'.[2]

The main concern of this chapter is not, therefore, to examine the intra-systemic philosophical questions which the process of dialogue raises, nor to analyse the empirical 'results' of dialogue, the changes and formations which it encourages.[3] It is to consider the significance of the inter-religious relationship itself – a project which, I shall argue, can only be pursued from the perspective of a particular religious tradition. The move from the supposedly disinterested world of the scholarly presentation of religious phenomena to the more risky demands of the *theological* interpretation of their engagement is not easy. Attempts to simplify the messy reality of particular encounters range from the outwardly eirenic to the more blatantly polemical. Troeltsch's Hegelian move, for example, which would relativise religious difference in an ordered hierarchy, subordinates all inter-religious encounter to the demands of the great historical dialectic.[4] Barth, on the other hand, with his antagonistic polarising of religion and revelation, reinstates the 'event' of the Word of God as the ultimate arbiter of religious truth but has little to say about troublesome 'other words'.[5] If forms of Barthian biblicism tend to reinforce interests which are narrowly confessional, Troeltsch's influence encourages a more universalising world or 'global' theology.[6] It is in reaction to the former and in continuity with the latter that in so much of Europe and North America 'religious pluralism' has acquired a very particular connotation.

The term is often taken in a normative sense to refer to a specific stance in philosophy and theology, that associated with the name of John Hick and the thinkers of what might be called the 'Myth of Christian Uniqueness' school.[7] In this chapter I propose a brief account and critique of this approach to religious pluralism. Hick's work is important because it raises many complex ethical and philosophical issues that attend the dialogue of religions. But I shall argue that ultimately it fails to address the crucial question of the *significance for religious faith of the engagement with 'the other'*. This will entail some attention being given to a re-reading of the Christian theology of religions which in important respects Hick misrepresents.[8]

The growth of a hypothesis

The first aim of this chapter is to identify some of the presuppositions that have led to the paradigm shift proclaimed by the Myth school. Two major contributions to the growth of this normative hypothesis can be noted, if not completely distinguished. On the one hand, an awareness of the relativity of all religions invalidates claims to superiority and exclusiveness on the part of one. On the other, the greater contact between, and increasing knowledge of, particular traditions makes arguments for a common core or essence increasingly plausible. The growth of religious studies as an academic discipline committed to discerning the various dimensions of the world's religions has clearly been influential in uniting the two.[9] These developments are treated at length in other chapters in this volume.

The same two themes run consistently through Hick's work.[10] His version of the pluralist hypothesis builds on various considerations, especially the phenomenological 'family resemblance' argument, which rule out an a priori 'Christianity-centred' theology. One is an appreciation of the spiritual and moral values present in the world religions; the other an account of the destructive effect of Christian claims to superiority. Hick thus reads the history of theological accounts of the other as a move from intolerant 'exclusivism' through a more liberal 'inclusivism' to his own move, a 'theological crossing of the Rubicon' into what he considers the theologically more straightforward world of pluralism. Calling for a radical reconstruction or relativising of Christian claims, Hick argues persuasively that traditional christocentric and ecclesiocentric positions that have dominated the agenda for centuries need to be replaced by a theocentric position if theologians are to give an adequate account of the modern experience of the plurality of religions. According to Hick, the only appropriate way of understanding the plurality of religious beliefs and practices in today's world must be based on a reflection on the total religious experience of humankind.

This historical overview is backed up with a realist account of religious experience.[11] Rejecting both the sceptical view that religious experience is delusory and what he sees as a dogmatic view that it is delusory except for what is mediated through one's own tradition, Hick develops a third view – that all major religions are different ways of experiencing the Divine or Real. Religions are alternative soteriological 'spaces' through which people find the way from self-centredness to 'Reality-centredness', different configurations of divine phenomena which are instantiated as myths or stories that change or direct people's lives.

This thesis is developed on the basis of a distinction (noted in some form in all religions but as developed by Hick owing more to Kant) between the Real as such and the Real as humanly thought-and-experienced. Invoking Kant's thesis that the mind contributes to the character of the perceived environment, Hick distinguishes between the phenomenal world of the religions and the noumenal world that exists independent of our perception of it. Like Kant he seeks to be both a 'transcendental idealist' and an 'empirical realist'. But Hick goes beyond Kant – for whom God is postulated as the pre-supposition of *moral* obligation – by postulating the Absolute or the Real as the condition of possibility of all religious experience. Thus the Absolute in collaboration with the experiencing subject is responsible for the phenomenal world which religious persons experience. In Kantian terms, the Absolute or Real is the unknowable *noumenon* 'behind' the known *phenomena*. Faith affirms the Absolute – but only *that* it is, not *what* it is. The 'content' of the act of faith is derived from the particular language of a tradition – in Christianity the language that speaks of 'God in Christ', in Buddhism the language derived ultimately from the Buddha's enlightenment experience. While various developments in Hick's thought can be noted, particularly a nuancing of language about the Absolute, he adheres consistently to the terms of what he calls a 'Copernican Revolution' in the theology of religious pluralism.[12] The same Absolute, however identified in personal or impersonal terms, is equivalently manifested in the various forms of human religiosity. Underlying all such forms is a common unthematised religious experience, which the religions refer to in terms of the different languages of faith.

The plausibility of the hypothesis

There is no doubt about the attractiveness of a single hypothesis to explain the phenomenon of religious pluralism. But such a panoptic overview, however idealistic in its intentions, is by no means unproblematic. 'Universal' theologies and comprehensive theories generally beg the same questions about method and coherence as various versions of the *'philosophia perennis'*.[13] Whose 'data' are being considered? And from whose perspective? The very shift in meaning from a purely descriptive to a normative account of 'the other' raises political and ethical issues, about the nature of power and control in theological and philosophical discourse generally. Pluralists such as are represented by the 'Myth school' are right to draw attention to the innate chauvinism of much traditional Christian thinking; their call for respect, openness and understanding is the *sine qua non* of any theology of religions. There is, therefore, a strong ethical basis for some version of pluralism. But the extent to which the hypothesis can be made *normative*, that is to say can be held with philosophical consistency, let alone theological integrity, is open to doubt. Some of the more obvious points can be noted here.

In order to ensure that pluralism does not descend into some form of relativism it becomes necessary to abstract from the particularity of languages some sort of common 'meta-language'. But it quickly becomes problematic to argue for a correspondence between religious phenomena – the concepts, symbols or stories – and the Absolute to which they supposedly point. How does one *know* there is a correspondence? Might not all be as equally false as equally true? The not-so-hidden assumption is that religious languages are equivalent, equally effective *soteriologically*, since they appear to perform the same function in their respective traditions in pointing the way to the same unknowable Absolute. But for this argument to work, the point of reference, the Absolute, must be capable of identification while yet remaining, by definition, the unknowable. It seems highly plausible to make different expressions of the Absolute identical; that is to say, to prescind from the particularity of the phenomenal names and to identify together the single noumenal reality to which they supposedly point. But the argument is invalid. One cannot make two 'unknowables' equivalent. As Keith Ward points out, 'it is rather like saying, "I do not know what X is; and I do not know what Y is; therefore X must be the same as Y". If I do not know what either is, I *ipso facto* do not know whether they are the same or different'.[14] The most we can say is that very different languages and concepts may be speaking of the same unknowable. But again they may not. There is, in short, an important point to be made in using the term religious pluralism in its purely descriptive sense to signify a phenomenon of contemporary experience. But it is illegitimate to turn the 'given' into a theory which somehow accounts for the given.

The point is that there is no vantage-point 'above the action', as it were, which is not itself historically or culturally conditioned. This is where the apparent strength of the pluralist case masks real weakness; the assumption of the moral high ground can quickly become ideological. While it is not the case that pluralists hold that all religions are talking in different ways about the same thing, there is, nevertheless, a tendency to a certain sort of reductionist universalism. This determination to search out common values and essences tends almost inevitably to short-circuit the highly complex ways in which people of faith seek to identify themselves. Such a universalism fails to take seriously the variety of religions and the differences between them and turns out to be covertly élitist. In fact, on closer inspection what purports to be an objective, neutral and universal perspective looks suspiciously like a contradiction in terms. On the one hand, each religion is given equal soteriological value; on the other, a privilege is assumed for the pluralist 'system' itself.

Pluralists rightly draw attention to the way perceptions of specific religious traditions have been formed by Orientalist types of discourse; popular stereotypes, such as 'mystic India' or 'primitive Africa', not to mention reifications such as 'Hinduism' and 'Buddhism', have been largely constructed by Eurocentric concerns. But a residual Orientalism, the tendency to project unexamined Western stereotypes on to what is properly 'other', is only too apparent in pluralist versions of the history of religions which seek to inscribe the plurality of creeds and culture within a single scheme.[15]

There is an ambiguity here. This drive for theoretical mastery is quite at variance not just with the post-modern awareness of the historicity of all discourse about the other but with the much more diffuse and ill-defined practice of inter-faith relations. There can be little doubt about the influence of post-colonialist and post-Shoah discourse on the pluralist hypothesis; the challenge put to Western thought generally by the liberation movements of the past half-century has focussed attention on salvation and liberation themes as the single goal of all religions, thus giving rise to a more ethically nuanced approach to 'common essence' theories of religion.[16] At the same time, the context within which liberation themes have been developed has now shifted from socio-economic analysis to the broader cultural considerations which attend post-modern thought generally.[17] Given that proponents of the normative hypothesis perceive the 'problem' of religious pluralism to lie with a 'Christianity-centred' view of reality and the false sense of superiority which it supposedly encourages, it is not altogether surprising that they have tended to ignore this dimension.

Identifying presuppositions

Two inter-related comments are in order here. The first is that there is nothing intrinsically dishonourable about the desire to mould others in one's own image; the properly ethical question, as Talal Asad indicates, is about the exercise of power and the means which are used in developing relations with the other.[18] Second, while it is obviously true that appalling things have been done in the name of religion – the Crusades and the conquest of the Americas are usually mentioned – it is one thing to recognise the failure of religious practice, another to lay it at the door of inherent defects within theory or the system of belief. There are, of course, significant links to be discerned between them, but any attempt to critique or re-read a religious tradition begs complex hermeneutical questions about language and method. Methods of correlation, bringing the texts of tradition into some sort of creative engagement with the exigencies of situation, are never value-free. Indeed the whole concept of a value-free universalism is itself deeply problematic. Self-confessedly neutral positions usually turn out, on closer inspection, to be dominated by very specific ideas of what makes for the 'humanum', human fulfilment or even the very nature of human being itself.[19]

Perhaps the most important – because intractable – of the unexamined presuppositions lurking behind the normative hypothesis is the concept of 'religion' itself. The idea that there are a number of identifiable entities called 'religions', different species of a common genus, is itself a construction of the Enlightenment.[20] During the Age of Reason 'religion' came to designate not the life of faith and the proper worship offered to God, but the external 'system' of practice, an object of scientific study with all the paraphernalia of diverse transcendent beings, myths, rituals and other data of the category 'religion'. With the growth of knowledge of other continents the discovery of analogous systems of belief and practice created a religious geography – subsequently immortalised by Hick, using more astronomical terminology, as the 'Universe of Faiths'. The model by which the discrete 'religions' were identified, however, was the rationalist deism that dominated the debate about the nature of Christian faith in the seventeenth and eighteenth centuries. This, of course, gave a privileged place to a transcendent Absolute reality, the ultimate object of human understanding, and was rooted in what developed into an all-pervading dualism of sacred and profane. As God was set apart from the world, so the practices of religion came to be divorced from everyday living. The result has been, as Lash observes, that 'the role of religion as a medium of truth has been privatised'.[21]

The desire to map all forms of knowledge on to a single manipulable grid finds its most celebrated exponent in Descartes but runs through so much of modern culture.[22] The drive to develop a normative 'religious pluralism' shares in a similar foundationalism. Similar presuppositions are at work: that 'religious' phenomena can be distinguished and categorised, that all point toward a single overarching truth, and that a comprehensive theory of all religious phenomena is possible. Theories about what holds such phenomena together, whether emerging directly from a philosophical critique such as Feuerbach's, or finding a more derivative form in the psychology of Freud or the sociology of Durkheim, can all be traced back to the Enlightenment desire to impose a structure of thought on the data of consciousness. But, like the blander versions of the modern normative thesis, they are all more or less reductionist.

At least in theory the Enlightenment view of rationality encourages pluralism. In practice it can be quite limiting, espousing not a plurality of equally plausible positions but a neutral vantage-point, a 'view from nowhere'. A concept of truth defined largely in terms of abstract, timeless principles has little space for the broader uses to which human language is usually put – forms of rhetoric and poetics, for instance. Similarly the pluralist hypothesis ignores the diversity and richness of religious literature, obscuring the different purposes to which stories, parables and myths can be put, in favour of what D'Costa calls 'an entirely instrumental use of religious language'.[23] All religion has but a single aim: to turn away from Self towards the Divine, or, in Hick's Kantian language, the noumenal Real. It is not difficult to recognise here an example of what Foucault defined as the aim of modern Western philosophy: 'to preserve, against all decenterings, the sovereignty of the subject'.[24] This tendency to define human selfhood in terms of self-knowledge makes God one more, albeit the supreme, human value, begging the question about the origin, not to say the interpretation of such values. Still less does it take into account the extent to which ethical value is to be understood within the particularity of distinct historical and cultural forms. There is always a danger, as Milbank observes, of an 'ascription to modern liberal Western values [that] does not acknowledge the traditional and continuing political sub-structures which perpetuate these values'.[25] Despite a degree of support, not just from a growing number of Asian theologians but also from a few Jewish and Muslim thinkers which give the hypothesis a certain moral force and plausibility, it remains very much a product of Anglo-American empiricist rationality.

In summary, what the pluralist hypothesis misses is a critical sense of itself being part of the historical and cultural complexity which has formed not just the different religious communities through their fraught and often destructive relations with each other but, more significantly, the particular post-Enlightenment universalist mindset which it has inherited. The desire to 'stand above the action', the drive to replace the diffuseness of local diversity with the neatness of a comprehensive system, is itself bound up with ill-defined cultural shifts of consciousness about that most ancient of philosophical questions, the relationship between same and other. Thus McGrane, in his anthropological survey of European accounts of the other, concludes that in the twentieth century, due to the modern experience of the great diversity of cultures, the other is regarded as 'merely different' – thus opening the way to a form of cultural relativism, 'a great trivialization of the encounter with the Other' which reaffirms 'the Eurocentric idea of the progress of knowledge'.[26] In other words, the pluralist hypothesis, Hick's route across the Rubicon, is less a royal road cutting majestically through mountains of theological obfuscation than a short cut which misses the richness and variety of the landscape in its anxiety to get to the end of the journey. If McGrane is right, then it is clearly naive – not to say tautological – to regard the pluralist hypothesis as a solution to the 'problem' of pluralism.

My point is that the pluralist paradigm should be understood as a dimension of the history of inter-religious relations, but *not* as its explanation.[27] Any work of critique is itself situated (including, of course, this one). In asking, therefore, what the *significance* of religious pluralism is for people of faith, it is important not to repeat the fallacy of a magisterial view from nowhere. This does not, however, entail replacing theology with genealogical deconstruction. Surin's acerbic attack on all forms of Christian theology of religions, on the ground that they serve up abstract unitary theories instead of identifying political and cultural self-interest, is surely a polemic too far.[28] Theological questions are rooted not in the defence of some 'given' tradition which promises to explain the totality of truth, but in an originating sense of wonder before a world regarded as, at once, familiar and strange, same and other. In some sense, that must be true of all religious traditions.

What follows, therefore, is not a theological *apologia* for Christianity, still less an attempt to rewrite the history of Christian mission. It is, in the first place, a re-reading of a few aspects of the story of Christian relations with people of other faiths. This story, largely dismissed by pluralists as the outmoded 'Christianity-centred' positions of so-called 'exclusivism' and 'inclusivism', is usually made to focus on the question of the salvation of the non-believer. That Christian discourse has often been dominated by such a problematic is clear. This, however, is not the whole story. If, as I suggested in the introduction, religious pluralism raises hermeneutical and ethical questions about the meaning of inter-religious engagement, then the theological task is essentially a collaborative or dialogical exercise. It is clearly not 'a view from nowhere'; but neither is it a defence of an all-encompassing somewhere. For Christians to account for the diversity of religions entails the retrieval of the proper status of the Christian tradition as genuinely 'other-centred', a tradition always charged with learning how to witness to what is discerned of God's purposes in the world of a rich and perplexing diversity.[29]

Revisiting theological positions

A dominant theme of many early Fathers of the Church, for instance, was to see the mystery of God's self-revelation in Christ as fulfilling what was only partially revealed elsewhere. Thus apologists like Justin showed an open universalist approach to the other, seeking the signs of the *Logos* at work before the historical coming of Christ and in the world of Graeco-Roman 'pagan' religion.[30] Clement of Alexandria was quite ready to recognise signs of the Spirit as a sort of 'divine pedagogy', leading pagan philosophers – even Indian thinkers – to a fullness in Christ.[31] Such openness was expressive of one side of the Church's self-understanding, the conviction that the whole of humankind has been redeemed in Christ and that this community of faith, by the witness of its life of faith, makes present this new creation. But for much of the Church's history this principle goes hand in hand with another – its more active witness to the way God's revelation has become known. The Church is also charged with proclaiming the particular Christian experience of a God whose purposes are revealed in the fateful and continuing clash between God's purposes and human sinfulness and misunderstanding. The crucifixion of God's Messiah, in other words, is central to Christian experience, raising a question mark over all claims to understand the nature of God. This story, the story of Christian origins, is rooted in the ambivalence of Christian relations with the Jewish people. Paul's wrestling with a dual inheritance, his Jewish faith in the God of the Covenant and his own conviction that in Christ God has acted in a new way, is in many ways paradigmatic of the Church's never-ending struggle to express the distinctiveness of a faith which it yet sees reflected elsewhere – in what the Fathers, invoking Stoic terminology, could speak of as 'seeds of the Word'.[32]

How to practise this 'double' witness, a sense of continuity and discontinuity? The tension runs throughout the history of Christian relations with the other. Many of the Fathers express a concern for the internal unity of the Church; attention to its relations *ad intra* are as important as those *ad extra*, if the constant danger of schism is to be avoided. Thus Ignatius and later Irenaeus insist that the fullness of truth, and therefore salvation, is only to be found by maintaining communion between the various communities if the Church as a whole is to be a credible sign of the harmony of humankind.[33] This is the context for understanding the well-known – to some notorious – axiom *Extra Ecclesiam Nulla Salus*.[34] Its original application needs to be noted carefully. Ascribed to Cyprian, it was invoked in the middle of the third century to defend Christian identity against schism at a time when Christianity was a persecuted minority. Cyprian held that the Church was essentially a community of love; hence anyone who violated this unity cut themselves off from the love of God. In other words, the axiom is not to be understood as a 'catch-all' condemnation of pagans and non-Christians but refers very specifically to those who have deliberately broken the unity of God's Church. More positively, it expresses a thesis about the Church as the sign or sacrament of God's salvific love.

Of course, it came to be used differently – in a much more polemical sense. Augustine argued expansively that wherever there is truth there is Christ. For him the Church is the community of the elect which in some sense can be said to pre-exist the coming of Christ in the flesh – the *ecclesia ab Abel* which includes righteous Jews and gentiles.[35] The primary emphasis, as with Cyprian, is very much on the Church as the community held together by the virtue of love; anyone who broke this principle was guilty of grave sin. At the same time, Augustine's insistence that all participate in original sin means that he finds it difficult to answer the question of how God can will all to be saved when manifestly many reject the Christian mystery. However, some of his followers were less ambiguous, emphasising more than Augustine himself human responsibility for sin. At the end of the fifth century, Fulgentius of Ruspe went so far as to consign to hell 'all Jews, all heretics and all schismatics who die outside the Catholic Church'.[36] What had changed, however, was not so much the reading of Augustine on the possibility of universal salvation but the political position of a Church which had become the official religion of the Roman Empire. The alliance of Church and State led to the assumption that the Christian Gospel was now manifestly known and understood everywhere. Everyone had had the opportunity to hear the Gospel; therefore anyone rejecting God's Church was *ipso facto* guilty of rejecting Christ. Fulgentius's extension of the *nulla salus* axiom to Jews and pagans dominated thinking throughout the Middle Ages and ended up in a decree of the Council of Florence in 1442.[37] The 'other' was clearly perceived as Jew or Muslim, essentially infidels who refused to believe, and even revolted against, the truth of the Gospel.

In this form it is difficult not to apply the term 'exclusivist' to a position that tends, almost inevitably, to make a very sharp distinction between Christian revelation and what may or may not be there in the world of the other. However, a mere fifty years after the Council of Florence, any idea that the complete geographical extension of Christianity had been achieved was shattered by the 'discovery' of America by Columbus. Christianity came face to face with people who had never known anything of Christ. The theological debate which ensued, especially in Spain provoked by the persistence of Bartolomé de Las Casas (1484–1566), marked a decisive return to the more traditional vision of the Apologists which saw in the religious belief and practice of others a *praeparatio evangelica*, a limited or imperfect version of what was fully revealed in the Gospel.[38] The missionary strategy of early Jesuit missionaries like Matteo Ricci (1552–1610) and Roberto de Nobili (1577–1656) reflected the same principles of justice and pastoral responsibility which motivated Las Casas.[39] This was given support by the soteriology of Bellarmine (1542–1621) and Suarez (1548–1619) who followed Aquinas's principle that God grants the means for saving faith to all persons unless they deliberately put obstacles in the way of grace.[40] But what most prevailed throughout the seventeenth century was the spirit of Renaissance humanism. The Roman College where Jesuit missionaries trained was famous for classical learning as well as for theological controversy.[41] It was thus understandable that men like Ricci and de Nobili should value local culture and learning. To some extent this was a matter of achieving effective contact through translation into local language. Thus an English Jesuit, Thomas Stephens, is famous even today for having produced the *Krista Purana*, a retelling of the Bible in traditional *puranic* or epic style, in Marathi.[42] But it also reflects the new experience of encountering a sophisticated society with clear parallels in the classical culture of Europe. This was not to be opposed but engaged in a dialogue that involved a complete translation not just of language, but of dress, lifestyle and even religious practice.

Taken with full seriousness, radical adaptation raised – and continues to raise – serious conceptual issues for the presentation of a faith which claims to be fully catholic or universal.[43] De Nobili's defence before nervous Roman authorities was that he was only following in a tradition which could be traced back to St Paul's practice on the Areopagus: building on what was already there in the faith of local people. In many ways he expresses the typically Catholic 'instinct' with regard to the other, and faced the same questions which were raised by the Second Vatican Council with its recognition of the 'truths and values' present in other religions. The fundamental theological principle at work here is a retrieval of the Apologists' sense of the continuity between God's presence within the created order and God's self-revelation in Christ. Where evangelical theology has taken its stand on what has been revealed by God's Word, the Catholic tradition has always taken a broader view of the action of God in the world; no one may put an arbitrary limit to the extent of grace. Vatican II, which in its theology of religions marks something of a return to the earlier tradition, affirms the universal call to salvation, but in the more traditional sense of a future sharing in the divine life.[44]

An 'other' pluralist reading

According to Hick's pluralist hypothesis this 'inclusivist' soteriology is to be super-seded by a normative pluralism which posits that all religions are in some way com-plementary to each other, each more or less soteriologically effective, and therefore sharing in some common essence or form. However, as argued earlier, the *extra eccle-siam* adage is fundamentally a thesis about the nature of the Church as the mediator of salvation.[45] In an uncontroversial sense all Christian theology is concerned with pluralism, with the relationship of the Church to the other. In practice, of course, responses vary. Some theologians seek to maintain the integrity of the Church against non-Christians; others more openly affirm the identity of persons of faith and see them as representing at least the *possibility* that there exist outside the visible bounds of the Church 'truths of religious significance'.[46] This latter perspective has led to some important historical retrievals. St Francis of Assisi, for instance, has become almost a patron of inter-faith dialogue.[47] In the wake of the First Crusade, in a Church obsessed with the Muslim menace, Francis proposed a mission of friendship and peace. In the early rule that he formulated for the order (1221) he distinguishes two ways in which the brothers who are sent among the Muslims can live:

> One way is not to engage in arguments or disputes, but to be subject "to every human creature for God's sake" (1 Peter 2:13), and to acknowledge that they are Christians. Another way is to proclaim the word of God when they see that it pleases the Lord . . .[48]

Some years after Francis, a Franciscan tertiary, the Catalan mystic Ramon Llull (1233–1315), wrote an extraordinary account of an imaginary dialogue between an enquiring gentile and representatives of the three semitic monotheistic religions. The work is remarkable for the eirenic spirit of the conversation. Llull emphasises what Judaism, Christianity and Islam have in common. But the decision about which to choose is left with the gentile. When the three wise men eventually take leave of each other, one of them asks:

> Would you like to meet once a day . . . and have our discussions last until all three of us have only one faith, one religion . . . ? For war, turmoil, ill will, injury, and shame prevent men from agreeing on one belief.

They ask forgiveness of each other for any disrespectful word they may have uttered and go on their way giving praise to God.[49]

What Francis and Llull introduce into a debate which has become fixated on ownership of place – particularly the holy places of Jerusalem – is some attention to the time which it takes to establish the truth which lies behind the reality of the plurality of religions. They tell us that inter-faith dialogue is necessarily open-ended; but for the sake of the peace and harmony of humankind such conversations must be continued. Nicholas of Cusa's *De Pace Fidei*, written in the immediate aftermath of the Fall of Constantinople in 1453 is remarkable for its optimistic vision of a lasting peace between warring religions. Cusanus imagines a heavenly dialogue between seventeen major regions or peoples in which the *Logos* explains that there is only 'one religion in the variety of rites'.[50] This dialogue finishes with the command of God that the

> wise men return and lead the nations to the unity of true worship . . . that with the full power of all they come together in Jerusalem as to a common centre and accept one faith in the name of all.[51]

Cusanus is sometimes claimed as a precursor of the Reformation, sometimes as representing Enlightenment values in a dark age. More accurately he stands in a tradition of Christian theology that has wrestled with the meaning of religious pluralism since the earliest times.[52]

Theological positions and virtues

Such a mystical vision of the harmony of all creation in Christ is a far cry from contemporary forms of a more *normative* pluralism. The great 'question of the other' is conceived quite differently – not as a problem to be solved but, more positively, as a relationship to be explored. After two decades of pluralist-dominated theology of religions the three-fold paradigm is looking a little dog-eared.[53] The reason for such dissatisfaction is to be sought not in millennial nostalgia for the more comforting solutions of yester-year but in a growing awareness that modern 'possessive individualism' fails to address the political, and therefore theological, issues which are raised by the interaction of different communities of faith in modern society. A pluralism that has already accepted a version of 'religion' as marginal to the public realm can produce little more than well-intentioned exhortations to a bland tolerance. Only by careful attention to the role religious practice plays in the formation and growth of communities of faith, and therefore to the ways it both encourages and discourages engagement and dialogue with others, can the significance of difference and otherness be appreciated. These are theological issues not because they are 'Christianity-centred' in the narrow sense, but because they address the challenge which inter-faith dialogue makes to all claims to self-sufficiency. In short: other persons disclose something of the mystery of *the* other, of God.[54]

The point to be stressed is that a normative account of religious pluralism does not encourage dialogue because it fails in the end to take otherness seriously. Whatever else religions may be about, they clearly respond to the human need for meaning. At some point all human beings, whether followers of recognised religious traditions or not, seek some sort of coherence in their living, what MacIntyre calls 'a life that can be conceived and evaluated as a whole'.[55] Supporters of the normative paradigm are undoubtedly correct that some theory of meaning is necessary to the understanding of religious diversity. Where the hypothesis appears curiously dated is in seeking to surmount diversity by assuming some sort of Archimedean 'place to stand'. My argument has been that there can be no such place which is not value- and theory-laden. The question, therefore, is how to shift attention from particular theories, which tend almost inevitably to assume the position of all-encompassing master narratives, to the skills, dispositions and virtues that sustain persons in their pursuit of meaning. As MacIntyre has shown, where the practice of such virtues is learned is in the living out of the heritage that grounds and gives coherence to the faith of communities. This begins with the liturgical celebration of memories and the transmission and re-imaging of life-giving stories, which are passed from one generation to another. It continues with the various practices of faith – study and prayer as well as social exchange and dialogue with others – which they support and which give rise to a hermeneutical sensitivity to what in the Christian tradition have been referred to as 'seeds of the Word'.

The three-fold paradigm, the heart of the normative pluralist mis-reading of theo- logical history, subordinates the life-giving practice of religious faith to a single value or virtue of tolerance, openness or respect. Admirable in its intentions, it neverthe- less begs the question of motivation. The story I have tried to tell reverses the order. There is a value in each of the three positions of the paradigm but it is distinctly *not* the value of the neat hierarchy. Rather than link so-called 'exclusivism', 'inclusivism' and 'pluralism' together as carefully graduated theological positions, ranked according to their openness to the other, it makes better sense to understand them as each embodying a theological virtue or value essential to the understanding of the rela- tionship between *any* faith community and those which it perceives as other. Exclusivism witnesses to that faith which speaks of what it knows through the speci- ficity of tradition. Inclusivism looks forward in hope to the fulfilment of all authenti- cally religious truth and value. Pluralism expresses that love which seeks always to affirm those values in the present.[56] This shift of attention – from consideration of the specific *objects* of theological study to the nature of the theological *subject*, the com- munity of faith which exists by seeking to articulate its relationship with God – makes for a more ethically and theologically nuanced account of the rich complexity of inter-religious relations than is allowed by a theory of normative religious pluralism.

Notes

1   See the discussion in Griffiths 2001: 21–65; also Yandell 1993.
2   O'Leary 1996: 15.
3   An increasing amount of attention is being given to the philosophical and theological questions which arise from *within the actual dialogue itself*. See, for example, Tracy 1990, 1993, Di Noia 1992, D'Costa 2000, Griffiths 2001, Heim 2001, as well as the more idio- syncratic but ever-influential work of Raimon Panikkar, especially 1993. For a theology of religions that focuses on the experience of dialogue itself see Barnes 2002.
4   See especially *The Absoluteness of Christianity and the History of Religions*, SCM: London: 1972, Knitter 1985: 23–36, Coakley 1988, Barnes 1989: 15–18.
5   A shift of perspective is, however, apparent – from *Church Dogmatics* Volume 1/2, 'The Revelation of God as the Abolition of Religion', to Volume 4 which concentrates on the humanity of Christ and the role of the Spirit. See Barnes 1989: 29–34.
6   See Cantwell Smith 1981 and Swidler 1987, especially pp. 4–50.
7   See Hick and Knitter 1987 and the response in D'Costa 1990a.
8   The line taken here is in broad agreement with that developed in recent years by Dupuis, especially 1997, 2002, a position neatly represented as 'open inclusivism' by Griffiths 2001.

9   See, for example, Smart 1989: 12–21.
10 Hick's account of religious pluralism is most fully developed in Hick 1989. See also Hick 1977 and 1980a. A selection of the vast literature which has been provoked: Byrne 1991, D'Costa 1986, 1987, 1990a, 1990b, 2000, Loughlin 1990, Rowe 1999, Surin 1990, Wainwright 1999.
11 See especially Hick 1989: 129–227.
12 For the development of Hick's philosophy of religious pluralism see D'Costa 1987. The shift from the 'Ptolemaic' to 'Copernican' versions occurs first in Hick 1973: 120–132.
13 See Swidler 1987. The classic account of the *philosophia perennis* in its modern pluralist form is Frithjof Schuon's *The Transcendent Unity of Religions*, New York: Harper & Row, 1975. See Smith 1988.
14 Ward 1990: 5
15 See, for example, Hick 1980b with its inscription of the religions within Jaspers' discourse of the 'axial age'.
16 The liberation perspective within the Myth school is represented particularly by the work of Paul Knitter and Aloysius Pieris. See especially Hick and Knitter 1987: 178ff., Knitter 1995, Pieris 1988, Swidler 1990: 19ff., May 1998: 75ff. For critique of Pieris see Ramachandra 1996: 38ff.
17 See especially de Schrijver 1998: 3–83.
18 Talal Asad 1993: 12.
19 See especially Surin 1990, Loughlin 1990, D'Costa 1996.
20 On the genealogy of 'religion' see Lash 1996, who draws particularly on the historical work of Harrison 1990. See also Cantwell Smith 1978, Smith 1998.
21 Lash 1996: 16.
22 See especially Toulmin 1990, Pickstock 1998: 47–61.
23 D'Costa 1990b: 532.
24 Michel Foucault, *The Archaeology of Knowledge*, New York: Harper & Row, 1972: 12.
25 Milbank 1990: 175.
26 McGrane 1989: 129.
27 A point developed at greater length in Barnes 2002.
28 Surin 1990.
29 See especially Rowan Williams's critique of Panikkar in Williams 2000: 167–180.
30 For a magisterial overview of the Christian tradition's response to religious pluralism see Dupuis 1997. See also Saldanha 1984, Sullivan 1992.
31 *Stromata* I, 15, quoted in Dupuis 1997: 68.
32 See especially Dupuis 1997: 57–60 on 'Saint Justin and the Logos-Sower'.
33 See Sullivan 1992: 18.
34 See Sullivan 1992: 18–27, Dupuis 1997: 84–109.
35 Dupuis 1997: 90f, Sullivan 1992: 28ff.
36 Quoted by Dupuis 1997: 92.
37 See text in *The Teaching of the Catholic Church*, compiled by Karl Rahner, edited by Heinrich Roos and Joseph Neuner, Cork: Mercier, 1967: 206.
38 See especially Las Casas's classic text on the just evangelisation of the Indians: *The Only Way*, edited by Helen Rand Parish, New York: Paulist, 1992.
39 The historical connection between Las Casas and the Jesuit missions of the seventeenth and eighteenth centuries is noted in Parish's introduction to *The Only Way*, p. 56.
40 See Sullivan 1992: 88ff.
41 See texts and introduction in Clooney and Amaladass 2000.
42 See Falco 2003.
43 Halbfass 1988: 38–43.
44 See *Nostra Aetate* (Other religions) 2, *Ad Gentes* (Missions) 7, *Gaudium et Spes* (Church in today's world) 18. For comment on Vatican II's emergent theology of religions see Barnes 2002: 29ff.
45 Sullivan 1992: 199–204.
46 Griffiths 2001: 63.
47 Dupuis 1997: 104–105.

48 These words are quoted in the 1984 document from the Vatican's Secretariat for non-Christians on the topic of Dialogue and Mission. See the Secretariat's *Bulletin*, XIX/2, p. 129. Francis's experience is linked with that of Charles de Foucauld who 'carried out mission in a humble and silent attitude of union with God, in communion with the poor, and in universal brotherhood' (p. 132).

49 From 'The Book of the Gentile and the Three Wise Men', abridged version edited and translated by Eve Bonner in *Doctor Illuminatus: a Ramon Lull Reader*, Princeton: Princeton University Press. 1993: 169–170.

50 *Nicholas of Cusa on Interreligious Harmony: Text, Concordance and Translation of 'De Pace Fidei'*, edited by James E. Biechler and H. Lawrence Bond, Edwin Mellen Press: Lampeter, 1990. Quotation from I.6.

51 Op cit. XIX.68.

52 See the introduction to 'De Pace Fidei', op cit. p. xxiv-xxv.

53 See Mathewes 1998, D'Costa in Ford 1997: 626ff., Barnes 2002: 3ff. A number of attempts have been made to develop a 'fourth paradigm', including Ogden 1992: 79ff. and Di Noia 1992: 47ff.

54 A point made by David Tracy, see e.g. 1990: 73ff.,95ff.

55 MacIntyre 1985: 205.

56 This correlation of the three-fold paradigm and the theological virtues is made in Mathewes 1998, see also Barnes 2002: 182ff.

References

Barnes, Michael (1989), *Religions in Conversation: Christian Identity and Religious Pluralism*, London: SPCK.

——— (2002), *Theology and the Dialogue of Religions*, Cambridge, Cambridge University Press.

Byrne, Peter (1991), 'A Religious Theory of Religion', *Religious Studies*, 27: 121–132.

Cantwell Smith, Wilfred (1978), *The Meaning and End of Religion*, London: SPCK.

——— (1981), *Towards a World Theology*, Philadelphia: Westminster.

Clooney, Francis and Amaladass, Anand (2000), *Preaching Wisdom to the Wise*, St Louis: Institute of Jesuit Sources.

Coakley, Sarah (1988), *Christ without Absolutes: a critical study of the christology of Ernst Troeltsch*, Oxford: Clarendon Press.

D'Costa, Gavin (1986), *Theology and Religious Pluralism*, Oxford: Blackwell.

——— (1987), *John Hick's Theology of Religions: a critical evaluation*, Lanham: Catholic University of America Press.

——— (ed.) (1990a), *Religious Uniqueness Reconsidered: the myth of a pluralistic theology of religions*, Maryknoll NY: Orbis.

——— (1990b), 'Taking Other Religions Seriously: Some Ironies in the Current Debate on a Christian Theology of Religions, *The Thomist*, 54: 519–529.

——— (1996), 'The Impossibility of a Pluralist View of Religions', *Religious Studies*, 32: 223–232.

——— (2000), *The Meeting of Religions and the Trinity*, Edinburgh: T. & T. Clark.

de Schrijver, George (ed.) (1998), *Liberation Theologies on Shifting Ground: a Clash of Socio-Economic and Cultural Paradigms*, Leuven: Leuven University Press.

di Noia, Joseph (1992), *The Diversity of Religions: a Christian perspective*, Washington DC: Catholic University of America Press.

Dupuis, Jacques (1997), *Toward a Christian Theology of Religious Pluralism*, Maryknoll NY: Orbis.

——— (2002), *Christianity and the Religions: from confrontation to dialogue*, Maryknoll NY: Orbis.

Falco, Nelson (2003), *Kristapurana: a Christian-Hindu encounter*, Anand: Gujarat Sahitya Prakash.

Ford, David (ed.) (1997), *The Modern Theologians*, Oxford: Blackwell.

Foucault, Michel, *The Archaeology of Knowledge*, New York: Harper & Row.

Griffiths, Paul (1990), *An Apology for Apologetics: a study in the logic of inter-religious dialogue*, Maryknoll NY: Orbis.

—— (2001), *Problems of Religious Diversity*, Oxford: Blackwell.

Halbfass, Wilhelm (1988), *India and Europe: an essay in understanding*, Albany: State University of New York Press.

Harrison, Peter (1990), *'Religion' and the Religions in the English Enlightenment*, Cambridge: Cambridge University Press.

Heim, S. Mark (2001), *The Depth of the Riches*, Grand Rapids: Eerdmans.

Hewitt, Harold (ed.) (1991), *Problems in the Philosophy of Religion: critical studies of the work of John Hick*, Basingstoke: Macmillan.

Hick, John (1973), *God and the Universe of Faiths*, London: Macmillan.

—— (1977), *God and the Universe of Faiths*, London: Fount.

—— (1980a), *God has Many Names*, London: Macmillan.

—— (1980b), 'Whatever path men choose is mine', in John Hick and Brian Hebblethwaite (eds), *Christianity and Other Religions: selected readings*, London: Fount.

—— (1989), *An Interpretation of Religion*, Basingstoke: Macmillan.

—— and Knitter, Paul (eds) (1987), *The Myth of Christian Uniqueness*, London: SCM.

Knitter, Paul (1985), *No Other Name? A Critical Study of Christian Attitudes towards the World Religions*, London: SCM.

—— (1995), *One Earth Many Religions: multifaith dialogue and global responsibility*, Maryknoll NY: Orbis.

Lash, Nicholas (1996), *The Beginning and the End of 'Religion'*, Cambridge: Cambridge University Press.

Loughlin, Gerard (1990), 'Prefacing Pluralism: John Hick and the Mastery of Religion', *Modern Theology*, 7.1: 29–55.

McGrane, Bernard (1989), *Beyond Anthropology: society and the other*, New York: Columbia University Press.

MacIntyre, Alasdair (2nd edn 1985), *After Virtue*, London: Duckworth.

Mathewes, Charles T. (1998), 'Pluralism, Otherness and the Augustinian Tradition', *Modern Theology*, 14.1: 83–112.

May, John D'Arcy (1998), *Pluralism and the Religions: the theological and political dimension*, London: Cassell.

Milbank, John (1990), 'The end of dialogue', in Gavin D'Costa, (ed.) *Christian Uniqueness Reconsidered*, New York: Orbis: 174–91.

Ogden, Schubert (1992), *Is there only one true religion or are there many?* Dallas: Southern Methodist University Press.

O'Leary, Joseph S. (1996), *Religious Pluralism and Christian Truth*, Edinburgh: Edinburgh University Press.

Panikkar, Raimon (1978), *The Intra-religious Dialogue*, New York: Paulist.

—— (1984), *Myth, Faith and Hermeneutics*, Bangalore: Asian Trading Corporation.

—— (1993), *The Cosmotheandric Experience*, Maryknoll NY: Orbis.

Pickstock, Catherine (1998), *After Writing: on the liturgical consummation of philosophy*, Oxford: Blackwell.

Pieris, Aloysius (1988), *An Asian Theology of Liberation*, Edinburgh: T. & T. Clark.

Ramachandra, Vinoth (1996), *The Recovery of Mission*, Carlisle: Paternoster.

Rowe, William (1999), 'Religious Pluralism', *Religious Studies*, 35; 129–150.

Saldanha, C. (1984), *Divine Pedagogy: a patristic view of non-Christian religions*, Rome: Libreria Ateneo Salesiano.

Schuon, Frithjof (1975), *The Transcendent Unity of Religions*, New York: Harper & Row.

Smart, Ninian (1989), *The World's Religions*, Cambridge: Cambridge University Press.

Smith, Huston (1988), 'Is there a Perennial Philosophy?', *JAAR*, January 1988: 553–566.

Smith, Jonathan Z. (1998), 'Religion, Religions, Religious', in Mark C. Taylor (ed.)*Critical Terms for Religious Studies*, Chicago: Chicago University Press: 269–284.

Sullivan, Francis (1992), *No Salvation Outside the Church? Tracing the History of the Catholic Response*, London: Chapman.

Surin, Kenneth (1990), 'A certain "politics of speech": "religious pluralism" in the age of the McDonald's Hamburger', *Modern Theology*, 7.1: 67–100.

Swidler, Leonard (ed.) (1987), *Toward a Universal Theology of Religion*, Maryknoll NY: Orbis.

—— (ed.) (1990), *Death or Dialogue? From the Age of Monologue to the Age of Dialogue*, London: SCM.

Talal Asad (1993), *Genealogies of Religion*, Baltimore: Johns Hopkins University Press.

Toulmin, Stephen (1990), *Cosmopolis: the Hidden Agenda of Modernity*, Chicago: Chicago University Press.

Tracy, David (1990), *Dialogue with the Other: the inter-religious dialogue*, Louvain: Peeters Press; Grand Rapids: Eerdmans.

—— (1994), *On Naming the Present: God, Hermeneutics and Church*, Maryknoll NY: Orbis.

Troeltsch, Ernst (1921), *The Absoluteness of Christianity and the History of Religions*, London: SCM.

Wainwright, William (2nd edn 1999), *Philosophy of Religion*, Belmont CA: Wadsworth.

Ward, Keith (1990), 'Truth and the Diversity of Religions', *Religious Studies*, 26: 1–18.

Williams, Rowan (2000), *On Christian Theology*, Oxford: Blackwell.

Yandell, Keith (1993), 'Some Varieties of Religious Pluralism', in J. Kellenberger (ed.) *Inter-religious Models and Criteria*, Basingstoke: Macmillan: 187–211.

Chapter 24

Religion and politics

George Moyser

One of the most interesting features of the study of religion in recent years has been the resurgence of interest in its relationship with the political world. Many scholars now recognize that earlier assumptions, at least in Western academic circles, about the fading of religion from political life have not been borne out (Westerlund 1996; Sahliyeh 1990). To the contrary, instead of a gradual marginalization and privatization of religion, in many parts of the world the opposite has occurred. Even in the West, religion has retained or even reasserted its presence in public debate, not least in the United States.

The result has been a substantial reassessment of the relationship of religion and politics in the modern world. Studies have appeared examining the way in which religious phenomena – ideas, symbols, individuals, institutions – influence the whole system of governance at local, national and international levels. Equally, attention is now being given to the ways in which the political system – leaders and institutions – respond to these religious claims. In short, the issue of the relationship between religion and politics is now a matter of serious academic attention (Wuthnow 1998). There is a growing recognition that religion and politics are not now, and in fact never have been, separate and hermetically sealed spheres of human thought and action. In the modern world, albeit in different ways from early times, religion and politics continue to combine in important ways to shape the public arena in which the many issues about the human predicament are debated and acted upon.

'Religion' and 'politics'

The intertwining of religion and politics, both as a descriptive reality and as a subject for prescriptive reflection, has an exceedingly long history that extends back to the earliest eras of intellectual discussion. This reflects the inherent qualities of 'religion' and 'politics' that seemingly inevitably drive them together into a complex, varied and dynamic relationship. From an historical point of view, as Finer points out, in the earliest times, religion formed part of a 'vast cosmology . . . into which all things are fitted' (Finer 1997: 23; see also Bellah 1969). This cosmology included matters religious, having to do with the divine, and matters political, having to do with the exercise of power. Within this context, those who monopolized political power also typically claimed religious authority, resulting in such offices as the Egyptian pharaoh who was considered as both king and divine. In this way, a pattern evolved bringing religion into the most intimate association with politics, the two forming a single or monistic whole.

With the advent of historical religions, such as Judaism, Islam, Buddhism and Christianity, a more complex pattern began to emerge. Here, the religious sphere was gradually differentiated as being concerned with a supernatural order associated with the divine, as distinguished from a secular and natural order associated with mortal humanity. In short, a cosmological dualism appeared. Now, religious activity and belief began to carry with it the idea that there was a higher and better reality above and beyond ordinary reality to which all were in principle subject, including the king, the wielder of political power within that natural order. Thus there arose the possibility for some separation between the religious and political spheres, but also the possibility of tension and rivalry. For in articulating the imperatives of the divine and supernatural, the religious sphere prescribed specific values and behaviors within what was viewed as a subordinate order. In response, there emerged a variety of religio-political patterns. Some entailed very close relationships indeed where each supported and reinforced the claims of the other, or at least an accommodation was reached not to undermine the other's position. In other contexts, an adversarial pattern developed whereby religion provided the institutional framework or ideological rationale for political revolution and reform by invoking the superiority of the divine and supernatural reality.

Within and between the two, many variations have arisen in the course of human history, as all the major religions have had a concern for the political realm. In so doing, of course, this has led the political realm to have a concern for religion. This dialectic has been particularly intense where the religious sphere has articulated its concerns through specific institutions such as churches, temples, mosques and synagogues, and expressed them through religious functionaries such as rabbis, mullahs, monks or priests. How all this worked out in specific historical patterns has been the intent of scholars through the ages to understand and explain, or to advocate for particular idealized relationships.

Religion and politics in the pre-modern period

In the lengthy era between the advent of the historical religions and modern times, much was written about the relationship between religion and politics, largely of a prescriptive variety. Religion loomed large in the wider culture and society and hence its manifestations were of considerable moment for the political realm.

In Judaism, a very substantial tradition exists of reflection on ideal political relationships from a religious perspective. These have their origins in the understandings of the nature and role of politics and religion as set out by the authors of the Hebrew Bible. Those authors were writing for a people who felt themselves in a close relationship with the divine and formed a community which, for much of its history, had a degree of political autonomy. As a result, much was written about the way that political life should be ordered, political affairs conducted, public policies formed and rulers rule (see Bauckham 1989). Fundamental was the idea that God was the sole creative source of all reality, supernatural and natural, and had entered into a special relationship with the people through a covenant, spelled out in laws, set out in the Pentateuch, that governed all aspects of life, religious, social, economic and political. Provision was made, in other words, for a very close and intimate relationship between the religious sphere and the political. Indeed, the notion of the divine covenant was the main principle of cohesion for what was otherwise a relatively loosely articulated tribal confederation. Political power was exercised in different specific forms, an assembly of adult males in earlier times, judges and kings later. But all operated within a framework that was substantially religious. Kings, however, were not of the pharaonic type – they were primarily secular political figures confirmed and legitimated by religiously conveyed gifts. This in turn allowed some prophetic writers to be highly critical of the way in which kingly political leadership was undertaken.

Later Jewish political organization and prescriptive political writing built on this tradition. Ben Joseph Gaon Saadiah (882–942), for example, set out prescriptive principles for Jewish life, in his *Book of Beliefs and Opinions* (1948), that sustained the idea of the Torah as the appropriate framework for a Jewish political constitution (see Elazar and Cohen 1985). Later still, other Jewish writers such as Moses Maimonides (1135–1204) advocated a form of prophetic political leadership. The common pattern of such writings, however, is the idea of a nation or community that was both political and religious, thereby closely interweaving religious and political ideas within one overarching system of thought.

The immediate context for writings in the Christian tradition was the presence of the Roman Empire, bitterly resented by many Jews. Within this emerged a Galilean Jew, Jesus, with remarkable gifts as a prophet and teacher whose attacks on established Jewish religious codes embroiled him in political as well as religious controversy. Some scholars, indeed, have cast him pre-eminently as a political revolutionary (Brandon 1967; Bammel and Moule 1984). From the New Testament record, however, his political views were essentially accommodationist, or neutralist, rather than adversarial. He is depicted as espousing a certain separation between politics and religion, and as expressing little direct interest in political affairs, and certainly not as encouraging nationalistic rebellion against the Romans.

In this vein, early Christian writings, represented by Paul (Romans 13: 1–13) and Peter (1 Peter: 2–3), reflect a fundamentally positive, or at least neutral, view of the Roman state (Cullmann 1957). Their concerns were with an 'other-worldly' agenda of conversion and awaiting the *Parousia*, Christ's soon-expected second coming. In this framework, mundane politics played little part. But, as the Church spread and grew, it increasingly attracted the attention of the governmental authorities as an unauthorized and potentially seditionist association. Some interpret passages in the Book of Revelation as cryptic responses to the persecution of the Church under Nero and Domitian (Rev. 17: 3–6, 18). As such attacks were periodically renewed, Christian writers such as Justin Martyr sought to explain and defend the Church, attacking the injustice and irrationality of the state in punishing believers. These 'apologists' claimed that the Church was not seeking to undermine Roman authority but looked to promote peace and decency in building 'God's Kingdom'. (Walker *et al.* 1985: 53–6). Their posture, in short, was largely apolitical and pacifist (Bainton 1960: 53–84) but, as in other historical and religious contexts, this does not always produce a policy of neutralism or neglect on the part of government.

In any event, the whole context changed radically with the coming to power of Constantine. In contrast to his predecessor Diocletian, who had a pursued a policy of persecution, under Constantine (312–37) the State and Church entered into a most intimate and mutually supportive relationship (Armstrong 1993). In short, there emerged in Western culture the model of the sacrilized Christian polity, or 'Christendom', which has provided the framework for debates about Church–State relations ever since, not least in the United States where public religious observances and favorable tax treatment of religious groups, for example, remain topics of public debate.

Reactions to this Constantinian settlement varied. Eusebius of Caesarea (c.260–c.340) occupies an important place as perhaps the first political theologian in that his central problem was to expound the virtues of a Christianized civilization and polity. To him, the close association of Church and Empire allowed for the possibility of realizing the image of the heavenly city on earth (Cranz 1993). In practice, however, by espousing Christianity, Constantine had moved to co-opt and control the Church for his own political purposes. In reaction, St Gelasius, Pope from 392 to 396, developed his notion of 'two swords', one to the emperor as a symbol of secular power, but the other to the Pope and Church as a symbol of spiritual authority. Indeed, he not only denied that secular power could be exerted over the Church, but also asserted the superiority of the ecclesiastical power to the civil, in the tradition of Israelite theocracy (Ziegler 1942). As such, his writings became the basis for later medieval papal claims to both religious and political authority – to hold both swords simultaneously.

Yet another response came from St Augustine of Hippo (354–430) in his celebrated *De Civitate Dei* (On the City of God). This, however, was heavily influenced by an Empire already falling into disarray with the collapse of Rome before the pagan Visigoths in 410. Augustine posited two 'cities', the 'City of God', which entails the establishment of a perfect peace and justice through fellowship with God, and a 'City of man', instanced for Augustine by the Roman Empire. Rooted, in his view, in materialism, violence and injustice, the 'City of man' can never be the subject of Christian sacrilization. At best it is capable of only a partial and temporary good. As such, his position on Church–State relations was a mixed one, advocating what might be called a semi-accommodationist posture (Figgis 1921).

Building upon Galasius, the theocratic claims of the medieval papacy in their turn produced a reaction, most notably perhaps in the writings of Marsilius (or Marsiglio) of Padua (c.1275–1342). In his *Defensor Pacis* (1522), he argued that it was the State, not the Church, which should be the unifying presence in society. Indeed, the Church should be subordinated to the State, not the other way around, with the Church's decisions made through conciliar, rather than Papal, institutions. However, by this period, the whole medieval religio-political system was beginning to break down by the onset of the Reformation and the emergence of secular national political power.

What was unleashed was a whole range of arrangements and prescriptions about the relationship of Christianity to politics. On the one hand, in the Lutheran and Anglican traditions, close relationships were advocated with the Church typically subordinated to the State. This is known as Erastianism after the Swiss theologian Thomas Erastus who defended the supremacy of the secular power in his *Ecclesiastical Polity* (1594). But the Reformation also gave rise to more radical ideas about Church–State patterns. Calvin's political views, for example, influenced developments in many parts of Protestant Europe including Scotland, England and Holland (Hunt 1965; Ridley 1968) that in turn influenced Puritan politics in New England and later the founding of the American republic (Davies 1955; Kelly 1992). What all of this demonstrates is that, within the historic Christian tradition, a wide variety of

Church–State patterns have been both advocated and institutionalized. These range from a monistic closeness and accommodation, on the one hand, to a dualistic tension and even adversarial separation, on the other, representing a diversity that persists through to the modern period.

The other major historical religions also developed distinctive views about the political realm. In traditional Islam, its core idea was the sovereignty of God over the entire community (the *ummah*), manifested in public witness through prayer, fasting, tithing and pilgrimage. In other words, it emphasized a whole way of life embracing all facets of society, both 'religious' and 'political'. As such, the Islamic tradition is analogous to biblical Judaism in that the two spheres, though distinguishable in principle, are in practice brought into a very close monistic relationship. Governing that relationship is a body of Holy Scripture (the *Qur'an*) and body of sacred law (the *sharia*).

Over the centuries since Muhammad (*c*.570–632), a number of writers developed these ideas in various ways. Ibn Khaldan (1332–1406), in his *Muqaddimah*, for example, argued that political rule was not *directly* drawn from divine sources, but arose from social solidarity within the *ummah* (Gibb 1962). Thus, while not espousing theocracy, he nevertheless saw a close relationship of politics, religion and law through their common roots in the *ummah*. Ahmad Ibn Taimiyya (1263–1328), on the other hand, developed a more direct and superordinate relationship between Islam and politics in which the *Qur'an*, the *sharia*, and the *hadith* (Muhammad's sayings and actions) provided the framework for government. For Taimiyya, religion provided legitimacy to Islamic rulers while the state provided security and protection to the religious authorities. His ideas have since inspired the political ideas of modern Islamic religious leaders such as Hasan al-Banna (1906–49), founder of the Muslim Brethren movement, Sayyid Abu al-Ala Mawdudi (1903–79) who established Pakistan's Islamic Party and, not least, Ruholla Musavi Khomeini (1902–89), who inaugurated a theocratic system of government in Iran in 1979 (Sivan 1985).

Buddhism also has a lengthy history of close entanglements with the political sphere. Buddha was himself, according to tradition, a political leader from Northern India who turned to an ascetic lifestyle and developed a set of teachings or truths about human existence (the *dharma*). Critically, for its relationship with the political realm, Buddha attracted a set of followers, or 'sons', committed to the 'Noble Eightfold Path', a disciplined way of attaining the Buddhist ideal of Nirvana. These monks or clergy, known as the *sangha*, formed the core of Buddhism as an institutionalized religion. However, Buddha's emphasis on ascetic detachment from worldly possessions led the *sangha* into dependency on worldly leaders with wealth and power to provide them support. Thus in Buddhist societies too there arose a close and mutually supportive relationship between the religious and political domains. The religious sphere, the *sangha*, provided political rulers with moral legitimacy while the political rulers provided Buddhist clergy with protection.

Such arrangements emerged in areas of South and Southeast Asia where Buddhism gained ascendancy. The earliest model is provided in India by Asoka who provided patronage to the *sangha* during his rule from 270 to 230 BCE. It was further realized elsewhere, notably in Ceylon (Sri Lanka), Burma (Myanmar), Siam (Thailand) and Tibet. In Sri Lanka, for example, a Buddhist dynasty was, according to tradition, established by Asoka's son and survived until its abolition by British colonialist intervention in 1815 (see Juergensmeyer 1989; Gombrich 1988). But the tradition of a close association between Buddhism and polity has remained and become a major element within modern Sinhalese nationalism (see Smith 1978).

Similarly close ties developed in Tibet where Mahayana Buddhism became the central motif of political rule. Tibetan rulers came together with religious leaders (lamas) in a close system of mutual accommodation. The Dalai Lama emerged as the most powerful among the latter to become a cornerstone of state rule in Lhasa, the Tibetan capital, from the seventeenth century onwards. Until the arrival of the Communist Chinese after the 1949 Revolution, Buddhist monks formed a core part of Tibetan government, with the Dalai Lama acting as spiritual guide to the lay political leadership. Not surprisingly, therefore, after his flight to India in 1959, Tenzin Gyatso, the fourteenth Dalai Lama (1935–), set up a Tibetan government-in-exile, upholding Tibetan culture and the traditional association of Buddhism with the exercise of political power (see Goldstein 1989).

In Hinduism, the religion of some 800 million adherents mainly in India, there is also a tradition of very close associations with the political realm. Indeed, as in Islamic and Buddhist thought, Hinduism sees no clear distinction between the two. Both are part of a common overarching set of cultural assumptions. Politics is seen as a moral activity and morality is a matter of religion. Hence, religion has a legitimate claim over the political order. In Hindu thought, this comes about through the notion of *purushartha* – that all action should conform to a set of moral or spiritual values that form the controlling framework for economic, social and political pursuits.

Such traditions, set out in classical Hindu texts as the *Arthashastra* of Kautilya from around 300 BCE, provided the basis for Hindu princely states right down to the modern period of British colonial rule. They also informed Hindu revivalist movements in the nineteenth century, such as the *Arya Samaj*, or Society of the Aryas, founded in 1876, which helped establish the Indian nationalist movement. Subsequent writers such as Bankimchandra Chattopadhyay (1839–94) and Bal Gangadhar Tilak (1856–1920) explicitly used religious ideas to link Hindu resurgence with political aspiration (see Jones 1989). And, of course, Mohandas K. Gandhi, who led the independence movement in the twentieth century, was himself a deeply spiritual Hindu and espoused a strong personal moral code as the basis for his political activity (see Chatterji 1983; Parekh 1989).

What these historical circumstances reveal is a common pattern in which religion, be it Jewish, Christian, Islamic, Buddhist or Hindu, has typically, but not uniformly, maintained a prescriptive claim over the workings of the political sphere. Similarly, such claims have aroused strong political responses, again often resulting in the religious sphere being drawn within the orbit of the State. As such, in the pre-modern period, there is a wide, indeed global, pattern of intense if varying relationships between the religious and the political in which at times any demarcation between the two seems hard to discern. It is in the context of that legacy that the relationship between religion and politics in the modern period must be situated.

Religion and politics in the modern period

Amidst all the immense changes that mark off the modern context, religion still continues its claim to political relevance. Religion's essential character claiming to be the prescriptive arbiter of political and public morality and the repository of received, indeed, divinely inspired wisdom, has not changed with the onset of modernity. Indeed, there has been much in the history of modern politics that has provoked, and continues to provoke, an affirmation of that claim. The scale and destructive capacity of modern warfare, the invention of nuclear weapons, the experience of the Holocaust and ethnic cleansing, the invention of new medical reproductive technologies, the recent phenomenon of global warning, the chronic disparities of material conditions within and between societies, are all examples of issues that have evoked a strong religious concern for the direction of public policy. Not least, the modern phenomenon of secularization has itself provoked a political response from the religious sphere. The whole movement of fundamentalism has been seen as a confrontation by traditionalists of those believed to be responsible for replacing a religious moral framework for politics and government by one that is humanistic, and therefore, in their view, anti-religious (see Kepel 1994; Marty and Appleby 1991 and 1995).

Christian fundamentalism has been a significant presence in the United States throughout the twentieth century. First emerging in response to Darwin's evolutionist ideas, the movement's political influence rose but then declined following the 1925 Scopes Monkey Trial in Tennessee. Until the 1960s, fundamentalists focused on building up educational and media institutions within their sub-culture. Then, with the rise of new issues evidencing a further erosion of the traditional religious and moral fabric of public life in the banning of prayer in public (state) schools by the Supreme Court in 1962–3, and the legalization of abortion on demand in 1973, they re-entered the political arena led by Jerry Falwell's Moral Majority. Since then, Christian fundamentalism has been a significant political presence, latterly in the organizational form of Pat Robertson's Christian Coalition.

In taking, generally speaking, a strictly literalist and inerrant view of Holy Scripture, emphasizing being 'born again' as a marker of faith, and adopting uncompromising political stances, Christian fundamentalists form at best a large minority of America's Protestant constituency, and far less than that in other Western countries. Nevertheless, there is no doubt that, contrary to the expectations of many scholars, it is a form of politicized religion that maintains a wide appeal (see Martin 1996; Wilcox 1996).

Fundamentalist religious ideas also have a significant resonance within contemporary Islam (Esposito 1997; Husain 1995). Here, however, the political marginalization of Islam is associated with the importation of Western secular values, which are viewed as having corrupted the community. Hence, to Muslim fundamentalists, what is needed is a rigorous re-establishment of Islamic law as the sole framework for national political life. Such ideas were first articulated by Hasan al-Banna who decried Western influence in Egyptian culture in the inter-war period. Through the Muslim Brotherhood, his ideas have since spread throughout the Islamic world. In Algeria, for example, they inspired the formation of the Islamic Salvation Front, which was only deprived of taking power in 1992 by military intervention (Vandewalle 1997). In the United States, they have surfaced through Shaykh Umar Abdal-Rahman who was convicted in 1996 of participation in the conspiracy to blow up the World Trade Center in New York City.

Perhaps the most enduring presence of Islamic fundamentalism is the regime established in Iran by Ayatollah Khomeini in replacement of the modernizing leadership of the shahs. Under their rule, a French-based legal code was substituted for the *Shari'a* and the educational system partly secularized. Khomeini then led a revolution that enabled him to put into effect his traditional Islamic ideas, set out in his *Islam and Revolution* (1981). To him, Islamic teaching demanded the merging of religion and politics and the establishment of a theocratic state. In this way, in Iran as in many other countries, fundamentalism has been a major modality for religion's seeking a central place in contemporary politics and public life.

The present era has also seen the development of a renewed relationship between Christianity and the political sphere through 'political theology' (Forrester 1988). Its founder was Johannes B. Metz whose *Theology of the World* (1969) was an attempt to correct the privatizing influence of modern Western culture which had led, in his view, to a neglect of the public and political sphere in favor of the private and individual. It also was an attempt to provide a faith-based assessment of the basic precepts that should govern the public pronouncements of religious institutions and leaders (see also Moltmann 1974; Kee 1978). For Metz, the Church has always been a political force in history and to him all theology, being in part a critique of the 'political implicatedness' of the Church, is necessarily political. In the past, he argues, the Church allowed itself to become politically engaged uncritically with Constantinian Christendom not the outcome of an evangelizing imperative but the product of a political policy for unification presented as if it were the will of God.

Similar but contemporary examples of the political exploitation of Christianity could be found, from this perspective, in Nazi Germany, in apartheid South Africa and, indeed, in its association with the political Right in the United States. In the latter case, what Christian fundamentalists would see as religiously authentic, here is viewed as a conservative political coalition co-opting religion to legitimate its values and goals. Such views have in turn developed into a number of situationally defined sub-species, such as black theology (Cone 1975; Wilmore 1972) and feminist theology (Reuther 1983) both of which have been influential in shaping new understandings of racial and gender issues in America.

Those understandings have focused around the theme of liberation, which has itself become a significant theological and political current in its own right. The term 'liberation theology' originated in Latin America with the publication of *A Theology of Liberation* by Gustavo Gutiérrez (1974). With Bonino (1975), Segundo (1976), Boff (1978) and others, a powerful and radical religious critique of economic and social conditions was developed, focused on a commitment to the materially poor and the urgent need for political action to transform a fundamentally unjust society. Through the development of religious and social networks among the non-elite in Latin America called base communities and, not least, strategic alliances with Marxist-inspired groups, liberation theology gave a whole new dimension to the way religion engaged with the Latin American political process.

A high-point was the Second General Conference of the Latin American Bishops (CELAM) in Medellín, Colombia in 1968, which approved documents articulating a preferential option for the poor (1970). At the same time, however, it resulted in a clash with conservative religious and political leaders. Not least, the linkage with Marxist analyses aroused opposition from the Vatican and the late Pope John Paul II whose experience of Communism in his Polish homeland had made him extremely hostile to such associations. For these and other reasons, since then the political impact of liberation theology in Latin America has seemingly diminished. Nevertheless, it has left a legacy in providing religious legitimacy for human rights that has resonated in other parts of the world, for example in Asia (Kee 1978: 127–50) and in South Africa.

In the latter case, there was a long history of human rights abuse, racism and oppression through the system of apartheid set up by the Nationalist Party when it came to power in 1948 and legitimated by the (white) Dutch Reformed Church in documents such as *Human Relations and the South African Scene in the Light of Scripture* (1976). Gradually, however, seeing this as a 'pseudo-gospel' religious groups became engaged with the resistance movement led by the African National Congress. Liberationist ideas influenced their contribution, especially in the *Kairos Document* (1985), which rejected both a 'State theology' of support for (white) political authority and a quietist 'Church theology' of focusing exclusively on saving souls. Instead, it called on the churches to engage directly in political action to challenge the satanic evil of apartheid (see Walshe 1991; Elphrick and Davenport 1997).

Outside of South Africa, however, liberation theology has had only a limited influence in African politics (Gifford 1998: 30). Instead, as in Latin America, Pentecostalism has recently had much greater sway and its political influence has generally been indirect, operating more within the cultural than the political arena (see Martin 1990). In its American roots at the turn of the twentieth century, Pentecostal movements were concerned above all with the imminent end of the world in divine judgment and the consequent need to evangelize (see Bloch-Hoell 1964). As such, Pentecostal churches, such as the Assemblies of God and the Church of God in Christ, were little concerned with worldly politics. Since World War II, however, and the non-arrival of judgment day, Pentecostalists became more open to political action, broadly defined. Black Pentecostalists, such as Al Sharpton and Eugene Rivers, stimulated by the 1960s Civil Rights Movement, turned to community involvement, tackling problems of juvenile delinquency and social welfare. But white Pentecostalists, such as Oral Roberts and Pat Robertson, inclined towards supporting the Christian Right, advocating prayer in public schools, and opposing abortion and homosexuality. It is this tradition which has, through missionary action, had a greater influence on the shape of Pentecostalism elsewhere. In Brazil, Guatemala and Chile, for example, Pentecostal leaders have tended to support conservative agendas, although a minority has also associated itself with calls for social and economic justice. In Africa, the 'Faith Gospel' of Kenneth Copeland (1974) and Kenneth Hagin (1985) has also led to a stress on individualistic and personalized prosperity, this-worldly success through faith now, rather than on any directly political agenda. By default, therefore, it has had a substantially conservative influence (Gifford 1998).

Of course, the contemporary relationship between religion and politics has not only been influenced by ideas and issues emanating from the religious sphere. Modern political thought has also had an immense influence, not the least being liberalism. Stressing, at its core, the value of liberty, and in particular a conception of personal freedom from external interference, liberalism provided much of the ideological framework within which Western Church–State relations are now conducted. Through its roots in the Reformation and the Enlightenment, liberalism developed a powerful critique of traditional arrangements. The idea of an established church, for example, was seen in the emergent pluralistic culture as a threat to individual religious freedom. What was needed was a disentangling of Church and State and the creation of a private sphere in which religion could prosper.

These ideas found their strongest expression in the United States where figures such as Thomas Jefferson and James Madison were instrumental in providing for both the disestablishment of churches and the protection of religious freedom in the First Amendment to the Constitution. But, as the decisions of the Supreme Court in subsequent years have made clear, it is an ambiguous and conflict-ridden provision. Weber (1998), for example, articulates five distinct interpretations of what separation of Church and State might mean, various combinations of which have been used to justify differing judicial outcomes. Thus, the Court tolerates paid chaplains for Congress and state legislatures, and official prayers at the opening of their daily sessions, but has prohibited similar prayers in state schools. Indeed, the school prayer issue is still alive as the Court continues to find a balance between the imperatives of non-establishment and religious freedom. All in all, the whole American model remains much contested (see Audi and Wolterstorff 1997), in part for the confusion and uncertainty it has produced, in part for the way it seems in practice to support secularism by restricting a public place for religion which puts in jeopardy the very religious freedom separation is supposed to procure.

Not surprisingly, therefore, other countries have adopted Church–State models based upon neutrality through pluralism rather than neutrality through separation, that is an acceptance by the State of a public role for religion but competing alongside other secular ideas for influence (see Monsma and Soper 1997). At the same time, however, American liberalism has clearly influenced constitutional arrangements concerning religion in many parts of the world including Turkey (Zürcher 1993), India (Brass 1990) and Japan (O'Brien 1996), all cases where the constitutions have been secularized and religious freedom mandated. Indeed, its pervasive influence is attested to by the rise of fundamentalism.

Marxism represents another modern political ideology that has had a major impact on the relationship between religion and politics. For Marx, the central value was equality, or rather the absence of it within capitalism, which engendered gross inequality, exploitation and alienation. To him, religion was a symptom of more fundamental social and economic problems, it was 'the opium of the people', a form of cultural distortion that veiled a deeper material alienation. Such a fundamental antipathy toward religion led Communists in the Soviet Union to espouse a policy of hostile Erastian control over, and restriction of, all public religious activity. Under Stalin, religious liberty was effectively dissolved. All churches had to be registered, public religious education was barred, many seminaries closed and much Church property confiscated. The Russian Orthodox Church was reduced to the role of a political puppet (Ramet 1988).

Following the Soviet lead, the Communist countries of Eastern Europe adopted similarly hostile state religious policies. Albania became the extreme case with the Communist authorities proclaiming the abolition of religion in 1967 (Beeson 1982). But, the collapse of communist rule in 1989–91, has led to an institutional revitalization of religion and a renewal of its autonomy and political presence throughout the region. In Russia, the Orthodox Church has sought to provide support and legitimacy for the new regime as well as seeking the reassertion of its traditional privileges amidst the flowering of religious pluralism. In Poland, the Czech Republic and East

Germany, the churches entered the post-Communist era with considerable prestige and influence, having actively assisted in the overthrow of Communist rule. In Romania, Hungary and Bulgaria, however, such was the compliant closeness of the churches' relationship with the Communist state that the new political era is less accommodating.

Meanwhile, the Marxist legacy continues in a number of countries still Communist ruled. In Cuba, after the Castro Revolution of 1959, the new regime expelled priests, shut down churches, nationalized private schools and inducted seminarians into the military. And though Church–State tensions have eased in recent years, culminating in a papal visit in 1998, the political authorities still remain wary of any Church comment that might be deemed critical (see Kirk 1989). Similarly in the People's Republic of China, a hostile Erastian religious policy is still in place. The State tightly controls religious institutions and restricts religious liberty. Indeed, the Cultural Revolution of 1966–76 led to thousands of religious adherents being jailed or killed. With the subsequent ascent to power of reformists, however, a slightly more liberal approach has gradually been taken. But the recent resurgence of religious activity, especially of Protestantism, has ensured that the State maintains strict limits on what is permitted (see Hunter and Chan 1993). In short, though now muted and even transformed, Marxism retains an important influence over contemporary relationships between religion and politics.

The Enlightenment also gave birth to nationalism which similarly contributes much to current relationships between religion and politics. For nationalism, the central value is 'nationhood' and loyalty to its manifestation in the nation-state. It has witnessed myriad different relationships with the religious sphere. In some cases, nationalism has remained largely secular, for example in Scotland, the Basque Country and Quebec. In other countries, however, religion has been woven into it. In the United States, Christian (and especially Protestant) religious symbols and images have been used to help form a 'civil religion', a political culture in which connections are drawn between national identity and the sacred (see Bellah 1970). These range from mythic religious ideas about America's founding, through religiously defined views of political authority, to religiously informed political rituals and discourse (see Hutcheson 1988).

In other contexts, religion has clashed violently with secular nationalism and the State by being the basis for a radical form of religious nationalism. Such has been the outcome in many parts of the Muslim world. For example, in Egypt an attempt was made by the Muslim Brethren to assassinate Gamal Abdel Nasser for his brand of secular nationalism in 1954. A radical offshoot of the Brethren succeeded in killing his successor, President Anwar al-Sadat, in 1981 (Kepel 1985). Similar tense confrontations have occurred in Afghanistan where Muslim groups overthrew the Communist government in 1992, to then be replaced by the even more radical Taliban who established a strict and autocratic Muslim state (Rashid 2000) that was only overthrown by American military intervention following the terrorist attacks of September 11, 2001. And in Gaza and the West Bank, a movement of Muslim nationalists, founded as Hamas by Sheik Ahmed Yassin in 1987, confronted the secular nationalism of Yasser Arafat and his ruling Palestine Liberation Organization.

In South Asia, religious nationalism is at the root of continuing international tension between Pakistan and India over Kashmir. In India itself, Hindu nationalism has long been a militant force confronting both the religiously accommodationist nationalism of Mohandas K. Gandhi (who was assassinated) and the once-dominant Congress Party he led. In recent years, operating through a cultural organization, the Rashtriya Swayamsevak Sangh, and the powerful Bharatiya Janata Party (Indian People's Party), Hindu nationalists have also been in bloody confrontations with Sikhs in the Punjab, and with Muslims at Ayodya in Northern India (Van der Veer 1994).

Nationalism is also an important element in the politics of Israel and the West Bank. Zionism is a modern movement of Jewish nationalism, rooted in European anti-Semitism and persecution, which helped found the Israeli state in 1948 (Alverini 1981). It has subsequently been represented in Israeli electoral politics by the National Religious Party which, in turn, gave rise to *Gush Emunim* ('Bloc of the Faithful'), a movement dedicated to the extension of Jewish territorial sovereignty in 'the Holy Land' through annexation and settlement (Gideon 1991). A particularly extreme form of Jewish nationalism was developed by Rabbi Meir Kahane, founder of the Kach Party, who argued for the Torah being the basis for Israeli law and clashed with both secularized Jews and all he perceived to oppose the establishment of a Jewish nation-state. Needless to say, the presence of such movements among both Jews and Arab Muslims has made finding solutions to the Palestinian question that much more violent and intractable. In 1995, Prime Minister Yitzak Rabin was assassinated by a follower of Rabbi Kahane for being too accommodating to the Palestinians.

Christianity too has been appropriated for nationalist causes in Europe for many centuries. Protestantism helped form British national identity and undergirded wars with Catholic France (Colley 1992). National identity and religion continue to be closely interwoven within Northern Ireland. The majority Protestant community sees the Roman Catholicism of the minority as a threat to its culture and way of life, not least because the latter wish to see the North reunified with the South where their co-religionists are in the vast majority. The inter-communal political conflict, and the search for a peaceful resolution, has, as in the Middle East, been made that much more elusive by the presence of the religious element in the two rival identities. It has deepened the sense of distrust and difference, and provided symbols and rhetoric to castigate the opposition. Among the Protestants, for example, Church and other cultural organizations such as the Free Presbyterians led by Ian Paisley, the Orange Order, and the Apprentice Boys of Londonderry, have mobilized support for militant political parties dedicated to the preserving of 'a Protestant state for a Protestant people' (Bruce 1986 and 1994; Fulton 1991).

Similar problems have afflicted Yugoslavia. The legacy of history left the country with three rival religious traditions, each intertwined with local communal identities. Orthodoxy has been a central element of Serbian nationalism; Roman Catholicism has historically been linked with Croatian and Slovenian identities, and Islam in Bosnia and Kosovo. After the collapse of Communism in 1990, these antagonistic forces surfaced again and the country fell apart amidst intense conflict and programs of ethnic cleansing. The worst experiences were in Bosnia, now effectively partitioned between the three communities under UN and NATO auspices, and Kosovo. Although with a Muslim majority, Kosovo contains a Serb minority together with holy orthodox sites strongly associated with Serb nationalism. This led the

Yugoslav government to try to evict the Muslim population by force in order to maintain its grip on the province. The genocidal carnage that resulted has again been stopped only through NATO military action and presence as peacekeepers on the ground.

It is clear that, while secularizing tendencies are discernible within contemporary politics, especially in the West, religion remains a significant element within modern politics, locally, nationally and internationally. Contrary to the expectations of those who thought religion would fade from political life, this has not happened in the modern era. Religion continues as a source of authority and guidance for political action around the globe, while political leaders, for their part, have to devise strategies that take those religious claims into account. The result is to perpetuate the relationship between religion and politics in ever-changing and complex patterns in the present and, no doubt, in the future.

This can, perhaps, be seen most dramatically in the recent rise of the fundamentalist Islamic group, al Qaeda, led by a Saudi exile, Osama bin Laden. Their orchestrated attacks on the World Trade Center in New York and the Pentagon in Washington DC signaled a new era in international affairs, dubbed by President George W. Bush 'the War on Terrorism'. The response of the United States, in initiating armed intervention in Afghanistan, the base of operations for al Qaeda, in late 2001, followed by the war to depose the regime of Iraqi president Saddam Hussein in 2003, brought religiously motivated violence to new heights of concern within the international community.

As later detailed analysis clearly shows, however (*The 9/11 Commission Report* 2004: 47–70) the historical roots and religious dimensions of this act of immense violence are substantial. For bin Laden and al Qaeda, the struggle is not just against the infidels of the West but, perhaps more importantly, it is also to promote 'the cause of Islamic revolution within the Islamic world itself, in the Arab lands especially and in Saudi Arabia above all' (Doran 2001). Regimes like that of Saudi Arabia, in allying themselves with the United States, have in their view betrayed Islam itself. Al Qaeda is itself part of a broader fundamentalist religious movement called *Salafiyya*, whose adherents, *Salafis*, encompassing Saudi Wahhabis, the Taliban and the Muslim Brotherhood, among others, share a common desire to see the restoration of a stricter and more literalist form of Islamic law throughout the Muslim world – for some of the more extreme by *jihad* (holy war) and martyrdom, if necessary. In doing so, they draw on a tradition of criticism of corrupt rulers that extends back centuries. It is that corruption that, again in their view, led to Islam's decline leaving it vulnerable to infidel regimes from the West 'eager to steal their land, wealth, and even their souls' (*The 9/11 Commission Report* 2004: 50).

It is perhaps doubtful that, in engaging in the war in Iraq, the leaders of the United States, Great Britain and allied Western powers, were fully cognizant of the religious ramifications of their actions. On the contrary, it seemed that President Bush, for one, was eager to downplay this element in favor of justifications cast almost entirely in military and political terms. But, fully recognized or not, the world of the twenty-first century is now embroiled in an open-ended international conflict that has deep connections to the religious sphere. As such it is but the latest manifestation of the abiding association of religion and politics in the affairs of human society.

References

Alverini, S., *The Making of Modern Zionism: The Intellectual Origins of the Jewish State* (New York, Basic Books, 1981).

Armstrong, G.T., 'Church and State Relations: The Changes Wrought by Constantine,' in E. Ferguson (ed.), *Church and State in the Early Church* (New York, Garland, 1993).

Audi, R. and N. Wolterstorff, *Religion in the Public Square: The Place of Religious Convictions in Political Debate* (Lanham, Rowman and Littlefield, 1997).

Bainton, R.H., *Christian Attitudes toward War and Peace: a Historical Survey and Critical Re-evaluation* (New York, Abingdon Press, 1960).

Bammel, E. and C.F.D. Moule (eds), *Jesus and the Politics of his Day* (Cambridge, Cambridge University Press, 1984).

Bauckham, R., *The Bible in Politics: How to Read the Bible Politically* (Louisville, Westminster/John Knox Press, 1989).

Beeson, T., *Discretion and Valour: Religious Conditions in Russia and Eastern Europe*, rev. edn (London, Fount Paperbacks, 1982).

Bellah, R.N. 'Religious Evolution', in R. Robertson (ed.), *Sociology of Religion* (Harmondsworth, Penguin, 1969).

—— *Beyond Belief: Essays on Religion in a Post-traditional World* (New York, Harper & Row, 1970).

Bloch-Hoell, N., *The Pentecostal Movement: Its Origin, Development and Distinctive Character* (New York, Humanities Press, 1964).

Boff, L., *Jesus Christ Liberator* (Maryknoll, Orbis, 1978).

Bonino, J.M., *Doing Theology in a Revolutionary Situation* (London, SPCK, 1975).

Brandon, S.G.F., *Jesus and the Zealots: a Study of the Political Factor in Primitive Christianity* (Manchester, Manchester University Press, 1967).

Brass, P., *The Politics of India since Independence* (Cambridge, Cambridge University Press, 1990).

Bruce, S., *God Save Ulster: The Religion and Politics of Paisleyism* (Oxford, Clarendon Press, 1986).

—— *The Edge of the Union: The Ulster Loyalist Political Vision* (Oxford, Oxford University Press, 1994).

Chatterji, M., *Gandhi's Religious Thought* (Notre Dame, University of Notre Dame Press, 1983).

Colley, L., *Britons: Forging the Nation 1707–1837* (New Haven, Yale University Press, 1992).

Cone, J.H., *God of the Oppressed* (New York, Crossroad Books, 1975).

Copeland, K., *The Laws of Prosperity* (Fort Worth, Kenneth Copeland Ministries, 1974).

Cranz, F.E. 'Kingdom and Polity in Eusebius of Caesarea', in E. Ferguson (ed.), *Church and State in the Early Church* (New York, Garland Publishing, 1993).

Cullmann, O., *The State in the New Testament* (London, SCM Press, 1957).

Davies, A.M., *Foundation of American Freedom* (New York, Abingdon, 1955).

Doran, Michael Scott, 'Somebody Else's Civil War', in James F. Hoge, Jr and Gideon Rose (eds), *How Did This Happen: Terrorism and the New War* (New York, Public Affairs, 2001).

Elazar, D. and S.A. Cohen, *The Jewish Polity: Jewish Political Organization from Biblical Times to the Present* (Bloomington, Indiana University Press, 1985).

Elphrick, R. and T. Davenport, *Christianity in South Africa: A Political, Social and Cultural History* (Cape Town, David Philip Publishers, 1997).

Esposito, J.L. (ed.), *Political Islam: Revolution, Radicalism or Reform?* (Boulder, Lynne Rienner Publishers, 1997).

Figgis, J.N., *The Political Aspects of St. Augustine's 'City of God'* (New York, Longmans, Green, 1921).

Finer, S., *The History of Government from the Earliest Times*, 3 vols (Oxford, Oxford University Press, 1997).

Forrester, D., *Theology and Politics* (Oxford, Blackwell, 1988).

Fulton, J., *The Tragedy of Belief: Division, Politics, and Religion in Ireland* (Oxford, Clarendon Press, 1991).

Gibb, H.A.R., 'The Islamic Background of Ibn Khaldun's Political Theory', in S.J. Shaw and W.R. Polk (eds), *Studies on the Civilization of Islam: Collected Essays* (London, Routledge & Kegan Paul, 1962).

Gideon, A., 'Jewish Zionist Fundamentalism: The Bloc of the Faithful in Israel', in M.E. Marty and S. Appleby (eds), *Fundamentalism Observed* (Chicago, University of Chicago Press, 1991).

Gifford, P., *African Christianity: Its Public Role* (London, Hurst, 1998).

Goldstein, M., *A History of Modern Tibet* (Berkeley, University of California Press, 1989).

Gombrich, R., *Theravada Buddhism: A Social History from Ancient Benares to Modern Colombo* (London, Routledge & Kegan Paul, 1988).

Gutiérrez, G., *A Theology of Liberation: History, Politics and Salvation* (Maryknoll, Orbis, 1974).

Hagin, K.E., *How God Taught Me About Prosperity* (Tulsa, Kenneth Hagin Ministries, 1985).

Human Relations and the South African Scene in the Light of Scripture (Cape Town, Dutch Reformed Church Publishers, 1976).

Hunt, G.L. (ed.), *Calvinism and the Political Order* (Philadelphia, Westminster Press, 1965).

Hunter, A. and K.-K. Chan, *Protestantism in Contemporary China* (Cambridge, Cambridge University Press, 1993).

Husain, M.Z., *Global Islamic Politics* (New York, HarperCollins, 1995).

Hutcheson, R.G. Jr, *God in the White House: How Religion Has Changed the Modern Presidency* (New York, Macmillan, 1988).

Jones, K.W., *Socio-religious Reform Movements in British India* (Cambridge, Cambridge University Press, 1989).

Juergensmeyer, M., 'Sri Lanka', in S. Mews (ed.), *Religion in Politics: A World Guide* (Harlow, Longman, 1989).

Kairos Document: Challenge to the Church: a Theological Comment on the Political Crisis in South Africa (Braamfontein, The Kairos Theologians, 1985).

Kee, A., *The Scope of Political Theology* (London, SCM Press, 1978).

Kelly, D.F., *The Emergence of Liberty in the Modern World: The Influence of Calvin on Five Governments from the Sixteenth through the Eighteenth Centuries* (Phillipsburg, Presbyterian and Reformed, 1992).

Kepel, G., *Muslim Extremism in Egypt* (Berkeley, University of California Press, 1985).

—— *The Revenge of God: The Resurgence of Islam, Christianity, and Judaism in the Modern World* (University Park, Pennsylvania State University Press, 1994).

Khomeini, R.M., *Islam and Revolution: Writings and Declarations of Imam Khomeini*, translated and edited by H. Algar (Berkeley, Mizan Press, 1981).

Kirk, J.M., *Between God and the Party: Religion and Politics in Revolutionary Cuba* (Tampa, University of South Florida Press, 1989).

Martin, D., *Tongues of Fire: The Explosion of Protestantism in Latin America* (Oxford, Basil Blackwell, 1990).

Martin, W., *With God on Our Side: The Rise of the Religious Right in America* (New York, Broadway Books, 1996).

Marty, M.E. and R.S. Appleby (eds), *Fundamentalisms Observed* (Chicago, University of Chicago Press, 1991).

—— *Fundamentalisms Comprehended* (Chicago, University of Chicago Press, 1995).

Metz, J.B., *Theology of the World* (London, Burns & Oates, 1969).

Moltmann, J., *The Crucified God: the Cross of Christ as the Foundation and Criticism of Christian Theology* (London, SCM Press, 1974).

Monsma, S.V. and J.C. Soper, *The Challenge of Pluralism: Church and State in Five Democracies* (Lanham, Rowman & Littlefield, 1997.)

O'Brien, D.M. with Y. Ohkoshi, *To Dream of Dreams: Religious Freedom and Constitutional Politics in Postwar Japan* (Honolulu, University of Hawaii Press, 1996).

Parekh, B., *Ghandi's Political Philosophy* (London, Macmillan, 1989).

Ramet, P. (ed.), *Eastern Christianity and Politics in the Twentieth Century* (Durham, Duke University Press, 1988).

Rashid, Ahmed, *Taliban: Militant Islam, Oil and Fundamentalism in Central Asia* (New Haven, Yale University Press, 2000).

Reuther, R.R., *Sexism and God-Talk: Toward a Feminist Theology* (Boston, Beacon Press, 1983).

Ridley, J., *John Knox* (Oxford, Oxford University Press, 1968).

Saadiah, B.J. Gaon, *The Book of Beliefs and Opinions*, translated by S. Rosenblatt (New Haven, Yale University Press, 1948).

Sahliyeh, E. (ed.), *Religious Resurgence and Politics in the Contemporary World* (Albany, State University of New York Press, 1990).

Second General Conference of Latin American Bishops, *Position Papers and Conclusions: The Church in the Present-Day Transformation of Latin America in the Light of the Council*, 2 vols (Bogotá, General Secretariat of CELAM, 1970).

Segundo, J.L., *The Liberation of Theology* (Maryknoll, Orbis Books, 1976).

Sivan, E., *Radical Islam: Medieval Theology and Modern Politics* (New Haven, Yale University Press, 1985).

Smith, B.L., *Religion and Legitimation of Power in Sri Lanka* (Chambersburg, Anima Books, 1978).

The 9/11 Commission Report: Final Report of the National Commission on Terrorist Attacks Upon the United States, (New York, W.W. Norton, 2004).

Van der Veer, P., *Religious Nationalism: Hindus and Muslims in India* (Berkeley, University of California Press, 1994).

Vandewalle, D., 'Islam in Algeria: Religion, Culture, and Opposition in a Rentier State', in J. Esposito (ed.), *Political Islam* (Boulder, Lynne Reiner, 1997).

Walker, W., R.A. Norris, D.W. Lotz and R.T. Handy, *A History of the Christian Church*, 4th edn,(New York, Charles Scribner's, 1985).

Walshe, P., 'South Africa: Prophetic Christianity and the Liberation Movement', *Journal of Modern African Studies* 29, no. 1 (1991), pp. 27–60.

Weber, P.J., 'Separation of Church and State: a Potent, Dynamic Idea in Political Theory', in R. Wuthnow (ed.), *The Encyclopedia of Politics and Religion* (Washington D.C., Congressional Quarterly, 1998).

Westerlund, D. (ed.), *Questioning the Secular State: The Worldwide Resurgence of Religion in Politics* (New York, St Martin's Press, 1996).

Wilcox, C., *Onward Christian Soldiers? The Religious Right in American Politics* (Boulder, Westview Press, 1996).

Wilmore, G.S., *Black Religion and Black Radicalism* (Garden City, Doubleday, 1972).

Wuthnow, R. (ed.), *The Encyclopedia of Politics and Religion* (Washington, D.C., Congressional Quarterly Press, 1998).

Ziegler, A.K., 'Pope Gelasius I and his Teaching on the Relation of Church and State', *Catholic Historical Review* 27 (1942), pp. 412–37.

Zürcher, E.J., *Turkey: A Modern History* (London, I.B. Taurus, 1993).

Chapter 25

Religion and geography

Chris Park

Introduction

Geography rarely appears in books on religion, and religion rarely appears in books on geography. So why include this chapter? The main reason is that some of the many interesting questions about how religions develop, spread and impact on people's lives are rooted in geographical factors (what happens where), and they can be studied from a geographical perspective.

This chapter focuses on two central themes that are both defined in terms of space and place. The first theme is the distribution of religion. This can be approached at various scales, from the global to the local. At the global scale the important questions are 'which religions are strongest in different places?' and 'why might this be so?'. Answers to such questions are often provided by more detailed studies of smaller scale distributions and dynamics. Here the key questions include 'how do religious groups and new religions spread across space?', 'how do they change through time?' and 'what processes might account for observed patterns of change through space and time?'. The second central theme of the chapter is sacred places and sacred spaces, and how in turn they influence movements of people. A key questions are 'why are some places regarded as sacred and special, and why is everywhere not regarded as sacred?'. In many religions people are actively encouraged to visit sacred places, and this gives rise to pilgrimage. The movement of large numbers of pilgrims to and within sacred sites is a special religious dynamic that can have very significant impacts on local economies and environments.

Distributions

The first of our two central themes is distribution and dynamics of religion at various scales. In this section we focus on the global distribution of major religions (with a particular emphasis on Christianity), consider what factors might account for the observed patterns, and look in closer detail at the patterns and processes of religious change in North America.

There are various ways of classifying religions, and the most commonly used ones reflect differences in belief. From a geographical perspective it is more useful to distinguish universal and ethnic religions. *Universal* (or *universalising*) *religions* – such as Christianity, Islam and the various forms of Buddhism – seek worldwide acceptance by actively looking for and attracting new members (converts). *Ethnic* (or *cultural*) *religions* are very different in that they do not seek converts. Each is identified with a particular tribal or ethnic group. *Tribal* (or *traditional*) *religions* involve belief in some power or powers beyond humans, to which they can appeal for help. Examples include the souls of the departed, and spirits living on mountains, in stones, trees or animals. More broadly based *ethnic religions* include Judaism, Shintoism, Hinduism and the Chinese moral-religious system (embracing Confucianism and Taoism), which mainly dominate one particular national culture.

It would be nice to be able to construct maps showing different dimensions of religion at different scales, but quite often the data simply do not exist. The most useful collection of statistics on contemporary religious distributions is contained in Barrett's (1982) monumental *World Christian Encyclopedia; a Comparative Study of Churches and Religions in the Modern World, AD 1900–2000.*

Global distribution

Although at the start of the third millennium roughly one in three people on earth are classed as Christian, the spatial distribution is uneven. Thus, according to Barrett (1982), a high percentage of the population in Europe (84 per cent), the Americas (91 per cent) and Oceania (84 per cent) is Christian, whereas the figure drops to 8 per cent in Asia and 45 per cent in Africa. Conversely, the great majority of Muslims (72 per cent) are in Asia, and most of the rest (26 per cent) are in Africa. Perhaps not surprisingly both Hinduism and Buddhism (both over 99 per cent) are overwhelmingly confined to Asia. Judaism, by far the smallest (numerically) of the five main world religions, has a much more dispersed pattern than the others.

The distinction between the universal and ethnic religions has a strong influence on their spatial distributions. Universal religions – as the name implies – are widely distributed. The ultimate goal of the three universal religions is to convert all people on earth. Believers are encouraged to share their beliefs with non-believers, and each universal religion engages in missionary activities and admits new members through individual symbolic acts of commitment. Christianity has an almost global pattern at the start of the third millennium, and Islam is dominant through much of Africa and Asia. Although Buddhism transcends cultural and political boundaries, it still has a marked concentration in Southeast and East Asia, although there is growing number of white Anglo-Saxons in Britain and North America.

Ethnic religions are often confined to particular countries. Thus, for example, Hinduism is particularly strong in India, Confucianism and Taoism are largely confined to China and Shintoism is concentrated in Japan. Unlike the universal religions – where diffusion is a primary objective – the spread of ethnic religions is limited and takes place only slowly because they do not actively seek converts. Although in the historic past Judaism engaged in missionary activity, in principle (and largely in practice today) membership is reserved for the in-group by inheritance. In other ethnic religions, individuals are not accepted until they are fully assimilated into the community. India and China, for example, gradually absorbed foreign tribes into their dominant culture, which expanded accordingly.

Traditional religions still persist in many less developed parts of the world, including much of Africa, South America, parts of Southeast Asia, New Guinea and northern Australia.

Distribution of Christianity

Christianity can be singled out for special treatment for three main reasons – it has more followers than any other religion, they are more widely distributed, and it is better documented, particularly in terms of statistical information.

The largest concentrations of Christians are in Europe and Latin America, where over half of the world's 1.5 thousand million Christians live, accounting for around 17 per cent of the global population. About one person in seven in North America and Africa is classed as Christian, accounting for nearly another half a billion individuals (just under a tenth of the world population).

Like all other major religions, Christianity is not monolithic and it is perhaps not surprising that the numerical strength (both absolute and relative) of different Christian sub-groups varies from place to place. The Eastern Orthodox Church is particularly strong in the former Soviet Union, and in parts of Europe and Africa (particularly North Africa). Roman Catholicism – altogether much larger and more widely dispersed than the Orthodox Church – has its strongest presence, at least numerically, in South America and Europe. In South America almost all Christians belong to the Roman Catholic Church; in Europe well over half do.

Protestantism remains numerically quite strong in Europe, where it accounts for nearly one in five of all Christians. It has its strongest base in North America, where it accounts for over 40 per cent of Christians. About a quarter of the large and growing number of Christians in Africa is associated with the Protestant churches. The Anglican Communion – representing the Church of England, the Church of Ireland, the Episcopal Church in Scotland, the Church in Wales, the Episcopal Church in the United States, and other churches that are in full communion with each other – has most (70 per cent) of its members in Europe.

Emergence and evolution

The mosaic of the world's religions raises interesting questions about how this pattern came into being, and what factors influenced it. Clearly, some components of the distribution are largely endemic. What some scholars call 'Animism', for example, is common among traditional societies and the archaeological evidence suggests that it was present in most cultures before more modern forms of religion took hold. Other components reflect religious persistence in or close to areas where those religions first appeared. Hinduism has dominated India since its birth, and Buddhism retains its foothold in the area where it first spread and became important. A third set of components reflects the spread of major religions from original source areas over time. Christianity is a good example – from its origins in the Middle East, it now spans the globe.

Present-day distributions of religions are merely snapshots in a continuously unfolding moving film. At the global scale, two factors are particularly important in accounting for the distribution of the major religions at any point in time – the places where religions originated, and the processes by which they were dispersed and diffused.

One particularly striking aspect of the geography of religions is that all of the main religions originated within a relatively small area in what is today south-western and southern Asia. Late nineteenth- and early twentieth-century attempts to explain such puzzling geographical phenomena relied heavily on environmental determinism, which is founded on the somewhat simplistic notion that human activities are controlled or determined by the environment.

Patterns and processes in North America

More studies have been undertaken into the geography of religion in the United States than in any other country, partly because more information is available for analysis. But cultural geographers there have long had an interest in religion as a cornerstone of cultural diversity, and this has inspired numerous studies. A particularly useful data source is the *US Church Membership Study*, which has collected county level statistics for the entire country in 1951, 1971 and 1980. A number of studies have examined spatial patterns and changes through time using this data set. Note, however, that the data relate to church membership rather than religious activism – the two are related but not the same thing.

Present-day patterns are very striking. American Jews are almost entirely concentrated in cities, and Roman Catholics, Episcopalians and Unitarians are also predominantly urban. The Baptists, on the other hand, tend to be more heavily concentrated in rural areas, along with other smaller sects (such as the Mennonites, including Amish) and fundamentalist groups derived from Puritan settlers.

One hallmark of religion within the United States is its diversity. This melting pot of a country boasts an almost unrivalled variety of religions, reflecting both historic factors (particularly migration) and contemporary socio-economic processes.

The distribution of church members shows some quite distinct patterns, which can be used to define religious regions. It is easy to pick out a strongly Catholic area in New England, and a broad region extending from the Middle Atlantic in the east to the Mormon region in the west with a mixture of denominations dominated by no single church (although Methodism is the largest single group). The Upper Middle West is dominated by Lutheran churches, and the Mormon region centred on Utah provides a distinctly separate religious (and cultural) unit. Baptists are the leading denomination in the South, where – together with other conservative fundamentalist denominations – they have give rise to the so-called 'Bible Belt'. Spanish Catholics dominate the Southwest. No single denomination dominates the West, but some studies identify two sub-regions there – the Pacific Southwest Region (strongly Catholic, with a large Jewish population in the Los Angeles area), and the Pacific Northwest (with even lower religious affiliation and Protestant dominance).

Interpretations of the national pattern usually place heavy emphasis on migration history. Thus, for example, the distribution of Roman Catholics partly reflects waves of immigrants from Europe and other parts of the Americas. A concentration of Catholics along the Mexican border in Texas, New Mexico and Arizona might reflect the legacy of the Spanish-Mexican influence, along with recent immigration from across the border. Similarly, the Roman Catholic enclave in the coastal region of Louisiana betrays the area's French heritage. Large numbers of Catholic immigrants from Ireland and central and southern Europe have swamped the original Protestant stronghold of New England.

The distribution of Protestant church members also owes as much to history as to contemporary socio-economic factors. The South is strongly dominated by Baptists, and Lutherans dominate parts of the Mid-West farm belt. Congregational churches are still strong in New England, and are scattered throughout the Mid-West. The most widely dispersed of the Protestant denominations are the Methodists, Presbyterians and Episcopalians. The main centre of Methodism runs through the Middle Atlantic states and the southern part of the Mid-West to the Rocky Mountains, while the main centre of Episcopalians stretches from their original core area in southern New England to Virginia.

American Jews also figure prominently in the religious scene. Since the 1950s the distribution of Jews across and within the United States has increased, although the Jewish population remained highly concentrated in metropolitan area counties. Regardless of their size, Jewish communities were overwhelmingly situated in areas characterised by high degrees of religious pluralism.

One of the problems of compiling maps of religious distributions is the impression given that patterns are unchanging through time. This is not necessarily so. Studies of changes in church membership between the 1950s and 1980s have shown remarkable stable patterns in denominational data, despite the high mobility of the US population (in a typical year one in five Americans changes their place of residence). This suggests that Americans do not carry their denominational affiliations with them when they move, but that they adopt the religious organisations of their new environment. The results are surprising, given that one might logically assume that a highly mobile population leads to religious mixing and, in turn, decreases the sharpness with which religious regions can be defined.

Regional culture in the United States appears to be not only strong, but also persistent. Some studies have uncovered a twentieth-century trend towards regional divergence between the main Protestant groups in the United States. For example, Baptists in the South, Lutherans in the upper Mid-West and Mormons in the West all dominated their regions more thoroughly in the early 1980s than they did at the turn of the century.

Dynamics – diffusion and dispersion

In this section we consider the general processes involved in spreading ideas spatially between people, examine how the global pattern appears to have evolved, and by means of some small-scale case studies reflect on detailed processes and resultant patterns.

Religion is in many ways like any other set of ideas or values that can be spread among and between groups of people, often separated by considerable distances. This involves processes of diffusion, which rest on two key principles – that anything that moves must be carried in some way, and that the rate at which some things move over geographic space will be influenced by other things that get in the way. As a result, we must recognise the existence and operation of both carriers (which promote diffusion) and barriers (which inhibit diffusion).

There are two basic types of diffusion process:

1   *expansion diffusion*: in which the number of people who adopt the innovation grows by direct contact, usually *in situ*. For example, an idea is communicated by a person who knows about it to one who does not, and through time the total number of knowers increases.

2   *relocation diffusion*: this involves the initial group of carriers themselves moving, so they are diffused through time and space to a new set of locations. Migration is a classic relocation diffusion mechanism, because those who migrate take their beliefs, values, attitudes and behaviour with them to new places. Missionaries who deliberately introduce religion into new areas fall into this category.

Expansion diffusion can be further sub-divided into:

a   *contagious diffusion*: this is diffusion through a population by direct contact. Diseases spread this way. Such diffusion expands and spreads, and the speed of expansion is strongly influenced by the frictional effect of distance. This operates like a series of concentric waves moving over the surface of a pond after a stone has been thrown in – places close to the points of diffusion normally adopt the innovation first, and more distant places adopt after a time lag during which intervening places have adopted. In human terms, ideas are passed to people close to those who already have them. Much religious diffusion is of this contagious type, and takes place by contact conversion as a product of everyday contact between believers and non-believers.
b   *hierarchical diffusion*: here the idea or innovation is implanted at the top of a society and it appears to leap over intervening people and places. Innovations are adopted or received from the top of the hierarchy down. Hierarchical diffusion of religion has occurred through history when missionaries deliberately sought to convert kings or tribal leaders, in the hope that their people would follow.

The most common type of diffusion process for most innovations, including religious ideas and practices, is contagious expansion diffusion. Traditionally this has taken place mainly through the physical relocation of people as carriers of the innovation (in this case a new religion). Modern telecommunications has opened up the prospect of using radio and television to spread religious messages across much bigger areas more quickly. Such processes underlie the evolution of tele-evangelism in the United States.

Emergence of the global pattern

The source areas or cradle lands of the main religions are well established through detailed historical and archaeological research. Northern India provides the core area of Hinduism in the Punjab, and Buddhism (an offshoot of Hinduism) in the Ganges Plain. From here both religions spread through the Indian subcontinent, but Hinduism (an ethnic religion) extended little further while Buddhism (a universal religion) dispersed across much of central and eastern Asia. Judaism and Christianity originated in Palestine, and Islam (partly based on both Judaism and Christianity) began in western Arabia. Both Christianity and Islam – the great universal monotheistic religions – dispersed widely through the Old World. Christianity gained a particular stronghold in Europe, and Islam spread through north and east Africa, as well as further east into central and southern Asia.

Geographers describe the two areas where the main religions originated as 'religious hearths' or 'religious heartlands'. The two areas share two important properties. First, they closely match the core locations of the major ancient civilisations in Mesopotamia and the Nile and Indus valleys. This makes cultural evolution of religion a distinct possibility (although spatial correspondence does not in itself establish cause-effect). Second, and equally importantly, the religions emerged on the margins not the centres of the great civilisations. This hints at a more complex interplay between religion and culture, involving factors such as innovation and cultural diffusion, religious adaptation, and exchanges of ideas, beliefs and values along migration and trade routes.

Whatever the reasons for the emergence of religions within such a small area, the fact remains that many religions have spread far beyond their original homeland. Paradoxically, many religions are stronger today in countries other than their source areas. Many religions have changed a great deal as they have spread and grown, so that the form they display today is often far removed from their original form. Through dispersion the main religions have come into contact with and been influenced by different cultures and customs, some have divided into sub-groups (sects), and many have changed forms of worship and organisation. Modern Christianity, for example, is different to what it was like in the first century after Christ. Similarly, Hinduism has evolved a great deal over nearly thirty centuries.

Religions of the Indo-Gangetic hearth

This important religious source area is based on the lowland plains of the northern edge of the Indian subcontinent that are drained by the Indus and Ganges rivers. Hinduism, Sikhism and Buddhism were born there. Hinduism had no single founder, and the reasons why it emerged here around 2000 BCE remain unclear. Buddhism and Sikhism evolved from Hinduism as reform movements, the former around 500 BC and the latter in the fifteenth century.

Once a religion is born, the quickest and easiest way in which it can spread is by diffusion. Throughout history India has been an important cultural crossroads and a centre from which cultures, beliefs and values were scattered far and wide.

Hinduism

Hinduism was the earliest major religion to emerge in this area, at least 4,000 years ago. It is known to have originated in the Punjab, in north-west. It later stretched from Afghanistan and Kashmir to Sarayu in the east, followed by a major wave of expansion across the Ganges to occupy the region between the Sutlej and the Jumna. From here it spread eastward down the Ganges and southward into the peninsula, absorbing and adopting other indigenous beliefs and practices as it spread. It was eventually to dominate the whole of the Indian subcontinent. Hindu missionaries later carried the faith overseas, during its major universalising phase, although most of the convert regions were subsequently lost. During the colonial period many hundreds of thousands of Indians were transported to other countries, including East and South Africa, the Caribbean, northern South America, and Pacific islands (particularly Fiji). This relocation diffusion effectively spread Hinduism far beyond its source area.

Buddhism

Buddhism began in the foothills bordering the Ganges Plain about 500 BC, as an offshoot from Hinduism. Its founder was Prince Gautama (traditionally said to have been born in 644 BC), who found Enlightenment while sitting under a pipal (Bodhi) tree. He later decided to make known to others the way of salvation he had found (the Middle Way between the two extremes of self-indulgence and self-mortification), initially in the Deer Park at Isapatana (now called Sarnath, near Benares). Starting with five converts who became disciples (monks), the Buddha soon gathered around him sixty monks who were sent out to preach and teach. During the Buddha's life-time his preaching activities were confined to northern India and a few small communities in the west of India. During the next two centuries Buddhism spread into other parts of India, although it was to remain confined to the Indian subcon-tinent for centuries after that. Missionaries and traders later carried Buddhism to China (100 BCE to 200 CE), Korea and Japan (300 to 500 CE), Southeast Asia (400 to 600 CE), Tibet (700 CE) and Mongolia (1500 CE). As it spread, Buddhism developed many regional forms. Ironically, it was subsequently to die out in the very area it had originated, and was re-absorbed into Hinduism in India in the seventh century (although it has survived among the mountain people of the Himalayas and on the island of Sri Lanka).

Sikhism

Sikhism originated in Punjab at the end of the fifteenth century in a reform move-ment initiated by a spiritual leader called Nanak. Before long he was being regarded as a holy man (guru), his ideas found widespread support, and he was preaching to large numbers, many of who had travelled especially to hear him. The new religion was widely adopted in the Punjab because it offered a fresh spiritual idea that people found attractive, particularly its criticism of the caste system that was so central a part of Hinduism. It grew fastest when peaceful conditions prevailed, which was not always the case (especially because of disturbance by Muslim invaders), and its consol-idation and expansion were greatly aided by initial political patronage. During the first two centuries Sikhism remained confined to its source area in the Punjab, mainly because successive gurus were chosen in accordance with family lines. Between about 1850 and 1971 there was considerable diffusion of Sikhism. Sometimes this occurred by voluntary migration, because the Sikh community was notoriously adventurous. Often the diffusion followed forced migration caused by political unrest. This was so especially with the creation of Pakistan after the partition of India in 1947, which divided the Punjab into an Islamic western half and a dominantly Hindu eastern half. Large numbers of Sikhs embarked on a mass exodus to India from the former West Punjab and other states in Pakistan. Since partition there has been an almost complete shift of the Sikh population from West Pakistan to India. Many of the immigrants settled in Punjab, where nationalism based on both religion and language led to the eventual formation of Punjabi Suba (state) in 1966.

Religions of the Semitic hearth

Judaism, Christianity and Islam – the three great monotheistic religions – all devel-oped first among the Semitic-speaking people in or on the margins of the deserts of south-western Asia in what is today the Middle East. Like the religions of the Indo-Gangetic hearth, these three have family ties. Judaism originated about 4,000 years ago, and Christianity emerged from within Judaism 2,000 years ago. Islam was born in western Arabia about 1,300 years ago. Many writers have questioned why it should be that the three great monotheistic religions all developed in the same basic core area but at different times. Environmental factors cannot be ruled out, as the determinists enthusiastically argued before about the 1950s, but it is much too simplistic to seek one single or even one dominant cause or explanation.

Monotheism has spread throughout the world, and between them Christianity and Islam have nearly 2.4 thousand million believers, accounting for half of the world population. Christianity and Islam, two dominant universalising religions, have played key roles in the dispersion of monotheism from their initial Middle East heartland. Judaism, the oldest Semitic religion that does not seek new converts and thus remains an ethnic religion, has played a more minor role, at least numerically.

Judaism

Judaism developed out of the cultures and beliefs of Bronze Age people who wandered through the deserts of the Middle East nearly 4,000 years ago. Like all major religions, Judaism spread and was quickly dispersed over a wide area. By 586 BC, when King Solomon's Holy Temple was destroyed, the ten tribes that constituted the northern kingdom of Israel had already been resettled in northern Assyria for four generations. This diffusion and scattering were to become a prominent feature of Judaism through the rest of its history. The Jewish diaspora (dispersion) began some time before 550 BC, and it was led by Jewish refugees and immigrants who refused to give up their faith when persecuted by pagan neighbours. Judaism spread into Europe by the forced and voluntary migration of Jews, starting with the forced dispersal from Palestine in Roman times that scattered Jews throughout the Mediterranean Basin. Through time most European Jews became concentrated around the present Russian-Polish border in an area that became known as the 'Jewish Pale'. In 1939 well over half the world's Jews were living in Europe and the Soviet Union (almost ten million). Poland housed over three million, and there were other concentrations in the Soviet Union, Romania and Germany. Modern Zionism (the political movement for the establishment of a national homeland for Jews in Palestine) has roots in medieval Jewish migrations to the Holy Land. But the most important catalyst was a series of shocks that shattered the life of Jews in Europe, the most prominent of which was the rise of Nazism in 1933 and its attempt to annihilate totally the Jews in its conquered territories from 1939 to 1945 (the Holocaust).

Christianity

Christianity began in Jerusalem when disciples of Jesus of Nazareth proclaimed that he was the expected Messiah. The movement spread slowly while Jesus was alive, but after Jesus' death it spread more rapidly. The diffusion was greatly assisted by Christian preachers and missionaries. It spread first to Samaria (in northern ancient Palestine), then to Phoenicia to the north-west, and south to Gaza and Egypt. Afterwards it was adopted in the Syrian cities of Antioch and Damascus, then subsequently in Cyprus, modern Turkey, modern Greece, Malta and Rome. It spread fast, and numbers quickly grew. Within the first century there were an estimated one million Christians, comprising less than 1 per cent of the total world population. But within 400 years over forty million people, nearly a quarter of the total population, had adopted Christianity. Imperial sponsorship of Christianity in the fourth century accounted for its rapid increase in influence and membership. The early spread of Christianity through the Roman Empire was achieved mainly by relocation diffusion aided by the well-developed system of imperial roads. Christian missionaries like Paul travelled from town to town spreading the gospel message.

In later centuries the pattern of Christianity reflected hierarchical expansion diffusion; early congregations were largely confined to towns and cities while the countryside remained largely pagan. Once planted in an area, Christianity spread further via contagious diffusion (contact conversion). Christianity diffused through Europe along a number of different routes, mainly via missionaries initially. Diffusion and adoption were slow during the first 300 years, and most early converts were town dwellers. Progress speeded up after 313 when the Christian Roman Emperor Constantine issued an edict of toleration for Christianity that led eventually to its status as state religion. The Roman Catholic church emerged in the fifth century, presided over by the bishop of Rome (the Pope). During the fourth and fifth centuries the Roman church spread rapidly in the western Mediterranean. Roman Catholic missionaries introduced Christianity to northern Europe. Between the fifth and seventh centuries Roman Catholicism gained a stronghold throughout Britain. Monks were an important and effective vehicle in the spread of Christianity around Europe, and monasteries were hubs in a network of diffusion points.

While Christianity was winning its battle against paganism in northern Europe, Islam was making inroads into the already Christianised Mediterranean region. In the eighth century North Africa was won by Islam, and has remained Muslim ever since. A sizeable area within the Iberian Peninsula (Spain and Portugal) was under Muslim rule for many centuries.

The worldwide dispersion of Christianity coincides with the era of colonial acquisition by European countries. Roman Catholicism was introduced into Middle and South America by the Spanish, after they had invaded the continent in the mid-sixteenth century. Much of Africa and small parts of India were converted by Christian missionaries, who were particularly active there during the nineteenth centuries (although many Indian Christians assert that Christianity was first brought to India by the Apostle Thomas). The Reformation in the sixteenth century served to intensify rather than diminish the enthusiasm of the Christian church for evangelism. Jesuits introduced Christianity into many areas including Ethiopia, Morocco, Egypt, India, China, Japan, the Philippines, Persia, Tibet, Ceylon, Malaya, Siam, Indochina and the East Indies. Many Protestant refugees from the seventeenth century onwards emigrated to North America to escape conflict and oppression in Europe, taking their Calvinist brand of Christianity with them and planting it firmly there. Christianity has remained a universalising religion, with an abiding commitment to active proselytism (the conversion of non-believers). A different form and rival to Catholic Christianity the Eastern Orthodox was powerful in Greece and northwards in Russia. It is estimated that it is the second largest Christian denomination in the twenty-first century to the Catholic church.

Islam

Islam means 'submission to God', and this strict monotheistic religion was founded by Mohammed in Medina in 622 (the year taken as the start of the Islamic calendar). By the time Mohammed died in 632, he ruled the whole of Arabia (in both religious and political terms). Islam spread and expanded mostly by force initially, because conversion of the mainly Christian populations it encountered usually required political control. Within less than a hundred years, Arab Muslims had conquered lands over a vast area – stretching from the Atlantic Ocean in western Europe to the borders of India, and including Spain, North Africa, Egypt, Syria, Mesopotamia and Persia. Today's distribution of Islam reflects a significant retreat from this early core emirate or territory, although the spread of Islam into India, Central Asia, the Sudan and the margins of East Africa has left an enduring legacy. Islam also has a strong presence in Southeast Asia.

One important factor in the rapid spread of Islam was its emergence at the hub of a series of important trade routes, including caravan trails leading from the Middle East through Central Asia to North China, and across the Sahara to the Sudan. Many Muslim traders were also effective missionaries, acting as multiple diffusion nuclei, who travelled widely. Expansion diffusion accounts for the spread of Islam from its Arabian source area, and relocation diffusion accounts for its subsequent dispersal to Malaysia, Indonesia, South Africa and the New World. Unlike Hinduism, Islam attracted converts wherever it took hold. New core areas soon turned into effective source areas for further dispersion, by a combination of contagious and hierarchical diffusion. In recent years Islam has once again started to spread into Europe, caused not by military invasion but by the immigration of dispossessed Muslims from North Africa, the Middle East and southern Asia.

Europe now houses an estimated 7.5 million practising or cultural Muslims, many of them in France, Germany and Britain. Muslims constitute the second largest population group within the former Soviet Union, and their numbers are rising at a rate four times as fast as the Soviet population as a whole. Separatist movements quickly emerged in the dying days of Communist rule, and by 1990 the peoples of the Soviet Union's Muslim republics (Azerbaijan, Kazakstan, Kirgizia, Tajakstan, Turkmenia and Uzbekistan) were seeking to regain control of their own destinies.

Relocation diffusion on a global scale

In the period since the Second World War there has been relocation diffusion of religions on an unprecedented scale. First through the recruitment of forces for the war, then for labour force reasons. This was first evident in Britain with the recruitment of manual workers from India, Pakistan and the Caribbean to help rebuild British industry not only devastated by bombing, but also the loss of so many young men to undertake the necessary work. The migrants were employed in manual labour. In the early 1970s first Canada and then the United States eased their previously very strict immigrations laws, but they accepted only those who would benefit the state predominantly highly educated professionals, e.g. in medical professions. Australia followed approximately a decade later, reversing its previously ruthless 'Whites Only' policy. At the same time most Asians working in Africa were expelled, e.g. from Kenya and notoriously by Idi Amin from Uganda. In this global relocation diffusion many religious groups were relocated so that the countries mentioned became more multi-religious than ever before with Sikhs, Hindus, East Asian Buddhists, South Asian and Eastern Mediterranean Muslims all gradually recreating something of their traditional culture and religions in the 'New World'.

Small-scale case study: the Old Order Amish

Small-scale case studies are useful for illustrating some of the detailed processes by which religion spreads from one place to another. They show what sorts of diffusion and dispersion processes are at work, and suggest key components of the dynamics involved. A particularly interesting example is the diffusion, growth and survival of one small religious sect, the Old Order Amish (Crowley 1978).

The Amish started life in Switzerland as a conservative reformist group within the Mennonite Anabaptist movement, under the leadership of Jakob Amman between 1693–7. In the early years of the Amish movement, congregations grew and spread largely through conversion, by contagious expansion diffusion. But during the eighteenth and early nineteenth centuries religious persecution was to cause them to move a number of times. This triggered a phase of relocation diffusion, initially within Europe but subsequently across the Atlantic. Through time in Europe many surviving Amish eventually relaxed the strict Amish code of conduct, which prohibited contact with outsiders, and associated with local non-Amish and even intermarried with them, and gradually the sect all but disappeared.

Two main phases of Amish immigrants arrived in North America, the first lasting from about 1717 to 1750. It involved about 500 people, mainly from the Palatinate, who settled in Pennsylvania largely because of attractive land offers from William Penn's agents. Around 1,500 Amish, almost entirely from Alsace and Lorraine, arrived in the second wave between 1817 and 1861. They settled in Canada and the United States, but most chose Ohio, Illinois, Iowa and southern Ontario where land was cheaper and more available than in Pennsylvania. Both migration waves gave rise to new Amish settlements in the United States, in five quite distinct phases of diffusion and settlement. During the 'first phase' (1717–1816) Amish settlements were established by newly arrived immigrant groups in south-eastern Pennsylvania. The 'second phase' (1817–61) saw the arrival of the second group of immigrants, mainly from Alsace. The new arrivals founded colonies in western Ohio, central Illinois and south-eastern Iowa. Many of the 'first phase' settlements continued to expand, with new settlements started in Ohio and north-eastern Indiana. Phase three (1862–99) brought to a close the 'Westward Advance' as the supply of virgin frontier land started to run out. But the Amish continued to expand westwards into North Dakota, Nebraska, Kansas, Oklahoma and Colorado (the Great Plains) and into more southern states (Maryland, Missouri, Mississippi, Arkansas, Tennessee and Virginia). The establishment of new Amish settlements continued at a similar rate during the 'early modern era' (1900–44), but patterns of expansion changed significantly. Little colonisation occurred within the core area, and most new settlements were located in Great Plains and Southern states surrounding the core. The impetus to start new Amish settlements survived into the 'modern era' (1945–70s), when 42 per cent of all recorded Amish settlements attempted in the United States were founded. Most new colonies were founded in states that already had an Amish presence, particularly Pennsylvania where twenty-three new communities were started over that thirty-year period.

The diffusion of the Amish, initially within Europe and subsequently within the United States, illustrates some interesting aspects of the diffusion process. One is the continued relocation diffusion that has caused Amish groups to migrate a number of times both within and between countries. Second, the evolution of the pattern of Amish settlements, particularly in the United States, has been neither unidirectional nor linear. Settlements were established and abandoned, and the distribution changed markedly through time. A third property of the Amish diffusion is the way in which its objectives have changed through time, from an initial enthusiasm for growth via conversion to a more long-term commitment to survive and grow through natural increase.

Sacred space and place

One of the more prominent geographical dimensions of religious expression is the notion of sacred space. Most religions designate certain places as sacred or holy, and this designation often encourages believers to visit those places in pilgrimage and puts responsibilities on religious authorities to protect them for the benefit of future generations.

Sacred sites

There is no easy answer to the question of what defines the holiness or sanctity of a place, although sacred places share two important properties – they are not transferable (they are valued because of their associated holiness), and they do not need to be re-established with each new generation (there is an inherited appreciation of the holiness of the site).

Some sacred sites are selected because they are associated with people who have some particular religious significance or credibility. For example, many individual pilgrimage sites in Islam and Hinduism mark significant places in the lives of religious founders or leaders. Sites associated with the life of the Buddha – such as his birthplace at Lumbini in Nepal, Bodh-Gaya in India where he received enlightenment and Sarnath (near Varanasi) where he first preached – are both sacred and heavily visited.

Many sacred sites are recycled earlier religious sites. There are many examples, including Christian chapels in Egypt converted from pre-Christian rock-tombs, ancient Egyptian temples converted to Christian use and early Christian churches built within ancient temples in Egypt and Cyprus. Many early British churches were sited either on or adjoining prehistoric or other pagan monuments.

The location of sacred sites in India largely reflects historic and topographic factors. One topographic factor of particular importance in Hinduism is proximity to water. Many sacred sites are concentrated along the seven sacred rivers of the Hindus – the Ganga (Ganges), the Yamuna, the Saraswati, the Narmada, the Indus (Sindhu), the Cauvery and the Godavari. The Ganges is India's holiest of holy rivers and there are many sacred shrines on its banks.

Sacred directions

Sacredness is not confined to particular places, because many religions also favour certain sacred directions and orientations. Ancient religions based on sun worship had particular reverence for east. Passages in the Hebrew Bible show that the ancient Jews also favoured the direction of Jerusalem (the City of God) and regarded north as unfavourable. The Prophet Mohammed originally followed Jewish tradition and prayed towards Jerusalem, until he received a revelation from God instructing him to turn his back upon it and face Mecca. Since then the sense of Holy Direction (towards Mecca) has had a pervasive influence on the everyday life of Muslims. Throughout the world of Islam the faithful turn towards Mecca to pray, and they are forbidden to spit or relieve nature facing in that sacred direction.

Sacred directions are also reflected in the orientation of churches, mosques and synagogues. In the west Jewish synagogues are mostly aligned from west to east, with worshippers facing the Ark towards Jerusalem (in the east they are aligned in the opposite direction towards Jerusalem). Since the eighth century Christian churches have been oriented with the altar (viewed as paradise) facing east. Orthodox Christian churches also have their altar at the eastern end. In Muslim mosques, a special niche (the *mihrab*) is built it a wall so that the prayers of those facing it will be addressed toward Mecca. These sacred directions continue to be important in the various diasporas.

Pilgrimage

The notion of sacred space is clearly very important in both theory and practice. It demarcates certain places and spaces as having some particular religious association, and by definition sets them apart from the rest of geographical space. The dynamics of sacred space are even more interesting to geographers, who have shown great interest in how and why pilgrims travel to sacred sites, and how their pilgrimages affect environment and society particularly in and around their destinations.

The *Collins English Dictionary* (1979) defines *pilgrimage* as 'a journey to a shrine or other sacred place', and a *pilgrim* as 'a person who undertakes a journey to a sacred place as an act of religious devotion'. Such journeys often involve large number of people, who travel long distances by a variety of means, often for specific religious festivals. Pilgrimages are typical of both ethnic and universalising religions, and they are found in all the major historical religions.

Pilgrimage is motivated by different factors in different places. Some pilgrim trips are made out of duty, whereas others are made in the hope of receiving special blessings or healing. Yet others are made to increase personal holiness, or just simply to escape temporarily from the pressures of modern society. It is important to distinguish between pilgrimage that is obligatory (as in modern Islamic pilgrimage to Mecca) and pilgrimage that is a voluntary act involving a vow or promise (such as early Christian sacred travel to Palestine or Rome). Obligatory pilgrimage inevitably involves larger numbers, guarantees the survival of the pilgrimage route and destinations, and has its own in-built dynamics.

New pilgrimage sites are beginning to appear in the diaspora as people undertake pilgrimages around major temples, mosques, gurdwaras, etc. How to relocate religious space in the New World is a major dimension to resettling in the New World.

Recent years have seen the emergence of new postmodern conceptions of pilgrimage to sacred places, which challenge traditional perspectives (Eade and Sallnow 1991). In the traditional view, some places are inherently sacred and the act of pilgrimage bestows inherent benefits. In postmodern terms, people bring their own perceptions and meanings to the sacred place, which thus has projected onto it a range of meanings and interpretations, even among believers.

Islamic pilgrimage to Mecca

Without doubt the best-known large-scale pilgrimage in the world is the annual pilgrimage of Muslims to Mecca, the *Hajj*. It represents a remarkable movement of people in the Middle East in terms of both size and durability. It has survived the thirteen centuries of Islam virtually without interruption. Its influence extends to all the countries of Islam, and for one month every year the city of Mecca in Saudi Arabia (with a resident population of around 150,000) has more visitors (over a million) than any other city in the world. The *Hajj* is a major source of income for Saudi Arabia (the third largest earner after oil exports and spending by oil companies). Indeed, before oil was discovered in Saudi Arabia in 1938, spending by pilgrims was the country's largest source of foreign exchange earnings.

To Muslims the pilgrimage to Mecca is not simply an act of religious obedience, it is a duty. It is the fifth pillar (foundation of faith) of Islam – along with declaration of faith, prayer, charity and fasting – although it is the only one that is not obligatory. Islam requires that every adult Muslim perform the pilgrimage to Mecca and to nearby Arafat and Mina (where they receive the grace of Allah) at least once in a lifetime. But the obligation is deferred for four groups of people – those who cannot afford to make the pilgrimage; those who are constrained by physical disability, hazardous conditions or political barriers; slaves and those of unsound minds; and women without a husband or male relative to accompany them. Most Muslims do make the pilgrimage at least once, and for many of them the trip is the culmination of a lifetime's saving. For many Muslims (*hajjees*) the pilgrimage is a time of great hardship and personal suffering, and until recently many pilgrims died along the way (from exhaustion, hunger, thirst, disease). Death during the pilgrimage is regarded as particularly honourable and is believed to guarantee entry into the afterlife.

The *Hajj* commences on the eighth day of the twelfth month (*Dhu'l-Hijja*) of the Muslim lunar year and ends on the thirteenth day of *Dhu'l-Hijja*. Prescribed rites are performed that follow the order of the farewell pilgrimage in prayers and physical movement to the various sites as performed by the Prophet Mohammed in 632 CE. The rites and rituals are performed in a tightly defined sequence. The *Hajj* pilgrimage is multidimensional, involving the visit to and walk around the Kaaba (the holy shrine in Mecca, containing the black stone), visits to various other holy sites in and around Mecca, the walk between the two hills of al-Safa and al-Marwah, and finally the return to Mecca for a last visit to the Kabaa.

Most pilgrims stay in Mecca for about a month, although the actual ceremonies take only a few days. Pilgrims who have travelled far to reach Mecca often stay a year or longer. Many also visit Medina – Islam's second holy city, 300 km north of Mecca – where the Prophet Mohammed died and is buried. Both Mecca and Medina are forbidden to non-Muslims. Boundary stones on all routes leading into the cities mark the point (30 km out) beyond which non-believers must not pass.

Large numbers of animals are slaughtered annually during the *Hajj*. It is estimated that about a million animals (mainly sheep, goats, camels and cattle) are transported to Mina (near Mecca) and slaughtered there according to strict rituals. Disposal of the vast number of carcasses, within seven days, has to be carefully planned and managed to avoid sanitary problems in the hot, dry environment.

Traditionally many pilgrims travelled overland to Mecca, using two main caravan routes, from Syria and Egypt. A popular pilgrim caravan travelled across Central Africa from the west coast eastwards to Nigeria. Many African pilgrims spent up to three years on their journey, trading, working or begging along the way, travelling mostly on foot with their families. It was not uncommon for children to be born along the way, and for many pilgrims to die before they reached their holy goal.

The growth in significance of the *Hajj* has affected transport in a number of ways. New pilgrimage routes were established linking Mecca with Iraq, Iran and Oman, and the overall pattern of transport within Saudi Arabia became highly focused on Mecca. Pilgrim traffic is heavily concentrated at one time in the year, and it is unidirectional in nature (towards Mecca before the pilgrimage, away from Mecca afterwards). The movement of vast numbers of pilgrims towards Mecca has also encouraged the expansion of settlements and oases along pilgrim routes.

Numbers attending the *Hajj* have fluctuated through time, largely in harmony with waves of economic and political change around the world. Analyses have shown that the estimated 152,000 pilgrims in 1929 had fallen to 20,000 in 1933 because of world depression, and then recovered to 67,000 in 1936 and 100,000 in 1937. The Second World War saw a fall in the number of pilgrims (there were an estimated 9,000 non-Arab pilgrims in 1939). Since 1945 numbers have risen progressively, with minor downturns associated with Arab wars (such as the 1967 Arab–Israeli War, when many Muslims are reported to have given their *Hajj* savings to the Arab cause).

Conclusions

Despite the relative lack of interest in religion among geographers, and in geography within religious studies, there are many interesting and important points of contact between the two disciplines. Spatial variations in religion within and between countries, and the global pattern of religion, are interesting in their own right because they illustrate cultural diversity. Such patterns generally reflect the interplay of many different factors, and they provide interesting opportunities for the study of the diffusion of ideas and the movement of people and the dynamics of human populations. At the smaller scale, patterns and diffusion of religion reveal interesting properties of human persistence, tolerance and motivation. But the interest extends beyond people and their belief systems, because it embraces themes such as sacred space and sacred directions. Religious beliefs also fuel religious practices that have spatial expressions, such as pilgrimage and visits to sacred places.

Bibliography

al-Faruqi, I. and D. Sopher (eds) (1974) *Historical Atlas of the Religions of the World*. Macmillan, New York.

Barrett, D.B. (ed.) (1982) *World Christian Encyclopedia; a Comparative Study of Churches and Religions in the Modern World, AD 1900–2000*. Oxford University Press, Nairobi.

Chidester, D. (1998) *Christianity*, Allen Lane Books, London.

Crowley, W.K. (1978) Old Order Amish settlements; diffusion and growth. *Annals of the Association of American Geographers* 68; 249–64.

Eade, J. and M. Sallnow (eds) (1991) *Contesting the Sacred*. Routledge, London.

Gaustad, E.S. (1976) *Historical Atlas of Religion in America*. Harper & Row, New York.

Kong, L. (1990) Geography and religion; trends and prospects. *Progress in Human Geography* 14; 355–71.

Nolan, M.L. and S. Nolan (1989) *Religious Pilgrimage in Modern Western Europe*. University of North Carolina Press, Chapel Hill.

Park, C. (1994) *Sacred Worlds: an Introduction to Geography and Religion*. Routledge, London.

Parry, K., Melling D.J. Brady, D. *et al.* (eds) (1999) *The Blackwells Dictionary of Eastern Christianity*. Blackwell, Oxford.

Sopher, D. (1967) *Geography of Religions*. Prentice-Hall, New York.

Chapter 26

Religion and science

Thomas Dixon

Introduction: the two books

From one point of view, religion and science simply have nothing to do with each other. Religions are concerned with scriptural traditions and rituals, with which all members of a community engage, in order to give themselves a sense of identity, history, moral values and spirituality; they are practised by billions of people world-wide, from the most to the least educated, richest to poorest. Science, in contrast, is an elite, educated, professional activity involving expensive high-tech instruments and complex mathematics; it is engaged in by a group of intellectual, expert researchers and theoreticians who push back the frontiers of human knowledge and discover the true nature of the universe. On this view, taking a course on 'religion and science' might seem like studying 'football chants and electronic engineering' or 'modern dance and nuclear physics' – an absurd attempt to bring together and compare two totally unrelated subjects.

In fact, of course, religion and science have much more in common than this initial caricature suggests. Specifically, religion and science share an interest in the same fundamental questions about the origins and nature of the physical universe in general, and of human beings in particular. It is when religion and science have found themselves giving different answers to these questions, whether in Renaissance Italy or in modern-day America, that conflicts have arisen. Since modern science was born into a European culture in which the Christian Church and its teachings held considerable political and intellectual influence, it has largely been in Christian countries that conflicts between scripture and science have been keenly felt and contested. As a result, in this section and the one that follows, although I talk about 'religion' and science, the examples I use are all cases of interaction specifically between *Christian* religion and science; I will discuss the problems this raises in the third section, on criticisms of the 'dialogue' project.

For some, the whole history of modern thought can be summarised as a battle between religion and science, which science has won. One of the most famous proponents of this idea was Thomas Huxley. Huxley was the archetypical Victorian agnostic and man of science. His determined assaults on Christian theology in the name of evolution earned him the nickname 'Darwin's bulldog'. In his review of Darwin's *On the Origin of Species* (1859), Huxley wrote as follows:

> Extinguished theologians lie about the cradle of every science as the strangled snakes beside that of Hercules; and history records that whenever science and

orthodoxy have been fairly opposed, the latter has been forced to retire from the lists, bleeding and crushed if not annihilated; scotched, if not slain.

(Huxley 1893: 52)

It is not difficult to think of examples that seem to substantiate this idea of the history of religion and science as a perpetual battleground. We might think of Galileo's condemnation by the Roman Catholic Church in the seventeenth century. In this case, the Bible taught that the earth was stationary and the sun orbited around it. For example, the book of Joshua (10: 12–14) stated that God made the sun stand still in the middle of the sky until Joshua and his troops were victorious in battle against the Amorites. This seemed to contradict the claim of the new Copernican astronomy, that the sun was static at the centre of the cosmos, while the earth and the other planets orbited around it. If the scriptures were the word of an omniscient God, and it was true that the earth orbited round the sun, then surely the book of Joshua should have stated that God had made the *earth* stand still to prolong the day, rather than that he had made the sun stand still. Either the religious text or the scientific theory must be wrong.

Or we might think about a conflict that is still hotly contested in modern America, namely that between the Bible and the theory of evolution. The first chapter of Genesis says that God made all the creatures of the sea, the birds, the wild animals, the livestock and the creatures that move along the ground, each 'according to their kinds', and that he created human beings in his own likeness to rule over them. This picture of the separate creation of many distinct kinds is directly contradicted by the Darwinian claim that all living things, including we humans, are descended from a common ancestor, only gradually evolving into the myriad species we now see around us.

Studying 'religion and science', then, could seem to involve thinking about a long list of conflicts: Galileo versus the Church; Darwinism versus Creationism; Bible versus science; superstition versus rationality; dogma versus empirical evidence; and so on. Certainly, any serious attempt to think about this subject must involve some account of the true nature and causes of these apparent conflicts. However, equally, any such attempt would not rest content with such a simplistically polarised account. Historical studies reveal that more complicated issues were at stake, often to do not only with the interpretation of scripture, but also with the question of the relative authority of Church and state over science and education. Struggles over the relationship between religion and science have often been political, rather than merely intellectual. Knowledge is a form of power, and there is much at stake, for both Church and state, in settling what sorts of knowledge should be taught in schools and universities, and by whom.

The main focus of any book or university course on 'religion and science' is likely to be the modern period (from around the seventeenth century onwards), since it is that period that saw the birth of the institutions, methods and theories that are representative of modern 'science'. However, the fundamental questions at issue are ancient and enduring. Perhaps the most fundamental of all is the question of the relationship between the observable and the unobservable. The Nicene Creed states that God made 'all that is, seen and unseen'. The Apostle Paul wrote, in his letter to the Romans, that 'since the creation of the world God's invisible qualities – his eternal power and divine nature – have been clearly seen, being understood from what has been made' (Romans 1: 20). But what exactly can the observable world tell us about the unobservable? The desire to answer this question motivates the whole immense variety of enterprises that might come under the umbrella of 'religion and science'. A second ancient question is about the relative authority of the different sources of human knowledge: our senses, our reason, the testimony of others and the testimony of scripture. This problem has surfaced in a number of different guises. Philosophers and theologians have written about the relationship between faith and reason, whether these are opposed routes to knowledge, and which should be given priority. Another way that this epistemological question has been discussed is to think about God's two books – the book of nature and the book of scripture. Do these books tell the same story? Do you need to be an expert to be able to read them properly, or can anyone understand them? Can they be read in the same way? One of the things that historians of science have shown is that the way these two books were read, and by whom, underwent significant changes as the modern period unfolded, and that this was one of the central factors in developing relationships between religion and science.

The emergence of 'religion and science' as an academic field

Considerations of the ways to relate knowledge of nature and knowledge of God, prior to the nineteenth century, were frequently undertaken in works of 'natural theology'. Authors of such works, echoing the opening lines of Psalm 19, 'The heavens declare the glory of God; the skies proclaim the work of his hands', reassured their readers that new scientific experiments, theories and technologies were supports and not hindrances to religious faith (see Brooke 1991; Brooke and Cantor 1998). Such writers agreed with Galileo, who had said that the book of nature and the book of scripture, since they had the same divine author, could not contain contradictory truths. Any apparent contradiction must result from faulty reading. William Paley's celebrated work, entitled simply *Natural Theology* (1802), was the classic expression of the view that the study of natural contrivances confirmed what was already known through revelation, namely that the world was the product of a divine contriver. As the nineteenth century wore on, however, discussions about the relationship between religion and science became more urgent and agonised. Works of natural theology continued to be written, arguing that the scientific study of all aspects of nature revealed it to be the handiwork of a wise, powerful and benevolent God. But the tone was becoming increasingly defensive. Theologians confronted a bewildering array of perceived threats – to biblical chronology, to mind–body dualism, to the possibility of miracles – posed by developments in the sciences of geology, physiology, neurology, psychology, sociology and evolutionary biology. 'Religion and science' was emerging as a lively intellectual arena in which a variety of different contests could be played out.

The first half of the twentieth century saw a steady stream of books on the relationship between religion and science, produced by scientists, historians, philosophers and theologians. Dominating themes included philosophical and scientific interpretations of evolution, including Henri Bergson's influential *Creative Evolution* (first published in French in 1907) as well as debates specifically about Darwinism, and about new developments in physics and cosmology. However, it was only in the second half of the century that 'religion and science' became organised as a distinct and recognisable academic field, with its own university courses and textbooks, and a specialist journal. One year in particular – 1966 – might be considered the watershed. That was the year that saw both the foundation, in Chicago, of *Zygon: Journal of Religion and Science*, the first academic journal in the area, and also the publication of British physicist-theologian Ian Barbour's important and substantial book, *Issues in Science and Religion*.

Barbour's work has set the agenda, the tone and the standard for much subsequent writing on the subject. *Issues in Science and Religion* was divided into three sections: 'Religion and the History of Science', covering Galileo, Newton, Enlightenment rationalism, Darwinian debates and twentieth-century 'process' thought; 'Religion and the Methods of Science', which looked at the roles of empirical evidence and authority in constructing and choosing between theories in both science and religion; and 'Religion and the Theories of Science', focusing on theological issues raised by developments in particular scientific areas including quantum physics, genetics and artificial intelligence. More recent books on religion and science (and, indeed, the rest of this chapter too) still tend to be organised along much the same lines. In his more recent work, Barbour (1997) has developed an analysis of four different possible ways of relating science and religion: conflict, independence, dialogue and integration. He argues in favour of 'dialogue' and 'integration' as his own preferred models. Like most writers in the field, Barbour's ethos is pluralist yet apologetic, rejecting the idea of an essential conflict between religion and science and seeking a more conciliatory and constructive interaction. Many authors have developed this approach further in the forty years since Barbour's seminal book. In Britain, John Polkinghorne (1994) and Arthur Peacocke (1984, 1993) have produced notable work in this tradition, as have Nancey Murphy (1990) and Robert J. Russell (1999) in the United States. In recent years, very substantial financial and institutional support for work seeking creative 'dialogue' and 'integration' between science and religion has been provided by the John Templeton Foundation, and by the Center for Theology and the Natural Sciences (CTNS) in Berkeley, California, which, in 2003, launched the journal *Theology and Science*.

Criticisms of the 'dialogue' project

While recognising the importance, for many practical, ethical and political reasons, of encouraging constructive dialogue between scientists and representatives of religious traditions, there are nonetheless several important criticisms that have been made of this 'dialogue' project. I should say at the outset that advocates of such dialogue would be the first to acknowledge the weight of these criticisms, and have certainly recognised and responded to them. It will be useful to articulate them nonetheless. Perhaps the three most important are: that the supposed 'dialogue' is one-sided; that it neglects the plurality of both science and religion; and that it does not acknowledge the fact that it is largely just about Christianity.

The first concern challenges the idea that there is really a balanced 'dialogue' between religion and science, or that work on religion and science has built a two-way 'bridge', allowing traffic to cross between theological and scientific communities. The reality seems much less balanced than either of these metaphors suggests. If it is a conversation, it is one in which science does all the talking and theology all the listening; if it is a bridge, the traffic across it seems to go just one way (compare Russell (2003), who favours the 'bridge' metaphor, with Drees (2003) who is more critical). It is generally scientific theories, and the philosophy of scientific method, that set the terms of the interaction, and religion and theology that are required to fit in with the theories, and to mimic the methods. Professional theologians write books and organise conferences about how their work should be shaped and constrained by the latest developments in the sciences. Professional scientists, even those with a religious commitment and a sympathy for the 'dialogue' project, only rarely seem to find their decisions about experimental and theoretical work being affected by theological or religious considerations.

The second criticism – that the 'religion and science' project overlooks plurality – is a particularly important one. Too frequently in the pages of books about religion and science one encounters statements about 'the relationship' between two 'disciplines' called 'science' and 'religion', or, indeed, about building a bridge between 'the religious community' and 'the scientific community', as if these were all singular items. In reality, of course, there are, and have been historically, an almost infinitely wide array of different sciences and different religions. It is, further, virtually impossible to reach definitive answers to questions about what counts as 'science' and what as 'religion'. Although we can all agree that physics, chemistry and biology are sciences, what about psychology and sociology? Even if we agree about those, what about economics, history, psychoanalysis, philosophy, theology? Are any or all of these scientific disciplines? What about 'creation science'? Similarly with 'religion': perhaps, from a Western perspective, the monotheistic faiths of Judaism, Christianity and Islam are what we have in mind when we talk about 'religion'. But what about Eastern traditions such as Buddhism and Confucianism? Is it accurate to put them into the same category? And what about New Age movements; or cults surrounding dead celebrities; or humanistic and atheistic traditions; or political ideologies such as Socialism or Nazism; or popular protest groups such as the anti-globalisation movement? Do any or all of these count as religions? Perhaps, for some people, science itself, or some form of scientific naturalism, can fulfil religious functions (see Dixon 2002; Drees 1996; Midgley 2002). Not only is it difficult to know how far the boundaries of 'science' and 'religion' extend, but also some enterprises and individuals have been simultaneously religious and scientific. How, in these cases, can we construe the idea of a 'dialogue'? Finally, we must remember that 'science' and 'religion' are, in any case, not real things or agents that can literally engage in a dialogue. They are abstractions that stand for a plurality of individuals, communities, institutions and practices, as well as ideas and theories. Which of these are being brought together in a 'dialogue' or 'integration'? Although (as this chapter itself amply demonstrates) it is difficult to eliminate general statements about 'science' or 'religion' from one's writing altogether, more specific statements, and ones that replace singulars with plurals, will often be more accurate and informative.

The third criticism follows on from this point. One of the ways in which discussions of science and religion are in danger of talking in misleadingly general terms rather than attending to particularities is when the terms 'religion' or 'theology' are used when what is actually being discussed is exclusively *Christian* religion or *Christian* theology. The overwhelming majority of academic contributions to the area of 'religion and science' in the last forty years or so have been written by individuals who profess some form of Christian faith (and of these, many are members or ministers of Protestant churches, whether Anglican, Reformed or Lutheran). The problem is not that most discussions of 'religion and science' are parts of specifically Christian, often Protestant, theological projects. The problem arises only when it seems that this particular context is being obscured or hidden by the use of very general language. Although talking about 'religion' and 'theology' in general terms might help to foster inclusiveness and pluralism in academic discussions, it could also have quite the opposite effect. Non-Christian readers might feel that the usage implies not an openness to plurality, but rather an arrogant assumption that 'religion' and 'theology' are synonymous with a particular kind of Christianity. And, looking at it from the other direction, members of particular religious traditions might feel that the distinctive values and beliefs of their traditions are being obliterated in general statements about an all-purpose, lowest-common-denominator 'religion'. For these reasons, some would say that, if the subject at hand is essentially the relationship between modern physics and Anglican theology, or between evolutionary theory and American evangelicalism, it would be best simply to say so, rather than conducting a more general discussion about 'religion', or 'theology', and 'science'.

There is awareness in the academic field of 'religion and science' that non-Christian religions have generally been excluded. Members of the 'Abrahamic', monotheistic traditions (Judaism, Christianity and Islam), by virtue of having in common certain prophets, teachings, historical contexts and basic theological assumptions about the Creator and his creation, can engage in a degree of shared discussion about relationships between science and religion. The very general questions alluded to in the introduction to this chapter, for instance, about relationships between the book of nature and the book of scripture; between faith and reason; and between the seen and the unseen, would make some sense to Jews, Christians and Muslims alike. The answers given to those questions would differ widely, not only between these faiths, but also within each tradition, but the questions could be discussed with some integrity nonetheless. But can the dialogue be extended even further? Robert Russell, in the editorial of the first issue of *Theology and Science*, expresses the hope that it can. He envisages the bridge-building project being extended to connect 'cosmology, physics, biology, and genetics and other religious traditions, such as Buddhism, Taoism, and Hinduism' (Russell 2003: 3). However, it is hard to imagine that the preoccupations of writers in the field of 'religion and science' will be very easily exported beyond the pale of Western monotheism. As historians have shown, those preoccupations have arisen from a very particular set of intellectual, social and political circumstances in Western Europe and North America, especially from the seventeenth century onwards. It might be better for proponents of science–religion dialogue to focus on articulating more precisely their own particular political agendas and theological commitments, rather than trying to stretch the boundaries and the senses of 'science' and 'religion' yet further in an attempt to create a universal dialogue.

Religion and the history of science

Some of the most interesting academic work of recent years on relationships between religion and science has been produced by historians. Their work has often highlighted the sorts of concerns about the 'dialogue' project mentioned earlier. They have particularly warned against the tendency to over-general, essentialist and schematic treatments of religion and science (Brooke 1991; Brooke and Cantor 1998; Cantor and Kenny 2001). 'Serious scholarship in the history of science', John Hedley Brooke wrote, in his 1991 book, *Science and Religion: Some Historical Perspectives*, 'has revealed so extraordinarily rich and complex a relationship between science and religion in the past that general theses are difficult to sustain' (Brooke 1991: 5). Brooke is one of many historians who have used historical examples to falsify generalisations about science and religion. Simple overarching stories about either war or peace, about either the building of walls or the building of bridges, are no longer tenable. Historians have taught us to ask, when confronted with a statement about relations between science and religion, to whose religion, which science, and what time and place, the statement refers (or belongs). The conclusion we must draw, according to Brooke, is that there is 'no such thing as *the* relationship between science and religion. It is what different individuals and communities have made of it in a plethora of different contexts' (Brooke 1991: 321). Jews, Christians and Muslims at different times and in different places, have all contributed to the development of modern science, and have reacted to that development in particular ways (see Ferngren 2000: Part IV). Pre-modern and early-modern Islamic culture, for example, provided a particularly fertile environment for the growth of the sciences of mathematics and astronomy, which were used, among other things, to calculate the correct times of prayer and the direction of Mecca from different locations. The experience of Jews in relation to modern science was different again. Excluded from the leading European universities in the early-modern period, Jews still developed a strong connection with the science and practice of medicine, and, once exclusions from academic institutions were finally removed, subsequently were able to contribute significantly in all areas of the sciences.

The 'complexity thesis' has become the prevailing orthodoxy among scholars writing about the history of science–religion engagements. Grand narratives are to be replaced with local histories; sweeping generalisations are to be falsified by way of thorough and historically sensitive case studies (Dixon (2003) reflects further on this 'antiessentialist consensus'). The last twenty-five years have seen the production of an impressive array of studies, which together provide those interested in religion and science with the materials to throw doubt on almost any generalisation with a well-chosen counterexample (for a flavour of these, see Brooke 1991; Brooke and Cantor 1998; Ferngren 2000; Lindberg and Numbers 2003; Moore 1979).

Celebrated episodes that had previously been cited, by writers sympathetic to Huxley's 'extinguished theologians' history of science, as examples of a conflict between religion and science, have now been reappraised. The Galileo affair, for example, can be understood as comprising several different conflicts. There was a theological conflict: between those who thought that only bishops and church councils had the authority to reinterpret the scriptures, and those who, like Galileo, thought that an individual layman could decide a particular passage, which seemed to conflict with scientific knowledge, should be read figuratively. This was a particularly sensitive issue in the wake of the Reformation. There was a scientific conflict: between believers in the old Aristotelian world-view and the Ptolemaic astronomy and defenders of the new Copernican system. There was a philosophical conflict: between those who thought that the Copernican system was merely a useful device for making astronomical calculations and predictions and those who thought that it actually described the true arrangement of the planets. There was a political conflict: between Galileo's friends, patrons and supporters and those who felt he was an arrogant and untrustworthy character whose influence needed to be curbed. Historians have thus looked for deeper causes of tension and conflict in the politics and theology of the seventeenth-century Roman Catholic Church. The Galileo affair, from this perspective, looks less like a conflict between a man of science on the one hand and church leaders on the other, and more like a tense and politically charged discussion among Catholics about biblical interpretation, Aristotelian science, and the relationship between individual believers and the church hierarchy (see Brooke and Cantor 1998: Chapter 4; Lindberg 2003).

More recent conflicts about evolution have also been reinterpreted. Victorian confrontations between Darwinians and Anglicans have become legendary. At a packed meeting of the British Association for the Advancement of Science in 1860, in front of an audience composed of many leading men of science as well as other ladies and gentlemen with an informed interest in scientific questions, the bishop of Oxford, 'Soapy Sam' Wilberforce, sarcastically asked Thomas Huxley whether he was descended from an ape on the side of his grandmother or his grandfather. Huxley, apparently white with rage, rose to his feet and tremulously responded that he would rather be descended from an ape than from a bishop, especially one who used his intellectual abilities to try to block the progress of science. This exchange caused such excitement that one woman was reported even to have fainted and been carried from the room. Behind this colourful legend, however, was much more than a simple conflict between a champion of science and a conservative defender of religion. As in the Galileo case, there were theological, scientific, philosophical and political dimensions to the conflict. Liberal theologians had no problem with accepting the Darwinian theory as an explanation of how God had brought plants and animals into existence. But other Christian writers saw the acceptance of Darwinism as tantamount to atheism. Scientists disagreed over whether there was enough evidence to accept the Darwinian theory of evolution; and philosophers over whether it had been produced according to the proper inductive scientific method. There was also an important political dimension to the Victorian conflict: Huxley and others were engaged in a campaign to separate scientific research and teaching at schools and universities from the influence of the established Church of England. High-profile assaults on bishops and theologians were useful rhetorical weapons in this battle to create an autonomous and secular scientific profession (see Brooke 1991, 2003; Moore 1979; Turner 1993).

Turning to early twentieth-century America, a disturbance that appeared on the surface to be a conflict between science and religion again turns out to have resulted from tensions running along deeper social and political fault-lines. In Dayton, Tennessee in a swelteringly hot courtroom in the summer of 1925, a local schoolteacher, John Scopes, was successfully prosecuted under new legislation for teaching his pupils that humans had evolved from lower animals. The prosecution was led by the three-times Democratic presidential candidate, William Jennings Bryan, and the defence by the most celebrated lawyer of the age, the agnostic Clarence Darrow. While many at the time (including Bryan and Darrow) saw the Scopes 'monkey trial' as a classic case of the conflict between religion and science, the reasons for the amount of political heat generated were more complicated. These included the continuing political hostilities between North and South, even sixty years after the Civil War; a popular resentment at the perceived autocracy of a Northern intellectual elite; tensions between the ideals of intellectual freedom and majoritarian democracy; and conflicts between the rights of individual states and the authority of the federal government (see Larson 1997).

What historians of science and religion have demonstrated is that for every individual who argues that a particular scientific advance is a threat to their religious faith, there will be another who can explain why, on the contrary, it is compatible or even confirmatory of that faith. One of the most interesting questions to ask, both historically and with reference to present-day debates, is what the broader political motives are for presenting such developments as either in conflict or in harmony with a particular kind of religion.

Philosophy of science and theological method

Philosophers of science interested in the project of demarcating science from other activities (including religion and theology) have often focused on the scientific method. Some have emphasised the inductive nature of scientific work – the way that it produces laws and generalisations only after painstakingly collecting empirical data from which to generalise. On this view, scientific theories can be verified by collecting a sufficient amount of confirmatory empirical evidence. Others, such as Karl Popper, have been less optimistic and argued that the hallmark of science is the quest not for verification but for falsification. No matter how many black ravens you observe, you cannot conclusively prove that all ravens are black simply by accumulating observations. The next one you see could be white. However, the observation of a single white raven is sufficient to falsify conclusively the hypothesis that all ravens are black. Thus the scientist can expect evidence to provide certain falsification of unsuccessful theories but, in the case of apparently successful hypotheses, the best that she can hope for is provisional corroboration. Even very well confirmed theories are sometimes eventually falsified, partially or completely. Imre Lakatos, and the highly influential Thomas Kuhn, subsequently suggested more sophisticated accounts of falsification, which acknowledged that the lack of a match between theory and data more often results in a rejection (or at least reinterpretation) of the data, or a questioning of the competence of the experimenter, than in a rejection of the theory that was being tested. The way that Lakatos put this was to say that every research programme has a 'hard core' of assumptions that are never discarded, no matter what the empirical evidence, and a 'protective belt' of auxiliary assumptions (about calibration of measuring instruments, possible sources of interference in the experimental set-up, and so on). The latter are more likely to be modified or discarded when experimental observations fail to match up with theoretical predictions.

Popper, Kuhn and Lakatos are just three of many philosophers of science to whom theologians have looked when formulating their arguments about the differences and similarities between theological and scientific methods (see Barbour 1966, 1997; Knight 2001; McGrath 1998). One of the central issues has been the question of whether science and religion can both be considered rational activities. According to one familiar caricature, scientific theories are rational because they are based on the facts, but religious beliefs represent an irrational sort of wish-fulfilment; science demands strong empirical evidence, but religion encourages blind faith in the complete absence of evidence; the scientist is the very embodiment of objectivity and reason, but the religious practitioner is, by contrast, a creature of irrational emotions and obscure mystical experiences. There are some grains of truth in all this. Certainly there has been a strand of thought within Christian theology that has celebrated the rejection of worldly wisdom, and has emphasised the contrast between the logic of secular reason and the ineffability of religious faith. However, it is unfair to suggest that most religions encourage people to believe things in the absence of any good evidence. Most theologians would see faith and reason as being more closely connected than that.

Writers on 'religion and science' have tried to overcome the stereotyped idea that science is supremely rational and religion is the opposite in two ways: talking down the rationality of science, and talking up the rationality of religion. Appealing to post-positivist philosophers of science, including Popper, Lakatos and Kuhn, those following the first strategy have noted that science is not quite the value-free, fact-based, truth-producing machine that it was once thought to be. They point to the fact that scientific observations are more loaded with theoretical assumptions than was previously supposed, that scientists are sometimes prone to be as dogmatic and inflexible in the face of recalcitrant evidence as the most doctrinaire of theologians, and that non-scientific factors (such as social and political concerns) seem to have a considerable impact on theory-choice in scientific communities. Writers following the second strategy have tried to draw close analogies between theological and scientific methods. Arthur Peacocke and Nancey Murphy have argued, each in their own way, that theology is very much like a scientific discipline: it makes inferences from the observable realm to the unobservable; it deploys models and metaphors to represent the unobservable, just as the natural sciences do (for instance, when physicists use models of 'waves' and 'particles' to understand the subatomic realm); and it has a set of hard-core theoretical commitments, which, just as in the natural sciences, are surrounded and supported by a belt of more flexible 'auxiliary hypotheses' (see Murphy 1990; Peacocke 1984).

Taken together, these strategies would be self-defeating, since the former questions the superior rationality of science, while the latter takes it for granted. There are problems with each of the strategies taken on its own too. Most religious traditions have a strong commitment to the careful study of nature and the rigorous application of human reason. In such traditions it is important that the rationality and success of the sciences are nurtured and encouraged. Talking down the sciences, in any case, does nothing to enhance the rationality of religion and theology, which are equally vulnerable to critiques that draw attention to hidden assumptions, prejudices and political interests. The problem, on the other hand, with suggesting a close analogy between scientific and theological methods is that it can look too much as though theologians have abandoned the distinctive skills and prophetic voice of religion in an attempt to mimic the high-prestige methods of the sciences. For many, this represents too much of an intellectual and cultural surrender to an anti-theological and scientistic world-view.

Physics and divine action

Early modern debates about the physical sciences (specifically about astronomy and cosmology) provided the centrepiece for one of the most well-known controversies concerning religion and science, namely the Galileo affair. For most of the modern period, however, physical science has frequently provided the basis for a more positive engagement. One of the pre-eminent figures in the history of modern science, Isaac Newton, is a case in point. Newton's laws of motion and gravitation laid the foundations for modern physics and were taken, by some, to depict a deterministic universe from which God had been banished. Newton himself, however, was devoutly religious and believed that there were many points in the system he described at which divine intervention was not only possible, but absolutely essential. He invoked the hand of the Deity to explain, for example, the rotation of the planets on their own axes, and the fact that matter was spread evenly throughout the universe rather than collapsing into a single great mass through the force of gravity. In the eighteenth and nineteenth centuries, alongside the development of explicitly atheistic and deterministic cosmologies by some French Newtonians, more pious writers on the physical sciences continued to discern divine authorship in the elegant mathematical laws that governed the movements and interactions of terrestrial and celestial bodies. In the later nineteenth century, physicists interested in the ways that different sorts of energy could be converted into one another, and in the role of the 'ether' as a vehicle for electromagnetic forces, became fascinated by psychical research, and the controversial idea that the human spirit could be understood as some sort of physical or electromagnetic phenomenon. Physicists in late Victorian Britain accordingly undertook investigations of the fundamental forces of nature in darkened seance rooms as well as in experimental laboratories (see Oppenheim 1985).

The twentieth century saw an explosion of new ideas in the physical sciences. The theory of relativity, quantum physics, chaos theory and 'Big Bang' cosmology all brought with them suggestive new religious and theological ideas. The fuzzy, indeterminate mathematics of quantum theory seemed to indicate that physical reality was not, after all, closed and deterministic. The central role of the observer in determining the outcome of quantum events challenged the modernist dichotomy between subject and object. Big Bang cosmology could be interpreted as confirming something like a biblical view of a moment of creation out of nothing, or alternatively as describing a closed system with no boundaries and no need for a Creator. This all opened up new possibilities in debates about divine activity, which continue to be discussed by theologians and scientists (see Drees 1990; Polkinghorne 1994; Russell *et al.* 1999; Saunders 2002). A key danger of which such writers are constantly aware is that they might end up constructing a 'God of the gaps' – in other words, locating God simply in gaps in current scientific knowledge. If those gaps turn out to be temporary ones that disappear with advances in science, rather than being permanent, metaphysical gaps, then the cause of theism will have been weakened rather than strengthened.

Darwinism and design

There is a stark contrast between the images of God and nature suggested by the physical sciences on the one hand and those conjured up by the biological sciences on the other. Physicists have often found it natural to infer the existence of an intelligent designer from the awesome scale and mathematical beauty of the universe, and from the apparent fine-tuning of its fundamental laws and constants, as discovered by modern physics. The biological sciences, on the other hand, deal not with immense expanses of space and time, nor with grand, elegant and satisfying mathematical proofs, but rather with the messy, violent realities of the Darwinian struggle for existence. A famously gruesome example of this struggle is to be found in the case of the parasitic ichneumon wasp. The female ichneumon lays her eggs inside the body of a caterpillar, with the result that, for their first meal, her offspring eat their host alive. Having observed this phenomenon, the young Charles Darwin wrote to a friend: 'What a book a devil's chaplain might write on the clumsy, wasteful, blundering, low, and horribly cruel works of nature!' And since the publication in 1859 of Darwin's book, *On the Origin of Species*, others too have found it harder to discern in the natural world the benign and intelligent Deity of Newton or Paley.

Indeed, for many, the question of evolution, especially human evolution, remains the central one in discussions of religion and science. It is certainly a question that polarises opinion, especially in the United States. Polls have found that about 45 per cent of the population of the US believe that man was created in roughly his present state at some time in the last 10,000 years; about 40 per cent prefer to say that humans were the result of a divinely guided process of evolution; and only about 10 per cent believe that human beings evolved in an entirely natural way over millions of years through a process in which God had no part. Among professional scientists, of course, the vast majority would believe in the minority view – that humans have a common ancestry with all other animals and have evolved in an entirely natural way. The philosophical question of the demarcation of science from pseudo-science takes on a new political urgency in the context of debates about creationism and evolutionism. Creationists, from the early twentieth century onwards, have claimed that the theory of evolution is scientifically unsound and, in reality, is merely a dangerous atheistic ideology dressed up in scientific clothing – a new pied piper leading the children of America into a pit of unbelief and immorality. Evolutionists return the compliment, arguing that 'creation science' is nothing more nor less than fundamentalist Christianity mischievously masquerading as science, in an attempt to confer on itself a bogus academic credibility. Arguments on both sides range from partisan bluster to careful philosophical and scientific argumentation. The most recent incarnation of this debate has focused on the scientific, philosophical and religious credentials of the new 'intelligent design' movement (see Dembski 2004; Shanks 2004). The way that these confrontations are resolved has particularly important implications since what is most often at issue is the practical question of who should determine the content of the science curriculum in public schools, and what should be on it. Thus, deciding how to answer the question of whether the biological sciences reveal a world of design or of chance, of divine purpose or of meaningless strife, continues to have concrete political consequences (see Larson 1997; Numbers 1992; Ruse 2001, 2003).

Science and the soul

While some reactions to Darwinism have centred on the difficulty of reconciling the theory of evolution by natural selection with the teachings of the Bible about the creation of separate species, the sticking point for others has been the question of the existence and status of the human soul. The problem of how to combine an evolutionary understanding of human origins with anything other than a materialistic understanding of the soul is a difficult one. If the brain is the organ of the mind, and the brain, like all our other organs, gradually evolved from much more basic beginnings, it is hard to see how an immaterial or supernatural 'soul' can be inserted into the process. If human beings are nothing more than large-brained apes who live in particularly complex and violent societies, what sense can be made of religious ideas about the dignity or even immortality of the human spirit? Scientific writers from Darwin himself, in *The Descent of Man* (1871), up to popular writers of our own day such as E. O. Wilson and Richard Dawkins, have produced intriguing accounts of the evolutionary origins, and genetic basis, of moral and religious feelings. For many theologians, however, the human soul, created in the image of God, with its faculties of will and intellect, is something that marks human beings out as quite different sorts of creatures from other animals. For them, the soul is the seat of reason and morality, which are both lacked by non-human animals.

It is not only modern evolutionary science that has posed problems for traditional understandings of the soul. Developments in medicine, psychiatry, psychology and neuroscience during the eighteenth and nineteenth centuries had already illustrated ever-closer links between the physical structures of the brain and nervous system and the healthy or pathological functioning of the human mind. As these links were made with ever greater precision and certainty through the twentieth century, theologians were confronted with difficult questions about the relationship between the body, on the one hand, and the mind, soul or spirit on the other (see Watts 2002). The simplest explanation, that all our thoughts and feelings were simply states of the brain, seemed incompatible with religious ideas about an immaterial soul and a freely acting will. One response to these questions was the development of a philosophical position termed 'non-reductive physicalism' (see Brown *et al.* 1998). Proponents of this view favoured a holistic understanding of human nature instead of the sort of soul–body dualism that modern science seemed to make untenable. As well as seeking consonance with scientific views of mind and brain, these writers also invoked biblical teachings about the indissolubility of the soul–body unity to support their case for physicalism, seeing the doctrine of the bodily resurrection, for instance, as more authentically biblical than belief in an immortal and immaterial spirit. In short, Hebrew holism was to be preferred, they said, to Hellenistic dualism. Others still need further convincing that a totally physicalist understanding of human beings can really do justice to traditional religious teachings about the soul.

From theory to practice: technology, ethics, politics

Many academic discussions about religion and science have taken place at an intellectual level. Religion and science are both, however, fundamentally practical activities. They both seek not only to describe the world, but also to change it. The prophetic voice in religion denounces injustices and abuses of the present day and calls for personal and social regeneration, reform, rebirth. Similarly, one of the leading justifications of the funding of scientific research is that it will provide the means of material improvement, for both rich and poor, through all sorts of new technologies, especially in the areas of communications, agriculture and medicine. In their different ways, religion and science both offer salvation. The leading questions driving academic discussions of religion and science have therefore often been about technology, ethics and politics rather than simply about competing intellectual positions. Historically, it has frequently been the spokespeople of religious traditions who have led the way in raising ethical concerns about such practices as experimentation on animals, the use of contraceptives, the development of nuclear weapons, the cloning of human beings or the patenting of genes. Religions can also provide resources for those concerned with ecology and the 'stewardship' of the natural world.

Religion and science both have fraught and ambiguous relationships with the political world. Scientists have often claimed to be ethically neutral creatures, driven only by the pursuit of truth. On this view, it is down to elected politicians or, indeed, religious leaders, to form committees and make decisions about moral and political questions arising from science. Such a simple view, however, does not stand very close scrutiny. All scientific research programmes have to be funded, either commercially or from public money. Such funding generally has strings attached. The decision to accept funding from a pharmaceuticals company, an arms manufacturer or even a charity, a campaign group or a government agency is always an ethical and political one. Scientists have a good deal of cultural and political clout as a result of the status of their profession. That status, in turn, rests very heavily on the belief that scientists are objective and detached, motivated by purer motives than, for instance, party politics or sectarian religious views. One of the most interesting lessons of the history of science is that in the modern world few more powerful rhetorical strategies exist than claiming scientific status for one's political ideology. Laissez-faire individualists, Socialists, Nazis and Communists have all claimed scientific authority for their political creeds. But while scientists and politicians today are quick to denounce such examples from history as perversions of both science and politics, they are not always so quick to notice cases in the present when science and politics have become closely intertwined. Interpreting scientific findings relating to physical and intellectual differences between different races, or between the sexes, for instance, is inevitably a political activity, no matter how much people, on all sides, try to present their case as purely scientific or empirical, while depicting their opponent's case as ideologically loaded.

Connections between religion and politics are similarly double-edged. One of the most important functions of religious leaders has been to draw attention to the failings of political rulers. For such complaints to seem authentic, they must be seen to come from outside the political system itself. While scientists can appeal to the authority of nature and of scientific objectivity, religious writers can invoke a moral, spiritual, even divine authority which is, like the authority of the scientists, based on something beyond and above the messy and corrupt world of human affairs. Indeed, if any single rhetorical strategy has been more effective in political debates through history than the appeal to nature or science, it has been the appeal to God and morality. Disputes over the teaching of evolution and creation science in schools in the United States in the twentieth century illustrate perfectly these complex relationships between religion, science and politics.

Concluding remarks

Even in this brief survey of issues arising in the study of interactions between the worlds of religion and science, we have seen how many different philosophical, theological, ethical and political interpretations can be given to the results of scientific research. From the gruesome habits of the ichneumon wasp to the mysteries of psychic phenomena – from parasitology to parapsychology – there has always been controversy about what the natural can reveal about the divine, and how such revelations should shape our actions. Scientific understandings of the universe and our place in it, together with the technological advances that come with them, will undoubtedly continue to provide material for a wide range of intellectual and political controversies as long as human civilisations survive. Students of 'religion and science', through their attempts to get to grips with the huge variety of engagements to which these fundamental human endeavours have given rise, will perhaps be less surprised than others to find, lying around the cradle of every science in the future, as the strangled snakes beside that of Hercules, extinguished scientists and their defunct research programmes, extinguished ethicists and their superseded philosophies, extinguished politicians and their exploded ideologies and, no doubt, one or two extinguished theologians too.

Further reading

Barbour, Ian (1997), *Religion and Science: Historical and Contemporary Issues*, San Francisco: HarperSanFrancisco (In the UK as: London: SCM Press, 1998). A thorough and wide-ranging survey by one of the central figures in the field.

Brooke, John Hedley (1991), *Science and Religion: Some Historical Perspectives*, Cambridge: Cambridge University Press. An excellent place to start: an erudite, engaging, informative and thought-provoking historical survey.

Brown, Warren S., Nancey Murphy and H. Newton Malony (eds) (1998), *Whatever Happened to the Soul? Scientific and Theological Portraits of Human Nature*, Minneapolis: Fortress Press. A collective attempt to harmonise scientific physicalism with Christian teachings on the soul.

Clark, Stephen (2000), *Biology and Christian Ethics*, Cambridge and New York: Cambridge University Press. A philosophically, historically and theologically sophisticated study of the ethical implications of evolutionary theory and modern biotechnology.

Ferngren, Gary B. (ed.) (2000), *The History of Science and Religion in the Western Tradition: An Encyclopedia*, New York and London: Garland. An invaluable reference work with contributions by leading scholars on historical, philosophical, religious and scientific themes coming right up to the present day and paying attention to particularities of time and place. Also available in condensed form as: Gary B. Ferngren (ed.) (2002), *Science and Religion: A Historical Introduction*, Baltimore, MD: Johns Hopkins University Press.

Larson, Edward J. (1997), *Summer for the Gods: The Scopes Trial and America's Continuing Debate over Science and Religion*, New York: Basic Books. A Pulitzer Prize-winning study, combining a vivid account of the Scopes trial with perceptive broader reflections.

Lindberg, David C. and Ronald L. Numbers (eds) (2003), *When Science and Christianity Meet*, Chicago and London: University of Chicago Press. A recent collection of studies by leading historians in the field, aimed at a broad readership.

Polkinghorne, John (1994), *The Faith of a Physicist*, Princeton, NJ: Princeton University Press (In the UK as: *Science and Christian Belief*, London: SPCK). An engaging and sophisticated study by an eminent theoretical physicist now ordained in the Anglican church.

Post, Stephen G. *et al.* (eds) (2002), *Altruism and Altruistic Love: Science, Philosophy and Religion in Dialogue*, Oxford and New York: Oxford University Press. A substantial interdisciplinary

work seeking answers from scientists, philosophers and theologians to fundamental questions about human nature and human morality.

Ruse, Michael (2003), *Darwin and Design: Does Evolution Have a Purpose?* Cambridge, MA:
Harvard University Press, 2003. A lively guide to debates about Darwinism and design from
the nineteenth century to the present.

Russell, Robert J., Nancey Murphy, Theo C. Meyering and Michael A. Arbib (eds) (1999),
Neuroscience and the Person: Scientific Perspectives on Divine Action, Vatican City State:
Vatican Observatory; Berkeley, CA: Center for Theology and the Natural Sciences. A
collection of reflections, by leading academics from a range of disciplines, on the theological implications of neuroscience.

Saunders, Nicholas (2002), *Divine Action and Modern Science*, Cambridge: Cambridge
University Press. A careful analysis of the theological and scientific issues at stake in discussions of modern physics and God's activity in the world.

Watts, Fraser (2002), *Theology and Psychology*, Aldershot: Ashgate. An engaging and accessible survey of the theological implications of scientific accounts of the human mind, from
evolutionary psychology to artificial intelligence.

Other works cited

Barbour, Ian (1966), *Issues in Science and Religion*, London: SCM Press.

Brooke, John H. (2003), 'Darwin and Victorian Christianity', in Jonathan Hodge and Gregory
Radick (eds), *The Cambridge Companion to Darwin*, Cambridge and New York: Cambridge
University Press, pp. 192–213.

—— and Geoffrey Cantor (1998), *Reconstructing Nature: The Engagement of Science and
Religion*, Edinburgh: T. & T. Clark.

Cantor, Geoffrey and Chris Kenny (2001), 'Barbour's Fourfold Way: Problems with his
Taxonomy of Science-Religion Relationships', *Zygon* 36: 765–81.

Dembski, William A. (2004), *The Design Revolution: Answering the Toughest Questions About
Intelligent Design*, Downers Grove, IL: Intervarsity Press.

Dixon, Thomas (2002), 'Scientific Atheism as a Faith Tradition', *Studies in History and
Philosophy of Biological and Biomedical Sciences*, 33: 337–59.

—— (2003) 'Looking Beyond "The Rumpus about Moses and Monkeys": Religion and the
Sciences in the Nineteenth Century', *Nineteenth-century Studies* 17: 25–33.

Drees, Willem B. (1990), *Beyond the Big Bang: Quantum Cosmologies and God*, La Salle, IL:
Open Court.

—— (1996), *Religion, Science and Naturalism*, Cambridge and New York: Cambridge University Press.

—— (2003), '"Religion and Science" Without Symmetry, Plausibility, and Harmony',
Theology and Science 1: 113–28.

Huxley, Thomas H. (1893), *Collected Essays, Volume 2: Darwiniana*, London: Macmillan.

Knight, Christopher C. (2001), *Wrestling with the Divine: Religion, Science, and Revelation*,
Minneapolis: Fortress Press.

Lindberg, David C. (2003), 'Galileo, the Church, and the Cosmos', in David C. Lindberg
and Ronald L. Numbers (eds), *When Science and Christianity Meet*, Chicago and London:
University of Chicago Press, pp. 33–60.

McGrath, Alister E. (1998), *The Foundations of Dialogue in Science and Religion*, Oxford, UK;
Malden, MA: Blackwell.

Midgley, Mary (2002), *Evolution as a Religion: Strange Hopes and Stranger Fears*, revised edition,
London and New York: Routledge.

Moore, James R. (1979), *The Post-Darwinian Controversies: A Study of the Protestant Struggle
to Come to Terms with Darwin in Great Britain and America, 1870–1900*, Cambridge:
Cambridge University Press.

Murphy, Nancey (1990), *Theology in the Age of Scientific Reasoning*, Ithaca: Cornell University Press.

Numbers, Ronald L. (1992), *The Creationists: The Evolution of Scientific Creationism*, Berkeley and Los Angeles: University of California Press.

Oppenheim, Janet (1985), *The Other World: Spiritualism and Psychical Research in Britain, 1850–1914*, Cambridge: Cambridge University Press.

Peacocke, Arthur (1984), *Intimations of Reality: Critical Realism in Science and Religion*, Notre Dame, IN: University of Notre Dame Press.

—— (1993), *Theology for a Scientific Age: Being and Becoming – Natural, Divine, and Human*, enlarged edition, Minneapolis: Fortress Press (In the UK as: London: SCM Press).

Ruse, Michael (2001), *Can a Darwinian be a Christian? The Relationship Between Science and Religion*, Cambridge and New York: Cambridge University Press.

Russell, Robert J. (2003), 'Bridging Theology and Science: The CTNS Logo', *Theology and Science* 1: 1–3.

Shanks, Niall (2004), *God, the Devil and Darwin: A Crititque of Intelligent Design Theory*, with a foreword by Richard Dawkins, Oxford and New York: Oxford University Press.

Turner, Frank M. (1993), *Contesting Cultural Authority: Essays in Victorian Intellectual Life*, Cambridge: Cambridge University Press.

Chapter 27

Religion and cognition

Luther H. Martin

Whereas the twentieth century has been characterized in terms of biological achievements, culminating with the mapping of the human genome, the twenty-first century is forecast as that of the brain and its relationship to cognition. The understanding of this most complex of human organs and an explanation for its mental functions is a daunting interdisciplinary project that includes evolutionary biologists and psychologists, computer scientists and neuroscientists, linguists and philosophers, researchers into cybernetics and artificial intelligence, as well as social and cultural anthropologists, historians and ethnographers. Researchers from across this broad range of disciplines have already initiated major investigations into how our evolved genetic endowment expresses itself in the physiology of the brain, in its various specialized systems, and in the relationships and interactions of these systems. They are also exploring internal (hormonal and chemical) effects upon these systems as well as the external import of our environment. These researchers anticipate that a comprehensive explanation of our neurological structures and their functions, and how they enable but also constrain our cognitive processes, will be one of the outcomes of this research over the coming century. And they anticipate that this explanation for the workings of our brain will be based solely upon material conditions – including, perhaps, a naturalistic explanation for consciousness itself. This predicted material explanation for mental functions has been termed the identity of 'brain' and 'mind'. In the meantime, cognitive scientists are contributing to this long-term task by focusing on the general properties, organization and functions of human cognition, including those associated with 'religion'.

What is cognitive science?

Cognitive scientists seek to explain the kinds of perceptual and conceptual representations that the mental processing of sensory input allows, the memory, transmission and transformations of these mental representations, the relationships among them, and the ways in which some of these mental representations become public ones. Everything that we perceive and conceive is, of course, the outcome of processing by the human mind. Much mental processing occurs, however, below the threshold of consciousness and, consequently, has only recently become recognized as an area of investigation. For example, human beings perceive their environment as a rich tapestry of color and represent it as such – to ourselves, to others, in decorative and artistic expressions, etc. What we experience as color is not, however, an innate property of objects in our environment, but is the mental representation of our sensory discernment of light waves as they are differentially refracted from these objects. This representational capacity to discern color is an adaptive and evolved function of the human mind – and also of the minds of some other species – to help discriminate, for example, which fauna and flora are good to eat, an ability upon which survival may well depend. The point is that the chromatic representation of our environment is the effect of a significant but non-conscious mental processing of sensory input. And there is any number of additional non-conscious cognitive processes upon which we depend every day and throughout our lives. In other words, non-conscious biocognitive systems control such physiological functions as the regular patterns of heartbeat and breathing, regulate such social proficiencies as instantaneous face recognition, or manage and coordinate complex mental functions such as those that orient us in space and time.

In addition to such non-conscious mental functionings, humans also have the ability of intentional representation, i.e. the ability deliberately to recognize and portray objects or events from our environment, or to recall certain objects or events from our past (from explicitly learned information or from experienced events). And we have the ability to communicate such representations among ourselves and to transmit them over time. We even have the ability to represent objects and events that have no natural existence. Common examples of fabricated and fabulous representations include monsters, unicorns, imaginary friends, the dramatis personae of novels and myths, UFOs and their alien personnel, etc. From the adaptive perspective of natural selection, this ability to imagine allows us to anticipate and plan for possibilities in a projected future.

Finally, we have the ability of metarepresentation – the ability to represent our representations, whether intentionally produced or not, both to ourselves (constituting a component of self-consciousness) and to others (establishing a basis for communication and sociality). It allows us, consequently, to categorize our representations, to compare them with others, to judge them, and to discriminate, thereby, between 'fact' and 'fiction'. This discriminatory capacity allows for a successfully adaptive relationship to our environment as well as for an appreciation and enjoyment of fiction and the creative arts. When this 'critical' ability is activated, however, it often exhibits environmental biases, for example, by relying upon socially transmitted 'common sense' (e.g. stereotypes) or upon ethnocentric cultural values rather than upon intersubjective and lawful criteria, as is the ideal, for example, in scientific inquiry. To the extent that the representational processes of human cognition can be described and their effects mapped, we have a basis for explaining common human capacities for and constraints upon the production of all human mental representations, past and present.

History of cognitive science

Until the mid-nineteenth century, the workings of the human mind were dominated by anecdotal evidence, a legacy of the philosophy of mind tradition that had long privileged first-person accounts of mental activity. This introspective tradition reached a psychological apogee in the psychoanalytic movements of the late nineteenth and early twentieth centuries. With the increasing availability of more advanced medical care during the twentieth century, a more objective alternative proved to be third-person accounts of mental capacities that were based upon neuro-physiological studies of subjects who had survived brain damage or pathology. These studies, along with advances in experimental psychology, showed that first-person accounts were insufficient to explain the increasingly sophisticated insights into the nature of mental processes, and were, in many cases, illusory.

First-person accounts as the basis for understanding mental activity were further challenged by the rise of behavioral psychology and its insistence upon *systematic*, experimental evidence for human behavior. Simply put, the behaviorists considered the human brain to be, at birth, a tabula rasa, or blank slate upon which was writ a cultural input, that, it was concluded, not only might be observed but that could, subsequently, be manipulated (by conditioning or by learning). Scientific controls on the stimulus-response methodology upon which behaviorism depended proved to be, however, imperfect. Even simple sensory stimuli are subject to a wide variety of interpretive responses that, consequently, are not reproducible. And as long as stimuli are capable of arousing a range of human response, they are simply not experimentally neutral.

The most significant challenge to the mind-blind premise of behaviorism were findings that the mental processing abilities of the brain itself contribute to the kinds of mental representations we are able to make. For example, by the mid-twentieth century linguists had concluded that young children exhibit a sophisticated use of syntactic rules in their verbal constructions long before they receive any instruction about these rules. This conclusion about the undetermination of linguistic competence by environmental input is perhaps the single most well-known development contributing to what came to be termed the 'cognitive revolution'. In turn, this conclusion gave focus to other findings that were emerging during this period. Advances in computer technology suggested that the human brain is a computational system for information processing. Developments in information theory itself, which explored how information is encoded and transmitted, offered analogies for how mental information might be encoded and transmitted. And a resurgence in memory research described discrete systems of human memory and the workings and limitations of these different systems. Finally, the development of non-invasive technologies for a direct imaging of brain activity, e.g. positron emission tomography (PET), magnetic resonance imagery (MRI) and functional magnetic resonance imagery (fMRI), contributed to an explosion in brain research during the final decades of the twentieth century.

Why a cognitive science of religion?

When an academic, in contrast to a theological, study of religion was first proposed in the late nineteenth century, it was envisioned, along with such new disciplines as anthropology, history, psychology and sociology, as one of the new human sciences. These human sciences all sought to discover and describe universal laws of human behavior and change. While some anthropological studies of religion did embrace such emergent scientific paradigms as natural selection (although generally misappropriated in terms of the social Darwinism of the time), the study of religion itself steadfastly resisted any scientific basis for its work, preferring instead to retain its theological agendas.

A general disenchantment with the optimistic views of scientific and technological advances, and with the concomitant views of social and cultural progress, followed upon the ravages of the First World War. This disillusionment, together with a correlative recognition of the fallacy of social Darwinism, reinforced the traditional anti-scientism of religious scholars. Ironically, it was again the effects of political history that gave rise to a new focus among the human sciences. As a consequence of the Cold War, many scholars turned their attention to 'area studies' – especially to those areas considered of strategic concern to national securities – and to the unique histories of these areas, to their subjectivities and to the specificities of their cultures, including their religions.

But religious attributions and practices seem to be a human universal. Along with paleoanthropologists, evolutionary biologists and psychologists, cognitivists argue that the representational capacities of and constraints upon the human brain are, like the functioning(s) of any of our organs or systems, the naturally selected consequences of adaptation. And because of our shared evolutionary history, such mental functions are, consequently, common to the species *Homo sapiens* (Tooby and Cosmides 1992; Mithen 1996; Atran 2002). Is religion, therefore, an evolved capacity of humans?

Whereas cognitivists agree that many specifically human capacities, such as sociality and linguistic competence, are explicable as evolutionary products, most consider religion, like any cultural form, to be only understandable as an evolutionary by-product. This conclusion does not diminish the historical and social significance of religion. It does mean, however, that those human capacities that are products of evolution and those cultural productions that are evolutionary by-products are subject to different levels of explanation. Whatever the perceived social or cultural value of religion, there is, in other words, no evolutionary basis, i.e. no reproductive or survivalist (metabolic) mandate, for its development (see, however, Wilson 2002). Even though religion is an evolutionary by-product, it is nevertheless still constrained by the mental 'landscape' of evolved possibilities and is subject, therefore, to 'naturalistic' explanations (Atran 2002). In contrast to supernaturalistic speculations, the possibility for naturalistic explanations lie at the core of all cognitive studies of religion.

The cognitive science of religion

The cognitive science of religion is the application of the findings of cognitive scientists to the study of religious practices and claims. Although a cognitive science of religion was first proposed in 1980 (Guthrie) and has produced a number of applied studies, only a few cognitive theories of religion have actually been proposed. These theories are focused on the areas of religious rituals, religious claims and religious transmission. While there are, of course, significant differences among these three areas of theoretical attention, together they lay the foundation for a comprehensive study of religion from the cognitive perspective.

Religious actions

In 1990, the scholar of comparative religion, E. Thomas Lawson, and his colleague, the philosopher Robert N. McCauley, proposed the first systematically formulated cognitive theory in the area of religion, specifically, a theory of religious ritual

(Lawson and McCauley 1990; McCauley and Lawson 2002). Whatever else religious rituals are, they argued, they are human actions. Consequently, religious rituals can be understood formally in terms of the ways by which humans represent any human action. This 'human action representation system', simply stated, is a set of relations that includes an 'actor' or agent, an 'act' and 'a recipient of the action' (which Lawson and McCauley term 'the patient'). This formal structure, in terms of which all human actions are represented, generates the possibility for two categories of actions – those in which the agent acts upon the patient and those in which the agent is acted upon by the patient (i.e. when the 'patient' is the 'actor').

What qualifies either of these ordinary types of action as religious are culturally postulated claims about the presence of a superhuman agent (or agents) or of their authorized surrogates in this formal structure. What qualifies the agent as superhuman (whether understood in negative or in positive terms, e.g. as a god or as a demon) is an attribution of the intentional ability to accomplish a desirable result considered unobtainable by ordinary means. What qualifies either of these types of religious actions as *ritual* is that something significant is understood to have transpired in the act, again whether the result is viewed as positive (e.g. a blessing) or negative (e.g. a curse). Thus, for example, when a Roman Catholic priest – an authorized surrogate of Jesus – baptizes an infant, that infant is henceforth officially considered to be a member of the Roman Catholic communion.

Lawson and McCauley further contend that the role assigned to superhuman agents determines certain predictable features of all religious ritual. When a superhuman agent, or the surrogate of a superhuman agent, is represented as the actor, what Lawson and McCauley term 'special agent rituals', then that act, as an action of superhuman agency, is understood to be altogether effectual and, as such, requires little or no repetition. It is, however, typically invested with memorable emotional salience, as, e.g. a wedding. If, on the other hand, a superhuman agent is not represented as the actor but as the recipient of the action, what Lawson and McCauley term 'special patient rituals', then the effects of that action will be less permanent and, consequently, they must be repeated more frequently. Periodic sacrifices or weekly offerings are examples of such special patient rituals. And in contrast to the heightened sensory pageantry of special agent rituals, Lawson and McCauley predict that the regular performance and consequent routinization characteristic of special patient rituals will result in a diminution of their emotional salience.

Lawson and McCauley readily acknowledge the limits of their theory. It addresses only religious rituals while (deliberately) avoiding the wider issues in the study of religion, and it offers a view of religious ritual which may exclude from their analysis other forms of religious action that do not conform to their model, such as prayer. Their very careful formulations, however, are the strength of the theory. Whereas religious scholars have heretofore understood ritual as an inclusive designation for sets of repetitive and patterned behavior, the Lawson and McCauley theory differentiates religious from otherwise ordinary kinds of human behavior, while explaining the common cognitive basis of both. Further, their theory differentiates among kinds of religious rituals that have often been viewed synoptically as aspects of a single ritual, e.g. the Roman Catholic Mass. And, finally, the Lawson and McCauley theory of religious ritual brings to the study of religion an analytical precision previously absent from religious studies.

Religious ideas

If ordinary human actions are predicated as 'religious' by claims to such ideas as those about superhuman agents, then the basis for such ideas must themselves be accounted for. The anthropologist Pascal Boyer has argued that ideas such as superhuman agency, documented from virtually every human society, are in fact as 'natural' as are the actions they predicate; such 'counterintuitive' ideas are, in other words, readily and easily produced by our ordinary cognitive equipment (Boyer 2001). Thus, the fundamental concept of 'agent' as a self-motivating, intentional object in the world is distinguished from inanimate objects already by infants. This innate (or at least developmentally very early) ability or propensity to distinguish intentional agency becomes generalized as the tendency to represent objects and events in our environments anthropomorphically, i.e. in terms of human features and attributes (Guthrie 1993).

Anthropomorphism is such an exquisitely tuned feature of our cognitive processing that we often conclude there is agency all around us, which of course there is, even when, however, no agent may actually be present (e.g. faces in the clouds, bumps in the night, etc.). There is, of course, an adaptive survival advantage for any organism to be able to react quickly, even automatically (i.e. non-consciously) to incomplete information from its environment, such as the fleeting perception of an unexplained movement, since this information may indicate the presence of a predator or foe. Even if it turns out, upon reflection, that the inferred presence was that of a friend or even incorrect – a blowing in the wind, as it were – 'it is better to be safe', the old adage holds, 'than sorry'.

There is, in other words, little cognitive difference between attributing agency to actual, intentional agents (friend or foe) and to non-agentic effects, especially when they are deemed to be potentially significant for our lives. And if otherwise inexplicable events are judged significant for our lives, again whether those effects are positive or negative, it is natural to conclude that they also may be the instigation of unexplainable, i.e. of superhuman, agency.

The category of agency belongs to what cognitivists refer to as our 'intuitive ontology', that is to say, to universal human expectations about the world. Thus, when an idea like superhuman agent is introduced, a great deal of information is already inferred about those agents, apart from any learned knowledge. Because of the capacity of the human mind to entertain the realm of possibility as well as to represent actuality, these categories are, in the absence of complete information, sometimes 'violated'. A common example in which the category of agent or person is violated to generate a superhuman agent is that of ghosts. Ghosts are ordinary agents in most expectations. They are, for example, intentional beings who act and react in terms of expected sensory information, e.g. sight, sound, smell, touch, they exist in time and hold memories of the past, they communicate and can be communicated with, etc. However, they also manifest a few unexpected characteristics, such as the capability of invisibility or of walking through physical barriers such as walls. Whereas such counterintuitive beliefs and claims about ghosts violate ordinary expectations about agents, they are not so excessive as to be judged bizarre (like the Godzilla of Japanese film) and dismissed, thereby, as a fantasy or as a popular diversion (at least, not by many). Such violations are, in other words, attention-grabbing and, consequently, highly memorable and readily transmissible while being, at the same time, ordinary enough to be easily accepted and readily understood (Boyer

2001). Most of the Christian Bible, for example, contains a collection of rather mundane, some might even say boring, stories – genealogies, family intrigues, accounts of kings and battles, insightful but unexceptional teachings, etc. – rendered memorable, however, by 'acts (and words) of God' that are interspersed throughout. It is these 'acts (and words)' attributed to God (or to His Son) that attract and retain the attention of Christians, many of whom admit never having read the 'ordinary' portions of the Bible at all.

In addition to an 'agent' (or person), cognitivists also refer to intuitive categories of 'substances' or 'physical objects', both natural and man-made, of 'animals' and 'plants' (Boyer 2001; Atran 2002). By investing any of these ordinary categories with some qualities that defy expectations, attention is drawn to the information embedded in the violated categories and that information tends, thereby, to be selected for and considered more valuable than others in the marketplace of possible human ideas.

Religious persistence

Initial occasions for attributing superhuman intentionality to effects considered to be especially meaningful often prove to be historically inaccessible or, if known, of little significance – that is to say, any number of ambiguous possibilities can provoke representations of superhuman intentionality. Is the hearing of voices, for example, to be interpreted as a divine call or as schizophrenia? Do feelings of exaltation indicate spirituality or mania? Are sensations of internal fullness the consequence of overeating or of possession by a superhuman agent? And if possession by a superhuman agent, is it by God or the Devil, the symptoms of which, according to Roman Catholic doctrine, are identical? Whereas naturalistic explanations for such experiences garner little attention, their interpretations as counterintuitive or religious are at least noticeable and, once introduced, tend to be transmitted in predictable ways. Cognitivists are interested in these modes of transmission.

The anthropologist Harvey Whitehouse has identified two divergent modes of religious transmission which he terms 'imagistic' and 'doctrinal' (Whitehouse 2004). The 'imagistic mode of religiosity' does not refer, in Whitehouse's description, to religious traditions that trade in images – a trait of virtually all religions. Rather, 'imagistic' is Whitehouse's designation for a convergence of practices by which religious knowledge is transmitted through infrequently performed rituals that – like Lawson's and McCauley's special agent rituals – are rendered especially memorable through intense sensory pageantry and heightened emotionality. The dramatic, often traumatic, character of these rituals (e.g. of some initiation rites) typically occasions a personal and spontaneous exegesis of that experience among its participants as well as an enduring cohesion among them in small, face-to-face communities. By contrast, Whitehouse contends that an alternative clustering of variables characterizes a 'doctrinal' mode of religiosity. Religious knowledge in this mode is formulated as a coherent set of 'orthodox' beliefs or doctrines maintained by a dynamic and hierarchically organized leadership. This coherent corpus of teachings is transmitted by repetitive and routinized instruction that supports the retention of these teachings and allows for their wide dissemination by authorized teachers and missionaries. The widespread distribution of religious knowledge that is characteristic of this mode of religiosity is constitutive of large, imagined communities – mainstream Protestantism, for example

– in which group affinities are largely anonymous. While this doctrinal modality may be found in non-literate contexts, it is more often characteristic of literate societies or of those influenced by them.

The transmission of religious knowledge involves processes of memory and these processes are selective – we don't remember everything nor do we remember anything in the same way. The two modes of religious transmission proposed by Whitehouse rely on and are constrained by different systems of memory that are selected by the alternative ways in which religious knowledge is encoded and by the different forms of ritual transmission. The catechetical instruction in and the repetitive reinforcement of beliefs that are characteristic of the doctrinal mode of religiosity are encoded in the explicit memory system as generalized scripts or schemas of knowledge and are transmitted as coherent systems of belief. The unique and personalized experiences characteristic of the imagistic mode are, on the other hand, encoded in episodic or autobiographical memory, the contents of which are only recalled by the rememberer when presented with stimuli associated with his/her own participation in a particular event. This remembered material is organized (and transmitted) only in terms of those personal associations and not in terms of any shared belief system.

A particularly salient type of episodic memory, sometimes referred to as 'flash-bulb' memory, often results from participation in a particularly traumatic or consequential event. This effect is especially characteristic of the abrupt and overwhelming emotional experience that is a feature of many initiation rites both ancient and modern, e.g. initiations among the Hellenistic mystery cults, a number of tribal societies, contemporary 'fundamentalist' religious groups, pseudo-religious fraternal organizations or revolutionary cells. Such events tend to create strong memories that, while incomplete, nevertheless retain many details that are especially long lasting.

Religious traditions – like any cultural materials – are collective or public products of cultural input only as that input has been processed by individual minds. The anthropologist Dan Sperber has acknowledged this cognitive in contrast to cultural processing and has emphasized that the transmission of religious knowledge is from mind to mind. Such transmission also inevitably involves the transformation by which 'remembered' traditions are, at the same time, the consequence of constructive cognitive processes (Sperber 1996). This transformative inevitability is illustrated, at a non-profound level, by the children's game known variously as 'Chinese Whispers' or 'Telephone' in which a message that is whispered from one person to another around the room becomes transformed, sometimes radically, by the time it reaches the final participant. Anything significant enough to be encoded in neural networks may also be considered significant enough to be inscribed and conserved in material culture as well (Debray 2000). Such inscribings – from the first flint tools to writing itself – provide way stations for the continuing mnemonic and reflexive traditions of transmission and exegesis.

Related theoretical initiatives

Cognitive theories of religious behavior, religious ideas and religious persistence have generated, and continue to generate, a wealth of experimental, analytic and applied research. Related research from the social sciences, remain, however, relatively unexploited by cognitivists, e.g. that of ethology and sociobiology.

Ethologists employ animal behavior as a basis for explaining the cultural – including the religious – behavior of humans. Sociobiologists seek to explain both animal and human behavior on the basis of evolutionary history and genetic makeup. The reason these approaches have been neglected is that both sociobiologists and ethologists have tended to overstate their case by suggesting direct, causal relationships between their data and culture. In other words, they take little account of intermediate steps such as the cognitive in the complex process of cultural production. On the other hand, fundamental conclusions by sociobiologists – those about the genetic basis for and consequent constraints upon human sociality, for example – concur with similar conclusions by cognitivists, such as those based on the constraints of short-term memory upon optimal group size. And ethological research, especially primatology, offers a wealth of insight concerning human cognitive potentialities and their evolutionary basis.

The role of emotion in religion should also be mentioned. Emotion (and its related senses of 'significant experience' or 'emotion-laden thought and perception') is, today, perhaps the single most widespread popular 'theory' of religion. Religions have their origin, or their 'essence', according to this view, in religious experience or in feelings of spirituality, the paradigm of which is mysticism. Whereas this popular view is largely a Protestant theological sentiment about the importance of an inward experience of grace in contrast to ecclesiastical and institutional externalities, religious claims and practices are universally correlated with heightened emotional display. Although the significance of emotion for religion has been acknowledged in connection with 'special agent rituals' and with the mnemonic strategies of the 'imagistic' mode of religious transmission, a comprehensive theory of the relation between emotion and religious cognition has yet to be fully undertaken (but see Pyysiäinen 2004: v).

The significance of cognitive science for the study of religion

What exactly can a cognitive science of religion contribute to the study of religion that has otherwise been lacking? A cognitive science of religion cannot, of course, explain all religious data. While, for example, cognitive science has little to say about the claimed meanings of specific cultural constructions, it *can* explain the ubiquity of religion among virtually all human societies, past and present. It can offer naturalistic explanations for the similarities that have long been noted among the diversities of religious expressions. It can offer explanations for the modes of transmission and conservation employed by those particular constructions and for individual commitments to them. And it can express these explanations with some precision in ways that are testable. For example, the cognitive theories of religious behavior, of religious ideas, and of religious persistence that have been previously discussed, have all been, and continue to be, the objects of experimental research by developmental and cognitive psychologists as well as being subject to systematic assessments by anthropologists, archaeologists and historians. Results of this research to date broadly confirm the predictions of cognitive theories of religion (Barrett 2004; Whitehouse 2004; Whitehouse and Laidlaw 2004; Whitehouse and Martin 2004).

In addition to proposing specifically *cognitive theories of religion*, the cognitive sciences can also contribute to three issues in the larger study of religion. They can help to define the kinds of data that might be included – and excluded – from such an area of study, they can provide a framework for organizing and evaluating the history of religions, and they can offer a non-ethnocentric basis for comparing religions.

Defining 'religion'

A comprehensive definition of religion – and consequently the focus and scope of its study – has long been debated. Proposals for such a definition have ranged from those with parochial (theological or confessional) biases, to those with a universalizing but still quasi-theological ('sacred' or 'spiritual') basis, to those shaped, however unintentionally, by Western conceptual categories (such as philosophical dualism) and/or political policies (colonialism). On the other hand, some functionalist definitions of religion (such as 'ultimate concern') are so broad as to include virtually anything and exclude nothing. Some recent scholars have even conceded defeat in the definitional endeavor and advocate collapsing the study of religion into that of culture(s) – posing then, of course, the even more daunting task of defining 'culture'.

There is, of course, no disembodied 'thing' as 'religion' out there for which a 'correct' definition might be agreed. 'Religion', however, is no less susceptible to definition as an *analytic category* than are other domains of culture. Analytic, in contrast to representational, categories must be theoretically formulated in a clear and explicit manner (which is not to say that representational categories don't present their own theoretical problems) and, consequently, be subject to assessment as to their validity and serviceability rather than simply be idiosyncratically confessed or asserted.

From a cognitivist perspective, a definition for what counts as 'religious' data can be stipulated, as we have seen, as those mental representations or set of mental representations that involve or make claims on the authority of superhuman (or counterintuitive) agents. In some form or another, such claims seems to be a human universal. This definition, adapted from E. B. Tylor's classic 'minimum definition of religion',[1] has the advantage of stipulating what religion is *not*. Ideologies such as Marxism, for example, are excluded from considerations of religion, as are world views such as Freudianism, and those patterned, repetitive human acts characteristic of such sports as football and often analyzed as 'ritual'. Whatever the functional similarities to religious ideas and practices that may be exhibited by such cultural expressions, they make no place for or claim to superhuman agency.

Further, the minimum definition of religion differentiates those representations commonly considered the domain of religion from other social functions. Many have argued, for example, that religion provides the basis for morality within human societies. The case of ancient Greece, however, where representations of deities exhibited a wide moral latitude in contrast to the ethical authority of the philosophers, provides a familiar historical example in which religion and morality are not necessarily associated. Rather, evolutionary biologists have argued that morality is the expression of evolved behavioral tendencies, however such tendencies become codified in particular contexts. They refer to such behavior as mutual altruism, an innate sense of fairness or justice, an ability to detect cheaters, etc. Rather than religion providing the basis for morality, it seems more likely that a 'natural' human morality provides the evolutionary basis for a social elaboration and religious reinforcement of ethical codes (Boyer 2001).

Some may object that the minimalist definition of religion also excludes certain forms of 'atheistic' religious thought, such as Buddhist, Taoist or Confucian. However, anyone with minimal experience – even as tourists – 'in the field' will recognize that the actual practices of the overwhelming majority of participants in such traditions involve a recognition of and devotion to superhuman agency. Such 'atheistic' beliefs, if held at all, are espoused by a relatively small number of intellectuals in these traditions. In fact, cognitivists have demonstrated that a dissonance between intellectual adherence and actual practice is a common feature of all religions. Confessional acceptance of a deity as omniscient, for example, does not negate a confessor's impulse to convey information to that deity through prayer (Barrett 2004; Slone 2004).

But how are those superhuman agents considered by a particular culture to be 'religious' to be distinguished from the proliferation of other counterintuitive agents that are 'naturally' produced by the mind but held by that same culture to be insignificant? How are gods to be distinguished from figures of folklore such as ghosts or demons, from popular cultural diversions such as Mickey Mouse or Superman? How are the 'true' (culturally accepted) deities to be distinguished from 'false' gods, from 'inauthentic' newly revealed deities or from alien 'imposters' imported from another cultural context?

In addition to Tylor's minimal definition of religion, an additional 'Durkheimian' caveat stipulates that religious representations are those that are bestowed with a clearly defined 'costliness' (in terms of time, labor, cognitive effort, etc.) not characteristic of other postulated claims and practices.[2] This cultural endowment of value on some but not on all available counterintuitive agents, based on judgments about their significance, can further differentiate what are considered to be religious practices and ideas from postulations of alternative superhuman agents within a particular context.

The stipulation of religious data as costly claims to the authority of superhuman agency emphasizes that the study of religion requires no privileged approach or method but rather is the study of ordinary human activities of attribution, the 'supernatural' inflections of which prove to be quite natural (Boyer 2001). Ironically, this cognitively informed definition of religion returns to and builds upon proposals by the nineteenth-century founders of a scientific study of religion, but it contributes a naturalistic foundation, a theoretical formulation and an analytic precision that are absent from earlier definitions. It is this more precise definition, whether universally accepted or not, that nevertheless provides a clearly stipulated subject, heretofore absent, for historical and comparative studies of religion.

The historical study of religions

In addition to providing historians of religion with a clearly defined theoretical object, cognitive science can provide them with a common human framework for explaining and understanding past expressions of religion. Cognitive archeologists and evolutionary psychologists have taught us that the fundamental architecture of human cognition is the product of our evolutionary history. The capacities and constraints that are characteristic of this organic architecture, consequently, can allow historians to discriminate between and organize their data in ways that are consonant with differences in human cognitive processes rather than conflating such data as the singular product of a common time and place. Thus, the different types of rituals described by Lawson and McCauley or the divergent modes of religious transmission described by Whitehouse may well support differing configurations of data within a common cultural context that may generate different histories. For example, a particular religion judged to be an example Whitehouse's description of an imagistic mode of religiosity might well have a history incommensurable with that of one judged to be doctrinal – even if those two histories have conventionally been considered of the 'same' tradition. Or the successful spread and establishment of one religion in the face of its alternatives might be explicable in terms of its adopted modality rather than in terms of its contents, which, in a common cultural context, are likely to be similar.

Further, cognitive science can contribute insights into how and why some historical events and representations but not others that may have been historically possible were selected (remembered) and how they were transmitted over time. For example, the acceptance of a new or imported religion might be attributed, in part at least, to the balancing appeal of one type of ritual form – special agent or special patient ritual, for example – in face of a relative absence of the other type from the traditional ritual system. Or the successful spread of a new religion might be attributed to its balance between these ritual forms or contribute to such a balance within a common cultural context.

The historical record is, in other words, not only limited by historical antecedents but by cognitive constraints. Based upon the predictable patterns of the latter, historians can construct historical trajectories that can help to fill in the gaps of historical knowledge – even when the historical data are incomplete or fragmentary, as is the case, of course, with most historical data. And they can do so with greater accuracy and with more nuance than they could if working from historical remains alone. Such a pursuit has already begun to produce significant research in the historical study of religion (see e.g. Whitehouse and Martin 2004).

The comparative study of religion

The nineteenth-century scholarly recognition of different religious traditions from around the world and the desire in some way to compare these historical traditions provided the very impetus for founding the academic study of religion. For many, this comparative perspective is what defined – and continues to define – the academic study of religion. If, however, our own past is, as the saying goes, a foreign country, how much more so is the past – and the present – of others. Unlike historians of religion, whose theoretical object is a particular religious tradition or several within a common cultural context, comparativists must question what, in any cross-cultural comparison, is in fact comparable?

As scholars of religion began to amass detailed knowledge of the various cultures of the world and of their local religious traditions and expressions, they produced ever-growing compilations of their 'phenomenal' characteristics. The emphasis on cultural studies in the latter half of the twentieth century revealed that the innumerable traits cataloged in these phenomenologies of religion were largely organized in Western, if not specifically of Christian, categories. Such scholarly biases, together with a focus on the autonomy of particular cultural formations, correctly called the comparative method into question.

It is simply unproductive, if not completely misleading, to compare, for example, a ritual from one culture with those from others, especially when that 'ritual' is more likely to be constitutive of a ritual set within which are embedded a number of different ritual forms. The kinds of ritual forms identified by comparativists can, however, be differentiated within a cultural ritual system and, as examples of a common 'human action representation systems', these forms and their cognitive functions *are* comparable from culture to culture. It is similarly unproductive to attempt to conflate divergent modes of religiosity, whether within the same culture or between different cultures. However, well-documented cases of one or the other of these religious modalities may well offer insight into a less well-documented instance of the same modality.

The evolved capacities and constraints of human cognition can, in other words, provide a blueprint of universal human possibilities in terms of which the vast diversity of human cultures – and their religious expressions – have been historically and socially constructed. And this cognitive blueprint of human possibilities can provide a non-ethnocentric framework for comparing the diverse architecture of cultural forms constructed upon it and, consequently, a common basis for the comparative studies of religion (see e.g. Whitehouse and Laidlaw 2004).

A comparative study of religions cannot, in other words, be pursued productively at the level of their cultural expressions and meanings but must be based in the generative level of their cognitive structure. Starkly put, any study of religion, past or present, must be a scientific study of religion.

Challenges and conclusion

The cognitive sciences are a relatively new area of study. They have, however, firmly established their basic principles and are poised to make dramatic breakthroughs over the coming century, both in new areas of discovery and application as well as in an integration of their fundamental theoretical premises. This is no less the case with the even more recent cognitive science of religion. As with any new discipline, however, basic challenges remain.

Challenges

If the cognitive sciences, including the cognitive science of religion, are to realize a comprehensive set of scientific explanations, then the relationship of cognitive organization and function to its biological base, to neurochemical/hormonal effects, etc., must ultimately be clarified. While cognitivists acknowledge the neurophysiological basis of cognition, the present state of knowledge does not yet allow for a comprehensive modeling of this relationship – although plausible theories are being proposed and significant research is beginning to emerge. Different memory functions, for example, have been associated with specific areas of the brain. The exact neural mechanisms of these areas for producing what we experience as memory are, however, considerably less well understood.

On the other hand, caution must be exercised about interpreting neurophysiological functions – those revealed by brain imaging – for example, as causal rather than
as correlative data for cultural phenomena such as religious experiences or states of
mind. This identity of particular mental representations with neurophysiological
activity neglects mediating levels of cognitive functioning as well as the individuated significance of environmental states for those mental representations and their
transmission. Such correlative data have even been evoked as proofs for the objective validity of specific religious claims, a fallacy of the so-called neurotheology that
is also characteristic of many sociobiological and ethological conclusions about
religious practices and ideas.

If a comprehensive explanation for the organization and functions of human cognition based upon the material conditions of brain activity has not yet been fully
realized, neither has a comprehensive explanation for the connection between cognition and culture. If cognitive science is finally to be applicable to a study of 'religion',
then those cognitive processes that generate cultural formations, such as the
'religious', must also be clarified further.

Although cognitivists readily acknowledge that religion cannot be explained solely
from a cognitive perspective, scholars who have devoted their professional life to the
validity of cultural studies have questioned, least constructively, the reductionistic
character of cognitive studies and, more positively, the precise nature of the connections between cognition and culture. Some of these scholars, who nevertheless wish
to include human cognition in their considerations, have been drawn to theories
that are less reductive than those previously discussed. Such theories emphasize,
rather, cognitive activities that are more congenial to conventional cultural studies,
those associated with narrativity and imagination, for example (e.g. Turner 1996;
Fauconnier and Turner 2002).

Of the first, reductionistic, concern, it might simply be noted that, from a scientific perspective, theoretical reduction (in contrast to a reduction of the data) is what
is recognized as progress in knowledge. The second concern about a theoretical
disconnect between cognition and culture seems to arise from perceptions that cognitivists are neglecting culture in favor of researches into the significance of cognition.
This is a somewhat surprising concern since leading cognitive scientists of religion
have, in fact, addressed and emphasized just this connection and have offered plausible if novel suggestions for how this connection is made (e.g. Sperber 1996; Lawson
and McCauley 1990; Boyer 2001; Atran 2002; Whitehouse 2004). If comprehensive
suggestions for the exact connections between cognition and culture remain tentative, it is because cognitive science is a new science, and it is important for this new
science to map precisely the forms and functions of human cognition before they
are connected to anything. And although they may have to relinquish certain of
their conventional presumptions, about the *sui generis* autonomy of culture, for
example (Tooby and Codmides 1992; Atran 2002), social and cultural theorists are
as capable of addressing the connection between cognition and culture as are cognitivists – a potential contribution presciently noted by one of the founders of
sociological studies.[3]

Conclusion

Religious actions derive from the basic repertoire of ordinary human behavior that are predicated by counterintuitive ideas that are, in turn, the natural products of human cognition. The ready grasp of such ideas and behaviors from a very early age attests to this 'naturalness', i.e. to the cognitive ease whereby they are produced and to the readiness of our cognitive acceptance of, and even commitment to, their cultural valuations and manipulations. Despite the predictions of many social scientists, consequently, it is unlikely that religiosity will ever wither away from, at least some of, the activities and ideas of our species. Because of this naturalness, however, religious ideas and behavior continue to persist as an 'intuitive' category of religious scholars and as part of their culture. Culturally based studies of 'religion' have proved, consequently, to be unproductive as an academic pursuit, especially in any scientific sense envisioned by its founders. The cognitive science of religion, on the other hand, can approach such questions theoretically, formulating generalizable answers as intersubjectively testable predictions, not only by experimentalists but also by ethnographic and historical assessment. Such a study, like the cognitive sciences generally, is an incredibly broad field of interdisciplinary research and study; its achievements will be those of a community of scholars working together over the coming decades.

Notes

1   E. B. Tylor's well-known 'minimum definition of Religion' is 'the Belief in Spiritual Beings' (E. B. Tylor, *Primitive Culture, Part II: Religion in Primitive Culture*. New York: Harper & Brothers, 1958, p. 8).

2   For Durkheim, religion 'always presupposes that the worshipper gives some of his substance or his goods to the gods' (Émile Durkheim, *The Elementary Forms of the Religious Life*, trans. J. W. Swain. New York: The Free Press, 1915, p. 385).

3   'Society exists and lives only in and through . . . individual minds', Durkheim wrote. 'If . . . the beliefs, traditions and aspirations of the group were no longer felt and shared by the individuals, society would die' (Durkheim, ibid., p. 359).

Bibliography

Atran, Scott (2002) *In Gods We Trust: The Evolutionary Landscape of Religions*. Oxford and New York: Oxford University Press. A comprehensive view of religion as an evolutionary by-product, by a leading cultural anthropologist.

Barrett, Justin L. (2004) *Why Would Anyone Believe in God?* Walnut Creek, CA: AltaMira Press. An examination of religious ideas about god(s) by an experimental psychologist.

Boyer, Pascal (2001) *Religion Explained: The Evolutionary Origins of Religious Thought*. London: Heineman and New York: Basic Books. A comprehensive view of religion, and one of the most important, by an anthropologist who is one of the pioneers of the cognitive science of religion.

Debray, Régis (2000) *Transmitting Culture*, trans. E. Rauth. New York: Columbia University Press. An argument for the significance of material culture as a mnemonic aid.

Fauconnier, Gilles and Mark Turner (2002) *The Way We Think: Conceptual Blending and the Mind's Hidden Complexities*. New York: Basic Books. A study of conceptual blending (and reblending) as the basis of human imagination.

Guthrie, Stewart (1980) 'A Cognitive Theory of Religion', *Current Anthropology*, 21 (2): 181–203.

——— (1993) *Faces in the Clouds: A New Theory of Religion*. Oxford and New York: Oxford University Press. A view of religion as an innate tendency of humans to anthropomorphize their environment, by a cultural anthropologist.

Lawson, E. Thomas and McCauley, Robert N. (1990) *Rethinking Religion: Connecting Cognition and Culture*. Cambridge: Cambridge University Press. A cognitively generated theory of religious ritual and one of the most important theories for the cognitive science of religion, by two of the pioneers in the field.

McCauley, Robert N. and Lawson, E. Thomas (2002) *Bringing Ritual to Mind: Psychological Foundations of Cultural Forms*. Cambridge: Cambridge University Press. An important continuation and extension of the arguments presented in Lawson and McCauley 1990.

Mithen, Steven (1996) *The Prehistory of the Mind: The Cognitive Origins of Art and Science*. London: Thames & Hudson. A fascinating and highly plausible reconstruction of the evolution of the human mind, by a cognitive archaeologist.

Pyysiäinen, Ilkka (2004) *Magic, Miracles, and Religion: A Scientist's Perspective*. Walnut Creek, CA: AltaMira Press. A comprehensive overview of the cognitive science of religion to date.

Slone, D. Jason (2004) *Theological Incorrectness: Why Religious People Believe What They Shouldn't*. Oxford and New York: Oxford University Press. A brief and accessible introduction to the cognitive science of religion, with examples and applications from Buddhism and Christianity.

Sperber, Dan (1996) *Explaining Culture: A Naturalistic Approach*. Oxford and Cambridge, MA: Blackwell. An important and influential theory of culture and of cultural transmission based on the micro-processes of human cognition, by a cultural anthropologist.

Tooby, John and Cosmides, Leda (1992) 'The Psychological Foundations of Culture'. In *The Adapted Mind: Evolutionary Psychology and the Generation of Culture*, J. H. Barkow, L. Cosmides, J. Tooby, eds. Oxford and New York: Oxford University Press, pp. 19–136. This classic article is the 'charter' for an evolutionary approach to the study of cultural phenomena.

Turner, Mark (1996) *The Literary Mind: The Origins of Thought and Language*. New York: Oxford University Press. Argues that a basic principle of the mind is story or narrativity and that linguistic competence derives from this principle.

Whitehouse, Harvey (2004) *Modes of Religiosity: A Cognitive Theory of Religious Transmission*. Walnut Creek, CA: AltaMira Press. An important and influential theory of different modes of culture and of cultural transmission, especially religious, by a leading cultural anthropologist.

——— and Laidlaw, James A., eds (2004) *Ritual and Memory: Towards a Comparative Anthropology of Religion*. Walnut Creek, CA: AltaMira Press. An exploration by anthropologists of comparative studies based in the cognitive sciences.

——— and Martin, Luther H., eds (2004) *Theorizing Religions Past: Archaeology, History, and Cognition*. Walnut Creek, CA: AltaMira Press. An exploration by archeologists and historians of historical approaches to religion based in the cognitive sciences.

Wilson, David Sloan (2002) *Darwin's Cathedral: Evolution, Religion, and the Nature of Society*. Chicago: The University of Chicago Press. An evolutionary argument for religious groups as culturally evolved adaptations, by an eminent biologist/anthropologist.

For recent overviews of the field of the cognitive science of religion, with good Bibliographies, see Ilkka Pyysiäinen, *How Religion Works: Towards a New Cognitive Science of Religion*. Leiden: E. J. Brill, 2001; and Pyysiäinen, Ikka *Magic, Miracles, and Religion: A Scientist's Perspective*. Walnut Creek, CA: AltaMira Press, 2004.

For specialized topics in the cognitive sciences, see *The MIT Encyclopedia of the Cognitive Sciences*, R. A. Wilson and F. C. Keil, eds. Cambridge, MA: The MIT Press, 1999.

Chapter 28

Religion and culture

Mark Hulsether

How do we begin to consider a subject so broad as 'religion and culture'? Starting from common usages of the term 'culture,' one could make an umbrella category covering every topic in this book. At the least, this umbrella would encompass religion and the arts, religion and anthropology, and postmodernism and the study of religion. Beyond this, cultural analysis commonly refers to work on language and other forms of symbolic communication: textual studies, linguistics, theology, ritual studies, and media studies. By extension, culture may refer to anything that we can analyze like a language (including dreams, conventions of visual art, or universal structures of cognition), read as a cultural text (including material artifacts, forms of entertainment, or social dramas such as revolutions), or understand as a discourse (including systems of law and medicine, sexual practices, or issues of colonialism).

Obviously, scholars who can claim expertise in 'religion and culture' have a license to pursue many fascinating topics. Unfortunately, this also means that the term 'culture' can lose all precision. By taking culture as our subject, we enter a zone in which it is hard to draw lines between anthropology, literature, history, sociology, philosophy, ethnic studies, and media studies. The idea of 'cultural studies' can dissolve into 'all studies with a foot somewhere in the humanities.' At an extreme, one UNESCO discussion about cultural policy failed because, for some participants, 'culture permeated the whole social fabric and its role was so pre-eminent . . . that it might indeed be confused with life itself' (Tomlinson 1991: 5).

This essay explores some of the key things that 'studying culture' means in the field of religious studies. It is divided into three sections: approaches from the social sciences, approaches from the study of arts and literature, and reflections on the relations between culture and religion. The point is not that any given reader should aspire to use all the approaches we will discuss. In fact, one cannot use all of them, at least at the same time. The goal is to help readers clarify which subfields of religion and culture best address their specific concerns.

Let us begin with two simple questions. First, can we identify any aspects of life that are more 'cultural' than others, toward which 'cultural analysis' directs our attention? If not, then culture refers to everything in general but nothing in particular, and we would be better off abandoning the term; there would be no difference between 'cultural practice' and 'practice' or 'cultural interpretation' and 'interpretation.' Second, suppose we can answer the first question in ways that offer a focus for analysis – but we can give numerous answers that are mutually exclusive. Are some of these answers more useful than others?

Two common-sense responses to the first question will provide our center of gravity: cultures can be understood as whole ways of life, or as especially valorized literature and art. However, there are complications. These approaches are often defined in opposition to each other. Moreover, some critics suggest that anyone who thinks with these approaches will overstress social consensus and moral regulations, underplay struggles for power and changes over time, and obscure aspects of life that cut across multiple groups. In light of such critiques, cultural theory has become a battlefield on which some scholars repudiate the idea of using culture as an analytical category at all. In response, other scholars refine the concept to give greater attention to history, power, and difference as part of cultural analysis. Meanwhile, some people have begun to use the name 'cultural studies' for a specific movement within this larger field. We must try to clarify all these matters.

Turning to my second question – whether some ways of studying culture are better than others – we will assume that approaches have varying strengths and weaknesses. There are good reasons to use certain approaches for specific purposes. However, no one can offer such reasons from a value-free standpoint outside culture. Determining what counts as a strength emerges from the processes of debate and struggle within specific contexts – what scholars call 'cultural contestation.' Does it reflect wisdom or elitist irrelevance to valorize canons of high culture as strongholds of spiritual insight and social critique, distinct from popular culture? Does it demonstrate minimal competence or disreputable arrogance to discuss the rise of human civilization or the need for cultural consensus? Are scholars who explore what is changing under postmodern conditions trendy nihilists? Are scholars passé if they do not explore such changes? Such disagreements are pervasive in current debates. The main issue at stake is not whether Professor X or Y does a better job at studying a given problem, but the strengths and weaknesses of different forms of inquiry.

The fascination and frustration of working in the field of religion and culture is its lack of agreement about how to judge such issues. True, we can clarify a range of approaches and analyze it with as much fair-mindedness as we can muster, given our human limitations. We can resist the temptation to use the complexity of our world as an excuse to replace critical and comparative thought with mere assertions of opinion about religious beliefs or scholarly methods. We can gain enough perspective to repudiate the type of academic gamesmanship – sadly popular among cultural theorists – wherein one 'wins' by comparing the strongest applications of one's favored approach to the least flattering implications that can possibly be attributed to opposing approaches. Still, at the end of the day we cannot gain enough focus to begin cultural analysis without choosing (explicitly or implicitly) certain working definitions and analytical priorities. These choices have ethical implications; they reflect certain values over others.

For example, when studying any given aspect of culture, one comes into dialog (at least implicitly) with the dominant attitudes and expectations related to this topic, as viewed from the standpoint of elite groups. Thus, scholarship will have implications for the outcome of debates between people who endorse the dominant cultural standpoints and people who critique them from other standpoints. Becoming self-conscious about this dynamic does not require us to become obsessed with it to the exclusion of all other concerns. Nevertheless, contrary to scholars who argue that entanglement with values should be out of bounds for the study of religion –

the self-defeating idea that the study of religion would be better if it purged categories such as 'better' – we should acknowledge that we are inevitably entangled with values whenever we clarify our priorities. We should discuss (forthrightly rather than implicitly) how to make our scholarship more constructive and critical – and indeed what 'constructive' and 'critical' should mean. As we will see, building bridges between religious studies and the interdisciplinary study of culture holds significant promise for deepening such discussions.

Cultures as whole ways of life – a few approaches and their critics

Does cultural analysis focus on some aspects of life more than others? When I asked my young children what culture is, they answered matter-of-factly: the ways of a people. People are different in how they work, dress, eat, organize families, and so on. Culture can be a name for talking about these differences as whole patterns. When I pressed my children harder – what is a 'people' and how could they tell? – their response was equally matter-of-fact: people had different cultures. These answers formed such a tight circle that it seemed obvious. Yet culture is not a stable thing waiting out there to be recorded. Until recently, there was no category of culture to interpret practices we now call cultural. We should understand culture less as a neutral category and more as 'an argument, a theoretical object that comes with a certain discipline, persuasions, and admonitions' (Masuzawa in Taylor 1998: 87). What does this argument argue? What exactly are we looking for if we look for the 'ways of a people' – and in that moment what might we *fail* to notice?

A leading approach to this problem is Clifford Geertz's anthropology, which analyzes cultures as sets of symbolic meanings shared among groups – 'webs of signification' which constitute their ways of life, especially through creating meaning and value. Geertz interprets symbols through 'thick description' with a goal of 'enlarg[ing] the possibility of intelligible discourse between people quite different from each other' (1988: 147). He offers a famous definition of religion as a cultural system: 'a system of symbols' which 'establish powerful, pervasive, and long-lasting moods and motivations' and naturalize 'conceptions of a general order of existence' (1973: 91). This definition is useful both for scholars who celebrate how religions can center quests for meaning and order, as well as for scholars who stress more pernicious aspects of religious 'moods and motivations' – for example, their capacity to 'invest specific human preferences with transcendent status by misrepresenting them as revealed truths, primordial traditions, divine commandments and so forth' (Lincoln, in Braun and McCutcheon 2000: 416). Geertz's methods can blend with sociological approaches such as Max Weber's, or with approaches from comparative religion such as Mircea Eliade's; both blends are common in religious studies.

Notwithstanding Geertz's wide range of allies, we should distinguish his interpretive (read: 'cultural') anthropology from other social scientific approaches to culture. Self-styled 'harder' social scientists paint Geertz as a humanistic 'softie' weakened by reading too many literary critics. Interpreting symbols seems hopelessly imprecise to scholars who march under banners such as quantitative sociology or materialist cultural ecology. For Geertz, such approaches are not wrong, but are too thin to account for the richness of culture. However, critics charge that his thick description stresses secondary issues at the expense of fundamental structural ones, and blurs important distinctions between science and literary analysis. Thus, a zone of broadly Geertzian cultural analysis of the 'ways of a people' comes into relief – as distinguishable from 'less cultural' forms of social science such as cognitive and physical anthropology or quantitative political science (Harris 1999; Lemert 1998; McCauley and Lawson 1996; Morris 1987). In practice, this may amount to the difference between digging up bones versus analyzing rituals or counting attendance at Hollywood films versus exploring why a film is popular.

For the moment, let us restrict our attention to symbolic or cultural anthropology. By no means does this conclude our quest for focus, because there remain worlds within this narrower world. To begin, we can distinguish between a 'sweeping, up-from-the-ape, study-of-mankind sort of business' and a 'focus on particular people as crystal wholes, isolate and entire' (Geertz 1988: 146). Scholars trace the roots of the former approach to E. B. Tylor's 1871 book *Primitive Culture*, which defined culture as a 'complex whole which includes knowledge, belief, art, morals, law, custom, and any other capabilities acquired by man as member of society.' Tylor discussed the evolutionary progress of 'man's culture' from a primitive and magical stage to a modern and scientific one. Compared to alternatives during his lifetime, his approach had strengths.[1] However, later scholars stress its weaknesses. They see Tylor and his colleagues such as James Frazer as 'armchair anthropologists' who overgeneralized and took data out of context. For example, creation myths of different languages, from various centuries and continents, might be torn from the societies that produced them and juxtaposed to illustrate some abstract point. Tylor overplayed the intellectual aspects of change from magical to scientific worldviews – and he did so with strong Eurocentric biases, as when he stated that 'few would dispute that the following races are rightly in order of culture: Australian, Tahitian, Aztec, Chinese, Italian' (cited in Stocking 1968: 81). In short, 'Tylor took data from all over the world out of context and arranged it in a sequential scheme according to a preconceived plan' (Morris 1987: 99).

Although no contemporary scholar would endorse Tylor's methods without extensive qualification, his scale of ambition and way of framing questions have continuing resonance. One can underline problems with Tylor's methods but respond by seeking better arguments on a similar scale. Thus, Robert Bellah (1970) offers an evolutionary panorama of growing 'differentiation' on a world-historical stage – a presentation overlapping with research on secularization and globalization. Much work in Eliade's tradition extends Tylor's sweeping comparative approach.[2] For better or worse, inquiries on this scale will remain significant in religious studies as long as textbooks keep trying to survey changes from primal to modern religions or mount catch-all chapters on things such as ritual, and as long as syllabi try to satisfy (rather than reorient) students who seek to learn a body of knowledge in line with such global appetites.

More important to the common sense of religious studies, however, is the anthropology pioneered by scholars such as Franz Boas and Bronislaw Malinowski. Geertz works within this tradition, which addressed the limitations of scholars such as Tylor through grounded research on specific groups using ethnographic methods. This means studying people through participant-observation at one slice of time, rather than across broad sweeps of time. It also means studying one group at a time and discussing its holistic coherence – for example, relating Mayan creation myths to other practices and artifacts of the Mayans, rather than to myths from more and less 'advanced' people. Although ethnographers sought dispassionate scientific knowledge, their work had ethical dimensions. They championed cultural pluralism against prevailing assumptions that groups such as the Mayans were 'backward' and racially inferior. Often they used cross-cultural comparison as a form of cultural critique – for example, by calling into question the givenness and universality of Western gender systems (Hegeman 1999; Marcus and Fischer 1986).

Both of these frameworks for studying cultures as whole ways of life – those that stress 'up-from-the-ape' evolution with limited appreciation for cultural pluralism, and those that champion the pluralism of 'isolate and entire' peoples with limited attention to change over time – have been strongly criticized by a generation of critics. These critics stress internal conflict and complexity rather than consensus within whatever remains of 'cultural wholeness' by the time the critics have finished. They underline historical changes, now approached not as sweeping evolution but as the local dynamics of the history of colonialism (Asad 1973; Hymes 1969; Clifford 1988). One author advocates 'writing against culture' in order to evade three assumptions embedded in the concept: (1) positing *stability and coherence* in the group being analyzed, (2) the *ahistorical* quality of culture as a conceptual frame, and (3) the *discreteness* of cultural boundaries as opposed to the ways that real life includes transnational migrations, hybrid identities, and global flows of information and commodities – in short, a kaleidoscope of local, regional, national, and global forces. For such critics, thinking with the concept of culture drastically oversimplifies complexity. It does so in a way that 'inevitably carries a sense of hierarchy.' Culture 'is the prime anthropological tool for making "Other"' (Abu-Lughod in Fox 1991: 147; see also Appadurai 1996; Clifford 1997).

Such critics worry when cultural analysis dovetails with colonization – as in the case of E.E. Evans-Pritchard's research on the Nuer during a British war against them, or as discussed in David Chidester's (1996) history of religious studies in Southern Africa. They also worry when efforts to study 'authentic' cultures before modernity transforms them beyond recognition (so-called 'salvage anthropology') are informed by imperialist nostalgia. This is a habit of thinking about cultural difference that emphasizes the noble but doomed ways of 'exotic others.' Scholars with this habit prefer to think about victims of colonialism as untouched by colonialism – however, if questions arise about resisting colonization, scholars focus on past defeats (which they lament as tragic) rather than ongoing resistance (which they treat as irrelevant to their scholarly priorities.) Imperialist nostalgia – which commonly informs not only books but also museums, tourism, and popular films – enables people who are complicit in imperialism, or who fail to address the legacies of imperialism, to transform their guilt into self-congratulation about their liberal sensitivity (Lutz and Collins 1993; Rosaldo 1989; Haraway in Dirks *et al.* 1994: 49–95). The practice of writing in an 'ethnographic present' – for example, one might read that 'the Lakota hunt buffalo on horses' although this was only true for one century of Lakota history – appears less quaint and more troubling when approached in this context.

Even if scholars evade such problems, there are further questions. If one works with the concept of cultural wholes at all – even anti-colonial wholes, or wholes that are clearly not static essences, such as an interpretation of Moroccan culture that does not posit 'any deep Moroccanity . . . struggling to get out of history'

(Geertz 1995: 23) – what is the analytical standpoint needed to imagine such wholes? Is it the standpoint of a Western observer in a colonial encounter trying to impose narrative order (read: 'cultural wholeness') on the shreds and patches of a reality that is complex enough to defeat such order? Even if the resulting narrative wholes might unravel by themselves without any help, is it the job of cultural theorists to hasten such unravelling? If so, culture begins to appear less as a stable source of meaning and more as a rhetorical strategy; it changes from a fact that allows children to study 'the ways of the Lakota' to a mere fig leaf masking difference and conflict. Is cultural analysis simply a way for outside analysts to express their 'superstitions' while intervening in other people's business in self-interested ways?[3] Scholars can no longer 'write culture' without arousing such suspicions (Clifford and Marcus 1986).

The high tide of the rage to treat every claim about culture as a narrative construction and then call every narrative into question appears to be passing (Fox 1991; Clifford 2000). For all its important contributions, this approach (often called 'deconstructive' or 'postmodern') produces diminishing returns in certain contexts.[4] Pervasive suspicion toward overarching narratives can create a void, so that scholarship only 'escorts one to the edge of one's ignorance and then leave[s] one to contemplate the vacancy' (Limerick cited in Tweed 1996: 130). What starts by critiquing problems that are internal to cultural discourses (for example, imperialist nostalgia) can end by losing track of other forms of power besides discursive ones, so that cultural critique in effect becomes a parasite on the discourses it criticizes – it is able to attack their internal weaknesses but not able to imagine critiques from other frames of reference. The radical celebration of cultural difference and complexity sometimes (which is not to say always) functions to depoliticize people and dissolve group solidarities into a form of liberal individualism (Eagleton 2000). Although postmodern critics see themselves as the cutting edge of an advancing critique of power, their history might equally well be traced to elitist and apolitical textual criticism (Hegeman 1999).

Importantly, if we use deconstructive approaches to dissolve all stable identities, we undermine not only dominant discourses, but also the standpoints from which underdogs in social conflicts stake their claims – for example, both ideologies of white supremacy and 'black' identities that are rallying points for anti-racism. One response is to defend 'strategic essentialism' – positive cultural identifications that appeal not to monolithic essences of groups such as races and sexes, but rather to evolving identities inherited from historical processes and embraced in specific contexts (Omi and Winant 1992; Rajchman 1995). Another response is to lament the erosion of universal values such as democracy and human rights (Palmer 1990).

In weighing such challenges, it is crucial not to dismiss the strongest postmodern insights in light of their least helpful applications. Rather, we need to discern in what contexts postmodern approaches do – and do not – produce diminishing returns. In any case, patterns of difference among human groups will not disappear simply because scholars can point out serious flaws and oversimplifications in past efforts to conceptualize these patterns. If we refuse to trust the most sophisticated forms of cultural analysis to chart such patterns, we may wind up reinventing something very much like cultural analysis under a new name.

Scholars who hope to refine (rather than abandon) the study of culture in light of the above critiques must be alert to a dispute that informs much recent debate.

Both the 'hard' social scientists introduced above and scholars grounded in structuralist and poststructuralist theory have a longstanding concern about scholars who approach culture as a tool or resource that people can deploy to accomplish their goals.[5] If one thinks this way, what understandings of the self and models of social change are being presupposed? Do common-sense assumptions about culture overestimate human agency? Suppose that culture is not like a tool to wield; suppose it is a structural matrix that shapes people's subjectivity before they pick up their tools and limits their ability to attain their goals. If so, it is misleading to talk about autonomous actors who use culture to create identities or change history. In fact, some critics use the term 'culturalism' for wishful enthusiasm about social change and naïve assumptions about individual autonomy. 'Even the inmates of a concentration camp are able . . . to live by their own cultural logic,' Talal Asad notes. 'But one may be forgiven for doubting that they are therefore "making their own history"' (1993: 4). 'Choices and desires make actions before action can make "history,"' he continues. 'But predefined social relations and language . . . shape the person to whom "normal" desires and choices can be attributed' (1993: 13).

Anyone who uses the category of culture must grapple with this challenge, and indeed stress it in many contexts. But on balance this challenge does not discredit cultural analysis in general, nor cultural agency in particular. In response to critics such as Asad, Sherry Ortner offers solid arguments for continuing to explore cultural agency and symbolic meaning, as long as scholars also give careful attention to sociohistorical power structures and the complexities of cultural hybridity. She also responds to Asad's complaint (1993: 27–54) that a Geertzian approach to culture is static and focussed too much on ideas that create social consensus. According to Ortner, one can draw on Geertz but see culture as an active communicative practice; that is, it involves not consensus, but conflict and negotiation over fluid and contested meanings. Ortner refuses a zero-sum choice between culture as agency and culture as a structural matrix that constitutes agents. Any approach that cannot account for agency and resistance carries the burden of proof for her (Ortner in Dirks et al. 1994: 372–411; Ortner 1999; see also Nye 2000). We could build a broad consensus for this abstract proposal, although the devil is in the details.

From culture as arts and literature to interdisciplinary cultural studies

I was not surprised when my children needed prompting to appreciate how many choices they had, if they wanted to study 'the ways of a people' – approaches that stress sweeping evolution, ethnographic wholes, instability and deconstruction, imperialist nostalgia, history and power, hybrid and diasporic identities, agency or structure, and so on. However, I was surprised when they did not mention arts and literature. Is it not common sense that 'cultural' analysis – as opposed, say, to sociopolitical or ecological analysis – pays special attention to this? Such common sense leads toward a second range of things that we could study if we are studying culture: literature versus science, literary theorists versus novelists, canonical works versus popular culture, written texts versus electronic media, specific forms of art (music, film, etc.) versus other forms, meanings intended by writers versus meanings discovered by readers, and many others. For every anthropologist who claims the high ground of cultural analysis because literature is shaped by whole ways of life, there are two literary theorists who respond that cultures are built of language and anthropologists must communicate through narratives.

Raymond Williams (1983) shows how the word 'culture' developed in this context, starting from the Latin word *colere* that was also the root of 'cultus' and 'colonize.' Originally, culture referred to cultivating crops and animals. Gradually, its meaning extended to a process of human development (the cultivation of people), an abstract state of achieved development (culture as a trait of educated people), and a body of artistic works exemplifying such development (culture as canon.) We have seen how anthropologists have used the term 'culture' both in universal evolutionary narratives and to focus on groups such as the Maya. A related distinction between universal and particular cultures operates in literary and philosophical scholars. Notably, the idea of culture was used by Johann Gottfried von Herder to draw contrasts between the distinctive virtues of German *Kultur* and the universal civilization propounded by the *philosophes* of the French Enlightenment.

Following Herder, literary scholars have distinguished many particular cultures from 'universal' contexts, or at least wider contexts. For example, students of US literature discuss how an 'American' cultural identity was imagined in opposition to an 'Old World' European civilization. Extending further, we could identify a 'culture of rock and roll' or an 'African-American culture' distinct from the wider US culture. In each case, scholars can analyze the focused culture or subculture through its representative art forms. At this point, literary variants of criticisms we have already discussed take hold. What groups are 'made other' by books that valorize German identity or Enlightenment progress? If deconstructive critics are willing to grant that an 'American' literary canon exists, what groups does it exclude and how does this relate to US imperialism? What theories of strategic essentialism or cultural hybridity are needed to understand hip-hop music?

But we are getting ahead of ourselves. Williams (1958) shows how the tradition of distinguishing literary/artistic cultures from larger 'whole ways of life' – as opposed to approaching cultures *as* whole ways of life – evolved in relation to conflicts inside Western societies during the rise of capitalism. Writers such as Matthew Arnold, the author of *Culture and Anarchy*, presented culture as a bulwark against the spiritual impoverishment of modern life. Culture was 'a pursuit of our total perfection by means of getting to know . . . the best which has been thought and said in the world,' thus 'turning a stream of fresh and free thought on our stock notions and habits' (Arnold 1993: 190). Williams traces Arnold's influence to the present through Edmund Burke, T.S. Eliot, and many others – all of whom contrasted 'cultured' people not so much with 'primitive' foreigners (as in Tylor's vision of the higher versus the lower stages of evolution) as with the 'mechanical' aspects of industrial society at home.

Arnold transmuted conservative religion into half-secular cultural conservatism. For him, culture and religion sought 'identical' goals; culture simply did so 'through *all* the voices of human experience,' including 'the arts, science, and history,' in order to 'give a greater fullness and certainty to its solution' (1993: 61). Although Arnold criticized the middle class and was more liberal than the aristocracy, his conservatism was unambiguous as he championed culture against the 'anarchy' he saw threatened by a rising working class. In this connection, Terry Eagleton (1996:

20) suggests that a major reason for the rise of English Studies – a field that Arnold helped to found – was 'the failure of religion.' (He has in mind conservative religions that are 'closed to rational demonstration and thus absolute in their claims.') Eagleton sees much textual study carrying forward similar work as conservative religion, because it creates a discourse framed in ahistorical categories, linked to the values of a 'cultured' elite. However, Eagleton argues that literary canons (much like religious values) do not simply exist out there waiting to be described. Rather, he asks three questions: (1) Which texts do scholars valorize as literature? (2) How do they interpret them? (3) What social purpose does this accomplish?

Williams presents much evidence in this same vein, but he stresses that literature can be also used as a mode of critique from the left. This is a matter of no small concern, since Williams is offering far more than a genealogy for today's cultural conservatives; he is seeking the roots of the general logic used to explain why students should be liberally educated (read: 'cultured') in liberal arts departments of universities. He shows that formally similar appeals to artistic value can express many kinds of politics. Thus, William Morris, whose socialist politics contrasted sharply with Arnold's, wrote about his love of life, then continued:

> Think of it! Was it all to end in a counting-house on top of a cinder heap . . . [with a committee] dealing out champagne to the rich and margarine to the poor? . . . Civilization has reduced the workman to such a skinny and pitiful existence, that he scarcely knows how to frame a desire for [a better] life . . . It is the province of art to set the true ideal of a full and reasonable life before him.
>
> (Williams 1958: 149–50)

Many artists and intellectuals found no satisfying place for themselves in modern society and tried to create such a place (a 'cultural' one) imaginatively. If we approach Arnold in this light – allowing different readers to select the works of art they find essential, then use this art to critique the aspects of society that they most dislike – we can better appreciate Arnold's view of culture. After introducing us to people who 'believe that our greatness and welfare are proved by our being so very rich,' Arnold asks us to

> consider these people, then, their way of life, their habits . . . the very tones of their voice . . . [Observe] the things which come forth out of their mouths, the thoughts which make the furniture of their minds; would any amount of wealth be worth having with the consideration that one was to become just like these people by having it?
>
> (1993: 65)

Many scholars who work with religious literature, or with other canonical texts that can be approached as strongholds of insight, pursue this sort of argument doggedly against aspects of life that they wish to critique.

Williams and Eagleton both argue that literary studies have often been too conservative and circumscribed, especially when they focus on narrow canons rooted in the past and/or do not explore how texts are embedded in dynamic historical processes.[6] Nevertheless, Williams wants to know under what conditions, and in what imaginative forms, literature can give voice to emergent 'structures of feeling' – his term for shared cultural sensibilities that include the 'moods and motivations' that readers may recall from Geertz, blended with the concept of hegemony from neo-Marxian theory. Hegemony roughly means ideas and practices that are taken for granted as common sense by a group, but which work to the power advantage of certain people (hegemonic elites) more than others. Williams describes hegemony as 'culture which has also to be seen as the lived dominance and subordination of particular classes' (1977: 110; see also Harris 1992; Nelson and Grossberg 1988). Those who seek a different kind of society must develop different (counter-hege-monic) forms of common sense. Structures of feeling do not always take the emergent and counter-hegemonic forms that Williams desires; they may extend traditions rooted in the past ('residual' traditions) or reinforce hegemonic values. However, insofar as social transformations unfold, changes in literary/artistic culture are part of this process. They may even play a leading role, insofar as one precondition for change is imagining such change in the first place.

Charting tendencies in the study of literary/artistic culture is far beyond the scope of this essay. We could pursue endless forking paths to explore literary variations on every distinction we have already introduced – universal versus particular, residual versus emergent, culturalist versus structuralist, deconstructive versus traditional, and so on – plus dozens of others (Eagleton 1996; Lentricchia et al. 1995; Payne 1997). However, just as one might consider Geertz 'more cultural' than a flat-footed func-tionalist who studies economics – so that in some sense he is paradigmatic for the social scientific analysis of culture – similarly, one might understand Williams as a paradigmatically *cultural* scholar within literary studies because of the connections he makes with social science and history. Although Williams grants that specialized definitions of culture may be needed for certain inquiries, he contends that 'in general it is the range and overlap of meanings that is significant.' He objects to books on culture in which 'usage in North American anthropology is in effect taken as the norm' (1983: 91, citing Kroeber and Kluckhorn 1952). For Williams, cultural analysis should chart 'relations between general human development and a particular way of life,' and between both of these anthropological matters and the 'works and prac-tices of art and intelligence.' Overstressing differences among these meanings of culture 'conceals the central question of the relations between "material" and "symbolic" production, which . . . have always to be related rather than contrasted' (1983: 91).

Although we have noted how Williams criticizes scholars who approach texts as autonomous worlds of meaning, this does not imply that he neglects the nuances and complexities of textual meanings, much less reduces them to simple reflections of sociohistorical contexts. On the contrary, he attacks scholars who theorize that a material base creates a dependent cultural superstructure. For him, this is an inverted version of the same problem he sees with conservatives: culture as a 'constitutive social process' is reduced to 'a realm of "mere" ideas' separate from the concrete prac-tice of those who produce it (1977: 19).

Thus we arrive – not as the end-point of all the forking paths mentioned above, but along one path of special interest – at the movement that currently claims the name 'cultural studies' for itself. This scholarly network traces its genealogy to work in the 1950s by Williams and colleagues such as E.P. Thompson in history and Stuart

Hall in the sociology of media. (As the movement spread around the world by the 1980s, its subcurrents often rebelled against these founders or blended their influence with others, but they remain a touchstone.) Although defining this proudly decentered field is risky, we can identify some common themes (Storey 1996; During 1999; Morley and Chen 1996). Cultural Studies (hereafter CS) focuses on symbolic communication – not only literature but also many forms of everyday rituals, popular media, body art, subcultural identities, and other practices from both sides of the collapsing divide between high art and popular culture. It favors multi-layered analyses that draw on many disciplines – especially sociology, literary studies, ethnography, and media studies – and pays attention to both producers and consumers of texts. A key emphasis is on the relation between symbols and power, when power is conceptualized within broad neo-Marxian traditions. Often CS uses the concept of cultural hegemony to analyze not only class, but also race, sexuality, empire, and other issues. It frequently emphasizes postmodern themes such as those we discussed in relation to anthropology: questioning received understandings of power in light of cultural difference, interrogating 'culturalist' understandings of agency, investigating global culture flows, and studying emergent media cultures. Finally, CS accents how scholarship relates to political struggles beyond academia; it promotes various forms of social activism and cultural critique.

Unfortunately, scholars in CS tend to treat religious identities as optional additions to longer lists beginning with race, class, and gender. Frequently, they approach religions as monolithic models of hegemony and fail to appreciate religions that are equally complex and internally diverse as other cultural forms. Although this creates obvious challenges for alliances with religious studies, it does not prevent students of religion from using CS categories (e.g. King 1999; Tanner 1997; Hoover and Lundby 1997; Jakobsen 2000; Hulsether 2004). In fact, this situation represents an opportunity for students of religion to fill a key gap in the literature.

Beyond these points it is hard to generalize about CS. Some find it too theoretical, although it focuses more on concrete cases than do many literary theorists, philosophers, and theorists in the social sciences. Some find it too postmodern, although it uses modern categories like democracy and economic justice as often as postmodern ones like difference and hybridity. Indeed, many postmodernists detect a permanent stench of working-class white maleness in its Marxian lineage. Some consider CS ungrounded and inattentive to economic class, even though it relates thick cultural descriptions to analyses of power; simply because it treats culture as one factor of power, this need not deny that other forms of power exist. In general, the work accomplished by 'doing CS' depends on which of its scholars are in view and what alternatives one compares to them. The movement hangs together as a loose network exploring intersections of culture and power. More than a body of work, it is a way of framing questions.

On the relations between religions, cultures, and cultural theory

Let us return to our opening query – is anything more cultural than anything else? – and relate it to another concept that we could define so broadly as to lose all focus. Is anything more *religious* than anything else? And how does studying culture fit together with studying religion?

One might hope that by shifting from a question about defining culture to one about defining religion, we could narrow our focus. After starting with a term broad enough to be confused with life itself, is it safe to assume that religious culture is a subset of culture at large, with meanings that are distinguishable from (although over-lapping with) other subsets such as political culture or media culture? Alas, even this minimal narrowing is contentious. Many scholars associate culture with concepts such as the secular, profane, or 'merely human'; they contrast these ideas with religion, thus conceiving religion as something that can be analyzed only using incommen-surate categories. Some see religion standing in judgment upon culture from a transcendent standpoint. For example, H. Richard Niebuhr's influential study, *Christ and Culture* (1951), builds on categories of 'Christ' (meaning Christian identity and practice, understood as a response to revelation) and culture (meaning broad socio-historical experience) that are basically opposed to each other. Niebuhr presents these categories as entangled, but typically in creative tension or sharp conflict. He criticizes religions that lack such tension – notably his 'Christ of Culture' model in which religion is trivialized through making peace with modernity.

Other scholars put less stress on religion transcending culture, but still understand the territory covered by religion to be as broad as culture, if not broader. For them, religion may refer both to human constructions and overarching categories tran-scending them: life *and* afterlife, things experienced through language or sense perception *and* mysteries stretching beyond them. Catherine Albanese's umbrella category for religious diversity encompasses both 'ordinary religions' which she describes as 'more or less synonymous with culture,' and 'extraordinary religions' which 'help people transcend, or move beyond, their everyday culture and concerns' (1999: 6). In effect, culture becomes a subset of religion in approaches such as those of Niebuhr and Albanese. Scholars may explore how religion relativizes culture, serves as a principle to ground culture, or moves beyond cultural limitations.

Is culture a subset of religion or vice versa? We cannot ride both these definitional horses at the same time. I propose to ride just one horse for the rest of this chapter – religion as a subset of culture – and bracket any further inquiries about how reli-gion may extend beyond culture. If some readers are nervous about this suggestion, they might consider that we can remain agnostic about possible senses in which reli-gion may transcend culture. We can explore case by case whether the religious parts of culture are significantly smaller than culture at large, or are more nearly coex-tensive with it – although at times we will definitely need to distinguish between more and less religious parts of culture, since this distinction is important for some religious groups. Nor does my suggestion prevent us from thinking about transcen-dence. For example, we can interpret Niebuhr's arguments as a form of cultural discourse – a form that uses the language of prophecy to critique other aspects of society.[7] We can interpret Albanese as speaking about two forms of culture – one that distinguishes between the religious and the ordinary and another that does not. We can approach religions as subsets of culture that often seek to ground cultural claims, deepen their resonance, or test their limits.

For better or worse, let us move forward with a premise that culture is an umbrella category with religious culture as a subset. We have seen that religious subsets of culture may overlap extensively with the umbrella category, sometimes to a point where for practical purposes they coincide. Because of these overlaps, there is a major benefit in approaching religious studies as the study of religious *cultures*. It allows us to translate analyses of religions – their genealogies, relations with power, prospects within postmodern society, and so on – into analyses of culture. At present, many scholarly conversations under the rubric of culture are more sophisticated than conversations under the rubric of religion per se. In such cases, translating from 'religion' to 'religious culture' to 'culture' and back again can save scholars of religion much effort at reinventing the wheel, and it can insert analyses of religion into fresher debates. Moreover, since many subjects besides religion can be approached in this same way, cultural theory has become a lingua franca for work from many disciplines. A common language of culture can translate between incommensurate vocabularies used in different disciplines, thus bringing diverse research to bear on particular problems.

This situation has both advantages and disadvantages. At worst, it merely leads back to our original problem – culture as a boundless field in which to flounder – and shifts incommensurable vocabularies to a new place – namely, incompatible approaches to culture. Even at best, the level of abstraction required for cross-disciplinary conversation can be off-putting. Learning to use cultural theory to bridge disciplines may feel like trying to decode an obscure train timetable in an unfamiliar city – and it does not help that some theorists are notorious for writing in a way that disrespects their readers. One may prefer the quiet predictability of home to the noise and novelty of travel, or know of books that are more gracefully written than the train schedules. Many scholars of religion have no desire to become 'theorists' who live full-time in a train station. They feel that, even though someone may need to work there, too many people who live in train stations are homeless.

Nevertheless, the skill of using cultural theory like a rail network to connect scholarly places – to move between different homes for constructive purposes – is extremely useful. This remains true even for scholars who do not wish to travel extensively, since the network connects their research to wider discussions. It remains true even though terrorists may also ride the trains. There is no reason to be excessively bullish about cultural theory, as if train stations were the only hip place to live, only virtuous people rode trains, and modern technology cannot tear apart communities as well improve them. But by the same token, there is no reason to treat the least helpful examples of cultural theory as typical. On balance, it is clear that fluency in cultural theory has become important for thriving in today's academy. If we ask *how* one thrives – for what purposes – we return to the question we posed at the outset: how scholarly priorities relate to specific problems. There are no simple answers to this question.

One example of how cultural debates may inform overlapping religious ones is the discussion about the status of insider perspectives in religious studies. Such controversy is by no means unique to religious subfields of the study of culture. Other fields have extensively discussed matters such as the prospects for objective scholarship, the challenge of clarifying subject positions from which to speak, and the risks of trying to speak for others. Can committed feminists be trustworthy scholars of gender? Do musicians have knowledge that is useful for academic studies of music? Does participation in a racial subculture enable scholarship? Anyone can cite examples that suggest a need for caution – brittle appeals to racial essences, puff pieces masquerading as music criticism, sermons in the guise of scholarship on religion, and so on. But it is all too easy to play tit-for-tat once this sort of criticism begins, pointing to more traditional scholars who make unconvincing claims of neutrality or defend noxious political ends in the name of universal values. On balance, scholars of culture widely accept that one can be a critical scholar of music and still love to listen to it, a critical scholar of politics with strong political commitments, and so on. One might not even trust scholars who fail to situate themselves explicitly, nor be deeply interested in reading scholars who are not themselves deeply interested in an issue. Insofar as the study of religion denies that scholars can be critical about religious practices that they may share, just as they can be critical about other cultural identities that they may embrace, scholarship on religion will be conspicuously out of step with trends in the interdisciplinary study of culture.

These considerations lead back to the problem of focus. One way to address the challenge we have confronted throughout this chapter – that 'religion and culture' may refer to almost anything but nothing in particular – is to begin from grounded case studies of practices that are conventionally understood as religious, and to take our cues for how we focus our analyses from the self-understandings of the people involved. This is a fundamental part of the repertoire of religious studies method. Of course, it is not enough by itself. At a minimum we also need comparative categories that can relate specific cases to a wider spectrum of religion. Beyond this, we may meet people who do not use the category of religion at all; we may also mistrust insider understandings or need to sort out conflicting insider definitions. We cannot clarify our focus solely through letting it emerge from analyzing cases in the 'real world,' because the priorities and interpretive frames we bring to our inquiry will help to determine both how we select our cases in the first place and what we notice as we study them. 'Religion is not an independent subject matter just sitting there for all to see, but a *term* that its user chooses to associate with certain kinds of phenomena' (Paden 1992: 5; see Idinopolus and Wilson 1998; Taylor 1998; Nye 2003).

At the same time, simply because we must clarify our categories, it does not follow that 'religious culture' can simply mean whatever scholars stipulate it to mean. Such an approach cannot solve the field's overall problem of focus (although obviously it could help focus a specific study.) More importantly, people have long done things that we know as religious without scholars from religious studies to interpret them. They have engaged in rituals reflecting their social priorities, described interactions with supernatural forces, used dreams to cope with death, and so on. If scholarly inquiries bring such activities into focus, there is concrete information to analyze. This may lead to a back-and-forth dialog in which scholarly interpretations are tested and revised toward such goals as accuracy, depth of insight, or contribution to analyzing a given problem. Such dialog is especially important when scholars do not analyze inert data, but living people who propose their own interpretive frames for understanding their religious practice – frames which may be fully commensurate with scholarly ones and/or call scholarly ones into question. Often different people from the same religious group have conflicting ideas; in such cases, scholars may not be able to avoid taking positions that affect the outcome of intra-religious competition.

None of this denies the value of a broad distinction between theological studies, and critical and comparative religious studies, although hard boundaries do blur once we acknowledge that insiders can be critical and outside scholars cannot be neutral. Nor does it deny that scholars may pursue scholarly inquiries for which insider claims are unhelpful, and may sometimes find insider religious claims unintelligible and/or dangerous. In such cases, the best scholarly option may be to think less about dialog and more about redescribing insider claims within alternative frames of reference. A key trend in the study of culture, however, is to criticize anyone who attempts this sort of redescription without first wrestling with a problem that has bedeviled much past research – that scholars and the people they study may have very different ideas about what should count as 'the best scholarly option.' As we have seen, scholarly approaches have often been entwined with exercising power and misrepresenting others.

In short, no one has a monopoly on critical skills, nor can we predict in advance whether any given encounter between people – including their concerns and priorities related to culture and religion – will lead to overlapping consensus or to misunderstanding and conflict. Since there is no court of last resort to judge which concerns and priorities trump others, the field of religion and culture is best understood as a multi-leveled dialog about these concerns, carried on by many kinds of scholars (some of whom practice religion) and the religious practitioners they study (some of whom are scholars). This dialog is not neutral with respect to values. Rather, it is a process of cultural contestation focusing on what the study of religion should be: what it is good for, and for whom. Translation among cultural discourses in light of contextual issues, rather than a search for final explanation or universal adequacy, becomes the watchword for scholarship. The study of religion and culture becomes a broad field of debate structured by the ways that people talk about their concerns – and by the ways they use power to promote their concerns, since this is certainly not a level playing-field, whether or not we wish it could be.

Although some might describe such a field as postmodern because of its diversity and lack of universal ground-rules, the fear that this situation implies a formless relativism will only come true to whatever extent that relativists dominate emergent discussions.[8] The situation does imply that if someone believes that a given concern must not be neglected in any vision of religious studies worth sustaining into the future – for example, I contend that one such issue is how religions relate to survival in the face of oppression – then one must insert the issues into the conversation and offer good reasons for others to share these concerns.

Conclusions

What has been the point of these reflections? Does it matter if we can clarify a few approaches to our question, 'Is anything more cultural than anything else?' Suppose we want to relate the term 'culture' to the following sentence: 'At this stage of history, our country needs social norms that encourage goal X; thus, artists should create works to strengthen people who pursue goal X.' Does it help that we are now prepared to rewrite this sentence using the word 'culture' indiscriminately? 'At this stage of global culture, our culture needs a culture of X; thus, cultural workers should create culture to strengthen subcultures that pursue X.' By reviewing the above sections, we could reflect on the scholarly traditions that inform various parts of this sentence: evolutionary theorists for stages of history, literary critics for art, CS for activists, and so on. Still, one might ask whether this has all been a game – whether our inquiry has been like touring a train station when we would rather be traveling.

Although we have noted the drawbacks of living in such a train station full-time, the ability to navigate within it matters a great deal. Fluency in cultural theory allows one to pursue a wide range of important topics, bring them into dialog, and relate them to larger scholarly debates. It offers one of the best vocabularies to enable research that integrates multiple disciplines. Framing questions with cultural theory is only the beginning of analysis – a platform from which to embark and a map that might keep us from losing the forest for the trees during later stages of research. Nevertheless, no one should underestimate the value of clarifying how different approaches lead one to focus on certain issues and *not* to focus on others. We should pay as much attention to this matter as travelers do to boarding the right train. Clarifying these issues is crucial for scholars who seek not only to thrive amid interdisciplinary debates, but also to thrive in ways that minimize their complicity with oppression and combat the complacency that declares scholars immune from worrying about such matters.

As we have seen, there are pitfalls in the study of religion and culture that no one should ignore. Scholars informed by common-sense notions of culture have often found it natural – with the best of intentions – to travel to foreign lands under conditions of colonialism and spend years writing books that abstract from issues of power and change. Their books have reinforced elitist hierarchies of high versus low culture that do not stand up under scrutiny, and they have made dubious assumptions (often linked to nostalgic sensibilities) that abstract art from its social contexts. They have presented hegemonic ideals as inevitable forms of consensus, and have undermined traditions under attack by colonialism. At times they have displayed an 'astonishing sense of weightlessness with regard to the gravity of history' (Said 1993: 278–9).

Should we then give up on cultural analysis and move to other approaches? No doubt we should approach this question case by case. However, we often need frameworks for comparing interdisciplinary perspectives and translating among practices that involve local, national, and transnational flows of ideas, technologies, and people. If we do not use culture as our lingua franca for such work, we may have to reinvent something very much like it. And why go to this trouble? If we are careful, we can conceptualize culture and power at the same time and relate them both to historical processes. Cross-cultural comparisons can destabilize hegemonic common sense. Artistic culture can nurture profound insights vis-à-vis other parts of life – and surely it is important to have approaches that are flexible enough to engage with music and literature, alongside approaches that declare such topics off-limits for 'value-neutral' science. Despite the risk that cultural analysis may oversimplify or harden human boundaries, sometimes it is crucial to understand that people live amid intelligible patterns of difference, rather than to pretend that postmodern complexity defeats every effort to interpret such patterns. We can learn to think about all these matters in light of the gravity of history, rather than as a distraction from it.

In short, we need to learn how to choose wisely among approaches to culture. It is because such choices are important in people's lives – as applied toward specific goals in concrete cases – that the field of religion and culture matters and we need good maps to navigate within it.

Notes

1   We are stressing a change from evolutionary approaches to later methods, but other maps of this terrain are possible. Tylor was in dialog with scholars who explained human difference as decline from a common culture suspiciously reminiscent of the Garden of Eden, or who stressed racial difference even to an extreme of denying the unity of humanity (Stocking 1968). Within evolutionary theories, it mattered whether one understood Darwinian natural selection as condemning 'backward' groups, or used a rhetoric (more like Tylor's) of 'older school chums rooting for them' (Lutz and Collins 1993: 27).

2   As noted above, Eliade's categories may be blended with Geertz's and deployed within more focused contextual studies. However, a broadly comparative and decontextualized approach is common. In some ways Eliade repudiates Tylor's stress on change over time, but he shares Tylor's contrast between modernity and earlier periods – Eliade's sensibility is simply nostalgic whereas Tylor's is progressive.

3   Herbert (1991) argues that 'superstitions of culture' is a more accurate term for Émile Durkheim's work than 'social science.' He presents Durkheim's core idea of social consensus keeping anomie in check as rearticulating the ideals of missionaries (Christianity keeping sin in check) and dovetailing with Matthew Arnold's vision dicussed below (literary culture keeping anarchy in check).

4   We cannot fully treat *postmodernity*, one aspect of which is a breakdown in the ability to take for granted universal narratives about things such as reason or progress – a breakdown which is related to changes in the world system and which is happening whether or not one considers it warranted. Nor can we chart the many forms of *postmodernism* that clear space – through rupture and/or organic development – from things that are labeled modern in various discourses (Best and Kellner, 1991; Connor 1989; Harvey 1990; Jameson 1998; Nicholson 1990). However, we can note two common patterns within this tangled discourse: (1) analyzing certain dominant practices as modern, then using deconstructive arguments to undermine them, and (2) analyzing postmodernism itself as dominant – perhaps reflecting a hypermodernism that dovetails with postindustrial consumerism or a hyper-reflexivity that disables moral commitments. So far, our argument has mainly discussed the first of these patterns, but we will consider both as we proceed.

5   Treating the complexities of structuralist and post-structuralist theory is beyond the scope of this article. Both stress how structures of language shape consciousness and society; for structuralists discourses are relatively stable and generalizable, while poststructuralists stress that meanings cannot be pinned down and subjectivities are fluid and unstable. See Morris 1987; Nicholson 1990; Harris 1992; Zizek 1994.

6   Consider how Williams responds to Eliot's suggestion that 'culture includes all the characteristic activities and interests of a people: Derby Day . . . dog races . . . the dart board . . . boiled cabbage cut into sections . . . Gothic churches, and the music of Elgar.' He points out that Eliot includes only 'sport, food, and a little art' but not 'steel-making . . . mixed farming, the Stock Exchange, coal-mining, and London Transport.' Eliot only expands to popular culture from 'the older specialized sense of "culture" (arts, philosophy)'; he should explore how art relates to the ordinary lives of working people (1983: 233–34).

7   In this regard it is interesting to compare what Niebuhr says about Christ as a critique of culture to what Matthew Arnold says about culture as a critique of middle-class 'Philistinism.'

8   Scholars who see postmodernism as hegemonic (see note 4) often fear relativism in two forms – liberal individualism and nihilism. However, a postmodern lack of consensus about universal standards opens the door not solely to this specter, but to *whatever* one fears: bloodthirsty fundamentalism, humorless structural Marxism, narcissistic media criticism, sadly limited masculine Euro-centrism, beleaguered humanism which cannot shake its nostalgia for universals, etc. Postmodernity is a condition in which none of these tendencies can be silenced even if one wishes they could. Taking this context for granted, most scholars informed by postmodernism do not see themselves as nihilistic; they are simply trying to make the most constructive moral interventions that they can.

Bibliography

Albanese, C. (1999) *America: Religion and Religions*, 3rd edn, Belmont, CA, Wadsworth Publishing.

√ Appadurai, A. (1996). *Modernity at Large: Cultural Dimensions of Globalization*, Minneapolis, University of Minnesota Press.

Arnold, M. (1993) *Culture and Anarchy and Other Writings*, New York, Cambridge University Press.

Asad, T. (ed.) (1973) *Anthropology and the Colonial Encounter*, London, Ithaca Press.

—— (1993) *Genealogies of Religion: Discipline and Reasons of Power in Christianity and Islam*, Baltimore, Johns Hopkins University Press.

Bellah, R. (1970) 'Religious Evolution' in *Beyond Belief: Essays on Religion in a Post-Traditional World*, New York, Harper & Row, pp. 21–50.

Best, S. and Kellner, D., (1991) *Postmodern Theory*, New York, Guilford.

Braun, W. and McCutcheon, R. (eds) (2000) *Guide to the Study of Religion*, London, Cassell.

Chidester, D. (1996) *Savage Systems: Colonialism and Comparative Religion in Southern Africa*, Charlottesville, University Press of Virginia.

√ Clifford, J. (1988) *The Predicament of Culture*, Cambridge, MA, Harvard University Press.

—— (1997) *Routes: Travel and Translation in the Late Twentieth Century*, Cambridge, MA, Harvard University Press.

—— (2000) 'Taking Identity Politics Seriously,' in P. Gilroy, L. Grossberg, and A. McRobbie (eds), *Without Guarantees: In Honour of Stuart Hall*, New York, Verso, pp. 94–112.

—— and Marcus, G. (eds.) (1986) *Writing Culture: the Poetics and Politics of Ethnography*, Berkeley, University of California Press.

√ Connor, S. (1989) *Postmodernist Culture: an Introduction to Theories of the Contemporary*, 2nd edn, Cambridge, Blackwell.

√ Dirks, N., Eley, G., and Ortner, S. (eds) (1994) *Culture/Power/History: a Reader in Contemporary Social Theory*, Princeton, Princeton University Press.

√ During, Simon (ed.) (1999) *The Cultural Studies Reader*, 2nd edn, New York, Routledge.

Eagleton, T. (1996) *Literary Theory: an Introduction*, 2nd edn, Minneapolis, University of Minnesota Press.

√ —— (2000) *The Idea of Culture*, Oxford, Blackwell Publishers.

Fox, R. G. (ed.) (1991) *Recapturing Anthropology*, Santa Fe, School of American Research.

Geertz, C. (1973) *The Interpretation of Cultures*, New York, Basic Books.

—— (1988) *Works and Lives: the Anthropologist as Author*, Stanford, Stanford University Press.

—— (1995) *After the Fact: Two Countries, Four Decades, One Anthropologist*, Cambridge, MA, Harvard University Press.

Harris, D. (1992) *From Class Struggle to The Politics of Pleasure: The Effects of Gramscianism on Cultural Studies*, London, Routledge.

√ Harris, M. (1999) *Theories of Culture in Postmodern Times*, Walnut Creek, CA: Altamira.

Harvey, D. (1990) *The Condition of Postmodernity*, Cambridge, Basil Blackwell.

Hegeman, S. (1999) *Patterns for America: Modernism and the Concept of Culture*, Princeton, Princeton University Press.

√ Herbert, C. (1991) *Culture and Anomie: Ethnographic Imagination in the Nineteenth Century*, Chicago, University of Chicago Press.

√ Hoover, S. and Lundby, K. (eds) (1997) *Rethinking Media, Religion, and Culture*, Thousand Oaks: Sage.

√ Hulsether, M. (2004) 'New Approaches to the Study of Religion and Culture,' *New Approaches to the Study of Religion*, eds Peter Antes, Armin Geertz, and Randi Warne. Berlin: Verlag de Gruyter, pp. 344–82.

Hymes, D. (ed.) (1969) *Reinventing Anthropology*, New York, Pantheon.

Idinopolus, T. and Wilson, B. (eds) (1998) *What is Religion? Origins, Definitions, and Explanation*, Leiden, Brill.

✓ Jakobsen, J. with Pelligrini, A. (2000) 'Dreaming Secularism,' *Social Text*, vol. 18, no. 3), pp. 1–27.

✓ Jameson, F. (1998) *The Cultural Turn: Selected Writings on the Postmodern, 1983–1998*, New York, Verso.

King, R. (1999) *Orientalism and Religion: Postcolonial Theory, India and the 'Mystic East,'* New York, Routledge.

✓ Kroeber, A. L. and C. Kluckhohn (1952) *Culture: a Critical Review of Concepts and Definitions*, New York, Vintage.

Lemert, C. (1998) *Social Theory: the Multicultural and Classic Readings*, 2nd edn, Boulder: Westview Press.

Lentricchia, F. and McLaughlin T. (eds) (1995) *Critical Terms for Literary Study*, 2nd edn, Chicago, University of Chicago Press.

Lutz, C. and Collins, J. (1993) *Reading National Geographic*, Chicago, University of Chicago Press.

✓ McCauley, R. and Lawson, T. (1996) 'Who Owns 'Culture,'' *Method and Theory in the Study of Religion*, vol. 8, no. 2, pp. 171–90.

✓ Marcus, G. and Fischer, M. (1986) *Anthropology as Cultural Critique*, Chicago, University of Chicago Press.

✓ Morley, D. and Chen, K. (eds) (1996) *Stuart Hall: Critical Dialogues in Cultural Studies*, New York, Routledge.

Morris, B. (1987) *Anthropological Studies of Religion*, New York, Cambridge University Press.

✓ Nelson C. and Grossberg, L. (eds) (1988) *Marxism and the Interpretation of Culture*, Urbana, University of Illinois Press.

Nicholson, L. (ed.) (1990) *Feminism/Postmodernism*, New York, Routledge.

Niebuhr, H. R. (1951) *Christ and Culture*, New York, Harper & Row.

✓ Nye, M. (2000) Religion, Post-Religionism, and Religioning: Religious Studies and Contemporary Cultural Debates. *Method and Theory in the Study of Religion*, 12 (4): 447–76.

—— (2003) *Religion: the Basics*, New York: Routledge.

Omi M. and Winant, H. (1992) *Racial Formation in the United States*, 2nd edn, New York, Routledge.

✓ Ortner, S. (ed.) (1999) *The Fate of 'Culture': Geertz and Beyond*, Berkeley, University of California Press.

Paden, W. (1992) *Interpreting the Sacred: Ways of Viewing Religion*, Boston, Beacon Press.

Palmer, B. (1990) *Descent Into Discourse: the Reification of Language and the Writing of Social History*, Philadelphia, Temple University Press.

✓ Payne, M. (ed.) (1997) *Dictionary of Cultural and Critical Theory*, Oxford, Blackwell Publishers.

Rajchman, J. (ed.) (1995) *The Identity in Question*, New York, Routledge.

✓ Rosaldo, R. (1989) *Culture and Truth*, Boston, Beacon Press.

✓ Rowe, J. (ed.) (1998) *'Culture' and the Problem of the Disciplines*, New York, Columbia University Press.

✓ Said, E. (1993) *Culture and Imperialism*, New York, Vintage.

✓ Stocking, G. (1968) *Race, Culture, and Evolution: Essays in the History of Anthropology*, New York, Free Press.

✓ Storey, J. (ed.) (1996) *What Is Cultural Studies?* New York, Arnold Press.

✓ Tanner, K. (1997) *Theories of Culture: A New Agenda for Theology*, Minneapolis, Fortress Press.

Taylor, M. C. (ed.) (1998) *Critical Terms for Religious Studies*, Chicago, University of Chicago Press.

✓ Tomlinson, J. (1991) *Cultural Imperialism: a Critical Introduction*, Baltimore, Johns Hopkins University Press.

Tweed, T. (ed.) (1996) *Retelling U.S. Religious History*, Berkeley, University of California Press.
Williams, R. (1983 [1958]) *Culture and Society, 1780–1950*, New York, Columbia University Press.
—— (1977) *Marxism and Literature*, New York, Oxford University Press.
—— (1983) *Keywords: A Vocabulary of Culture and Society*, 2nd edn, New York, Oxford University Press.
Zizek, S. (ed.) (1994) *Mapping Ideology*, New York, Verso.

Chapter 29

Religion and the arts

John R. Hinnells

Introduction

Religious studies courses commonly focus on texts and the social sciences as do the student text books written for them. Few undertake any substantial study of the arts. I want to argue that these should be a primary focus. Viewed across history and around the globe, the vast majority of religious people have been illiterate, so why study the texts that were cut off from the direct religious practice of most religious people? Even in the literate West, children in schools commonly learn about their religion through drawing, painting, dance or school plays. So the first contact most contemporary westerners have with a religion is through its arts. In historical terms, arts were primary – Paleolithic cave paintings long predated any texts. The reason for this traditional approach is that scholars and students who are themselves very literate prioritize in their subject what they value in the own lives – reading, statistics etc. But those issues, I argue, are not what are prominent in the daily life of most religious practitioners.

The purpose of this chapter is to highlight the importance of understanding diverse art forms in religions. Examples are taken from different religions, but clearly it is impossible to give even an overview of the range of religious arts in any one tradition, much less cross-culturally, in the space available. Even within one subject area, e.g. European art, I have focused on what I know a little more about (and enjoy most!), namely the Renaissance rather than North European art. I have omitted many areas that actually provide excellent examples of my themes, namely the traditional arts of Africa, North America and the Pacific, because I am not competent to discuss them (see Moore 1995; Williams 1974; Hackett 1996). Nevertheless, I hope that, by highlighting some key issues, with examples, readers may be provoked to explore the arts in their study of specific religions. I will first discuss some key terms, consider the different roles that the arts play in religions, and will then focus on arts and religious emotions, looking in particular at architecture. In order to look at the study of symbolism, I will compare the use of one symbol, the nude, in three religions, arguing that its use is not what one might logically have expected and pointing out how symbols allude inexplicitly – but powerfully – to important unwritten values, ideas or theologies. This leads on to a discussion of the role of the artist and finally the use of religious symbols in the contemporary world. There have been numerous theoretical debates concerning both secular and religious arts, especially among anthropologists (e.g. Layton 1991), but I have not attempted to discuss these; here my focus is on how religious studies not only could but should include the significant arts of the region or cultures being studied. In order to keep the references to a manageable size across such a huge topic, I have taken as many examples from one book as possible, e.g. Snellgrove (1978) for the Buddha image and Levey (1968) for western art, rather than attempt a comprehensive bibliography.

It is increasingly common in religious studies, as in other subjects, to 'situate' one's self. In this case it is important that I do so. My original career was as an artist. I studied at art college, taught art and made my living for a couple of years as an artist (mostly oil painting). That might make me biased, but it will explain why I ask some of the questions that I do in what follows.

Some terms

The definition of 'religion' has consumed many book and articles, so that I do not have to rehearse that particular question. But it is important to ask when is 'art' 'religious art'? It is common to identify, for example, Leonardo da Vinci's painting of *Madonna and Child with St Anne and St John* or his *Virgin of the Rocks* (late fifteenth century; see Levey 1968: pls 173, 174). In the former, Leonardo was fascinated mostly by the portraiture of the two women and the folds of their dresses (Gombrich 1971: 58–63). In the latter, Leonardo did countless studies of the plants in the bottom left of the painting and the perspective of the landscape and the numerous patterns of circles in the composition of the rock faces behind the figures. When these works are exhibited in art galleries, to what extent are they 'works of religious art'?

In contrast, in one of my paintings (I am not claiming to be a great artist like Leonardo!) I undertook a study of patterns of light and shade that fascinated me as I was walking home one evening, when a couple walked in front of me with the street light in front of them throwing strong elongated shadows and highlights in the road and in the trees at the side. An art critic looking at the result in an exhibition commented that one could see a strong religious theme in the composition as the couple strived to reach the light at the end of the dark tunnel. This was news to me, but I accepted that explanation when a church purchased it as a work of religious art and hung it in a side chapel. It has never been hung in an art gallery, but perhaps my study of patterns of light and dark functioned as a piece of religious art while it was in the church. Leaving aside the comparison of a second-rate artist with the work of a great master, in function surely the *Virgin of the Rocks* in the galleries in London and Paris (there are debates about which is the original!) is not a work of religious art just because of the names given to the figures in the painting. My study in light and shade became religious when hung in a church. Similarly, a piece of music when played in a secular auditorium is a secular production, but when used as part of a liturgy becomes an example of religious music. Is it not the function of a piece of art, not the artist – or composer's – intentions, nor its title, that make it religious? All this would imply that the classification of a piece of art can change. If a fine painting or statue is removed from a sacred space and put in the antiseptic atmosphere of a gallery or museum, then perhaps it follows that it changes from being a religious piece of art to a secular object. Picasso is reputed to have said that the 'picture hook is the ruination of painting' and 'A painting is done for as soon as it is bought and hung on a wall' (Honour and Fleming 1982: 9) – for then he thought it became simply decoration, not something with a purpose or use. A further question: can a work of art be religious because of its theme even if that was not the artist's intention? One example of this may be Picasso's *Guernica* – a powerful protest against war and the associated violence (twentieth century; Honour and Fleming 1982: 602, pl. 20.20).

The word 'art' also merits comment. For the purpose of religious studies the distinction between 'high' and 'popular' art is inappropriate. The fact that I personally consider Michelangelo's paintings on the ceiling of the Sistine Chapel in the Vatican (1508 CE; see Levey 1968: pl. 176) to be brilliant art, whereas the many images of the bleeding heart of Jesus in most Catholic churches I find to be the opposite, does not matter. When a work of art stimulates religious emotions or thoughts it merits serious attention in religious studies. The same is true of the contrast between some of the finest Hindu sculptures and the decorated stones in a village shrine (Elgood 1999: pls 3.5, 4.10; cf. 6.3, 6.11). The relatively few writers on religion and the arts in Christianity commonly focus on the 'great' art rather than what was probably the focus of daily life (e.g. Apostolos-Cappadona 1985 and Dillenburger 1986).

Although it does not appear in the title of this chapter a word that must inevitably be used is 'symbol'. This is a contested word in the study of religions (see the discussion in Morris (1987: 218–63)). Here I take 'symbol' to mean a word or motif that points to something beyond itself and I am concerned with what the symbol means for religious people. There are two main 'types' of symbol – iconic and aniconic. The former bears some resemblance to the subject, for example a Buddha *rupa*, or Buddha image, depicting a figure in traditional Indian monk's garb and shown meditating. An aniconic symbol would be where the Buddha (or Buddhahood) is represented by a wheel (the message) or tree (under which Buddha is said to have meditated), or a footprint representing his preaching mission (Snellgrove 1978: 39–44). In Christianity an iconic image would be a crucifix depicting the crucified Jesus, whereas the cross does not, though normally the motif still alludes to the work and crucifixion of Jesus. Fish and lambs are other common aniconic Christian symbols.

What constitutes 'the arts'?

The boundaries of the subject require comment. Not only should we look at the visual arts, such as paintings and statues, but at many other art forms also, e.g. the structure and function(s) of sacred space (i.e. architecture) and the performing arts – music and dance. Drama also in my opinion is a major dimension of religious practice in most if not all religions, whether it be the drama of the mass, *puja* in the temple, the Friday prayers in a mosque or much Jewish liturgy, especially great events celebrated in the home, such as Pesach. This is far from an exhaustive list. The arts are yet more diverse. Poetry is clearly an important art form, but I have omitted this because textual studies often include poetry. Dress is an important part of many religions, whether it be the head covering in Islam, the skull cap in Judaism, or the sacred shirt and cord (*sudre* and *kusti*) worn next to the skin at all times by most Parsis as the armour of Ohrmazd in their war against the evil Ahriman. Similarly food is a major part of many religious traditions, e.g. the Friday evening meal at the start of the Sabbath in Judaism, or the food shared by all present after Sikh worship. Many religions have food associated with some of their major liturgies, e.g. bread and wine for Christians in the Eucharist, or the offering of food to Hindu deities in a temple or domestic shrine. In my global survey of the Zoroastrian diaspora I found that diaspora Zoroastrians wanted to preserve their customs associated with food almost as much as they did the religion (Hinnells 2004). All the main seasonal festivals (*gahambars*) and above all their New Year (*No Ruz*) are associated with food as are such joyful occasions as initiations and weddings. (For Parsi food and customs see Manekshaw (1996).) Some scholars would want to emphasize other art forms, for example body painting or the role of masks and many arts associated with religious books, notably calligraphy in Islam. Also in Islam, gardens and tombs have considerable religious significance. Liturgy is included in many studies of religion(s), but generally in terms of the doctrinal structure of the liturgy rather than of what is almost certainly more important for the worshipper, namely its powerful emotional impact and its role as a source of spiritual inspiration. The last point for me highlights a key issue with religious arts: I suspect that most religious people consider the important aspect of their own religion to be the spiritual, emotional and personal dimensions usually experienced through one or other art forms rather than through the religion's texts.

However, this should not imply that religion and the arts have always had a mutually positive relationship – far from it. The Christian Church, for example, has been one of the most ruthless suppressors of diverse art forms. After the Reformation many Protestants associated fine arts with 'popery' – one of their greatest condemnations of religious practice – and destroyed them. Many evangelicals have dammed artists as heathens; for example, the religious preacher Savonarola (late fifteenth century) demanded (successfully, unfortunately) that Botticelli destroy much of his earlier work because it dealt with pagan themes. I share the common view that Botticelli's earlier work, represented among his extant works by *The Birth of Venus*, to be far greater than his religious works, such as his crucifixion, which seems to me sentimental as Jesus almost floats on the cross against a blue sky with angels peacefully flying by (Levey 1968: 43, pl. 59). Piety all too often has been the destroyer of the arts. Similarly, Muslims have generally held that artists – especially sculptors – were evil because of their associations with the worship of idols and the belief that God alone can create. Conquering religions have usually destroyed the art and culture of the vanquished, and thereby much religious art around the world has been lost. Nevertheless, religions have also encouraged the reproduction of what is considered beautiful, but the concept of what is beautiful changes over time, even within the same culture (another contested word! – see Geertz, a pioneering but now a more controversial scholar).

The roles of the arts in religions

The various arts play different roles in different contexts. Perhaps the most obvious is their didactic or teaching role. Pictures tell the stories of the religions, whether it is the life, death and resurrection of Jesus as in the Ravenna mosaics (fifth-sixth centuries CE); the paintings of Giotto at Padua (early fourteenth century; Honour and Fleming 1982: 307); cave paintings of the lives of the Buddhas (Snellgrove 1978: 108–223); or the life and work of the Gurus in Sikhism (K. Brown 1999: 52–71). Islam is something of an exception as it, like Judaism, rejects images. Yet even here there are exceptions, as with the Persian and Indian traditions of miniature paintings (Gray 1961, 1981). Most Persian miniatures depict scenes from the great Persian epic, the *Shah-nama*, but there are Islamic scenes, for example the ascent of Muhammad (B. W. Robinson 1980: pl. 407 (p. 73); Welch 1976: 96ff. in colour).

One of the most common examples of the didactic role in art is drama – the school Christmas play in Britain or Festivals in Hindu temples (Jackson and Nesbitt 1993), or the Kathakali dancers retelling the epic stories of Hinduism (Gaston 1985). Both in India and in the diaspora in the 1980s and 1990s it was Bollywood films and videos of the two great epics that unwittingly provoked the aggressive expressions of Hindu nationalism and inspired – among many other things – the BJP. The producers of those epics could never have foreseen the huge political impact of their work (see Van der Veer 1994: 174–8).

The teaching function of the arts, however, is not merely storytelling; it can involve far more fundamental theology. For example, following the Enlightenment and the Renaissance, Trinitarian doctrine emphasized the humanity of Jesus, whereas his divine status had previously been the focus of teaching. In the painters of the early Renaissance, notably Giotto (early fourteenth century), Jesus is no longer located in a heavenly setting of gold – the background for earlier paintings of religious figures – but appears in an Italianate geography of hills, houses and trees, and, with the growing interest in perspective and form, Jesus is shown as a solid figure depicted in light and dark shading, which gave him the solid bodily form that theologians were then emphasizing (Levey 1968: 15; cf. Giotto's annunciation, pl. 3, with that of his contemporary Simone Martini, pl. 14). Giotto and his successors made real for Christians that which theologians debated in learned tomes. Similarly, it is through Indian and Persian miniatures – as well as from the oral tradition – that some of the great epics, such as the *Shah-nama*, the *Ramayana* and the *Mahabharata*, are taught to successive generations, and from which people learn about their role models, heroes and villains, values and ideals. The visual – and especially the performing – arts are key transmitters of knowledge in a religious setting.

Another example of the arts conveying underlying theology is with the representation of God. Christianity – especially in its western form – is one of the most anthropomorphic religions in this regard. Perhaps that is proper in a religion that teaches that man is made in the image of God, and moreover that God took human form in the person of Jesus. This theology is reflected in – and reinforced by – many of the images of God, such as Michelangelo's paintings in the Sistine Chapel and the paintings of William Blake in both of which God is an old man with a long white beard (1509 and late eighteenth century respectively; see Levey 1968: pls 176ff., 460). The level of anthropomorphism is indicated by the outcry in America in the 1960s and 1970s when a picture depicted God in female form; some of the critics argued that only the male form could be used.

In Indian art, by contrast, if the artists wanted to stress the power and wisdom of God, then an elephant's head could be used in a statue (the widely popular Ganesha), or God may be incarnated in animal form, for example as a boar (Michell *et al.* 1982: 202; Blurton 1992: 121, 146; Michell 1977: 28), and other nonhuman forms – for all life is sacred. The creative dimension of divinity is often depicted in female form, as the destructive, and therefore in a cyclical view of time the regenerative, force; for example, Kali was sometimes depicted with her tongue dripping with blood walking on the prostrate figure of her husband (on Ganesha see Courtright (1985) and on Kali see Mookerjee (1988)). Yet it is she to whom mothers commonly pray for the gift of a child. Some Indian sculptures depict the divine as half male and half female, transcending human gender (Blurton 1992: 96). Even dramatic stones or trees can be sacred locations (Michell *et al.* 1982: 214; Blurton 1992: 79–81 and 11 respectively). Different forms/images express different aspects of the ultimate in Indian art. There is no element of portraiture in divine imagery – the power of the divine may be depicted by many arms, or the all-seeing nature may be illustrated by many eyes, or many heads. Why should the divine be restricted to mere human form? (See Elgood 1999: 44–92; Michell 1977: 20–48.)

In some ways Zoroastrians went further, rejecting any element of anthropomorphism in their 'image' of God (Ohrmazd) in fire: that might be the fire of the sun in the heavens, the great fires in temples, or an oil lamp at home. One common Parsi refrain is 'What better symbol is there of He who is pure light than the flame of the fire?' Others see much more in the flame of the ritual fire, namely the presence of the divine creative power on earth and in the ancient Avestan phrase venerating the fire as 'the Son of God', for example in the pre-Christian Litany to the fire (Dhalla 1908: 134–87). The High Priest with whom I have worked in Mumbai for 30 years answered my question, 'Can you put into words what you feel as you pray before the fire in the temple?', by saying 'I stand in the presence of God'. Fire is formless, but, throughout the ancient history of Zoroastrianism on the Asian steppes, fire gave protective warmth, enabled them to cook their food, protected them from wild animals, and was also a means of trial by fire to determine, in certain cases, the innocence or guilt of the accused. It is inevitable that such crucial roles should in ancient society affect how people viewed ultimate issues of life; it also means that there are many levels to the symbol of fire – one symbol having various meanings is called 'multivalent symbolism'. There is not the slightest element of anthropomorphism in the Zoroastrian imagery, theology or art, in what is a profound spiritual vision of God but which Christians and Muslims have dismissed over the centuries as mere 'fire worship'.

The art of the book

This heading indicates not textual studies but the significant artistic role of the holy book in some traditions, notably Judaism, Christianity in certain eras (e.g. illustrated manuscripts), the Sikhs, but perhaps most of all Islam. Calligraphy, along with architecture, is probably the characteristic form of Islamic art. Arabic script was woven into highly ornate form and lush foliate features, with birds and animals and highly ornate patterns on the walls of mosques, and on countless types of artefacts, e.g. rugs. Calligraphers who worked on texts had a long training with a master and held a high social position. There was a strong link between highly developed calligraphy and Sufism; mystics in various countries, notably Turkey and Persia, worked in distinct regional styles (Schimmel 1970 and her more technical 1984). The writing would not simply be pen and ink on paper, but carved in stone or wood with a vivid and highly symbolic colouring, enmeshed with the common theme of walls of light and shade in fine tracery with complex geometric shapes and foliate designs (see especially Dalu Jones in Michell (1978: 145–75), and on pp. 145–57 a superb set of illustrations to demonstrate the points made; see also Thackston in Frishman and Khan (1994: 48–53)). In many places these patterns were linked deliberately to reflections in water, thus enlarging the space and extending patterns. Surface decoration – of objects and buildings – is a crucial feature of Islamic art, although, with mosques as with homes, it is the decoration facing into the courtyard rather than the view from the outside world that is important. But on the inward facing walls run highly elaborated key texts from the Qur'an to inspire the worshipper. As Qadi Ahmad wrote (Schimmel 1984: 33), 'If someone, whether he can read or not, sees good writing, he likes to enjoy the sight of it'. The Qur'an – and other holy utterances – envelops the worshipper in the mosque. The Qur'an thereby might be said to become the book, or the holy word – on the wall, artefacts, prayer mats or carpets which surround the Muslim's life, or as Thackston puts it: '[the inscription] equivalent to a Christian icon: it serves as a visible representation of supernatural reality' (Frishman and Khan 1994: 45). In Islam, therefore, the book is not merely a matter of paper and ink, but of something visibly prevalent in all decoration and in diverse building forms. The Qur'an is part of the lived environment, not only a book. Looking only at texts students get no idea of how the word of God enfolds Muslims physically.

The 'transformatory' role of the arts

A different function of the arts in religions is what might be called their 'transformatory' role. Ordinary secular objects can by their decoration play this role. In Catholic and Orthodox Christianity the use of vestments highlights the spiritual power and role of the priest; he is no longer a mere ordinary human being but can re-enact, say in the Mass or Eucharist, the work of Jesus; just as a judge's garments transform him from the mere Mr Jones to the worshipful Judge, Mr Justice Jones. In many cultures masks are used to transform the 'ordinary' person into a powerful spiritual being who can bless, curse or inspire their followers commonly in dramatic dance and music (see especially Hackett (1996) on Africa). In most religions what is sacred is marked out with dramatic art forms.

'Ordinary' locations can at, say, festival time be considered to be, or to represent, a 'holy place'. For example, in my native county in England, Derbyshire, there is maintained what was almost certainly a pre-Christian practice of well dressings. This celebrates the coming of fertility in the early part of the agricultural cycle, Spring. For geological reasons, in Derbyshire springs, even rivers, disappear beneath the ground, to reappear elsewhere apparently from nowhere as the geology changes. Sites where waters sprang from the earth were decorated with flowers to celebrate the rebirth cycle of nature with prayers seeking an abundant harvest. This has been taken over by the Christian Church, so the pictures in petals from flowers, leaves or seeds (pressed into a large block of damp clay) depict sacred events, mostly from the life story of Jesus; they are blessed by the priest and become the focal point of week-long village celebrations. The site, which has lain devoid of any decoration or marker of significance all year, becomes a temporary holy site of blessing and fertility. The secular temporarily becomes the sacred as represented by the traditional art of decoration. A similar longer-lasting example would be demarcated shrine areas in Hinduism (Elgood 1999: 193, 195, 221).

Arts and protection

Religious art can also have a protective role, especially in popular art. Lorries carrying heavy loads in Afghanistan and Pakistan frequently have religious symbols painted on them to protect them on their journey. The most common are Qur'anic quotations in ornate Arabic or the depiction of what is sometimes known as 'the Evil eye', which shields them from harmful powers. In Mumbai, taxi drivers regularly have a Hindu or Sikh image on their dashboards similarly protecting them in their work, as in the West images/necklaces of St Christopher, the patron saint of travellers, are there to protect their wearers.

Emotion and religious arts

In my opinion one of the most important roles of the arts in religion is their emotive impact. A colleague (a philosopher) once commented that religion is to do with concepts. I totally disagree with that statement. Sometimes people dismiss issues as 'mere' emotion. I maintain that emotion is of crucial importance in religion, indeed in all life. Our emotions commonly govern our actions in daily life, and especially in religion. Worship in many religions – Christianity, Judaism, Islam, Hinduism and Sikhism – is generally expressed in art forms. (How one characterizes the goals of Buddhist meditation or of Zoroastrian prayers before the sacred fire I am less certain.) For most people, emotions are at the heart of their religious experience. I suggest that few Christians, Muslims, Sikhs etc. go to a centre of worship because of their concepts of God, but because worship makes them feel better. The emotional impact of architecture, the beautiful clothing, such as vestments, the uplifting singing or chanting of a group worshipping together inspire any but the most cynical. Of course some rituals express the reverse: funerals or memorial services are frequently communal expressions of the emotions of grief, loss and sadness – and maybe, at times of conflict, outrage or the desire for protection. Music, be it in the form of marching bands or wailing relatives and friends, gives vent to (or excites) powerful emotions.

In discussions of the emotions and religious arts there are – in my opinion – two especially important areas for discussion: architecture and the representation of people/god(s). (If I knew more about it I would add music. Of course, there could have been many other examples.)

Religious architecture

Architecture determines the nature of worship conducted therein. Sometimes this conflicts with what one might imagine should logically be the spirit of worship. In Christianity, for example, the saying attributed to Jesus, 'where two or three are gathered together in my name, there am I in the midst of them', should logically imply the intimacy of Christian worship. The doctrine of the incarnation, that God became man in Jesus, should for believers naturally suggest that worship involves the closeness of the congregation and the divine. Gothic is the most common architectural form of churches in Western Europe. The distinguishing feature of early Gothic (to summarize almost to the point of oversimplifying) was that, with technological development, thick walls and heavy buttresses were no longer needed to support the roof so that tall graceful columns and large windows that admitted much more light into the liturgy became widely popular. Gothic churches or cathedrals are beautiful and awesome. But, in practice, the first instinct of most people entering them is to whisper, because, rather than stressing the closeness of God and his people, God is made to look far away 'up there', distant and remote, so that worshippers feel small and dwarfed. The symbolism of a Gothic church is complex, for example the ground plan is shaped as a cross. The richly coloured stained-glass windows and east-facing windows looking to the rising sun invoke the beauty and light of heaven. Their beauty and colours may have made them seem like heaven; they can also make God feel beyond reach. But this essay has to be too short to follow up all the symbolism of any one form of religious art in a tradition. (A standard work on Gothic architecture is Focillon (1963), but see also Honour and Fleming (1982: 293–301) and Gombrich (1972: 138–41).)

The experience of whispering in a Gothic church is the very opposite of the typical form of worship in a Hindu temple. Whether a temple is large or small, it has three basic elements: an entrance hall or chamber, a spire representing the cosmic mountain, Mt Meru (the *shikhara*), and, directly beneath that spire, the womb chamber (*garbhagriha*). The spire can be immense, depicting many ranks of sacred beings in the cosmos, for in Hindu thought all life is lived on the same mountain. Animals may be on the lowest level, and humans above them with heavenly beings above them, but all life is on the one mountain. The temple is the home of the deity; worshippers come as their guests, bearing gifts (flowers, garlands, coconuts, etc.). They announce their arrival by ringing the bell, and saying prayers, offer gifts to God by handing them to the attendant priest, perhaps circumambulating the shrine in the larger temples, and then praying silently before God. At the heart of Hindu worship is the conviction that, where people worship God, there divinity 'really' dwells. The divine powers are more likely to dwell in a beautiful location; hence the representations of the gods in the temples conform to the ideals of beauty as conceived within the Hindu tradition. Temple worship is, therefore, lively, the setting bright and beautiful. However splendid, huge and ornate the exterior of the building, in the womb chamber all is simple and rough, like a cave, and in that simple space the worshipper stands alone before God, offers devotion and receives blessing. The Indian temples enact in daily practice what one might have thought would be the purpose of Christian churches. (An old but standard work is Kramrisch (1946); see also Michell (1977, 1989) and Elgood (1999: 93–134).) The bustle, colour and noise of a Hindu temple are totally different from western stereotypes of Hindu holy men meditating in solitude. There are such holy men (and some women), but the Hindu daily religious life is very different. The great scholar on India, A. L. Basham, underlined this point:

> In our opinion the usual inspiration of Indian art is not so much a ceaseless quest for the Absolute as a delight in the world as the artist found it, a sensual vitality, and a feeling of growth and movement as regular and organic as the growth of living things upon earth.

(1982: 349)

The mosque is different again. There are several types and functions of mosques; here I am focusing on the mosque used for communal Friday prayers. Again it is important to emphasize 'where I am coming from'. Although I have visited mosques in India, Pakistan and the West, most of my mosque experience has been in Iran. I am therefore influenced by one regional form of mosque architecture (and its decoration). The basic function of a mosque is to provide a pure space where Muslims can assemble together. In Islam the congregational dimension is vital, whereas Hindu temple worship is a pilgrimage of the self alone to God, even though others may happen to be present. To preserve the purity of the mosque it is necessary first to wash exposed parts of the body, and offer preliminary prayers; shoes are left outside to avoid bringing the pollution of the outside world into the pure sacred space. In contrast with the Hindu temple, the external decoration and design is generally unimportant; it is the inside that is crucial. Two internal features are essential; the *quibla*, which shows the direction of Mecca because that must be the orientation of prayer, and a pulpit for the sermon that is part of Friday prayers. The prayer leader at the front acts almost like the conductor of an orchestra, ensuring that sounds and movements are in harmony. The Friday mosque brings people together to make jointly their submission to, and worship of, Allah and receive his blessing. In much of Central Asia, but especially in Iran, the mosque has important decorative features. There is a belief that symmetry represents the harmony of heaven, so that in both big architectural forms (e.g. the colonnades), and the detailed tile work, there will be symmetry even in the largest mosques. Over the *quibla* is a dome, the symbol of the power of Islam, and within that an abstract pattern of the tree of life may be shown growing outwards and downwards. There can be no depiction of humans. The tile work symbolically represents the abundant life of heaven with elaborate floral arabesque; the walls are rich in colour. Any reader who has been to Iran will realize that I am influenced by one mosque in particular – what was known at the time of my visits (pre-1979) as the Shah mosque in Isfahan. There the central courtyard has a huge expanse of water, making the symmetry not only horizontal in the tile work, but vertical as the water reflects the sky above. The domes themselves are in an exquisite blue, giving an ethereal effect that transforms the believer from the mundane world outside to closeness with God. On my first visit to the Shah mosque in the early 1970s I was so transfixed that – apparently – I remained unmoving, and unmovable, for almost five hours (I was consequently five hours late for a meeting with a very senior member of government – but in the circumstances was forgiven!). I am not a Muslim, but the power of that experience remains vividly with me. I cannot accept my colleague's idea that religion is to do with concepts; rather I think it is to do with personal emotions, experiences transmitted for many by the arts of the religion. A book or course that ignores such subjects fails to communicate what is the lived experience of the religion concerned. It is impossible to understand what prayer means to a Muslim without seeing and studying the mosque. (On mosque design, architecture, structure and decoration see especially Michell (1978), Frishman and Khan (1994), Ettinghausen *et al.* in Lewis (1976), and Grubbe (1966), which covers a wide range of the arts and is superbly illustrated. The mosque I wrote about above is on pp. 123 and 143ff. and on the front cover of Grubbe; see also Frishman and Khan (1994: 129–31) and Michell (1978: 25, 253ff). The garden tomb of the Taj Mahal at Agra displays similar qualities and in my experience inspires similar feelings; see Michell (1978: 255).)

The representation of humans and gods: the body in religious art

The representation of the human form is common in many religions. Here I look at just three: Christian, Hindu and (Indian) Buddhist. They illustrate three different ways of representing humanity and its relationship to God. I am focusing on this motif/symbol because, throughout history, various cultures have represented the human form differently but frequently. The nude has been a theme in art from Paleolithic cave paintings down to this day. Although artists have studied countless subjects, the most common has been the nude. At art college and afterwards one of my favourite subjects was life (or figure) drawing. From an artistic perspective, the body is one of the most complex and challenging forms to draw, paint or sculpt. The slightest change in pose can express different moods, from ecstasy to fear, from tension to exhilaration, from restful to strenuous, in a way that no clothed figure – or any other subject – can. No two models, no two poses, are the same. It is the most common and the most demanding subject to draw. Of course its representation in religious art is different from that of the secular life studio in a college.

In Christian art one might logically have expected that the human body would have been the symbol of God for the reasons given on worship above – the teaching that humans are made in the image of God, and with the doctrine of God becoming man. Furthermore the nude was a common form in Greek and Roman art and in the former especially the (generally male) nude represented something of the perfection of the ideal form and even what might now be termed the 'erotic' (Johns 1982). Early Christian art encompassed numerous aspects of Greek and Roman art, but the use and symbolism of the nude was not one of them (P. Brown 1988). The nude rarely figures in Christian art. Occasionally it is used when depicting classical Greek and Roman subjects, pre-pubescent cherubs, or Adam and Eve in the garden of Eden (though a falling fig leaf often conveniently covers the genitals; see, for example, Levey (1968: pl. 36)). Steinberg, in his discussion of Jesus' sexuality in Renaissance art, emphasized the significance of artists depicting Jesus' genitals. This was undoubtedly an outcome of belief in the incarnation, but the examples are of the infant, pre-pubescent child only. Depictions of genitalia in the adult Jesus are extremely rare (see the discussion by Miles in Adams and Apostolos-Cappadona (1987)). The main use of the nude is the figure of Jesus in scenes of the flagellation, crucifixion and deposition from the cross and perhaps the resurrection. But he is almost always depicted only semi-nude, for a loin cloth covers his genitals, a totally unhistorical draping for, in crucifixions, the victims were not given such 'privacy' (see Schiller 1972). If I had focused on themes of (semi-)naked young men in bondage and being whipped questions might have been asked about my motivation. Some of the depictions of Saint Sebastian almost enjoying being shot with arrows have provoked suggestions that there is an element of pornography here (see, for example, Levey 1968: pls 39, 94; Gombrich 1972: pl. 171; Honour and Fleming 1982: 342, pl. 10.33). The nude became more acceptable with the high Renaissance, for example Michelangelo and his masterpiece of David – though still not for Jesus (Honour and Fleming 1982: 363, pl. 11.15). With some exceptions, such as Michelangelo, western religious art (as opposed to the modern phenomenon of secular art) restricted the nude to the female form, depictions of themes from Greek and Latin classics and pre-pubescent children. The Renaissance inspired numerous fine paintings of the human Jesus, but could – or would – not address the issue of his sexuality. Later western artists, in predominantly secular art, depicted the nude, which for some became perhaps the ideal form. The famous art historian, Kenneth Clark (1956), sought to distinguish between the naked and the nude, where naked represented the vulnerable, undressed figure, the nude the confident ideal – a distinction that became popular in the history of art though more recently it has been questioned (see Need (1992) and Gill (1989)). For a discussion of Foucault's *History of Sexuality*, and of earlier Christianity, see Culianu in Law (1995)). But in Christianity, however, the nude has remained the naked – the symbol of degradation, humiliation, sin (in depicting Eden) and brutality (with the flagellation). Christian art has avoided sexuality as in practice the religion has commonly had problems with sex.

Logically one would not have expected the nude in Indian art to have been a positive symbol of the good, in view of the belief in reincarnation, wherein the immortal 'soul' is imprisoned in the material world, while seeking release from rebirth so that the blissful state beyond the material might be achieved. But the body is not used in most Indian art to represent sin, degradation or humiliation. Instead, the human body is generally depicted virtually – if not completely – naked, almost always full of life, vigour, beauty and energy; indeed it often involves scenes on temple walls of ecstatic copulation – sometimes in pairs, sometimes in groups (*maithuna*). In the temples, the phallus and the vagina are common motifs in the sanctuary (see Elgood (1999: 105, 107); Michell *et al.* (1992: 54); on the nude in tantric art and practice, see Rawson (1973)). How can this be? The nineteenth-century missionaries were disgusted at such scenes and interpreted them as evidence of the degradation of Hindus. For many Hindus, however, it is natural to use representations of the source of human life as symbols of the divine creative power. Happy copulating couples were symbols of the generation of life and of the love of God for the soul and vice versa. Despite contemporary Asian attitudes to displaying the body, much classical Indian art used the human form as the obvious religious symbol for the gods. Human beauty is based on traditionally defined proportions – the body should be 'x' times the length of the head, similarly the width of shoulders and hips. Beauty is represented by wide shoulders, narrow waists and round pendulous breasts for the women. By using these proportions, the beauty of the figure is assured (Michell 1977: 36–9). If Clark's polarization were accepted, then one might say there are no naked, only nude, forms in virtually all Indian art. The individual identity of the deities depicted is not always clear, because many figures are depicted in a similar beautiful pose (notably the 's' or threefold alignment of shoulders, hips and lower limbs), though the dancing Shiva is different, and virtually all follow the same canons of beauty. Instead, they are identified by the attributes they carry (for example a trident) or by their hand gestures (*mudras*), as they also are in Indian dance – an art form closely related to sculpture (Gaston 1985: *passim*; see also Neuman *et al.* in F. Robinson 1989: 445–56). Divinity dwells where it is worshipped, so it is thought that, when the worshipper approaches the image in purity and with devotion, then the gods indwell that beautiful form. As the devotee sees the image with the eye of knowledge the deity comes to dwell within the worshipper. When an image is made the last step is always 'the opening' of the image's eyes by the priest, for not only does the worshipper see the image, so also the divine sees, and thereby blesses, the worshipper (Eck 1985). It is impossible to understand Hindu devotion without studying the divine image bringing the divine into the person of the worshipper.

In Buddhism the theory and practice varies between the two great branches of Theravada and Mahayana, and even between different countries of each branch. The focus here is on the image of the Buddha in the Theravada tradition, which grew out of and retained many traditional Indian principles of art. In what follows, I am not discussing how Theravada Buddhism viewed the human body (for that see Hamilton in Law 1995), but rather the Buddha *rupa*; I am not even discussing Shakhyamuni before he was enlightened, but more Buddhahood; that is, the ideal, the role model, the figure that 'drives' religious belief and practice. There is debate over the issue of whether the aniconic or the iconic forms of the Buddha image were used first, but in the early years the aniconic was dominant; the Buddha, having passed beyond all human categories, could not be depicted in merely mortal form. He was therefore represented by the wheel depicting his religious journeys, an empty throne from which he might have preached, or two footprints depicting his teaching mission. When the Buddha image took iconic form he was widely depicted sitting cross-legged, in the yoga pose, evidently deep in meditation. Iconic Buddhist art in India broadly followed Indian canons of beauty, i.e. using standard proportions. The Buddha, standing or meditating, is shown with marks of Buddhahood – e.g. elongated ears or a bump (of knowledge) on his head. The face is typically calm, eyes half-closed suggesting tranquillity, and he is clothed in a light garment from neck to below the knee (Snellgrove 1978: 23–82). For me personally, the seated Buddha from Sarnath (fifth–sixth centuries CE) is one of the most exquisite pieces of sculpture anywhere. Even in its current museum location the simple beauty alone inspires peaceful reflection (Snellgrove 1978: 99). Such images are designed for use in visualization meditation, where by concentrating attention on different parts of the image one becomes one with the Buddha essence. Many, if not most, Buddha images are nowadays to be found in museums, but their purpose was to aid devotional practice. Their nature cannot be understood apart from their use in practice. In both Hindu and Buddhist art there are examples of didactic and narrative art, for example in the life of Krishna and of Shakyamuni, but in India images are commonly for use in meditation, not for 'mere' decoration. One cannot understand Buddhist spiritual practice without studying the art and the process of visualization.

The point behind this discussion is that statues and other visual representations differ in function from each other, from religion to religion. Leaving aside the secular artist's depiction of the nude, the Christian/western role of the image is didactic, decorative or, with statues in churches, more commemorative. With stained-glass windows the figures are commonly symbols to evoke a known story, for example the image of a sheep to allude to the doctrine of Jesus as the paschal lamb. The Orthodox icon is different for that is itself a holy object, a means of direct apprehension of God. It has a more 'sacramental' role than figures in stained-glass windows (see Stewart in Parry *et al.* 1999: 243–7). In Hinduism and Buddhism, the figures are representations of divine powers, which through meditation can enter the individual worshipper. Whereas the nude has generally been used in Christian art to portray sin or humiliation, in Hinduism it is expressive of life, vitality, creation or birth. In Buddhism the image is functional (however beautiful), to achieve the fulfilment of meditation and to point to something beyond human experience (Snellgrove 1978: 403–38). The one symbol, the human body, is used for totally different purposes and in ways at variance with what one might logically have expected of the religion.

The artist

Many books distinguish between 'artist' and 'craftsman', reserving the former for someone who is an original creator of a work of art and the latter for people who reproduce what others have done or designed. In religious studies I question the value of this distinction. As noted above, works of art in India (and icons in the Greek and Russian Orthodox Churches) are produced according to clearly defined and precise canons of religious principle and the 'producers' might therefore be referred to as craftsmen, but the beauty of many artefacts (for example the Sarnath Buddha referred to on p. 521) is such that the term 'artist' seems entirely appropriate. (Obviously some artists reproduced the grace and beauty more effectively than others; even some of the 'copies' of great art, for example the images used daily in the home, may not reproduce the beauty of the original – as in Christianity.) Whereas in western art it is normal for the artist to sign his or her work, because it is a personal individual creation, this was not the case in classical India. It is precisely because the Indian artist is thought to be reproducing visions that the figures produced are so spiritually powerful. Normally the paintings or statues are beautiful. Some depictions of Kali apart, there is little like the torture depicted in many flagellations or crucifixions. (See, for example, the crucifixion painted by Grunewald in the early sixteenth century – Levey (1968: pl. 149); Honour and Fleming (1982: 352). See also Schiller (1972: *passim*), the standard work on the Passion of Jesus.) Two of the characteristic features of Indian arts are: first, beauty as an affirmation of the vitality of the divine; and, second, beautiful images as a means of uniting oneself with the deity that dwells within the image when (but normally only when) being worshipped. The Orthodox icon apart, there is nothing comparable in Christianity.

It should be noted that western artists have never been as free and independent in their work as imagined. Even where the church – or any religious body – has patronized the arts, strict guidelines have often been laid down. The patron is virtually always the one who determines what shall be done. To illustrate the point from my own experience, I was once commissioned by a theologian to do a painting of the Trinity. Dozens of sketches of the proposed painting were approved of artistically, but rejected as being heretical in the symbolic relationship of one member of the Trinity to another. I am not sure whose product the final outcome was! The power of a western patron's wishes can be almost as binding as ancient Hindu texts are for their artists – at least if one needs to earn a living!

Religious arts in the modern world

Both in the West and in Asia many of the arts nowadays have a wholly secular purpose and origin, although ecclesiastical commissions still occur, and diaspora communities periodically employ Indian craftsmen to reproduce centres of worship in the West fashioned closely on classical temples. Religion in some ways has become yet more important in diaspora groups than in the old country. In a fascinating article, Naficy (1999) studied the Iranian exiles in Los Angeles and their diverse art forms (including their own TV and radio stations and videos). He considers in particular the (re)creation of the image of Iran in a way that seems to me to be appropriate for many other diaspora groups. He writes of the imaginary geography as a construction created by exile narratives. But this creation is not hermetic, since the 'real' past threatens to reproduce itself as a lack or loss; it is against the threat of such a loss that the nostalgic past must be turned into a series of nostalgic objects, in fetish souvenirs that can be displayed and consumed repeatedly. Photo albums, letters, diaries, and telephones . . . The exiles construct their difference through not just what they see and hear but through their senses of smell, taste and touch.

He goes on to emphasize how festivals and their celebrations become boundaries round a community and stresses the importance of the old rituals. What he writes concerning a group of Iranians in California is replicated in many communities, especially the importance of touch, taste and smell. Two British studies of Hindu children (Jackson and Nesbit 1993; Gillespie 1995) have stressed how they commonly spend time with the extended family looking at Indian art, or watching videos of Bollywood films, Asian channels on television or camcorder films of visits back the old country, of weddings and of other celebrations linking families and friends across continents. From these sources, and from posters, calendars and domestic shrines, rather than books, the children learn about the values and ideals of their heritage. The nearest publications to conventional books that influence young children of Indian parentage are comic-style magazines telling the lives of the gods and heroes, not just of Hindu figures, but from other religions in India; for example, there are 'comics' of the lives of Zoroaster and of Jesus. These visual resources, plus the sharing of Indian food, the wearing of traditional dress, the burning of incense sticks and standing in veneration, even the offering of *puja* when the gods appear in the video (Gillespie 1995: 85–106), create an Indian world in another culture. The sources least used by Indian communities in the West are the books written about Hinduism by western or even Indian academics. If courses on religions are to give a balanced account of the living religion their focus needs to change dramatically from the current emphases of student textbooks. I question whether any religion or culture can be properly understood if its characteristic art forms are neglected. Texts are commonly generated by educated intellectuals for educated intellectuals; it is the arts that form the core of most lived religious experience.

A concluding speculative note

Might it be that for some (not all, not even for most) it is pointless to distinguish between the artistic and the religious experience? Would some people interpret my experience at the Shah mosque as a religious experience, while others might call it an artistic experience? Might it be the case that some use a religious vocabulary to describe an experience, whereas others might use a vocabulary drawn from the arts? A famous ballerina is said to have been asked by a rapturous reviewer what she was trying to say with a particular (and perhaps her best) performance, to which she is said to have replied, 'if I could put it into words would I have exhausted myself with that long performance?' (at least that is the discreet account of what I was told by my dancing informant who used much more robust language!). Not only dancers but painters or sculptors may sometimes be trying 'to say' something they cannot put into words. Most of my paintings were, bluntly, done to earn money (at least when

I left art college) – one does have to live! – but when I painted some works for myself, then occasionally I was trying to convey a feeling, an emotion or an experience for which I could not find words. For example, on one occasion I was asked to produce a painting for a room for Anglicans to meditate in. I was not asked to do a crucifixion or any specific subject, but something that conveyed or inspired an appropriate mood. I therefore went to a beautiful place in the country near my home, which I had always found peaceful and tranquil. I stayed there for most of the day for several days before I began work. I doubt if anyone would have recognized the place from my painting (it was fairly abstract), but I think, hope and was assured it communicated the mood I had experienced. Nothing I could say would have done that.

Some writers have tried to take the link between religious experience and the arts much further than that (Dillenberger (1986), Coleman (1998), Martland (1981), Pattison (1991) and the essays edited by Apostolos-Cappadona (1985)). Although I cannot go as far as some of these authors, what I am convinced of is that one cannot understand a religion or culture without a serious study of the diverse arts associated with that religion, which have inspired people, or through which they have sought to communicate their experiences and through which they have lived and learned about the religion. But few courses and textbooks take them into account.

References

Adams D. and Apostolos-Cappadona, D., 1987, *Art as Religious Studies*, New York: Crossroad Publishing.

Apostolos-Cappadona, D. (ed.), 1985, *Art, Creativity, and the Sacred*, New York: Crossroad Publishing.

Basham, A. L., 1982, *The Wonder That Was India*, London: Fontana.

Blurton, T. R., 1992, *Hindu Art*, London: British Museum.

Brown, K. (ed.), 1999, *Sikh Art and Literature*, London: Routledge.

Brown P., 1988, *The Body and Society: Men, Women, and Sexual Renunciation in Early Christianity*, New York: Columbia University Press.

Clark, K., 1956, *The Nude*, London: John Murray.

Coleman, E. J., 1998, *Creativity and Spirituality: Bonds Between Art and Religion*, New York: State University of New York Press.

Courtright, P. B., 1985, *Ganesa, Lord of Obstacles, Lord of Beginnings*, Oxford: Oxford University Press.

Dhalla, M. N., 1908, *The Nyaishes or Zoroastrian Litanies*, New York: AMS Press.

Dillenberger, J., 1986, *A Theology of Artistic Sensibilities, The Visual and the Church*, New York: Crossroad Publishing.

Eck, D. L., 1985, *Darsan: Seeing the Divine Image in India*, 2nd edn, Pennsylvania: Anima Books.

Elgood, H., 1999, *Hinduism and the Religious Arts*, London/New York: Cassell.

Focillon, H., 1963, *The Art of the West II: Gothic*, Oxford: Phaidon (English translation by D. King).

Frishman, M. and Hasan-Uddin Khan, 1994, *The Mosque: History, Architectural Development and Regional Diversity*, London: Thames & Hudson.

Gaston, A., 1985, *Siva in Dance, Myth and Iconography*, Delhi: Oxford University Press.

Geertz, C., 1973, *The Interpretation of Cultures*, London: Fontana.

Gill, M., 1989, *Image of the Body*, New York: Doubleday.

Gillespie, M., 1995, *Television, Ethnicity and Cultural Change*, London: Routledge.

Gombrich, E. H., 1971, *Norm and Form: Studies in the Art of the Renaissance*, 2nd edn, London: Phaidon.

—— 1972, *The Story of Art*, 12th edn, London: Phaidon.

Gray, B., 1961, *Persian Painting*, 1st edn, Geneva: Editions d'art.

—— (ed.), 1981, *The Arts of India*, Oxford: Phaidon.

Grubbe, E. J., 1966, *The World of Islam*, London: Hamlyn.

Hackett, R., 1996, *Art and Religion in Africa*, London/New York: Cassell.

Hinnells, J. R., 2004, *The Zoroastrian Diaspora*, Oxford: Clarendon Press.

Honour, H. and Fleming, J., 1982, *A World History of Art*, London: Macmillan.

Jackson R. and Nesbitt, E., 1993, *Hindu Children in Britain*, Stoke on Trent: Trentham Books.

Johns, C., 1982, *Sex or Symbol: Erotic Images of Greece and Rome*, London: British Museum.

Kramrisch, S., 1946, *The Hindu Temple*, reprinted 1980, London/Calcutta: Motilal Banarsidass.

Law, J. M. (ed.), 1995, *Religious Reflections on the Human Body*, Bloomington, IN: Indiana University Press.

Layton, R., 1991, *The Anthropology of Art*, 2nd edn, Cambridge: Cambridge University Press.

Levey, M., 1968, *From Giotto to Cezanne: A Concise History of Painting*, London: Thames & Hudson.

Lewis, B., 1976, *The World of Islam*, London: Thames & Hudson.

Manekshaw, B. J., 1996, *Parsi Food and Customs*, Delhi: Penguin Books.

Martland, T. R. 1981, *Religion as Art, An Interpretation*, Albany: SUNY.

Michell, G., 1977, *The Hindu Temple*, London: Paul Elek.

—— (ed.), 1978, *Architecture of the Islamic World: Its History and Social Meaning*, London: Thames & Hudson.

—— 1989, *Monuments of India*, London: Viking.

—— Lampert, C. and Holland, T. (eds), 1982, *In the Image of Man*, London: Weidenfeld & Nicholson.

Mookerjee A., 1988, *Kali: The Feminine Force*, London: Thames & Hudson.

Moore, A. C., 1995, *Arts in the Religions of the Pacific*, London/New York: Cassell.

Morris B., 1987, *Anthropological Studies of Religion: An Introductory Text*, Cambridge: Cambridge University Press.

Naficy, H., 1999, 'The Poetics and Practice of Iranian Nostalgia in Exile,' *Diaspora* 1 (33): 285–302.

Need, L., 1992, *The Female Nude: Art, Obscenity and Sexuality*, London: Routledge.

Parry, K., Melling, D., Brady, D., Griffith, S. H. and Healey, J. F., 1999, *Dictionary of Eastern Christianity*, Oxford: Blackwells.

Pattison, G., 1991, *Art, Modernity and Faith: Restoring the Image*, Basingstoke: Macmillan.

Rawson, P., 1973, *The Art of Tantra*, London: Thames & Hudson.

Robinson, B. W., 1980, *Persian Paintings in the John Rylands Library*, London/New York: Sotheby Parke Bernet.

Robinson, F., 1989, *Cambridge Encyclopedia of India*, Cambridge: Cambridge University Press.

Schiller, G., 1972, *Iconography of Christian Art, vol II: The Passion of Jesus Christ*, London: Lund Humphries (English translation by J. Seligman).

Schimmel, A., 1970, *Islamic Calligraphy*, Iconography of Religions, Leiden: Brill.

—— 1984, *Calligraphy and Islamic Culture*, London: I. B. Tauris.

Snellgrove, D. L., 1978, *The Image of the Buddha*, Paris, London and Tokyo: UNESCO.

Van der Veer, P., 1994, *Religious Nationalism: Hindus and Muslims in India*, Berkeley, CA: University of California Press.

Welch, S. C., 1976, *Royal Persian Manuscripts*, London: Thames & Hudson.

Williams, D., 1974, *Icon and Image: A Study of Sacred and Secular Forms of African Classical Art*, London: Allen Lane.

Chapter 30

Migration, diaspora and transnationalism

Transformations of religion and culture in a globalising age

Seán McLoughlin

Autobiographical out-takes: Irish Catholics and Punjabi Sikhs overseas

As an undergraduate student during the late 1980s, I encountered (what was still called) 'comparative religion' for the first time. As part of the course, students were introduced to the religions and cultures of so-called 'ethnic minorities', especially South Asian heritage Muslims, Hindus, Sikhs and Parsis. While preparing for end-of-term examinations, I remember very clearly a long, early summer's day spent reading a study of migration from rural India. An educationalist's account of the significance of family, home, language and religion for the children of Indians overseas, it explores 'how far the social traditions of the Punjabi villages are being maintained in Sikh households' (James 1974: 2).[1] This early study of how religion and culture 'travel', how they alter and change as people move, mix and remake their lives in new settings, what they 'preserve', 'lose' and 'gain', and the impact of all this on their identification with 'homes' new and old, really captured my interest. Although, I did not consciously make such a connection at the time, I imagine now that it had much to do with my own sense of identity. As with so many people, in so many different places, during the modern period, my family history has been shaped by forces of international migration.

Like the Punjabi Sikhs described by James, I grew up with a strong sense of religious and cultural distinctiveness. In a small market town in the English Midlands I did not experience the overt hostility often shown to 'people of colour'. However, against the general context of John Paul II's papal visits and a 'civil war' in 'the North', growing up in a nationalist family from rural Ireland ensured a very ambiguous sense of belonging to 'Protestant' England. My early life and socialisation in the 1970s and 1980s revolved around various Catholic institutions: a church with an Irish parish priest; three schools often staffed by Irish teachers; and a social club where the 'navvies' drank and Irish bands played ballads about rebellion and the migrant's sense of opportunity and loss. A deep connection with Catholic Ireland was reinforced by visits 'home' every summer and the regular arrival, from across the water, of St Patrick's Day cards and religious paraphernalia from rosaries to relics. Broader but less intense links were maintained with 'the Yanks' (unfamiliar Irish-American relatives) who arrived periodically for weddings and funerals and Catholic missionaries who returned from India or Africa to raise funds and remind us that 'the poor' would eventually be sending missions back to us.[2] The latter, in particular, pointed beyond attempts to reproduce and encapsulate Irish Catholic 'tradition' in a alien setting, attempts that could not resist broader and more organic processes of cultural exchange and 'translation'. My local 'community' included some Catholics who were not Irish – Italians, Poles, Yugoslavs, even one or two Africans and Pakistanis – and, as a teenager especially, I was acculturated to (increasingly commodified and globalised forms of) English popular culture (mostly music and football).

Deciding to study theology and religious studies at university opened up more cosmopolitan experiences. In multi-racial, multi-cultural, multi-faith Manchester I found myself embracing the diversity of the city both intellectually and emotionally and my intended focus on Christian theology was soon dropped in favour of comparative religion. Towards the end of a vacation spent packing eggs back in Nottinghamshire, 'inter-railing' around Europe, and meeting my future (English, non-Catholic) wife, I was also given the chance to spend one week studying religion more intensively 'in the field'. John R. Hinnells, Professor of Comparative Religion in Manchester at the time, had arranged for a small group of interested students to *practise* what John always preached, that is, '*get your hands dirty with religion*'. We would stay at a United Reformed Church under the supervision of the resident minister, someone who was actively engaged in multi- and interfaith work in the West London suburb of Southall.

Doing Comparative Religion in '*chota* (little) Punjab'

Southall, perhaps like parts of Houston, Washington DC or Northern California in the United States (Jurgensmeyer 2002: 3), is one of any number of the world's '*chota* (little) Punjabs'. It is seen by some as a 'ghetto' and by others as the busy, if slightly tatty, 'capital' of South Asian Britain (Baumann 1996: 38). In 1991, just a few years after my stay, the decennial national census suggested that around 60 per cent of Southall's 61,000 population were of South Asian heritage (1996: 48). Sikhs are the largest single religious grouping in the town, representing around 40 per cent of the population (1996: 73). Like so many 'Chinatowns' or 'Little Italys' in today's global cities, institutions, organisations and businesses owned, and run, by people who trace their cultural heritage overseas have transformed the ecology of Southall's main streets. As well as *gurdwaras* (Sikh temples), *mandirs* (Hindu temples) and Muslim mosques, there are numerous 'Asian' grocers, pubs, butchers, video and music stores, jewellers, curry houses, *sari* shops and the offices of *Des Pardes* (*Home and Abroad*), the largest Punjabi language newspaper in Britain. Southall, then, is what anthropologists sometimes call 'institutionally complete' – it is 'a home abroad' to all things South Asian. Because of this, the town is a magnet for Asian family and visitors from the rest of England. It has even featured heavily in so-called 'Asian cool' movies, such as *Bend It Like Beckham* (2002).

With all this on the doorstep, and briefed with a little local knowledge, I was encouraged to go out into Southall and simply '*do*' comparative religion. I should attempt to produce, in outline, my own 'religious map' of the area, visiting places of worship and community organisations, observing and talking to people as best I could about such matters as:

- the background to, and history of, their migration;
- places of worship and their associated rituals;

- different religious movements, organisations and their leaderships;
- issues of gender and generation;
- the question of public recognition and multi-cultural/interfaith relations;
- and, finally, continuing links with the Indian subcontinent and beyond.

Looking back now, there was a danger of becoming a 'comparative religion tourist' and unreflectively 'consuming' the 'difference' and 'exotica' around me. After all, 'why should people want to talk to me?', 'what did I have to offer?' and 'could I possibly hope to give anything back?'. Nevertheless, somewhere in between the fear and the exhilaration of awkwardly made dialogues and connections, I was able to reflect that, given a general concern to 'maintain' religious and cultural identifications while all the time adapting to new circumstances, something that set them apart from the (ir)religious 'ethnic' majority in Britain, the South Asian heritage people I had met and spoken to in Southall probably had much in common with the parents and grandparents of the (admittedly increasingly assimilated) O'Sullivans, Passaseos and Heidukewitschs I had been to school with.

Where do we go from here? Reflection and overview

My experiences as a Catholic of Irish heritage, and those of Southall Sikhs of Punjabi heritage, provide just two ethnographic 'snapshots' of a diverse and complex global phenomenon, which, since the 1990s especially, has often been described as 'diaspora religion' (Hinnells 1997). The examples I have given locate both me and my academic career firmly in England, however 'diaspora religion' is, of course, 'everywhere'. In the United States, for example, The Pluralism Project at Harvard University has sought to map the changing religious landscape of America since the early 1990s. As the director of the project, Professor Diana L. Eck (2002), argues, diversity is now a feature of 'Main Street' USA.[3] In Boston, The Pluralism Project has documented the history of 13 traditions and interfaith groups. One of the most prominent and long-standing of these is, undoubtedly, Irish-American Catholicism. Between 1820 and 1920, a massive four and a half million people left poverty and famine in Ireland for life in a modern American city in the making. Dominated by the 'New England' Protestant establishment, Boston in the nineteenth century was nevertheless increasingly the home of Italian and other Catholics from Southern and Eastern Europe, as well as Jews and Orthodox Christians. Today Irish Catholics in Boston are themselves part of the 'establishment', but they still share something of a 'transnational' tradition with newcomers, such as the Vietnamese who have arrived in the city since the Immigration Act of 1965. While Irish Catholics in Boston and the English Midlands have quite different histories, I have no doubt that many of the themes in 'my story' would still have much resonance there.

Whether taken in America or in England, my 'snapshots' of 'diaspora religion' are intended to give a certain depth and texture to a topic that, after all, is primarily concerned with the 'living religions' of 'real people'. 'We' are these people, or at least many of us will meet 'these people' on an everyday basis. Therefore, just as my own account reveals something of 'who I am' and 'where I'm coming from', I hope readers will be prompted to reflect on how they and their families, or at least the neighbourhoods, cities and countries in which they live, have been impacted by migration, diaspora and transnationalism. At its best, the study of religions and cultures should always provoke us to ponder the risks and rewards of learning about our 'selves' as we encounter the 'difference' of 'others'. Moreover, as we are beginning to see, diaspora religion is by no means confined to the experiences of 'people of colour' or the 'visible minorities' who have migrated from Asia, Africa and the Middle East in the post-war period. Discussions that mention both Irish and Vietnamese Catholics in the same breath, never mind Punjabi Sikhs, may be rare. However, history teaches us that migrants and diasporas do share many continuities of experience for all their differences. Indeed, what remains perhaps most interesting are the products of 'our' interactions, whoever 'we' may now be.

In the rest of this chapter I will explore how the relatively new field of 'diaspora religion' has evolved and developed within what is variously identified as comparative religion, the history of religions, religious studies and the study of religion. For pragmatic reasons, I draw no particular distinctions between these different labels here. Indeed, I tend to use them interchangeably. The chapter continues with some general definitions of 'migration', 'diaspora' and 'transnationalism', drawing out the distinctions made by Professor Steven Vertovec (2000a), director of the recently completed Transnational Communities Programme at the University of Oxford.[4] Vertovec's key points are illustrated with further reference to James' *Sikh Children in Britain* (1974: 30–52).

My next task is to contextualise the current prominence of diaspora and transnational studies in the academy. While Professor Robin Cohen's excellent survey, *Global Diasporas* (1997), demonstrates that the field has a long history often associated with Judaism, its contemporary high profile is closely linked to recent developments in globalisation and postmodern theory. Whereas, hitherto, there was a focus on the study of *migrants and minorities within particular states*, the emphasis now is on the way that *diasporas* sustain both imagined and actual connections *across borders*, challenging the very idea of the *nation*. At this point I shall also move beyond commonsense definitions of other vocabulary I have begun to use, for example: 'culture', 'identity', 'hybridity', 'race', 'ethnicity', 'community' and 'multiculturalism'.

In terms of beginning to locate the study of religion in the context of these developments, an extremely helpful account is provided by Martin Baumann (2001), Professor of the History of Religions at the University of Lucerne, Switzerland.[5] In current genealogies the late Professor Ninian Smart (1987), of Lancaster and Santa Barbara Universities, is identified as the first to use the term. However, this fact should not obscure, as it sometimes does, that the roots of a distinctive research agenda for religious studies in this field actually lie elsewhere. My focus here is on the early work of one of the religious studies scholars working on migration and ethnicity during the 1980s, my colleague at the University of Leeds, and Director of the Community Religions Project, Professor Kim Knott (1986, 1992).[6]

The final parts of this chapter return us to an account of some of the main theoretical debates and empirical patterns and trends of the last decade or so. I explore the question of whether 'religions' can truly be considered 'diasporas', reflecting on the distinctions that are sometimes made between so-called 'ethnic' and 'universal' traditions. However, I also argue that it is the truly *comparative* mapping of migrant, diasporic and transnational *religion* that stands as the major achievement of scholars such as Professor Hinnells, both in *The New Handbook of Living Religions* (1998) and elsewhere.[7] By way of conclusion, I shall be arguing that, in the future, the study of religion should pay greater attention to theorising the different types of 'work' done by religions in spaces of migration, diaspora and transnationalism.

Migration, diaspora and transnationalism: distinctions and illustrations

> Diasporas arise from some form of migration, but not all migration involves diasporic consciousness; all transnational communities comprise diasporas, but not all diasporas develop transnationalism.
>
> (Vertovec 2000a: 12)

Having outlined the general thrust of this chapter, my first task now is to suggest certain definitions and distinctions in terms of our main vocabulary of 'migration', 'diaspora' and 'transnationalism'. In this respect it will be useful to begin by reflecting on the significance of the above quotation from Vertovec (2000a). At first glance, perhaps, it seems to resemble a riddle. However, in essence, what Vertovec is suggesting here is that 'migration', 'diaspora' and 'transnationalism' are three separate, but related, terms. Each can be associated with particular patterns of socio-religious continuity and transformation, and scholars and students alike should seek to distinguish between them more carefully.

For Vertovec '*migration*' involves movement and relocation from one place to another, something that has prompted people throughout the ages to 'reconstruct', or 'remake', their life-worlds in new contexts. Migrants very often form a 'minority', marked out from the 'ethnic' majority in terms of 'race', language, culture and/or religion. While '*diaspora*' also suggests a community 'dispersed' or 'scattered' away from the homeland, Vertovec insists that it should be defined in terms of the continuing 'consciousness' of a connection, 'real' or 'imagined', to that homeland and 'co-ethnics' in other parts of the world. In the present age of accelerated globalisation, time and space are compressed by advances in communications technology to such an extent that people increasingly experience the world as 'a global village' or 'a single place'. Under these conditions diasporas can become '*trans-national*', in the sense that social, economic, political and cultural 'circulations' or 'flows' between the homeland and its diasporas become very real indeed. However, this was not always the case historically and diasporas may have struggled to maintain contact and communication with the homeland while still imagining a sense of connection to it.

While lacking the more discriminating theoretical framework of Vertovec, James' study of Sikhs in a northern British town illustrates the distinctive notions of 'migrant', 'diasporic' and 'transnational' religion very well. In the early stages of settlement during the late 1950s and 1960s, the people James lived among had not sufficiently reconstructed their 'religious worlds' to be able to celebrate Diwali (the winter festival of light). This was because, living away from India, they lacked access to the knowledge of when it should 'properly' be observed (1974: 42). As wives and children began to join their husbands and fathers in England, some Punjabis acculturated to life in Britain by taking on various local customs, such as marking birthdays, Christmas and Easter. Into the 1970s, by which time the 'community' was well established, the main Sikh festivals were being commemorated but, interestingly, many highly localised ritual celebrations linked to particular villages of the Punjab had not survived (1974: 42). Religious and cultural reconstruction can therefore involve processes of 'standardisation', whereby those practices that command 'particular' rather than 'universal' allegiance do not 'travel' very well and are lost.

In a similar fashion, many Sikhs who had observed *kesh* (uncut hair) in the Punjab actually cut their hair and shaved their beards in Britain so as to look less conspicuous (1974: 49). However, as the numbers of migrants grew and families reunited, communities became more confident and keeping *kesh* became increasingly common. Moreover, when the wearing of turbans at work became a matter of controversy with employers, there were mass *khande di pahal* (Sikh 'initiation' or 'baptism') ceremonies in places like Southall (1974: 47–8). Observed rigorously by only the minority in India, these became ritual and symbolic vehicles for the assertion of collective pride and resistance in the face of discrimination in Britain. Indeed, while never the whole story, the politicisation of religious identity can play an important role in the growth of 'revivalism' among migrant communities.

James suggests that, in theory at least, there are no specifically religious reasons for Sikhs to 'remember' the Punjab (1974: 43). Indeed there is a general question about whether 'religious' (as opposed to 'ethno-national') groupings can truly be considered diasporas, a debate we shall return to in due course. Nevertheless, from their arrival in Britain, Sikhs have sustained numerous imagined and more tangible connections with the subcontinent. They are not required to make pilgrimage to the Punjab but many British Sikhs do return for this purpose, especially to the symbolic centre of the faith, the Golden Temple at Amritsar (1974: 43–4). In the age of international jet travel, Sikhs from Britain were also able to charter aeroplanes to travel to Talwandi (in modern Pakistan) on the five-hundredth anniversary of Guru Nanak's birth in 1969 (1974: 44). However, even in the 1970s the traffic between Britain and the Punjab was never 'one-way'. For example, *sants* (saints) from the subcontinent would tour Britain, giving sermons, leading devotions and collecting donations and gifts, both to fund their trips but also to finance educational institutions and charitable concerns back in India (1974: 42–3). Coupled with the obvious importance of migrants' remittances, this underlines the reliance of the homeland on the diaspora, as well as vice versa.

'Babylon' and beyond: the study of diaspora and transnationalism

Now that we have some feel for the complexity and texture of our subject, there is a need to contextualise the growth, particularly in diaspora studies, over the last few decades. Describing something of a 'takeover' in the humanities and social sciences especially, Baumann (2001: 2) cites Khachig Tölöyan, the editor of *Diaspora: A Journal of Transnational Studies* (launched 1991). Tölöyan argues that the new surge of popularity in diaspora studies has been accompanied by a 'decisive shift' in focus for the field. The term 'diaspora' was once used only in relation to the 'classical' Jewish, Greek and Armenian diasporas. However, its meaning now has expanded to encompass a much wider 'semantic domain' (Baumann 2001: 2). Those social groups hitherto identified as 'immigrants', 'ethnic minorities', 'exiles', 'expatriates', 'refugees', 'guest-workers' and so on, have all been re-imagined as 'diasporas' today.

Cohen suggests that 'The word "diaspora" is derived from the Greek verb *speiro* (to sow) and the preposition *dia* (over)' (1997: ix). The ancient Greeks thought of this 'sowing over' mainly in terms of migration and colonisation. However, for the Jews especially, it had the more negative connotation of enforced exile, whereas still others who have lived 'at home abroad', can be categorised neither as 'colonists' nor as 'victims'. Therefore the characteristics of 'diasporas' settled in specific places at specific points in time vary significantly. Indeed, Cohen (1997: x) produces a typology of diasporas, each 'type' exemplified by the experiences of particular 'ethnic groups':

- *victim diasporas* (e.g. Jews, Africans and Armenians);
- *labour diasporas* (e.g. Indians);
- *trade diasporas* (e.g. Chinese and Lebanese);
- *imperial diasporas* (e.g. British);
- *cultural diasporas* (e.g Caribbeans).

Here Cohen is not implying that the Jews can only be regarded as a 'victim diaspora'. At different times in history, they have been successful labour, trade and cultural diasporas (1997: xi). Indeed, given the variety of experiences subsumed by the term, he judges 'a grand overarching theory . . . impossible' (1997: xii). Nevertheless, Cohen still accumulates a list of what he regards as diasporas' 'common features' (1997: 26). This is reproduced here in a somewhat abbreviated form:

(i)   dispersal from a homeland to two or more foreign regions;
(ii)   or, expansion from a homeland in search of work, trade or empire;
(iii) a collective memory and myth about the homeland;
(iv)   an idealization of the ancestral home and collective commitment to it;
(v)   a return movement;
(vi)   a strong ethnic group consciousness of distinctiveness over a long period;
(vii) a troubled relationship with host societies, suggesting a lack of acceptance;
(viii) a sense of empathy and solidarity with co-ethnics elsewhere;
(ix)   the possibility of enrichment in host countries tolerant of pluralism.

While all of the above suggests that it is no longer necessary to take Jewish experiences as the only paradigm of diaspora, it is clear from the literature that Judaism has a special place in diaspora studies.[8] For example, of 106 results produced in a search for 'religion and diaspora' titles at the Amazon online bookstore (30 April 2004), 47 (nearly 50 per cent) related to Jewish studies. Of course, Jews were made captives and exiles after Jerusalem was captured by the Babylonians in the sixth century BCE and thereafter the idea of 'Babylon' became synonymous with oppression and exile in an alien land. However, as both Cohen (1997) and Ter Haar (1998) remark, even as the Jews of the diaspora 'remembered Zion', there was opportunity and creativity in 'Babylon' as many integrated and made their home there. Indeed, 'the Jewish communities in Alexandria, Antioch, Damascus, Asia Minor and Babylon became centres of civilisation, culture and learning' (Cohen, 1997: 5). For example, 'the term 'diaspora' itself became widely 'used in the Septuagint, the Greek translation of the Hebrew scriptures explicitly intended for the Hellenic Jewish communities in Alexandria (circa third century BCE)' (Braziel and Mannur 2003: 2). In a similar way, reflecting on the time of St Paul, Jurgensmeyer describes Rome, Antioch and Corinth as 'multi-ethnic . . . urban melting pots', where Roman, Greek, Egyptian and Persian religions competed with, and left their mark upon, both Judaism and Christianity (2002: 4–5).

Before the 1960s, however, the study of diaspora was largely confined to more traditional approaches to Jewish and Christian studies. Baumann suggests that much of this scholarship was 'historically descriptive' (2001: 2) and demonstrated little interest in the sort of theory or comparison that occupies many scholars today. In other academic circles, the study of diaspora first came to prominence in African studies during the 1950s and 1960s. However, Baumann remarks that it took until the mid-1970s for interest to mushroom as 'diaspora' became associated with contemporary 'black' politics and memories of the impact of the transatlantic slave trade.[9] Clearly there are a number of parallels with the Jewish experience here, including the biblical symbolism of living under oppression in 'Babylon' and the emergence of modern 'return' movements, which often found a religio-nationalist expression, for example in Rastafarianism.

It was from African studies that the term 'diaspora' entered the social sciences in the 1980s. By the 1990s, sociologists, anthropologists, political scientists and cultural studies scholars were all using the term to refer to various 'transnational communities'. A key feature of this and related literature has been close attention to the theorisation of such concepts as 'culture', 'identity', 'hybridity', 'race', 'ethnicity', 'community' and 'multiculturalism'. What follows next is a brief outline of some of these ideas.

Diaspora and the global postmodern: culture, hybridity and ethnicity

The current salience of diaspora studies cannot be understood without reference to recent developments in globalisation and postmodern theory. As well as reproducing 'uneven' power relations between 'the Rest and the West', Hall (1992: 304–5) argues that the impact of globalisation has been contradictory. On the one hand, it has given rise to processes of cultural *homogenisation*, whereby transnational corporations have exported the consumer-capitalism of the West worldwide. For obvious reasons, this is often known as the 'McWorld' phenomenon. On the other hand, because globalisation has also had the effect of *relativising the discreteness of different 'cultures'*, it has given rise to a *defence of particularistic identities* (Hall 1992: 304). This second set of processes is what concerns us especially here and we shall now explore the twin notions of *hybridity* and *ethnicity* in more detail. *Hybridity* can be seen in terms of 'the fusion and intermixture of cultures', whereas *ethnicity* represents 'the reassertion of cultural distinctiveness'. In both cases, theorisations of *culture* are key.

Globalisation has intensified the 'de-territorialisation of *culture*'. That is, 'cultures' have become separated from any absolute connection with localities, regions or nations 'of origin'. In very general terms, earlier theories tended to conceive culture as 'some*thing*' unified and undivided, a list of essentially unchanging traits and customs contained by social structures and boundaries. However, anthropologists now speak of 'travelling cultures' (Clifford 1994), breaking any necessary link between 'culture' and 'place'. Today, culture is understood as a *practice* rather than a *characteristic*, something people are in the continuous process of *making* and *remaking*, rather than something they *have* (Baumann 1996, 1999).

Such a perspective reflects the influence of 'postmodernism'. Put simply, this suggests that the 'old certainties' and 'universal claims' associated with post-Enlightenment thinking are now in crisis. They are giving way to an acknowledgement of more uncertain and relative, more plural and contingent, constructions of identity and ways of knowing the world. For example, in modernist thinking *identity* was seen as relatively unified, stable and autonomous (Hall 1992). However, such a view has gradually been replaced by more social and dialectical notions, where 'self' identifications are shaped and modified contextually in relation to the (often false) ascriptions of 'others'. Indeed, in the postmodern age, it is usual to talk about 'multiple' and 'criss-crossing' identities constantly under revision.

As 'migrants', 'diasporas' and 'transnationals' cross the borders of contemporary nation-states, their cultural identities are unconsciously *hybridised*. Bhabha (1994) suggests that this renegotiation takes place in the 'translated' spaces *in between* 'cultures'. It is here that 'newness enters the world'. Indeed, it is now common to speak of 'hyphenated' 'African-American' or 'British-Asian' identities. Rather than the youth of diasporic communities being 'caught between two cultures', this suggests the emergence of a generation of 'skilled multi-cultural navigators' whose practices cannot be contained by assumptions about their 'roots' as they improvise 'routes' in new directions (Gilroy 1993; Ballard 1994).

Moreover, the hybridity associated with boundary crossing also unsettles the powerful and highly politicised ideas about 'purity' and 'origins' still prevalent in society today (Gilroy 1993; Brah 1996). Modern genetics has shown that there are no separate 'racial' groups within humankind. In fact, the arguments of nineteenth-century 'scientific-racism', which maintained that there was a hierarchy of 'races' among the people of the world, each with their own hereditary characteristics, are worthless. Nevertheless, in contemporary 'racisms', 'nationalisms', 'ethnic absolutisms' and 'religious fundamentalisms', it is common to find the mistaken suggestion that there are 'innate' *cultural*, as opposed to *biological*, differences between certain 'peoples', 'communities' and 'civilisations'.

There is no doubt, then, that hybridity alerts us to the ways in which apparently 'unified' cultural traditions are actually 'invented', reflecting specific historical contexts and power relations (Asad 1993). It illuminates that significant exchanges have long existed between 'black' and 'white', 'the West' and 'the Rest'. However, for those not part of the cosmopolitan jet-setting elite that selfconsciously 'celebrates difference', the intermixing and fusion of cultures can appear somewhat threatening (Werbner and Modood 1997). Not least for diasporas, hybridity can be experienced in terms of transgression, doubt, crisis and alienation. In such a context, nostalgic emphasis on the particular 'chains of memory' and social networks associated with 'tradition' and 'community' can restore certainty in the face of cultural 'translation' (Hall 1992).

What is equally clear, here, is that an effective 'politics', one that seriously challenges the uneven distribution of power and resources between 'majorities' and 'minorities', especially in the ghettoes of the world's global cities, has not emerged from the endless shifting of cultural boundaries (Asad 1993). To be sure, we all have multiple identities (Hall 1992). However, we must also 'speak from somewhere'. 'Being heard' requires an act of prioritising, of naming oneself, of coming into representation, if only momentarily. So, often 'blocked out' of identifying with countries of settlement because of racisms and nationalisms, Eastern European Jews, Irish Catholics, African Caribbean Christians and South Asian Muslims have all turned to 'invented traditions' to find a political voice in diaspora (Hall 1992). Such a response represents no literal 'return' to the past or simple 'reproduction' of traditional culture. Rather, what social anthropologists call *ethnicity* involves a dynamic 'remaking' of cultural distinctiveness' in a new context. Notions of communal identity are organised symbolically through the construction of boundaries marked by signifiers such as language, custom and/or religion. It is the resulting solidarities that help groups to advance their own interests in competition with others outside the boundary.

In the plural societies of liberal democracies, for example, these 'fictions of *ethnic unity*' have been useful in binding individuals together periodically, not least when diasporas have addressed themselves to the state or wider society (Werbner and Modood 1997). Indeed, for both pragmatic and political reasons, the main vehicle for the public recognition of 'ethnic minorities', *multicultural* policy-making, has tended to promote the idea of 'communities', each with its own distinctive 'culture'. Nevertheless, *communities*, whether ethnic, national or religious, are routinely made up of individual differences, conflicting constituencies and relations of power that silence women and young men especially. Indeed, as Cohen (1985) argues, it is only their 'symbolic form', and not their 'content', that is held in common. This means that the multiple interpretations and meanings attached to such symbols can be reconciled.

Depending on the dynamics of any given context, then, and who one might be interacting with, people both *hybridise* and *ethnicise* their identities, that is, routinely cross and dissolve, as well as remake and fix boundaries (Baumann 1996, 1999). They take part in a wide range of overlapping 'cultures' and 'communities'. My contention is that only against the context of such theorising can an adequate account of 'diaspora religion' be given. In the second half of this chapter we trace the recent impact of diaspora studies on the study of religion.

The study of 'diaspora religion'

In 1997, Hinnells' *New Handbook of Living Religions* was published. Since its first publication in 1984 the *Handbook* had acquired seven additional chapters 'on the subject of religion in migration, or diaspora religion' (1997: 1). By contrast, the 1984 edition had restricted any mention of diaspora to just two index entries ('Diaspora China' and 'Diaspora Jews'), while fleeting references to 'emigration', 'ethnic communities' and 'Asian immigrants' pointed only to a general chapter on the increasingly pluralistic and post-Christian patterns of religiosity in the West. If the *New Handbook* is anything to go by, then, 'diaspora' would seem to have arrived in religious studies.

Hinnells explains why he thinks the study of religion should take 'diaspora religion' seriously. In terms of promoting the relevance of the study of religion per se, both to potential students and those who fund education at all levels, he insists that the challenges posed to plural societies by recognising religious and cultural differences have been tremendously important (1997: 1–2). Indeed, elsewhere in the *New Handbook*, Hinnells argues that the presence of 'world religions' in global cities has raised the profile of religion generally, both encouraging new religious movements and reinforcing the public position of historic churches (1997: 845). However, despite this, and the fact that, contrary to many expectations, 'migrants are more rather than less religious after migration' (1997: 683), Hinnells observes that scholars of migration and diaspora in other disciplines have tended to overlook the significance of religion. Moreover, he also laments that, despite their growing size and evidence of their impact on migrants' homelands, diasporas are still of 'marginal' interest within religious studies (1997: 682).[10]

Hinnells is not alone in making these observations. Baumann, for example, suggests that in other disciplines the significance of religion is underplayed 'in favour of ethnicity and ethnic adherence' (2001: 7), while, for its part, 'The discipline of the history of religions is a real late-comer in adopting the diaspora term' (2000: 1).[11] We shall return to Baumann's point about religion and ethnicity in due course, but his remarks about the history of religions are worth pursuing briefly. He insightfully observes that, for sound academic reasons, many in this area of the field have been reluctant to embrace a term that they still associate with Jewish Studies: 'the caution was (and is) in many cases also based on the knowledge of the term's origins and soteriological connotations, stirring up various problems for a cross-cultural, generalized application' (2001: 4). Such comments begin to reveal the broad differences in attitude and approach that exist between the different methodological sub-fields of the study of religion, from mainly textual and historical, to mainly empirical and socio-cultural, studies. Despite the reticence of the former, by the mid to late 1990s diaspora had become the 'self-evident' term to describe religious communities settled overseas for the latter (2001: 4).

Notwithstanding the relatively late appearance of 'diaspora' in the study of religion, recent surveys are unanimous in tracing the first discussion of its significance to Ninian Smart. Baumann (2000, 2001), Vertovec (2000b) and Hinnells (2005) all follow Cohen (1997) in mentioning a short paper, 'The Importance of Diasporas', published in 1987. As Cohen suggests, the contribution is 'not fully theorized' (1997: 187). Indeed, there is perhaps an assumption that 'religious homelands' are the equivalent of 'ethno-national homelands' and little attempt is made to differentiate 'diaspora' from 'globalisation'. Nevertheless, both in this 'somewhat hidden article' (Baumann 2000: 1) and a more easily accessible textbook of the late 1980s (Smart 1989), patterns and trends in 'diaspora religion' are identified that other religious studies scholars would ultimately research in more depth.

Smart (1987) argues that, given the global communications revolution, more than ever before, religious communities are in a position to sustain contacts, not only with their homelands, but also with the sacred centres of their faith. Globalisation has intensified the possibilities for religions to both imagine and actively reproduce a sense of 'community' amongst co-religionists, for example during great pilgrimages such as the Muslim *Hajj*. As we have seen already, religions exhibit both continuity and transformation as they adapt to new contexts. However, Smart (1987) underlines that, generally speaking, rather than assimilate or liberalise, under the pluralising conditions of contemporary globalisation, diasporas tend to emphasise 'universalising' religious tendencies such as 'ecumenism', 'orthodoxy' or 'fundamentalism'. Certainly, this chimes with what we heard about 'hybridity' and 'ethnicity', 'translation' and 'tradition', in the previous section. Indeed, Smart (1987) maintains that 'universalising' processes can be observed even among Hindu traditions, often characterised as essentially pluralistic and resistive of singular definitions. The selfconsciousness of 'difference' provoked by interactions with 'others' in a diasporic context, with the state, wider society and a broader range of co-religionists, has seen diasporas in 'the West' produce increasingly 'rationalised' and 'homogenising' accounts of their traditions. As Smart aptly puts it: 'though "Buddhism" [my emphasis] may not quite have existed before, it does now; and the same for all the other religions. Self-definition is becoming the order of the day' (1989: 556). Finally, Smart (1987) suggests that the centres of gravity within traditions are shifting and that it is unnecessary, now, for 'Western' scholars of religion to travel 'East' to study the various dimensions of Hinduism, Buddhism or other world faiths. Instead, there is no reason why they should not be studied 'at home'.

Since the publication of Smart (1987) the study of 'diaspora religion' has been elaborated significantly. Baumann notes that 'the term was applied with more rigor . . . during the mid-1990s' (2001: 4). In his *New Handbook*, for example, Hinnells (1997) 'named factors for a religion's change and continuity in diaspora situations and differentiated seven areas of research' (Baumann 2001: 4). However, Baumann does not acknowledge that this agenda for research was adopted from those scholars who pioneered the study of religion, migration and ethnicity during the 1980s. In many respects all that has changed in the shift from 'migration' to 'diaspora', at least in religious studies, is the vocabulary. So, to suggest that the study of 'diaspora religion' was 'new' in the 1990s, as many scholars do, requires further qualification. However, before we say any more about the 1990s, I want to discuss some of the early work of my colleague, Professor Kim Knott, who has worked on the Community Religions Project at the University of Leeds since the mid-1980s. Knott did not especially anticipate the 'decisive shift' to 'diaspora' associated with globalisation and postmodernist theory. However, as we shall see, she was among the first to systematically analyse (1) the theoretical relationship between religion, ethnicity and identity and (2) how the empirical 'content' of religion was changing, having been 'transplanted' overseas.

Religion, migration and ethnicity: research agendas for religious studies

> [T]here have been relatively few accounts of migration and settlement in which religion has been described as having any significance for individuals and communities beyond its role in assisting them to organise, to reap material benefit or to enter dialogue or competition with the wider society . . . religions do perform these functions in many situations. However, they also have their own dynamics which, though related to social, political and economic contexts, are explained from within rather than from without (with recourse to their historical development, texts, value systems, ritual practices, socio-religious organisation etc).
>
> (Knott 1992: 13)

These comments are taken from Knott's research paper, *The Role of Religious Studies in Understanding the Ethnic Experience*, first presented at a conference in Warsaw, Poland, in September 1989. Foreshadowing a similar assessment by both Hinnells (1997) and Baumann (2001), they represent a plea to religious studies scholars to be more active in the study of 'ethnic minority' religions, at least in part because the accounts of other disciplines have proved limited. Reflecting on the work of sociologists and anthropologists, Knott argues that 'with a few notable exceptions, they have failed to provide plausible accounts of the role and significance of religions in the lives of the groups they have described' (1992: 4–5). At the same time, Knott admits that, 'The discipline of Religious Studies in Britain or elsewhere has not so far developed a coherent perspective on ethnicity' (1992: 11). She suggests that this is partly because the study of 'migrant religion' is still new to the discipline, as is the idea of taking the 'social context of religion' seriously. Moreover, the dominant paradigm of religious studies, phenomenology, had also tended to emphasise description over explanation. As a result, social scientific assumptions about religion have often gone unchallenged.

In this respect Knott's main concern is that the literature on religion and ethnicity generally fails to distinguish sufficiently between the two. Religion is often seen merely 'as the passive instrument of ethnic identity' or 'in the service of ethnicity' (1992: 12). For Knott, while there is no doubt that religion can operate in this way, such an approach has obvious limitations: 'there are times when religion plays a more active role in the definition of an ethnic group's identity and behaviour than many of these accounts suggest ' (1992: 12). Knott identifies the work of Hans Mol, a sociologist of religion, as of particular use here. She finds his notion of religion as 'harnesser of change' and 'sacralizer of identity' especially suggestive. Mol is perhaps too quick to generalise about the 'essential function of religion', its 'most universal form', 'basic human needs' and so on (1979: 34). Nevertheless, he clearly elaborates on the remarks we have encountered so far about the significance of 'tradition':

> Religion ... seems to have more to do with an already established system of meaning, a stable tradition, an orderly delineation of a potentially disorderly existence. The essential function of religion cannot therefore be exhaustively summarized in terms of 'creative change'. Rather religion in its most universal form seems to function as an antidote to change, or as the 'harnesser' of change. If religion then somehow is bound up with a basic human need for delineation, order, one may define it as 'the sacralization of identity'.
>
> (1979: 34)

> It directs the attention to the boundary maintenance of an embattled ethnic culture in a strange environment. Religion seems to be always bound up with the clearer delineation of a culture ... it also provides ... an island of meaning, tradition and belonging in the sea of anomie of modern industrial societies.
>
> (1979: 37)

For Mol, religion, as a 'resource' with which to 'mark' ethnic identity, offers something that other 'cultural stuff' cannot. Backed by 'sacred' authority, religious boundaries would seem to provide more 'universal', and so less readily negotiable, vehicles for the articulation of distinctiveness than those associated with the customs of particular peoples and places. According to Mol, the function of religion is at least as much to do with an 'orderly delineation' and 'harnessing of change' as opposed to 'creative change', a comment we might relate, once again, to the contrast between ethnicity and hybridity, tradition and translation, discussed earlier. In contrast to Mol, I would suggest that even the reproduction of a 'stable tradition' is always a creative act – to say the same thing in a new context is always to say something different (Baumann 1996, 1999). Nevertheless, Mol's work very effectively underlines the fact that an emphasis on 'tradition' among many migrants, at least initially, represents no simple 'refusal to change', as sometimes suggested, but rather a dynamic adaptation strategy in the undeniable face of change.

If Mol's emphasis is on the *function* of religion in contexts of migration, elsewhere Knott (1986) argues that religious studies scholars must also be attentive to what happens to its specific *content* in such circumstances. 'How does a religion and the religiousness of its people change in an alien milieu? How are they different from their parent traditions in the homeland?' (1986: 8). Further to this empirical 'comparative religion exercise' (1986: 8), Knott has proposed a much cited and elaborated framework (see, for example, Hinnells 1997, 2005), which allows us to 'map' the range of *factors* that might contribute to 'new patterns and forms of religious behaviour, organisation, experience and self-understanding' (1986: 10). These are the very factors that, as noted in the previous section, Baumann (2001) traces back only as far as Hinnells (1997). Indeed, writing slightly earlier, Knott covers the same ground as Smart (1987) only in more detail. The only difference would seem to be in terminology – 'migration' instead of 'diaspora'. In any case, Knott's (1986: 10–12) 'original factors' can be summarised thus:

(a) '*Home traditions*' – (i) the nature of the religion itself (e.g. its universality or ethnic particularity) and (ii) the nature [and impact] of other cultural factors such as language, customs, food and dress, etc.
(b) '*Host traditions*' – cultural, political, legal, educational, welfare, immigration and settlement procedures [e.g. the place of religion in society].[12]
(c) '*Nature of migration process*' – from the homeland or other migration contexts [e.g. people who are 'twice migrants']; are migrants sojourners or settlers, economic migrants, exiles or refugees?
(d) '*Nature of migrant group*' – religious and ethnic diversity, group size, geographical dispersion, division and cohesion (origin, history of settlement, caste and kinship, [social class and educational background]).
(e) '*Nature of host response*' – social attitudes [discourses and practices] rather than cultural traditions, e.g. racism, attitudes to assimilation and integration, ecumenism.

For Knott, it is the complex relationships between these different factors that begin to explain the sheer diversity of expressions and trajectories of religions in contexts of migration. As well as choosing 'to standardize their beliefs and practices, to reject their "little" traditions at the expense of their "great" traditions' (1986: 13), religious individuals and communities may opt for, 'Increased traditionalism, new sects, unlikely religious unions, conversion and mission' (1992: 10). All form part of the remaking of religious traditions in new contexts. Looking to the future Knott argues that 'the Religious Studies approach . . . [is] in great need of unleashing' (1986: 13). However, in the mid- to late 1980s, the project of mapping the evolution of religious continuity and transformation had only just begun. In our penultimate two sections we trace how Knott's agenda for the study of migration and ethnicity in religious studies has developed since the 1980s, first in theoretical terms and then in more empirical terms.

Theorising 'diaspora religion': 'ethnic' and 'universal' traditions?

> In general, I would argue that religions can provide *additional cement to bind* a diasporic consciousness, but they do not constitute diasporas in and of themselves . . . an overlap between faith and ethnicity is likely to *enhance social cohesion* . . . [but] The myth and idealization of a *homeland and a return movement are also conspicuously absent* in the case of world religions. Indeed one might suggest that their programmes are *extraterritorial* rather than territorial . . . On the other hand . . . spiritual affinity may generate a bond analogous to that of a diaspora.
>
> (Cohen 1997: 189; my emphasis)

The question of whether a particular tradition, or religions in general, can properly be described in terms of 'diaspora' has been one of the more obvious theoretical issues to occupy scholars in the last decade or so. However, ironically, perhaps the first thing to say about Cohen's discussion of religion and diaspora here is that it is immediately reminiscent of the social scientific conceptions of religion, migration and ethnicity examined by Knott (1986, 1992). In the same way that religion 'reinforced' ethnicity', Cohen suggests that religion provides 'additional cement' to diasporas and 'is likely to enhance social cohesion'. Indeed, for Cohen, diaspora is essentially an ethno-national phenomenon, something to do with peoples and places. Therefore, religion can only ever be a supplementary factor, one of a number of 'cognate phenomena' (1997: 187). Referring to Hinnells' work on the Parsis, for example, Cohen argues that those Zoroastrians who migrated from Persia to India so as to 'survive' the Islamisation of early Muslim Iran, represent 'not so much a travelling nation then, as a travelling religion . . . Parsees . . . do not seek to return to, or to recreate, a homeland (1997: 188–9).

In his most recent monograph Hinnells (2005) takes issue with Cohen's arguments about the Parsis and religion per se. First, he notes that orientation to the homeland can be manifest in many ways to various degrees of intensity and, for some, cultural identification with the homeland may be far more important than return (Brah 1996). Hinnells insists that many Parsis do still speak of themselves as 'Persians' and not 'Indians'. Not least because of the Islamic Republic in contemporary Iran, few currently consider 'returning' to live there. Nevertheless, the Parsis do express their 'love for Persia' in various ways. For example, they furnish their homes with books, artefacts and symbols of ancient Iran and organise religious tours as and when possible. Second, Hinnells suggests that Cohen's comments also raise questions about what is meant by the term 'world religions'. If this simply suggests a tradition to be found in many countries around the world, and so is related to globalisation and international migration, then Zoroastrianism would 'qualify', as would most other 'faiths' today. However, if, as Cohen suggests (1997: 188), a 'world religion' is a tradition open to all people in the world, then Hinnells (2005) is clear that not only Zoroastrianism, but also Judaism, Hinduism and Sikhism are not really 'world religions'.

Vertovec (2000a) takes up this debate in a somewhat different way. He is less concerned with what constitutes a 'world religion' than the distinctions that can be made between different 'types' of traditions. For example, Vertovec reminds us that, given the existence of the 'Zionist' and 'Khalistani' movements, Judaism and Sikhism are both exceptions to Cohen's general 'rule' about religions and homelands. Both 'religions' are in effect 'discrete ethnic groups' (2000a: 10). Indeed, he argues that, if Judaism and Sikhism can be considered 'exceptions', as Cohen agrees they can, then so, too, can Hinduism. The emphasis here is on 'a place' as much as 'a people': 'no matter where in the world they live, most Hindus tend to sacralize India . . . [as] a spiritual homeland' (Vertovec 2000a: 10).[13] As Hinnells (2005) remarks, Cohen's 'rule' is clearly one with a lot of exceptions. Nevertheless, if, following Knott (1986:11) and others, we differentiate between so-called 'ethnic' and 'universal' traditions, then Vertovec's distinctions make good sense. 'Ethnic' religions may properly represent 'diasporas'. However, for other, more 'universal' and missionary religions, less obviously tied to particular peoples or places, for example Christianity, Islam and Buddhism, the relationship with ethnicity can be very different:

> It broadens the term far too much too much to talk – as many scholars do – about the "Muslim diaspora", "Catholic diaspora" . . . and so forth. These are of course world traditions that span many ethnic groups and nationalities . . . Hinnells (1997) himself flags up one problem . . . are Muslims in Pakistan part of a diaspora religion because Islam is derived from and broadly centred on Mecca?
>
> (Vertovec 2000a: 11)

Perhaps, in the case of 'universal' religions, then, it would be better to speak only of 'migration' or 'transnationalism'? However, Vertovec does not make such a suggestion. Indeed, accounts that explicitly identify 'transnational religion' are still quite small in number.[14] Moreover, it also seems clear that apparently 'ethnic' and 'universal' traditions can 'behave like each other' in different situations. For example, we have seen already how Smart (1987) argues that plural Hindu traditions are exhibiting a tendency to 'universalise'. Similarly, traditions such as Christianity and Islam have always been 'ethnicised' and 'territorialised' in practice.[15] To spread their messages successfully and stay meaningful through time and across space, both have had to be flexible enough to adapt to local circumstances. Indeed, once people are gradually 'born into' universal traditions, religion becomes 'indigenised' and so, for many adherents, essentially a matter of custom and descent.

Of course, religion remains a matter of custom and descent for many in the world today, with only limited efforts to distinguish the two. However, in the diaspora especially, many second- and third-generation youth are disentangling what they see as the 'universals of religion' from the 'localised custom' they associate with their parents' and grandparents' homelands. One way of analysing this situation is to relate it to

Mol's (1979) conception of religion as the 'sacralizer of identity' and 'harnesser of change'. Because religion, backed by 'sacred' authority, has such great potential for articulating distinctiveness in its own right, this can open the way for other potential markers of 'ethnic' identity to become more negotiable as time passes and those born in the diaspora establish their own priorities. So long as religious boundaries are maintained – and, recalling Cohen (1985), this does not require unchanging 'content' – language and aspects of custom, as well as attachment to the 'homeland' per se, can become relatively less important. All this without the 'risk' of losing continuity with the past, all the threads in a chain of memory. Indeed, the prioritisation of 'religion' over 'custom', especially for those with most invested in new contexts, can facilitate adaptation and acculturation, while all the time retaining a sense of pride in 'distinctiveness' and rejecting outright 'assimilation'. Ter Haar (1998), for example, shows how many African Christians in Europe are 'forward-', rather than 'backward-', looking. They see themselves as part of an 'international', rather than an 'ethnic', church, deliberately using religion as a 'bridge' to reach out beyond the 'bonding' provided by cultural heritage.[16]

In a roundabout way then, Cohen's account of religion does actually strike the right chord, even though, perhaps not surprisingly, he shows little real awareness of the significance of what he says for the study of religion. On the one hand, religions (both supposedly 'ethnic' and 'universal') can and do provide 'additional cement' and 'cohesion' to 'territorial' ethno-national diasporas (1997: 189). However, in different contexts, the very same traditions can challenge and transcend ethnicity (as well as the nation-state) by forging multi-ethnic and more universalising networks and linkages. They can point beyond the 'territorial' to the 'extraterritorial' (1997: 189), whether that be in terms of the convergences of a global 'ethics' and 'civil society' or the conflicts of 'transnational terrorism' (Jurgensmeyer 2002). In either case, 'ethnic' or 'universal', the shift in emphasis here is from what religions 'are' to what work they 'do', that is, the 'uses' of religious symbols, discourses and practices in particular contexts. In our penultimate section I briefly outline how religious studies' more empirical agenda, in terms of mapping contemporary patterns and trends, has evolved in the last decade or so.

Mapping 'diaspora religion': contemporary patterns and trends

Perhaps the main characteristic of contemporary scholarship on 'diaspora religion' has been the growth of studies documenting the 'content' of religious continuity and transformation in various local, national and international contexts. In many ways this is more representative of the research that has been completed than the theoretical debates considered in the previous section. To give a flavour of this empirical work, and provide an opportunity for further reading, studies of contemporary Sikhs, Christians, Jews, Hindus, Zoroastrians, Buddhists and Muslims have all been cited in footnotes throughout this chapter. The majority focus on North America and Europe, although the processes described are by no means confined to 'the West'. With just a few exceptions, all were written in the 1990s or 2000s. This reflects the fact that, in the last decade or so, diasporas established in the post-war period have begun to 'mature' and are increasingly 'visible' in public life (Coward et al. 2000). Most accounts tend to focus on one religious tradition and/or ethnic community.

However, some scholars have sought to analyse the more general patterns and trends that emerge from comparison across traditions, communities and contexts. Indeed, Hinnells (2005) argues that comparative studies should be more of a priority. It is this sort of analysis that I want to dwell on in this section.

In the same way that Knott's (1986, 1992) theoretical agenda for religious studies is closely related to current debates, so too her framework for mapping the factors affecting religions in migration remains a starting point today. Instead of Knott's five 'factors', mentioned earlier, for example, Hinnells (1997) produces a ten-point framework and Vertovec (2000b: 21–3) goes even further, reminding us of a seventeen-point framework he and others first devised back in 1990. However, as both Hinnells and Vertovec cite Knott with approval, and her framework is the most manageable, I do not propose to elaborate these further here. All that remains to be said is that attention to such factors in a comparative perspective begins to reveal important differences within and between traditions, depending upon the particularity of different migrant groups and local as well as national contexts. What may be more useful is to turn our attention to patterns and trends in contemporary empirical research.

Writing in the mid- to late 1980s, Knott understood that, although already established for two to three decades, the dynamics of post-war migration to, and settlement in, the West were still very much unfolding. Therefore in various publications she listed potential topics for future studies. In the 1990s and 2000s, others have adopted many of these.[17] Hinnells, for example, draws upon themes identified by Knott to elaborate an ambitious international comparison across the major religious traditions of South Asian diasporas in Australia, Britain, Canada and the United States.[18] We have already mentioned some of these, notably 'individual identity', 'group identity', 'leadership' and 'universalisation'. However, other trends that Hinnells takes up – 'the place of language', 'the transmission of the tradition' and 'the impact of western religious ideas' (1997: 826–35) – are also worthy of brief discussion.[19]

Hinnells, for example, argues that, in general, South Asian diaspora traditions have been impacted by 'Western' perceptions of the category 'religion', so much so that they often exhibit a syncretistic tendency towards 'Protestantization' (1997: 829). In this regard, he cites the increasing desire for English language 'translations' allowing access to the 'meaning' of sacred texts and rituals, the liberal project of interfaith relations, as well as the influence of rationalised and decontextualised accounts of 'world religions' routinely reproduced in school-based religious education. Hinnells also compares the dynamics of different national contexts. For example, since the 1960s, when South Asian migration to Canada and the United States began, newcomers have tended to be educated professionals more likely to integrate and produce innovative religious scholarship (1997: 837, 840). In Britain, by contrast, because of its colonial connections to the subcontinent, diasporas are longer-standing and comprise a higher percentage of unskilled workers, although this is rapidly changing, especially amongst Hindus and Sikhs (1997: 836). Finally, Hinnells compares the 'experiences' of the various religious traditions associated with South Asian diasporas. For example, Muslims are most ethnically diverse in the United States and Canada, whereas in Britain South Asians predominate (1997: 841). Of the Jains, Hinnells remarks that, given their low public profile and numbers, for pragmatic reasons they will often tolerate the 'outsiders' perception of them as part of the Indian, or Hindu, scene rather than as something different' (1997: 843).

Clearly, it is extremely difficult in a general survey to do justice to the numerous empirical studies that have been conducted, or even Hinnells' more comparative synthesis of such material. Nevertheless, by way of drawing different threads together, and so dealing rather more systematically with the empirical realities of 'diaspora religion' only alluded to in this chapter, I want now to present my own rather tentative summary of various theories, factors and trends. My starting point for this was initially a list of the things I thought I had learned while involved in the religious mapping of Southall back in the late 1980s. For example, I will never forget being told how, when during 1984 the Indian government stormed the Golden Temple at Amritsar in their attempt to capture religious nationalists hidden within, media footage of demonstrations in Southall had provoked a further upturn in tensions back in the Punjab. However, once I began to write it was, of course, impossible to exclude my subsequent experiences as a researcher and teacher across Islamic, South Asian and religious studies or, indeed, new insights gleaned from reading and rereading the likes of Hinnells, Knott, Vertovec and Baumann while preparing this piece.

1   The context of migration, migrants' socio-economic and cultural backgrounds – their social or cultural 'capital' – as well as the timing and circumstances of their migration, all have consequences in the diaspora. For example, initially at least, rural uneducated migrants who move to urban contexts tend to emphasise 'tradition' over 'translation', 'ethnicity' over 'hybridity'. Those 'twice migrants', who already have experience of life in the diaspora, may prosper because they are well practised in developing effective adaptation strategies.

2   Similarly, the context of settlement also has massive consequences in shaping the dynamics of a diaspora. Factors deserving of consideration include the legacy of colonialism, the extent of citizenship rights, the nature of immigration legislation and levels of protection from discrimination, the status of religion in a society, employment and educational patterns, social attitudes to cultural pluralism, the numbers of 'co-ethnics' and 'co-religionists' settled in an area, and the size and presence of other 'religious' and 'ethnic' groups.

3   Religious beliefs and practices have been pivotal to many ordinary people in terms of adapting to, and reorganising, both their domestic and public lives in a new environment. For example, the idea of a 'congregation' can become more significant than in the homeland, as public meetings for worship provide an opportunity for socialising. Similarly, amongst women especially, domestic rituals performed collectively can be an important part of reproducing the 'community'.

4   Huge moral and economic investments have been made by diasporic communities to establish and sustain religious institutions, movements, organisations and associations. These often represent quite different and competing denominations and orientations. Such investments were often accelerated with the emergence of generations born in the diaspora as the need to transmit traditions overseas was brought sharply into focus.

5   Facilitating an imagined sense of continuity with the past is an important function of religion in diaspora. In the first stages of settlement at least, people have tended to become 'more religious'. Nevertheless, compared to what was commonplace in the homeland, traditional practices can be elaborated or abbreviated, and even disappear, overseas. Innovation may ease transmission but such changes are also part of global processes of religious homogenisation and universalisation.

6 Religious communities are divided among themselves, so much so that ethnic, sectarian and other divisions can result in open conflicts. So, while communal 'fusion' and cooperation is another feature of early settlement, 'fission' and fragmentation is quick to develop as 'communities' mature. Nevertheless, as leaderships seek to present a common front to outsiders, especially when seeking recognition from the state in respect of planning permission, animal sacrifice, school uniforms, burial or cremation arrangements, 'fusion' reasserts itself temporarily in the shape of local, national and international 'umbrella' organisations.

7 Leaders (both religious specialists and communal representatives) can marginalise the interests of women and young men in their 'communities', especially over such matters as education, marriage and work. Similarly, despite young people's protestations about their lack of appropriate skills, 'elders' may still prefer to 'import' functionaries from the homeland. Traditional male leaderships are also being challenged by the political participation of well-educated professional women in public spaces.

8 While religion can undoubtedly reinforce ethnicity, the children and grandchildren of migrants, born and socialised in quite different contexts to their parents, increasingly produce their own local-global interpretations of traditions, often arguing for the separation of religious 'universals' from cultural 'particulars' in ways their parents and grandparents rarely did. Cosmopolitan encounters with 'others' of the same faith tradition in diaspora have broadened awareness and self-conscious explorations of global religious identities at the expense of ethnicity. This is manifest in religious dress, student societies, camps, magazines, websites and so on.

9 In a globalising world, transnational contacts are maintained between diasporas, ethno-national 'homelands' and sacred 'centres' of faith traditions. Such networks are sustained by pilgrimages and holidays, various media, including satellite television, and the visits of religious and political leaders, as well as international movements and world organisations. Political crises 'there' continue to impact communities and identities 'here' and vice versa. Indeed, perhaps because of nostalgia, or a lack of access to power, diasporas have played a significant role in supporting not only homeland movements, but also religious nationalism and even transnational terrorism.

10 For good or ill 'religion', at least as much as 'race' or ethnicity, has become one of the main ways of identifying the 'difference' of migrants, diasporas and transnationals among both 'insiders' and 'outsiders' in contemporary societies.

Conclusion

The project of empirical mapping remains a hugely important one. To cite the editor of this collection one last time, all students of comparative religion should seek to 'get their hands dirty with religion'. Indeed, with its emphasis on the complex continuities and transformations of lived experience, the study of 'diaspora religion' has already played a significant, but rarely acknowledged, role in taking religious studies beyond the outdated 'world religions' paradigm. Nevertheless, as Hinnells (1997: 683) himself implies, compared to fieldwork-based studies, theoretical discussions have not been taken up as vigorously as they might. Recent interventions have to some extent 'replayed' the debate about religion and ethnicity, although it is now much clearer that religion has become 'disembedded' from, and can work 'against', ethnicity at least as much as it works 'with' it (as it does with and against the nation-state). By way of conclusion, then, I want to argue that there is now an opportunity and a need for more intense theoretical reflection on the significant body of data that has been collected over the last 20 years or so.

Flood (1999) maintains that 'after phenomenology' religious studies is at something of a theoretical and methodological crossroads and needs to engage more openly across disciplinary boundaries. Given the wide-ranging interest of other disciplines in migration, disapora and transnationalism, and the continuing salience of religion for these issues and related public policies, the study of 'diaspora religion' ought to be one area where the prospects for such engagement are good. However, it is striking that most of the literature considered here, whether produced by scholars of religious studies or the social sciences, *still* rarely theorises religion with the same level of sophistication as culture, hybridity, ethnicity and so on. Therefore, while religious studies may begin to relocate in terms of broader disciplinary contexts, it must also start to 'export' more sophisticated accounts of religion to those for whom such a task is less of a priority. Future success in this respect will involve building upon the empirical mapping of religion as 'content' and thinking seriously about its relationships to other concepts discussed in this chapter. This could begin to reveal more clearly the particular sorts of 'work' that religions 'do' in a wide variety of socially, politically, economically and culturally constructed spaces.

Notes

1 For other accounts of the Sikh diaspora see the relevant chapters in Ballard (1994), Hinnells (1997), Cohen (1997) and Coward et al. (2000), as well as Tatla (1999).

2 For an account of the Irish Catholic diaspora in England see Fielding (1993) and in America see McCaffrey (1997).

3 A number of other resources have been produced, including a CD-ROM, *On Common Ground: World Religions in America*, Columbia University Press, 1996/2000. See http://www.pluralism.org.

4 See http://www.transcomm.ox.ac.uk/. A number of papers referring to religion and transnationalism, including Vertovec (2000a), can be downloaded from this site.

5 For an online copy of this and other papers on diaspora and migration, as well as materials on Buddhism in the West and Tamil Hindus in Germany, see Baumann's well-stocked homepage, http://www.baumann-martin.de/. See also Prebish and Baumann (2002) on Buddhism in the West.

6 For a list of the Community Religions Project's publications see http://www.leeds.ac.uk/trs/respub/crp.htm. Notably, globalisation theory led Knott not so much into the study of diaspora but the study of locality and thence to the study of space. See *The Location of Religion: A Spatial Analysis*, London, Equinox Books, 2005.

7 See also Hinnells' (2005) account of the Zoroastrian diaspora in 11 countries.

8 For the Jewish diaspora, historical and contemporary, see the relevant chapters in Cohen (1997) and Ter Haar (1998) as well as Barclay (1996), Kaplan (2000) and Gilman (2003). See also the website of 'Beth Hatefutsoth', the Museum of the Jewish Diaspora, at http://www.bh.org.il.

9 Ter Haar (1998) notes that the African diaspora in Europe, as opposed to America and the Caribbean, has had rather different experiences. For religion in the African diaspora see also the chapter in Hinnells (1997), as well as Pitts (1993), Murphy (1994) and McCarthy Brown (2001).

10 For example, Braun and McCutcheon (2000) include entries on 'Ethnicity' and 'Culture' and Taylor (1998) includes 'Culture' and 'Territory' as well as a mentioning 'nomadization' in his introduction. However, there is no reference to migration, diaspora or transnationalism in either.

11 Sharpe (1975/1986) does not mention the study of religion and migration, even in a footnote. A new chapter, added to map the field of Comparative Religion since 1970, was written in the mid-1980s, a time when 'diasporas' were beginning to make demands for recognition in respect of public services. Nevertheless, Sharpe does anticipate something of postmodernism and especially post-colonialism, trends that would ultimately make some areas of Comparative Religion hospitable to this new field.

12 The idea of 'host' societies is now inappropriate given the emergence of second and third generations born in the diaspora (Hinnells 1997).

13 Vertovec's arguments are expanded in 2000b. For other accounts of the Hindu diaspora see the relevant chapters in Ballard (1994), Hinnells (1997), Ter Haar (1998) and Coward et al. (2000), as well as Burghart (1987) and Baumann (2000).

14 While my search for 'religion and diaspora' at the Amazon online bookstore (30 April 2004) produced 106 results, 'religion and transnational' produced just 20. Of that 20, 60 per cent were studies of the more 'universalising' traditions, especially Islam and Christianity (mainly Catholicism in America, Europe and China, as well as Pentecostalism in Africa and Latin America). The rest were general collections, e.g. Hoeber (1997). Only 25 per cent were published prior to 2000.

15 For Muslim heritage 'diasporas' and 'transnational' Islam, see chapters in Ballard (1994), Hinnells (1997) and Coward et al. (2000), as well as Fischer and Abedi (1990), Metcalf (1996), Mandaville (2001) and McLoughlin (forthcoming).

16 Indeed, Ter Haar (1998) argues that 'diaspora' can itself re-inscribe a focus on overseas 'origins' that places people outside the nations in which they live.

17 Baumann (2000) traces the different 'stages' or 'phases' in the process of religious continuity and transformation, which for present purposes can be summarised very briefly thus: (1) migration and arrival; (2) 'communities' become established; (3) gradual engagement with the 'host'; (4) acculturation or retreat depending on 'host' response; (5) simultaneous efforts to both adapt and maintain difference.

18 This comparison, minus its Australian dimension, where developments are at an earlier stage, is further developed in Coward et al. (2000). Elsewhere, Ter Haar (1998) attempts a smaller-scale mapping of Africans in Europe (Germany, Britain and the Netherlands) and Vertovec (2000b) of Hindus in the Caribbean and Britain.

19 To this list Knott (1992: 20–1) adds: the impact of ethnicity on religion, including its ability to survive and grow; stages in the process of religious change following migration; how religions cope with change, e.g. generational change; interfaith dialogue; the use of places of worship; mission; and sectarianism.

References

Asad, T., 1993, *Genealogies of Religion: Discipline and Reasons of Power in Christianity and Islam*, Baltimore, MA, and London: The Johns Hopkins University Press.

Ballard, Roger (ed.), 1994, *Desh Pardesh: The South Asian Presence in Britain*, London: Hurst & Co.

Barclay, John M. G., 1996, *Jews in the Mediterranean Diaspora: From Alexander to Trajan*, London and New York: Continuum International Publishing Group.

Baumann, Gerd, 1996, *Contesting Culture: Discourses of Identity in Multi-ethnic London*, Cambridge: Cambridge University Press.

—— 1999, *The Multicultural Riddle: Rethinking National, Ethnic and Religious Identities*, New York and London: Routledge.

Baumann, Martin, 2000, 'Becoming a colour of the rainbow: Indian Hindus in Trinidad analysed along a phase model of diaspora', paper presented at the 18th Congress of the IAHR, Durban,

South Africa, 6–11 August, posted at http://-user.uni-bremen.de/~mbaumann/lectures/durb-dia.htm.

—— 2001, 'What you always wanted to know about the origins and usage of that word "diaspora"', paper posted on irishdiaspora.net, http://www.sobolstones.com/papers/vp01.cfm?outfit=ids&folder=46&paper=59.

Bhabha, Homi, 1994, *The Location of Culture*, London: Routledge.

Brah, Avtar, 1996, *Cartographies of Diaspora*, London: Routledge.

Braun, Willi and McCutcheon, Russell T., 2000, *Guide to the Study of Religion*, London and New York: Cassell.

Braziel, Jana Evans and Mannur, Anita (eds), 2003, *Theorizing Diaspora: A Reader*, Malden, MA, and Oxford: Blackwell.

Burghart, Richard (ed.), 1987, *Hinduism in Great Britain: The Perpetuation of Religion in an Alien Cultural Milieu*, London and New York: Tavistock Publications.

Clifford, James, 1994, 'Diasporas', *Current Anthropology*, 9 (3): 302–38.

Cohen, Anthony P., 1985, *The Symbolic Construction of Community*, London: Routledge.

Cohen, Robin, 1997, *Global Diasporas: An Introduction*, London: Routledge.

Coward, Harold, Hinnells, John R. and Williams, Raymond Brady, 2000, *The South Asian Religious Diaspora in Britain, Canada, and the United States*, New York: State University of New York Press.

Eck, Diana L., 2002, *A New Religious America*, San Francisco, CA: Harper.

Fielding, Steven, 1993, *Class and Ethnicity: Irish Catholics in England 1880–1939*, Buckingham: Open University Press.

Fischer, Michael M. J. and Abedi, Mehdi, 1990, *Debating Muslims: Cultural Dialogues in Postmodernity and Tradition*, Madison, WI: University of Wisconsin Press.

Flood, Gavin, 1999, *Beyond Phenomenology: Rethinking the Study of Religion*, London and New York: Cassell.

Gilman, Sander L., 2003, *Jewish Frontiers: Essays on Bodies, Histories and Identities*, New York and Basingstoke: Palgrave Macmillan.

Gilroy, Paul, 1993, *The Black Atlantic: Modernity and Double Consciousness*, London: Verso.

Hall, S., 1992, 'The question of cultural identity', in Hall, S., Held, D. and McGrew, T. (eds) *Modernity and Its Futures*, Cambridge: Polity Press, in association with Blackwell Publishers, Oxford and The Open University, pp. 273–325.

Hinnells, John R., 1984, *A Handbook of Living Religions*, London: Penguin Books.

—— 1998, *The New Handbook of Living Religions*, London: Penguin Books.

—— 2005, *The Zoroastrian Diaspora: Religion and Migration*, Oxford: Oxford University Press.

Hoeber, Susanne (ed.), 1997, *Transnational Religion and Fading States*, Boulder, CO: Westview Press.

James, Allan G., 1974, *Sikh Children in Britain*, London and New York: Oxford University Press.

Jurgensmeyer, Mark, 2002, 'Thinking globally about religion', paper posted at the eScholarship Repository, University of California, Santa Barbara, http://repositories.cdlib.org/gis/1.

Kaplan, Yosef, 2000, *An Alternative Path to Modernity: The Western Sephardi Diaspora in the Seventeenth Century*, Leiden: Brill.

Knott, Kim, 1986, *Religion and Identity, and the Study of Ethnic Minority Religions in Britain*, Community Religions Project Research Papers No. 3, Leeds: Department of Theology and Religious Studies, The University of Leeds.

—— 1992, *The Role of Religious Studies in Understanding the Ethnic Experience*, Community Religions Project Research Papers No. 7, Leeds: Department of Theology and Religious Studies, The University of Leeds.

Mandaville, Peter, 2001, *Transnational Muslim Politics: Reimagining the Umma*, London and New York: Routledge.

McCaffrey, Lawrence J. 1997, *The Irish Catholic Diaspora in America*, Washington, DC: Catholic University of America Press.

McCarthy Brown, Karen, 2001, *Mama Lola: A Vodou Priestess in Brooklyn*, Berkeley, CA: University of California Press (updated and expanded edition).

McLoughlin, Seán, forthcoming, *Representing Muslims: Religion, Ethnicity and the Politics of Identity*, London: Pluto Press.

Metcalf, Barbara Daly (ed.), 1996, *Making Muslim Space in North America and Europe*, Berkeley/Los Angeles, CA, and London: University of California Press.

Mol, Hans, 1979, 'Theory and data on the religious behaviour of migrants', *Social Compass*, XXVI (1): 31–9.

Murphy, Joseph M., 1994, *Working the Spirit: Ceremonies of the African Diaspora*, Boston, MA: Beacon Press.

Pitts, Walter F., 1993, *Old Ship of Zion: Afro-Baptist Ritual in the African Diaspora*, New York and Oxford: Oxford University Press.

Prebish, Charles, S. and Baumann, Martin (eds), 2002, *Westward Dharma: Buddhism Beyond Asia*, Berkeley, CA: University of California Press.

Sharpe, Eric J., 1975/1986, *Comparative Religion: A History*, 2nd edn, London: Duckworth.

Smart, Ninian, 1987, 'The importance of diasporas', in Shaked, S., Werblovsky, R. Y., Shulman, D. D. and Strounka, G. A. G. (eds) *Gilgul: Essays on Transformation, Revolution and Permanence in the History of Religions*, Leiden: Brill, pp. 288–95.

—— 1989, *The World's Religions*, Cambridge: Cambridge University Press.

Tatla, Darshan Singh, 1999, *The Sikh Diaspora: The Search for Statehood*, London: University College London Press.

Taylor, Mark C., 1998, *Critical Terms for Religious Studies*, Chicago, IL, and London: The University of Chicago Press.

Ter Haar, Gerrie (ed.), 1998, *Strangers and Sojourners: Religious Communities in the Diaspora*, Leuven: Peeters.

Vertovec, Steven, 2000a, 'Religion and diaspora', paper presented at the conference on *New Landscapes of Religion in the West*, Oxford: School of Geography and the Environment, University of Oxford, 27–29 September.

—— 2000b, *The Hindu Diaspora: Comparative Patterns*, London and New York: Routledge.

Werbner, P. and Modood, T. (eds), 1997, *Debating Cultural Hybridity: Multi-cultural Identities and the Politics of Anti-racism*, London and Atlantic Highlands, NJ: Zed Books.

Index